*Bertolt Brecht's Dramatic Theory*

*Studies in German Literature, Linguistics, and Culture*

Edited by James Hardin
(*South Carolina*)

# Bertolt Brecht's Dramatic Theory

John J. White

CAMDEN HOUSE

First published 2004 by Camden House
Transferred to digital printing 2007
Reprinted in paperback 2010

Camden House is an imprint of Boydell & Brewer Inc.
668 Mt. Hope Avenue, Rochester, NY 14620, USA
www.camden-house.com
and of Boydell & Brewer Limited
PO Box 9, Woodbridge, Suffolk IP12 3DF, UK
www.boydellandbrewer.com

Paperback ISBN-13: 978-1-57113-473-8
Paperback ISBN-10: 1-57113-473-5
Hardback ISBN-13: 978-1-57113-076-1
Hardback ISBN-10: 1-57113-076-4

**Library of Congress Cataloging-in-Publication Data**

White, John J.
    Bertolt Brecht's dramatic theory / John J. White.
      p. cm. — (Studies in German literature, linguistics, and culture)
    Includes bibliographical references and index.
    ISBN 1-57113-076-4 (hardcover: alk. paper)
      1. Brecht, Bertolt, 1898–1956—Aesthetics. 2. Brecht, Bertolt, 1898–
    1956—Knowledge—Performing arts. 3. Theater—History—20th cen-
    tury. I. Title. II. Series: Studies in German literature, linguistics, and
    culture (Unnumbered).

PT2603.R397Z8996 2004
832'.912—dc22                                                                  2004014263

A catalogue record for this title is available from the British Library.

This publication is printed on acid-free paper.

Cover image: Undated portrait of Brecht courtesy of Ullstein Bild, Berlin.

# Contents

# Acknowledgments

M Y LONGEST STANDING THANKS go to Hugh Powell (Indiana) for introducing me to Brecht's *Schriften zum Theater* and for the combination of eye-twinkling inquisitiveness and skepticism with which he took his class meticulously through various theoretical statements. In subsequent years, I have gratefully received substantial help, answers to my questions, and other forms of assistance from a number of friends, colleagues, and institutions. Above all from the much missed and much loved Philip Brady † (Birkbeck College London) who always maintained that the twentieth century should be called the Age of Brecht. Thanks also go to Aase Funding Andersen, Shami Ghosh (Harvard), Didi Hopkins, David Jenkinson (formerly Goldsmiths College London) and Victoria Jones (currently Goldsmiths College London), Ania Kepka, Joanne Leal (Birkbeck College London), Stephen Parker (Manchester), Matthew Philpotts (Manchester), Ronald Speirs (Birmingham), Christine Anhut, Matthew Bell, Derek Glass †, and Chris Thornhill (King's College London), and Erdmut Wizisla of the Bertolt Brecht Archive, Berlin. I should also like to record my gratitude to the graduate students taking the King's College London/Royal Academy of Dramatic Art MA course in "Text and Performance Studies" who attended my seminars on the theory of drama and Brecht. Their actor, producer, and audience perspectives, as well as their lively reactions, have over the years been a greatly appreciated challenge to my more "bookishly" academic relationship to Brecht's dramatic theory. Anyone who has worked on Brecht during the past three decades has accumulated an immense intellectual debt to the indefatigable Jan Knopf (Arbeitsstelle Bertolt Brecht, Karlsruhe). In his multiple capacities as editor, commentator, and leading Brecht scholar, he has transformed our picture of Brecht's work and done much to secure the textual basis of current Brecht scholarship and systematize the information available on the playwright's writings and their reception. My own debts to Knopf and his fellow editors and collaborators — and the occasional disagreements — are amply documented in the chapters that follow. However, on a more personal note, I should like to express my thanks to him for making available the proofs of the theory volume of the new *Brecht Handbuch* at a dark time when I was beginning to become increasingly aware of how foolhardy it would be to go to press without being able to absorb the new material. My thanks also go to Jim Hardin and Jim Walker at Camden House for their patience and for encouraging the present project, as well as to Sue Innes for her meticulous copy-editing, valuable searching questions, and help with presentation. My greatest thanks, as always, go to my family: to my wife and colleague Ann White (Royal Holloway College London) and to Jonathan White (European University Institute, Florence). Both have unstintingly assisted and supported me in my work on Brecht in a variety of ways. For this and many other reasons this volume is dedicated to them.

J. J. W.
August 2004

# Abbreviations of Works Frequently Cited

BHB      *Brecht Handbuch in fünf Bänden*. Ed. Jan Knopf. Stuttgart-Weimar: Metzler, 2001–3. By volume and page number. Details of the individual volumes are given under Works Consulted.

BT      *Brecht on Theatre: The Development of an Aesthetic*. Ed. and trans. by John Willett. New York: Hill and Wang. London: Methuen, 1964.

GBA      Bertolt Brecht. *Werke: Große kommentierte Berliner und Frankfurter Ausgabe*. Ed. by Werner Hecht, Jan Knopf, Werner Mittenzwei, and Klaus-Detlef Müller. 30 vols + *Registerband*. Berlin-Weimar: Aufbau. Frankfurt a. M.: Suhrkamp, 1988–2000. Paperback special limited edition with same pagination: 2003.

GW      Bertolt Brecht: *Gesammelte Werke: Werkausgabe*. Ed. by Suhrkamp Verlag in collaboration with Elisabeth Hauptmann. 20 vols. Frankfurt a. M.: Suhrkamp, 1967. Abbreviated in *BHB* and *GBA* as *WA* (*Werkausgabe*). A raised asterisk after page-reference to this edition indicates that the quotation comes from the "Anmerkungen" section of the relevant volume.

Theaterarbeit      *Theaterarbeit: 6 Aufführungen des Berliner Ensembles*. Ed. by Berliner Ensemble and Helene Weigel. Second, revised edition. Berlin: Henschel, 1961.

## Note

References to titles of individual theoretical works that were not given to them by Brecht follow the *GBA* convention of indicating this by putting them in square brackets.

# Introduction

THE PRESENT STUDY OFFERS the first detailed commentary in English on Bertolt Brecht's major theoretical writings on the theater. It is not intended as an introduction to the plays or as a basic guide to his main dramaturgical concepts (fortunately a number of general studies of Brecht's work already perform that task admirably). Rather, my aim is to provide in-depth critical analysis of Brecht's thinking on the subject, discussed both with reference to the intellectual context of the time and in the light of subsequent dramatic and aesthetic theory. This will be coupled with an exploration of his methods of argumentation and an evaluation of the strengths and weaknesses of his evolving theoretical position on the problems he confronts at different stages of his theoretical development.

Throughout his entire creative life, from "Zur Ästhetik des Dramas" (On the Aesthetics of Drama, 1920) to the essays on "Dialektik auf dem Theater" (Dialectics in the Theater, 1956), Brecht theorized prolifically: on theater as an institution, on contemporary drama, and, above all, on Epic Theater, "Verfremdung," and his works' sociopolitical role. Although his theoretical statements on film, radio, poetry, and the novel also exerted considerable influence, the dramaturgical writings far outstrip these in quantity and significance. Indeed, the theoretical works of few modern playwrights can have shaped their plays' reception and our thinking about modern drama to a comparable degree. Yet few bodies of theoretical writing have also remained so contentious, been treated so selectively, or been so blatantly manipulated for ideological purposes. And it was not just his detractors who misunderstood or falsified them. As we shall see, two of his most ardent American admirers, Eric Bentley and Mordecai Gorelik, left Brecht somewhat disappointed with their largely supportive accounts of what they took to be his position. Writing of his experiences with one less sophisticated admirer, Brecht confessed: "Es ist mir dann zumute, wie es einem Mathematiker zumute wäre, wenn er läse: Ich bin mit Ihnen ganz einverstanden, daß zwei mal zwei fünf ist" (*GBA*, 23:171).

One of the last occasions on which Brecht substantially re-thought his theoretical position was in 1953. In January 1953 the GDR's State Commission for Artistic Affairs had announced that a Stanislavsky Conference would be held in the East German capital later that same year. It was an event stage-managed to bring together dramatists, practical theater people, academics, and *Kulturpolitiker* to debate just what East German theater could — that is, should — learn from the methods of the late Konstantin Sergeyevich Stanislavsky (1863–1938). This furnished a pretext for the further polarization of the Russian's work (by now officially appropriated as theater of Socialist Realism) and Brecht's own in order to demonize Brecht's Epic Theater as decadent formalism. In the words of a recent commentator, the planned Stanislavsky Conference "came to represent a very real threat to the continued existence of the Berliner Ensemble" (Philpotts 2003, 59). It was imperative for Brecht, Helene Weigel, and the Berliner Ensemble that their position be made clear before, during, and after the event (which took place between 17 and 19 April). The Ensemble was coming under increasing pressure from those whom Brecht referred to as "die Leute [. . .], die das *Kleine Organon* angreifen" (*GBA*, 25:580) to reposition itself *vis-à-vis* the twin artistic orthodoxies of the time: the Stanislavskian system of dramatic production and the content-oriented Soviet aesthetic of Socialist Realism. The establishment in 1947 of an Institute for the Methodical Renewal of German Theater at Weimar under the directorship of the then arch-Stanislavskian Maxim Vallentin had given a clear signal regarding the direction the Soviet Military Administration in Germany expected East German theater to take. The Berliner Ensemble, "das einzige große Theater der Welt, das von einem Schriftsteller geleitet wird" (*GBA*, 23:383), could not be seen to dissent from the Soviet cultural program. Having suffered much during the anti-formalism campaigns of the early 1950s, it was now about to come under a fresh concerted attack.

Brecht was prepared for the gathering storm. During the latter part of 1952 he had collaborated with Erwin Strittmatter (1912–94, best-known for his 1963 novel *Ole Bienkopp*) on a production of the young writer's first play, *Katzgraben*, a social comedy subtitled *Szenen aus dem Bauernleben*. This prudent, though by no means merely expedient,[1] move offered the Ensemble the opportunity to produce an exemplary work of Socialist Realism involving a politically correct picture of village life in the Soviet Zone of Occupation during the turbulent land-reform period (1947–49). As significant as the signals sent to the Establishment by the mere fact of Brecht's work with Strittmatter was an accompanying series of theoretical writings entitled "*Katzgraben*-Notate 1953." These, together with the work they documented, became part of a robust response to the campaign of vilification in the build-up to a conference that risked becoming theater's

---

[1] Philpotts (2003) challenges the interpretation of Brecht's behavior in 1953 as merely an opportunistic response to threats to the Berliner Ensemble. Brecht's admiration for Strittmatter is shown to date back to 1951 and to continue long after the anti-formalist furor had subsided. These insights represent a salutary warning against what Philpotts sees as the "tendency in Brecht criticism to over-privilege tactical explanations for his behavior in the GDR" (56).

equivalent of a show trial. A companion piece, "Erwin Strittmatters *Katzgraben*" (*GBA*, 24:437–41), published in *Sinn und Form* earlier in the same year, has also been read as part of a counter-campaign on Brecht's part, although recent scholarship (Philpotts 2003) has demonstrated that any tactical significance Brecht's collaboration with Strittmatter may have had needs to be seen in the context of his part in a campaign to launch promising young GDR writers, evidence which puts in question any crude reading of the adoption of Strittmatter's work as a mere self-serving ploy. Added to which, as has been pointed out (Mumford 1995), the Berliner Ensemble's production of *Katzgraben* offered Brecht the opportunity to test Stanislavsky's practice and assumptions against his own approach, as well as to re-visit his last major theoretical work, *Kleines Organon für das Theater* (1948), in the light of ongoing production experiences with Epic and Aristotelian Theater. As all this suggests, one can hardly do justice to the *Katzgraben* notes by considering them independently of the context in which they were written, in this instance a particularly complex situation that has generated diametrically opposite readings. Context is important for an appreciation of the theoretical works written at all stages of Brecht's life. Theory does not come into being in a vacuum.

The "*Katzgraben*-Notate 1953" represent Brecht's most important attempt to record his rehearsal procedures and offer detailed insights into Epic Theater, not through his usual analysis of features of the end product or via a photographically documented *Modellbuch,* but by focusing on the process of evolving a production concept through rehearsal discussions focusing in detail on what Epic Theater could learn from the state-sanctioned Stanislavsky System. An editorial note records that this work soon assumed "den Charakter eines exemplarischen 'Proben-Modells'" (*GBA,* 25:586). Unfortunately, the production of Strittmatter's play was not a success (*GBA,* 25:585–86), and as a consequence the notes were not published in their entirety until considerably later.[2] To complement the rehearsal notes, other Ensemble members set down independent accounts (material now housed in the Bertolt Brecht Archive). Brecht's own notes were at the time transcribed by Käthe Rülicke in such a way as to allow space for intercalated information about the various rehearsals (63 days in all), thus giving the documentation the appearance of a rehearsal diary. Yet, in a manner typical of Brecht's way with quasi-documentation, the dialogues that make up the *Katzgraben* complex, though based on discussions that had actually taken place during rehearsals, were progressively reformulated and reordered, with

---

[2] *Sinn und Form: Sonderheft Bertolt Brecht,* Potsdam, 1949, 11–41. East and West German *Versuche* versions were only published after the death of Stalin, although a GDR *Versuche* publication had originally been planned for Aufbau's Heft 10 of 1950 (cf. *GBA,* 23:459). This was in the event canceled for unspecified reasons.

words being put into the participants' mouths to allow them to act as foils to Brecht's own stringently formulated and often non-negotiable views. Such hybrid forms — in this case, part orchestrated dialogue, part production chronicle, but always involving a high degree of retrospective rescripting — were a feature of many of the theoretical writings we shall shortly be considering.

The first *Katzgraben* note touches on a question of central importance to the present study. It begins with a character, identified simply as "P.," asking the playwright: "Wie kommt es, daß man so oft Beschreibungen Ihres Theaters liest — meist in ablehnenden Beurteilungen —, aus denen sich niemand ein Bild machen könnte, wie es wirklich ist?" (*GBA*, 25:401). P. (modeled on Peter Palitzsch, a member of the Berliner Ensemble since 1949) is told by B. (Brecht) that he considers himself at fault for having placed such emphasis on theory. But he also points an accusing finger at his detractors, especially the powerful GDR Stanislavskians and anti-formalists who were currently after his blood: "Mein Fehler. Diese Beschreibungen und viele der Beurteilungen gelten nicht dem Theater, das ich mache, sondern dem Theater, das sich für meine Kritiker aus der Lektüre meiner Traktate ergibt. Ich kann es nicht lassen, die Leser und die Zuschauer in meine Technik und in meine Absichten einzuweihen, das rächt sich" (ibid.). Despite the confessional "Ich kann es nicht lassen," Brecht theorized less out of compulsion than from sheer necessity. What he refers to as his "Traktate" had invariably been produced because the situation demanded them. "Die meisten dieser Äußerungen, wenn nicht alle," Brecht had observed two years before the work on *Katzgraben*, "sind als Bemerkungen zu meinen Stücken geschrieben, damit die Stücke richtig aufgeführt würden. Das gibt ihnen einen etwas trockenen, handwerklichen Ton" (*GBA*, 23:171). Radical innovators often feel called upon to explain their experiments; the predicament of exile forces once famous dramatists to introduce themselves in new cultural environments; and those under attack, which in Brecht's case was often from the Lukácses, Erpenbecks, and Kurellas on the Left, need theory to defend their positions. On occasions, Brecht's intended "trockener, handwerklicher Ton" would give way to more aggressive forms of self-justification, but while he was in protracted exile, much of his output did not even enter the public domain. It remained what the composer and Brecht's collaborator Hanns Eisler (1897–1968) once referred to as "Schreiben für die Schublade" (Bunge, 70–71), its function often being to help the writer think through his position on some question in a written form equivalent to what Heinrich von Kleist saw as "die allmähliche Verfertigung der Gedanken beim Reden." Nevertheless, what lingered for some time in a bottom drawer had a habit of eventually finding its way into print, in expanded form or cannibalized for fragmentary publication. Theory conceived under such circumstances could in any case often be more radical than what Brecht did succeed in getting into print. For as he once observed, "für die Schublade braucht man keine Konzessionen" (*GBA*, 26:332).

In the "Episches Theater" section of the *Katzgraben* notes, Brecht tries once more, but not for the last time, to combat an unfortunate situation where his theories had an unforeseen effect on the public perception of his work. He reminds his readers that one of his favorite English proverbs is that "the proof of the pudding lies in the eating." In other words, theories and programs will always be less important than the resultant (or prior) creation. He also tries to counter any assumption that his theorizing is either difficult or offputtingly "Teutonic": "Meine ganzen Theorien sind überhaupt viel naiver, als man denkt und — als meine Ausdrucksweise vermuten läßt" (*GBA*, 25:401). Yet Brecht never disowns the vast body of writings that had been a part of his self-presentation and self-understanding from the second half of the Weimar Republic onwards. When proposing a postwar edition of his works to the Suhrkamp Verlag in 1953, he is above all interested in having his major dramas back in print, but at the same time he stresses that any such collection should be theoretically underpinned ("mit einem theoretischen Band dazu" [*GBA*, 30:221]). Brecht repeatedly draws attention to theory's crucial role, while at the same time keeping it in its proper subservient place. Abandon your prejudices and go and see my plays, he advises "die Kritiker":

> Sähen sich die Kritiker mein Theater an, wie es die Zuschauer ja tun, ohne meinen Theorien zunächst dabei Gewicht beizulegen, so würden sie wohl einfach Theater vor sich sehen, Theater, wie ich hoffe, mit Phantasie, Humor und Sinn, und erst bei einer Analyse der Wirkung fiele ihnen einiges Neue auf — das sie dann in meinen theoretischen Ausführungen erklärt finden könnten. Ich glaube, die Kalamität begann dadurch, daß meine Stücke richtig aufgeführt werden mußten, damit sie wirkten, und so mußte ich, für eine nichtaristotelische Dramatik — o Kummer! — ein episches Theater — o Elend! — beschreiben. ("Episches Theater," *GBA*, 25:401–2)

The reference to the point at which an "Analyse der Wirkung" is attempted as the stage when theory could prove most useful suggests it is the place of feelings in Epic Theater that was expected to give most difficulty. Indeed, from the *Mahagonny* notes of 1930 until his final years, explaining the complicated role of emotions in a theater of critical distance remained one of the greatest challenges Brecht had to face.

In more respects than he concedes, Brecht had himself to blame for much of the hostile reception. His lead concepts were not always well defined or adequately related to one another; and they seldom find full expression in any one single document. A further problem was that Brecht preferred the high-risk strategy of resorting to an innovative terminology, provocative neologisms even, or idiosyncratically redefined terms rather than the familiar conceptual repertoire of his contemporaries. What is more, the pronounced role played by an arsenal of high-profile concepts in the reception of Epic Theater was not without its dangers. As Walter H. Sokel has warned, to approach Brecht's plays using the yardstick of his own seductive terminology can have an inhibiting effect (Sokel 1973, 548), especially if his conceptual framework is subjected to insufficient scrutiny. Another source of misunderstandings has been a tendency to underestimate the need to make his underlying assumptions (political as well as artistic) explicit: "Ich glaube, gewisse Äußerungen werden mißverstanden, weil ich Wichtiges vorausgesetzt habe, statt es zu formulieren" (*GBA*, 23:171). This admission will be of especial relevance to the consideration of *Der Messingkauf.*

Although one finds Brecht on occasion referring to his theory as if it were some monolithic entity, the individual writings that made up the amorphous "Schriften zum Theater" were usually the product of continually changing circumstances. From 1919 to 1921 the young Brecht did his theoretical apprenticeship as cub drama-reviewer for the local Augsburg USPD-oriented newspaper *Der Volkswille,* and from 1922 onwards he wrote regular commissioned reviews and literary essays for the prestigious *Die literarische Welt* and the *Berliner Börsen-Courier,* the theater section of which was in the hands of his powerful friend and ally Herbert Ihering. From here on, his disquisitions on drama tend to home in on his own work rather than that of contemporaries or precursors. Even when early reviews served as pegs for pronouncements about the dire state of Weimar theater or the failure of German Naturalism and Expressionism to confront social problems adequately — and could thus be read as justifications of the "Neue Dramatik" of which Brecht's work was the main example — they gave little hint of the powerful propagandizing on his own behalf that was to emerge in the wake of his 1926 conversion to Marxism and the runaway success of *Die Dreigroschenoper.* Many of his canonical theoretical statements from the 1930s and 1940s had to wait years for publication in the German original or in an appropriately influential organ. What are now regarded as Brecht's major dramaturgical writings often suffered from unpropitious beginnings. His most important pre-exile statement on Epic Theater, "Anmerkungen zur Oper *Aufstieg und Fall der Stadt Mahagonny*" (Notes to the Opera *The Rise and Fall of the City of Mahagonny,* 1930), had the misfortune of being published less than thirty months before Hitler's coming to power, after which few Germans with any sense would have wanted to be found in possession of *Versuche* 2, in which the notes appeared. The publication of the revised *Mahagonny* notes by the then London-based Malik Verlag within a year of the outbreak of the Second World War was also hardly propitious timing, but rather a matter of Brecht's need to avail himself of one of the few leading exile publishing outlets still relatively safe from German invasion. In fact,

throughout the exile period Brecht was forced to become more opportunistic, seeking possibilities for promoting Epic Theater wherever they might
arise, allowing himself to be interviewed, published (above all in English
translation) and talked about in the international press.[3]

Brecht's account of "Verfremdungseffekte in der chinesischen Schauspielkunst" (Alienation Effects in Chinese Acting, 1936), not published in
German until 1957, first appeared in English in the London magazine *Life
and Letters To-Day* in the year it was written. The script of a radio talk entitled "Radiovortrag Bertolt Brecht" (1935), although probably never broadcast, became the starting-point for "Das deutsche Drama vor Hitler,"
written with Margarete Steffin in preparation for visits to London and New
York and published as "The German Drama: Pre-Hitler" in the *New York
Times* (November 1935) and the following year in the London *Left Review*.
"Über experimentelles Theater" (On Experimental Theater, 1939), "Kurze
Beschreibung einer neuen Technik der Schauspielkunst, die einen Verfremdungseffekt hervorbringt" (Short Description of a New Technique of Acting
Which Creates an Alienation Effect, 1940), and many other seminal theoretical writings from the exile period did not appear in any language until after Brecht's return to Europe, and in many cases posthumously. His most
ambitious theoretical project, the fragmentary *Der Messingkauf* (The Messingkauf Dialogues, 1939–55), had to wait until 1993 for an acceptably authoritative edition (*GBA,* 22:695–869). Its fortunes in English are even
more curious. In 1964, John Willett included a brief account of the material
in *Brecht on Theatre* (*BT,* 169–75) in an attempt to give "a rough indication
of the subjects covered by *Der Messingkauf* in the confused and fragmentary
state in which Brecht left it" (*BT,* 175). Yet 1965 saw Willett produce a 95-
page translation (*The Messingkauf Dialogues*), presumably because the material had been released for translation after Suhrkamp's publication of it in
Elisabeth Hauptmann's 1963 "Lese-Fassung" of the incomplete project.
Even though Brecht had, from the early 1930s on, set about systematically
disseminating his theoretical writings alongside the literary works in his *Versuche* series, launched in 1930 in the Weimar Republic and revived in both
GDR and FRG editions from 1951 until 1977, coverage was highly selective
and individual essays often fell victim to the vicissitudes of a volatile exile
predicament, the ravages of war, and thereafter the cultural politics of Stalin-
ism and the Cold War. What those of us who came after ("die Nachgeborenen" of the last half century) think of as an agreed canon of theoretical

---

[3] It would be wrong to associate the campaign for international recognition exclusively with the exile years. As early as 1928, *Die Weltbühne* published "Bertolt Brecht,
dargestellt für Engländer" by Lion Feuchtwanger. The improbable choice of a Berlin
periodical for a piece with such a title suggests that it must have been written primarily for English-language publication.

writings had often from the outset suffered an incredibly tortuous fate. Even in our own time, only those with access to that increasingly rare commodity, a well-stocked academic library, or who are in a position to be able to buy the expensive *Große kommentierte Berliner und Frankfurter Ausgabe* for themselves, are able to come to terms with the substantial number of first publications and new findings made accessible in what has become the standard edition. Yet although the volumes containing the theoretical writings (*GBA*, vols. 21–25) have been in print for over a decade, findings are only gradually percolating via recent scholarship (above all, *BHB*, vol. 4) down to the wider group of those interested in Brecht's work. Virtually all the leading monographs on, or dealing in part with, Brecht's dramatic theory were published before the present edition.[4]

Of the initial impact of National Socialism and exile on his own life and work, Brecht notes: "Sie haben mir nicht nur mein Haus, meinen Fischteich und meinen Wagen abgenommen, sie haben mir meine Bühne und mein Publikum geraubt" (Benjamin 1978, 170). If "*Ein Theater ohne Kontakt mit dem Publikum*" had always for Brecht been "*ein Nonsens*" (*GBA*, 21:121), the exile predicament of seldom having either an audience or access to a theater in which to experiment compounded what he referred to as "meine Isolierung, was die Produktion betrifft" (*GBA*, 26:414). "Es ist unmöglich," he complains, "ohne die Bühne ein Stück fertig zu machen" (*GBA*, 26:395). A remark he made of Helene Weigel's predicament — "Durch ihr Bestreben, vor vielen spielen zu dürfen, war sie dazu gelangt, nur noch vor ganz wenigen spielen zu dürfen" (*GBA*, 22:798) — shows the isolation was not his alone. Brecht had also been deprived of most of his publishing outlets and his chosen cultural environment of Berlin. He found himself repeatedly having to establish a fresh foothold in new countries, some at the time hostile to things German, others with a growing suspicion of what could be interpreted as Soviet-inspired culture, and all by and large unsympathetic towards the avant-garde of the by then politically discredited Weimar Republic. This bleak picture is part of the received wisdom communicated over the years by the playwright's biographers, his published correspondence, and his journals. However, as the present study tries to show, there are respects in which one feature of exile, that is to say, having to establish himself afresh in a variety of host countries, had a distinctly beneficial effect on the nature and construction of Brecht's theoretical position. To claim this is neither the token of unquestioning optimism nor the corollary of a view predicated on the ideological assumption that all adversity will have a dialec-

---

[4] Notably those by Brüggemann, Claas, Fischer, Hecht (1972 and 1986), Hinck, Hultberg, Knopf (1974 and 1980a), Ludwig (1975), Voigts, and Willett (*BT*, 1964), all written before *GBA*'s substantial body of new material and *BHB*, vol. 4 became available.

tically productive result. It is simply to recognize that Brecht's theorizing thrived on adversity. The present study will seek to question the view that the exile period produced little more than a "Bestandsaufnahme und nochmalige Vergewisserung" of earlier theoretical positions (*BHB*, 4:225, 285). However, this does not mean either that I subscribe to Walter Hinck's view that Epic Theater is itself a product of the exile years (Hinck 1966, cf. *BHB*, 4:283). Nevertheless, with the exception of the *Mahagonny* notes and the "Lehrstück" theory, almost all of Brecht's most important theoretical writings stem from the exile period. As Voges has pointed out, "Auf Dauer gesehen waren die Auswirkungen der Exilsituation für den Stückeschreiber ambivalent" (Voges 1985, 214). The remark about not having to make concessions when writing for the bottom drawer was made in connection with *Der gute Mensch von Sezuan* (The Good Person of Setzuan, 1938–40), a work Brecht hoped would be uncompromising ("ich kann [. . .] dabei die epische Technik entwickeln *und so endlich wieder auf den Standard kommen*" (*GBA*, 26:332, my emphasis). Voges (ibid.) argues that Brecht was producing such high caliber avant-garde work in the 1930s and 1940s that it would be wrong to think of his prolific theoretical writings as "die Kompensation für eine fehlende künstlerische Praxis." And since so much of this theory was written for the bottom drawer, it is hardly surprising that the results often show greater vision than some of the compromise plays that were also the product of the exile period.

In one very obvious yet important respect, theory was the exiled Brecht's visiting card. He repeatedly found himself in the predicament of being a relatively unknown quantity, a fish out of water, in situations where he had to explain himself — as was the case in each of his three Scandinavian host countries — while at the same time needing to prepare for an even longer-term campaign of self-presentation in respect of the United States, the country which was gradually crystallizing in his mind as the only logical destination for someone needing to escape the long arm of National Socialism and the continuing Soviet purges. Thus, while Brecht was still in Danish exile, many of his public (rather than bottom-drawer) dramaturgical pronouncements became more than just a way of explaining himself to hoped-for Copenhagen audiences and theater groups with whom he wished to work. As we shall see in chapter 2, he was at the same time paving the way for a move on to fresh and safer pastures. Much of the theorizing surrounding the New York production of *Die Mutter* (The Mother, 1932), as well as the English publication of his essay on alienation effects in Chinese acting, and the approach adopted in "Kurze Beschreibung einer neuen Technik der Schauspielkunst, die einen Verfremdungseffekt hervorbringt," make more sense when seen against this backcloth. Similarly, "Über experimentelles Theater" represents an attempt to redefine in European terms the historical significance of Epic Theater — first for Brecht's prospective Swedish hosts and subsequently, as his plans included the need to establish a foothold in Helsinki. *Kleines Organon für das Theater* (Short Organum for the Theater, 1948) and the related *Messingkauf* complex are also closely bound up with the exigencies of the exile situation. To say this is not to seek to relativize their importance as theory, but simply to contextualize them, even if not always in Brecht's sense of "Historisierung." As the war continued, however, it became increasingly clear to Brecht, now from his Californian perspective, that what he had thought of as a kind of limbo ("die *Inzwischenzeit*" [*GBA*, 26:414]) would soon come to an end. From then on, the completion of a theoretical *magnum opus,* be it *Der Messingkauf* or *Kleines Organon für das Theater,* was no longer seen as part of the preparations for moving on to another makeshift place of sojourn, but for a definitive return to East Germany: to the Soviet Zone of Occupation, soon to become the German Democratic Republic. Given the dangerous quicksands of cultural politics in such a Stalinist environment, it was crucial for Brecht to establish his theoretical position. There was an urgent need to produce a succinct, clearly formulated statement of his aesthetic ideas (a statement that was now *aesthetic,* rather than merely dramaturgical) and to place it in the only GDR publication defiantly liberal enough to serve as a vehicle: Peter Huchel's *Sinn und Form.* That way, he hoped that he would be able to influence the choice of ground on which the polemics about his work would be conducted. The subsequent anti-formalist debates of the GDR "Aufbau" years were by and large reprises of the hostile reception of Brecht's theoretical work in exile, above all of the "Expressionismusdebatte" of the late 1930s. But this time, instead of introducing himself by establishing what he was for and against, Brecht had to position his ideas in a constructive relationship to the dominant Marxist aesthetic. This he had always done, though often in ways too subtle for his opponents' grasp.

The presentational methods adopted to put his ideas across were often related to the ones Brecht used in his plays. As he was well aware, analytical theory inevitably de-familiarizes praxis. In the seventeenth appendix note to "Kurze Beschreibung einer neuen Technik der Schauspielkunst, die einen Verfremdungseffekt hervorbringt," he observes: "Der Verfremdungseffekt selber ist durch die vorliegende Darstellung in gewissem Sinn verfremdet worden, wir haben eine tausendfache, gewöhnliche, überall vorliegende Operation, indem wir sie als eine besondere beleuchteten, zum Verständnis zu bringen versucht" (*GBA,* 22:657). However, Brecht's theoretical writings defamiliarize his dramatic practice more than "in gewissem Sinn"; he is, as we shall see, extremely ingenious in the ways he applies what might be thought of as specifically "Brechtian" strategies of defamiliarization to the theoretical points he wishes to get across. Of special relevance in this respect is the rich diversity of paradigms and text-types chosen to communicate dramaturgical ideas. One commentator called Brecht's notes to *Die Dreigro-*

*schenoper* "eine Abhandlung," others have been referred to as "Traktate,"[5] but we shall find in chapter 1 that no such conventional academic categorization does justice to the early theoretical writings on opera. And as chapters 2 to 5 demonstrate, Brecht makes effective use, for purposes of "Episierung" and "Verfremdung," of a wide spectrum of genres, including fictive dialogue, poetological letters, reflective poetry, responses to newspaper questionnaires both real and invented, *aides-mémoire* and what would now be thought of as "Thesenpapiere." Conceivably, the fine body of dramaturgical poems that form the subject of chapter 3 of the present study was a response to an awareness that much of the early theory had been "trocken" and off-puttingly "handwerklich." In other words, the bare "Neue Sachlichkeit" style of the Weimar period was not always necessarily an advantage, when it came to winning minds. It says much about Brecht's general sensitivity to questions of presentational strategy that he made the following comment about genre's importance for effective communication in a letter to his publisher in February 1950: "was das Buch über das *Courage*-Modell angeht, habe ich jetzt, wie ich denke, eine Form gefunden, die nicht zu pedantisch ist" (*GBA*, 30:16). Very often the choice of genre or text-type was a combination of appropriation and innovation. Yet the more important his later theoretical statements become, the more intent Brecht appears to be on signaling his consciousness of working within time-honored aesthetic traditions. Witness the relationship of *Kleines Organon* to Aristotle's *Organon* and Francis Bacon's *Novum organum,* that of *Der Messingkauf* to Galileo's *Discorsi,* of the dramaturgical poems to Horace's *Ars poetica,* as well as the interface between the *Katzgraben* notes and Stanislavsky's use of quasi-fictive dialogues in *An Actor Prepares.* In other words, theory could be generically "defamiliarized," as well as contextually estranged by the exile situation. Noticeably, not one of the theoretical intertexts mentioned above is German. Even Brecht's interest in Gottsched's Enlightenment poetic is more an indirect concern with Horace's *Ars poetica.*

Writing from Switzerland to Karl Korsch (1886–1961) in April 1948, Brecht, then putting the finishing touches to *Kleines Organon,* confides his thoughts about the kind of scholarly work he would ideally like to see his former mentor attempt: "Manchmal wünschte ich, Sie hielten ein Journal mit vielen Eintragungen in der Baconischen Form über alle die Gegenstände, die Sie gerade interessieren, unmethodisch im ganzen, ich meine antisystemisch. Solche wissenschaftlichen Aphorismen könnte man einzeln, in der oder jener Zusammenstellung, zu diesem oder jenem Zweck, verwerten,

---

[5] Hultberg (1962, 105) and Klaus-Detlef Müller (1967, 72) use the term "Abhandlung" for Brecht's longer theoretical writings. On Brecht and the "Textsorte Traktat," see *BHB,* 4:275.

sie wären alle fertig zu jeder Zeit; anstatt einen davon umzubauen, könnten Sie einen neuen bauen usw. — Es wäre sozusagen epische Wissenschaft!" (*GBA*, 29:449–50). This passage is much more than a displaced rumination on the structure and method of *Kleines Organon* and parts of *Der Messingkauf*; it is evidence of an awareness that, as a matter of general principle, theory could be most effectively formulated using epic structures able to create critical distance, curiosity and methodological doubt; in short, to encourage productive reading. Almost two decades earlier, Brecht himself had, as the analysis in chapter 1 will show, embarked on an embryonic essay in "epische Wissenschaft" with his "Anmerkungen zur Oper *Aufstieg und Fall der Stadt Mahagonny*." This first major theoretical work displays a rudimentary recognition of the fact that methods of distantiation used on the stage could also be employed on the page. Later, Brecht extends the same principle to the use of conceptual "Verfremdung." For while the plays may be primarily associated with two techniques ("Episierung" and "Verfremdung"), Brecht experimented with a number of further theoretical concepts, partly to help clarify his thinking, but also for the defamiliarizing impact on the reception of his ideas: "man [soll] neue Begriffe reichlich einströmen lassen, so das Denkmaterial vermehren, denn viel liegt an dem zu zähen Beibehalten des alten Begriffsmaterials, das die Realität nicht mehr zu fassen vermag" (*GBA*, 21:508). Clinging to ossified concepts is, of course, the very behavior that "Verfremdung" was intended to combat.

The predicament of the European exile repeatedly moving on to find new places of asylum, not necessarily changing his theoretical position as often as his shoes, but nevertheless needing to present it afresh — or in some cases reinvent himself — has much to do with general processes of defamiliarization and the "Gestus des Zeigens." Brecht the dialectician and arch-experimenter, in his theories as much as in his theatrical practice, was usually reluctant to have his previous theoretical works simply translated into Danish, Swedish, Finnish, or English. In general, each new context became the catalyst for a newly formulated pronouncement and for theoretical advances. This accounts for the similarity within the patterns of theory to processes Brecht referred to as "gegenseitige Verfremdung" and "geographische Verfremdung." Brecht in exile was Brecht geographically "verfremdet": needing to introduce his elsewhere familiar thoughts to a new, alien audience or readership. And his latest theoretical utterances also stand in a relationship of "gegenseitige Verfremdung" to his previous ones. It is the particular historical context of the prolonged "Inzwischenzeit," in other words, that of virtually all his major theoretical writings, which has a bearing on the extraordinary agility and freshness with which Brecht rethinks and expresses his ideas on theater and progressively develops a wider system — though not anti-system, in the Korsch letter's sense.

If the image of a Brecht moving on time after time, constantly needing to re-define his theoretical position and to accommodate it to new audiences, can come across as fragmentedly "epic" in its intellectual discontinuity, those concerned with his theoretical writings have at times attempted to offset this by identifying certain continuities and patterns of development within the apparent discontinuity. Willett's influential *Brecht on Theatre* (1964) bears the subtitle *The Development of an Aesthetic*. An afterword states that the volume's purpose is to bring together the playwright's "main texts [. . .] in chronological order so as to show how his ideas evolved, gradually forming them into a quite personal aesthetic" (*BT*, 179). Too often, Willett observes, "the theory is treated as if it were a coherent whole which sprang from Brecht's head ready-made. The endless working and re-working it underwent, the nagging at a particular notion until it could be fitted in, the progress from an embryo to an often very differently formulated final concept, the amendments and the after-thoughts, all this is something that tends to be overlooked" (*BT*, 179). In his endeavor to provide a corrective to the received static, monolithic picture of Brecht's theory, Willett, however, soon found himself charged with having imposed too procrustean a teleology. Even such expressions as "gradually forming into a quite personal aesthetic," making notions "fit in" or the suggestion of a "progress from an embryo to an often very differently formulated final concept" risk creating the impression of a project eventually coming to rest and being brought to a conclusion, rather than something open-ended, consisting of "Teile eines 'work in progress'" (*BHB*, 4:3) and merely "in Bruchstücken fixiert" (*GBA*, 22:166). Even in the last months of his life, Brecht was toying with the idea of moving on from the concept of a "Dialektisches Theater" to one of "Naives Theater," a proposal which would, had Brecht lived long enough, doubtless have generated a further wave of tentative theorizing in its wake.[6] Clearly, Brecht's writings on theater were not based on a series of key concepts that eventually became clarified to the author's satisfaction. Nor did they comprise a body of preliminary sketches, notes and preparatory essays that eventually culminated in definitive statements. Probably for this reason, there are places where Willett veers in the direction of a counter-image to that suggested by his subtitle, as he conjures up a picture of the relatively uncontrolled nature of Brecht's theorizing:

> Theoretical notes and essays of this type are something of a snowball: a statement is made, then another statement has to follow to explain what the first statement means, and in the end a whole agglomeration seems to have set itself in motion, without the direction always being

---

[6] Wekwerth (1957, 260–68) documents the genesis of Brecht's "Asthetik des Naiven," and Schöttker 1989 explores its theoretical and practical significance.

what the author wants. [. . .] Brecht had to qualify certain of his ideas, to insist, for instance, that "renouncing empathy in no way meant re-nouncing the emotions [. . .]" or to point out that "the actual practice of the V-Effekt is not half so unnatural as its description." (*BT*, 179)

This may overstate the case, but the possibility of an ongoing process of never-ending theory building through correctives does nevertheless strike a chord when one examines the ratio of fragments to completed works in the theoretical corpus. We should perhaps bear in mind what Brecht himself once said of political processes: "Prozesse kommen in Wirklichkeit überhaupt nicht zu Abschlüssen" ("[Über Dialektik 6]," *GBA*, 21:523). His theoretical works raise the question of whether they also generally obey the same law.

Criticism of the evolutionary narrative implicit in Willett's selection of and commentary on his material tends to concentrate on three main issues: whether there is any consistent development to the theoretical writings, whether some final optimal resting-point was ever reached, and whether the dramaturgical theorizing can at any stage be thought of as forming part of a larger unitary "aesthetic."

The fear that Willett's corrective to the previous ahistorical picture might have imposed too rigid a teleology was first expressed in Eric Bentley's 1964 *TLS* review "Brecht on Brecht," republished in his *Brecht Commentaries, 1943–1980,* under the title "A New Aestheticism." Taking issue with Willett's subtitle, Bentley remarks:

> The attempt to demonstrate such a development gives the volume ex-citement and unity. Of the result, it can be said at best: almost thou persuadest me. It is of interest to trace the mind of Brecht through the radical skepticism of his early years to the theory of Epic Theater in its first, narrow form, and thence to the broadening of this theory and its tentative replacement by Dialectical Theater. [. . .] At the same time Mr Willett's treatment may be said to subject the aesthetics of Brecht to a scrutiny they cannot well survive and were probably never meant to en-counter. Aesthetics? Do we have an aesthetician here whose work can stand beside that of the chief philosophers in the field, or their more adept pupils and expositors, or even beside the playwrights who have also been outstanding theorists, such as Schiller and Hebbel? [. . .] if Brecht's way of putting his theory actually makes it impossible for peo-ple to see what the theory is like, it would seem to be a mistake to re-print his theoretical writings at all, let alone try to show that "an aesthetic" is developing in them year by year, and article by article. (Bentley 1981, 132)

Bentley's bleak verdict was that "perhaps what Mr Willett has done had to be done if only to show that it cannot be done" (134).[7]

Those who claim that Brecht's writings are less systematically formulated and involve, at most, sporadic traces of a development, can always turn to the writer himself for support. His emphasis on the experimental, on proceeding inductively, the sheer generic and thematic diversity of his writings and the number of times key concepts are criticized and disowned hardly suggest a simple evolution. Nevertheless, that the writings do undergo changes and could thus be subject to grouping by period was for a long time generally taken for granted. As the analysis in Fischer's *Brechts Theatertheorie* (Fischer 1989, 134–39) has shown, in nearly all surveys of the theoretical writings up to the mid-1970s three phases are proposed to Brecht's development as a writer of dramatic theory,[8] even though, as Knopf points out, the "Lehrstücktheorie" — in which Reiner Steinweg's first monograph did so much to awaken interest — drove a coach and horses through the so-called "Dreiphasentheorie."[9] Yet this was not the main reason why the tri-partite model gradually fell from favor: "die Abwendung von der Phasentheorie hängt [. . .] auch damit zusammen, daß — angesichts der kaum mehr überschaubaren Forschungsliteratur — zunehmend Spezialthemen gewählt werden, die zu einer zeitlichen Begrenzung des Gegenstands führen" (Fischer 1989, 138). Yet the waning confidence in what Fischer dismisses as the "traditionelle verflachende Phasentheorie" (ibid.) need not result in a total lack of concern for the possible stages of Brecht's theoretical

[7] There is a certain irony to Bentley's being the originator of such a charge since it has been suggested that "the discovery that a sympathetic collaborator and promoter of his works like Bentley did not understand his theories well enough to explain them to Brecht's satisfaction [the reference is to Bentley's *The Playwright as Thinker*] seems to have been the catalyst for Brecht's writing [the] early version of the *Short Organum*" (Lyon 1980, 163). Willett's thesis and Bentley's response should be judged in the light of the limited amount of published theory then available to them. As one commentator points out, "durch die Auswahl der sich ergänzenden Schriften in der WA [=GW] wurde [Brecht] ideologisch an einer theoretischen Konsistenz gemessen, die er selbst nicht anstrebte" (*BHB*, 4:1).

[8] Grimm, concentrating on "Verfremdung," divides the theoretical writings into three main phases: the pre-1926 apolitical pieces, the stridently didactic publications of the Berlin phase up to 1933, and the subsequent period of the canonical plays and accompanying theory (Grimm 1959, 74; 1961, 67). So too, with minor variations, do Klotz (1957, 115) and Fradkin (1974, 60).

[9] "Die Theorie von den drei Phasen in Brechts Entwicklung wird hinfällig, da Brecht zu einer Zeit, in der er, wie sonst angenommen wird, allmählich und vulgär zum Marxismus fand, ein sozialistisches Theater entwarf, das vom späteren Theater nicht mehr eingeholt wird" (Knopf 1974, 96–97; cf. Steinweg 1976, 79 for the source document).

development. The prevalence of particular lead concepts at different phases of his writing itself indicates that changes, and by that token a rudimentary development, in Brecht's theoretical position, do occur.

In September 1920, the twenty-two-year-old playwright made an entry in his diary that has never ceased to attract the attention of those wanting to stress the lack of coherent evolving system to his theorizing: "Ein Mann mit einer Theorie ist verloren. Er muß mehrere haben, vier, viele! Er muß sie sich in die Taschen stopfen wie Zeitungen, immer die neuesten, es lebt sich gut zwischen ihnen, man haust angenehm zwischen den Theorien" (*GBA*, 26:160). Availing oneself eclectically — often heuristically — of the theory appropriate to the task in hand was one thing, but adhering to a rigorously systematized theory, and one only, was at the time for Brecht a cardinal mistake. "Zweifellos gibt es zuwenig Theorien," he was to declare a little later ("Über die Operette" [c. 1928], *GBA*, 21:239). According to one of his GDR collaborators, Manfred Wekwerth: "Brecht haßte nichts mehr als übereilte Systematisierungen [. . .], er untersagte uns Schülern die Verwendung des Begriffs 'System' für seine eigene Theatertheorie und verwies auf Stanislawski, der diesen Begriff immer nur mit Gänsefüßchen verwendete" (Wekwerth 1973, 4).[10] Klaus-Detlef Müller comments on the repercussions of this attitude: "Es ist eine kennzeichnende Eigenart der Brechtschen Theatertheorie, daß sie kein geschlossenes System darstellt. Bei den zahlreichen Schriften und Beiträgen, deren Umfang vom Aphorismus bis zur Abhandlung reicht und unter denen sich auffallend viele Fragmente befinden, handelt es sich vielmehr um Erörterungen von Einzelaspekten, die aus aktuellem Anlaß notwendig wurden und die das Ganze nur insoweit ausführen, wie es der Anlaß erforderte" (Müller 1967, 72). Although elsewhere, in a discussion of *Der Messingkauf*, Müller argues that, while the work may appear not to exhibit an explicit set of organized theoretical assumptions, Brecht's Marxism supplies the implicit (binding) political theory: "die systematischen Gesichtspunkte [liegen] nicht in der Theorie selbst, sondern außerhalb von ihr im dialektischen Materialismus [. . .]. Die Ganzheit ist ihr immer schon vorgegeben" (Müller 1972, 47). Knopf echoes Müller's general characterization of the theoretical writings in a reference to the *Nachlass* fragments: "Brecht [hat] diese Schriften, vor allem die zum Theater, weitgehend unsystematisch geführt, wobei auch vieles fragmentarisch blieb, und [. . .] sie [galten] vornehmlich der theoretischen Selbstverständigung in der praktischen Theaterarbeit [. . .]. Eine »Theorie«

---

[10] Brecht was less consistent than this suggests. He often refers to his own "System" without resorting to scare-quotes or other caveats. Thus, in "Stanislawski und Brecht," he initially allows his interlocutor to use quotation-marks ("Ihr 'System'" [*GBA*, 25, 461]), but subsequently to make repeated reference to "beide Systeme" without such marking.

im strengen Sinn ergibt sich daraus nicht" (Knopf 2000, 77). That conceded, the picture may look rather different, if one concentrates on the principal theoretical statements from any given phase. While there may not be a fully worked-out aesthetic macro-theory, one can still seek to ascertain just how structured Brecht's individual statements were and whether they really merit the epithet "unsystematisch." Initial impressions would suggest a complex picture, with some works, including "Kurze Beschreibung" and *Kleines Organon,* displaying a combination of systematic organization and epic strategies and others, most notoriously *Der Messingkauf,* vitiated by the lack of any adequate delivery system.

A further question raised by Bentley is whether the sum of Brecht's writings amounts to an "Ästhetik." Willett was not the only one to assume they did. Herbert Claas (1977) refers to *Die politische Ästhetik Bertolt Brechts,* as does Busch 1982; and Peter Hacks (in Mittenzwei 1977, 477) and Günter Hartung (1982) also use the term "Ästhetik." In 1986 the East German Akademie der Künste published an entire volume on the subject: *Brecht 85: Zur Ästhetik Brechts* (Brecht-Zentrum der DDR 1986). Initially, Brecht was skeptical of the concept's relevance. The year 1929 finds him adamantly declaring: "Die Möglichkeit, eine neue Ästhetik zu schaffen, ist zu verneinen" ("Forderungen an eine neue Kritik," *GBA,* 21:331). Later, he shifts his ground. A journal entry for May 1942 characterizes his notes to individual plays as "Bruchstücke einer Ästhetik des Theaters, die nicht geschrieben ist" (*GBA,* 27:94); in "Über experimentelles Theater" he declares his aim to be to explore "die Entwicklung der Krise des Theaters im Bezirk der Ästhetik" (*GBA,* 22:544). This makes it surprising that one of the earliest monographs on Brecht's theoretical writings declares that what Brecht succeeded in producing was not so much an "Ästhetik" as an "Anti-Ästhetik" and that none of his theoretical principles can be interpreted "rein ästhetisch" (Hultberg 1962, 18–19, 187). Hultberg nevertheless goes on to quote Brecht on the goals of his "Ästhetik" (using that very word[11]). Brecht had been cited a few pages earlier defining his conception of Epic Theater as

---

[11] "Über literarische Formen muß man die Realität befragen, nicht die Ästhetik, auch nicht die des Realismus. Die Wahrheit kann auf viele Arten verschwiegen und auf viele Arten gesagt werden. Wir leiten unsere Ästhetik, wie unsere Sittlichkeit, von den Bedürfnissen unseres Kampfes ab" (*GBA,* 22:433). The terms of the reference to "unsere Sittlichkeit" are intended to align Brechtian aesthetics with Lenin's infamous "morality of expediency," as outlined in his October 1920 address to the Third All-Russian Congress of the Komsomol, in particular the declaration (which Brecht knew in German translation): "Unsere Sittlichkeit leiten wir aus den Interessen des proletarischen Klassenkampfes ab. [. . .] Wir glauben an keine ewige Sittlichkeit." (Lenin, "Der 'Radikalismus,' die Kinderkrankheit des Kommunismus," in Lenin, *Sämtliche Werke,* 25 (Vienna-Berlin, 1930), 240. For details, see *GBA,* 3:445–46.

"eine Kategorie des Gesellschaftlichen und nicht des Ästhetisch-Formalen" (Hultberg 1962, 184). But this cautiously formulated disclaimer does not substantiate Hultberg's argument. For it needs to be borne in mind that Brecht uses the noun "Ästhetik" and the adjective "ästhetisch" with two distinct connotations.[12] First, from the 1920s onwards, to refer pejoratively to non-political, "bourgeois" aesthetics: for example, in his attack on "ewige ästhetiche Gesetze" (*GBA*, 22:408) or his rejection of "die herrschende Ästhetik" (*GBA*, 24:128). In respect of this hostile referential sense and here alone, there is some justification in calling Brecht's writings a form of "Anti-Ästhetik." But elsewhere the term is appropriated and used in a different way by Brecht to refer to his own politicized concerns. For this reason, it is crucial to distinguish between occasions when Brecht refers to the narrowly conceived, non-political "bourgeois" aesthetic he never ceased to oppose[13] and when the term refers to his own Marxist position, a form of counter-aesthetic both to the bourgeois variety and also to the aesthetic of Socialist Realism.

The *locus classicus* for Brecht's appropriation of the term "Ästhetik" in respect of his own theoretical writings is the "Vorrede" to *Kleines Organon für das Theater,* a work which will, the reader is promised, offer "Umrisse einer denkbaren Ästhetik" (*GBA*, 23:66):

> In der Folge wird untersucht, wie eine Ästhetik aussähe, bezogen von einer bestimmten Art, Theater zu spielen, die seit einigen Jahrzehnten praktisch entwickelt wird. In den gelegentlichen theoretischen Äußerungen, Ausfällen, technischen Anweisungen, publiziert in der Form von Anmerkungen zu Stücken des Verfassers, wurde das Ästhetische nur beiläufig und verhältnismäßig uninteressiert berührt. [. . .] die Häufung von Neuerungen bei dem Fortfall praktischer Demonstrationsmöglichkeiten in der Nazizeit und im Krieg legen nun den Versuch nahe, diese Spezies Theater auf seine Stellung in der Ästhetik hin zu prüfen oder jedenfalls Umrisse einer denkbaren

---

[12] In the Cologne radio discussion of 1929, Brecht declares: "die ganze Ästhetik [. . .] hilft uns da gar nicht. Wir können mit Hilfe der Ästhetik allein nichts gegen das bestehende Theater ausrichten" (*GBA*, 21:270). In "Primat des Apparates," the reference to "die außerordentliche Verwirrung, in die die bürgerliche Ästhetik geraten ist" (*GBA*, 21:226) is spelled out by reference to such an aesthetic's lack of political value-center: "Wer von unsern nur ästhetisch geschulten Kritikern wäre imstande, zu begreifen, daß die selbstverständliche Praktik der bürgerlichen Kritik, in ästhetischen Fragen in jedem einzigen Fall den Theatern gegen die Produktion Recht zu geben, eine *politische* Ursache hat?" (*GBA*, 21:226).

[13] As his attack on the at the time obligatory "Ästhetik des Realismus" (i.e. Socialist Realism) makes clear, such a prescriptive aesthetic could be construed as being the opposite of an interventionist aesthetic.

Ästhetik für diese Spezies anzudeuten. Es wäre zu schwierig, etwa die Theorie der theatralischen Verfremdung außerhalb einer Ästhetik darzustellen. (*GBA*, 23:65–66)

Although he had set himself the goal of defining the new aesthetic of the Theater of the Scientific Age and presenting Epic Theater as a place of entertainment ("wie es sich in einer Ästhetik gehört" [*GBA*, 23:66]), Brecht still feels no compunction to refrain from referring to the traditional "Ästhetik, das Erbstück einer depravierten und parasitär gewordenen Klasse" (ibid.). In seeking to locate his pragmatic theoretical concerns within a wider aesthetic framework, Brecht was evidently unwilling to abandon such a central traditional concept as "Ästhetik." Instead, he merely attempted to renegotiate it.

A further issue, often prominent in debates about the status and value of Brecht's theoretical utterances, concerns their relationship to his literary works. There is a revealing moment in a radio discussion where, in a response to the remark "Sie haben [. . .] eine ganz bestimmte Theorie entwickelt, Ihre Theorie des epischen Dramas," Brecht replies: "Ja, diese Theorie vom epischen Drama ist allerdings von uns," adding: "Wir haben auch versucht, einige epische Dramen herzustellen" (*GBA*, 21:273). Strangely, perhaps because of the functionalist verb "herstellen," the dramas come across as little more than illustrations of a set of dramaturgical principles. Not surprisingly, few have seen the relationship this way, and neither did Brecht usually. Think of his injunction: "Man darf nicht über den Überbau — die Theorie — herangehen, sondern über die praktische Probenarbeit" (*GBA*, 23:225). According to Volker Klotz: "Brechts Äußerungen sind als sekundär anzusehen gegenüber dem Werk, bedeutungsmäßig wie zeitlich" (Klotz 1957, 131). Brecht himself can at times appear to be adopting a dissenting stance. "In der Praxis," he wrote in 1929, "muß man einen Schritt nach dem andern machen — die Theorie muß den ganzen Marsch enthalten" ("Über Stoffe und Formen," *GBA*, 21:302). But since the specific context makes it clear that "Theorie" refers to "Theatertheorie" and "Praxis" signifies "Theaterpraxis," there is as yet no hint of the more important theory-praxis dimension of a theater of "Veränderung." But when Brecht came to write "Dialektik und Verfremdung" (c. 1938), the dialectical relationship between the two is more authoritatively formulated. Point 9 reads: "*Praktizierbarkeit des Wissens* (Einheit von Theorie und Praxis)" (*GBA*, 22:402).

In the theoretical writings themselves, praxis often clarifies points of principle. For example, we are told that "der zeigende Laughton verschwindet nicht in dem gezeigten Galilei" (*Kleines Organon* §49); and the claim in the "Vorrede" to *Kleines Organon* that the work documents "eine bestimmte Art, Theater zu spielen, die seit einigen Jahrzehnten entwickelt wird" (*GBA*, 23:65) is underwritten by references to sequences in

*Leben des Galilei* (§§49, 63), and, in *Der Messingkauf,* to *Furcht und Elend des III. Reiches, Mutter Courage und ihre Kinder,* and Piscator's theater, all of which lend weight to the general points made. Praxis in this sense legitimizes the theory that illuminates it. In such a dialectical context, the traffic is moving in both directions, though it is worth recalling that for many years the Berliner Ensemble had a "Theorie-Brigade," but not, at least not by name, a "Theorie-Praxis-Brigade."

In a list of common misconceptions about Epic Theater composed in 1937 in response to attacks on him in *Internationale Literatur* and *Das Wort,* Brecht cites two frequently encountered hostile allegations concerning the relationship of his particular theory to praxis:

> 1) Es ist eine ausgeklügelte, abstrakte, intellektualistische Theorie, die nichts mit dem wirklichen Leben zu tun hat. [ . . .]
>
> 2) Man soll nicht Theorie machen, sondern Dramen schreiben. Alles andere ist unmarxistisch (*GBA,* 22:315).

He refutes the first charge by describing his theory as "entstanden in und verbunden mit langjähriger Praxis," which must above all mean "Theaterpraxis," though not exclusively. He then attempts a two-pronged rebuttal. The claim that slogans from his works were used "als headlines politischer Leitartikel" (*GBA,* 22:315), as well as being quoted in famous court cases, and that some plays were banned is meant to give force to the idea that Brecht's work does actually relate to the real world and is not just a matter of "ivory tower" dramaturgical concerns. This is more important to Brecht than the fact that "die Theorie wurde in Universitätsseminaren durchgenommen" (ibid.). The recommendation that one should write plays rather than theory is deflected with the assertion that this represents a "primitive Verwechslung der Begriffe Ideologie und Theorie," a position usually paraded with support from Marx or Engels in passages which, Brecht gleefully observes, are themselves usually of a theoretical nature. Brecht may not have mounted an adequate defense against the attacks in the late 1930s from various intellectuals associated with the Moscow periodical *Das Wort,* but he does effectively bring out the dual relationship between theory and praxis: i.e. between dramatic theory and "Theaterpraxis," as well as between his plays (as part of the superstructure) and praxis.

In his review of Hultberg's *Die ästhetischen Anschauungen Bertolt Brechts,* Grimm set out the orthodox position on the theory-praxis relationship in Brecht's work:

> Theorie und Praxis lassen sich [ . . .] nicht trennen; sie gehören bei Brecht unlösbar zusammen. Das ist nicht nur die Auffassung, zu der jeder unvoreingenommener Betrachter kommen muß, sondern vor allem die Überzeugung des Dichters selbst.[ . . .] Wekwerth [ . . .] überliefert noch eine weitere Bestätigung aus dem Munde Brechts: "Zu

unserer Spielweise gibt es keinen rein theoretischen Zugang" [*GBA*, 25:386]. Der Ton liegt selbstverständlich auf dem "rein," d.h. auf dem In- und Miteinander von Schauspieltheorie und Spielweise. Nicht zufällig ist ja ein gut Teil der theoretischen Schriften als Anmerkungen zu Brechts eigenem Schaffen entstanden. Ebenso bezeichnend dürfte es sein, daß immer wieder (selbst in dem geschlossensten theoretischen Werk, dem *Kleinen Organon*) praktische Beispiele aus den Aufführungen und Stücken zum Vergleich herangezogen werden. (Grimm 1965, 106–7)[14]

In the GDR, a land with a more strongly ideological conception of the theory-praxis relationship, the point was also made that "Brechts literarische, theoretische und theaterpraktische Arbeiten bilden ein Ganzes und sind schwer verständlich, wenn ein Teil davon isoliert betrachtet wird. [. . .] Eine Einzeluntersuchung über die Entwicklung der Brechtschen Theatertheorie wäre demnach ein fragwürdiges Unternehmen" (Hecht 1972, 45). Yet if the theoretical writings and the plays do logically form "ein Ganzes" (and one would not need to invoke dialectics to make a similar point about the work of many other German dramatists), it would still be hermeneutically desirable to look at the parts and gauge how they contribute to the whole. And since no adequately detailed reading of the theory against the background of Brecht's theater practice yet exists, the relationship of the parts to the whole must for that reason remain a contentious issue. The solution to the present impasse is arguably to proceed via an interim series of more modest steps. Thus, given that Brecht's theory does grow out of practical concerns and does include substantial illustration from his own work, this would involve a preliminary close analysis of the theory *in relative isolation*, while acknowledging that this can only be a first stage towards contextualizing dramaturgical theory (about which there is still much to be said) within theater practice (about which a great deal has been written). Subjecting the theory to close scrutiny is not a strategy to be confused with Hultberg's doggedly isolationist approach; after all, Brecht manages to discuss theater as "eingreifendes Denken" with only a limited reference to his own work and explains "Historisierung" more in the context of Shakespeare and Dreiser than with examples from Epic Theater. And in any case, anyone interested enough to want to study Brecht's theory in depth, or read such a study, will have been sent to the theory by the plays, just as Brecht suggested ought to

---

[14] Hultberg is castigated for his belief that theory and praxis can be unproblematically uncoupled from one another in this way, but also for prioritizing theory: "Der Verf. ist [. . .] nicht nur davon überzeugt, daß man bei Brecht dialektisch verfahren und dennoch Theorie und Praxis fein säuberlich trennen könne; er glaubt offensichtlich sogar, die Theorie gehe als Programm dem künstlerischen Schaffen voraus" (Grimm 1965, 90).

be the case. Arguably, Hultberg's radically isolating "semantic" approach has created a climate of unwarranted skepticism about whether the theoretical writings, which were usually published in isolation from the works, could be considered in their own right as important parts of the wider jigsaw puzzle. And the fact that theory and practice (both in the specialized connotation of "Theatertheorie" and "Theaterpraxis" and in the wider political sense suggested by Brecht's reference to "*praktikable Abbilder*") stand in a dialectical relationship to one another does not in any case mean that praxis axiomatically becomes the yardstick of theory or *vice versa*. (In the history of Marxism both positions have been adopted.[15]) Whereas Hultberg on occasion makes theory the arbiter of praxis, many have adopted the contrary position. What is beyond dispute is that, as Grimm pointed out, Brecht's theoretical writings were often produced in connection with specific works and should not be divorced from this context.

The notion of theater as "eingreifendes Denken," associated by Brecht with "der Zweifel an der Diktatur der sozialen Faktoren" (*GBA*, 21:524), offers one important way, not discussed by Hultberg or Grimm, of bridging the gap between theory and praxis in the wider social arena by interpreting them as a dialectical unity of "Begreifen" and "Eingreifen." "Es ist eine Lust unseres Zeitalters," §46 of *Kleines Organon* declares, "alles so zu begreifen, daß wir eingreifen können" (*GBA*, 23:82). "Wir können den andern nur begreifen, wenn wir in ihn eingreifen können. Auch uns selbst können wir nur begreifen, indem wir in uns eingreifen" (*GBA*, 24:182). Similarly, in the "Episches Theater" section of the *Katzgraben* notes, one finds B. echoing Marx's eleventh "Feuerbach-Thesis": "Ich wollte auf das Theater den Satz anwenden, daß es nicht nur darauf ankommt, die Welt zu interpretieren, sondern sie zu verändern" (*GBA*, 23:340). With less overt siting within the Marxist-Leninist tradition of interventionist thinking, Brecht's written contribution to the 1955 Darmstadt colloquium on the question "Kann die heutige Welt durch Theater wiedergegeben werden?" answers with the declaration: "Die heutige Welt ist den heutigen Menschen nur beschreibbar, wenn sie als eine veränderbare Welt beschrieben wird" (*GBA*, 23:340). Just what such a conception of activist-interventionist drama implies has been the subject of much debate and we shall be returning to this contentious issue in a number of the chapters that follow. The point to be stressed here is that the concept of "eingreifendes Denken" is as central to Brecht's theorizing

---

[15] An instructive comparison between the ways in which various radically divergent relationships between theory and praxis are handled in the following works would show that, even during Brecht's lifetime, there was no consensus on the question of primacy: Lukács: *Geschichte und Klassenbewußtsein*; Korsch: *Marxismus und Philosophie*; Kautsky: *Neue Programme*; and Thalheimer, "Über den Stoff der Dialektik," and *Einführung in den dialektischen Materialismus*.

about the theory-praxis aspect of his work as are "Historisierung" and "Dialektik." That he was not invoking the phrase merely to explain the theory-praxis relationship in Epic Theater can be seen from the following remarks from his journal for 1 November 1940 about the relationship between what he liked to call "praktikable Abbilder" and "eingreifendes Denken":

> Diese *praktikablen Abbilder* von Vorgängen unter Menschen, welche das nichtaristotelische Theater liefern will, machen dieses Theater noch nicht zu einem rein utilitären. Beabsichtigt sind nur Abbilder, welche die Welt einem nicht nur betrachtenden, sondern auch praktischen Menschen abbilden, d. h. die Welt wird als änderbare gefaßt. Ein moralischer Imperativ "Ändert sie!" braucht nicht wirksam zu werden. [. . .] Es muß sich natürlich nicht darum handeln, daß jeder Zuschauer eine Patentlösung der Welträtsel ausgehändigt bekommt. Nur als Mitglied der Gesellschaft wird er instand gesetzt zu praktizieren. Und der Begriff *Praxis* bekommt eine ganz neue mächtige Bedeutung. (*GBA*, 26:439)

With the publication of the *Große kommentierte Berliner und Frankfurter Ausgabe*, Brecht scholars now have an indispensable tool at their disposal. The volumes devoted to the theoretical writings bring together some 1700 works, of which only 300 were published in the writer's lifetime. Over 400 items appear here in print for the first time. Yet unfortunately, because of the editorial principles applied to the entire edition, the theory volumes exclude many further relevant remarks to be found in Brecht's published and unpublished correspondence and in his journals. In presenting this material, the editorial team also found itself obliged to compromise between the principle of strict chronological ordering of the theoretical writings of almost four decades and the logistical advantages of separating out utterances relating to specific works by Brecht, including the *Modellbücher*. As a result, what figures in my chapter 1 as Brecht's first major statement on Epic Theater, "Anmerkungen zur Oper *Aufstieg und Fall der Stadt Mahagonny*," comes in the volume of "Texte zu Stücken" (*GBA*, 24:74–84) and not alongside Brecht's other theoretical utterances of the time where it would have helped reinforce the thematic context afforded by such writings as "Dialog über Schauspielkunst" (to which one of Brecht's notes refers the reader), "Sollten wir nicht die Ästhetik liquidieren?," "Die Not des Theaters," "Ist die heutige Bühne überhaupt noch brauchbar?" and "Das Theater und die neue Produktion," all of which contribute to our understanding of the climate in which the *Mahagonny* notes were written. The *GBA* edition is, nevertheless, invaluable for more than the wealth of newly published theoretical writings and drafts it brings together. It also provides copious genetic data, details of later versions and reception, as well as information about Brecht's sources and intertexts. No one concerned with the theory can afford to ignore this mine of new information (now available in a paperback limited special edition), to which the sections of *BHB*, vol. 4 refer exclusively. The present volume lays claim to being the first English-language study of Brecht's dramaturgical and aesthetic writings to have worked with the new edition, albeit selectively and aware that this can only be but the first step. The fact that there is little likelihood of *GBA* appearing in an English translation in the near future means that there will continue to be a specific need for mediation between state-of-the-art information available in the German-speaking world and a continuing reliance on Willett's *Brecht on Theatre* and *The Messingkauf Dialogues*.

One feature of Hultberg's monograph singled out for comment was the very fact that it subjected individual theoretical writings to detailed exegesis: "Es gibt, was Brechts Theorien betrifft, keine andere *explication de texte,* die eingehender Zeugnis um Zeugnis sichtete, prüfte, vergliche" (Grimm 1965, 111). The present study attempts to continue in that tradition of exegetical close reading, a practice more prevalent in the case of theoretical works from earlier centuries, yet one that later ones also require. The difficulty in Brecht's case is the need to take into account not simply single canonical documents, but a vast theoretical *œuvre*. The most detailed examination to date of one specific theoretical work is Steve Giles's *Bertolt Brecht and Critical Theory* (1997). Yet perversely, this admirable combination of meticulous close reading and contextual information concerning *Der Dreigroschenprozeß* demonstrates how difficult it would be to adopt a similar in-depth approach to all of Brecht's theoretical works within the confines of a single volume. (The *GBA* theory volumes number some 3,800 pages, compared with the 290 pages of Willett's *Brecht on Theatre*.) The present solution is to approach the corpus via a series of soundings; "soundings" in two respects. First, soundings will be taken by means of a selective focus on the most influential writings and some that have been unwarrantedly underestimated (including Brecht's dramaturgical poems and his discussions of "Historisierung"). And second, the material in these texts, especially in *Kleines Organon* and *Der Messingkauf*, will be approached by taking further detailed sampling probes, thus enabling focused close readings of chosen passages and arguments while passing over areas where Brecht is once more merely presenting well established points to new readerships. In the first respect, taking strategically planned soundings frees up space for the intellectual and historical contextualization of Brecht's theoretical writings. In the second, subjecting chosen passages to close reading creates the opportunity to explore the stages of Brecht's argument and examine his rhetoric. It also enables us to subject his theoretical ideas to critical scrutiny in the light of later thinking, rather than continuing the longstanding practice of simply saying what Brecht was trying to say.

Some preliminary caveats and statements of intention are called for at the outset. As has just been indicated, my main concern in this study is with Brecht's canonical theoretical writings. In the process of exploring these works, I shall inevitably have recourse to a large number of related essays, journal entries, letters, interviews and notes. However, I shall be little concerned with the literary dogfighting and polemical feuds that were a feature of much of Brecht's life. Brecht's relations with the dominant contemporary Marxist cultural theorist writing in German, Georg Lukács (1885–1971), and in particular feuds with the Bund Proletarisch-Revolutionärer Schriftsteller (BPRS) and later GDR Zhdanovites like Fritz Erpenbeck (who organized the Stanislavsky Conference) and Alexander Abusch, will be no more central to my approach than they were to the theoretical writings themselves. In his main dramaturgical works, Brecht tended to engage more with other writers and theater practitioners like Stanislavsky and Piscator than with entrenched ideological opponents and *Kulturpolitiker*. The Brecht-Lukács relationship and the so-called "Expressionismusdebatte" have in any case been admirably documented and analyzed in recent decades, as has Brecht's part in the often cruder "Formalismus-" and "Realismusdebatten" during the Stalinist phase of the GDR's early history. I therefore propose to touch on them only when they are of direct relevance to Brecht's repositioning of himself *vis-à-vis* Stanislavsky and in connection with the differentiated concept of "Realismus" that cleverly sanctioned the use of "Verfremdung" and other experimental techniques associated with Epic Theater. For different reasons, I am reluctant to enter the minefield surrounding Brecht's early "Lehrstück" theory, partly on the grounds that, as has often been pointed out, it involves reconstructing a putative theoretical position out of a series of inconclusive fragments, but also because others, more convinced of the genre's significance, have already been there in considerable numbers and effectively established the main areas of agreement and debate. Of all Brecht's major concepts, "Gestus" and "das Gestische" will receive less, and more guarded, treatment. These ambiguous and for many unhelpful terms have led to more confusion than explanatory concepts have the right to do. As has been pointed out, "Brecht selbst liefert keine klare Definition wie im Fall der 'Verfremdung'" (Knopf 1980a, 392). In short, the soundings that follow have been decided both on the criterion of each individual theoretical work's status within Brecht-reception and also on my personal evaluation of their importance within Brecht's prolific theorizing.

# 1: Epic Opera and Epic Theater: "Anmerkungen zur Oper *Aufstieg und Fall der Stadt Mahagonny*" (1930)

IN JULY 1939, NOW IN EXILE on the Swedish island of Lidingö, Brecht drafted a letter concerning the hostile reception of his theoretical writings. Addressed to "Genosse M.,"[1] it proposed to offer, "da Sie gerade meine theoretischen Dinge durcharbeiten, einige Bemerkungen, die Ihnen vielleicht Umwege ersparen können":

> Die Ausführungen, die gedruckt vorliegen [. . .], sind als Anmerkungen zu Theateraufführungen und daher mehr oder weniger polemisch geschrieben. Sie enthalten nicht komplette Definitionen und rufen deshalb bei dem sie Studierenden oft Mißverständnisse hervor, die ihn hindern, produktiv theoretisch mitzuarbeiten. Besonders der *Opernaufsatz* zu "Mahagonny" bedarf einiger Zusätze, damit die Diskussion fruchtbar werden kann. Man hat aus ihm herausgelesen, daß ich "gegen das Gefühlsmäßige für das Verstandesmäßige" Stellung nehme. Das ist natürlich nicht der Fall. [. . .] Daß ich mich nur an den Verstand wenden wolle, finden meist die Leute, welche bei meinen Arbeiten nur verstandesmäßig mitkommen (oder jedenfalls glauben, sie kämen mit), gefühlsmäßig aber streiken. [. . .] Ähnlich verhält es sich mit dem Gegensatz, in dem in meinen Ausführungen sich das belehrende Element mit dem unterhaltenden befinden soll. In Wirklichkeit habe ich nicht den geringsten Grund, von einer der beiden Diderotschen die Kunst beherrschenden Konstituanten [*sic*] *Unterhaltung* und *Belehrung* abzugehen.[2] Nur ist, was z.B. das Proletariat belehrt oder was das Proletariat lehrt, für das Bürgertum nicht besonders unterhaltend [. . .]. Ich würde Ihnen all das nicht schreiben,

---

[1] *Schriften* 4 (*GBA*, 24:479) assumes the addressee to be the Danish journalist Fredrik Martner (real name: Knud Rasmussen), whereas *Briefe* 2 (*GBA*, 29:149) proposes Götz Mayer, then working in Parisian exile on a study of Brecht's work. Brecht usually addressed Martner either as "Herr Rasmussen" or by his pseudonym "Crassus." Whoever the intended recipient was, the phrases "Lieber Genosse" and "Mit kameradschaftlichem Gruß" indicate beyond doubt that it was a fellow socialist.

[2] The reference is to Diderot's *Discours sur la poésie dramatique* (1758). Diderot's influence on Brecht, especially on his theory of acting, is treated skeptically in Barthes 1977 and persuasively in Buck 1971.

wenn nicht meine Arbeiten tatsächlich Formulierungen enthielten, die geeignet sind, die Diskussion auf diese Basis zu schieben, wo gar nichts herauskommt. Die Diskussion *Gefühl oder Verstand* verdunkelt nämlich nur die Hauptsache, die sich aus meinen Arbeiten (besser Versuchen) ergibt für die Ästhetik: *daß ein bisher als konstituierend angesehenes Phänomen, die Einfühlung, neuerdings in einigen künstlerischen Werken mehr oder weniger ausgeschaltet wurde.* (Das Gefühl ist damit ja keineswegs ausgeschaltet worden.) (*GBA*, 29:149–50)

Like many of his dramaturgical pronouncements, this letter is something of a damage-limitation exercise. Less characteristically it apportions blame to the author's own infelicitous formulations as well as to his readers' prejudices. Brecht must have been reminded of his own part in such confusions while recently seeing an edition of his work through the press for the Malik Verlag. Added to which, he was probably still smarting from earlier attacks from a number of largely predictable quarters on the Left.[3] Two years before the Lidingö letter, Brecht had drawn up a list of common misconceptions about Epic Theater, accompanied by his latest answer to the question "Was ist episches Theater?" (*GBA*, 22:15–17). Yet as long ago as 1927, he had pointed out that it was not possible to set out the principles of Epic Theater "in wenigen Schlagworten" (*GBA*, 21:210). But that was precisely what he had repeatedly tried to do, above all in the work with which his Lidingö letter is mainly concerned: the "Anmerkungen zur Oper *Aufstieg und Fall der Stadt Mahagonny*" of 1930. Given his desire to set the record straight, one might wonder why the *Mahagonny* notes had ever been allowed to appear in a form liable to give rise to so many misinterpretations. Had serious problems arisen, as the Lidingö letter suggests, because of their aggressively antagonistic style? Or did some unforeseen conflict between manifesto rhetoric and rational exposition account for misunderstandings on the part of foes and sympathizers alike?[4] Had Brecht perhaps misjudged his readership? Such questions remained as pertinent to his reception during the Cold War and beyond as they had been in the Weimar Republic. Years after his death, an

---

[3] Under the pretext of a review of Ernst Ottwalt's novel *Denn sie wissen, was sie tun* (1931), Georg Lukács launched a broadside attack on Brecht's Epic Theater (Lukács 1932). This was followed in the same issue of *Die Linkskurve* by Andor Gábor's equally polemical "Zwei Bühnenereignisse" with its criticisms of the "starre Gegenüberstellung" of Dramatic and Epic Theater in the *Mahagonny* notes "Schema" (Gábor 1932): two attacks in a campaign of vilification, matched only by the viciousness of the "Expressionismusdebatte" towards the end of the 1930s.

[4] Brecht was always refining previous theoretical positions and offering supplementary clarifications. In some contexts, claiming to have been misunderstood and wanting to set the record straight became a favorite rhetorical strategy in order to present a re-invented self. The *Mahagonny* notes appear not to be an example of this ploy.

authoritative verdict on the "Schema" in the *Mahagonny* notes, describing it as rightly famous but all too frequently misunderstood, summed up the predicament (Hecht 1972, 52).[5]

## Matters Editorial

The *Mahagonny* notes stand out from the bulk of Brecht's theoretical utterances dating from the twenties and thirties for a variety of reasons. Unlike most of his theoretical works ("im Gegensatz zu seinen künstlerischen Texten hat [Brecht] seine Schriften kaum überarbeitet" [*BHB*, 4:14]), they had appeared in print soon after completion and were subsequently repeatedly repackaged and recycled. Another rare feature is the fact that the *Versuche* 2 version had Peter Suhrkamp as co-author.[6] Suhrkamp's involvement was not commented on at the time, nor has it been adequately clarified since; but then, the even greater enigma of Kurt Weill's contribution to the notes has not been solved either.[7] During the Hitler years it would have been politic for Suhrkamp to erase all traces of collaboration with such an infamous enemy of the state as Brecht. So the notes became Brecht's alone. Few of his theoretical works can have sailed under so many different colors. They had first been published in late summer 1930, in the recently inaugurated journal *Musik und Gesellschaft*.[8] There

---

[5] *GW* does not include the revised "Schema" in its postwar republication of "Vergnügungstheater oder Lehrtheater?" Of the three versions, only that in *Versuche* 2 is adequately represented in the *GW* edition.

[6] Best known as founder of the postwar Suhrkamp Verlag, Peter Suhrkamp (1891–1959) had been *Dramaturg* and Director of the Landestheater Darmstadt until 1925. He moved to Berlin in 1929. When the table contrasting Dramatic and Epic Theater was reproduced in Arno Schirokauer's *Der Kampf um den Himmel* (Schirokauer 1931, 121), Suhrkamp was for tactical reasons named as sole author, his collaboration with Brecht being played down after Brecht's emigration so as not to jeopardize his position as director of the Fischer Verlag. Suhrkamp was sent to Sachsenhausen concentration camp in April 1944.

[7] Kurt Weill (1900–1950). *BHB* 4:54 refers to "Weill, dessen (indirekter) Beitrag zu den *Anmerkungen* schwer feststellbar und daher umstritten ist, da er sich vermutlich in Gesprächen während der Periode seiner engen, produktiven Kooperation mit Brecht [. . .] herauskristallisierte." Brecht published the *Mahagonny* notes and Weill his "Anmerkungen zu meiner Oper *Mahagonny*" (1930) and the *Vorwort zum Regiebuch der Oper "Aufstieg und Fall der Stadt* Mahagonny*"* (1930), "ohne Mitwirkung des jeweiligen Partners" (Dümling 1985, 223). Brecht's *Mahagonny* notes and Weill's stated position in the above works and in "Über den gestischen Charakter in der Musik" (1929) are briefly examined in *BHB*, 4:54–55.

[8] *Musik und Gesellschaft* 3 (1930), 5–12. Published under the editorship of Hans Boettcher and Fritz Jöde, author of *Musik und Erziehung* (1919), *Musik und Gesell-*

they appeared, in a slightly different form from that which shortly thereafter appeared in *Versuche* 2,[9] as "Zur Soziologie der Oper — Anmerkungen zu *Mahagonny*," the main title being singularly appropriate to the work's first section. The subsequent *Versuche* 2 version was prefaced by the announcement that it offered "eine Untersuchung über die Möglichkeit von Neuerungen in der Oper" (44). The volume's table of contents refers to the notes by the short title "Über die Oper," possibly meaning "On Opera," but this time more probably "On *the* Opera," i.e. Brecht-Weill's *Mahagonny,* the libretto of which precedes the notes in *Versuche* 2. In other words, "Über die Oper" is not a further alternative title, but simply an abbreviated reference. The full *Versuche* title, "Anmerkungen zur Oper *Aufstieg und Fall der Stadt Mahagonny*," eventually found itself demoted to mere subtitle: Unseld's *Schriften zum Theater* anthology (1957) and the seven-volume collection of the same title (1963–64), as well as Willett's *Brecht on Theatre,* all have as their main title "Das moderne Theater ist das epische Theater," a claim taken from the third section of the notes. Yet this upbeat apodictic pronouncement remains something of an anomaly, for at this stage Brecht appears reluctant to use terms like "episches Theater" and "epische Oper" in his titles. In all probability it was his collaborator Elisabeth Hauptmann who added it to posthumous reprintings.

The *Mahagonny* notes eventually acquired a uniquely canonical status, having become one of the staple sources of material for introductions to Brecht, largely thanks to the table contrasting the "*Dramatische Form des Theaters*" with the "*Epische Form,*" a feature which readily lent itself to separate reproduction and was to remain a "fortwährender Stein des Anstoßes" (*BHB,* 4:56) for decades to come. Yet the table's status and value was not helped by its continually shifting contours. In its immediate context, the full "Anmerkungen zur Oper *Aufstieg und Fall der Stadt Mahagonny*," it survives in three versions (*Musik und Gesellschaft, Versuche* 2 and the Malik edition), while the "Schema" of contrasts is itself published in three distinct forms.[10] Those in *Musik und Gesellschaft* and *Versuche* 2 are identical on all

---

*schaft* was to become the leading organ of the "linksbürgerliche Flügel der Schulmusikbewegung" (Voigts 1977, 132). Voigts's account of the movement (131–37) concentrates on its importance for Brecht's *Lehrstücke.* Although it does not indicate that the notes first appeared in *Musik und Gesellschaft,* Voigts's study does help explain why Brecht chose this particular publication to present musicologists with the theory behind *Mahagonny* at the same time as *Versuche* 2 was targeting the literary world.

[9] The differences are documented in *GBA,* 24:476–78.

[10] Brecht republished the *Versuche* 2 "Schema" in *Die Szene* 8 (1931) and in his program notes for the Berlin première of *Die Mutter* (January 1932), as well as in a number of later contexts (detailed in *BHB,* 4:56–57). However, when "The German Drama: Pre-Hitler" was re-issued the following year in the London *Left Review* (10, 504–8), a new footnote was added giving no more than a truncated version.

major points, but thereafter the contents were revised twice. First, for the essay "Vergnügungstheater oder Lehrtheater?" (*GBA*, 22:106–16) and subsequently for the Malik edition, although this is something about which most editions are singularly uninformative.[11]

Despite such a complex pedigree, the persistence with which the *Mahagonny* notes remain associated with the more prestigious of the two 1930 versions is understandable. For generations this had been the most accessible one — available in the *Versuche* series, as well as various postwar editions. It has probably had more impact on people's conceptions of Epic Theater than any other theoretical pronouncement by Brecht; and the vast majority of those conversant with the table will know it from reprintings of the second (*Versuche*) version. This means that an important document on one of Brecht's central concepts has remained stubbornly identified with its earliest articulation; a fact not without problematic repercussions. For particularly in the case of the table of contrasts, it has led to the freezing in time of a progressively evolving conception. *Schriften zum Theater* and *Brecht on Theatre* offer the older (1930) version, whereas *GW* (also referred to as "*WA*" [Werkausgabe]) presents the subsequent (1938) Malik version. Sadly, none of these acknowledges the role played by "Vergnügungstheater oder Lehrtheater?" in bringing about the table's most substantial reformulation. The new edition of Brecht's works departs from the time-honored, though in this case particularly problematic, editorial principle of giving pride of place to the last version approved and published during an author's lifetime ("die Ausgabe letzter Hand"), instead preferring "die Ausgabe früher [albeit not always "frühester"] Hand."[12] The danger in such a situation is that Brecht's revisions are lost sight of and central seminal statements become de-historicized.

---

[11] According to *GW*, "die Anmerkungen erschienen zuerst 1930 im 2. Heft der *Versuche*. Da die Schemata dieser Ausgabe zu Mißverständnissen geführt hatten, *veränderte und ergänzte sie Brecht für den zweiten Druck in der Malik-Ausgabe 1938*" (*GW*, 17:4*, my emphasis). The mistake is repeated in Hecht 1972, 52 and in the relevant secondary literature of the time.

[12] Unseld states "wenn Texte mehrfach veröffentlicht wurden, bezieht sich die Quellenangabe möglichst auf die 'Stücke' und die 'Versuche,' *die am weitesten verbreitet sind*" (*Schriften zum Theater*, 1957, 287, my italics). By contrast, *GW* gives precedence to final versions. The editorial principles underlying the new edition are set out in the *GBA Registerband* (805–10). Having made a case for giving precedence to the "Ausgabe früher Hand," the editors nevertheless add a rider: "Der Vorzug war den Fassungen zu geben, mit denen Brecht an die Öffentlichkeit getreten ist, mit denen er öffentliche Diskussionen ausgelöst und also 'Geschichte' gemacht hat" (807). The question "in welcher Textgestalt [die Werke] Streit oder Zustimmung ausgelöst haben" (806) is, the editors state, intended to establish "die Brechts Werk angemessene Historisierung" (807).

Almost as intriguing as the tenacity with which the 1930 *Mahagonny* notes continue to hold center-stage are the contours of their reception, in particular, the frequency with which his remarks on theatrical innovation have been discussed with little reference to the discursive framework in which they were made. Although reaction to the Brecht-Weill opera was indubitably influenced by Brecht's notes (Voigts 1977, 162), one could scarcely claim that the notes had themselves suffered from being read restrictively with reference to *Mahagonny*. On the contrary, it is as if there had been a conspiracy to assume that Brecht, rather than basing his arguments on this specific opera, chose to operate with an illustrative model that could equally well elucidate the rationale behind *Die Dreigroschenoper, Die Mutter, Die heilige Johanna der Schlachthöfe, Turandot* or even Brecht's entire *œuvre*. The sweeping claim "Das moderne Theater ist das epische Theater" must bear some of the blame. Yet more unfortunate than the problems caused by assuming such imprecise referentiality has been the general reluctance to engage with the notes in their entirety, to subject their arguments to scrutiny or take account of the strategies Brecht uses to put his ideas across.[13] Thanks to the new edition and the impetus provided by *BHB*, vol. 4, now seems an appropriate time to return to Brecht's first major theoretical statement and try to do justice to its content and see it in context.

## On the Sociology of Opera

The title's modest formulation "Anmerkungen zur Oper [. . .]"[14] hardly leads the reader to expect the kind of totalizing theory and macroscopic statements contained in some parts of the *Mahagonny* notes. The alternative titles — "Zur Soziologie der Oper" and "Das moderne Theater ist das epische Theater" — give a very different impression. The *Ur*-title, "Zur Soziologie der Oper," was evidently consonant with the editorial policy of a journal the very name of which (*Musik und Gesellschaft*) proclaimed a broad interdisciplinary remit. It also reflected the first section's concern with the sociopolitical significance of contemporary opera and theater *as institutions*. In fact, the first section's primary task is to diagnose the predicament of opera as a paradigmatic "late capitalist" cultural phenomenon and at the same time assess the specific function of intellectuals and artists in late capitalist Weimar Republic society. Any serious suggestion of a diffident young

[13] Outside the valuable work of Giles 1997, Knopf 2000, Voigts 1977, Willett 1964 and 1965, and *BHB*, vol. 4, approaches to Brecht's theoretical writings have tended to be concept-oriented, rather than viewing the canonical essays as coherent entities in their own right.

[14] "Schon der Titel besagt, dass es nicht um die Grundlegung einer Theorie handelt, sondern um Erläuterungen zur Oper" (Knopf 2000, 78).

Brecht, cautious about engaging in macroscopic pronouncements and large-scale sociopolitical theorizing, is dispelled by such magisterial pronouncements as "Die großen Apparate wie Oper, Schaubühne, Presse usw. setzen ihre Auffassung sozusagen inkognito durch" ( *GBA,* 24:74). Or the verdict on intellectuals operating within such dehumanizing "Apparate" as "mitverdienend" and "ökonomisch betrachtet [. . .] mitherrschende, gesellschaftlich betrachtet schon proletaroide — Kopfarbeiter" ( *GBA,* 24:74). Or the claim that, "in der Meinung, sie seien im Besitz eines Apparates, der in Wirklichkeit sie besitzt, verteidigen sie einen Apparat, über den sie keine Kontrolle mehr haben, der nicht mehr, wie sie noch glauben, Mittel für die Produzenten ist, sondern Mittel gegen die Produzenten wurde" ( *GBA,* 24:75). Any putative rhetoric of self-effacement would seem to be little in evidence in these instances.[15]

The explanatory paradigm underlying Brecht's picture of theater's commodification and its misrepresentation by those involved in it derives from the assumption that the agencies whose attitudes the notes are examining are the victims of what Friedrich Engels referred to as "falsches Bewußtsein" or the Brecht of *Der Messingkauf* would call "die Unwissenheit." The other paradigm informing the first section of the *Mahagonny* notes, that of theater *qua* "Produktion" within a complex system of supply and demand, is presented in an equally apodictic manner. This is the case, for example, with the interconnected claims that "Ihre Produktion [i.e. that of musicians, writers, and critics] gewinnt Lieferantencharakter" and that the result is "allgemein der Usus, jedes Kunstwerk auf seine Eignung für den Apparat, niemals aber den Apparat auf seine Eignung für das Kunstwerk hin zu überprüfen" ( *GBA,* 24:75). This is as totalizing in its ideological scope as one of the key works on which it depended for its methodology: Georg Lukács's *Geschichte und Klassenbewußtsein* (especially the section "Das Problem der Verdinglichung": Lukács 1923, 170–209). No wonder Brecht, who had already declared that the state of affairs he was about to describe had "ungeheure Folgen, die viel zu wenig beachtet werden" ( *GBA,* 24:74–75), felt entitled to charge recent reformers of opera with timidity — timidity of political vision as well as in their compromises with artistic radicalism. (He later refers to "Fortschritte, welche die Folge von nichts sind und nichts zur Folge haben, welche nicht aus neuen Bedürfnissen kommen, sondern nur mit neuen Reizen alte Bedürfnisse befriedigen, also eine rein konservierende

---

[15] The material in this first, "sociological" section of the *Mahagonny* notes was so important to Brecht that he took much of it across, almost verbatim, into "Über die Verwendung von Musik für ein episches Theater" (cf. *GBA,* 22:160–61). As has been pointed out ( *BHB,* 4:50) this section carries the germs of Brecht's "Tui"-critique in *Der Tuiroman* ( *GBA,* 17:9–161), where Stravinsky and Schoenberg are dismissed as "zwei große Musiktuis" ( *GBA,* 17:159).

Aufgabe haben" [*GBA,* 24:82].) As the final section of the *Mahagonny* notes makes clear, any such narrowly "aesthetic" perspective is deemed to be politically myopic, whereas Brecht, in his newfound indebtedness to *Kultursoziologie,* sees himself as scientifically "objective" and immune to "Verdinglichung."

One might well ask why a playwright who had but recently turned to opera[16] and had, even more recently, claimed to have discovered that Karl Marx was his ideal audience,[17] should place such emphasis on the *sociology* of opera. What were the specific connotations of "sociology" for him at this time?

Crucial evidence is to be found in an open letter to a certain "Herr X.," entitled "Sollten wir nicht die Ästhetik liquidieren?" (*GBA* 21:202–4[18]). Published below Brecht's name in the *Berliner Börsen-Courier* of 2 June 1927, this represents part of what the paper billed as "ein polemischer Briefwechsel über das gegenwärtige Drama," with Brecht now replying to the opening salvo of 12 May: Herr X.'s "Brief an einen Dramatiker. Der Niedergang des Dramas." Herr X.'s tactic of addressing an open letter about the parlous state of contemporary drama to a "young" man who persisted in remaining a dramatist was designed to cause maximum personal provocation, given that the two correspondents knew each other's positions extremely well by that time. For as many of the *Börsen-Courier*'s readers would have known, Herr X. was none other than the Marxist sociologist Fritz Sternberg, his "first mentor," as Brecht called him in a 1927 dedication copy of his play *Mann ist Mann* (A Man's a Man). Sternberg was later to participate in the milestone Cologne radio discussion of January 1929 ("[Neue Dramatik]," *GBA,* 21:270–77) which began with Ernst Hardt, *Intendant* of the Westdeutscher Rundfunk, posing the question "Warum Soziologie?" which the orchestrated exchange has Sternberg, Herbert Ihering, and Brecht

---

[16] Evidence has come to light (*GBA Registerband,* 757) of *Mahagonny*'s completion before *Die Dreigroschenoper.*

[17] In "[Der einzige Zuschauer für meine Stücke]," c. 1928, Brecht recalls that when he initially read *Das Kapital* he understood his own work for the first time: "dieser Marx war der einzige Zuschauer für meine Stücke, den ich je gesehen hatte. Denn einen Mann mit solchen Interessen mußten gerade diese Stücke interessieren. Nicht wegen ihrer Intelligenz, sondern wegen der seinigen. Es war Anschauungsmaterial für ihn" (*GBA,* 21:256–57).

[18] Willett renders "liquidieren" with "abolish." However, the presence of this business term in other configurations in Brecht's writing of the period, e.g. "Die Liquidierung der Jungen Bühne" and "Liquidierung darf kein Akt sein" (*GBA,* 21:290–93), suggests that contemporary theater's prospects are assessed very much with an eye to the hard economic facts of life in the late 1920s, even if the vocabulary of the Soviet purges is prefigured in such a metaphor.

endeavoring in their various ways to answer. Many parts of the ensuing discussion offer little more than a reprise of Sternberg's and Brecht's earlier *Berliner Börsen-Courier* exchange, although this time the writing is less polemical and there is more constructive clarification of positions. As planned, Sternberg is allowed in the radio discussion to reiterate the substance of his original letter, with Brecht replying in kind, this time with conclusive support from Ihering. But there is one important difference between the two clashes of minds. Brecht now pegs what had previously been a rather abstract defense of the sociological value of his work on the best of all possible arguments: his *Mann ist Mann*. In similar vein, the *Mahagonny* notes answer Brecht's rhetorical question "Sollten wir nicht die Ästhetik liquidieren?" — albeit somewhat belatedly, but all the more forcefully — by citing Exhibit A for the defense of Epic Theater: his and Weill's *Mahagonny*. He could just as well have cited *Mann ist Mann* and *Die Dreigroschenoper,* because the existence and social critical power of these works meant that liquidation would have to be rejected as an option, as far as Brecht was concerned. Such a context makes it clear why Brecht felt obliged first to question and then defend his own artistic legitimacy, as well as that of his theories intended to legitimize Epic Theater.

Even at the time of the *Börsen-Courier* exchange, Sternberg seemed intent on provoking someone who had regularly attended his Marxist seminars throughout 1927 and whose thinking had been strongly influenced by his own published work on the subject of the relationship between the cultural superstructure and its societal base. A draft note by Brecht, entitled "Soziologische Betrachtungsweise" (c.1928), advocated submitting German theater's current predicament to examination from a sociological point of view (*GBA,* 21:233–34). "Soziologische Betrachtungsweise" reads like a blueprint for the first section of the *Mahagonny* notes. Even as late as 1932, Brecht was still working on a piece entitled "Der soziologische Raum des bürgerlichen Theaters" (*GBA,* 21:557–59)[19] where one can still discern much common ground with Sternberg, even if signs of a widening gulf are beginning to show.[20] The paths of Sternberg and Brecht may have started to

---

[19] The term "soziologischer Raum" is borrowed from the title of chapter 6 of Sternberg's *Der Imperialismus* (1925): "Der soziologische Raum der materialistischen Geschichtsauffassung."

[20] Fritz Sternberg (1895–1963) "Diese Differenz zwischen dem Wissenschaftler Sternberg und dem Künstler Brecht ist, weil sie die erste einer Reihe Begegnungen von Wissenschaft und Kunst war, von großer Bedeutung. Daß Brecht den Standpunkt der Produktion notfalls auch gegen den der wissenschaftlichen Analyse aufrechterhielt, war eine Grundentscheidung, der er Zeit seines Lebens treu blieb" (Voigts 1977, 96). The exchange, as strong echoes of it in the Cologne radio discussion suggest, retained its importance for both participants. Its significance for Brecht

diverge by the late 1920s, with the latter coming progressively under Karl Korsch's influence, but as has frequently been pointed out, Brecht the syncretist did not simply abandon sociological analysis in order to align his conception of "eingreifendes Denken" with Korsch's call for "geistige Aktion."[21] He still took what he needed from Sternberg's methodology and uncompromising diagnosis. Seen in the terms of Marx's eleventh "Feuerbach-Thesis," Sternberg offered tools for its *interpretation,* but since Brecht wanted to *change* society, he needed something more politically interventionist than his mentor's academic sociological approach provided.

The aspect of Sternberg's thinking relevant to the *Mahagonny* notes is its unmitigatedly pessimistic, mechanical determinist diagnosis of the decline of modern drama, a phenomenon interpreted as the "barometer" of the climate of a whole period. Brecht remains suitably impressed by a sociological method that sought to evaluate literature, not by adopting narrow aesthetic criteria, but diagnostically with reference to the society that produced it, a society represented by institutions ("Apparate"), the presence and hold of which both Sternberg and Brecht associated with the marginalization and even "Liquidierung" of the individual.[22] In Brecht's words, "Der Soziologe weiß, daß es Situationen gibt, wo Verbesserungen nichts mehr helfen" (*GBA,* 21:203). He concedes that it may be sociology's "einfache und radikale Funktion" to prove that "dieses Drama keine Existenzberechtigung mehr hat" (*GBA,* 21:202). But he refuses to let the matter rest there — understandably, since in Sternberg's diagnosis "dieses Drama" means *all* drama. In a move calculated to accentuate the incompatibility of their views (but evidently intended to persuade Brecht to abandon his position and return to the purely sociological fold), Sternberg had concluded his open letter with the specific charge already intimated in his title: namely, that Brecht himself, who is assumed for argument's sake to share Sternberg's diagnosis, is at the same time *part of the problem.* He is roundly criticized for failing to draw the obvious conclusion from their shared assessment of the moribund state of modern theater and for his unwillingness "dieses Drama, das nichts *als eine Photographie des Gestern, ein historischer Überrest* ist, zu liquidieren"

---

can be gauged from the fact that he allowed it to be republished in the *Schwäbische Thalia der Stuttgarter Dramaturgischen Blätter* 41 (1927), 325–28 and in the Hamburg journal *Der Freihafen* 3 (1928), 8–11.

[21] Karl Korsch (1886–1961). In the wake of "Bertolt Brechts marxistischer Lehrer" (Rasch 1963), a body of conflicting opinion has grown up on Korsch's importance for Brecht: Brüggemann 1973a and 1973b (76–138); *alternative* 41 (1965); Voigts 1977 (118–22); Knopf 1974 (149–64); and Knopf 1980a (413–15). Although Knopf 1980a (44) differentiates between Korsch's "geistige Aktion" (Korsch 1966, 135) and Brecht's "eingreifendes Denken," this does not necessarily invalidate the former's importance for Brecht's dialectical concept of interventionist thinking.

[22] Cf. Sternberg 1963 (63) and Sternberg 1925 (107).

(*GBA,* 21:675). "Liquidating" drama would, in the *ad hominem* sense intended, have entailed giving up writing plays, as well as all other cultural activity. Brecht was not prepared to accept what Sternberg presented as the next logical step and decamp from drama and aesthetics and pitch his tent on the territory of critical sociology proper. The contrast in the *Börsen-Courier* exchange is therefore between Sternberg the sociologist, laying claim to objective insights, and Brecht the dramatist, by and large agreeing with his diagnosis, but not with his publicly announced remedy.[23] Brecht in fact refuses to draw any conclusions that would have amounted to artistic suicide; more important, he refuses to accept that drama is unable to contribute to radical social change.

The positions expressed here by Sternberg and Brecht supply an important subtext to the *Mahagonny* notes. Brecht continues to align himself with Sternberg's bleak assessment, but when it comes to the challenge to abandon drama and liquidate aesthetics, he draws a line in the sand. In his open letter, Brecht bows dutifully in his mentor's direction with the claim that "keine andere Wissenschaft als die Ihre besitzt genügend Freiheit des Denkens, jede andere ist allzusehr interessiert und beteiligt an der Verewigung des allgemeinen zivilatorischen Niveaus unserer Epoche. [. . .] Der Soziologe ist unser Mann" (*GBA,* 21:202–4). Yet while such a sociological standpoint may be an adequate tool for an assessment of the situation, in Brecht's eyes drama still had not lost "die Verpflichtung und die Möglichkeit, das Theater einem *anderen* Publikum zu erobern. Die neue Produktion, die mehr und mehr das große epische Theater heraufführt, das der soziologischen Situation entspricht, kann zunächst ihrem Inhalt wie ihrer Form nach nur von denjenigen verstanden werden, die diese Situation verstehen" (*GBA,* 21:204). Using a familiar intellectual ju-jitsu move (the metaphor is the playwright's own), Brecht informs his readers that Sternberg had been invited — whether by Brecht himself or by Ihering on behalf of the *Berliner Börsen-Courier* is not said — to present a diagnosis of drama's condition "weil ich von der Soziologie erwartete, daß sie *das heutige Drama* liquidierte."[24] But when Sternberg delivers what he has been asked to deliver,

---

[23] Ironically, Brecht's *Berliner Börsen-Courier* reply lectures Sternberg on ideas Brecht has only recently acquired from him. For example, the suggestion that the sociologist's "Skala [der] Schätzungen liegt nicht zwischen 'gut' und 'schlecht,' sondern zwischen 'richtig' und 'falsch.' Er wird ein Drama, wenn es 'falsch' ist, nicht loben, weil es 'gut' (oder 'schön') ist" (*GBA,* 21:203) is, for example, pure Sternberg.

[24] The unfolding exchange is marred by a number of confusions of expression, for which Brecht is largely responsible. In his original letter, Sternberg advocated the liquidation of "dieses [i.e. contemporary] Drama" (*GBA,* 21:675), yet although the title of Brecht's reply talks about liquidating "die Ästhetik," the target changes to

Brecht adopts an antagonistic counter-position. For Voigts,[25] the fundamental difference between the two is that between cultural analyst and practising artist (1977, 96). While he may well have put his finger on the problem,[26] Sternberg has failed to appreciate that Epic Theater has the panacea. This helps explain Brecht's assertion that the new work being produced "wird die alte Ästhetik nicht befriedigen, sondern sie wird sie vernichten." That is to say, Epic Theater will be unacceptable to bourgeois aesthetics, but it is bourgeois aesthetics itself that will go under in the resultant struggle. Prefigured here are also later ideological differences between the perspectives of East and West German commentators on this transitional phase of Brecht's development.[27]

Rebuilding, as well as demolition, is the task Brecht allots to his and Weill's opera and even to the accompanying notes. The word "liquidation" does not appear in the new context, not even in the early sections where it might have offered a stepping-stone to Brecht's remarks about the state of contemporary opera. Nor is there any explicit reference to Sternberg's particular brand of cultural sociology. The rejection of the title "Zur Soziologie der Oper" for the second (*Versuche*) version can be interpreted as evidence of a widening rift between the two men. Even in *Musik und Gesellschaft*,

---

"das heutige Drama" in the very first sentence. This is followed by an unhelpful proliferation of terms, all presumably intended to echo the noun "die Ästhetik": "der Ästhet," "ästhetischer Reiz," "der ästhetische Standpunkt," and "die alte Ästhetik" (*GBA*, 21:202–4).

[25] Despite this altercation, in 1928 Brecht continued to collaborate with Sternberg and Erwin Piscator (1893–1966) on a project to rework Shakespeare's *Julius Caesar* from a modern sociological point of view ("Das Stück enthielt so vieles, was in eine neue soziologische Konzeption nicht hineinpaßte" [Sternberg 1963, 35]). The collaboration is documented in Claas 1977.

[26] Sternberg had the distinct attraction of applying the sociological approach to theater and hence giving Brecht the opportunity to suggest that his own theoretical writings were beginning to build on current scholarly ideas.

[27] From Hecht's GDR vantage-point, the disagreement is not so much that between a representative of a pessimistically determinist "Soziologismus" and a *practicing writer* for whom Sternberg's thesis of the "Liquidierung des Individuums" need not as a corollary require the liquidation of either all contemporary drama or aesthetics. Rather, it is evidence of Sternberg's and the early Brecht's failure to allow for the "Wechselwirkung" between the subjective factor and social conditions: "es war undialektisch, wenn hier eine Einflußnahme des Menschen auf den Stoff rundweg übersehen wurde" (Hecht 1972, 32). By the time of *Mahagonny*, Brecht is shown to have progressed to a dialectical materialist position. Although Korsch has been airbrushed out of the picture, Hecht nevertheless offers a valuable account of Brecht's development from the vulgar determinist phase of *Mann ist Mann* to the dialectical position on the relationship between the individual and conditions in the *Mahagonny* notes and in his comments on *Die Mutter*.

Brecht may have been using "Soziologie" in his title to signal differences as
well as common ground. Nevertheless, the approach adopted in the first part
of the *Mahagonny* notes still bears traces of Sternberg's methodology, even if
the work ostentatiously begins with the more positive question of whether
and how opera can be revitalized. Only in piecemeal fashion does the connection between the aesthetic question and the underlying sociopolitical
conditions responsible for the current crisis in late capitalism emerge. On
one occasion Brecht does, however, echo his earlier response to Sternberg's
letter:

> Es wird gesagt: dies oder das Werk sei gut; und es wird gemeint, aber
> nicht gesagt: gut für den Apparat. *Dieser Apparat aber ist durch die*
> *bestehende Gesellschaft bestimmt und nimmt nur auf, was ihn in dieser*
> *Gesellschaft hält.* Jede Neuerung, welche die gesellschaftliche Funktion
> des Apparates, nämlich Abendunterhaltung, nicht bedrohte, könnte
> diskutiert werden. Nicht diskutiert werden können solche Neuerungen,
> die auf seinen Funktionswechsel drängten, die den Apparat also anders
> in die Gesellschaft stellen, etwa ihn den Lehranstalten oder den großen
> Publikationsorganen anschließen wollten. *Die Gesellschaft nimmt durch*
> *den Apparat auf, was sie braucht, um sich selbst zu reproduzieren.*
> Durchgehen kann also auch nur eine "Neuerung," welche zur
> Erneuerung, nicht aber Veränderung der bestehenden Gesellschaft
> führt — ob nun diese Gesellschaftsform gut oder schlecht ist. (*GBA*,
> 24:75, my emphasis)

Instead of endorsing Sternberg's sociological judgment that works produced
under such conditions have forfeited their "Existenzberechtigung," Brecht
now puts the counter-case in decidedly interventionist terms: "Der Fehler ist
nur, daß die Apparate heute noch nicht die der Allgemeinheit sind, daß die
Produktionsmittel nicht den Produzierenden gehören, und daß so die Arbeit
Warencharakter bekommt und den allgemeinen Gesetzen einer Ware
unterliegt" (*GBA*, 24:76). The "Dynamitstelle" in this passage (to borrow a
word from Ernst Bloch's *Dreigroschenoper* essay [Bloch 1960, 187]) is the
phrase "noch nicht." In 1930, this marks the key difference between Sternberg's position and Brecht's confidence that change is imminent.

## *"Oper — aber Neuerungen!"*

The first three sections of the *Mahagonny* notes are structured under a series
of interlocking headings:

> (1) *"Oper — aber Neuerungen!"*: making the case for a radical reas-
> sessment of opera as a cultural institution on the basis of a recognition
> of its socioeconomic function within the capitalist system of the Wei-
> mar Republic

(2) *"Oper —"*: a critical exposition of the preponderantly "culinary" nature of opera prior to *Mahagonny*, which is presented as a work exploring the status of opera as an affirmative form of escapist entertainment[28]

(3) *" — aber Neuerungen!"*: a survey of the main forms of innovation in Epic Theater and their political and aesthetic rationale. The structural and ideological innovations described take up the claim in (1) that the only acceptable innovations are those "Neuerungen" leading to a radical change ("Erneuerung") of society.

This triad of interrelated headings is obviously intended to foreground the historical dialectic that has given rise to epic forms of theater and opera. The initial, elliptically phrased heading *"Oper — aber Neuerungen!"* hinges on an apparent contradiction: "yes, keep opera," it seems to be saying, "it does not necessarily have to be 'liquidated' as a socially irrelevant anachronism, but if there is to be a reprieve, and not just a stay of execution, a radical re-think is called for." What began by looking like an unexpected concession on Brecht's part (in the rallying cry *"Oper —"*) is modified by what the following *"aber"* implies: i.e. that it can only be legitimate to retain opera if it is revolutionized. Just what innovations Brecht has in mind are only gradually revealed. In any case, to propose keeping something that can only be preserved after a radical change in character and function is a question-begging stance to adopt. The ensuing paragraph plays with the reader's expectations in further ways.

> Seit einiger Zeit ist man auf eine Erneuerung der Oper aus. Die Oper soll, ohne daß ihr kulinarischer Charakter geändert wird, inhaltlich *aktualisiert* und der Form nach *technifiziert* werden. Da die Oper ihrem Publikum gerade durch ihre Rückständigkeit teuer ist, müßte man auf den Zustrom neuer Schichten mit neuen Appetiten bedacht sein, und man ist es auch: man will *demokratisieren*, natürlich ohne daß der Charakter der Demokratie geändert wird, welcher darin besteht, daß dem "Volk" neue Rechte, aber nicht die Möglichkeit, sie wahrzunehmen, gegeben werden. Letzten Endes ist es dem Kellner gleich, wem serviert wird, es muß nur serviert werden! Es werden also — von den Fortgeschrittensten — Neuerungen verlangt oder verteidigt, die zur Erneuerung der Oper führen sollen — eine prinzipielle Diskussion der Oper (ihrer Funktion!) wird nicht verlangt und würde wohl nicht verteidigt. (*GBA*, 24:74)

---

[28] As the section on the *Mahagonny* notes in the *Brecht Handbuch* demonstrates, Brecht's and Weill's diagnoses of the contemporary malaise in opera have been seen as by and large accurate (*BHB*, 4:52–53).

Partly because of the programmatic section-title, the reader is initially expected to assume that Brecht wishes to associate his and Weill's collaborative work with various modish attempts to update opera. As the first paragraph implies, the issue was very much in the air at the time. In October 1927, the *Blätter der Staatsoper* (Berlin) organized an opinion poll on the theme "Wie denken Sie über die zeitgenössische Weiterentwicklung der Oper?" In February 1929, the *Berliner Börsen-Courier* had published "Über die Erneuerung der Oper," a topic to which *Das Kunstblatt* also devoted an entire number that same year. In such a climate of profound self-questioning, it was inevitable that certain figures on the contemporary musical scene would be perceived as part of a concerted project of renewal.[29] These ultra avant-garde experimenters must, in the public perception, have represented the sort of cultural developments that formed the context for *Mahagonny*.[30] Indeed, the impersonal subject "man" of Brecht's first sentence appears to include himself, Suhrkamp, and Weill in the project. What follows, however, disabuses us of any such assumption. At the time, the musical scene might well have been awash with modishly avant-garde works, its cultural organs and the feuilleton press buzzing with controversies and debates about the critical state of opera and theater, but for Brecht any such sense of progress remained illusory. The end of the essay's first paragraph is so formulated as to make Brecht seem like a lone voice in a deceptively avant-garde wilderness, isolated because of his call for a fundamental discussion of first principles. But even this is only part of the unfolding picture. As soon becomes clear, the only justifiable form of debate about opera is the currently unavailable one addressing the need for a fundamental "Funktionswechsel." The main thrust of the *Mahagonny* notes is summed up in two sentences: one in the first section and the other right at the end of the last

---

[29] These included Ernst Krenek with his topical *Zwingburg* (1925) and the jazz-inspired *Jonny spielt auf* (1926); Darius Milhaud and Egon Wellesz, whose *L'Enlèvement de l'Europe* had shared the Baden-Baden stage with Brecht-Weill's original *Mahagonny Songspiel* in 1927, a year that had also witnessed the premières of George Antheil's *Flight* and Stravinsky's *Oedipus Rex*, as well as Ernst Toch's experimental *Die Prinzessin auf der Erbse* (after Hans Christian Andersen), also performed at the Baden-Baden music festival. Max Brand's *Maschinist Hopkins* (1929) and Paul Hindemith's *Neues vom Tage* date from the same year. In a later comment, Brecht records his judgment that "Hindemith und Strawinsky [scheiterten] unvermeidlich am Opernapparat" (*GBA*, 22:160). For a fuller picture of the musical context, see *BHB*, 4:54–55.

[30] The references to "Lokomotiven, Maschinenhallen, Aeroplane, Badezimmer usw.," as well as to *Gebrauchsmusik* and the fact that "die Besseren verneinen den Inhalt überhaupt und tragen ihn in lateinischer Sprache vor oder vielmehr weg" (*GBA*, 24:82), allude, respectively, to works by Krenek, Brand, Antheil, Hindemith, and Stravinsky.

one. The first declares that the means of production are *not yet* in the right hands (*GBA*, 24:76). In the German original, the other reads: "Wirkliche Neuerungen greifen die Basis an" (*GBA*, 24:84), translated in Willett, presumably in an effort to attenuate the Marxist jargon, with a horticultural metaphor: "Real innovations attack the roots" (*BT*, 41). Yet as Brecht puts it more explicitly elsewhere: "Der Schrei nach einem neuen Theater ist der Schrei nach einer neuen Gesellschaftsordnung" (*GBA*, 21:238). Which is why he thought of *Die Maßnahme* as "Theater der Zukunft" in more than the simple sense that it was technically radical Epic Theater. In democratizing the theater as an institution, that work also prefigured a new form of egalitarian society (see Steinweg 1972, 196). But an attack on the "base" (as opposed to tinkering with the "superstructure") would hardly be achieved via *discussion* alone, even if discussion of the correct political kind would serve to clarify the need for intervention on a revolutionary scale.

Clearly what we have here is hardly the argument of someone still strongly influenced by Sternberg's sociological approach. Brecht is now explicitly availing himself of a more dialectical interpretive model. Its gradual establishment is the principal purpose of the first part of the *Mahagonny* notes. If genuine innovations attack the base, then the representatives of the avant-garde associated with the fashionable experiments of the time must be seen as little more than part of a pseudo-radical cultural epiphenomenon. This accounts for the sarcasm of the first paragraph's reference, using the superlative, to the would-be *dernier-cri* avant-garde ("die Fortgeschrittensten"), which becomes a rhetorical refrain in the following paragraphs: "Diese Bescheidenheit in den Forderungen der Fortgeschrittensten hat wirtschaftliche Gründe, die ihnen selbst teilweise unbekannt sind" (*GBA*, 24:74), "die Fortgeschrittensten denken nicht daran, den Apparat zu ändern" (*GBA*, 24:75). Having dissociated himself from such an avant-garde as categorically as he is about to hive off Epic Theater from its dramatic predecessors and contemporary rivals, Brecht effectively prepares the ground for interventionist innovation: in the shape of *Mahagonny* itself as well as on the theoretical front. For the terms in which Brecht-Weill's opera is discussed at the end of the *Mahagonny* notes apply just as much to the function of the accompanying notes: "es stellt eben das Kulinarische zur Diskussion, es greift die Gesellschaft an, die solche Opern benötigt; sozusagen sitzt es noch prächtig auf dem alten Ast, aber es sägt ihn wenigstens [. . .] ein wenig an" (*GBA*, 24:84).

The presentational technique used in the first section of the notes is all too familiar from Brecht's plays. First, we are tricked by a caption into a misguided assumption, only to be forced to abandon such a naive misreading in the light of textual counter-evidence. The third caption's afterthought "— *aber Neuerungen!*" (the mock-enthusiastic exclamation-mark no doubt there to alert us to the fact) is a trap. Innovation that fails to attack the base does little to countermand the present "culinary" nature of the medium.

To help anchor the main argument, various terms of contrast are introduced. The word "Neuerung" (coupled with the promise of social "Erneuerung") leads on to a distinction between acceptable and mere palliative ("culinary") innovations, well reflected in the way Willett's translation plays "innovation" off against mere "rejuvenation" and "renovation" (*BT*, 34, 41). Those who are deluded enough to think they possess the apparatus are in turn shown to be possessed *by it*. Whether a work is "gut" or "schlecht" is superseded by the question of whether the society that produced it is "gut" or "schlecht." Even the automatic assumption that the artist's current dependence on the apparatus must be a bad thing is brought into question: "An sich aber ist die Einschränkung der freien Erfindung des einzelnen ein fortschrittlicher Prozeß. Der einzelne wird mehr und mehr in große, die Welt verändernde Vorgänge einbezogen. Er kann nicht mehr sich lediglich 'ausdrücken.' Er wird angehalten und instand gesetzt, allgemeine Aufgaben zu lösen" (*GBA*, 24:76).

Culinary imagery plays a major role in the unfolding argument. The apparatus appropriates the "Kopfarbeit" of artists (seen as "Kopfarbeiter") in order to serve it up "zur Speisung[31] ihrer Publikumsorganisationen"; hence, what is required is audiences "mit neuen Appetiten" (*GBA*, 24:74), whereas the current apparatus merely puts on the table ("serviert") what artists have created to cater for undemanding palates (*GBA*, 24:75). In the case of the superficially avant-garde innovations Brecht treats with cynicism in both the first and last sections of the *Mahagonny* notes, we are assured that "der Kulinarismus war gerettet!" (*GBA*, 24:83). But this is no more than polemical sarcasm, for the implication is that society itself has not been saved. The initial antithesis "kulinarisch"/ "fortgeschritten" is now unmasked as a false dichotomy, for one of the argument's main tactics involves insinuating that even avant-garde artists can be culinary without being aware of the fact. It is essentially in the light of this extended metaphor's socioeconomic associations that we are expected to understand the repeated claims about the "culinary" nature of most opera. If deployed in isolation, such an image would give rise to a series of banal associations concerning pleasure and consumer-values. Hence, while the metaphor might be unobjectionable, it would remain tired and lacking in subtlety. Audiences, would be the implication, have "appetites" which operas (or plays) obligingly satisfy. This is the rather predictable way the subject of appetites is treated at the beginning of "Soll-

---

[31] Willett's pejorative "to make *fodder* for their public entertainment *machine*" (*BT*, 34, my emphasis) palpably misses Brecht's register. The German term "Speisung" is distinctly refined and helps continue the all too vivid metaphor of the (working-class) waiter serving food to an affluent diner.

ten wir nicht die Ästhetik liquidieren?" (*GBA*, 21:203) and in section 3 of "Kleines Privatissimum für meinen Freund Max Gorelik" (*GBA*, 23:37). Such an indiscriminate use amounts to little more than a modish variation on Marx's image of religion as "das Opium des Volkes" (in *Zur Kritik der Hegelschen Rechtsphilosophie*).[32] However, at this stage of the argument, Brecht inserts — between the charge that opera has hitherto been culinary and the above passage on such opera as a gratification of unworthy appetites — the claim that opera was "ein Genußmittel, lange bevor sie eine Ware war" (*GBA*, 24:76). As a consequence, the attack becomes less purely aesthetic (art as gratification) than sociopolitical (gratification as commodity).[33] This neat twist justifies the earlier focus on the attitude of waiter, not diner (to the meal or to the restaurant) or on that of the chef (to the recipes). It also throws light on why Brecht later turned his attention to another middleman in the complicated chain of commercialized artistic supply and demand: the "culinary critic." In a radio discussion of 15 April 1928, Brecht dismisses this figure as "der auf ästhetische Reize aller Art fliegende Genußmensch" (*GBA*, 21:232). The main target is Brecht's arch-enemy Alfred Kerr,[34] who, as Hecht has observed, is being patronizingly treated as a *type*, not that this prevents the polemic from being intensely personal. Kerr had in fact been one of the participants in the Cologne radio discussion, although he was allowed to play little more than the role of whipping boy. Yet the ease with which Brecht moves from the idea of culinary opera and culinary drama to

---

[32] E.g. the references to bourgeois culture's "Rauschgifthandel" (*GBA*, 22:162 and 164) and in the Preface to *Kleines Organon* (*GBA*, 23:65), where theater is charged with having degenerated into a branch of the bourgeois narcotics industry.

[33] In Voigts's reading (1977), "[die] Differenzierung von 'kulinarischem Genuß' und 'Appetit' zeigt, wie wichtig für Brecht der Kampf gegen die Ersatz-Funktion des Theaters war. Während der 'Appetit' allgemein mit der Aufstiegsphase des Kapitalismus assoziiert wird, ist der Kulinarismus Ergebnis des Niedergangs: 'Hier wird längst nicht mehr produziert, hier wird lediglich verbraucht, genossen und verteidigt.'" Hence: "Der Genuß erscheint nur in seiner zum 'Kulinarismus' verzerrten bürgerlichen Form als Ware und als Erholung" (85, 160).

[34] Cf. "Die dialektische Dramatik," an unsparing diatribe against the dyed-in-the-wool bourgeois culinary critic Alfred Kerr (*GBA*, 21:434–35) and Brecht's occasional pieces against Kerr in the same volume (323–25). In "Gespräch über Klassiker" "culinary thinking" is also discussed: "Das Bürgertum mußte seine rein geistigen Bemühungen so ziemlich liquidieren in einer Zeit, wo die Lust am Denken eine direkte Gefährdung seiner wirtschaftlichen Interessen bedeuten konnte. Wo das Denken nicht ganz eingestellt wurde, wurde es immer kulinarischer. Man machte zwar Gebrauch von den Klassikern, aber nur mehr kulinarischen Gebrauch" (*GBA*, 21:310). Audiences of the bourgeois theater of entertainment receive a similar broadside: "Die Zuschauer genießen den Menschenschmerz rein als Amüsement, sie haben eine rein kulinarische Auffassung" (*GBA*, 21:229).

the less predictable subject of the culinary critic reveals the extent to which he sees the latter, not as an independent arbiter, but very much as part of the cultural apparatus. "*Bloße Agenten der Theater*" had been Brecht's verdict on critics two years before the *Mahagonny* notes (*GBA*, 21:236). It is this part of the notes that is as indebted to the Lukács of *Geschichte und Klassenbewußtsein* as to Sternberg's influence.

The culinary metaphor of the waiter for whom it is all the same which customer he waits on, as long as he gets paid for performing his job, is satirically focused on the superficial, avant-garde innovators who come in for a further drubbing in the final section, not the more obvious targets — the purveyors of sentimental dramas, kitsch operettas or Wagnerian *Gesamtkunstwerke,* about whose irrelevance both Brecht and his readers are assumed to be in agreement. ("Saustück" had been his term of abuse for one such work in 1922.[35]) The further metaphorical linking of innovation with a process of democratization is to be understood as deliberately subversive, given that we are still in the world of what Brecht saw as the Weimar Republic's pseudo-liberties. For this reason, the notion of giving the people new rights, but no chance to exercise them, leaves opera on one side in order to launch an attack on the base. As all this shows, the first section's title is now less innocent than it was on an initial reading.

Despite Brecht's resorting in parts of the notes to the discourse of Marxist analysis (opera as "Ware," attacking "die Basis,"[36] and the controlling of works' reception as a form of manipulative "Bewußtseinsindustrie"), his most extended metaphor, that of "Kulinarismus," is less obviously part of a recently acquired Marxist model. And it tends to work via a cumulative process of satirical reduction and thus becomes, in this respect, interventionist rather than merely analytical. A related point is made elsewhere in the notes, not through abstract theorizing but by reference to *Mahagonny* itself, an operatic work whose subject matter Brecht once summed up as being "der Kulinarismus" (*GBA*, 22:159). The passage this time literally involves

---

[35] In Brecht's review of the Augsburg première of W. Meyer-Förster's *Alt-Heidelberg,* in *Der Volkswille,* 15 October 1920 (*GBA*, 21:77). As a result, he was banned from attending any performance of Albert Lortzing's *Zar und Zimmermann* for reviewing purposes.

[36] Like many of the points in the *Mahagonny* notes, this model (generally indebted to Marx's "Der achtzehnte Brumaire des Louis Bonaparte" [Marx-Engels 1958–68, vol.8 (1960), 111–94], and Georg Lukács's *Geschichte und Klassenbewußtsein*) had already appeared in an earlier form that was not as well worked out. Brecht had referred to theater, literature and art as the "ideologischer Überbau" as early as November 1927 ("[Schwierigkeiten des epischen Theaters]," *GBA*, 21:210). He also uses both "Basis" and "Unterbau" (sic) in "[Basis der Kunst]" c. 1930 (*GBA*, 21:375–76).

eating. Having reminded readers that *Mahagonny*'s content is pleasure, the notes underline the political implications of this by considering the potential impact of one particular episode in the work:

> Es soll nicht geleugnet werden, daß dieser Inhalt [der Genuß] zunächst provokatorisch wirken muß. Wenn zum Beispiel im dreizehnten Abschnitt der Vielfraß sich zu Tode frißt, so tut er dies, weil Hunger herrscht. Obgleich wir nicht einmal andeuten, daß andere hungerten, während dieser fraß, war die Wirkung dennoch provozierend. Denn wenn nicht jeder am Fressen stirbt, der zu fressen hat, so gibt es doch viele, die am Hunger sterben, weil er am Fressen stirbt. Sein Genuß provoziert, weil er so vieles enthält. In ähnlichen Zusammenhängen wirkt heute Oper als Genußmittel überhaupt provokatorisch. Freilich nicht auf ihre paar Zuhörer. Im Provokatorischen sehen wir die Realität wiederhergestellt. "Mahagonny" mag nicht sehr schmackhaft sein, es mag sogar (aus schlechtem Gewissen) seinen Ehrgeiz darein setzen, es nicht zu sein — es ist durch und durch kulinarisch. "Mahagonny" ist nichts anderes als eine Oper. (*GBA*, 24:77–78)

Mahagonny, the "Paradiesstadt" where appetites are satisfied, is often, as Knopf has complained, interpreted as a "Spiegelbild der kapitalistischen Welt."[37] Brecht is even reported to have told an American interviewer that *Mahagonny* was "set in an imaginary Florida" (Schevill 1961, 103). But as Knopf points out, such sloppy associations fail to do justice to the fact that Mahagonny was founded as a reaction against capitalism and the great cities (Knopf 2000, 105). The lure of consumables (whisky, food, adventure, women) is the main reason why the "Goldstadt" becomes a mecca for "DIE UNZUFRIEDENEN ALLER KONTINENTE," as the caption to scene 4 puts it. Yet even at plot-level, such indulgence has its dark side, as the image of the man dying of over-consumption shows.

The main significance of this episode for the *Mahagonny* notes exceeds mere plot-function. Brecht's concern is primarily with the requisite audience-response, one that would eventually be called dialectical, although for the time being he prefers to talk of "Provokation." What is said has meta-textual significance. The man depicted indulging in an act of gross self-gratification is watched by people observing the spectacle from the auditorium and meant to recognize an analogy to their own behavior as spectators of a calculatedly "culinary" performance. Consequently, as the commentary suggests, they are provoked into stepping out of their role as "culinary" spectators when, and because, they find the episode disturbing. That is to say, when they have realized that others must starve so that he can indulge himself, just as they are indulging in escapist enjoyment while what *Die*

---

[37] The phrase was originally Klaus Völker's (Völker and Pullem 1985, 112).

*Dreigroschenoper* calls "die im Dunkel" struggle to survive. As Brecht puts it in his most memorable formulation of the predicament in "An die Nachgeborenen" (*GBA*, 12:85):

> Man sagt mir: iß und trink du! Sei froh, daß du hast!
> Aber wie kann ich essen und trinken, wenn
> Ich es dem Hungernden entreiße, was ich esse, und
> Mein Glas Wasser einem Verdurstenden fehlt?

Rather than merely caricaturing capitalism, the city Mahagonny — like opera itself, or, more specifically, like the opera of that name — represents a surrogate world (a "Gegengründung"). But much more even than the fictive town, *Mahagonny* at the same time forces people to reflect on their behavior both in and outside the theater: "Selbst wenn man die Oper als solche (ihre Funktion!) zur Diskussion stellen wollte," the end of the first section of the notes declares, "müßte man eine Oper machen" (*GBA*, 24:76). That is: an opera designed, by *displaying* pronounced "culinary" features rather than *being* culinary, to engender discomfort and insight, not an uncritically escapist opera. Under such circumstances, audiences are forced to bring the real world into the picture, not exclude it as the notes claim most opera does. "Im Provokatorischen sehen wir die Realität wiederhergestellt."[38]

The words "kulinarisch" and "Kulinarismus" do not appear in the following section, although it hardly requires a great leap of the imagination to realize that what Brecht calls the "Dramatische Form des Theaters" has boundless culinary potential. The reason for such a lack of terminological continuity (at the same time as the section titles engage in an ongoing dialogue with one another) is that the *Mahagonny* notes are structured according to the selfsame "epic" principle of relative autonomy of parts that the third section will shortly elucidate. The sections looked at so far form part of a deliberately segmented structure, the first, largely on a Marxist sociology of opera, being followed by an aesthetically oriented analysis of the "culinary" nature of the medium and thus its affirmative function, then intercut by what looks to all intents and purposes like an excursus on the relationship between Epic and Dramatic Theater. Brecht does admittedly provide an explicit rationale for this last thematic shift, even if it hardly helps distract our attention from the fact that the new section differs radically from the preceding argument. Opera, "— *aber Neuerungen!*" announces, "war auf den

---

[38] Brüggemann 1973, 156–57, posits a relationship between montage and "Verfremdung" in which the formal elements of montage ("Distanz, Unterbrechung, Umfunktionierung") obey a defamiliarizing principle according to which they transcend theater's autonomy and separation from everyday life. This feature is prefigured in Brecht's remarks about scene 13 of *Mahagonny*.

technischen Standard des modernen Theaters zu bringen" (*GBA*, 24:78). To give substance to this declaration, Brecht explains just what kind of technical standard is meant. But to do so by no means "harmonizes" (in his pejorative sense) the relationship between the previous section and the material to come. On the contrary, the sudden shift of focus from opera to theater creates a disjunctive effect comparable to the one §74 of the *Kleines Organon* refers to as an act of "gegenseitige Verfremdung." From the point when the title of the notes became "Das moderne Theater ist das epische Theater," the discussion of opera was estranged by being approached via theater, with theater itself being estranged by having been placed within a context stressing the extreme "Kulinarismus" of opera. In embryonic form, we are exposed to the same processes of montage, reciprocal estrangement, and "Episierung" that characterize Epic Theater. Indeed, the section titles in these notes function in much the same way as Brecht's prefaces to the individual scenes of works of Epic Theater. (Perhaps this is one reason why the reader is referred by a footnote to the section on "*Titel und Tafeln*" in Brecht's notes to *Die Dreigroschenoper*.[39]) The section headings employed in the *Mahagonny* notes are not scholarly headings, with the task of structuring a complex argument. They primarily represent challenges to the reader; and in doing so they create space for critical reflection. The word "Neuerungen" used in two of the early section titles is clearly inserted to be deconstructed, to make some of its connotations appear questionable, and thus prepare the ground for a substantially more radical interpretation of what might constitute genuine innovation. The combination of italics and exclamation mark in the first heading, the way the second and third play with isolated parts of the first, and the use of a reporting (epic) preterite in a sub-section title within the third section ("*Musik, Wort und Bild mußten mehr Selbständigkeit erhalten*"[40]), all involve a dialectical play with expectations (not least because of the political metaphor of autonomy). They keep us on our toes in a way that

---

[39] "Literarisierung des Theaters" was written before the *Mahagonny* notes, and appeared in the *Programmblätter der Volksbühne* for the Berlin première of *Die Dreigroschenoper* in September 1928. The *Mahagonny* notes were written almost two years later.

[40] In Willett, the sentence loses much of its epic quality by being transposed into the present tense: "*Words, music and setting must become more independent of one another*" (*BT*, 38). In the new edition (*GBA*, 24:79), the following sub-subtitle — "*a) Musik*" — is indented to align it with the above sentence, which, since they are both italicized and there is no line-space between them, makes them together form part of a further sub-segmentalization of the argument.

has more in common with the techniques of Epic Theater than with the scholarly conventions of the time.[41]

One reason for such a strategy was hinted at in my earlier reference to "falsches Bewußtsein." By this I mean that a recurrent Brechtian method of combating the ideological inertia that false consciousness induces entails the creation of critical distance through carefully planted "epicizing" elements, some of which had already been identified in Brecht's notes to *Die Dreigroschenoper*. There are "Titel" in both the operas *Mahagonny* and *Die Dreigroschenoper* and in the notes to them, although "Tafeln" can hardly figure in a published work of theory. And in the *Mahagonny* notes as well as in many of Brecht's other theoretical works, techniques of framing can be seen as logical corollaries of his suggestion that "auch in die Dramatik ist die Fußnote und das vergleichende Blättern einzuführen" (*GBA*, 24:59). Methods of distancing that work in the theater can be equally effective in theoretical texts. After all, Brecht never tired of repeating his claim that the kind of defamiliarization he sought to achieve onstage was a phenomenon common in other walks of everyday life (witness "Die Straßenszene"[42]).

Immediately preceding his two-column table contrasting Dramatic and Epic Forms of Theater, Brecht inserts the most important footnote he ever wrote: "Dieses Schema zeigt nicht absolute Gegensätze, sondern lediglich Akzentverschiebungen. So kann innerhalb eines Mitteilungsvorgangs das gefühlsmäßig Suggestive oder das rein rationell Überredende bevorzugt werden" (*GBA*, 24:78). So anxious is Brecht to ensure that his readers realize that the table's task is to make visual not absolute antitheses but merely shifts in emphasis, that he rounds off the "Schema" with another footnote using the same metaphor: "Über die Gewichtsverschiebungen innerhalb der Darstellung siehe Versuch 'Dialog über Schauspielkunst'" (*GBA*, 24:79).[43] And, when presenting a second table contrasting Dramatic and Epic Opera, he reiterates the image ("für die Musik ergab sich folgende

---

[41] Giles 1997 adopts a similarly Brechtian "Gestus": individual "section headings [being] inspired by [Brecht's] conversations on Kafka with Walter Benjamin in 1931 and 1934" (33). Such headings as "Vor dem Gesetz," "Der Verschollene," "Der Prozeß," "Das Urteil," "Eine alltägliche Verwirrung," "Ein Bericht für eine Akademie," "Beschreibung eines Kampfes," "Zur Frage der Gesetze," and "Gib's auf!" are related to stages of the *Dreigroschenprozeß*.

[42] "Die Straßenszene. *Grundmodell einer Szene des epischen Theaters (1940)*" (*GBA*, 22:370–81).

[43] Although this note is deleted in the Malik edition, presumably because the final "Gefühl"/"Ratio" contrast has been removed, it arguably refers to the entire table, not just to its final contrast. More intriguingly, it is also missing from Unseld's *Schriften zum Theater* (*GW*, vol. 17) and *Brecht on Theatre*, although these reinstate the final contrast.

Gewichtsverschiebung" [*GBA*, 24:79]). To appreciate the strategy employed, it is necessary to bear in mind that the *Mahagonny* notes are something of a rarity among Brecht's theoretical writings because of both the frequency with which they resort to footnotes and the function that most of the notes serve. *Der Messingkauf*, more than fifteen times longer, has only five footnotes, *Kleines Organon* only one. Without exception, these all serve the conventional function of indicating a source. But when a source is signalled in the *Mahagonny* notes, for example in the perhaps surprising reference in note 10 to Freud's *Das Unbehagen in der Kultur* (*GBA*, 24:83), the argument is taken off in a substantially new unexplored direction and the failure of that footnote to indicate whether we are being offered a quotation from, or a paraphrase of, Freud means that readers will have to go and find out for themselves. (Which is what the editors of the new edition had to do before they could report that Brecht was quoting in abbreviated form from the 1930 Vienna edition of the work [*GBA*, 24:481].) The *Mahagonny* notes were not only the first of Brecht's theoretical writings to make intelligent use of an epicizing footnote strategy, they were also one of the last.[44]

Using a footnote to forewarn readers not to expect the "Schema" to offer a simple set of absolute antitheses would under some circumstances simply have been a prudent preemptive move on Brecht's part (which might have been the case, had not the footnote's caveat been so stubbornly ignored in the coming years). Yet although it contains an important rider, Brecht's note still appears to be disturbingly at odds with the rigorous contrast implied by the column-headings *"Dramatische Form des Theaters"* and *"Epische Form."* As has been suggested, "zur Verkennung von [Brechts] intendierter Schwerpunktsverlagerung mag der beim Lesen entstehende optische Eindruck der schlagwortartigen Gegenüberstellung zweier Formen des Theaters beigetragen haben" (*BHB*, 4:51). Although it has the appearance of a late caveat added to subsequent reprintings to fend off certain forms of misinterpretation, it was in fact already there in the *Musik und Gesellschaft* version. So we are left with a conundrum: why does Brecht use misleading absolutizing presentational strategies, if, as he claims, he is only concerned with shifts of accent? An alternative formulation such as "Die dramatische Tendenz im Theater" and "Die epische Tendenz" or recourse

---

[44] There are two major exceptions: the *Antigonemodell 1948* (where the notes are of a conventional scholarly kind) and some of Brecht's theoretical writings that appear not to have been written for immediate publication (e.g. "Über neue Musik" [*GBA*, 21:402–4], "Über den Erkennungsvorgang" [*GBA*, 22:410–12], and "Einige Gedanken zur Stanislawski-Konferenz" [*GBA*, 23:236–39].) Here the uncommon phenemenon of a writer adding footnotes to penned draft material can best be accounted for by assuming that they function primarily as *aides-mémoire*.

to the term "Element" might arguably have saved him a number of later difficulties. But this is to miss the point. The goal of such disjunction is primarily "epic" distancing. To be told in a footnote what the scheme *does not* show is on a par with Brecht's term "nicht-aristotelisches Theater." Making readers work *ex negativo* towards insights demands the kind of "productivity" that Brecht the dramatist expects of his theater audiences.[45] And in a more modest way, so too does the footnote appearing at the end of the "Schema" that refers us to "Dialog über Schauspielkunst." We are being invited to engage in the sort of intertextual "vergleichendes Blättern" invoked in the "Literarisierung des Theaters" section of the notes to *Die Dreigroschenoper*. At issue in this case is not the need to keep emotion at bay (feelings hardly represent a danger to someone consulting a table of contrasts in some notes on (an) opera). Rather, the purpose is to encourage what the sentence following immediately on from the one about footnotes in "Titel und Tafeln" refers to as "komplexes Sehen" (*GBA*, 24:59). Complex seeing, even if it is not yet necessarily synonymous with a dialectical response, is far removed from unthinkingly approaching theatrical developments in terms of simple antitheses. Like Epic Theater itself, the theorizing of Epic Theater evidently required new techniques of discursive presentation to facilitate the right kind of response.

## Scheming Brecht

Brecht's table contrasting Dramatic and Epic Theater has probably been reproduced more often than any of his other theoretical utterances. Reproduced, that is, but seldom subjected to detailed exegesis, the honorable exceptions being Hultberg 1962 and Hecht 1972. Brecht's "Schema" (*GBA*, 24:78–79) is reproduced below, with numbers added to the pairs of contrasting points, for the convenience of operating with the same reference-system as Hultberg uses.

---

[45] In *Kleines Organon* §23, Brecht speaks of "ein Theater, das die Produktivität zur Hauptquelle der Unterhaltung macht" (*GBA*, 23:74). The kind of productivity he has in mind is explained in "Die dialektische Dramatik" (written in the same year as the *Mahagonny* notes): "[Der moderne Zuschauer] wünscht nicht, bevormundet und vergewaltigt zu werden, sondern er will einfach menschliches Material vorgeworfen bekommen, *um es selber zu ordnen*. [. . .] er ist nicht nur mehr Konsument, sondern er muß produzieren" (*GBA*, 21:440–41).

| | Dramatische Form des Theaters | Epische Form des Theaters |
|---|---|---|
| (1) | handelnd | erzählend |
| (2) | verwickelt den Zuschauer in eine Bühnenaktion | macht den Zuschauer zum Betrachter, aber |
| (3) | verbraucht seine Aktivität | weckt seine Aktivität |
| (4) | ermöglicht ihm Gefühle | erzwingt von ihm Entscheidungen |
| (5) | Erlebnis | Weltbild |
| (6) | Der Zuschauer wird in etwas hineinversetzt | er wird gegenübergesetzt |
| (7) | Suggestion | Argument |
| (8) | Die Empfindungen werden konserviert | bis zu Erkenntnissen getrieben |
| (9) | Der Zuschauer steht mittendrin, miterlebt | Der Zuschauer steht gegenüber, studiert |
| (10) | Der Mensch als bekannt vorausgesetzt | Der Mensch ist Gegenstand der Untersuchung |
| (11) | Der unveränderliche Mensch | Der veränderliche und verändernde Mensch |
| (12) | Spannung auf den Ausgang | Spannung auf den Gang |
| (13) | Eine Szene für die andere | Jede Szene für sich |
| (14) | Wachstum | Montage |
| (15) | Geschehen linear | in Kurven |
| (16) | evolutionäre Zwangsläufigkeit | Sprünge |
| (17) | Der Mensch als Fixum | Der Mensch als Prozeß |
| (18) | Das Denken bestimmt das Sein | Das gesellschaftliche Sein bestimmt das Denken |
| (19) | Gefühl | Ratio |

Hultberg's commentary, the first of its kind, sets out to demonstrate that "dieses Schema ist nicht sonderlich klar":

> Mehrere Punkte scheinen überflüssig zu sein. So ist es schwer, zu sehen, daß 17 mehr sagt, als schon unter 11 gesagt ist; 2, 6 und 9 könnten auch unter einem Punkt zusammengefaßt werden, während dafür 4 und 19 widersprechend zu sein scheinen. (Entscheidungen und Ratio, die das epische Theater im Gegensatz zu dem Gefühl des dramatischen Theaters kennzeichnen sollen, sind zwar nicht Gegensätze, aber jedenfalls in keiner Weise identisch). Ferner ist es auch nicht klar, inwieweit die einzelnen Punkte auseinander folgen, oder ob sie ganz unabhängig voneinander sind, so daß man von einigen

von ihnen absehen könnte. Daß das Bild, das Brecht vom "dramatischen Theater" zeichnet, [. . .] überaus irreführend ist, bedarf keines näheren Nachweises; interessanter ist die Verwirrung, die das Bild des epischen Theaters prägt. Der entscheidende Punkt ist wohl *18*, der deutlich Brechts deterministische, vulgärmarxistische Haltung zeigt. Falls dieser Punkt absolut gesetzt wird, ist ein eigentlich didaktisches Theater ja unmöglich. In dem Falle hat der Zuschauer nur die Möglichkeit, die Welt zu studieren (*9*), eventuell zu gewissen Erkenntnissen zu gelangen (*8*), aber wirkliche Entscheidungen (*4*), eine echte Aktivität (*3*) kann im Theater nicht erreicht werden. Wenn das Bewußtsein des Menschen ausschließlich von den sozialen Verhältnissen geformt wird, so ist das Theater eine Belustigung ganz ohne Bedeutung wie z .B. Sportkämpfe, was Brecht bisher ja auch behauptet hat. (Hultberg 1962, 107)

Hultberg concludes: "Das *Mahagonny*-Schema ist der Versuch eines Kompromisses zwischen der alten und der neueren Auffassung, zwischen dem Sporttheater und dem Schultheater, und es ist daher höchst mißlich, daß es meist in kürzeren Darstellungen benutzt wird, um zu zeigen, was Brecht eigentlich mit seinem Theater wollte" (ibid.). Because of the seriousness of the points raised here, I should like to examine them in detail.

First, there is the damaging assertion that certain items are superfluous: that 17 says little more than had already been said in 11 and that 2, 6 and 9 could have profitably been conflated. Brecht could well have sensed a certain lack of economy in the 1930 version, for when he revised it for inclusion in "Vergnügungstheater oder Lehrtheater?" he removed some of the redundant elements that Hultberg was still complaining about some quarter of a century later.[46] Yet none of these changes takes account of the main problems Hultberg was to have with the "Schema." To explain why, we need to distinguish between a *vertical* reading of the material and a *horizontal* one.

In the case of at least one pair of contrasts, syntax clearly forces us to read from the left-hand column across to the directly opposite equivalent on the right-hand side: "Die Empfindungen werden konserviert / bis zu Erkenntnissen getrieben." In the second, less frequently quoted "Schema" contrasting Dramatic and Epic *Opera* (*GBA*, 24:80), the same shared subject

---

[46] Hultberg cannot have known this since *GW*, vol. 15 omits the "Schema," indicating the omission with ellipsis dots, and wrongly stating that they refer to "das Schema, das Brecht in der ersten Ausgabe der *Versuche*, H. 2, 1930, in den 'Anmerkungen zur Oper *Aufstieg und Fall der Stadt Mahagonny*' veröffentlichte" (Anmerkungen, 9*). The subsequent statement is equally misleading: "Da Brecht dieses Schema später in der Form für unzureichend hielt und für den zweiten Druck der Anmerkungen in der Malik-Ausgabe, 1938, redigierte und ergänzte, wurde der Text hier ausgelassen und auf das gültige Schema verwiesen" (ibid.).

again results in a situation where the reader can only make sense of the points by reading horizontally across from individual items in the left-hand column to their adjacant equivalents:

| | |
|---|---|
| Musik illustrierend | Stellung nehmend |
| Musik die psychische Situation malend | das Verhalten gebend (*GBA*, 24:80) |

But even where our reading is not a matter of being carried across by the syntax, entry by entry, from the left-hand column to the right-hand one, the horizontal paradigm (as in 6, 10, and 13 in the first "Schema") still tends to predominate:

| | |
|---|---|
| Der Zuschauer wird in etwas hineinversetzt | er wird gegenübergesetzt |
| Der Mensch als bekannt vorausgesetzt | Der Mensch ist Gegenstand der Untersuchung |
| Eine Szene für die andere | Jede Szene für sich |

Only once does a grammatical pointer invite the reader to drop directly down to the next entry *in the same column,* viz. at the end of 2, when the "aber" identifies an apparent contradiction between the passivity of "macht den Zuschauer zum Betrachter" and "weckt seine Aktivität." This pairing involves issues vital to an understanding of Brecht's conception of Epic Theater, hence the anomalous feature is best regarded as a pattern-breaking "Verfremdungseffekt."

Many of Hultberg's quibbles and objections remain explicable only when read as part of a *vertical* reading of the right-hand column, even though, from its two polarizing headings onwards, Brecht's actual "Schema" invites us to engage with the material by traversing from a characteristic in the left-hand column to its equivalent on the right. (Even the footnote denying absolute antitheses is predicated on the same linear paradigm.) Only someone bent on a vertical reading would have a modicum of justification in claiming "es [ist] schwer, zu sehen, daß *17* mehr sagt, als schon unter *11* gesagt ist." True, "Der unveränderliche Mensch" may on a cursory reading mean the same as "Der Mensch als Fixum," but as so often with this table of paired terms, it is what the characteristic in the one column is being set against that obviates any crude exercise in tautology. Brecht obviously refuses to pair "Der unveränderliche Mensch" with the predictable "Der veränderliche Mensch." Instead, he juxtaposes it with "Der veränderliche und verändernde Mensch." And since "verändernd" has no object, it remains for the reader to decide whether this means capable of altering himself or herself or possibly refers to "das gesellschaftliche Sein" mentioned in 18. This contrast's field of meaning is therefore not slavishly duplicated in 17. In any case, the German word in the left-hand column ("Fixum") is in a register significantly more technical — more scientific, even — than the phrase "fixed entity" offered in Willett's English translation. And that it has a technical quality is understandable, given that the new concept has the task of preparing for an ideological contrast between idealist and materialist conceptions of reality, one which certainly refers to the notion of changing social conditions and not just individual human beings, once the context is supplied by the Foreword to Marx's *Politische Ökonomie*.[47] Hultberg also worries about the fact that "Entscheidungen" (4) and "Ratio" (19), while being "zwar nicht Gegensätze," are "in keiner Weise identisch." But this merely raises the question of just what relationship is assumed to be the operative one. The "ermöglicht ihm Gefühle" and the single noun "Gefühl" of the left-hand column may appear synonymous, if one does not look too closely, but as Hultberg notes, the relationship between a theater leading to "Entscheidungen" and a theater of "Ratio" is a more complex one.

As the points looked at so far suggest, there is more than one way to respond to the *Mahagonny* "Schema." It can be read as proof of Brecht's incompetence when it comes to presenting important material in diagrammatic form (the breast-beating in his letter to "Genosse M." might seem like an invitation to view it thus). An alternative would be to treat it as part of an argument deliberately constructed according to a less discursive principle.[48] Hultberg unwittingly hints at what that principle might be when he complains: "es [ist] auch nicht klar, inwieweit die einzelnen Punkte auseinander folgen, oder ob sie ganz unabhängig voneinander sind, so daß man von einigen von ihnen absehen könnte" (Hultberg 1962, 107). Now this sounds very reminiscent of Point 13's contrast between the situation in the "*Dramatische Form des Theaters*" ("Eine Szene für die andere") and that in the "*Epische Form*" ("Jede Szene für sich"). One of the repercussions of Epic Theater's relative autonomy of parts is that some points could be either replaced or omitted, as in Willett's 1959 account, where only eight of the

---

[47] *GBA*, 24:479 cites Engels's — Friedrich Engels (1820–1895) — *Ludwig Feuerbach und der Ausgang der klassischen deutschen Philosophie* (Vienna-Berlin, 1927, 27–28) as source, no doubt because Brecht's "Nachlassbibliothek" contains a copy. But Engels's discussion of the relationship between "Denken" and "Sein" is not being quoted; the Foreword to the *Politische Ökonomie* is. Brecht could, however, have just as well made the point using Marx's and Engels's *Die Deutsche Ideologie*.

[48] In her discussion of analogous examples of seeming inconsistency in the various parts of *Kleines Organon*, Ana Kugli reminds her readers that "Unstimmigkeiten sind von der Forschung selten als eigene Qualität gewürdigt, vielmehr als eindeutige Unzulänglichkeit [. . .] herausgestellt worden, ohne dass dabei die [Brechtsche] Methodik reflektiert worden wäre" (*BHB*, 4:321). On this phenomenon, see also Kobel 1992.

"Schema"'s nineteen points are offered, or in the case of the *Left Review*'s new note to its reprint of "The German Drama: Pre-Hitler," where, again, only a small selection is offered. Compare this feature with two remarks Brecht made elsewhere about Epic Theater: "Eine gewisse Austauschbarkeit der Vorkommnisse und Umstände muß dem Zuschauer das Montieren, Experimentieren und Abstrahieren gestatten" (*GBA*, 24:182); and in the specific case of *Die Maßnahme*, "ganze Szenen können eingefügt werden" (*GBA*, 22:351). My working hypothesis in what follows is that Brecht's "Schema," like the *Mahagonny* notes in their entirety, displays features best understood as "epic." It is time to leave Hultberg on one side and look at this feature of the way the "Schema" is structured.

One salient characteristic is a visual rhythm whereby juxtaposed phrases of varying length are repeatedly punctuated in the two columns by single pairs of antithetical characteristics: "handelnd" / "erzählend," "Erlebnis" / "Weltbild," "Suggestion" / "Argument," "Wachstum" / "Montage." These (usually nominal) pairings have tended to become the main bones of contention in the table's reception. Apart from the fact that they are not invariably absolute antitheses, their reception has shown that Brecht's various contrasts are not always as lucid or without need of clarification as their reduction to single nouns might imply. The terms in the right-hand column identifying characteristics of Brechtian Epic Theater have been especially susceptible to divergent readings and in some instances possess a more specific connotation than might at first appear to be the case. Some are also more elevated (or more technical) in register than the English equivalents usually offered for them. Thus, for example, the contrast between "Suggestion" and "Argument" (in 7) acquires a far more specific referential framework once one realizes that in German "Suggestion" tends to occur in depth-psychological contexts. In "Dialog über Schauspielkunst" (which a footnote advises readers to consult), Brecht criticizes conventional empathic acting. Thespians of the old school, he complains, achieve their effects: "mit Zuhilfenahme der Suggestion. Sie versetzen sich selber und das Publikum in Trance. [. . .] Sie haben etwa den Abschied darzustellen. Was machen sie? Sie versetzen sich in Abschiedsstimmung. Sie wollen, daß das Publikum in Abschiedsstimmung gerät. Niemand sieht zuletzt, wenn die Séance glückt, mehr etwas, niemand lernt etwas kennen, im besten Fall erinnert sich jedermann, kurz: jedermann fühlt" (*GBA*, 21:280). The appearence here of the term "Suggestion" in close proximity to the words "Trance" and "Séance" establishes a connection between identificatory acting and hypnotism. The *Mahagonny* notes go on to declare: "alles, was Hypnotisierversuche darstellen soll, unwürdige Räusche erzeugen muß, benebelt, muß aufgegeben werden" (*GBA*, 24:79). In the revised version of the "Schema" from 1935 "Suggestion" has been expanded to: "Es wird mit Suggestion gearbeitet" (*GBA*, 22:109), yet it is unlikely that Brecht's readers, especially non-German ones, will perceive that this statement is intended to take up the earlier reference to "Suggestion" in the "Schema." The metaphor of hypnosis has taken over from the culinary as the main weapon in Brecht's polemical arsenal by this stage of the argument, and this long before Brecht has encountered the classic embodiment of such an approach: in the American reception of the Stanislavsky-System.

Other nouns in the German original possess different nuances or are in a different register to their standard English translations. "Montage" might seem to be the only technical loan-word in the "Schema" accurately reflected by its English equivalent, yet even it proves to be a false friend. Its primary association in German is with mechanical engineering rather than the dizzy heights of Dada and Surrealism. In *Mann ist Mann,* Galy Gay's transformation into a human fighting-machine is expressed using this connotation: "Hier wird heute abend ein Mensch wie ein Auto ummontiert" (*GBA*, 2:123), i.e. as if he were a piece of machinery which could be taken to pieces and re-functionalized, to become a "Kampfmaschine." Brecht reinforced the mechanical association in his notes to the play (*GBA*, 2:157); the idea is echoed in Hecht's account of the link between montage and alterability: "Die Veränderungen wurden in der ersten Fassung des Schemas noch als 'Montage'-Akte gesehen (in der Art, wie die Soldaten beispielsweise Galy Gay 'ummontierten')" (Hecht 1972, 53). Brecht in due course went on to use the cognate verb "einmontieren" to refer more specifically to a structural principle in Epic Theater. In "Über experimentelles Theater" (1939), he establishes a parallel between the insertion of didactic elements into a work and the technique of montage: "Die belehrenden Elemente in einer Piscator- oder einer 'Dreigroschenoper'-Aufführung waren sozusagen *einmontiert;* sie ergaben sich nicht organisch aus dem Ganzen, sie standen in einem Gegensatz zum Ganzen" (*GBA,* 22:546). The *Mahagonny* table's juxtaposition of "Wachstum" with "Montage" is replicated in the above observation, although the material inserted is now specifically defined as didactic. (Elsewhere Brecht speaks of the music and song being montage components.) Brüggemann (see note 38) relates the montage principle to the insertion of elements *from the real world* into an epic structure. Despite these highly specific interpretations, it is also possible to read "montage" as denoting, not the intercalating of some circumscribed category of material, but possessing an over-arching epic macro-structure. Indeed, the table's contrast between organic growth and montage would appear to indicate that it is primarily at such a level of generality that the term is meant to be understood. Immediate context in the "Schema" offers further support for such an assumption, for the contrast in 14 is sandwiched between a series of attempts at summing up differences between Epic Theater and Dramatic Theater in unambiguously structural terms:

| Eine Szene für die andere | Jede Szene für sich |
|---|---|
| [14]------------------------------------------------- | |
| Geschehen linear | in Kurven |
| evolutionäre Zwangsläufigkeit | Sprünge |

It is particularly this part of the "Schema" that invites the conclusion that Brecht's conception of Epic Theater is to some considerable extent a structural one, standing in a prestigious German cultural tradition of contrasting the epic and the dramatic.

Consider, for example, the following extracts from the correspondence between Goethe and Schiller in April 1797 and their similarity to Brecht's account of the differences between Epic and Dramatic Theater:

> daß sie [die poetische Fabel meines *Wallensteins*] ein stetiges Ganzes ist, daß alles durchgängig bestimmt ist (Schiller, 18 April).

> daß die Selbständigkeit seiner Teile einen Hauptcharakter des epischen Gedichtes ausmacht (Schiller, 21 April).

> daß man von einem guten [epischen] Gedicht den Ausgang wissen könne, ja wissen müsse, und daß eigentlich das *Wie* bloß das Interesse machen dürfe. Dadurch erhält die Neugierde gar keinen Anteil an einem solchen Werke und sein Zweck kann [. . .] in jedem Punkte seiner Bewegung liegen (Goethe, 22 April).

> [der tragische Dichter] steht unter der Kategorie der Kausalität, der Epiker unter der der Substantialität (Schiller, 25 April).

> das epische Gedicht [soll] keine Einheit haben (Goethe, 28 April).[49]

---

[49] *Briefwechsel zwischen Goethe und Schiller in den Jahren 1794 bis 1805.* In fact, Brecht makes repeated references to the correspondence during 1948, the year of his work on both *Kleines Organon* and the *Antigonemodell*. A note in *GBA*, 25:512 states that in the period leading up to the *Antigone* production in Chur that year, Brecht had been led by Lukács's 1934 essay "Der Briefwechsel zwischen Schiller und Goethe" to engage in a protracted study of the correspondence. However, the journal entry for 8 January 1948 (*GBA*, 27:263) to the effect that it is the first time that he has been struck by the way Goethe and Schiller handle their public implies that he had lived with the material for some considerable time before that. Similarly, the way the argument in "Vergnügungstheater oder Lehrtheater?" moves rapidly from the examples cited by Goethe and Schiller to a consideration of developments in the nineteenth-century bourgeois novel suggests that he was already familiar with Lukács's essay within a year of its first appearence, though whether he had read the actual correspondence by then seems more doubtful. There is no evidence that he had read Goethe's and Schiller's "Über epische und dramatische Dichtung," although Lukács emphasizes its importance.

Here is Brecht on the same subject in "Vergügnungstheater oder Lehr-theater?":

> Der Unterschied zwischen der dramatischen und der epischen Form wurde schon nach Aristoteles in der verschiedenen Bauart erblickt, deren Gesetze in zwei verschiedenen Zweigen der Ästhetik behandelt wurden. Diese Bauart hing von der verschiedenen Art ab, in der die Werke dem Publikum angeboten wurden, einmal durch die Bühne, einmal durch das Buch [. . .]. Der bürgerliche Roman entwickelte im vorigen Jahrhundert ziemlich viel "Dramatisches," und man verstand darunter *die starke Zentralisation einer Fabel, ein Moment des Aufeinandergewiesenseins der einzelnen Teile.* Eine gewisse Leidenschaftlichkeit des Vortrags, ein Herausarbeiten des Aufeinanderprallens der Kräfte kennzeichnete das "Dramatische." Der deutsche Epiker Döblin gab ein vorzügliches Kennzeichen, als er sagte, Epik könne man im Gegensatz zu Dramatik sozusagen mit der Schere in einzelne Stücke schneiden, welche durchaus lebensfähig bleiben. [. . .] [Die] Umwelt war natürlich auch im bisherigen Drama gezeigt worden, jedoch nicht als selbständiges Element, sondern nur von der Mittelpunktsfigur des Dramas aus. [. . .] Im epischen Theater sollte sie selbständig in Erscheinung treten. (*GBA*, 22:107–8; my emphasis)[50]

The idea is taken up and again modified a few years later in *Der Messingkauf*:

> Bei der aristotelischen Stückkomposition und der dazugehörigen Spielweise [. . .] wird die Täuschung des Zuschauers über die Art und Weise, wie die Vorgänge auf der Bühne sich im wirklichen Leben abspielen und dort zustande kommen, dadurch gefördert, daß der Vortrag der Fabel ein absolutes Ganzes bildet. Die Details können nicht einzeln mit ihren korrespondierenden Teilen im wirklichen Leben konfrontiert werden. Man darf nichts "aus dem Zusammen-hang reißen," um es etwa in den Zusammenhang der Wirklichkeit zu bringen. Das wird durch die verfremdende Spielweise abgestellt. *Die Fortführung der Fabel ist hier diskontinuierlich, das einheitliche Ganze besteht aus selbständigen Teilen,* die jeweils sofort mit den korrespondierenden Teilvorgängen in der Wirklichkeit konfrontiert werden können, ja müssen. Ständig zieht diese Spielweise alle Kraft aus dem Vergleich mit der Wirklichkeit, d.h. sie lenkt das Auge ständig auf die Kausalität der abgebildeten Vorgänge. (*GBA*, 22:701, my emphasis)

---

[50] "Bemerkungen zum Roman" (originally published in *Die Neue Rundschau*, March 1917), quoted here from Döblin 1963, 21. Brecht spares his more squeamish readers the fact that Döblin's metaphor concerns the cutting-up of a live "Regenwurm."

It is only at the point where the above observation shades into a consideration of epic montage's fragmentary referentiality that it departs radically from the contrasts Goethe and Schiller make. In doing so it picks up the traces of an idea that had already been present in the passage in the *Mahagonny* notes about the man gorging himself to death in scene 13.

One could sum up by concluding that in the 1930s one of the main characteristics of Brechtian Epic Theater was a particular discontinuous kind of (montage) structure and that his theorizing on the subject builds on ideas in Goethe's and Schiller's correspondence, even if the question of generic characteristics has now become politicized and more specifically related to twentieth-century concepts of "montage" in both engineering and the visual arts. But if, as some other parts of the table suggest, all Brecht means by "Episches Theater" is a theater of critical distance, then another area of unclarity still remains, for at times the table refers to means and at times to ends. Of course, there is no reason why it has to focus exclusively on just the one or the other. Indeed, such shifting between the two may be a further strategy intended to provoke the reader into a "productive" engagement with the material.

It was not until the late 1940s that Brecht returned to his earlier points about epic characteristics, now providing an account of them with reference to the Goethe-Schiller correspondence. In a journal entry for 3 January 1948, he notes:

> *Schiller* sieht erstaunlich deutlich die Dialektik (widersprüchliche Verknüpfung) in dem Verhältnis *Epos — Drama*. Meine eigenen Hinweise, das epische Theater betreffend, sind oft mißverständlich, da sie kritisch oppositioneller Natur sind und sich voll gegen das Dramatische meiner Zeit richten, das künstlich undialektisch gehandhabt wird. In der Tat soll einfach das epische Element in die dramatische Dichtart wieder hingebracht werden, freilich widersprüchlich. Die Freiheit der Kalkulation muß eben "in dem mitreißenden Strom" der Geschehnisse etabliert werden. (*GBA*, 27:260–61)

Surprisingly, this, like the reference to the Goethe-Schiller *Briefwechsel* in §50 of *Kleines Organon* (*GBA*, 23:84), shows total disregard for the structural issues touched on at the stage of the exchange that appears to have been so important to him in the early 1930s. Conceivably, Brecht was already moving towards his later stated position that a concern with epic *structure* was too formalist (*GBA*, 23:386) and that, as Lukács had shown, one needed to progress beyond an obsession with discontinuity and the relative autonomy of parts to a dialectical conception of the material's relationship to the world depicted. This will later be summed up in §67 of *Kleines Organon*, where the gaps between the individual components of an epic structure are said to allow the audience "mit dem Urteil dazwischen [zu] kommen" (*GBA*, 23:92). The archetype of a "non-epic" play as a monolithic whole to which all of its parts cumulatively contribute is based on an anachronistic image of structure-as-growth derived from botany and probably being used here for satirical effect.[51] Whether Brecht's unnamed target was the Wagnerian *Gesamtkunstwerk*,[52] Max Reinhardt's theater, or the "well-made" drama of the late nineteenth century, none of these is predicated on the metaphor of structure-as-growth offered as the contrast to epic structure.

One further, related feature of the *Mahagonny* "Schema" demands caution. When Brecht contrasts the "*Dramatische Form des Theaters*" with the "*Epische Form des Theaters*," the word "Form" probably means no more than "type" or "embodiment. The two headings do not necessarily imply that the contrasts are primarily between what in other contexts would be referred to as "tectonic" and "atectonic" or "closed" and "open" forms of drama. The structural debate did not end with Brecht's theory of Epic Theater and it was often conducted in equally antithetical terms. Certain items in the "Schema" are very close to what Volker Klotz has to say about the teleological "Zielstrebigkeit" of the "closed" — Aristotelian — form of drama or Emil Staiger's observations on the epic work's "Funktionalisierung der Teile."[53]

One element closely related to the issue of different kinds of structure, the initial contrast between the dramatic form of theater ("handelnd") and the epic form ("erzählend"), has itself proved open to a variety of readings. Although often translated into English by the nearest available nouns — cf. Willett's "plot" and "narrative" (*BT*, 37) — the German words are gerundival and would be more accurately rendered by some such formulation as "consisting of action" and "telling a story" (though this would go against the economy of the way the initial contrast is expressed). But it is not at the grammatical level that the principal difficulty lies. It may be self-evident that

[51] See Salm 1971 for a survey of the genesis and implications of this botanical metaphor. "Man sollte sich hüten," Brecht wrote at the time of work on the *Katzgraben* production, "in alten Bildern zu denken. Die Vorstellung von der Blüte ist einseitig. Den Wert, die Bestimmung der Kraft und der Größe darf man nicht an die idyllische Vorstellung des organischen Blühens fesseln" (*GBA*, 27:322–23).

[52] "Sein Angriff auf das Gesamtkunstwerk beruhte wahrscheinlich weniger auf genauer Kenntnis der programmatischen Schriften Richard Wagners wie *Oper und Drama* von 1851 [. . .] als auf seiner Kenntnis des Theaters und der Aufführungspraxis. [. . .] In der kurzen tabellarischen Gegenüberstellung [. . .] kam Wagner zweifellos als Hauptrepräsentant der ersteren Form in Betracht" (*BHB*, 4:52).

[53] Klotz 1968, 33; Staiger 1968, 168. Fundamental objections to the uncritical way in which Staiger derives abstract qualititative nouns (e.g. "das Epische") from genre-concepts such as "Epik" have been made in Ellis and Mowatt 1965.

Dramatic Theater consists of a "Handlung" made up of a plethora of actions and hence that it is logical to associate the theater of dramatic suspense with dramatic action. The gerundival form has been chosen to create such intertwined associations. While not commenting specifically on the *Mahagonny* notes, David Midgley's account of Brecht's innovations explains that Epic Theater chose "to adopt an approach which was 'epic' in the sense of *telling* audiences about the world in which they were living."[54] Such an explanation remains at a high level of generality; that is to say, entire epic plays are assumed to consist of single stories or parables that communicate political truths about the nature of society or demonstrate kinds of behavior. From *Die Maßnahme* to *Der kaukasische Kreidekreis,* Brecht's approach could be thought of as being parabolically "narrative" in this wide sense. But a work like *Die Maßnahme* also narrates in another, more specific respect, one that the Goethe-Schiller *Briefwechsel* identifies as a key difference between the epic and the dramatic: "Daß der Epiker seine Begebenheit als vollkommen vergangen, der Tragiker die seinige als vollkommen gegenwärtig zu behandeln habe" (Schiller to Goethe, 26 December 1797). With this temporal distinction in mind, one can see that individual scenes or local elements in Brecht's works stand out as being particularly epic, in the sense of narrating something as *completely past.* This is sometimes the method of entire plays (*Die Maßnahme* or *Die Ausnahme und die Regel*) or merely parts of works (scenes 2–5 of *Der kaukasische Kreidekreis* or the point in scene 10 of *Die Mutter* where Pelagea Wlassowa learns how her son Pawel died). What is more, "erzählend" is an epithet that could also be applied to many of the devices that Brecht was to treat as part of the "Literarisierung" of theater: for example, the use of captions, choruses, prologues and epilogues, reports, resumés, predictions, action-replays, and analyses. In "Vergnügungstheater oder Lehrtheater?" the section *"Die Bühne begann zu erzählen"* (*GBA,* 22:108) illustrates just how many ways there are for non-verbal forms of "Erzählen" to be achieved via stage props, décor, sound effects, and lighting. In some sense, all these relatively local devices are also part of a move from a drama of action to a theater based to some greater extent on "narrating events" as *completely past* or, in some instances, yet to happen. In many instances, "erzählend" has one further, equally important association: that of narrating things *to an audience.* In Epic Theater, it is not only characters who tell *each other* stories: narrating figures like the *Sänger* of *Der kaukasische Kreidekreis* or Wang in *Der gute Mensch von Sezuan* narrate directly *to the audience.* More important, this narrative function is also fulfilled by

---

[54] Midgley 2000, 123. Midgley is paraphrasing two essays of February 1929 ("Letzte Etappe: Ödipus" and "Dialog über Schauspielkunst," *GBA,* 21:278–82), pieces that prefigure a number of points in the *Mahagonny* notes.

"Spruchbände," symbolic costumes, body language, and stylized gesture. Once again, the idea in the left-hand column of the "Schema" is clearer than its counterpart. However, given that this particular contrast dates from 1930, it is unlikely that the description "handelnd" refers to the importance of "die Fabel" for Epic Theater. As we shall see in the chapter on *Kleines Organon,* the latter only gradually became central to Brecht's post-exile theorizing, as it was bound up with his interest in Stanislavsky's late work. "[Die Methode der 'physischen Handlungen' am Berliner Ensemble]" of 1953 stresses: "Brecht verlangt immer, daß der Schauspieler auf den ersten Proben hauptsächlich die Fabel, den Vorgang, die Beschäftigung zeigt [. . .]. Er bekämpft mit aller Kraft die üble Gewohnheit vieler Schauspieler, die Fabel des Stücks sozusagen nur als unbedeutende Voraussetzung ihrer Gefühlsakrobatik zu benutzen, wie der Turner den Barren benutzt, um seine Gewandtheit zu beweisen" (*GBA,* 23:229). The contrast here, between a psychological theater based on individual characters' — and actors' — emotions, and an Epic Theater where plot is of vital significance to a work's political statement, differs substantially from the "handelnd"/ "erzählend" contrast that begins the *Mahagonny* "Schema."

Just as the individual components of an epic structure tend not to be of equal value, so certain points in the *Mahagonny* "Schema" stand out as more important than their neighbors. For Hultberg, point 18 is assumed ("falls dieser Punkt absolut gesetzt wird" [?]) to put many of the other characteristics in question. The point's tacit reference to Marx's writings will, it is assumed, cancel out a number of other items that put the stress squarely on change. Vulgar determinism wins the day over "eingreifendes Denken" in such a scenario. By contrast, Hecht, who has little patience with non-dialectical determinism, chooses to attribute paramount importance to point 11, where man is seen as both "veränderlich" and "verändernd." These epithets become significant evidence in his account of Brecht's development towards a more mature Marxism, inasmuch as what Engels calls the "Wechselwirkung" between the subjective and determining factors is allowed for: "Tatsächlich befand sich Brecht, die Grenzen des Behaviorismus erkennend, auf dem Wege zu einer dialektischen Einschätzung des Bewußtseins" (Hecht 1972, 63). The fact that this contrast was only added to the "Schema" in the *Versuche* 2 version would appear to strengthen Hecht's reading. For the reference to Marx is inserted at a time when the title "Zur Soziologie der Oper," showing Sternberg's influence, has been abandoned. And in any case, according to recent work, the covert quotation from Marx is less vulgarly determinist than Hultberg would have his reader believe.[55] One of the clearest

---

[55] See Avineri 1968, 75–77, on the misreadings of this passage and for an account of what Marx really meant.

statements of his new position comes in the 1933 notes to *Die Mutter*, where it is claimed that the spectator's "Aufgabe seinen Mitmenschen gegenüber besteht darin, unter die determinierenden Faktoren sich selbst einzuschalten. Bei dieser Aufgabe hat ihn die Dramatik zu unterstützen. Die determinierenden Faktoren, wie soziales Milieu, spezielle Ereignisse usw., sind also als veränderliche darzustellen" (*GBA*, 24:127). In Hultberg's account, this appears to be little more than a brief explanation to point 11, while for Hecht it signals a new stage in Brecht's development. Thus, selective stress on one element in the table can lead to diametrically opposite conclusions: either Brecht is well on his way to a dialectical conception of Epic Theater (Hecht) — though the notes themselves are viewed as propounding "eine typische Übergangstheorie" (Hecht 1972, 46) — or he is a sad case of recidivism, unable to shake off the vestiges of his "behaviorist"/"vulgar determinist" past (Hultberg 1962). Since neither contentious element was removed from the 1935 and 1938 versions of the "Schema," it would be comforting to assume that they were retained for a purpose. For once, Brecht cannot hide behind his usual let-out clause that the "Schema" shows mere shifts of accent, not absolute antitheses, for it is difficult to see that such a defense applies to the totalizing formulations in 11 and 18.

It may help at this stage to note that Hultberg had himself also detected *contradictions* in the table and to recall how central the notion of "Widerspruch" is to Brecht's conception of Epic Theater. The true Brecht, it might therefore be argued, is not to be located in either 11 or 18. Which one he stands closer to may be less important for the table's impact than the fact that it confronts the reader with a contradiction (though one no more contradictory than the suggestion that "epic" is essentially a structural concept and that the main differences between Dramatic and Epic Theater are of an essentially ideological nature). The *Mahagonny* "Schema" does more than delineate mere shifts of emphasis rather than absolute antitheses; in places it also engages in a thought-provoking "gegenseitige Verfremdung" of internal antitheses in order to provoke a dialectical response in the reader.

Brecht's table is designed as an exposition of the characteristics of Epic Theater and Opera and the political rationale behind them. In such a context, "epic" means "*not* 'Einfühlungstheater'" (an *end*, inasmuch as a theater of distance is the *goal*); although also it signifies, as some parts of the "Schema" make clear, whatever means, structural or non-structural, have to be used to achieve it.

One further connotation of "epic," that suggesting an Olympian distance and hence an audience response based on cool, detached observation, caused Brecht the most problems. For over a quarter of a century, he repeatedly found himself having to define — and refine — his position, legislating which kinds of emotion Epic Theater rejected and which were permissible. His change of ground and the refinements to the original theoretical stance are well documented and analysed (in Dickson 1978, 233–38). The general picture is less the one of a wilfully misunderstood Brecht painted in the Lidingö letter than that of someone whose manifesto rhetoric initially resulted in an overstated position that subsequently had to be redefined. Removing the "Gefühl"/"Ratio" contrast from the table of course failed to make the problem disappear. Hence, Brecht's various attempts at differentiation, not only between various forms of feeling, but also between "Ratio" and intelligence, common sense, and what would now be thought of as a lateral thinker's perspective on a problem. But no amount of clarification seems to have helped. To claim, as Brecht did in the Lidingö letter, that there is much emotion in scientific discovery and in the joy of learning even risks blurring vital differences between an emotional response to the results of a process and the atmosphere of inquiry in which an experiment is conducted.[56] Even empathy will eventually be re-admitted to the domain of Epic Theater, provided it is framed in such a way as to make the emotional experience productive.

One principal objection to Brecht's longterm dialogue with the critics of this final contrast does not stem from the fact that the two nouns might erroneously be taken for absolute opposites, but results from his habit of changing the terms of the discussion. Although claiming that he is concerned with "*Akzent*verschiebungen," what is actually shifted in subsequent debates is the terminology. To substitute "Einfühlung" for "Gefühl," and to do so without offering a similar corrective to the other term in the pairing, is hardly likely to guarantee greater understanding of the original table. And as we shall see in the next chapter when we turn to the theory of the middle and late thirties, Brecht's position is not always helped by an undifferentiating concept of aesthetic distance. Whereas total identification might appear to be an absolute, the detachment implied in such items as "macht den Zuschauer zum Betrachter," "er wird gegenübergesetzt," "studiert," or the claim that he views something as "Gegenstand der Untersuchung" is less fixed than its contrastive function might lead one to suppose.

"Vergnügungstheater oder Lehrtheater?" offers an embryonic model of the way the "Gefühl"/"Ratio" contrast might have been more profitably handled. It comes in Brecht's observation that, independent of the fact that there are two different forms of dramatic structure and audience response, one still finds "'das Dramatische' auch in epischen Werken und 'das Epische'

---

[56] "Brecht tried to deny the inconsistency by claiming that science was actually not something unemotional, in that it involved the excitement of discovery. However, the analogy is quite unconvincing, for although it is possible to be emotional *about* science, emotions have no place in the procedures of science, whereas the theatre, even as Brecht himself practised it, is intrinsically bound up with the emotions" (Speirs 1987, 45).

in dramatischen" (*GBA*, 22:107). If, instead of substituting or redefining his lead concepts, Brecht had elaborated a similar gradational model where examples of both the theater of emotion and the theater of reason had been dissected more rigorously in terms of their various constituent parts, some of the misconceptions caused by the pairing of "Gefühl" and "Ratio" might have been avoided.[57] Although the more one moves from terms of contrast and simplifying juxtapositions to notions of the amalgamation of both dramatic elements within one overall dominant generic set of characteristics, the less likely it becomes that such a refinement could find adequate expression in tabular form. Or that it would make a sufficient splash. (When Brecht uses a "vielleicht" in "[Schwierigkeiten des epischen Theaters]" — "Das Wesentliche am epischen Theater ist es vielleicht, daß es nicht so sehr an das Gefühl, sondern mehr an die Ratio des Zuschauers appelliert" (*GBA*, 21:210) — one can sense how easily differentiation might suggest dilution.) Ironically, the paragraph coming immediately after the table, a paragraph that might conceivably have performed the function of further clarifying it, does operate with the terms "radikale *Trennung der Elemente*" and "*Schmelzprozeß*." But it does so, not in order to apply them to the mixture of dramatic and epic elements in all drama or to widen the scope to include the lyrical component that is so important in many of Brecht's plays. Instead, the emphasis is solely on the increased autonomy of "*Musik, Wort und Bild*" in order to avoid creating the kind of "Schmelzprozeß" that for Brecht was epitomized by the Wagnerian *Gesamtkunstwerk*. Regrettably, the discussion hurries quickly on at this point from an explanation of Epic Theater to a consideration of Epic Opera, formulated in such a way as to do little more than prepare for the discussion of music in the next section. This does for once look more like an example of one section "für die andere" than each section "für sich."

The other nominal pairing that has given rise to unclarity is the juxtaposition of "Erlebnis" and "Weltbild" in point 5. In *Versuche* 2, the kind of experience he was referring to had already been characterized at the beginning

---

[57] Not long after "Vergnügungstheater oder Lehrtheater?" Emil Staiger published his *Grundbegriffe der Poetik*, an attempt to dissect the ingredients of what he saw as the lyrical, the epic, and the dramatic. While conceding "daß jede echte Dichtung an allen Gattungsideen in verschiedenen Graden und Weisen beteiligt ist" (Staiger 1968, 10), he in practice focuses in turn on all the three genres in isolation and fails to do justice to the amalgam posited. An impure methodology, combined with a desire to relate generic concepts to an anthropological concern with "fundamentale Möglichkeiten des Daseins überhaupt" (Staiger 1968, 209), led to the work's dismissal as a "blind alley" (Duroche 1967, 105). See also Zutshi 1981. The failure of *Grundbegriffe der Poetik* in this respect mirrors Brecht's own unwillingness to pursue the posited shifts in emphasis into fine detail.

of the section in which the table occurs: "[kulinarische Oper] nähert sich selber jedem Gegenstand in genießerischer Haltung. Sie 'erlebt,' und sie dient als 'Erlebnis'" (*GBA*, 24:76). This is not an easy formulation, but it could refer to the aestheticizing cult of experience and the savoring of precious "Augenblicke" associated in the German-speaking world above all with the *fin-de-siècle* Viennese neo-Romanticism of Hugo von Hofmannsthal and his contemporaries. Opera's hedonism is essentially a matter of escapism, in other words; it is this association that the table refers back to, just as we shall find that *Der Messingkauf* describes forms of superficial realism as "Naturalist" to imply their anachronism. When the table was revised in 1935 exile for insertion into a new context, the strength of such a reference risked becoming obscure. Hence, the allusion is removed. The deficit is not substantial, however, even on the right-hand side of the table. For arguably *both* forms of theater mediate "Weltbilder" in the sense that any such worldview is either an embodiment of the assumption that "das Denken bestimmt das Sein" or that "das gesellschaftliche Sein bestimmt das Denken." In any case, a point recently made by Knopf has a bearing on the terminology used here: "Wichtig [. . .] ist zu betonen, dass [Brecht] nie von Weltanschauung spricht oder Weltanschauung meint — im Gegenteil: im *Buch der Wendungen* wendet er sich explizit dagegen ("Kein Weltbild machen"); (*GBA*, 18:60) [. . .]" (*BHB*, 4:269). "Weltbild," in other words, appears to relate to Brecht's revised "Abbild" theory and to his materialist aesthetic rather than to the kind of idealist conception implicit in the term "Weltanschauung." As all this demonstrates, Brecht not only expended considerable energy trying to put right the various misreadings of the "Schema" in the 1930 *Mahagonny* notes; he at the same time adjusted the material to its new context and to his own changed and still changing dramaturgical position.

## The "Schema" Redeployed

After substantial revision, the table of contrasts reappeared in "Vergnügungstheater oder Lehrtheater?" (1935). It now forms part of a different debate, signaled in the title, and no longer relates to *Mahagonny*. Nor is it primarily concerned with the differences between Dramatic and Epic Theater. Even the way in which it is presented — as one of "*Zwei Schemata*" (the section title) — frames the material differently. Nevertheless, few editions make this clear. In Willett, for example, the section does not appear as such. The "*Epic Theatre*" section is followed immediately by "*The Instructive Theatre*," though Willett is not to blame; he is merely the victim of a defective source: the multi-volume East and West German *Schriften zum Theater* edition of the 1960s.

Since only the new edition includes the section in its proper form, I quote the passage in full:

## *Zwei Schemata*

Einige kleine Schemata mögen zeigen, worin sich die Funktion des epischen von der des dramatischen Theaters unterscheidet.

**1.**

| *Dramatische Form des Theaters* | *Epische Form des Theaters* |
|---|---|
| Die Bühne "verkörpert" einen Vorgang | Sie erzählt ihn |
| verwickelt den Zuschauer in eine Aktion und | macht ihn zum Betrachter, aber |
| verbraucht seine Aktivität | weckt seine Aktivität |
| ermöglicht ihm Gefühle | erzwingt von ihm Entscheidungen |
| vermittelt ihm Erlebnisse | vermittelt ihm Kenntnisse |
| der Zuschauer wird in eine Handlung hineinversetzt | er wird ihr gegenübergesetzt |
| es wird mit Suggestion gearbeitet | es wird mit Argumenten gearbeitet |
| die Empfindungen werden konserviert | bis zu Erkenntnissen getrieben |
| der Mensch wird als bekannt vorausgesetzt | der Mensch ist Gegenstand der Untersuchung |
| der unveränderliche Mensch | der veränderliche und verändernde Mensch |
| die Geschehnisse verlaufen linear | in Kurven |
| natura non facit saltus | facit saltus |
| die Welt, wie sie ist | die Welt, wie sie wird |
| was der Mensch soll | was der Mensch muß |
| seine Triebe | seine Beweggründe |

**2.**

*Der Zuschauer des dramatischen Theaters sagt:* Ja, das habe ich auch schon gefühlt. — So bin ich. — Das ist natürlich. — Das wird immer so sein. — Das Leid dieses Menschen erschüttert mich, weil es keinen Ausweg für ihn gibt. — Das ist große Kunst: da ist alles selbstverständlich. — Ich weine mit den Weinenden, ich lache mit den Lachenden.

*Der Zuschauer des epischen Theaters sagt:* Das hätte ich nicht gedacht. — So darf man es nicht machen. — Das ist höchst auffällig, fast nicht zu glauben. — Das muß aufhören. — Das Leid dieses Menschen erschüttert mich, weil es doch einen Ausweg für ihn gäbe. — Das ist große Kunst, da ist nichts selbstverständlich. — Ich lache über den Weinenden, ich weine über den Lachenden. (*GBA*, 22:109–10)

Some of the changes made to the 1930 table to make it into "Schema 1" involve expansion and reformulation for the sake of greater clarity. The "handelnd"/"erzählend" contrast no longer suffers from indeterminacy; there is now a clear subject and object ("Die Bühne 'verkörpert' einen Vorgang" / "Sie erzählt ihn"). The earlier elliptical contrast between "Erlebnis" and "Weltbild" has also been elucidated to bring out a sharper distinction between "vermittelt [. . .] Erlebnisse" and "vermittelt [. . .] Kenntnisse." The potential objection to the first version (i.e. if one were not familiar with the connotations "Weltbild" and "Weltanschaung" had for Brecht, one could object that all theater communicates "Weltbilder") has now been met, even if the difficulties with the word "Erlebnis" remain. The further contrast between a theater of "Suggestion" and one of "Argument" has been rephrased to shift the emphasis to a contrast between two methods of presentation: "mit Suggestion gearbeitet" or "mit Argumenten." Brecht is not always content with merely reformulating his earlier points, though. In the 1935 version of the "Schema," there are also various significant omissions from, additions to, and regroupings of items in the *Mahagonny* material. What had always been the most troublesome contrast — between a theater of "Gefühl" and one of "Ratio" — has been prudently dropped, though the idea is still implied in some of the other pairings. The "Wachstum"/"Montage" antithesis has also disappeared. Brecht had conceivably realized that in the twentieth century it would be too trivializing a caricature to associate any manifestation of "Aristotelian" theater with such an outmoded botanical conception of form. Or possibly it was because the term "Montage" was itself not without its ambiguities, as well as implying unhelpful analogies with the visual arts. In a change of greater magnitude, the original contrast between a theater predicated on an idealist assumption ("Das Denken bestimmt das Sein") and one based on Marx's thesis that "das gesellschaftliche Sein bestimmt das Denken" has also been deleted. In light of Hultberg's criticism of its potentially devastating impact on the interpretation of the

1930 original, one might wonder whether this was because Brecht wanted to signal that he had transcended his earlier mechanical determinist position. If so, the fact that it reappeared in the Malik edition (1:154), and now, with the "Gefühl"/"Ratio" contrast excised, in prestigious final position, need not invalidate such a hypothesis. Brecht may have simply wished to document the fact that his original statement had worked with an explicitly Marxist component, one representing a vital bridge leading from the revised 1935 scheme back to the sociological and political analysis of theater as institution of the period leading up to the *Mahagonny* notes. In this connection, it is worth bearing in mind that after completing "Vergnügungstheater oder Lehrtheater?" Brecht had taken the manuscript with him to Moscow in 1935, in the hope of persuading Sergei Tretiakov to place it for him in a Soviet journal.[58] If the above-noted revisions had been made with this in mind, then any inclusion of such a contentious passage from Marx might well, after his mixed treatment at the hands of the Third International, have looked imprudent by this time.

The most striking addition to the original set of contrasts is that between "Natura non facit saltus" and "facit saltus." The source for the premise in the left-hand column, that nature does not proceed by leaps and bounds, is Aristotle's *Historia de animalibus*.[59] Having chosen a Latin quotation to signify an anachronistic "Aristotelian" thesis, Brecht is obliged to offer his antithesis by negating the same Latin sentence (the one in the right-hand column functioning as a "Verfremdung" of the first position). One effect of inserting (and subsequently retaining) this item is to widen the scope of the "Schema" beyond dramaturgical issues to what most readers would understand by the earlier version's use of the word "Weltbild." We shall later encounter Brecht's attempts to demonstrate that "Verfremdung" is a feature of our everyday experience, not just some dramaturgical method. Here, he appears to be trying to do something similar in the case of epic discontinuity. The use of the present tense (Aristotle has "fecit," not "facit") makes reality an ongoing process rather than consigning creation to some period in the past.[60]

---

[58] According to Mierau 1976 (264), Tretiakov complained that Brecht, having entrusted the manuscript to him, subsequently took it back with him to Denmark.

[59] *GBA*, 22:916 glosses Brecht's Latin with an equivalent passage from the German translation of Leibniz's *Nouveaux essais* (*Neue Versuche über den menschlichen Verstand*) of 1704. Here the philosopher explains what he calls his "Gesetz der Kontinuität": "Nichts geschieht auf einen Schlag, und es ist einer meiner wichtigsten Grundsätze, daß die Natur niemals Sprünge macht."

[60] This need to open out to larger philosophical issues may also lie behind Brecht's allusion to the same Latin phrase in the seventh of his 1938 notes on "Dialektik und

None of these changes appears especially designed to make the *Mahagonny* table more suited to the theme expressed in the 1935 essay's title. This becomes predominantly the task of the second of the two "Schemata." That the two paragraphs should be regarded as constituting a bipartite "Schema" and be treated as generically comparable to the one appropriated from the *Mahagonny* notes may come as a surprise. Admittedly, the paragraphs are constructed — both syntactically and in sequence of ideas — as *Kontrafakturen* of one another, though with Brecht now shifting the horizontal contrast structure of the first "Schema" to the vertical plane. Although the second "Schema" takes up the suggestion in the essay's title that a choice has to be made between "Vergnügungstheater" and "Lehrtheater," neither paragraph is exclusively confined to one of the two terms in which this dichotomy has been presented. Each represents a complex synthesizing of what Brecht by now held to be a false dichotomy. Like "Ratio" and "Gefühl" and "Lachen" and "Weinen," "Vergnügung" and "Lehre" are no longer the absolute antitheses they were for the earlier Brecht. The relationship between the one and its counterpart has beeen transposed onto a dialectical plane, inasmuch as the behavior being displayed onstage is designed first to elicit an antithetical response from the ideal audience of Epic Theater; but then, the ideal audience response will be to transcend such a simple antithesis. As his letter to Comrade M. implied, from the mid-thirties onwards Brecht was no longer concerned with playing two kinds of structure off against one another and artificially presenting polarized modes of audience response (empathy, critical distance). His interest is now more decidedly in highlighting the enjoyment that comes with learning.

In 1953 Brecht wrote a piece with a direct bearing on the second "Schema" in "Vergnügungstheater oder Lehrtheater?"[61] Entitled "Gespräch über die Nötigung zur Einfühlung," it reveals the principal source and intertext for some of the formulations used in the second 1935 "Schema." The semi-fictive conversation begins with B. (presumably Brecht) addressing W. (Weigel) and P. (Palitsch) on the subject of a passage from Horace's *Ars poetica* which Gottsched had included, in lieu of an introduction, in his *Versuch einer critischen Dichtkunst vor die Deutschen* of 1730:

---

Verfremdung": *"Der Sprung* (saltus naturae, epische Entwicklung mit Sprüngen)" (*GBA*, 22:402).

[61] In a debate after Mei Lan-fang's 1935 exhibition performance of Chinese acting, Brecht became the main target of an anti-formalist polemic, in the presence of Stanislavsky himself. For details see Kebir 2000.

Ich habe hier die "Poetik" des Horaz in Gottscheds Übertragung.[62] Er formuliert hübsch eine uns oft beschäftigende Theorie, die Aristoteles für das Theater aufgestellt hat.

> Du mußt des Lesers Brust bezaubern und gewinnen
> Man lacht mit Lachenden und läßt auch Tränen rinnen
> Wenn andre traurig sind. Drum, wenn ich weinen soll
> So zeige du mir erst dein Auge tränenvoll.

Gottsched verweist an der berühmten Stelle sogleich auf Cicero, der, über Redekunst schreibend, von dem römischen Schauspieler Polus berichtet, der die Elektra darstellen sollte, wie sie ihren Bruder beweint. Weil ihm eben sein einziger Sohn gestorben war, holte er dessen Aschenkrug auf die Bühne und sprach die betreffenden Verse "mit einer so kräftigen Zueignung auf sich selbst aus, daß ihm sein eigner Verlust wahrhafte Tränen erpreßte. Und da war kein Mensch auf dem Platze, der sich der Tränen hätte enthalten können." (*GBA*, 23:412)

B. adds: "Das muß doch wahrhaftig als ein barbarischer Vorgang bezeichnet werden," a judgment later explained by the comment "die Absicht jedenfalls ist es, uns mit irgendeinem Schmerz abzuspeisen, der transportabel ist, das heißt von seinem Anlaß entfernt und unbeschädigt einem anderen Anlaß zur Verfügung gestellt werden kann. Der eigentliche Vorgang der Dichtung verschwindet wie das Fleisch in einer schlau eingerührten Sauce von bestimmtem Geschmack" (*GBA*, 23:412–13).

What Brecht is referring to, albeit in a highly circuitous way, is something far more specific than the dubious practice of exploiting the "transposability" of private emotions for acting purposes. For Polus's strategy reads like a deliberate caricature of the Stanislavskian "Psycho-Technique," in particular what chapter 9 of *An Actor Prepares* refers to as "emotion memory" (Stanislavksy 1988, 163–92). Recourse to "emotion memory," a concept indebted to the work of the psychologist Théodule Ribot, involved the actor in tapping into the reservoir of subconsciously stored deep emotions from the past, deep-seated resources of intense feeling associated with the physical and sensory circumstances that accompanied the first occurrence of the emotion. Polus's bringing of his only son's funeral urn on to the stage could well serve as a classic illustration of what *An Actor Prepares* refers to as the exploitation of "sensation memory" to arouse "dormant feelings" capable of being rechanneled in the performance of a part: "Just as your visual memory can reconstruct an inner image of some forgotten thing, place or person, so your emotion memory can bring back feelings you have already experienced" (Stanislavsky 1988, 167–68). Hence Stanislavsky's advice: "Always act in

---

[62] "Horaz von der Dichtkunst, übersetzt und mit Anmerkungen erläutert" (Gottsched 1962, 21).

your own person," which means: "use your own feelings" and "we must play ourselves always" (177). The "Psycho-Technique" is a clear illustration of the Moscow Art Theater's "cardinal principle: through conscious means we reach the subconscious" (178). As has been pointed out (Counsell 1996, 29), "an important consequence [of the actor's resorting to the emotion memory strategy] is that the character's hypothetical psyche will always be based on the actor's, since it is the actor's emotions, experiences and responses that provide the bricks of which a role is built." As a further consequence, instead of material being "historisiert," in Brecht's sense, it is psychologized through the indiscriminate use of emotion memory. Indirectly, via Cicero via Horace via Gottsched, Brecht's phrase "ein barbarischer Vorgang" is being applied to the exploitation of emotion memory, and not just to Polus's approach to the challenge of registering grief. Nevertheless, the charge of barbarism does not have to represent an unequivocally hostile gesture towards all that Stanislavsky represents. By the early 1950s, much more was known about Stanislavsky's later development. Hence, while the above conversation may seem to be attacking the Stanislavsky of *An Actor Prepares,* it misses the mark when it comes to the work of the later Stanislavsky and the Moscow Art Theater's later work. The nature of that development is explored in Brecht's "Stanislawski-Studien" of the 1950s.

What "Gespräch über die Nötigung zur Einfühlung" and *"Schema 2"* have in common is something scarcely touched upon in the *Mahagonny* notes: a concern with the importance of a non-identificatory method of acting for combating empathy in the audience. The *Mahagonny* table's two main groupings of items focus on (i) the fact that Epic Theater is an antiempathic theater of aesthetic (though not necessarily yet critical) distance and (ii) the importance of an alternative kind of discontinuous structure for the right audience response. Although 1930 readers are referred to the "Dialog über Schauspielkunst," they would probably be left with the impression that Brecht was still placing considerable hopes on a structural solution to the empathy problem. The subsequent emphasis on a *"Trennung der Elemente"* and the requisite epic autonomy of word, music, and image would appear to expand the notion of epic discontinuity by relating it to a montage of different *kinds of art.* The failure of the original "Schema" to do justice to some of these matters may explain the presence of two "Schemata" in the 1935 essay. For the one is mainly confined to structural features, while the other is concerned with performance concepts. This would mean that the most important change made to the original *Mahagonny* "Schema" lay not in local modifications to its constituent parts, but in its being offset (or reciprocally estranged) by being juxtaposed with a second one. That crucial effect is lost in all but the *GBA* edition.

Three years later, the *Mahagonny* "Schema" was to appear in its final form. With the exception of the removal of the final contrast, most of the changes in the Malik reprint had been carried out in "Vergnügungs-theater oder Lehrtheater?" Brecht clearly had no wish to relinquish the revisions made there. However, deprived of that essay's new approach to pleasure — no longer dismissed as entertainment or mere "Kulinarismus" — and despite the removal of the original "Schema's" "Gefühl"/"Ratio" contrast, the final 1939 version lacks any explicit statement that learning is both an enjoyable experience and tends to involve strong emotions. Given that "Vergnügungstheater oder Lehrtheater?" was not published until 1957 (in truncated form, in Unseld's *Schriften zum Theater*), it was all too foreseeable that Brecht would continue to suffer for a long time from the misreadings that the 1930 "Schema" had occasioned.

## Words, Music, and Setting

The italicized statement "*Musik, Wort und Bild mußten mehr Selbständigkeit erhalten*" is not a section title for the penultimate part of the *Mahagonny* notes. Nevertheless, it behaves as though it ought to be one. It appears in italics and following immediately on from it are three subsections "a) Musik," "b) Wort" and "c) Bild," which elaborate the idea that the three had to be separated and allowed to comment in their various relatively autonomous ways on the material. Already, when revising the *Musik und Gesellschaft* version for *Versuche* 2, Brecht (or was it Weill?) had added the claim "die Musik ist der wichtigste Beitrag zum Thema" (*GBA*, 24:80). This may explain why music's new function within Epic Opera is the only aspect to be adumbrated with the help of a further "Schema" and why four out of its five points treat the complex issue of the relationship between music and text. While again nothing but the underlying principle is outlined, this additional "Schema" constitutes one of the most illuminating characterizations of core epic strategies in the entire notes. Obviously, Epic Theater could not have remained a parallel, rather than contrastive, point of reference at this late phase of the argument if over-specific illustrations from opera had been included. By remaining at the level of principles Brecht can still maintain the dominant comparison in the notes between Epic Theater and Epic Opera. The separation of elements is recognizable as a common procedure in both genres; the implied analogy between a music that interprets the text ("auslegend") by assuming a "Stellung" or a "Verhalten" towards it bridges the gap between a feature like the narrator in Epic Theater and the commenting role of music in Epic Opera. Similarly, it links the function of gesture and stage-props and the way in which the singer and the music draw attention to anti-illusionistic aspects of performance and adopt a stance to what is being displayed.

At the beginning of "*— aber Neuerungen!*" we encountered a situation where Epic Theater was being characterized in order to give a context for

Epic Opera and hence make it more understandable as part of a broader series of innovations. By the end of the section, however, it almost looks as if the converse is happening. Two out of the three headings under which Epic Opera is being discussed apply just as well to Epic Theater; and the "Schema" in the third part is noticeably briefer and less specific to such an extent that it could as well serve as a defamiliarizing model for demonstrating the function of songs in such plays as *Die Maßnahme* and *Die Mutter* or the role of literary commenting elements in Epic Theater. Brecht's method of theorizing here prefigures something that will later, in respect of his plays, be termed "stereometric."[63] In the *Mahagonny* notes the dual theater/opera focus is again a function of the need to encourage "komplexes Sehen." Indeed, a similar stereometric principle is shown to be in operation in the epic techniques of opera that are being discussed at this point. The music will no longer be permitted to heighten or illustrate the text or paint "die psychische Situation"; instead, audiences will receive the music and words stereometrically. The words will exhibit sentimentality, rather than being sentimental, and the double-take of Caspar Neher's backcloth showing a glutton gorging himself to death at the same time as this happens onstage is described as "Stellung nehmend" to events: "Sie [the words] bilden ihr Anschauungsmaterial." Insight is gained through comparison — between words and music, staged events and backdrop, and, in the theory, between the epic techniques of opera and theater. As we have recently been reminded, "Nach [Brecht] wird Erkenntnis durch Vergleichen produziert" (*BHB*, 4:119).

The final section title — *"Die Folgen der Neuerungen: Beschädigung der Oper?"* — pursues the same dialogic strategy to be found at a number of other places in the *Mahagonny* notes. A token reactionary or otherwise unacceptable view is expressed (or mimicked) so as to allow the main voice to elaborate the correct position. Here, the idea that audiences used to traditional opera might feel that it is in jeopardy becomes a pretext, not so much for a direct response as for a cameo caricature of demeaning audience behavior. That is to say: reactionary audiences stand condemned by their own conduct, rather than being dignified by receiving counterassurances from the Left:

> Herausstürzend aus dem Untergrundbahnhof, begierig, Wachs zu werden in den Händen der Magier, hasten erwachsene, im Daseinskampf erprobte und unerbittliche Männer an die Theaterkassen. Mit dem Hut geben sie in der Garderobe ihr gewohntes Benehmen, ihre Haltung "im Leben" ab; die Garderobe verlassend, nehmen sie ihre Plätze mit der Haltung von Königen ein. [. . .] Die Haltung dieser

---

[63] Wirth (1957, 346–87). As we shall shortly see, Brecht operates with comparable "stereometric" structures in a number of his subsequent theoretical writings.

Leute in der Oper ist ihrer unwürdig. Ist es möglich, daß sie sie ändern? Kann man sie veranlassen, ihre Zigarren herauszuziehen? (*GBA*, 24:81)

Brecht's answer, even to that question, remains oblique. Whatever members of the above kind of audience do or whatever they expect from opera, they must be replaced. And opera's *content* will have to become more relevant before fresh audiences can be legimately enticed into the theater. In order to show, once more *ex negativo*, what is the wrong way to conjure up the new audience, the notes launch into a final barbed attack on formal and thematic innovation for its own sake (a diatribe substantially expanded for *Versuche* 2, no doubt because it was now less counterproductive to imply specific targets than it might have been in *Musik und Gesellschaft*). *L'art pour l'art* becomes Brecht's dismissive verdict on innovation for innovation's sake. The flurry of avant-garde experiments evoked at the beginning of the notes is now seen as merely marking time. (Willett has "treading water.") An image of alienated modern man is conjured up suggesting that contemporary theater in all its various "culinary" manifestations, from "Saustück" to *dernier-cri* avant-garde, is equally alienated from its true social purpose and in dire need of refunctionalizing. Having moved from a characterization of Epic Theater and Opera to indications of what their new function will be, the notes have now, for purposes of provocation, reverted to polemicizing against contemporary audiences and the pseudo-avant-garde, a tactic which, as the Lidingö letter reveals, did not, on the whole, win Brecht many sympathizers.

The *Mahagonny* notes conclude by looking in both directions at once. The long penultimate section ends with a defamiliarizing pastiche of the end of Heinrich Heine's poem "Die Lorelei," with the avant-garde now playing the role of the siren-like Rhine-spirit: "Und das haben mit ihrem Singen die Neuerungen getan,"[64] harshly juxtaposing the seductive singing of culinary experimentation with the concluding bald statement: "Wirkliche Neuerungen greifen die Basis an." A brief postscript records that *Mahagonny* was written three years before and that it is time to look forward. The final stated goal of developing the means of pleasure into an object of instruction (*GBA*, 24:84) might, with hindsight, seem less related to *Mahagonny* or *Die Dreigroschenoper* than to the extreme didacticism of Brecht's "Lehrstücke" of the late twenties and early thirties. But such ideas as "entwickeln aus" and "umbauen" are kept deliberately imprecise: the process does not have to involve the abandoning of the one for the other; in particular, the demonizing of all pleasure as "culinary" or unworthy of the audience is avoided even at this early stage. In the notes, pleasure was never

---

[64] The intertext here is Heinrich Heine's couplet "Und das hat mit ihrem Singen / Die Lorelei getan," the last two lines of "Die Lorelei." For an alternative reading of Brecht's use of these lines, see Brüggemann 1973, 92.

the main target of this polemical word-field. "Genuß," "Spaß," and, above all, "Vergnügen," the term Brecht will soon prefer, are all kept distinct. The main program for the future, according to the final section of the notes, appears to leave the door open for a new politically interventionist synthesis of "Vergnügungstheater" and "Lehrtheater."

# 2: Conceptualizing the Exile Work: "Nicht-Aristotelisches Theater," "Verfremdung," and "Historisierung"

THE *MAHAGONNY* NOTES are characterized by an exuberant sense of living in an age of transition: "dieser (so kostbaren) Übergangszeit" (*GBA* 21:143). "Nach meiner Ansicht," Brecht wrote at the time of *Mann ist Mann*, "ist es sicher, daß der Sozialismus, und zwar der revolutionäre, das Gesicht unseres Landes noch zu unseren Lebzeiten verändern wird" (*GBA* 21:145). The picture is one of a society on the brink of revolution and, culturally, of a bourgeois institution not yet under the control of the progressive class, but whose appropriation is imminent, hence the thematic concerns of works like *Die Maßnahme, Kuhle Wampe,* and *Die Mutter.* This is coupled with an optimistic picture of an embryonic Marxist theater designed to *attack the base.* If the *Mahagonny* notes are colored by any sense of historical crisis, the analysis that they contain nevertheless focuses on the "Theater-Apparat" itself and on diagnosing the *culinary* wares and unproductive audience response Epic Theater needed to combat. As Kobel has pointed out, Brecht argues as if the audience of Aristotelian theater took no political views to the theater with them (Kobel 1992, 136). But the real problem in the early 1930s was that a large portion of potential theater audiences was of the radical political right. Yet we find little indication in Brecht's theoretical writings that the real enemy was by then not bourgeois culture, but National Socialism's totalizing program. Indeed, as the *Brecht Handbuch* states, National Socialism was a nearly nonexistent theme in Brecht's writings on politics and society until early 1933 (*BHB* 4:129). Soon after the *Mahagonny* notes, Brecht was to receive a savage reminder of the difference between the Weimar Republic's relatively *laissez-faire* theater practices and Goebbels's ruthless *Kulturpolitik.* Within the space of three years, National Socialism's hold on post-Weimar theater would be consolidated, Brecht would be driven into exile and German theaters *gleichgeschaltet.* All forms of innovation, not just those targeting the base, found themselves threatened with summary "liquidation," and now no longer in Fritz Sternberg's figurative sense. As Brecht was to put it two years after Hitler's coming to power: "Die Entwicklung des revolutionären deutschen Theaters und der deutschen revolutionären Dramatik wurde durch den Faschismus abgebrochen" ("Radiovortrag Bertolt Brecht," *GBA* 22:120).

Brecht comments in "Vergnügungstheater oder Lehrtheater?" (1935):

Nur an wenig Orten und nicht für lange Zeit waren [. . .] die Umstände einem epischen lehrhaften Theater günstig. In Berlin hat der Faschismus der Entwicklung eines solchen Theaters energisch Einhalt geboten. [Episches Theater] setzt außer einem bestimmten technischen Standard eine mächtige Bewegung im sozialen Leben voraus, die ein Interesse an der freien Erörterung der Lebensfragen zum Zwecke ihrer Lösung hat und dieses Interesse gegen alle gegensätzlichen Tendenzen verteidigen kann. (*GBA* 22:116)

Of course, the main problem in Germany at the time was not the absence of a "mächtige Bewegung im sozialen Leben," but the fact that there were *two* conflicting movements, and the one lacking in any interest in the open discussion of the vital questions in life in order to arrive at a solution to them was about to carry the day. As Peter Brooker has pointed out, the result was to be a "change of emphasis and orientation" in Brecht's dramatic theory: "a reversal of the priorities [. . .] announced in 1929, when he had said 'it is not the play's effect on the audience but its effect on the theatre that is decisive at the moment'" (Brooker 1988, 40). In Brooker's view, while these two effects are related and usually occur "in sequence" in Brecht's thinking, it is nevertheless possible to appreciate how

increasingly restricted opportunities for securing control of the "means of production," or even of a venue for such production in a Berlin experiencing Hitler's rise to power, would have turned Brecht's attention from the second to the first as a more practical possibility. His situation in exile from 1933 [. . .] would have put questions of economic and large-scale social change further beyond the realm of what was immediately and practically possible. (40)

This helps give the requisite context for what Brooker diagnoses as the

disappearance in subsequent essays of the themes of the theatre's economic basis and the socialisation of the means of cultural production. By the mid-1930s these interests had been overtaken by Brecht's development of the theory of *Verfremdung*. And this [. . .] implied a foreshortening of focus or change of tactics, since *Verfremdung* was designed to fulfil the drama's pedagogic function. [. . .] The success of a dialectising experience in the theatre had to wait upon the operations of the dialectic in history. (Brooker 1988, 40–41)

Brecht as a consequence "turned away from the project of expressly applying dialectical materialism to the theatre [in order] to consider more intrinsic questions of dramatic form and function" (Brooker 1988, 39). Other factors played a part in this radical change of orientation. The unorthodox nature of Epic Theater soon found itself under fire from Marxist BPRS cultural circles, with Brecht becoming increasingly obliged to defend Epic Theater rather than his core ideology. And this was not the sole reason why "caution" became the watchword from now on. If the impressive corpus of theoretical writings from the Scandinavian period is circumspect about political assumptions and long-term goals, and might at times appear to be laying Brecht open to the charge of showing more concern for artistic than political radicalism, there was one further key reason for this shift of emphasis: the conditions imposed on Brecht by his countries of asylum. Brecht was required to refrain from political activity, even in the aesthetic realm (Nørregaard 1993, 405–6). And while he usually refused to comply, the shadow of such an injunction nevertheless exercized a distorting effect on his theoretical writings during the Scandinavian years and in US exile.

In the majority of accounts of the exile period, 1935 is regarded as a watershed, with Brecht, during a visit to the USSR, being introduced to Viktor Shklovsky's Formalist concept *priem ostraneniya* ("making wondrous") and allegedly re-theorizing it in his own terms to become "Verfremdung." Willett's 1959 study *The Theatre of Bertolt Brecht* gave substantial impetus to this thesis. A decade and a half later, in 1974, Jan Knopf found it necessary to complain that Willett's tentative hypothesis had become virtually cast-iron fact.[1] According to Willett's scenario, Brecht's Soviet go-between, Sergei Tretiakov, had drawn his attention to the term as used in Shklovsky's 1917 essay: "Isskustvo kak priem" (Art as a Device). The assertion has by no means been laid to rest. Even in the face of evidence that Brecht had not used the term "Verfremdung" only (or immediately) *after* his 1935 Moscow

---

[1] Willett (1959, 163); Knopf (1974, 17). According to Willett: "there seems to me every reason to accept the view of Bernhard Reich [ *Im Wettlauf mit der Zeit*, 371–73] that he first heard the term *Verfremdung* used that year (1935) by Tretiakov, with Brecht present, and concluded that this inspired Brecht to adopt Shklovsky's formulation as a description first of the Chinese methods [he witnessed when seeing the actor Mei Lan-Fang perform in Moscow] and then of his own" (Willett 1984, 219). Booker (1988, 68–69 and 1994, 192–93) gives a critical evaluation of Willett's argument. The best detailed assessment of Mei Lan-fang's importance for Brecht's theory of "Verfremdung" remains Tatlow (1977, 303–17), who suggests that Brecht "probably saw the troupe's full performance in the theatre," as well as Mei Lan-fang's private demonstration before a small invited audience" (Tatlow 1977, 221; see also Kebir 2000, 142–45).

visit,[2] and despite the fact that Brecht's concept has radically different connotations from Shklovsky's, the claim persists.[3]

1935 was not just the year of Brecht's second Moscow visit, which also
gave rise to an instructive encounter with the Chinese actor Mei Lan-fang
that left its mark in an important essay on defamiliarization in oriental acting.
It was also the year of a production of *Mother,* Brecht's *Die Mutter* in translation, by the Theatre Union at the Civic Repertory Theatre in New York.[4]
The play's cavalier treatment at the hands of the Theatre Union was a hard
blow for Brecht who had begun to think of the United States as more auspi-
cious for his exile prospects than his current "Dänisch-Sibirien," as he called
it. Apart from the New World's obvious geopolitical advantages over an already threatened and soon to be occupied continental Europe, America had
for a long time held the lure of a European cultural capital-in-exile for
Brecht. "Dort würde er auf Eisler, Korsch, Piscator, Kortner und auch
Feuchtwanger treffen können" (*BHB* 4:298) It was also the land of John
Dos Passos and Theodore Dreiser, Sinclair Lewis, Thornton Wilder, Sher-
wood Anderson, John Steinbeck, Eugene O'Neill and, above all, Clifford
Odets (the great "white hope des amerikanischen Theaters" as Brecht had at
the time heralded him [*GBA* 27:100]). Although Odets's *Waiting for Lefty*
was a play Brecht held in high regard (*GBA* 28:545), much of the work by
the others mentioned above was known to him more by reputation than as
the result of any great familiarity with their writings. Brecht knew the work
of George Bernard Shaw, Rudyard Kipling, and Edgar Wallace more inti-
mately than he did that of any US novelist, dramatist, or poet. For a while he
even labored under the impression that his beloved Robert Louis Stevenson
was an American writer (*GBA* 21, 107).

[2] Shklovsky is nowhere mentioned in Brecht. The closest the *GBA* notes come to circumstantial evidence of an influence is with the suggestion that Brecht's term
"Kunstgriffe" might derive from Shklovsky's *Isskustvo kak priem* (*Kunstgriff* being
the German for *priem,* "device") (*GBA* 22:1024).

[3] For objections to the idea of a Shklovsky influence, see Rülicke-Weiler (239), Mittenzwei (1969, 420–21), Fradkin (65–66), and Knopf (1974, 16–19).

[4] According to Nørregaard 1993 (419–22), Brecht had been rehearsing *Die Mutter*
with Berlau's Revolutionært Teater in 1934. Although the troupe was scheduled to
stage Brecht's Gorky adaptation in Copenhagen the following year, another play that
was in repertoire there at the time ran for more than twelve months, so that Brecht
had to find an alternative solution: "Nachdem er nur einen flüchtigen Blick auf eine
definitivere Ausgabe von *Moderen* mit Ruth Berlaus R.T.-Amateuren geworfen hatte,
reiste Brecht im Oktober nach New York, um eine Inszenierung von *Mother* zu
überwachen. Hier zeigte sich klar und berechnet Brechts Unterscheidung zwischen
Wesentlichem und Unwesentlichem. Vor allem anderen ging es ihm darum, Zugang
zum amerikanischen Markt zu erhalten" (Nørregaard 1993, 421).

# "Mother" at the Theatre Union, New York

Thanks to the mediation of Hanns Eisler, who was at the time lecturing at the New School for Social Research in New York, Brecht agreed to grant permission for the staging of *Die Mutter* by the Theatre Union, described by him in a letter to Maxim Gorky as "das einzige ständige Arbeitertheater New Yorks" (*GBA*, 28:539). The story of what went wrong has been told many times, most acrimoniously in Brecht's various postmortems (*GBA*, 24:135–91), above all in his letters to the Theatre Union of 3 October and 9 November 1935 (*GBA*, 28:527–32); more even-handed versions can be found in the "Prologue to American Exile" chapter of *Bertolt Brecht in America* (Lyon 1980, 6–10) and in Lyon 1975.

At the time of the *Mahagonny* notes, "kulinarisches Theater" was little more than an abstract term of abuse, one seldom contextualized, except by innuendo, and rarely backed up with examples. Following in Sternberg's footsteps, Brecht regarded the crisis of mainstream bourgeois drama as a *fait accompli*. As a consequence, he preferred to concentrate his polemics closer to home: mainly on various forms of ill-conceived pseudo-avant-garde experimentation. In New York, however, he suddenly found himself on the receiving end of a salutary lesson, experiencing at first hand the hold the drama of manipulated empathy continued to exercise on large sections of the contemporary theater world. This helps explain why, of the 90 pages of Brecht's writings on *Die Mutter* in *GBA*, vol. 24, less than a quarter are devoted to the 1932 Berlin production; and even many of these involve afterthoughts in the light of the adverse New York experience. The bulk of the rest attempt to pinpoint the lessons to be learnt from the Theatre Union adaptation.[5]

Things started to go wrong almost from the outset. Although it was "one of America's most progressive workers' theaters" (Lyon 1980, 10), the Theatre Union was far from being the proletarian cooperative Brecht had enthused about to Gorky. Its "advisory and executive boards consisted of a cross-section of Stalinists, Trotskyists, socialists and liberals" and its procedures and dramaturgical principles hardly made it the "apparatus"[6] that

---

[5] "Empfehlung für die Theatre Union," "Memorandum über die Verstümmelung und Entstellung des Textes," "[Zur amerikanischen Aufführung der *Mutter*]," and the expanded Malik edition of the "Anmerkungen zur *Mutter* [1938]."

[6] "Die Theatre Union unterschied sich durch ihre politische Einstellung beträchtlich von den Theatern, welche die Oper *Mahagonny* aufführten. Dennoch reagierte der Apparat durchaus als ein Apparat zur Herstellung von Rauschwirkungen. Nicht nur das Stück, auch die Musik wurden dadurch verunstaltet, und der lehrhafte Zweck zum größten Teil verfehlt" (*GBA*, 22:161). The fact that two years before this Friedrich Wolf, the author of the highly "Aristotelian" play *Professor Mamlock*, had wanted

Brecht would ideally have chosen: "[It] followed no party line. Its aim was to present plays with a progressive, socially conscious message at drastically reduced ticket prices to as wide an audience as possible, which ranged from labor unions to upper-middle-class New York theater patrons" (Lyon 1980, 6–7). When the dramatist Paul Peters submitted his English translation for Brecht's approval, it was found to be a travesty. Peters, Brecht claimed, had transformed a major piece of Epic Theater into a sentimentalized drama of family relationships set against the mere façade of a revolutionary background. The underlying culture clash was interpreted by Brecht as a matter of aesthetics rather than geography, the adaptation being damaged by a "nicht besonders amerikanisches, sondern besonders naturalistisches Gepräge" (*GBA*, 28:522–23).[7] Without delay, Brecht set off for New York with the express purpose of taking the production in hand, while also "clearly hoping to introduce his name and theories to the theater world" there (Lyon 1980, 8). A campaign of self-promotion had also been set in motion. Brecht's article on "The German Drama: Pre-Hitler" (*GBA*, 22:939–44), published in *The New York Times* on 24 November 1935 — five days after the première of *Mother* — as well as his critique of the New York production (*GBA*, 24:169–73) which he had hoped to place in *New Masses*, were, in their different ways, further evidence of the beginnings of a concerted US promotional program.[8]

Initially unable to have the adaptation made sufficiently epic, Brecht ended up, after much hectoring, being banned, along with Eisler, from all rehearsals. Ground was eventually yielded on both sides, but the result was a hybrid that satisfied no one. "Mir kommt es vor," Brecht complained, "als wären in der Adaption vor ein Auto wieder Pferde gespannt worden, weil der Anlaßschlüssel nicht gefunden werden konnte" (*GBA*, 28:523). The panning Victor Wolfson's production received is documented in Brecht's miscellany of press responses to the play (*GBA*, 24:124–26). As part of a — by then typical — learning-from-defeat strategy, Brecht subjected these reviews to a critique. "Damit die Kunst kritisiert werden kann, muß die Kunstkritik kritisiert werden," as he once put it (*GBA*, 23:134). Legally pre-

---

to have the Theatre Union stage his work should have been warning enough. See Wolf 1968, 247–53.

[7] "Wie ich aus Ihrer Bearbeitung [. . .] entnehme, glauben Sie nicht, daß der amerikanische Arbeiter auf eine naturalistische Form verzichten kann" (Brecht to Peters, August 1935 [*GBA*, 28:520]).

[8] As Brecht noted with satisfaction, the *Times* piece "stand am Sonntag an prominentester Stelle und soll sehr gewirkt haben" (*GBA*, 28:537). He placed an expanded version in the *Left Review* (10 (1936): 504–8) and his "Principles of 'Educational' Theater" in *New Masses* (31 December 1935). A fictive "Selbstinterview" on the subject of Epic Theater also appeared in the US *Daily Worker* (31 October 1935).

vented in 1935 from remonstrating on the spot with the Theatre Union, by which time it was in any case too late to repair the damage, Brecht turned his attention to the long-term lessons to be learnt from the experience.

While engaged in a massive theoretical rethink, Brecht at least had the advantage of knowing that *Die Mutter* had recently been performed according to rigorous epic principles back in Denmark.[9] Such a successful production can only have reassured him that the work was not just a forgotten chapter in the annals of Weimar Republic theater history. According to Nørregaard (1993, 420), no copy of the Danish rehearsal script has been discovered and there are few hard-and-fast dates to go by. Ruth Berlau's "*Die Mutter*: Berlin 1932 — New York 1935 — Kopenhagen 1935 — Leipzig 1950 — Berlin 1951" (*Theaterarbeit*, 332–41) lists the Copenhagen production *after* the New York one, whereas a more recent authority (*GBA*, 25:512) refers to Berlau's production with the Arbejderenes Teater as taking place as early as autumn 1935. Berlau remarks disingenuously of the New York production that "die geplante naturalistische Inszenierung wurde aufgegeben und der Wunsch des Stückschreibers nach Benutzung des Modells erfüllt" (*Theaterarbeit*, 334). Her most revealing comments on the Copenhagen production allude more to the New York débâcle than their ostensible subject. We are told, for instance, that use of the 1932 Berlin "*Mutter*-Modell" helped the Danish group avoid amateurish effects ("dilettantische Entstellungen" had been one of Brecht's main complaints about the New York production [*GBA*, 28:531]). The Danish amateurs, Berlau records, had no difficulty in depicting working-class characters; and the *esprit de corps* engendered by collective work on the play was so contagious that some of the cast went off to fight in the International Brigade in the Spanish Civil War. Brecht was nevertheless unable to take comfort from the knowledge that the New York failure was compensated for by a Danish production. What the Theatre Union fiasco had brought to his attention demanded a more thorough-going response than any faithful production could ever offer.

---

[9] *Theaterarbeit* reproduces two production shots featuring Dagmar Andreasen as Wlassowa (one from the anti-war propaganda scene cut in New York). Nørregaard (1993) does not mention this production, but records that "Dank des Montagecharakters der *Mutter* eignete sich das Stück dafür in Auszügen gespielt zu werden, so daß die einzelnen Szenen, analog zu den üblichen Sketches des R.T., bei Parteiveranstaltungen mit politischen Reden und anderen Einlagen abwechseln konnten" (420).

## New Theaters for Old

Two factors weighed heavily with Brecht in the mid-1930s. The first was knowing that ideologically progressive theater-groups could also fail to grasp Epic Theater's innovative approach, and the second, an awareness that the American stage was becoming dominated by Stanislavskians to a far greater extent than he could have suspected from his European vantage point. His eyes had been been opened to the fact that he would need to clarify his theoretical position and perhaps even compromise if he was to make an impact in America.[10]

The most salutary thing to come out of the New York experience was a recognition of the tactical advantages Stanislavskians enjoyed over the proponents of Epic Theater. Not just in the sense that the Moscow Art Theater (MAT) had many disciples in America, whereas Brecht was something of a lone voice. That could be either the cause or merely a side-effect of more fundamental factors. But Stanislavsky and his fellow-artists at MAT were obviously increasing their hold on contemporary drama. In retrospect, Brecht did concede that "in den Staaten [bedeutete] der Stanislawskismus einen Protest gegen das merkantile Theater" (*GBA*, 27:246), but he did not at the time attenuate his position. On the basis of the two numbers of *Theatre Workshop* that Mordecai (Max) Gorelik of the Theatre Union had sent to put him in the picture, Brecht could see that an "erste Welle russischen Theaters" was inundating America and that it was "eine reichlich trübe Welle" (*GBA*, 22:990). He was quick to deduce that this new wave offered the twin attractions of methodically systematized rehearsal and performance techniques and a political rationale for the exploitation of feeling in left-wing theater:

> Das System Stanislawskis ist ein Fortschritt schon deswegen, weil es ein System ist. Die von ihm vorgeschlagene Spielweise erzwingt die Einfühlung des Zuschauers systematisch [. . .]. Es ist kein Zufall, daß z.B. in Amerika gerade die linken Theater sich mit dem System Stanislawskis auseinanderzusetzen beginnen. Diese Spielweise scheint ihnen eine bisher unerreichbare Einfühlung in den proletarischen Menschen zu gewährleisten. ("[Fortschrittlichkeit des Stanislawski-Systems]," *GBA*, 22:284–85)

Not by chance would Stanislavskian techniques soon be associated with "Method" acting. Indeed, Brecht uses both the phrase "Stanislawski-Methode" and "Stanislawski-System" as early as 1937.

---

[10] Baxandall (1967, 81) attributes the more conventional quality of *The Private Life of the Master Race* and *Señora Carrar's Rifles* to the Theatre Union experience.

Brecht promptly set about studying his adversary's writings. "Gibt es in Englisch das Buch Stanislawskis über sein System der Schauspielkunst?" (i.e. *My Life in Art* of 1924), he asks Margarete Steffin in February 1936. "Wenn nicht, könntest Du mir daraus übersetzen? Das wäre sehr wichtig" (*GBA*, 28:548). (As far as MAT writings of the 1930s in English are concerned, Brecht does not seem to have known of *The Soviet Theatre* [1934] by P. Markov or V. Nemirovich-Danchenko's *My Life in Russian Theatre* [1937].) Nevertheless, on the basis of limited information, Brecht drew up a list of the Stanislavsky system's advantages, beginning again with the fundamental observation: "Fortschrittlichkeit der Stanislawski-Methode: 1) Daß es eine Methode ist."[11] The numbers of *Theatre Workshop* that Gorelik had sent contained two lengthy accounts of the Stanislavskian approach: Josef Rapoport's "The Work of the Actor" (*Theatre Workshop* 1 (1936): 5–40) and "The Actor's Creative Work" by Ilya Sudakov, one of Stanislavsky's codirectors at MAT (*Theater Workshop* 2 (1937): 7–42). On the principle of "know thine enemy," Brecht noted down his reactions in "Zu Rapoport 'The Work of the Actor'" (*GBA*, 22:282), and "[Sudakow]" (*GBA*, 22:284). He embarked on a "nüchterne Betrachtung des Vokabulars des stanislawskischen Systems" (*GBA*, 22:280–81), resulting in the essay "Das verräterische Vokabular" (*GBA*, 22:279). If the exercise was also to be of practical value, Brecht realized, Epic Theater would need to learn from an analysis of what the Stanislavskians regarded as *distractions* from total identification (*GBA*, 22:282–83). What they wished to avoid was what Epic Theater needed to exploit for distancing purposes. As a corollary to this detailed study of the published theoretical writings of its adversaries, Epic Theater's theorizing needed to become more systematic in both methodology and self-presentation, if it was to compete. Although fundamentally opposed to the ideas and techniques that Stanislavsky and his followers promoted, Brecht clearly admired the way the Stanislavsky method was documented in a series of authoritative publications, thus identifying itself as a coherent and meticulously explained performance theory.

There followed a series of attempts at coming to terms with contemporary "Aristotelian," Stanislavsky-influenced theater, including "[Über die Krise der Einfühlung]," "Aufgeben der Einfühlung," "Über die

---

[11] "[Stanislawski — Wachtangow — Meyerhold]" (*GBA*, 22:285), written in 1937. Brecht gives thumbnail sketches of the "method" of all three directors, but the Stanislavsky section begins with the acknowledgment that his primary importance lies in having a method. The other features cited are "2) Intimere Kenntnis des Menschen, das Private, 3) Die widersprüchliche Psyche darstellbar (moralische Kategorien gut und böse aufgegeben), 4) Einflüsse des Milieus berücksichtigt, 5) Toleranz, 6) Natürlichkeit der Darstellung"; all except the last two tend to highlight points of contact between Brecht and Stanislavsky.

Bezeichnung 'restlose Verwandlung,'" and "Die nicht restlose Verwandlung ein scheinbarer Rückschritt" (*GBA*, 22:170–80), all dating from 1935. Having by 1936 read Stanislavsky's *My Life in Art* "mit Neid und Unruhe," Brecht wrote to Piscator in July 1936 that it was "grundfalsch, daß wir für unsere Art, Theater und Film aufzufassen, keine Propaganda machen." The reason for this observation emerges from a reference to Stanislavsky later in the same paragraph: "Der Mann hat sein System in Ordnung gebracht und die Folge ist, daß sie in Paris und New York Stanislawski-Schüler werden. Muß das sein? Wir sind wirklich weltfremde Träumer" (*GBA*, 28:558). Nevertheless, the significance of Brecht's preoccupation with Stanislavsky was obviously not just a matter of propaganda tactics. It also had heuristic value for his own theoretical self-understanding.

While noting that in far too many quarters a good play is measured by how fully an audience is able to identify with the central characters, Brecht remarks on how difficult the requisite "Einfühlung" apparently is for even a good actor to achieve: "eine ingeniöse Pädagogik mußte erfunden werden, damit der Schauspieler nicht 'aus der Rolle fiel'" (*GBA*, 22:280). On the basis of this, Brecht arrived at what was to become the extremely useful hypothesis that the Stanislavskian actor's "restlose Verwandlung" into the part to be played is vital to the achievement of absolute audience empathy, an idea he would adapt to distance Epic Theater's audiences by ensuring that his own actors *demonstrate* behavior rather than *identify* with a character. "Zeigen ist mehr als Sein" (*GBA*, 23:315) became the underlying premise.

Brecht's immediate reactions to Stanislavsky's writings are largely in the form of scattered aperçus and half-digested insights. The closest to a systematic approach comes with a reiteration, in "Thesen über die Aufgabe der Einfühlung in den theatralischen Künsten," of his and Sternberg's earlier position that there were cogent sociological reasons why empathy must be rejected: "Heute, wo die 'freie' Einzelpersönlichkeit zum Hindernis einer weiteren Entfaltung der Produktivkräfte geworden ist, hat die Einfühlungstechnik [. . .] ihre Berechtigung eingebüßt. Die Einzelpersönlichkeit hat ihre Funktion an die großen Kollektive abzutreten" (*GBA*, 22:175). On a more strictly aesthetic plane, one still finds little concern with the paradoxical fact that Stanislavsky's main aim is to encourage audiences to identify with characters who are making grave mistakes or whose vision is impaired by false consciousness. Nor does Brecht engage with the fact that Aristotelian catharsis is less central to the Stanislavskian conception of dramatic effect than is being implied. Brecht's exploration of the Stanislavsky phenomenon proceeds from the working hypothesis that empathy is ill-equipped to deliver political insights.

At the same time that he was studying Stanislavsky, Brecht embarked on a substantial reformulation of Epic Theater. While initially one finds little that is absolutely new in his writings on the subject apart from a more pronounced emphasis on the importance of epic acting,[12] there is evidence of the need to map such concepts as "Verfremdung," "experimentelles Theater," and "Historisierung" on to the larger territory previously occupied exclusively by the term "Episches Theater." For a while, there is indecision about which concept — or just how many — to privilege. Thus, although the "Anmerkungen [1933]" to *Die Mutter* present the play as "ein Stück antimetaphysischer, materialistischer, *nichtaristotelischer Dramatik*," the following paragraph goes on to offer an account of the "*Mittelbare Wirkung der epischen Bühne*" (*GBA*, 24:115), suggesting that "episch" still retains favor as the lead concept at the time when the notes were written early in 1932. The term "nichtaristotelisch" (a neologism already to be found in *Der Dreigroschenprozeß* of 1931 [*GBA*, 21:477]) gradually assumes greater importance in the theoretical writings. By 1933 a prefatory note declares that "Die *Anmerkungen* zur 'Mutter' gehören zum 9. Versuch *Über eine nichtaristotelische Dramatik* (*Versuche* H. 7)." It is indicative of that new term's growing importance that Brecht's most influential remarks about non-Aristotelian theater should be given pride of place in his American calling-card essay "The German Drama: Pre-Hitler" (*GBA*, 22:941–42). When this was reprinted the following year (1936) in the London *Left Review*, the term is further highlighted by the editor's accompanying explanation: "Since Brecht's works are practically unobtainable in published form, all available copies having been burnt by the Nazis, some further elucidation of what he means by non-Aristotelian or 'Epic' drama may be appended here" (*GBA*, 22:944). The term occurs ever more frequently, until it is eventually superseded by "Verfremdung." (Unseld 1957 muddies the waters by giving the entire one-volume Suhrkamp edition of Brecht's *Schriften zum Theater* the subtitle *Über eine nicht-aristotelische Dramatik*.) In "[Kritik der *Poetik* des Aristoteles]," written c. 1935, Brecht makes a detailed attempt to explain "aristotelisches Theater" with reference to Aristotle's *Poetics*: "Als aristotelische Dramatik [. . .] wird da alle Dramatik bezeichnet, auf welche die aristotelische Definition der Tragödie in der *Poetik* in dem, was wir für ihren Hauptpunkt halten, paßt. Die bekannte Forderung der drei Einheiten betrachten wir nicht als diesen Hauptpunkt, sie wird vom Aristoteles auch gar nicht erhoben, wie die neuere Forschung festgestellt hat. Uns erscheint von größtem gesellschaftlichem Interesse, was Aristoteles der Tragödie als Zweck setzt, nämlich die *Katharsis,* die Reinigung des Zuschauers von Furcht und Mitleid durch die Nachahmung von furcht- und

---

[12] The following appear in *GBA*, vol. 22: "Kleine Liste der beliebtesten, landläufigsten und banalsten Irrtümer über das epische Theater" (315–16), "Was ist episches Theater?" (317), "Historische Linie des epischen Theaters" (317–18), "Dialog über eine Schauspielerin des epischen Theaters" (353–55), and "Vorwort (Über ernsthafte Bemühungen um das Theater)" (381–83).

mitleiderregenden Handlungen. Diese Reinigung erfolgt auf Grund eines eigentümlichen psychischen Aktes, der *Einfühlung* des Zuschauers in die handelnden Personen, die von den Schauspielern nachgeahmt werden. Wir bezeichnen eine Dramatik als aristotelisch, wenn diese Einfühlung von ihr herbeigeführt wird, *ganz gleichgültig, ob unter Benutzung der vom Aristoteles dafür angeführten Regeln oder ohne deren Benutzung. Der eigentümliche psychische Akt der Einfühlung wird im Laufe der Jahrhunderte auf ganz verschiedene Art vollzogen"* (*GBA* 22:171, last emphasis mine). Given that a note to "Die Straßenszene" describes "das uns gewohnte Theater" (i.e. Aristotelian Theater) as "am klarsten entwickelt durch Stanislawski" (*GBA,* 22:377), it is tempting to speculate about why Brecht did not consider using the phrase "eine nicht-stanislawskische Dramatik." Of course, there were good cultural-political grounds for the use of such a term being impolitic for a Marxist, as well as further reasons why the presentation of his work as "anti-aristotelisch" helped give the impression of a substantially more radical paradigm shift. A subsequent note on catharsis among the fragments of *Der Messingkauf* spells this out: "Das Theater hat sich, seit Aristoteles dies schrieb, oft gewandelt, aber kaum in diesem Punkt. Man muß annehmen, daß es, wandelte es sich in diesem Punkt, nicht mehr Theater wäre" (*GBA,* 22:779). Brecht's inscription, dating from the mid-1930s, in an edition of Aristotle's *Poetics* makes the point even more emphatically:

> Mit recht hat LESSING die in der POETIK des A. aufgestellten lehr-
> sätze für so unfehlbar gehalten wie die elemente des EUKLID. Die herr-
> schaft beider doktrine erstreckt sich über 2 jahrtausende und für
> bestimmte funktionen haben die lehrsätze heute noch gültigkeit.
> Jedoch kann man und muss man ebenso wie eine NICHTEUKLIDISCHE
> GEOMETRIE heute eine NICHTARISTOTELISCHE DRAMATURGIE auf-
> stellen. (Wizisla 1998, 171)

While the process of bruised self-examination continued during the period 1936–38, Brecht's campaign for recognition in the English-speaking world progressed apace, though with less clear a sense of direction. In June 1937, "Epic Realism: Brecht's Notes on the *Threepenny Opera*" appeared in *Theatre Workshop*. As well as material from the "Anmerkungen zur *Dreigro-schenoper,*" there was a commentary by Gorelik. Poetry by Brecht, as well as the scene "Der Spitzel" from *Furcht und Elend des III. Reiches,* appeared in John Lehmann's *New Writing* (V, Spring 1938 and II, New Series, Spring 1939). And Gorelik's *New Theatres for Old* (1940) was to offer what has been called "the most advanced exposition of Brechtian theater [then] available in any language" (Lyon 1980, 14). It was little more than a Pyrrhic victory for Brecht to have to introduce himself to a sophisticated *Theatre Work-shop* readership with, of all things, thoughts about *Die Dreigroschenoper.* Weill's presence in the USA and a shortlived earlier American production of the work at the Empire Theatre in 1933 must have made this seem a logical move. And it could only have been something of an indignity to find himself figuring in *New Theatres for Old* alongside such a galaxy of competing forms of twentieth-century theater in a compendious work whose author was by all accounts largely sympathetic towards the theater of identification. As Brecht was later to remark, this was not the only bone of contention:

> *Max Gorelik,* der in seinem Buch *New Theaters for Old* [sic] über das epische Theater referiert hat, bringt mich mehr und mehr auf die theoretischen Lücken: Ich sehe seine Mißverständnisse. Ein eigentümlich puritanischer Geruch steigt von der Gorelikschen Reproduktion auf, etwas Laboratoriumhaftes. Die ästhetische Seite schrumpft zum Formalismus zusammen. (Das Theater eines wissenschaftlichen Zeitalters wird zum wissenschaftlichen Theater.) (*GBA,* 27:216)

Brecht was of course conscious of the need to explain the guiding concepts behind his theater to new audiences in the English-speaking world. The lead terms by this time associated with his Epic Theater, "Verfremdung," "Historisierung," "Theater des wissenschaftlichen Zeitalters," and "nicht-aristotelische Dramatik," relate mainly to his own experiments, whereas many of his older labels related to the things he was against. Sometimes key terms (e.g. in "Über experimentelles Theater") are introduced in passing in general expository accounts of his work. Elsewhere they are introduced almost clandestinely like Trojan Horses, which, as we shall shortly see, happened with "Historisierung" in "Verfremdungseffekte in der chinesischen Schauspielkunst." Gradually, all of these concepts become the topic of canonical passages on the new techniques and modes of theater. But because the discursive setting of these reconceptualizations of Brechtian theater is of some significance, I propose to look first at the three major essays written during the second half of the 1930s: "Verfremdungeffekte in der chinesischen Schauspielkunst" (1936), "Über experimentelles Theater" (1939), and "Kurze Beschreibung einer neuen Technik der Schauspielkunst, die einen Verfremdungseffekt hervorbringt" (1940). Since no one essay offers the classical exposition of a term, it will then be necessary to draw together Brecht's thinking on the various procedures in order to assess the theory emerging from the 1930s in the light of its reception. As such a compromise implies, Brecht was trying to launch a fresh series of unfamiliar (and sometimes unhelpfully neologistic) terms within a relatively short period. In his attempt to create the impression of a complex theory sophisticated enough to weigh in alongside Stanislavsky's writings, he appears reluctant to foreground single concepts in the theoretical writings from what Hecht has called the period of "die zweite Fassung der Theorie" (Hecht 1972, 134–35).

## "Verfremdungseffekte in der chinesischen Schauspielkunst" (1936)

Brecht saw a clear link between "Schauspielkunst" and "Verfremdung" well before he began to use the term "Verfremdung." Of characters in Epic Theater, he says: "Ihr Handeln wurde als nicht selbstverständlich, sondern als auffällig hingestellt" ("Die dialektische Dramatik" [1930], *GBA,* 21:439), using the terms of contrast he would later return to in his explanations of "Verfremdung." That same year a fragment records: "Die Schauspieler müssen dem Zuschauer Figuren und Vorgänge entfremden, so daß sie auffallen" ("[Die Große und die Kleine Pädagogik,]" *GBA,* 21:396). Between 1936 and 1938 Brecht wrote a series of notes and sketches on "Verfremdung," some referring to his own experiments, others to "Verfremdung" in various embryonic pre-Brechtian forms to be found *avant la lettre* in other cultural contexts or defamiliarization processes encountered in everyday life. Given that most of this work was not published in German at the time,[13] it may seem ironic that the first essay in which "Verfremdung" is discussed at any length should be about alienation effects in Chinese acting and that it should have come out in English, in a London magazine, rather than in *Theatre Workshop.*[14]

In "Verfremdungseffekte in der chinesischen Schauspielkunst" — or "The Fourth Wall of China: An Essay on the Effect of Disillusion in the

[13] See *GBA,* vol. 22: "Episches Theater, Entfremden" (211–12), "V-Effekt [1]" (212), "Verfremdung bestimmter Vorgänge durch eine Darstellungsart, die sonst Sitten und Gebräuche erfahren würden" (213), "V-Effekt [2]" (214), "Der V-Effekt auf dem alten Theater" (214–15), "[Der V-Effekt im älteren Theater]" (215–16), "Der V-Effekt" (216–17), "Politische Theorie der Verfremdung" (217–18), "Politische Theorie des V-Effekts auf dem Theater" (218–19), "Allgemeine Theorie der Verfremdung" (219), "Nützlichkeit des V-Effekts" (220), "Verfremdung des Autos" (220), "Der V-Effekt bei Mommsen und Feuchtwanger" (220–21), "V-Effekte bei Chaplin" (223), "[Der Verfremdungseffekt in anderen Künsten]" (223–24), "Hervorbringen des V-Effekts" (355–56), and "Dialekt und Verfremdung" (401–2). The majority of these pieces date from 1936.

[14] *Life and Letters To-Day,* 6 (1936), 116–23, reprinted in *GBA,* 22:960–68. The essay's translator, Eric Walter White, author of the first essay in English on Brecht (1935), also reviewed *A Penny for the Poor* (*Die Dreigroschenoper,* 1937), *The Expedient* (*Die Maßnahme,* 1937), and *The Private Life of the Master Race* (*Furcht und Elend des III. Reiches,* 1948) for the same journal. White's various contributions on music to *Life and Letters To-Day* suggest that he came to Brecht via *Die Dreigroschenoper* and the German music festivals; he was, after all, the author of *Stravinsky* as well as a book of *Studies in Ballet.* From 1928–33, when Desmond MacCarthy had been the editor of what was then simply entitled *Life and Letters,* the London monthly retained a strong interest in contemporary drama.

Chinese Theatre," to give it its full English title — we find Brecht, undaunted by the methodological problems underlying the project, confidently discussing techniques of "Verfremdung" in Chinese acting that require substantial reformulation before coming across as a plausible protoform of the distancing strategies of Epic Theater. For "Verfremdung" Brecht's translator, Eric White, uses "disillusion," a word which looks more like an English translation of "Enttäuschung" and is hardly synonymous with the German source term, even if the concepts share common ground. Brecht does refer, in White's sense, to "eine desillusionierende Bühne" in his "Anmerkungen zur *Mutter* [1938]" (*GBA*, 24:171). The translation's playful title, "The Fourth Wall of China" also shifts the essay's material perceptibly in the direction of Brechtian theater conventions, perhaps to downplay the political thrust of the final part of the essay.

Brecht begins with a more succinct statement of purpose than can be found in any of the theoretical writings hitherto:

> Im nachfolgenden soll kurz auf die Anwendung des *Verfremdungseffekts* in der alten chinesischen Schauspielkunst hingewiesen werden. Dieser Effekt wurde zuletzt in Deutschland, bei den Versuchen, zu einem *epischen Theater* zu kommen, für Stücke *nichtaristotelischer* (nicht auf Einfühlung beruhender) *Dramatik* angewendet. Es handelt sich hier um Versuche, so zu spielen, daß der Zuschauer gehindert wurde, sich in die Figuren des Stückes lediglich einzufühlen. Annahme oder Ablehnung ihrer Äußerungen oder Handlungen sollten im Bereich des Bewußtseins, anstatt wie bisher in dem des Unterbewußtseins des Zuschauers erfolgen. (*GBA*, 22:200)

As an introduction to a time-honored style of Chinese acting, this piece already goes off at a remarkable tangent by implying that, in the Chinese tradition, one of the technique's functions is to prevent the actor from identifying with a part. Indeed, the suggestion that "Verfremdung" in acting belongs essentially to the conscious realm, whereas until now theater's appeal had been more to the subconscious, has more to do with differences between Epic and Stanislavskian Theater, as perceived and valorized by Brecht.[15] Hardly a paragraph in the entire essay discusses "chinesische Schauspielkunst" without such contemporary European framing. The image of the missing "fourth wall" leads on to the remark: "Das entfernt sogleich eine bestimmte Illusion der europäischen Bühne" (*GBA*, 22:201), the one according to which characters onstage appear to be oblivious to the presence of an audience eavesdropping on a scene ostensibly from real life. Elsewhere, having described Chinese opera's treatment of a journey by boat (in *Ta-yü Sha chia* [*The Fisherman's Revenge*] *BHB*, 4:190), Brecht adds: "Die Szene

---

[15] E.g. "[Suggestive Technik]" (*GBA*, 22:283).

erinnerte uns an den Marsch nach Budweis in der Piscatorschen Aufführung des *Braven Soldaten Schwejk*" (*GBA*, 22:202).[16] Later, when speculating about how an oriental acting style will appear to Westerners — cold? bizarre? over-ritualistic? — Brecht adopts the polemical, as well as defamiliarizing, ploy of equating the Western audience with Stanislavskian, empathy-dominated assumptions and presenting the Chinese actor as the epitome of a longstanding convention of estrangement in acting. West-meets-East thus doubles as Stanislavskian acting versus Epic Theater's "Gestus des Zeigens," the gulf between the two traditions being assumed for rhetorical purposes to be just as wide. Such moving back and forth between Asiatic acting conventions and contemporary Western theater involves more than rapid shifts in perspective. The very choice of concepts (an even more complicated feature in the English translation where there is no Brechtian German precedent to build on) creates a clash between oriental practices and Western descriptive vocabulary.[17] The terms "Verfremdung" and "Verfremdungs-effekt," the presentation of the "Sich-selber-Zusehen" of the actor as "ein künstlicher und kunstvoller Akt der Selbstentfremdung" (*GBA*, 22:202), even the presence of Freudian psychological terms,[18] all come across as Western intrusions upon the essay's apparent subject matter, for they are deliberately couched in terms more appropriate to Epic Theater:

> Der Artist wünscht, dem Zuschauer fremd, ja befremdlich zu erscheinen. Er erreicht das dadurch, daß er sich selbst und seine Darbietungen mit Fremdheit betrachtet. So bekommen die Dinge, die er vorführt, etwas Erstaunliches. (*GBA*, 22:202)

> Es ist zunächst schon schwierig, sich, wenn man Chinesen spielen sieht, frei zu machen von dem Gefühl der Befremdung, das sie in uns, als in *Europäern*, erregen. Man muß sich also vorstellen können, daß sie den V-Effekt auch erzielen bei ihren chinesischen Zuschauern. (*GBA*, 22:206)

Such terminological hybridity loses some of its force in translation. Stanislavsky's "creative mood" (from the chapter "The Beginnings of my

---

[16] *Life and Letters To-Day* relegates this material to a modest "*Author's Note*," with the effect that it no longer formed part of the essay's dominant "stereometric" strategy.

[17] In "*Das 'asiatische' Vorbild*," a section of "[Der Weg zu großem zeitgenössischem Theater]" (*GBA*, 21:380–81), Brecht confronted the problem raised for many Western readers by the exotic nature of oriental terms. Apart from being an act of verbal "gegenseitige Verfremdung," the application of Western analytical vocabulary to Chinese acting techniques was intended to minimize such a risk.

[18] It may not be irrelevant here that the *Mahagonny* notes had based part of their argument on Freud's *Das Unbehagen in der Kultur* (see *GBA*, 24:83).

System," *My Life in Art*), a term montaged in a defamiliarizing way into the original German (*GBA*, 22:203), is deprived of much of this impact when merely appearing in quotation marks as English among English. "Der Versuch, dem Publikum die darzustellenden Vorgänge zu verfremden" (*GBA*, 22:200) is misleadingly rendered by "attempts to disillusion the audience about the events portrayed" (*GBA*, 22:960) and "V-Effekt" becomes "disillusion in the theatre" (*GBA*, 22:964). Brecht's deliberately estranging discourse is diluted to the point of resembling everyday English.[19]

More important, Brecht's translator was faced with the dilemma of having to choose which term to use for "Verfremdung": "alienation," "defamiliarization," "estrangement," or "distanciation"? Having opted for the more problematic word "disillusion," he was still left with the difficulty that Brecht uses "Verfremdung" in at least two senses. White's preferred "disillusion in the theatre" appears to refer to the effect on the audience (which is how many have understood the English term "A-effect"). However, the first paragraph's phrase "Der Versuch, dem Publikum die darzustellenden Vorgänge zu verfremden" would be better expressed by the verb "to estrange," in the sense of something being "made strange" (*verfremdet*). After all, the "V-Effekt" is referred to as "ein Verfahren" (*GBA*, 22:220).[20] If this were not the term's principal meaning, Brecht would not have been able to employ the noun in the plural: "die neuen Verfremdungen," in the sense of "the new alienation devices" (*Kleines Organon* §43, *GBA*, 23:81). Willett has tried to help English readers by pointing out that Brecht's "'Effekt' corresponded to our own stage use of the word 'effects': a means by which an effect of estrangement can be got" (Willett 1959, 177). But this still fails to address the further problem created by the fact that Brecht's usage is far from consistent. Compare "der V-Effekt hatte seine Wirkung bei ihnen verfehlt" (*GBA*, 22:206), applied to Mei Lan-fang's enactment of a deathbed scene, with "der Verfremdungseffekt tritt ein" (*GBA*, 22:204) and "den V-Effekt auslösen" (*GBA*, 22:205). The verbs "eintreten" and "auslösen" would hardly be appropriate to the deployment of a device, but they are to the effect on the audience. In English usage, one *estranges* or *de-*

---

[19] Whether Brecht vetted White's English version is not known. The insertion in "The Fourth Wall of China" of the declaration that "Only those who have learned to think dialectically will hold it possible that a technique derived from the realm of illusion can be used as a weapon in the struggle against illusion" (*GBA*, 22:965) does, however, suggest that additions may have been made at the German end of the proofreading process.

[20] A further distinction would be between the "V-Effekt" (the device) and "Verfremdung" (the alienation of the audience). But the title "Kurze Beschreibung einer neuen Technik der Schauspielkunst, die einen *Verfremdungseffekt* hervorbringt" makes it clear that no such distinction between means and ends is maintained.

*familiarizes* an object or some onstage activity, but *alienates* an audience. However, when Brecht says "Der Verfremdungseffekt wird auf dem chinesischen Theater auf folgende Weise erzielt" (*GBA*, 22:201), he once more refers unhelpfully to the *result*, the alienation of the audience. In other words, we have a further example of the blurring of the distinction between means and ends that was also a feature of the first *Mahagonny* "Schema." While such an ambiguity may not detract from the substance of the dominant contrast between stylized oriental acting and the Western tradition of empathy or make the assumed parallels between Chinese and epic acting seem any less convincing, it hardly augurs well for the proposed Diderot Society's program of systematizing terminology in the arts and sciences.[21]

Having surveyed an array of estranging devices in Chinese acting, Brecht turns to the question of their significance for Western theater: "Es ist nicht ganz einfach, den V-Effekt der chinesischen Schauspielkunst als ein *transportables Technikum* [. . .] zu erkennen" (*GBA*, 22:206). (At this point the translation inserts: "Only those who have learned to think dialectically will hold it possible that a technique derived from the realm of illusion can be used as a weapon in the struggle against illusion" [*GBA*, 22:965]). The eventual, unsurprising conclusion is that it ought only to be appropriated if used "für ganz bestimmte gesellschaftliche Zwecke" (*GBA*, 22:207).

Brecht's overall rhetorical strategy here should not pass without comment. If the essay's disclaimer is to be believed,[22] Brecht had not first discov-

---

[21] "Die Wissenschaften haben ihren gemeinsamen Standard, ihr gemeinsames Vokabular [. . .]. Die Diderot-Gesellschaft setzt sich die Aufgabe, [. . .] eine Terminologie zu schaffen" (*GBA* 22, 274). Brecht's attempt to found a "Gesellschaft für induktives Theater" (*GBA*, 22:274) stems from a similar desire to establish common methodological principles and nomenclature. The *Brecht Chronik* relates the project to Brecht's need to come to terms with Stanislavsky: "In der *Diderot-Gesellschaft* sieht Brecht u.a. die Möglichkeit, sich mit dem System Stanislawskis auseinanderzusetzen" (Hecht 1997, 505).

[22] In "[Der Weg zum zeitgenössischen Theater]" (1930), Brecht writes: "Wir müssen [. . .] auf Vorbilder bedacht sein. Sie sind nur schwer zu finden, und bestimmt nicht in unserer räumlichen oder zeitlichen Umgebung" (*GBA*, 21:379). The section, "Das 'asiatische Vorbild'" (*GBA*, 21:380–81), points in the direction of Japanese theater, as does "Über die japanische Schauspieltechnik" (*GBA*, 21:391–92), of the same year. Brecht's later assertion that "die Experimente des neuen deutschen Theaters entwickelten den V-Effekt ganz und gar selbständig, es fand bisher keine Beeinflussung durch die asiatische Schauspielkunst statt" (*GBA*, 22:207) remains ambiguous. The use of the adjective "asiatisch" may be intended to avoid any suggestion that his interest has been confined to Chinese conventions. But the phrase "keine Beeinflussung" only makes sense if one assumes Brecht means that his specifically political form of the "V-Effekt" is not indebted to oriental traditions. In Tatlow's words, "[Brechts] gesellschaftliche Interessen und Bezüge teilte das

ered estrangement in Chinese theater and only then raised the question of its possible value for Epic Theater. Yet that is precisely what the essay appears to suggest. There may well have been an element of organized chance to the Moscow encounter with Mei Lan-fang. After all, Tretiakov, Brecht's Soviet kindred spirit and author of the epic play known in German as *Brülle, China!*, had arranged the demonstration of Chinese acting at the house of the Chinese ambassador to the USSR. Yet the resultant essay involves a conscious presentational strategy on Brecht's part: that of drawing attention to an oriental analogue to his own theater in order to use the parallel as a means of explaining Epic Theater's experiments within a new defamiliarizing framework.

In any case, more was involved in Chinese acting than a series of simple techniques for "making strange." In an earlier draft "[Über ein Detail des chinesischen Theaters]," Brecht explains that the Chinese actor "legt Gewicht darauf, daß er es nicht als seine Hauptleistung betrachtet, wie eine Frau gehen und weinen zu können, sondern wie eine bestimmte Frau" (*GBA*, 22:127). In connection with this, Antony Tatlow notes: "In Mei Lan-fang's acting Brecht saw not just an externalization of the typical, but also an evaluation of the particular" (Tatlow 1977, 315). Which is tantamount to claiming that Brecht detected rudiments of a form of "Historisierung" in the acting style he had witnessed in Moscow.

Nevertheless, while an account of "Verfremdung" in Chinese acting might illustrate general techniques of "making strange" and attention to significant detail, it was hardly adequate for explaining Brecht's political conception of "Historisierung." Not just because Brecht was insufficiently versed in the Chinese tradition, but because Mei Lan-fang's style did not "historicize" its material in Brecht's sense. Brecht thus found himself obliged to turn to Western theater for an illustration of the technique's political potential. It is worth bearing in mind that an earlier draft dating from 1935 (*GBA*, 22:151–55) conveys the importance of Mei Lan-fang's performance without ever using the words "Verfremdung" and "Historisierung." Now, once the relationship of "Historisierung" to "Verfremdung" is required as part of the picture, the Chinese illustration can be little more than a stepping-stone to the essay's final perspectives.

---

chinesische Theater nicht" (*BHB*, 4:191). Note also the telling remark, when Brecht is describing the effect of Chinese acting on a Westerner: "Man muß sich also vorstellen können, daß sie den V-Effekt auch erzielen bei ihren chinesischen Zuschauern" (*GBA*, 22:206). If not, one would have thought, Brecht's guiding claim that "Auch die alte chinesische Schauspielkunst kennt den Verfremdungseffekt" (*GBA*, 22:200) loses its argumentative value.

Processes of "Verfremdung" and "Historisierung" need to be shown to be ways of treating the present, rather than just the past.[23] As Brecht puts it elsewhere, taking up Benjamin's concept of "Jetztzeit": "die Jetztzeit wird zur Historie" (*GBA*, 22:736). "Verfremdungseffekte in der chinesischen Schauspielkunst" now develops this idea:

> Der V-Effekt [. . .] bezweckte hauptsächlich die *Historisierung* der darzustellenden Vorgänge. Darunter ist folgendes zu verstehen:
>
> Das bürgerliche Theater [the English translator here adds "i.e. what we mean when we talk of 'the theatre'"] arbeitet an seinen Gegenständen das Zeitlose heraus. Die Darstellung des Menschen hält sich an das sogenannte Ewig-Menschliche. Durch die Anordnung der Fabel werden solche "allgemeine" Situationen geschaffen, daß der Mensch schlechthin, der Mensch aller Zeiten und jeder Hautfarbe, sich nunmehr ausdrücken kann. Alle Vorgänge sind nur das große Stichwort, und auf dieses Stichwort erfolgt die "ewige" Antwort, die unvermeidliche, gewohnte, natürliche, eben menschliche Antwort. Ein Beispiel: Der Mensch schwarzer Haut liebt wie der weiße Mensch, und erst wenn ihm von der Fabel der gleiche Ausdruck erpreßt ist, wie ihn der weiße liefert (sie können die Formel theoretisch angeblich umkehren), ist die Sphäre der Kunst geschaffen. Das Besondere, Unterschiedliche kann im Stichwort berücksichtigt werden: die Antwort ist gemeinsam; in der Antwort gibt es nichts Unterschiedliches. Diese Auffassung mag die Existenz einer Geschichte zugeben, aber es ist dennoch eine geschichtslose Auffassung. (*GBA*, 22:207–8)

If it is strange in an oriental context to find Brecht contrasting "Historisierung" with bourgeois theater's essentialist emphasis on timeless verities, it is even more unexpected to see him stressing the need to take account of cultural differences by comparing the way that "der Mensch schwarzer Haut" feels love with the way that a white Caucasian does. So far, while he may have admitted that there is a fundamental difference between non-political "disillusion-effects" in Chinese acting and socially focused experiments with "Verfremdung" in Epic Theater, he has offered no "historicization" of his oriental illustration. By introducing an American perspective,

---

[23] As Müller explains: "Durch das Historisieren wird ja ein Erkenntnisakt provoziert, der analog auf die Gegenwart übertragbar ist und hier praktisch wirksam werden soll. [. . .] Historisierung der Gegenwart bedeutet deren objektive Erkenntnis, aus der im Sinne des dialektischen Verhältnisses von Theorie und Praxis ein richtiges Verhalten folgt. Darum ist die Gegenwart der entscheidende Anwendungsbereich der Historisierung" (Klaus-Detlef Müller 1967, 40). Müller sees a parallel to Lukács's call "den Staat der kapitalischen Gesellschaft schon während seines Bestehens als historische Erscheinung zu betrachten und zu bewerten" (Lukács 1923, 266).

Brecht now removes the field of investigation further from the original Chinese context, thus encouraging even greater "komplexes Sehen." Once more a new term ("Historisierung") is presented by way of a preliminary account of a phenomenon ("eine geschichtslose Auffassung") to which it is an antidote. This *ex negativo* ploy is then brought to a sudden halt with the declaration that "die Auffassung des Menschen als einer Variablen des Milieus, des Milieus als einer Variablen des Menschen, d.h. die Auflösung des Milieus in Beziehungen zwischen Menschen, entspringt einem neuen Denken, dem historischen Denken" (*GBA*, 22:208). Dismissing his previous remarks about bourgeois theater's ahistoricity as a "geschichtsphilosophische Exkursion" (in actual fact they were a necessary stage in a process of "Historisierung"), Brecht moves on to an example of how the present can be historicized.

The seemingly archetypal situation chosen ("Ein junges Mädchen verläßt ihre Familie, um eine Stellung in einer größeren Stadt anzunehmen") could be played in an essentializing way or historicized. In a form of "doppelte Verfremdung," the reader is invited to relate the dramatic cliché to a specific episode in *An American Tragedy*, not Theodore Dreiser's original 1925 novel, but Piscator's 1935 stage adaptation (also known under the title *The Case of Clyde Griffiths*). The allusion to the Dreiser adaptation, like the earlier concern with color, suggests that "The Fourth Wall of China" was as much "für New York geschrieben" as Brecht's *Leben des Galilei* was to be. Yet it looks suspiciously as if Brecht had taken deliberate liberties with the material. For in Dreiser's novel neither Esta Griffiths nor her brother Clyde goes off into the big wide world under the circumstances conjured up in Brecht's scenario. Esta merely elopes, only to be abandoned on becoming pregnant, while Clyde leaves when suspected of being an accomplice to a road accident. Brecht has clearly grafted his argument onto a somewhat imaginative reconstruction of Piscator's *An American Tragedy*. And he may have had good reasons for doing so. The fact that the author of *Sister Carrie* and *An American Tragedy* was one of the principal representatives of American Naturalism and that Piscator was one of the early proponents of Epic Theater may have had more value for Brecht than any need to respect plot details in the rather "culinary" source novel or in a bold adaptation that few Americans would have seen.[24] Although neither sibling leaves Kansas City for purely economic reasons, Brecht's conception of "Historisierung" required this rather than infatuation or a car accident to be the main cause of their departure.

[24] A note in *GBA*, 22:969 describes Piscator's adaptation as "erst am Broadway realisiert," although it had already been put on in 1935, under the title *The Case of Clyde Griffiths*, at the Jasper Deeter Hedgerow Theatre, Moylan, Pennsylvania, and Lee Strasberg's Group Theatre staged it in New York the following year.

Brecht passes up a number of opportunities to attack the emotional socialism of Asa and Elvira Griffiths and the melodramatic tenor of Dreiser's account. He keeps his powder dry for the ensuing indication of what a "Historisierung" of such material would entail:

> Für das historisierende Theater liegt alles anders. Es wirft sich ganz und gar auf das Eigentümliche, Besondere, der Untersuchung Bedürftige des so alltäglichen Vorgangs. Wie, die Familie entläßt aus ihrer Hut ein Mitglied, damit es sich nunmehr selbständig, ohne Hilfe den Lebensunterhalt verdient? Ist es dazu imstande? Was es hier, als Familienmitglied, gelernt hat, wird ihm das helfen, den Unterhalt zu verdienen? Können Familien ihre Kinder nicht mehr behalten? Sind sie eine Last geworden oder geblieben? Ist das so bei allen Familien? War das immer so? Ist das der Lauf der Welt, der nicht zu beeinflussende? Wenn die Frucht reif ist, fällt sie vom Baum. Gilt hier dieser Satz? Machen sich die Kinder immer einmal selbständig? Taten sie es zu allen Zeiten? Wenn ja, wenn es etwas Biologisches ist, geschieht es immer in der gleichen Weise, aus demselben Grunde, mit den gleichen Folgen? Das sind die Fragen (oder ein Teil von ihnen), welche die Schauspieler zu beantworten haben, wenn sie den Vorgang als einen historischen, einmaligen darstellen wollen, wenn sie hier eine Sitte aufzeigen wollen, die Aufschluß gibt über das ganze Gefüge der Gesellschaft einer bestimmten (vergänglichen) Zeit. (*GBA,* 22:209)

Historicization's ability to provoke the correct political response is shown to depend on the careful choice of telling detail and through it a sense of historical specificity. But only through "Verfremdung" at the hands of the actor will the historical significance of the detail be held up for critical inspection.

> Wie soll aber ein solcher Vorgang dargestellt werden, daß sein historischer Charakter hervortritt? Wie kann die Wirrnis unserer unglücklichen Zeit auffällig gemacht werden? Wenn die Mutter unter Ermahnungen und moralischen Forderungen der Tochter den Koffer packt, der sehr klein ist — wie zeigt man das: So viele Forderungen und so wenig Wäsche? Sittliche Forderungen für ein ganzes Leben und Brot nur für fünf Stunden? Wie hat die Schauspielerin den Satz der Mutter zu sprechen, mit dem sie den so sehr kleinen Koffer übergibt: "So, ich denke, das reicht aus," damit er als historischer Ausspruch verstanden wird? Das kann nur erreicht werden, wenn der V-Effekt hervorgebracht wird. Die Schauspielerin darf den Satz nicht zu ihrer eigenen Sache machen, sie muß ihn der Kritik überantworten, sie muß das Verständnis seiner Motive ermöglichen und den Protest. (*GBA,* 22:208)

After the precision of the above points, the rallying ending to the essay comes as something of an anticlimax: "Bei der Aufstellung neuer künstlerischer Prinzipien und der Erarbeitung neuer Methoden der Darstellung," the essay concludes, "müssen wir ausgehen von den gebieterischen Aufgaben einer Zeit des Epochenwechsels, Möglichkeit und Notwendigkeit einer Neuformierung der Gesellschaft taucht auf. Alle Vorgänge unter Menschen werden geprüft, *alles* muß vom gesellschaftlichen Standpunkt aus gesehen werden" (*GBA*, 22:210). The tone is guardedly reformist rather than stridently revolutionary. The exiled Brecht was not only writing in a country that forbade his participation in political activity; he was also writing for another country that was beginning to become uncomfortable about Dreiser's later, more committed writings.[25] However much "Historisierung" implied a dialectical materialist conception of history and hence revolution, this was left understated.

Brecht's essay on "Verfremdung" in Chinese acting explicitly characterizes the Stanislavskian method as being a matter of working within "ein ganzes System" (*GBA*, 22:203–4), something for which Chinese acting, with its highly sophisticated system of conventions, offered a counterpart. However, Chinese acting is only treated eclectically and the focus of the second half of the essay is on the need for a process of "Historisierung"; although the actor's importance for the processes of "Verfremdung" and "Historisierung" is stressed, little sense of any Epic Theater countersystem emerges. Only in "Kurze Beschreibung einer neuen Technik der Schauspielkunst, die einen Verfremdungseffekt hervorbringt" (alternative title: "Neue Technik der Schauspielkunst") is the challenge of creating a *Kontrafaktur* to the Stanislavsky system confronted head-on. But the need to oppose Stanislavsky, already in evidence in the opening pages of "The Fourth Wall of China," will eventually lead to a major imbalance in Brecht's theoretical statements about the different types of "Verfremdung" in Epic Theater's repertoire. And there are often times when his need to measure himself against the Stanislavsky of *My Life in Art* had a distorting effect on the scope of the dramaturgical writings. This was hardly the case, however, with his second major theoretical work of the late 1930s.

## "Über experimentelles Theater" (1939)

Although not published until after the end of the Second World War,[26] "Über experimentelles Theater" played a part in Brecht's preparations to leave Denmark for a safer place of asylum. To pave the way for a move to Sweden, he declared himself prepared to give "eine Serie von Vorträgen über

---

[25] As his works *Dreiser Looks at Russia* (1928) and *Tragic America* (1931) reveal, Dreiser moved substantially to the left after his visit to the USSR in 1927.

[26] In the journal of the Schweizerischer Verband Sozialistischer Studenten: *Bewußtsein und Sein* 3 (July, 1948): 1–5.

die Themen *Volksbühne, Laientheater* und *experimentelles Theater*" (*GBA,* 29:133) in Stockholm. The only response led to what Brecht described as "ein erstes Verständnis des Prinzipiellen" (*GBA,* 29:144). The lecture "Über experimentelles Theater" was delivered twice in the Swedish capital in May 1939, initially to the "Studentenbühne" and subsequently to the Amatörteaterns Riksförbund. Encouraged by the response, Brecht repeated it the following year before a student audience in Helsinki. This time he was less impressed: "Nette junge Leute, anscheinend ganz ohne Interessen, weder am Studieren noch am Theater. Ein Grauen, zu denken, vor dieser Schicht so etwas wie nichtaristotelisches Theater etablieren zu wollen" (*GBA,* 22:1070). Nevertheless, the lecture format, coupled with a sense of how much depended on such an act of public self-advertisement, proved beneficial, for the result was a highly informative, broad-based survey of modern German theater up to the time of his own work, combining a lucid account of Epic Theater with a crusading sense of the need to continue in the direction taken, all communicated in a rare demonstration of Brecht's public oratorical skills. It was also, he noted, "Zum Aufsatz 'Über eine neue Technik der Schauspielkunst' [. . .] eine gute Einleitung" (*GBA,* 26:337). That is, it was a bridge between the two innovative accounts of acting: relating to the Chinese theater and to Epic Theater. Although the general impression is of a broad survey of contemporary drama, Brecht strikes a defensive note when it comes to Epic Theater: "[Unsere] Versuche konnten nicht so methodisch durchgeführt werden wie die (andersgearteten) der Stanislawski-, Meyerhold- und Wachtangowgruppe (es gab keine staatliche Unterstützung), aber sie wurden dafür auf breiterem Feld, nicht nur im professionellen Theater, ausgeführt" (*GBA,* 22:555). This last reference is to the "Lehrstücke," the only audience of which were the participating performers, and to Brecht's work with various socialist amateur theater groups, particularly in Denmark.

One finds a clearer sense of teleology in the Stockholm lecture than in the essay on Chinese acting. In the wake of a long line of experiments by other dramatists, Brecht's work is presented as the logical solution to a series of impasses. In that sense, he attempts to "historicize" his own work. When Brecht concludes by asking: "Ist dieser neue Darstellungsstil nun *der* neue Stil [. . .], das endgültige Resultat aller Experimente?" he answers with transparently diplomatic modesty: "Nein. Er ist *ein* Weg, der, den *wir* gegangen sind" (*GBA,* 22:557).

Much of the lecture's coherence is supplied by the elastic notion of "experiment." "Den üblen Klang, den der Begriff 'Experiment' heute hat, muß er in der vorbaconischen Ära gehabt haben," Brecht noted in his journal for 16 October 1940 (*GBA,* 26:436). Like the later *Kleines Organon,* "Über experimentelles Theater" was in Brecht's eyes immediately associated with Francis Bacon, his methodological forerunner, and the

Stockholm audience was clearly expected to make the connection between Bacon's concept of scientific experiment and Brecht's epic "Versuche." Recent work on Brecht's conception of a literary "experiment" has emphasized the difference between scientific experiments either designed to discover new facts or to corroborate hypotheses (in most hard sciences both are possible) and an analogically conceived literary "experiment" with a distinctly political agenda. "Diese Zwecksetzung [as set out in Brecht's prefatory note to the first number of *Versuche,* see note 27 below] beinhaltet einen veränderten Werk- und Kunstbegriff: die Suspendierung einer Vorstellung von Kunst als einmaliger Ausdruck 'individueller Erlebnisse,' der als 'Werk' sein vermeintlich autonomes Dasein jenseits aller Verwertungszusammenhänge habe. Das [literarische] Experiment dagegen hat seinen Zweck gerade als bewegendes/umwälzendes [i.e. revolutionary] Moment im Verwertungsprozess selbst" (*BHB,* 4:42). While not being a matter of the difference between a scientific experiment and a literary one, this does suggest that Brecht is using the experiment metaphor to minimize the distinction between a seemingly objective process and an ideologically driven one.

From Naturalism onwards, Brecht's argument runs, European theater has been (in some instances consciously) situated "in einer Epoche der Experimente." Its experiments fall into two main categories: "Experimente, die seine Amüsierkraft, und Experimente, die seinen Lehrwert erhöhen sollten" (*GBA,* 22:540). Such an account bypasses the contrast between "Vergnügungstheater" (now made to sound rather more frivolous by being reduced to its "Amüsierkraft") and a more serious-minded "Lehrtheater." That the theater of amusement is driven to find "immer neue Effekte [. . .], um seinen zerstreuten Zuschauer zu zerstreuen," may be making a familiar, yet in its formulation defamiliarizing, point about the built-in obsolescence of contemporary "Anstrengungen, immer neu zu erscheinen" (the concept of art as "Zerstreuung" is a major plank in the picture presented in Benjamin's "Das Kunstwerk im Zeitalter seiner technischen Reproduzierbarkeit"; cf. *BHB,* 4:183). Yet to stretch an already elastic metaphor by describing the search for new forms of largely emotion-based escapist appeal as "experiments" is to dignify the results of market processes with a false rationale. The effect of Brecht's application of the experiment model to such diverse material is in fact to highlight the difference between Epic Theater's serious agenda and the frivolity of novelty for novelty's sake (a phenomenon already satirized in the *Mahagonny* notes).

Brecht's concept of "experiment" may bear only a superficial resemblance to that of a Zola or a Holz,[27] but the Naturalists' concern with

---

[27] A prefatory note to the first issue of *Versuche* in June 1930 explains the title: "Die Publikation der Versuche erfolgt zu einem Zeitpunkt, wo gewisse Arbeiten nicht

*littérature expérimentale* still accounts in part for Brecht's point of departure. The innovations of Antoine, Brahm, Stanislavsky, Craig, and Reinhardt are credited with enhancing theater's "Ausbau der Maschinerie," as well as a more sophisticated general methodological concern with theater's expanding repertoire of effects. Advances in lighting, acoustics and staging techniques are presented as the fruits of systematic experimentation, in a technological sense that goes well beyond Naturalism's concept of literary experimentation. Although conceding that such advances are "sehr ungleichwertig" and that "die auffälligsten sind nicht immer die wertvollsten," Brecht concedes that "Das Theater im allgemeinen ist noch lange nicht auf den Standard der modernen Technik gebracht" (*GBA*, 22:542).[28]

---

mehr so sehr individuelle Erlebnisse sein (Werkcharakter haben) sollen, sondern mehr auf die Benutzung (Umgestaltung) bestimmter Institute und Institutionen gerichtet sind (Experimentcharakter haben) und zu dem Zweck, die einzelnen sehr verzweigten Unternehmungen kontinuierlich aus ihrem Zusammenhang zu erklären" (*Versuche* 1, 1). In the first half of the twentieth century, anyone using the word "experimental" in an aesthetic context invited comparison with Emile Zola's *roman expérimental*. Brecht once remarked that "Die Geschichte des neuen Theaters beginnt mit dem Naturalismus" (*GBA*, 26:449). Hultberg argues that *Le roman expérimental* offered a seminal model for Brecht's theory of Epic Theater (Hultberg 1962, 155–57). Müller, on the other hand, rightly counters that to try to place Brecht in the Naturalist tradition would be to underestimate the dialectic of his work (Klaus-Detlef Müller 1967, 189). Nevertheless, if Naturalism is to be admitted as a possible influence on, but not the source for, Brecht's idea of literature as experiment, then the scope of the discussion needs to be widened to encompass Arno Holz's critique of the notion of a literary "experiment" in "Zola als Theoretiker." While the chemist conducts actual experiments "in der Realität," the novelist, according to Holz, only experiments "in seinem Hirne": "Ein Experiment, das sich bloß im Hirne des Experimentators abspielt, ist eben gar kein Experiment" (1896, 104). The attack on Zola's concept of *littérature expérimentale*, which, as has been pointed out, was a common feature of German Naturalist theorizing (Brauneck and Müller 1987, 171–72), was as much a part of the Naturalist inheritance of the first half of the twentieth century as Holz's "Die Kunst: Ihr Wesen und ihre Gesetze" or Bölsche's *Die naturwissenschaftlichen Grundlagen der Poesie*. The discussion of Brecht's concept of "experiment" in "Der 'Experiment'-Begriff der *Versuche*" (*BHB*, 4:41–44) argues that "der von [Brecht] [in der programmatischen Notiz zur *Versuche*-Reihe] Experimentbegriff ist angemessen nur zu verstehen, wenn man von Assoziationen aus dem Bereich der exakten Wissenschaften absieht. [. . .] Experimentiert wird mit Strategien der Veränderung der kulturvermittelnden Institutionen" (*BHB*, 4:42). Which would suggest a radical shift in Brecht's concept of experimentation between the heady days of the early 1930s and the exile period of "Über experimentelles Theater," *Der Messingkauf,* and *Leben des Galilei*.

[28] The passage is omitted from *Brecht on Theatre*, which offers a draconianly edited version of "Über experimentelles Theater" (*BT*, 130–35). A complete English trans-

While Naturalism is credited with bringing about a "'Verwissenschaftlichung der Kunst,' die ihm sozialen Einfluß verschaffte" (*GBA*, 22:546), the main positivist disciplines involved (medicine, psychiatry, biology, social Darwinism) are accused of having offered "eine bloße Symptomatologie der sozialen Oberfläche" yielding few "Einblicke in das soziale Getriebe" (*GBA*, 22:543). Brecht had already had harsh words to say about Naturalism's failure to become interventionist: "Das Wort Naturalismus ist selber schon ein Verbrechen, die bei uns bestehenden Verhältnisse zwischen den Menschen als natürliche hinzustellen, wobei der Mensch als ein Stück Natur, also als unfähig, diese Verhältnisse zu ändern, betrachtet wird, ist eben verbrecherisch" ("Über die Verwertung der theatralischen Grundelemente" c. 1928, *GBA*, 21:232). The Theater of the Scientific Age, as conceived by Brecht, is in part characterized by the fact that it turned to different academic disciplines from those favored by the Naturalists. At the end of his sketch "[Benutzung der Wissenschaften für Kunstwerke]" (c. 1938, *GBA*, 22:480), Brecht identifies the main sciences as being "Psychologie / Ökonomie / Geschichte / Politik." But "Psychologie" here embraces Pavlovian behaviorism and sociology, the historical model is predicated on dialectical materialism and "Politik" means Marxism-Leninism. Given the two contexts of the lecture (Sweden was studiously neutral and Finland feared the Soviet Union more than Nazi Germany), Brecht is obliged to signal his political premises obliquely. He thus invokes a theater working with "Modelle des Zusammenlebens der Menschen, die es dem Zuschauer ermöglichen konnten, seine soziale Umwelt zu verstehen und sie verstandesmäßig und gefühlsmäßig zu beherrschen" (*GBA*, 22:548). And he declares that "der heutige Mensch weiß wenig über die Gesetzlichkeiten, die sein Leben beherrschen" (ibid.), without making explicit that the key to these laws of cause and effect is to be found in Marxism-Leninism. He has to slip in encoded political points while assuring his audience "Wir wollen uns [. . .] heute darauf beschränken, die Entwicklung der Krise des Theaters im Bezirk der Ästhetik zu verfolgen" (*GBA*, 22:544) at the same time as using veiled language to complain that contemporary theater offers "kein Bild dieser Welt, das stimmt" (*GBA*, 22:548).

> Daß die Menschen so wenig über sich selber wissen, ist schuld daran, daß ihr Wissen über die Natur ihnen so wenig hilft. In der Tat, die ungeheuerliche Unterdrückung und Ausbeutung von Menschen durch Menschen, die kriegerischen Schlächtereien und friedlichen Entwürdigungen aller Art über den ganzen Planeten hin haben zwar schon beinahe etwas Natürliches bekommen [. . .]. Die großen Kriege z.B. scheinen unzähligen wie Erdbeben, also wie Naturgewalten, aber

lation by Carl Richard Mueller ("On the Experimental Drama") can be found in *The Tulane Drama Review* 6, no.1 (1961): 3–17.

während sie mit den Erdbeben schon fertig werden, werden sie mit sich selber nicht fertig. Es ist klar, wieviel gewonnen wäre, wenn z.b. das Theater [. . .] imstande wäre, ein praktikables Weltbild zu geben. Eine Kunst, die das könnte, würde in die gesellschaftliche Entwicklung tief eingreifen können [. . .] dem fühlenden und denkenden Menschen die Welt, die Menschenwelt, für seine Praxis ausliefern. (*GBA*, 22:550)

Not only is this one of Brecht's classic evocations of false consciousness, but the judicious phrase "ein praktikables Weltbild" also makes an unmistakable plea for a dialectical theater of "eingreifendes Denken." "Über experimentelles Theater" thus establishes what a truly scientific theater would be *before* positioning Brecht's "experiments" in relation to the theater of "Einfühlung." And even if he tries to pretend that "experimental theater" is a matter of *theatrical* progress, he has nevertheless tacitly subordinated aesthetics to ideology and implied that any notion of the work of art's autonomy has to be abandoned. In retrospect, Brecht thought that the lecture had been "ein wenig allgemein gehalten" (*GBA*, 22:1069), a necessity under the circumstances.

The crisis of contemporary theater Brecht posits was one of which he had considerable experience, as it involved the problematic relationship between entertainment and didacticism, empathy and critical distance. "Je mehr wir das Publikum zum Mitgehen, Miterleben, Mitfühlen brachten, desto weniger sah es die Zusammenhänge, desto weniger lernte es, und je mehr es zu lernen gab, desto weniger kam Kunstgenuß zustande" (*GBA*, 22:547). Willett sees this lecture as "the first indication that Brecht wanted to strike a balance between didacticism and entertainment" (*BT*, 135). It is certainly one of the first of Brecht's major theoretical statements to admit to Epic Theater's earlier mistakes; for example, "In einer [. . .] Phase der Experimente führte jede neue Steigerung des Lehrwerts zu einer sofortigen Schwächung des Unterhaltungswerts. ('Das ist nicht mehr Theater, das ist Volkshochschule.')" (*GBA*, 22:547). In some respects, "Über experimentelles Theater" continues the thinking of "Vergnügungstheater oder Lehrtheater?" but now moves beyond the question of fundamental entertainment versus didacticism in order to explore various specific distancing techniques. Before he can do this, however, Brecht needs to convince his audience that empathy has to be unequivocally rejected as drama's guiding principle.

The case presented against empathy rests on three charges: that it sustains the notion of theater as a privileged autonomous realm under no constraint to offer a "Weltbild, das stimmt"; that the audience is cognitively tied to the false consciousness of characters onstage; and that with the new doctrine of social changeability, "Einfühlung in änderbare Menschen, vermeidbare Handlungen, überflüssigen Schmerz usw. ist nicht möglich" (*GBA*,

22:552).[29] In fact, even if one were to replace "nicht möglich" with "nicht legitim," this would remain one of the lecture's more contentious claims, mainly because it fails to spell out the underlying premises of such an assertion. Brecht returns to safer ground when declaring empathy to be "das große Kunstmittel einer Epoche, in der der Mensch die Variable, seine Umwelt die Konstante ist" (*GBA*, 22:553), inasmuch as a sense of inexorable fate risks increasing our capacity to empathize with people who feel unable to escape their predicament. The quasi-scientific appeal to constants and variables is one of the few occurrences of the use of a scientific model in "Über experimentelles Theater."

At this point, Brecht places the discussion in a wider context than a merely post-Naturalist one. "Was konnte an die Stelle von *Furcht* und *Mitleid* gesetzt werden, des klassischen Zwiegespanns zur Herbeiführung der aristotelischen Katharsis? Wenn man auf die Hypnose verzichtete, an was konnte man appellieren?" (*GBA*, 22:553). These are the "anti-Aristotelian" questions Brecht uses as a bridge to his own methods. Rejecting the terminology with which catharsis is explained in Aristotle's *Poetics*, Brecht now proposes a theater predicated on *Wissensbegierde* "anstelle der Furcht vor dem Schicksal" and *Hilfsbereitschaft* "anstelle des Mitleids" (*GBA*, 22:554), with the second compound transparently standing for socialism and the kind of (scientific) curiosity Brecht has in mind being aroused by processes of "Verfremdung" and "Historisierung." But it is the processes by which "Wissensbegierde" is encouraged that dominate the ensuing remarks about "Verfremdung." "Einen Vorgang oder einen Charakter verfremden heißt zunächst einfach, dem Vorgang oder dem Charakter das Selbstverständliche, Bekannte, Einleuchtende zu nehmen und über ihn Staunen und Neugierde zu erzeugen." Brecht's attempt to indicate what the procedure would mean in the case of *King Lear* has the advantage of using familiar material to illustrate two contrasting approaches: "den Zorn des Lear über die Undankbarkeit seiner Töchter [. . .] so darstellen, daß der Zuschauer ihn für die natürlichste Sache der Welt ansieht" or "Vermittels der Verfremdungstechnik [. . .] so [. . .], daß der Zuschauer über ihn staunen kann, daß er sich noch andere Reaktionen des Lear vorstellen kann als gerade die des Zornes. Die Haltung des Lear wird verfremdet, d.h. sie wird als eigentümlich, auffallend, bemerkenswert dargestellt, als gesellschaftliches Phänomen" (*GBA*, 22:554). Yet since the illustrative passage is to end with

---

[29] In the fourth of his "Thesen über die Aufgabe der Einfühlung in den theatralischen Künsten" (1935), Brecht had already noted, evidently with Socialist Realism in mind, that "Die Versuche, die Einfühlungstechnik so umzugestalten, daß die Identifikation nunmehr in Kollektiven (Klassen) vor sich geht, sind nicht aussichtsreich. Sie führen zu unrealistischen Vergröberungen und Abstraktionen der Personen und Kollektive zugleich" (*GBA*, 22:175).

the declaration "Verfremden heißt also Historisieren," the audience is offered surprisingly little concrete detail, in contrast to the earlier discussion of *An American Tragedy*, to show how this would be achieved. As Brecht noted, it is the general principle, not the detail that is the Stockholm lecture's main concern. That principle he sums up in the following way:

> daß der Zuschauer die Menschen auf der Bühne nicht mehr als ganz unänderbare, unbeeinflußbare, ihrem Schicksal hilflos ausgelieferte dargestellt sieht. Er sieht: dieser Mensch ist so und so, weil die Verhältnisse so und so sind. [. . .] Er bekommt den Abbildern der Menschenwelt au f der Bühne gegenüber jetzt dieselbe Haltung, die er, als Mensch dieses Jahrhunderts, der Natur gegenüber hat. (*GBA*, 22:555)

"Das Theater legt ihm nunmehr die Welt vor zum Zugriff" ("die Welt meistern" is the phrase with which the lecture ends) establishes a context for the earlier concept of "Hilfsbereitschaft."

Brecht evidently decided that an exposition via key Epic concepts was the safest way to present Epic Theater in the present context. The audience would hear little about the essay's most intractable term: "das *gestische Prinzip*," and even if familiar with the *Mahagonny* notes, they might have difficulty with "*epischer* Darstellungsstil" as a stylistic concept. Also, the inclusion of a technique Brecht refers to as "das *Nehersche* Prinzip" is at best likely to radiate a vague aura of general experimental activity rather than mean much in constructive terms. Nevertheless, three central concepts, "Verfremdung," "Historisierung," and "experimentelles Theater," have been clearly established both as innovative aesthetic principles and as responses to the crisis of an "Epoche der Experimente." And "experimentelles Theater" has been effectively contextualized by extensive reference to the predicament of a society in peril evoked by the quotation of Einstein's words for the time capsule buried at the time of the New York World Fair[30] and the references to nuclear fission's ambiguous powers (*GBA*, 22:549).

"Über experimentelles Theater" avoids too narrow a focus on Brecht's own experiments, while giving a sense of the social problems and dramatic developments to which they were a response. Although addressing audiences of amateur actors, it makes little of acting; indeed, in places it seems more fascinated by the potential of stage machinery. Elaborating on the concept of experiment behind the *Versuche* series and his notion of an "induktives Theater," Brecht has now repackaged it as experimental theater, with "Verfremdung" remaining one of the main characteristics. However, "Über experimentelles Theater" remains an introduction for the non-initiated.

---

[30] Compare *GBA*, 22:549 and Albert Einstein, *Über den Frieden: Weltordnung oder Weltuntergang?* ed. Otto Nathan and Heinz Norden (Bern, 1975, 299).

Brecht's next major essay appears to be preaching to those already converted and hence is able to concentrate on more specific features of Epic acting.

## "Kurze Beschreibung einer neuen Technik der Schauspielkunst, die einen Verfremdungseffekt hervorbringt" (1940)

In February 1937, Brecht was busy with the task of drawing together his theoretical thinking into a single "zusammenfassende" statement with the working title "Verfremdungseffekt beim epischen Theater" (*GBA*, 22:1098), clearly intended as a pendant to the Chinese essay. His journal for May also refers to a large-scale theoretical project ("Über eine neue Technik der Schauspielkunst"), observing that "Über experimentelles Theater" was "eine gute Einleitung," but adding: "natürlich sind keine so bewußten Fragen gestellt und keine so zielstrebigen Experimente gemacht worden, wie der Aufsatz vielleicht glauben läßt" (*GBA*, 26:337). If "Über experimentelles Theater" was a start, inasmuch as Brecht had begun to develop his dramaturgical theory more systematically than in "Vergnügungstheater oder Lehrtheater?" or "Verfremdungseffekte in der chinesischen Schauspielkunst," it was in other respects hardly what was now required. Too much of the Stockholm lecture had been taken up with surveying modern European drama in general, leaving comparatively little space for Epic Theater. The new essay, "Kurze Beschreibung einer neuen Technik der Schauspielkunst, die einen Verfremdungseffekt hervorbringt" (*GBA*, 22:641–59), concentrates on "Verfremdung" as mainly the responsibility of the actor. Little space is wasted polemicizing against other traditions; Brecht seems to have mastered, at least for the time being, his need to be defensively aggressive towards "Aristotelian" drama and Stanislavskian "Naturalism." And the result is his most important theoretical statement until *Kleines Organon* of 1948. Both serve a similar function: to clarify Brecht's aims and theoretical position prior to arrival in a new country — in the one case, the USA, in the other, East Germany. When first published in *Versuche* 11 (1951), it was prefaced by the statement that "Die *Kurze Beschreibung* [. . .], 1940 geschrieben, gehört zum 9. Versuch 'Über eine nichtaristotelische Dramatik.'" Although it was published after the more important *Kleines Organon*, late appearance is no gauge of the piece's significance. Until its publication, people had probably heard more about "dis-illusioning" techniques in Chinese theater than about Brecht's own "V-Effekte."

After the bravura Stockholm performance and the often provocative stance of Brecht's earlier writings, "Kurze Beschreibung" comes across as measured, scrupulous and economic. Whereas "Über experimentelles Theater" had devoted four out of seventeen pages to Brechtian theater (not much more than to Piscator's), "Kurze Beschreibung," which is scarcely much longer than the Stockholm lecture, concentrates exclusively on Brecht's work. The essay is a unique combination of overview[31] (six pages) and an "Anhang" twice that length, consisting of nineteen sections glossing key points in the main body of the account. As an attempt to impose order, such a structure prefigures the numbered paragraphs of *Kleines Organon,* while at the same time involving a form of attention-splitting reception not unlike "vergleichendes Blättern." The reference at one point to an epic strategy whereby events in a Brechtian play are first "in Worten bezeichnet und angekündigt" and then actually happen (*GBA,* 22:646) suggests a strategy similar to the interaction between text and appendix in "Kurze Beschreibung." However, the numbered parts of the appendix are not conventional footnotes. Rather, they flesh out the main argument, offering illustrative detail, including passages from Brecht's earlier theoretical writings (on *An American Tragedy,* on "Der Bühnenbau des epischen Theaters," and on "Verfremdungseffekte in der chinesischen Schauspielkunst") or drawing attention to symptomatic counterpositions. The amount of cross-referring to Brecht's earlier dramaturgical writings is doubtless intended to convey the impression that the present work is as much the logical consolidation of Brecht's thinking to date as a fresh breakthrough. Even when the writings in question had yet to find a publisher, Brecht is still able, by referring to them, to show that he has theorized more extensively than the scope of "Kurze Beschreibung" can do justice to.

In characteristically "epic" vein, the essay begins with a monumental "Gestus des Zeigens," once again allowing theory to illustrate the method in action:

> Im folgenden soll der Versuch gemacht werden, eine Technik der Schauspielkunst zu beschreiben, die auf einigen Theatern angewandt wurde [. . .], um darzustellende Vorgänge dem Zuschauer zu verfremden. Der Zweck dieser Technik des *Verfremdungseffekts* war es, dem Zuschauer eine untersuchende, kritische Haltung gegenüber dem darzustellenden Vorgang zu verleihen. Die Mittel waren künstlerische. (*GBA,* 22:641)

The overriding concern is with acting, which includes rehearsal and preparation techniques; even the claim that the means are "artistic" really means "theatrical." The rehearsal process is firmly established as a vital stage in the actor's achievement of "Distanz" from the specific part to be played.

---

[31] At the time of "Über experimentelles Theater," Brecht drafted a piece entitled "Überblick," consisting of eight numbered paragraphs (*GBA,* 22:557–61), material that was later incorporated into *Kleines Organon.* The sections here are much more discontinuous than the appendices to "Kurze Beschreibung."

A case can be made that uncritical empathy is just as unworthy of actors as of audiences. To have them totally "becoming" the people they play is "ihrer unwürdig," to employ a phrase Brecht had used in the context of culinary theater at the time of *Mahagonny* (*GBA*, 24:81). Here, however, the essay's concern with the actor's distance from a role is of a substantially different order. Brecht had always been fascinated by relationships of proportionality. In the case of culinary opera, for example, he claimed that "der Grad des Genusses hängt direkt vom Grad der Irrealität ab" (*GBA*, 24:77). Now he reasons that the audience's distance from characters and events onstage will be *directly proportional* to the actors' ability to maintain "die richtige distanzierte Haltung" to their parts. This, rather than any crude need to match Stanislavsky's system item-for-item or rescue his actors from unworthy practices, is the rationale behind Brecht's concern with innovative rehearsal techniques: "Ist die restlose Verwandlung aufgegeben, bringt der Schauspieler seinen Text nicht wie eine Improvisation, sondern wie ein Zitat" (*GBA*, 22:643). Although the formulation here suggests a *fait accompli,* Brecht's main concern is with the strategies that will bring this about. Techniques that are the actor's equivalent of "Literarisierung" are itemized systematically, but other possibilities are also referred to, as if to suggest that ensembles must build on the *principles* rather than mechanically take over Brechtian *solutions* to the problem of creating critical distance in the actor.

> Drei Hilfsmittel können bei einer Spielweise mit nicht restloser Verwandlung zu einer Verfremdung der Äußerungen und Handlungen der darzustellenden Personen dienen:
>
> 1. *Die Überführung in die dritte Person.*
> 2. *Die Überführung in die Vergangenheit.*
> 3. *Das Mitsprechen von Spielanweisungen und Kommentaren.*
> (GBA, 22:644)

Other recommended routines include role-swapping, "Proben am Tisch," rehearsing in dialect, and the insertion of spoken *verba dicendi* ("sagte er," "fragte sie er"), as well as exploiting tonal differences between the character's actual lines and impersonal stage directions. The impression given is one of confidence that such strategies will prove sufficient to prevent the "restlose Verwandlung" of actor and audience in an act of unchecked identification.

One particular aspect of preparation stands out because it is evidence of a dialectical conception of acting a part. It concerns the creation of an antithetical response on the part of the audience:

> Geht [der Schauspieler] auf die Bühne, so wird er bei allen wesentlichen Stellen zu dem, was er macht, noch etwas ausfindig, namhaft und ahnbar machen, was er nicht macht; das heißt er spielt so,

daß man die Alternative möglichst deutlich sieht, so, daß sein Spiel noch die anderen Möglichkeiten ahnen läßt, nur eine der möglichen Varianten darstellt. Er sagt zum Beispiel: "Das wirst du mir bezahlen" und er sagt *nicht*: "Ich verzeihe dir das." Er haßt seine Kinder und es steht *nicht* so, daß er sie liebt. Er geht nach links vorn und *nicht* nach rechts hinten. Das was er *nicht* macht, muß in dem enthalten und aufgehoben sein, was er macht. So bedeuten alle Sätze und Gesten Entscheidungen, bleibt die Person unter Kontrolle und wird getestet. (*GBA*, 22:643)

Rather surprisingly, given that this closely resembles the discussion of the "Historisierung" of *King Lear,* Brecht adds the claim: "Der technische Ausdruck für dieses Verfahren heißt: Fixieren des *Nicht — Sondern.*" There is no evidence that Brecht had used the term before (apart from in drafts of "Kurze Beschreibung"), and it seldom found subsequent favor, either with Brecht or with any of his collaborators.[32]

The way in which this strategy functions is far more complex than the lapidary " *Nicht — Sondern*" antithesis suggests. Initially, the "*Sondern*" does not denote a single alternative to what is happening at a given moment in the play, an "antithesis" to the staged or articulated "thesis." Instead, the theory invokes other possibilities in the plural ("die anderen Möglich-keiten"). The actor's "take" on the role only represents one of many possible variants. (Even in 1954, Brecht can still be found using a plural: "dichtet das Publikum im Geist andere Verhaltungsweisen und Situationen hinzu" [ *GBA,* 23:300]). What explains this discrepancy between a simple one-to-one an-tithesis and a contrast between a single given and a variety of conceivable al-ternatives is Brecht's assumption that actors need to engage critically with the stage material in order to "fix in their minds" which alternative the per-formance should communicate. There is a preparatory act of "Fixieren," pos-sibly even prior to the rehearsal stage, but certainly long before the audience is called upon to construct one single alternative to what is being shown. Whereas the dialectical negation of what is shown is a relatively simple opera-tion, the prior selection of the (politically) logical alternative involves a

---

[32] In "Anweisungen an die Schauspieler," the idea is set out using the same illustra-tions, though this time without reference to the technical term. The technique is simply presented as "Das *Nicht, Sondern*" (*GBA,* 22:667). The only new element, apart from adducing one further, contrived example ("Er fällt nicht in Ohnmacht, sondern er wird lebendig"), comes with the observation: "Gemeint ist: der Schauspieler spielt, was hinter dem *Sondern* steht; er soll es so spielen, daß man auch, was hinter dem *Nicht* steht, aufnimmt." Brecht also toyed with a variant model, "Das Ja-Nein": "Die Handhabbarkeit einer Beschreibung hängt davon ab, ob das Ja-Nein in ihr ist und ob das Ja-oder-Nein genügend bestimmt ist in ihr" (*GBA,* 22:669).

choice, presumably on the basis of ideological criteria not made explicit in the case of any of the examples offered.

One key to Brecht's presentational method here lies in his statement that "Allereinfachste Sätze, die den V-Effekt anwenden, sind Sätze mit 'nicht — sondern.'" In practice, this seldom refers to actual sentences heard by the audience, or even possibilities literally generated in the audience's mind by the performance. On the contrary, the alternatives represent *models* of audience reaction. Obviously, any crude form of dialectical response would involve no more than an awareness that someone who says "kommen Sie herein" could have said "geh weg" — or even "haben Sie geklopft?" Or, to take two illustrations from *Der Messingkauf:* "Sie [Helene Weigel] bat nicht die Unterdrücker um Mitleid mit den Unterdrückten, sondern die Unterdrückten um Selbstvertrauen" (*GBA,* 22:799), "[sie verstand es], den Menschen nicht nur Gefühle, sondern auch Gedanken zu erregen" (*GBA,* 22:797). Brecht's concern with using contrasts at sentence-level, and particularly his concentration on "allereinfachste Sätze," forms part of a more general technique of illustrating *points of principle* via models and schemata. And just as they involve processes of simplified antithesis offset by footnoted caveats, so here the focus on "allereinfachste Sätze" has to be treated with circumspection. When point 17 of the Appendix declares "es gab *nicht* nur eine Möglichkeit, *sondern* deren zweie, beide werden angeführt, zunächst wird die eine, die zweite, dann auch die erste verfremdet" (my emphasis), the initial spectrum of alternatives at the rehearsal stage has now evidently given rise to a model of the relationship between negation and not only antithetical thinking but also a reciprocal estrangement of both elements. This means that the audience has to be encouraged to move productively beyond mere antitheses, if "gegenseitige Verfremdung" is to lead to genuine insight. It is hardly by chance that Brecht uses the Hegelian term "aufgehoben" (sublated) in the passage quoted above.

The model character of Brecht's " *Nicht — Sondern*" becomes apparent when compared with the cognate estranging approach in Peter Handke's 1968 essay "Ein Beispiel für Verwendungsweisen grammatischer Modelle." Responding to what he objects to as the hypocrisy in certain responses to works shown at the Oberhausen Short Film Festival, Handke records the presence of "eine beachtliche Anzahl der handelsüblichen Rechtfertigungsfloskeln":

> Den meisten gemeinsam war jedenfalls das vielseitig brauchbare grammatische Modell des *Ja-aber:* wobei das *Ja,* die Bejahung, jeweils aus dem Bekräftigen eines allgemeinen und auch, weil allgemein, allgemein unverbindlichen Grundsatzes bestand, worauf dann im *Aber* die entkräftende Verneinung dieses allgemeinen, bejahten Grundsatzes durch die Aufzählung der besonderen, für diesen Fall verbindlichen

Grundsätze folgte. Auf das äußerste abstrahiert, aufs äußerste automatisiert [. . .] gab sich der Rechtfertigungssatz in der Regel dergestalt: Ich bin *ja* (wirklich, grundsätzlich, im allgemeinen) gegen die (jede) Zensur, *aber* — und hier folgten nun die in diesem Fall besonderen Grundsätze, die einer Macht, die ja immer auch das Recht, d.h. recht hat (sonst würde man sie wohl nicht als Macht, sondern als Gewalt bezeichnen) das Recht zum Eingreifen gaben, d.h. recht gaben. (Handke 1969, 298)

Handke's examples show that his model, while requiring a penetration to the deep structure of the actual quoted utterances, still reflects a predilection for the words "ja" and "aber" (or synonyms thereof) in such contradictory critical discourse. Although Handke's grammatical model simplifies contingent detail, the usual suspects stand condemned by the grammatical patterns they employ.

Brecht's "*Nicht — Sondern*" paradigm clearly belongs to a different class of model. There are hardly any instances where "nicht" and "sondern" figure among the words spoken, either in "Kurze Beschreibung" or in his plays. Instead, it is his commentary (or the structuring during the actor's preparation) that super-imposes a "*Nicht — Sondern*" schema of contrast between what is said or done and what could have happened. Brecht's model operates on a higher level of iconic abstraction than Handke's and might for that reason be expected to create more critical distance in both actors and audience. In fact, the more able they are to perceive the surface detail in terms of a "*Nicht — Sondern*" antithesis, the more defamiliarization will have been achieved through recognition of the underlying paradigm.

In *Modell, Modelltheorie und Formen der Modellbildung in der Literaturwissenschaft,* Horst Flaschka offers a stimulating account of various scientific model theories in order to explore the use of dramatic models in the work of Frisch, Brecht and Dürrenmatt. His main point is that modern model theory is able to differentiate in a more sophisticated way between such heterogeneous kinds of *Modellstück* and can supply a more precise analytical tool for drama criticism. The resultant testing of individual works against the established criteria for evaluating scientific models reveals the extent to which blanket terms like "Modellstück" and "Parabelstück" have had a leveling effect over the past half century. But if we appreciate the role played by "Strukturanalogien" in scientific models, we will read the astronomy lesson in scene 1 of *Leben des Galilei* rather differently. Also the distinction between a "heuristisches Analogon" (Flaschka 1976, 196) and a mere explanatory model helps throw new light on Brecht's dramatic procedures, especially in cases where the latter is being confused with the former. Flaschka also emphasizes the role of the "Modellbegriff" in Marxist aesthetics, highlighting in particular the links between Moissej Kagan's *Vorlesungen zur marxistisch-leninistischen Ästhetik* and the work of the Berliner Ensemble (see White 1998). However, following a brief look at "Die Straßenszene," Flaschka confines himself to the canonical plays and offers no consideration of modelling in other theoretical writings. Yet as we have already seen, the "*Nicht — Sondern*" approach is itself a syntactical template constructed to model the dialectical process by which actor and audience come to interpret a character's behavior. The way in which Brecht's argument moves from an image of one possibility among many to a simple "*Nicht — Sondern*" antithesis involves the process of streamlining common to most models. Even the refusal to identify the ideological factors that determine the "*Nicht — Sondern*" components is another feature of the model's ability to cut through its material's complexity. Arguably, many of Brecht's problems with the *Mahagonny* "Schema" resulted from a failure to acknowledge the theoretical table's model status.

The most frequent use of paradigmatic models in "Kurze Beschreibung" comes with the attempt to demonstrate that "Verfremdung" is "eine Prozedur des täglichen Lebens" (*GBA*, 22:655). The chosen real-life situations in turn become "verfremdet," since it is unlikely that people will have thought of them within such a conceptual framework. Moreover, some of Brecht's examples are so artificial that even allegedly "everyday" examples can scarcely conceal their convenient "Modellhaftigkeit." As we shall see when we come to consider "Die Straßenszene," the assumption that a "model" is derived from everyday experience often proves to be more deceptive (or disingenuously presented) than the surface material might suggest.

"Kurze Beschreibung" insists that estrangement is far from being only an aesthetic phenomenon: "[Der Schauspieler] benützt dieses Mittel eben so weit, als jede beliebige Person ohne schauspielerische Fähigkeiten [. . .] es benützen würde, um eine andere Person darzustellen, das heißt ihr Verhalten zu zeigen" (*GBA*, 22:642). Two common examples are initially flagged: "Zeugen eines Unfalls machen das Verhalten des Verunglückten neu Hinzutretenden vor, Spaßmacher imitieren den komischen Gang eines Freundes" (ibid.). The first is destined to become "Die Straßenszene." The second hardly needs embroidering on since it is the paradigm on which so many of Epic Theater's scenes are based. But the main emphasis is on the street, not the theater: "Vorgänge und Personen des Alltages, der unmittelbaren Umgebung, haben für uns etwas Natürliches, weil Gewohntes. Ihre Verfremdung dient dazu, sie uns auffällig zu machen. Die Technik des Irritiertseins gegenüber landläufigen, 'selbstverständlichen,' niemals angezweifelten Vorgängen ist von der Wissenschaft sorgfältig aufgebaut worden und es besteht kein Grund, warum die Kunst diese so unendlich nützliche Haltung nicht übernehmen sollte [. . .]" (*GBA*, 22:646).

In support of this contention, the appendix cites a number of examples:

Ein einfacher V-Effekt wird angewendet, wenn man jemandem sagt: Hast du dir schon einmal deine Uhr genau angesehen? Der mich das fragt, weiß, daß ich sie schon oft angesehen habe, nun, mit seiner Frage, entzieht er mir den gewohnten, daher mir nichts mehr sagenden Anblick. Ich sah sie an, um die Zeit festzustellen, nun stelle ich, auf eindringliche Art befragt, fest, daß ich die Uhr selber nicht mehr eines staunenden Blickes gewürdigt habe, sie ist nach vielen Richtungen hin ein erstaunlicher Mechanismus.

Ebenso handelt es sich um einen Verfremdungseffekt einfachster Art, wenn eine geschäftliche Besprechung eingeleitet wird mit dem Satz: Haben Sie sich schon einmal überlegt, was aus dem Abfall wird, der aus Ihrer Fabrik tagaus, tagein den Fluß hinunterschwimmt? Dieser Abfall ist bisher nicht unbemerkt den Fluß hinuntergeflossen, er ist sorgfältig in diesen geleitet worden, Menschen und Maschinen werden dazu verwendet, der Fluß ist schon ganz grün von ihm, er ist sehr bemerkbar weggeflossen, aber eben als Abfall. Bei der Fabrikation war er abfällig, jetzt soll er zum Gegenstand der Fabrikation werden, das Auge fällt interessiert auf ihn. Die Frage hat ihn verfremdet, und das sollte sie.

Damit ein Mann seine Mutter als Weib eines Mannes sieht, ist ein V-Effekt nötig, er tritt zum Beispiel ein, wenn er einen Stiefvater bekommt. Wenn einer seinen Lehrer vom Gerichtsvollzieher bedrängt sieht, entsteht ein V-Effekt; aus einem Zusammenhang gerissen, wo der Lehrer groß erscheint, ist er in einen Zusammenhang gerissen worden, wo er klein erscheint.

Eine Verfremdung des Autos tritt ein, wenn wir schon lange einen modernen Wagen gefahren haben, nun eines der alten T-Modelle H. Fords fahren. Wir hören plötzlich wieder Explosionen: Der Motor ist ein Explosionsmotor. Wir beginnen uns zu wundern, daß solch ein Gefährt, [. . .] ohne von tierischer Kraft gezogen zu sein, fahren kann, kurz, wir begreifen das Auto, indem wir es als etwas Fremdes, Neues, als einen Erfolg der Konstruktion, insofern etwas Unnatürliches begreifen. [. . .] Durch die Definition der Eskimos "das Auto ist ein flügelloses, auf dem Boden kriechendes Flugzeug" wird das Auto ebenfalls verfremdet. (*GBA*, 22:656–57)

One might inquire why, in the case of the art-life parallel, Brecht offers such a large number of examples and why most of them are non-political. Again, circumstances may have obliged him to make estrangement seem less a matter of ideology than it really was, possibly because he would be more likely to gain acceptance in America if he came across as a man of the theater without extreme political views. To create such an impression, the *principle* of "Verfremdung" could be explained with innocuous examples, even though Epic Theater's "Verfremdungeffekte" were deemed to possess "kämpferischen Charakter" (*GBA*, 23:294). There is no adversarial dimension to a Ford Model T, a watch, or the Inuit description of an airplane. In fact, such material risks violating one of Brecht's main caveats about "Verfremdung": "Es handelt sich [. . .] um eine Technik, mit der darzustellenden Vorgängen zwischen Menschen der Stempel des Auffallenden, des der Erklärung Bedürftigen, nicht Selbstverständlichen, nicht einfach Natürlichen verliehen werden kann. Der Zweck des Effekts ist, dem Zuschauer eine fruchtbare Kritik vom gesellschaftlichen Standpunkt zu ermöglichen" (*GBA*, 22:377).

There are other, less Machiavellian reasons for the emphasis in "Kurze Beschreibung" on "Verfremdung" being part and parcel of everyday experience. At stake is theater's relationship to life. If "Die Straßenszene" provides a *"Grundmodell,"* episodes from Epic Theater could in their turn provide basic models for understanding everyday behavior. Theater models and models from our everyday world can be juxtaposed to suggest their potential for reciprocal illumination. If Brecht's examples show the heuristic value of looking at something from a different perspective, then the principle becomes "transportable," i.e. translatable to politically less neutral spheres. Further advantages included the fact that Brecht (like Galileo) could stress people's common sense and the part played by "Vernunft" in emancipating perception from false consciousness. And to do this would protect "Verfremdung" from charges of philosophical idealism, as well as bridging the divide between theory and praxis.

A number of illustrations in "Kurze Beschreibung" involve technology: the watch as "ein erstaunlicher Mechanismus" or industrial effluent as a recyclable "Gegenstand der Produktion." Here, Brecht deliberately concentrates exceptionally on the role played by discovery in the amelioration of social conditions. One of his earliest examples of the cognitive value of "Verfremdung" is taken from an apocryphal account of Galileo's discovery of the laws of motion: "Der Mann, der eine an einem Seil schwingende Lampe zum ersten Mal mit Staunen betrachtete und es nicht selbstverständlich, sondern höchst auffällig fand, daß sie pendelte und daß sie gerade so und nicht anders pendelte, näherte sich mit dieser Festsetzung sehr dem Verständnis des Phänomens und damit seiner Beherrschung" (*GBA*, 22:207). Here the reader is offered an anecdote combining elements of "Verfremdung," the *"Nicht — Sondern"* model, and "Historisierung," for this illustration from the past is designed to assist contemporary readers with an idea of "Verfremdung" that will help them create a radically different world. We are not expected to react by saying simply: "die hier vorgeschlagene Haltung zieme sich der Wissenschaft, aber nicht der Kunst. Warum sollte die Kunst nicht versuchen, natürlich mit *ihren* Mitteln, der großen gesellschaftlichen Aufgabe der Beherrschung des Lebens zu dienen?" (ibid.). Like Galileo's discoveries, the examples from modern technology in turn become models of a theatrical approach to social problems, one already alluded to in the essay's contrast between the extent to which people have the means to control threats from nature, yet still understand little of the laws of social behavior. As we shall see in chapters 4 and 5, for any Marxist the overarching "science," the one where the laws of cause and effect are most important for the human race, is beyond doubt the dialectical materialist interpretation of history.[33] Although "Kurze Beschreibung" appears on the surface to be about "eine neue Technik der Schauspielkunst," its patient explanation of "Verfremdung" and "Historisierung" widens the ostensible subject's scope beyond purely aesthetic matters. It is not by chance that the sections of the appendix devoted to more sociopolitical ideas (16–19) are substantially longer than those explaining dramatic principles.

## Distance, Empathy, and Identification

"Der Zweck [der] Technik des *Verfremdungeffekts,*" according to the first paragraph of "Kurze Beschreibung," "war es, dem Zuschauer eine untersuchende, kritische Haltung gegenüber dem darzustellenden Vorgang zu verleihen" (*GBA,* 22:641). Estrangement is presented by reference to what it is intended to combat, rather than how it works or in the context of its politically constructive function. Borrowing a technical term from chemistry, Brecht talks of the way "Verfremdung" *neutralizes* "die Neigung des Publikums, sich in eine solche Illusion zu werfen" (ibid.). Yet while preventing total identification or minimizing *empathy* may be the way in which an attitude of inquiry and interventionist criticism is created, this does not mean that destroying illusions is the device's sole or principal function. Brecht claims that "die Technik, die den V-Effekt hervorbringt, [ist] der Technik, die die Einfühlung bezweckt, diametral entgegesetzt" (*GBA,* 22:642), but this reveals little about a process that is above all a "soziale Maßnahme" (*GBA,* 22:700). Given Brecht's association of Aristotelian theater with "Einfühlung," it is worth bearing in mind that the term has no equivalent in Aristotle's *Poetics* (Flashar 1974, 33). Nevertheless, "Vergnügungstheater oder Lehrtheater?" had sought to identify "Einfühlung" as the polar opposite of a critical response; this is the same assumption we find in embryonic form in the *Mahagonny* "Schema." Hence: "Von keiner Seite wurde es dem Zuschauer [des epischen Theaters] weiterhin ermöglicht, durch einfache Einfühlung in dramatische Personen sich kritiklos (und praktisch folgenlos) Erlebnissen hinzugeben" (*GBA,* 22:108–9). Even in

---

[33] Marx's *Capital,* vol. 1 (Moscow, 1961), 272, describes its approach as "the only materialist and therefore scientific method." In *Marxism and Philosophy,* Korsch observes that "for a Marxist, the task of scientific politics — a politics which describes causal connections — is to discover the[se] determinants of the will of classes" (55). Distinct echoes of both points occur in Brecht's theorizing about "Verfremdung."

"Über experimentelles Theater," the goal of "Verfremdung" was still being presented as an aesthetic one: "Das Prinzip besteht darin, anstelle der Einfühlung die *Verfremdung* herbeizuführen" (*GBA*, 22:554). But the terms of the discussion are not really antithetical. "Einfühlung," a relative term, points, like its absolute equivalent "restlose Verwandlung," to a state of mind, a type of audience response. It is an end. Estrangement, at least in the primary meaning of Brechtian "Verfremdung" (i.e. "making strange"), refers to the means of creating a different state of mind: a politicized critical distance.

Strictly speaking, extreme aesthetic (or psychic) *distance,* not "Verfremdung," is the opposite of empathy, except in cases where Brecht is using his ambiguous term in its secondary sense. Despite earlier problems with the schematic expression of different kinds of theater by means of oppositional pairings, Brecht once more operates with a dominant contrast. Apart from differences of kind between terms referring to *ends* and those specifying *means,* there is the further problem that "Einfühlung" is treated as if it signified an absolute, the total identification lampooned in Brecht's reference to bourgeois audiences' "Inkubusgewohnheiten" (*Kleines Organon für das Theater, GBA* 23:78).[34] To compound the problem, there is a lack of clarity about whether the audience is assumed to be empathizing with one central figure (what modern German calls a work's "Identifikationsfigur"), with a number of characters or even, as Brecht sometimes appears to claim, with events. "The Fourth Wall of China" refers to audiences "identifying themselves with the dramatis personae" (*GBA,* 22:960). In §28 of *Kleines Organon* Brecht writes that one of the main principles of "Einfühlung" is that "die Mittelpunktsfiguren müssen allgemein gehalten werden, damit der Zuschauer sich mit ihnen leichter identifizieren kann" (*GBA,* 23:76). The plural in this case probably means in general, in all the plays seen, but one cannot be sure whether identification with collectives is again being suggested. If a number of people are in the same predicament, it is theoretically feasible to identify with them as a collective. But the other possibility — that the audience can identify *with a situation* — means little more than that some scenes in a play stimulate heightened emotional involvement of an ill-focused kind. To theorize "distance" without being sufficiently explicit about the degree of distance could again be viewed, charitably, as a form of model-determined simplification intended to make the underlying principle clear. Thus, when one commentator (Ben Chaim 1981, 99) claimed that Brecht seems "unable or unwilling" to admit that all drama involves distance

---

[34] Willett translates "Inkubusgewohnheiten" with "deadweight of old habits." But the deliberately satirical analogy with being penetrated and physically possessed by the Devil is part of Brecht's strategy of associating empathy with the irrational.

of some kind, she was doing little more than pointing toward one further illustration of a tendency to present theoretical points via models and schemata.

Blurring the distinction between degrees of "Einfühlung" and "restlose Verwandlung" and thinking in dichotomies may be a rhetorically effective use of the "*Nicht — Sondern*" approach to dramatic theory; Brecht's antitheses are doubtless also intended to suggest those positions between the reactionary and the politically correct. But terms like "restlose Verwandlung," "totale Einfühlung," "Identifikation," and "Austilgung der eigenen Person" cannot but convey a false absolute. It was Arthur Koestler who suggested that "the process of identification [. . .] is transitory and partial, confined to certain climactic moments" (Koestler 1978, 76); it can never extend across an entire work.

Edward Bullough, Ben Chaim's mentor, indicates one important reason why any concept of "total identification" calls for differentiation and a more skeptical approach. What follows involves an example which would have been read very differently by Brecht:

> Suppose a man, who believes that he has cause to be jealous about his wife, witnesses a performance of *Othello*. He will the more perfectly appreciate the situation, conduct and character of Othello, the more exactly the feelings and experiences of Othello coincide with his own — at least he ought to on the principle of concordance. In point of fact, he will probably do anything but appreciate the play. In reality, the concordance will merely render him acutely conscious of his own jealousy; by a sudden reversal of perspective he will no longer see Othello apparently betrayed by Desdemona, but himself in an analogous situation with his own wife. This reversal of perspective is the consequence of the loss of Distance. (Bullough 1957, 99)

Empathy, according to Bullough, "should be as complete as is compatible with maintaining Distance" (ibid.). If this is accepted, it means that even the simpler term in Brecht's antithesis, "totale Einfühlung," calls for some reexamination.[35] Given that he was writing in 1912 with predominantly "Aristotelian" material in mind, Bullough understandably suggests that "what is [. . .] most desirable is the *utmost decrease of Distance without its disappear-*

---

[35] In "Levels of Identification of Hero and Audience," Jauß historicizes issues that Brecht's approach treats generically, e.g. by relating identification to contrasting Greek and Christian concepts of "pity" and distinguishing between individual, norm-creating, cathartic, and ironic forms of identification, as well as differentiating between various characters or situations open to identification and the various cultural values identification can embody. Most pertinently, he argues that aesthetic distance and identification "are by no means mutually exclusive" (286).

*ance*" (100). But "the work of Distance," as Bullough has already cautioned, "is [. . .] highly complex" (95). Clearly, Bullough's "Distance" and Brecht's "Distanz" are not the same thing. For the former, "Distance is a factor in all art" (ibid.) and for that reason too much concern with the general and eternal verities is assumed (in a manner alien to Brecht's reasoning) to create a surfeit of distance rather than encourage empathy. Bullough sees "Distance" as inhibiting our concern with "the cutting-edge of the practical side of things" (95), whereas Brecht arrives at the diametrically opposite conclusion. For Bullough, "it is Distance which makes the aesthetic object an 'end in itself'" (129), while for Brecht the creation of *critical* distance is intended as the antidote to a Kantian-Schillerian conception of art as an autonomous entity. Bullough's approach has the virtue of drawing attention to psychical distance's variability. Total identification, "zero distance" in Bullough's sense, might be conceivable, if not desirable, in either audience or actor. But there is no obvious opposite phenomenon in his scheme. Bullough's discussion of "under-distance" and "over-distance" (100–101) suggests that the term ought to inhabit some middle ground between extremes and hence a different space from that usurped by Brecht's *bêtes noires*: "totale Identifikation" and "restlose Verwandlung." While we may not agree with Bullough's criterion for objecting to over-distancing ("an excess of Distance produces the impression of improbability, artificiality, emptiness or absurdity" [101]) his assumption that distance is not static does highlight the constructedness of Brecht's theoretical approach.

The nearest we come to Bullough's position in Brecht is with point 13 of the appendix to "Kurze Beschreibung." Here a case is made for the actor's not treating his audience as a monolith, but playing off different factions against one another. To do this, it is suggested, he will have to adopt an antagonistic attitude to the part he is playing, that is, one of critical distance. But without making anything of his crucial point, Brecht adds in parenthesis: "Dies ist wenigstens die Grundhaltung, auch sie muß wechselnd sein, zu den verschiedenen Äußerungen der Figur verschieden" (*GBA*, 22:652). This is the closest Brecht comes to abandoning a conception of fixed distance in his schematic model of the empathy/distance antithesis.

"Kurze Beschreibung," like many of the theoretical writings that precede it, treats "Distanz" and "kritische Haltung" as if they were *de facto* synonyms, and as if the one were the inevitable result of the other. Thus, in the incomplete essay "Die dialektische Dramatik," written in the same year as the *Mahagonny* notes, one already finds a clear statement of Brecht's unquestioning assumption about the relationship between aesthetic and critical distance: "Aufgefordert, eine nicht willenlose (auf Magie, Hypnose beruhende), hingegebene, sondern eine beurteilende Haltung einzunehmen, nahmen die Zuhörer sofort [!] eine ganz bestimmte *politische* Haltung ein" (*GBA*, 21:442). Similarly, in a draft to the final section of the appendix to

"Kurze Beschreibung" ("Ist die kritische Haltung eine unkünstlerische Haltung?"), we hear: "Die Kritik erhebt sich dann nur, wenn die Einfühlung nicht zustande kommt oder aussetzt" (*GW*, 15:377). In the final version, Brecht adopts a more circumspect standpoint:

> Um diese kritische Haltung in die Kunst einzuführen, muß man das zweifellos vorhandene negative Moment in seiner Positivität zeigen: diese Kritik an der Welt ist eine aktive, handelnde, positive Kritik. Den Lauf eines Flusses kritisieren, heißt da, ihn verbessern, ihn korrigieren. Die Kritik der Gesellschaft ist die Revolution, das ist zu Ende gebrachte, exekutive Kritik. (*GBA*, 22:659)

But deflecting attention to interventionism by means of the river metaphor can hardly do justice to the question of just how aesthetic distance is convertible into "exekutive Kritik." In §37 of *Kleines Organon,* Brecht did concede that procedures of "Verfremdung" and "Historisierung" can only be "der Beginn der Kritik" (*GBA*, 23:79), not a guarantee that a critical position, let alone the correct critical position, will be achieved. But too often the easy equation of "Distanz" with "kritisches Denken" and, by extension, "eingreifendes Denken" remains little more than an article of aesthetic dogma.

In *Distance in the Theatre,* the first work to look at Brecht's conception of distancing within the framework of modern aesthetic theory, Ben Chaim shows Brecht's concern with distance to be "less ambitious, less complex" than Bullough's. Her verdict is that it "essentially probes at only one corner of the area that Bullough stakes out for the concept" (25).[36] That is to say, Brecht is really only concerned with the political implications of distancing *in a certain kind of theater.* Yet while Ben Chaim concedes that an "emphasis on the social and economic context presumably increases distance by widening the audience's perspective" and sees Brechtian "Historisierung" as "a specific distancing device that has special value for throwing a socioeconomic system into relief" (29–30), she remains suspicious of the way Brecht assumes distance automatically becomes *critical* distance. Equating "Verfremdung" too narrowly with "Antiillusionismus," she observes that "Brecht's distancing techniques are primarily devices to exaggerate what is inherent in art in order that art will be effective propaganda" (32). This for her further raises the question of whether "an increased awareness of the mechanics of the theater, its conventions and devices, [will] necessarily create a critical attitude" and "if it does, whether the response necessarily excludes all other responses (such as an empathic one)" (33). Even for those who interpret the

---

[36] Casebier charges Bullough with failing to distinguish between "attentional" and "emotional" distance. He argues that there is no necessary connection between the two, although Brecht seems to assume that the one is a prerequisite of the other.

primary function of "Verfremdung" in less procrusteanly aesthetic terms, this remains a crucial issue, and one which Brecht tends not to confront. Ben Chaim's answer is that, "rather than merely techniques, it becomes a matter of the fusion of techniques and *content*: a political consciousness, on the simplest level, is raised by the subject matter, to which attention is being drawn by the distancing devices. [. . .] The techniques are informed by a context which becomes potent by those techniques" (35).

Ben Chaim's emphasis on the content factor is welcome, inasmuch as there are clear indications in what Brecht says, especially in *Kleines Organon*, about "Historisierung" and the need to bring out the social "Gestus" of scenes, to suggest that he also considers "Verfremdung" to be the application of certain distancing devices to material that is already by definition political:

> Es ist der Zweck des V-Effekts, den allen Vorgängen unterliegenden gesellschaftlichen Gestus zu verfremden. Unter sozialem Gestus ist der mimische und gestische Ausdruck der gesellschaftlichen Beziehungen zu verstehen, in denen die Menschen einer bestimmten Epoche zueinander stehen. (*GBA*, 22:646)

Only by relating the concept "Verfremdung" to the material that undergoes a process of estrangement can the achievement of critical distance be adequately understood. This Brecht's theoretical writings for a long time failed to elucidate adequately.

## "Verfremdung"

The reception of "Verfremdung" has been dominated by three main issues: the concept's source(s) and range of connotations; the various ideological disputes during the "Expressionismus-," "Realismus-," and "Formalismus-debatten"; and the relative merits of what Matthias-Johannes Fischer terms the opposing schools of "werkimmanente" and "marxistische Interpretation," of which Reinhold Grimm and Ernst Schumacher are presented as being the respective founding fathers (Fischer 1989, 244).

On the third issue, Fischer claims that there is a tendency for these two rival approaches to emphasize different phases of Brecht's theoretical development, with the Marxists making much of the moment in 1935 when Brecht made his most famous, but not first (that was in "Zum Theater" [*GBA*, 21:396]) reference to the process of defamiliarization, using the noun "Entfremdung" (in lieu of "Verfremdung") in a section of "Vergnügungstheater oder Lehrtheater?" entitled "Das epische Theater": "Die Darstellung setzte die Stoffe und Vorgänge einem Entfremdungsprozeß aus. Es war die Entfremdung, welche nötig ist, damit verstanden werden kann" (*GBA*, 22:109). This is interpreted as *prima facie* evidence of the concept's ideological roots and its function as a device to counteract "alienation," in Marx's sense. In contrast, Fischer sees the "werkimmanent" school making more of the later Brecht, from *Kleines Organon* onwards, and focusing on the aesthetic device, not the politics behind it. Yet such a picture hardly squares with the fact that most of the more politically framed *Messingkauf* material dates from 1939 to 1940, and by the late 1940s one finds Brecht explicitly stating that "Verfremdung" is above all a political device. In fact, although two general tendencies may have been discernible at the time Fischer was writing, the findings of those adopting a "werkimmanent" approach, seen by Fischer as a "secularization" of a political concept, can in most instances still be mapped onto the latter's political territory. Indeed, the work of many of Fischer's allegedly "werkimmanent" commentators (Esslin, Grimm, Klotz and Jendreiek) often contains valuable insights into the way "Verfremdung" operates and into the device's taxonomy. On the other hand, many who have argued that "Verfremdung" has to be seen within the context of Brecht's Marxist conception of dialectics have nevertheless contributed less to our understanding of the way such distancing functions than, say, Ben Chaim or Grimm. Moreover, as we saw in the case of "Kurze Beschreibung," any neat distinction between "Verfremdung" as an apolitical aesthetic concept and "Verfremdung" as a process within a specifically Marxist dramaturgy becomes difficult to maintain in the light of the emphasis Brecht puts on the presence of defamiliarization processes in everyday life. This factor has been underrated in the majority of debates about the term's connotations, in part because dramaturgical poems like "Über alltägliches Theater" have seldom received their due, but also because the rationale behind Brecht's use of everyday illustrations in the appendix to "Kurze Beschreibung" has not been taken into account. Revealingly, the "Anhang" was not included in Unseld's one-volume miscellany of *Schriften zum Theater*.

Critical debate on the subject sometimes fails to allow for the possibility that Brecht's theoretical position is by no means fixed. At times, he presents "Verfremdung" either as simply one more addition to theater's repertoire of technical devices, or as a feature of everyday experience, or as a means to a political end, depending on the readership or audience he is addressing. Note the seemingly non-interventionist or apolitical, cognitive nature of the following definitions:

> Der V-Effekt besteht darin, daß das Ding, das zum Verständnis gebracht, auf welches das Augenmerk gelenkt werden soll, aus einem gewöhnlichen, bekannten, unmittelbar vorliegenden Ding zu einem besonderen, auffälligen, unerwarteten Ding gemacht wird. Das Selbstverständliche wird in gewisser Weise unverständlich gemacht, das geschieht aber nur, um es dann um so verständlicher zu machen. Damit

aus dem Bekannten etwas Erkanntes werden kann, muß es aus seiner Unauffälligkeit herauskommen; es muß mit der Gewohnheit gebrochen werden, das betreffende Ding bedärfe keiner Erläuterung. (*GBA*, 22:635)

*Verfremdung als ein Verstehen* (verstehen — nicht verstehen — verstehen), Negation der Negation. ("Dialektik und Verfremdung" [1938], *GBA*, 22:401)

Passages of the second kind (of which there are many examples) contain distinct traces of deriving from Hegel rather than Marx.[37] They echo the idea in the *Phänomenologie des Geistes* that "das Bekannte überhaupt ist darum, weil es bekannt ist, nicht erkannt" (Hegel 1969–71, V [1970], 28–29), as well as the Hegelian notion of a "Negation der Negation," albeit in the particular theatrical sense that something negative (deceptively familiar surface reality) is negated through the process of "Verfremdung" in order that true "Erkenntnis" can be achieved. And, as the noun "Erkenntnis" and Brecht's formulations imply, the insights gained are grounded in epistemology rather than politics.

Despite the concept's Hegelian origins, Brecht's framework for "Verfremdung" often becomes explicitly political. Even if Brecht's initial use of "Entfremdung" did not possess unequivocally Marxist connotations of "alienation," it would in many contexts soon be impossible for the device to be thought of except as a remedy for the condition that Marx diagnosed using the term "Entfremdung." As one Marxist commentator put it: "Um eine Einsicht in diese 'Entfremdung' zu ermöglichen und damit die Voraussetzungen für die Aufhebung schaffen zu helfen [. . .], ist auf dem Theater eine 'Verfremdung' dieser für selbstverständlich und unveränderbar empfundenen Welt nötig" (Schumacher 1955, 193). Hence, Brecht's later, more explicitly political definitions of "Verfremdung," including the following two explanations first published in the GDR:

Echte, tiefe, eingreifende Verwendung der Verfremdungseffekte [presumably as opposed to the popular misconception that the "A-Effect" is merely a theatrical device] setzt voraus, daß die Gesellschaft ihren Zustand als historisch und verbesserbar betrachtet. Die echten V-Effekte haben kämpferischen Charakter. ("[Weitere Nachträge zum *Kleinen Organon*]" [1954], *GBA*, 23:294)

Man wird daraufhin untersuchen müssen, wie denn nun der V-Effekt einzusetzen ist, was, für welche Zwecke da verfremdet werden soll. Gezeigt werden soll die Veränderbarkeit des Zusammenlebens der Menschen (und damit die Veränderbarkeit des Menschen selbst). Das

---

[37] See Schaefer 1956, Grimm 1961, Knopf 1974, 15–60, and 1980a, 378–402, Fankhauser 1971, 23–29, and Fischer (1989), 244–64.

> kann nur geschehen dadurch, daß man das Augenmerk auf alles
> Unfeste, Flüchtige, Bedingte richtet, kurz auf die Widersprüche in allen
> Zuständen, welche die Neigung haben, in andere widerspruchsvolle
> Zustände überzugehen. ("[Notizen über die Dialektik auf dem
> Theater]" [c.1954], *GBA*, 23:299)

The question is whether Brecht had radically changed his position between
the time of the first two definitions of "Verfremdung," explanations that, at
least on the surface, sound closer to Hegel (or even Shklovsky), and the later
two, about whose "kämpferischer Charakter" there can be no doubt. This is
not easy to decide, despite the wealth of theoretical evidence, because Brecht
does at times choose, for tactical reasons, to emphasize the general cognitive
value of "Verfremdung" and to illustrate the priniciple using material from
daily life. Given the stress on "Veränderbarkeit," even as early as the time of
the *Mahagonny* notes, coupled with the fact that he had already toyed with
the concept of "dialektisches Theater" in the early thirties, it seems unlikely
that a radical Marxist repositioning of "Verfremdung" only occurred at the
time *Der Messingkauf* was being prepared. *Der Messingkauf,* it could be argued, merely makes explicit what exile contexts at times obliged Brecht to
treat with discretion.

Hanns Eisler once described Brecht as "mit der Verfremdung [. . .]
geboren [. . .] die große Verfremdung des Kasperls, des Wurschtl-Theaters,
der Volkskunst. Brecht hat die Verfremdung nicht erfunden. Er hat sie nur
auf eine enorme Höhe gebracht und sie neu angewendet" (Bunge 1970,
150). Because the wider tradition, what Eisler calls "die große Verfremdung," is something Brecht himself often admitted to being influenced by,
the phrase "nicht erfunden [. . .] nur [. . .] neu gewendet" seems an uncon-
tentious verdict on the various artistic debts Brechtian "Verfremdung" entailed. Not that this has stopped some from indulging in a certain
*Schadenfreude* when trying to show that Brecht's ideas were far from new.
Usually the debate is conducted in a more circumscribed arena and revolves
around certain very specific debts: how much Brecht's "Verfremdungseffekt" owed to Galileo, Francis Bacon, German Romanticism's concept of
"Befremden," Hegel's *Phänomenologie des Geistes,* the idea of "Entfremdung" in Marx's *Deutsche Ideologie,* to Shklovsky, or to oriental theater.
All these possibilities have been explored,[38] though an undue preoccupation with provable influences and sources has on occasions led to examples
of what an earlier generation would have dismissed as a form of "genetic
fallacy."

One recurrent inference involves the assumption that if Brecht can be
shown to have been influenced in his terminology or his practice by either

---

[38] Hansen-Löve (1978), 19–42 and Fankhauser (1971), 23–30.

Shklovsky or Chinese theater, this must in some way be evidence that the concept means the same in his writings as it did in his source. Since Shklovsky's *priem ostranenya* refers to a characteristic of all art and both Brecht and Shklovsky use cognate theoretical terms, this has persuaded some (who often did not take much persuading) that he and Brecht must be talking about the same aesthetic phenomenon, others to conclude that Shklovsky cannot have influenced Brecht's thinking, and yet others to reject the "influence" scenario as a further feature of Cold War Brecht scholarship, since it would imply that Brecht's achievements were in some way connected with Russian Formalist ideas that had long since been criminalized in the USSR. As Tatlow remarks, "everything depends on the definition of influence. If we imagine 'influence' as something obvious, absolute and direct" (Tatlow 1977, 221), we are likely to arrive at one set of conclusions. If on the other hand, in the wake of *The Anxiety of Influence* and the large-scale reassessment of the concept for which Harold Bloom was the catalyst, one allows less positivistic models of "influence" to come into play, then the central issue of the term's provenance, "Transportabilität" and primary associations may not be as cut-and-dried as has sometimes been assumed. As a matter of principle, it might be assumed that if Brecht could talk about estrangement as "eine Prozedur des täglichen Lebens," yet radically politicize it in his own theatrical work and the accompanying theory, then there is no reason why he might not have been equally impressed by Shklovsky's exploration of "eine Prozedur der Kunst im allgemeinen," without necessarily being obliged to use the term in the same sense. In fact, although he saw many heterogeneous examples of "Verfremdung" around him and recognized that cultural history documented the device in many different forms, Brecht was insistent that his own brand of "Verfremdung" ("echte Verfremdung") was only distantly related to the estrangement to be seen in a Breughel painting, a Chaplin film or the work of Surrealist artists.[39] Likewise, the fact that a writer sporadically used a term prior to the time when he could have encountered it when used by a particular putative influence need not necessarily invalidate the possibility of his interest in the phenomenon being intensified by an idea that was received later. That too is influence, even if the mono-causal notion of one sole "source" is hardly pertinent.

At a more healthily pragmatic level, Reinhold Grimm distinguishes three main kinds of "Verfremdung": "einmal beim Schreiben eines Stückes, dann

---

[39] "Der V-Effekt ist ein altes Kunstmittel, bekannt aus der Komödie, gewissen Zweigen der Volkskunst und der Praxis des asiatischen Theaters" (*GBA*, 26:404). See also Brecht on the "V-Effekt in Breughel and Chaplin" (*GBA*, 22:223, 271) and his claim that "der Dadaismus und der Surrealismus benutzten Verfremdungseffekte extremster Art. Ihre Gegenstände kehren aus der Verfremdung nicht wieder zurück. Der klassische Verfremdungseffekt erzeugt erhöhtes Verständnis" (*GBA*, 22:224).

bei seiner Inszenierung [. . .] und schließlich im Spiel der Darsteller" (Grimm 1959, 13). One striking feature, in this connection, of Brecht's various theoretical discussions of "Verfremdung" is their asymmetry. Brecht pays much attention to the role of the actor in "Verfremdungseffekte in der chinesischen Schauspielkunst" and in "Kurze Beschreibung." He also has much to say about the importance of songs, music, narrator figures, stage sets, and the direct addressing of the audience in the theatrical process of "Verfremdung." But his theorizing says remarkably little about Grimm's first category of textual "Verfremdung." One result has been the replication of this asymmetry in much of the secondary literature on the subject. Discussions of staging-as-"Verfremdung" and of particular theatrical devices like half-curtains and anti-illusionist stage props far outnumber any theoretical analysis of verbal and other literary estranging devices, such as Brecht's use of clashing stylistic registers, bold metaphors and image patterns, stylistic anachronisms, word-plays, and verbal montage. The major exception has been at the level of genre: here, Brecht's own categories ("episches Theater," "epische Oper," "Lehrstück," "Songspiel," "Modellstück," and "Parabelstück") have with some justification determined dominant reception categories. Brecht himself may well have had good reasons for stressing the pragmatic aspects of stage "Verfremdung": for example, when seeking to establish an appropriate production concept on the part of producers and actors or when trying to ensure that his work was properly received by recidivist bourgeois audiences. If this was one of the main purposes of the theory, then verbal "Verfremdung" would inevitably receive less attention. After all, Brecht had written the script, and thus there was no real need to subject details to microscopic analysis to get across his general theoretical position. For reasons connected with the various chequered phases of Brecht's exile and post-exile creative work, theory targeted at producers, actors and potential audiences would always remain a vital ingredient in the playwright's self-presentation and the mediation of his aesthetic ideas.

## "Historisierung"

"Kurze Beschreibung" presents "Historisierung," the final — and most political — major new term in Brecht's conceptual arsenal of the late 1930s, as an "entscheidendes Technikum." It is explained, in more detail than in the discussion of a girl leaving home in *An American Tragedy,* as one of the responsibilities of an epic actor:

> Der Schauspieler muß die Vorgänge als historische Vorgänge spielen. Historische Vorgänge sind einmalige, vorübergehende, mit bestimmten Epochen verbundene Vorgänge. Das Verhalten der Personen in ihnen ist nicht ein schlechthin menschliches, unwandelbares, es hat bestimmte

Besonderheiten, es hat durch den Gang der Geschichte Überholtes und Überholbares und ist der Kritik vom Standpunkt der jeweilig darauffolgenden Epoche aus unterworfen. Die ständige Entwicklung entfremdet uns das Verhalten der vor uns Geborenen.

Der Schauspieler nun hat diesen Abstand zu den Ereignissen und Verhaltungsweisen, den der Historiker nimmt, zu den Ereignissen und Verhaltungsweisen der Jetztzeit zu nehmen. Er hat uns diese Vorgänge und Personen zu verfremden. (*GBA*, 22:646)

In order to discourage any automatic association of "Historisierung" with distant history, the passage begins disingenuously with a focus on what Brecht calls "historische Vorgänge." But it is the subsequent concern with "Vorgänge und Personen [der Jetztzeit]" that becomes the most important point in the entire "Kurze Beschreibung." This is meant to explain a device whose nature and function are less ambiguously formulated and for that reason could have been more crucial to an understanding of Brecht's work than even "Verfremdung" was to become. Unlike "Verfremdung," "Historisierung" did not give rise to complex debates about the semantic territory it occupied or about its pedigree. It occasioned no factional split between "textimmanent" and politically oriented scholars. And whenever Brecht writes about "Historisierung," there is invariably a coherence to the points made. He would later reject the term "episches Theater" as being "zu formal" (*GBA*, 23:386), preferring "dialektisches Theater," yet "Historisierung" arguably already contained the element missing from both "episches Theater" and his at times tactically apolitical definitions of "Verfremdung."[40] Moreover, his various explanations of "Historisierung" leave one in no doubt about their being predicated on a dialectical materialist

---

[40] A prefatory note to "Die Dialektik auf dem Theater" (early 1950s) expresses Brecht's "Vermutung [. . .], daß die Bezeichnung 'episches Theater' für das gemeinte (und zum Teil praktizierte) Theater zu formal ist. Episches Theater ist für diese Darbietungen wohl die Voraussetzung, jedoch erschließt es allein noch nicht die Produktivität und Änderbarkeit der Gesellschaft, aus welchen Quellen sie das Hauptvergnügen schöpfen müssen" (*GBA*, 23:386). Although Brecht adds "Die Bezeichnung muß daher als unzureichend bezeichnet werden," "[Vom epischen zum dialektischen Theater 1]" (c. 1954) records: "Es wird jetzt der Versuch gemacht, vom *epischen* Theater zum *dialektischen* Theater zu kommen. Unseres Erachtens und unserer Absicht nach waren die Praxis des epischen Theaters und sein ganzer Begriff keineswegs undialektisch, noch wird ein dialektisches Theater ohne das epische Element auskommen. Dennoch denken wir an eine ziemlich große Umgestaltung" (*GBA*, 23:299). Such comments could just as well have been made about "Verfremdung." Brecht had already talked of a "dialektische Dramatik" in the early 1930s; see *GBA*, 21:431–40, 763–64 and 790).

conception of history and not on some simple appropriation of Walter Benjamin's more mystical concept of the "Jetztzeit."[41]

The account of "Historisierung" in the "Zweiter Nachtrag zur Theorie des *Messingkaufs*" is not as succinct as some later ones: "*Bei der Historisierung* wird ein bestimmtes Gesellschaftssystem vom Standpunkt eines anderen Gesellschaftssystems aus betrachtet. Die Entwicklung der Gesellschaft ergibt die Gesichtspunkte" (*GBA*, 22:699). Just what these "Gesichtspunkte" might be is hinted at in a further "Nachtrag"[42] to the *Messingkauf* with the suggestion that "die Vorgänge werden *historisiert* und *sozial milieurisiert*" (*GBA*, 22:701). This new, more explicit emphasis on milieu gives a clearer focus to the device, since social and historical milieus demonstrably interact dialectically with the individual. This comes out clearly in "Über das Historisieren" (early 1940, eventually to become part of *Kleines Organon*):

> Vor dem Historisierenden hat der Mensch etwas Zweideutiges, Nicht-zu-Ende-Komponiertes. Er erscheint in mehr als einer Figur; er ist zwar so wie er ist, da es zureichend Gründe dafür in der Zeit gibt, aber er ist, sofern ihn die Zeit gebildet hat, auch zugleich ein anderer, wenn man nämlich von der Zeit absieht, ihn von einer anderen Zeit bilden läßt. [. . .]. Es steckt viel in ihm, was da entfaltet wurde und entfaltbar ist. Er hat sich schon geändert, kann sich also weiter ändern. (*GBA* 22, 689–90)

As is usual in Brecht's theoretical presentation of "Historiserung," there is a tendency to emphasize a lack of consistency in the way an actor should present a character: he contends that people should not be portrayed as frozen in time and as examples of a given monolithically conceived epoch, but should come across, like society itself, always at any moment in a state of flux.

Although still remaining at the level of general principles, the fictive conversation "Über die epische Schauspielkunst. *Der Wechsel*" (*GBA*, 22: 689–90) again emphasizes the actor's importance within the process of

---

[41] The "Jetztzeit" concept plays a central role in Benjamin's attempted dismantling of the myth of historical progress (see "Erkenntnistheoretisches, Theorie des Fortschritts" [Benjamin 1972–89, V-1: *Das Passagen-Werk* (1981), 570–611], and "Über den Begriff der Geschichte," [I-2 [1974], 691–704]). The pessimism that informs Benjamin's focus on the "Jetztzeit" is the diametrical opposite of the premises of Brecht's conception of "Historisierung."

[42] The reason for the pronounced concern with "Historisierung" in the "Nachträge" is that Brecht had considered including "Verfremdungseffekte in der chinesischen Schauspielkunst" in the complex and he was trying to elucidate points that are unclear there.

conveying a sense of flux through the process of "Historisierung." In this dialogue between a "Schauspieler" and a "Zuschauer," it is the representative of the audience (of *praxis*) who gives the actor lessons on how he should perform and whose superior insight is acknowledged in the actor's desire to learn from him.

The discussion proper gets underway when the actor says: "Du sagtest, der Schauspieler muß den Wechsel der Dinge zum Ausdruck bringen. Was heißt das?" Throughout the following question-and-answer routine, the "Zuschauer" remains closer to Brecht's position than the hapless thespian.

ZUSCHAUER:    Der Historiker interessiert sich für den Wechsel der Dinge.

SCHAUSPIELER:  Und wie spielt man für ihn?

ZUSCHAUER:    Indem man zeigt, was damals anders war als heute, und den Grund andeutet. Aber man muß auch zeigen, wie aus dem Gestern das Heute wurde. (*GBA*, 22:670)

SCHAUSPIELER:  Ich soll also eine Figur so anlegen, daß ich immerfort zeige: so war dieser Mensch zu dieser Zeit seines Lebens und so zu jener, und: das war sein Ausspruch, oder: so pflegte er zu jener Zeit zu sprechen [. . .].

ZUSCHAUER:    So ist es. Wenn ihr eure Rolle durchlest, dann findet zuerst Überschriften solch historischer Art. Aber vergeßt nicht, daß die Geschichte eine Geschichte von Klassenkämpfen ist, daß also die Überschriften gesellschaftlich wichtig sein müssen.

SCHAUSPIELER:  Also ist der Zuschauer ein Gesellschaftshistoriker?

ZUSCHAUER:    Ja. (GBA, 22:671–72)

On being informed that the "Zuschauer ist auch ein Historiker," the actor's immediate assumption is that they must be talking about historical drama. But his mentor's real point is that most "Stücke, die in der Vergangenheit spielen" are anything but plays for the new breed of Marxist historians, defined as people interested in "der Wechsel der Dinge." The point becomes clearer with the reference to "Historiker" who are at the same time "Gesellschaftskritiker." Brecht then rehearses his standard contrast between a bourgeois form of essentialist drama showing "das immer gleichbleibende Menschliche" and "Historisierung," underwritten by a view of history as an ever-changing continuum, rather than stasis or an entity that can be neatly divided into past, present and future.[43] This explicit emphasis on a dialectical

---

[43] On the subject of "[die] für Brechts Denken so wichtige Dreidimensionalität der Zeit," Müller sums up a relationship that privileges the present in the following

conception of history as change is a new plank in Brecht's justification of "Historisierung."

A sharper ethical focus is then introduced. First, with the objection that turning to the past for a paradigm based on eternal verities encourages "eine Gleichgültigkeit gegenüber der Form, in der wir Menschen leben, und damit eine Billigung der gerade eben vorkommenden" (*GBA*, 22:670). And second, with a point concerning the individual's status within such a type of theater: "Wird der Mensch selber so nicht allzu unwichtig?.," a question inserted to counter prejudices likely to arise as a result of the impersonal phrase "Wechsel der Dinge." The response from the "Zuschauer" is central to Brecht's conception of history: "Im Gegenteil. Er wird geehrt, indem alle Veränderungen, die an ihm und durch ihn sichtbar sind, festgestellt werden. Er wird ebenso ernst genommen, wie die Napoleons früherer Zeit" (*GBA*, 22:671). The assumption underlying the actor's present worry has itself been cleverly historicized to show that the values his spontaneous anxiety implies also have to be seen as part of history's dialectical flux. Any misguided actor harboring such doubts, it is implied, is as much an anachronism as those "Könige des 16. Jahrhunderts" who, according to the "Zuschauer," have to be depicted in such a way "daß solches Benehmen und solche Personen heute kaum noch vorkommen oder, wo sie vorkommen, Staunen verdienen" (*GBA*, 22:670).

Klaus-Detlef Müller has argued that since history is "die umfassende Wirklichkeit aller gesellschaftlichen Erscheinungen," "Historisierung [umfaßt] Ästhetisches (eine Theatertechnik) und Gehaltliches (Beziehung auf die Wirklichkeit schlechthin) zugleich" (Müller 1967, 30). On the surface, the dialogue "Über die epische Schauspielkunst. *Der Wechsel*" (even its dialectical subtitle) may still appear to emphasize the aesthetic aspect by laying such stress on the actor's role. But as the two parts of his title suggest, Brecht is as concerned to establish the political philosophy ("Wechsel der Dinge") underlying the dramaturgical discussion as he is to explain the technical repercussions of his Marxist conception of history for acting techniques ("die epische Schauspielkunst"). Müller defines the image of history presented in this context as "weniger ein Gegenstand als eine Kategorie des Wirklichkeitsverhältnisses [. . .], die sich als Vermittlung kennzeichnen läßt" (Müller 1967, 96), that "Vermittlung" being part of the process of "Historisierung" that has now become a central feature of Brechtian theater. "Durch das Historisieren wird ja ein Erkenntnisakt provoziert, der analog auf die Gegenwart übertragbar ist und hier praktisch wirksam werden

---

terms: "die Gegenwart befindet über das Vergangene, um von hier aus die Zukunft zu bestimmen. Vergangenheit und Zukunft sind diesseitig, die Gegenwart ist ein Heraustreten aus der unmittelbaren Geschichte in die urteilende Reflexion" (Klaus-Detlef Müller 1967, 143).

soll. Die Geschichte ist ein Medium der Erkenntnis, nicht primär ihr Gegenstand" (Müller 1967, 40).

Two particular aspects of Müller's discussion of "Historisierung" deserve special comment. First, the claim that historicization is "als Technik eine Vermittlung von Inhalt und Form, noch nicht selbst Form. Das ist erst die dramatische Parabel, um die sich alle mit der erörterten historischen Thematik gegebenen Gestaltungsfragen gruppieren" (Müller 1967, 147). Müller demonstrates the importance of the parable form for historicization, but the parable is not the only dramatic form with which historicization is associated in the theoretical writings. Brecht's remarks about *King Lear* and *An American Tragedy* would hardly lead to such a conclusion. And while one of Müller's most revealing examples of a "Historisierung der Jetztzeit" is the treatment of fascism in "Fünf Schwierigkeiten beim Schreiben der Wahrheit" (*GBA*, 22:74–89), a canonical dramatic embodiment of this interpretation would not be the parable play *Die Rundköpfe und die Spitzköpfe*, but *Furcht und Elend des III. Reiches*. As Müller's discussion of a "Historisierung der Gegenwart" (70–88) suggests, highlighting the impermanence of the present world is one of Brecht's major theoretical postulates. Yet the plays display a marked predilection for what Brecht saw as the "konkretisierte" model derived from the historical past rather than a "Historisierung der Jetztzeit" in all its complexity. In this respect, the practice of "Historisierung" was decidedly narrower than the potential implied by theoretical explanations of it.

The relationship between "Verfremdung" and "Historisierung" was to remain an elusive issue throughout this stage of Brecht's theorizing. The declaration in "Verfremdungseffekte in der chinesischen Schauspielkunst" that "Der V-Effekt [. . .] bezweckte hauptsächlich die *Historisierung* der darzustellenden Vorgänge" (*GBA*, 22:207) suggests one of a means to an end. However, Müller is more cautious: "Verfremden, historisieren und 'dialektisieren' sind drei Aspekte des Zentralbegriffs der Brechtschen Theatertheorie, sie beinhalten eine Entwicklung zu größerer Präzision, indem sie sich gegenseitig ergänzen" (46), a claim which makes it even more surprising how seldom this reciprocal illumination has played a part in discussions of the individual terms. What is clear, however, is that all such relationships will be in need of drastic reformulation at the point where Brecht focuses on the concept of "Dialektisches Theater" as the most appropriate term for his experiments.

# 3: The Dramaturgical Poems and Their Contexts

"WENN ICH MEINE letzten Stücke betrachte und vergleiche," Brecht wrote in 1941, "so finde ich sie enorm uneinheitlich in jeder Weise. Selbst die Genres wechseln unaufhörlich. Biographie, Gestarium, Parabel, Charakterlustspiel im Volkston, Historienfarce, die Stücke streben auseinander wie die Gestirne im neuen Weltbild der Physik, als sei auch hier irgendein Kern der Dramatik explodiert. Dabei ist die Theorie, die ihnen unterliegt oder abgezogen werden kann, ihrerseits sehr bestimmt gegenüber den anderen Theorien" (*GBA,* 26:477). There is much truth to this picture, but the theoretical writings are also "enorm uneinheitlich" and, here too, "die Genres wechseln unaufhörlich." Apart from conventional essay and article formats, one finds a skilfull exploitation of reviews, open letters, responses (both real and spoof) to journalistic questionnaires, new genres such as "Funkgespräch" and radio essay, self-interviews, and program notes, as well as detailed rehearsal diaries and "Materialien" on specific plays. Above all, there was what Brecht thought of as his "Hauptwerk" (*GBA,* 29:471): the extensive *Versuche* series of volumes containing a mixture of extracts from plays, accompanying musical scores, performance photographs, poems, and theoretical writings. This variegated output spans more than three decades of Brecht's creative life. Although Scandinavian and US exile restricted the range of available outlets, Brecht remained adept at placing flagship pieces in opinion-forming publications. In the Weimar years it might seem as if Brecht had merely used channels of communication open to any author in a modern, technologically advanced society. Yet he did so shrewdly and often with panache. Whenever his contributions appeared in feuilleton surveys on topics of the moment, it was alongside the great names of the time. While still in Weimar Germany, Brecht was in the thick of things. That would not happen again until his final years in the GDR. Exile, as far as his theoretical writings were concerned, was to some extent a period of consolidation and preparation for better times. Yet despite adverse conditions, the exile period was responsible for much of Brecht's most important dramaturgical and aesthetic writings and his most inventively presented theory.

The works looked at so far show how deceptive categorization on the basis of conventional genres can be. What looks like a set of notes to a single opera (*Mahagonny*) serves as the pretext for a diagnosis of the bourgeois theater "Apparat" and the cultural superstructure of the entire Weimar Republic. An essay, tucked away in a London monthly, drawing attention to defamiliarization in traditional Chinese acting became a vehicle for one of Brecht's most memorable treatments of "Historisierung." Likewise, while it is possible to pinpoint the salient themes and presentational strategies of "Kurze Beschreibung," the work's unprepossessing title would appear to be a calculated misnomer, not because of any lack of economy (Brecht, who had coined the phrase "dramatischer Taylorismus"[(*GBA*, 26:338] when working on some of his more austere parable plays, also practised a form of theoretical Taylorism[1]), but because "Beschreibung" suggests a more discursive, coherent approach than the "epic" technique adopted. It would be difficult to find a satisfactory generic label for such a work. Indeed, each of Brecht's dramaturgical statements appears to be formally unique.[2] Even when he does turn to specific available formats, he displays an ability to exploit the chosen paradigm as much for heuristic as for promotional purposes; they even become "verfremdet" each time Brecht works with them. His letter to the Berliner Ensemble on the eve of their 1956 London visit (*GBA*, 30:475) soon found its way into the London theater program.

As a public lecture, "Über experimentelles Theater" would appear to involve the most conventional of formats considered so far. Brecht's annotations regarding pacing and emphasis in the case of the 1932 talk "Rundfunk als Kommunikationsapparat" (*GBA*, 21:552–57) suggest great sensitivity to the niceties of public oratory. However, the impression that there is less "Episierung" or "Verfremdung" in "Über experimentelles Theater" is deceptive. Brecht's adoption there of the rhetorical stance of a German writer arriving hot-foot from Berlin with news of exciting developments in one of Europe's main theatrical centers is itself a form of defamiliarization. Brecht may choose to assume the mask of an outsider bearing tidings of "strange" developments to people anxious to hear about them, but in truth

---

[1] "Taylorism" is a system of labor time-and-motion study named after the US engineer Frederick Winslow Taylor (1856–1915), author of *Shop Management* (1903) and *The Principles of Scientific Management* (1911). By the 1920s Taylorism or the Taylor System had become a byword for rationalized industrial efficiency in both the Western world and the Soviet Union. It formed part of the cult of "Amerikanismus" in the Weimar Republic and also influenced the *Neue Sachlichkeit* functionalist aesthetic. See Midgley 2000, 315–17 on some of the cultural influences of Taylorism.

[2] *Kleines Organon* has been seen to be equally difficult to pigeon-hole: "Zugleich fallen Besonderheiten auf, die dieser theoretischen Schrift — legt man die üblichen Muster zu Grunde — unangemessen scheinen oder untypisch sind. Dazu gehört, dass statt exakter und klarer Abgrenzungen oder Inhaltsbestimmungen widersprüchliche bis paradoxe Feststellungen zu finden sind [. . .]" (*BHB*, 4:320).

he comes from the seclusion of Svendborg and (only indirectly) from a Berlin that no longer exists. This enables him to transform an apparent eyewitness account into an elaborate, distanciating outline of the cultural and historical context for his own experiments. Even in such a seemingly simple instance, Brecht comes across as a master of the art of subverting pre-existing discourse formats. His pioneering "Rundfunkgespräche," which were inevitably subject to the tyranny of the cultural agenda assigned to them, nevertheless tended to depart quite substantially from agreed norms. One often finds Brecht over-scripting or in other ways orchestrating things to highlight his own position. In the case of the Cologne radio talk with Sternberg and Ihering, we saw the former having his lines mapped out for him on the basis of an already-published open letter, but now being assigned the task of presenting it as a thesis to which Brecht constructed a carefully formulated counter-position. Ihering too was to receive comparably manipulative, though less hostile, treatment in "Gespräch über Klassiker" (GBA, 21:309–15), where his views were inserted into the script for him to parrot, the necessary material being drawn from a brochure published earlier that same year (Ihering 1929). The comment in the GBA notes on such a manipulative procedure merely states: "Vermutlich ist Brecht [. . .] wesentlich an der Zusammenstellung und Formulierung der Texte auch der anderen Gesprächspartner beteiligt" (GBA, 21:707). One wonders how the other participants saw things! Sketches for another radio discussion, "Die Not des Theaters" (GBA, 21:690–92), are equally manipulative, but this time it is Brecht's contributions that are pre-scripted in great detail, with other "Gesprächspartner" being reduced to playing walk-on parts. One only has to compare such manipulation with the fictive conversations on aesthetic issues that form part of Hugo von Hofmannsthal's literary essays to appreciate the extent to which Brecht departs from the established convention of using theory in dialogue form to permit a sophisticated interplay of ideas.

Even in the 1920s, Brecht had tended to manipulate the other available discourse opportunities in unpredictable ways. "An den Herrn im Parkett" (GBA, 21:117–18), for example, looks to all intents and purposes like an open letter (which may explain why, in GBA, it immediately precedes two bona fide "Offene Briefe"). But it was submitted in response to the Berliner Börsen-Courier's December 1925 survey "Was, glauben Sie, verlangt Ihr Publikum von Ihnen?" Instead of playing by the rules, as the other dramatists approached did — which would have been tantamount to engaging in a cultural dialogue behind the audience's back — Brecht opts for the provocative strategy of directly addressing the man in the stalls and having the resultant fictive letter published. His purpose appears to be to suggest that the views of the man who has paid for his theater seat urgently need to be considered, not just those of the author or the demands of the all-powerful theater "Apparat." For similar reasons, when, in November

1927, the "Literaturblatt" of the *Frankfurter Zeitung* approached him for a contribution to its column "Der Autor über sich selbst," Brecht responded with a seemingly incongruous contribution entitled "Schwierigkeiten des epischen Theaters" (*GBA*, 21:209–10). Although the piece was accepted, the literary editor advised readers that Brecht's observations, while not a direct response to the rubric's invitation, were intended to give "einen Einblick in sein besonderes Interessengebiet" (quoted in *GBA*, 21:681). The formulation used ("gewähren soll") leaves the editor sounding less than convinced that this was what had been asked for. Brecht was evidently not prepared to go on record "über sich selbst" in any narrowly self-promotional sense. Yet rather than decline to write a contribution, he turned the request to his advantage, cunningly implying that the topic "Schwierigkeiten des epischen Theaters" was of far wider significance than what would nowadays be presented as "Brecht über Brecht." Even seemingly autonomous theoretical pieces turn out to have begun life as answers to newspaper questionnaires, as was the case with "Über Stoffe und Form" (*GBA*, 21:302–4), a *Berliner Börsen-Courier* piece, part of a survey on the subject of "Das Theater von morgen." Brecht, along with a number of other German dramatists and *Theaterintendanten,* had been asked "Welche neuen Stoffgebiete können das Theater befruchten? Verlangen diese Stoffe eine neue Form des Dramas und des Spiels?" In the midst of launching and theorizing Epic Opera, Brecht must have seen another opening not to be turned down.

Although in the case of some writings the fictiveness is obvious, there are many others where it is not possible to make binding distinctions between authentic material (real interviews subsequently transcribed, published answers to actual journalistic questionnaires, and *bona fide* open letters to specific newspapers) and creative variations on the same sub-genres. The 1929 "Dialog über Schauspielkunst" (*GBA*, 21:279–82) consists of a series of routine question-and-answer set pieces with no assignation to specific speakers. In this respect, it differs from Brecht's tribute in dialogue form to Helene Weigel's acting in "Letzte Etappe: Ödipus" (*GBA*, 21:278–79). Yet even when real exchanges had taken place, they were often planned down to the last detail. One might think that if a genuine dialogue between specific, identified people had occurred on a particular occasion, it would be remarkable to find such extensive drafts for it. Yet as "Letzte Etappe: Ödipus" shows, even real dialogues can sometimes be meticulously sketched out in advance, reconstructed or written up after the event. Thus, while it is conceivable that Brecht's "Rede an die deutschen Arbeiter, Bauern und Intellektuellen" (*GBA*, 22:337) was prepared for transmission, it is just as likely that the script bearing that title is merely the blueprint for a fictive broadcast Brecht would have liked to have made. Fictiveness is certainly the case with the vast majority of the thirty or so other pieces listed in the *GBA Registerband* under such telltale titles as those beginning "Brief an," "Aus einem

Brief an," "Aus einem kleinen Gespräch," "Aus einem Traktat über," or "Aus einer Ansprache an."

Looking back at "Über die epische Schauspielkunst: *Der Wechsel,*" we can detect a generic quality that raises suspicions as to whether any such discussion ever did take place. No one is named: the participants are merely "der Zuschauer" and "der Schauspieler." And it would be hard to imagine an actor wanting to make a fool of himself by expressing the naive views attributed to the thespian in this stiltedly didactic exchange. He is more like the fictive Simplicio in Galileo's dialogue concerning two astronomical systems than a real historical "Gesprächspartner."[3] In the case of the *Messingkauf* complex, conceived at the start of Brecht's Swedish exile (1939), much of the preliminary material is in prose, a feature that has given rise to the assumption that it had simply not yet been transposed into dialogue. Thus an editorial note to "Verfremdungseffekte in der chinesischen Schauspielkunst" raises the question of whether it was intended for integration into *Der Messingkauf* in its present form or whether Brecht "[es] dafür dialogisieren wollte" (*GBA,* 22:959).

Well before embarking on *Der Messingkauf,* Brecht had written a number of fictive conversations that can best be thought of as "dialogisierte Theorie." One of the earliest, "Dialog über eine Schauspielerin des epischen Theaters" (*GBA,* 22:353–55), is between participants identified as "Ich" and "Der Schauspieler." The date of composition (1938) suggests that the actress could well have been Helene Weigel, at the time playing the lead part in Brecht's and Berlau's production of *Die Gewehre der Frau Carrar* (Señora

---

[3] The problem of fictive versus real has occasioned much debate, particularly in the case of so-called "literary conversation": "Die meisten 'Gespräche,' die von [Brecht] überliefert sind, stellen nachträgliche (oder auch vorbereitende) Aufzeichnungen [Brechts] dar; sind insofern keine authentischen Protokolle von tatsächlich stattgefundenen Gesprächen; es handelt sich vielmehr um Schriften, die sich zwar auf reale 'Gespräche' beziehen, nicht jedoch wiedergeben, was wirklich gesagt worden ist (wobei in nicht wenigen Fällen sogar damit gerechnet werden muss, dass [Brecht] seinen Gesprächspartnern Äußerungen in den Mund legte, die diese gar nicht vertreten hatten)" (*BHB,* 4:456). Seidel (1978, 109) makes a well-reasoned plea for a more rigorous classification, one differentiating between, *inter alia,* "Dialog" and "Gespräch" proper. On the basis of his distinction between fictive "Dialog" ("literarische Form") and "Gespräch" ("tatsächlich, protokolliert"), the Suhrkamp anthology *Brecht im Gespräch* (Hecht 1975) stands accused of creating a "terminologisches Allerlei" and even failing to record when "discussions" are merely Brecht's "Konstrukte" (*BHB,* 4:456). There are, however, more gray areas than even Seidel's proposed taxonomy suggests. The equally important need to distinguish between real (sent or unsent) letters and fictive missives, not to mention the *Briefgedicht,* or to differentiate between real public addresses and the *Anrede* poem raises a series of further problems of categorization, especially in the case of putative addressees.

Carrar's Rifles, 1938). Yet it is possible that the actor who participates in the discussion never existed. The relevant *GBA* note displays caution: "Möglicherweise liegen dem Texte Gespräche mit Per Knutzon (dem Regisseur der Uraufführung von *Die Rundköpfe und die Spitzköpfe* in Kopenhagen) zugrunde" (*GBA*, 22:1013). What is revealing here is the ambivalence: a modicum of fictiveness anchored in fact is conceded through the combination of the adverb "möglicherweise" and the verb "zugrundeliegen," yet there is obviously a reluctance to entertain the possibility that there may never have been any actual discussion and the entire piece could be pure invention. In some other instances, for example, "Gespräch über blaue Pferde" (*GBA*, 22:351) and "V-Effekte, Dreigespräch" (*GBA*, 22:398–401), the very names of the participants — Thomas, Lukas, and Karl — give rise to the suspicion of fictitiousness, especially given the number of times Brecht includes a "doubting Thomas" in his dialogues.

Another series of conversations involving a Karl (this time referred to colloquially as "Kalle"), *Flüchtlingsgespräche* (Conversations between Refugees, 1944; *GBA*, 18:195–327), may look like an exception to Brecht's tendency, while in Scandinavian exile, to locate his discussions in non-specified settings, for this time the exchanges take place in the "Bahnhofsrestaurant" of Helsinki's main station. Yet despite this token referentiality, the participants come across as invented. It may not be irrelevant that much of the material that ended up in the *Flüchtlingsgespräche* began life belonging to other genres, including Brecht's *Unpolitische Briefe* as well as a series of untitled prose sketches on topics of the moment and various paralipomena to the main themes of *Herr Puntila und sein Knecht Matti* (Mr Puntila and his Man Matti, 1940). These drafts were only gradually integrated into the eventual framework of the two exiles' regular weekly discussions held by mutual agreement at a convenient central meeting place. The participants are simply referred to as Kalle and Ziffel, names which sound as invented as the Mies and Meck (in an earlier draft, Kries and Mies) of another fragment from the same period (*GBA*, 18:329–38). Early drafts give no names at all, and even in later ones, some speeches are still not yet allocated to either speaker. In the case of the eventual *Flüchtlingsgespräche,* we are dealing with a genre that might at best be called "dialogisierte Tagespolitik" or dramatized *politique du trottoir.* Commenting on his method, Brecht cited his models: "Ich las in *Diderots* 'Jakob der Fatalist,' als mir eine neue Möglichkeit aufging, den alten *Ziffel*-Plan zu verwirklichen. Die Art, Zwiegespräche einzuflechten, hatte mir schon bei *Kivi*[4] gefallen. [. . .] Ich

---

[4] Aleksis Kivi (1834–72), author of *Seitsemän veljestä* (Seven Brothers, 1870), a novel Brecht read in the German translation *Die sieben Brüder* (1921). As Kalle and Ziffel would have known, Kivi's statue stands in the square adjoining Helsinki's main railroad station.

schrieb probeweise zwei kleine Kapitel und nannte das Ganze '*Flücht-lingsgespräche*'" (*GBA*, 26:430). For German readers, the affinity to Goethe's *Unterhaltungen deutscher Ausgewanderten* (Conversations of German Refugees, 1795) would also suggest fictionality, situating the *Flücht-lingsgespräche* in the context of the best-known German example of a European genre that stretches back to Boccaccio and Chaucer. Brecht, of course, had other models for his use of the fictive letter as a vehicle for bringing theory to life. A reference in *Der Dreigroschenprozeß* to "Schillers Vorschlag, die politische Erziehung zu einer Angelegenheit der Ästhetik zu machen" (*GBA*, 21:472) suggests familiarity with *Briefe über die ästhetische Erziehung des Menschen* (On the Aesthetic Education of Man, 1795). Yet, most important when it comes to fictive modes of theorizing, as has been pointed out (Licher 1984, 221–25), Brecht had been profoundly influenced at various stages of his life by Horace's *Epistulae* (above all, Book 2: *Ars poetica*), as well as the didactic poetry of Virgil's *Georgics* and Lucretius's *De rerum natura*.

Somewhere between the end of 1935 and spring 1936, Brecht wrote the short poem "Brief an den Stückeschreiber Odets" (*GBA*, 14:305–6). Its title applies to Clifford Odets (1906–63) the anti-auratic term "Stücke-schreiber" that Brecht frequently uses when talking about himself. Yet despite the clear signal that he is writing to a like-minded fellow dramatist, Brecht complains that the sympathy shown for the class enemy in Odets's 1935 play *Paradise Lost* was a betrayal of the socialism he so admired in *Waiting for Lefty* of earlier the same year. It seems unlikely that Brecht sent a German letter poem to the American (even though Odets was at the time married to the Austrian actress Luise Rainer). On the other hand, the poem's charge was echoed in an authenticated letter of February 1936 to Victor J. Jerome (written in English, but published in a German translation): "Welch ein verräterischer Schritt von *Waiting for Lefty* (das ich sehr schätze) zu *Paradise Lost*! Vom Mitleid mit den Chauffeuren zum Mitleid mit denen, die sich schon bald kein Taxi mehr leisten können — woran der verfluchte Kapitalismus schuld ist. Der unsichtbare Feind des kleinen Kapitalisten: der große Kapitalist" (*GBA*, 14:616). Understandably, the *GBA* notes use the authentic letter to Jerome to document the background to Brecht's *Briefge-dicht*. In Brecht's case, it is rare for fictive letter and genuine letter to exist side by side in this way.[5] If nothing else, this indicates that even when letter

---

[5] "Aus der Korrespondenz des Berliner Ensembles über Modelle: Fragen des Regie-kollektivs Döbeln" (*GBA*, 25:395–97), for example, also "fingiert" (*GBA*, 25:541), is a dialogue constructed on the basis of questions submitted to Brecht in a letter from the theater group of the GDR town of Döbeln. "Aus der Korrespondenz" in this case means *arising from* a letter to Brecht, one answered in a fictive dialogue rather than private correspondence.

poems have specified addressees, it may be unwise to leap to the conclusion that they must have been sent or (and this will be a more important point for the approach that follows) that the nominal addressee is necessarily the same as the intended readership. Rather than being too literal-minded on the question of a letter poem's status, we should recall that the *Briefgedicht* was a common literary form, not least in the Weimar Republic; witness the many letter poems by Erich Kästner, Walter Mehring, and Mascha Kaléko (with all of whose work Brecht must have been familiar). This popular sub-genre of *Neue Sachlichkeit* poetry had strong connections with the *chanson* and the cabaret *Rollengedicht*, genres where the convention was recognized as involving a fiction. The majority of Brecht's dramaturgical poems appear to follow the same convention. Neither of his two earliest dramaturgical poems — "Brief an das Arbeitertheater 'Theatre Union' in New York, das Stück 'Die Mutter' betreffend" and "Brief an den Stückeschreiber Odets" — employs more than minimal gestures towards the fiction of epistolarity implied in their titles. In any case, the nominal addressees shared little or no common language with the author, and in one instance it was a collective. As this suggests, the primary audience or readership was not the ostensible addressee. Instead, the two poems were part of a one-sided dialogue between a playwright and the theater-world at large.

In 1926, Brecht reportedly declared: "Meine Lyrik hat privaten Charakter. [...] Im Drama hingegen gebe ich nicht meine private Stimmung, sondern gleichsam die Stimmung der Welt."[6] Up until then, such a distinction had made sense, but by the time of the dramaturgical poems of the mid-1930s this was no longer the case. Admittedly, some of the poems associated with the *Messingkauf* complex were more private reminiscences or tributes[7] than dramaturgically focused pieces. It is inconceivable that these could have been integrated easily into *Der Messingkauf*, with its

---

[6] Bernard Guillemin, "Was arbeiten Sie? Gespräch mit Bertolt Brecht," *Die literarische Welt*, 50, July 1926: 2.

[7] From the *GBA* "Gedichte aus dem *Messingkauf*" section, I would want to single out "Die Requisiten der Weigel" and from the earlier *GW* corpus: "O Lust des Beginnens," "Begräbnis des Schauspielers," "Die Schauspielerin im Exil," "Beschreibung des Spiels der H. W.," "Helene Weigel als Frau Carrar," "Schminke," "Selbstgespräch einer Schauspielerin beim Schminken," "Lockerer Körper," "Das Vollführen der Bewegungen," and "Sparsames Auftreten der Meisterschauspieler." The majority of these are "Gelegenheitsgedichte," or personal tributes of a non-dramaturgical kind. Similarly, although the poem "Allgemeine Tendenzen, welche der Schauspieler bekämpfen sollte" (*Theaterarbeit*, 387; *GBA*, 23:170), has been referred to as "ein 'theoretisches' Gedicht" (*BHB*, 4:307), it is difficult to see why this catalog of things-not-to-do has sometimes been interpreted as a work with a *theoretical* — as opposed to merely practical — dimension.

program of establishing dramatic theory within an ideologically conceived aesthetic framework. But this was not the only problem. Of one example of Brecht's use of the letter-format, "Aus einem Brief an einen Schauspieler" (*Theaterarbeit*, 414), Willett recorded that "the Actor addressed has not been identified" (*BT*, 236). The new edition designates the work as "für *Theaterarbeit* geschrieben und an keinen bestimmten Adressaten gerichtet" (*GBA*, 23:503). Which means that we now have recognition that there is a difference of genre between a fictive poem like "Aus einem Brief an . . ." and a more intimate work like "Brief an den Schauspieler Charles Laughton, die Arbeit an dem Stück *Leben des Galilei* betreffend" (*GBA*, 23:37–39), a series of poetic fragments that Brecht no doubt shared with Laughton during their period of intensive collaboration.

Sometimes genre gives some clue to status. Nørregaard (1993 420) notes that although the title of Brecht's "Rede an dänische Arbeiterschauspieler über die Kunst der Beobachtung" implies a performative situation, there is no record of such a "Rede" ever having been delivered. Nor does it appear to have been pinned on some backstage notice board or passed on to Ruth Berlau to communicate its substance in Danish to the addressees in question. The sole record of any such use comes in a journal entry four years later: "*Stockholm*. 'Rede an Arbeiterschauspieler über die Kunst der Beobachtung.' Anläßlich von Sitzungen zur Gründung einer Amateurtheatergruppe für die sozialdemokratischen Gewerkschaften!" (May 1939, *GBA*, 26:338). The omission of "dänische" is explained by the new context, although what Brecht meant by "anläßlich" remains unclear. The note to this entry reads: "Vermutlich stellt Brecht sein 1935 entstandenes Gedicht [. . .] für die Sitzungen zur Verfügung" (*GBA*, 26:633). Whether it was translated for the purpose, circulated in the original, or just put at the unions' disposal is also not known.

The Brecht Archive holds many letters either never sent or in some instances with no indication of an addressee. Brecht may have on occasion thought twice about sending a particularly aggressive missive. On the other hand, the letter format was also one of his favorite methods of setting out embryonic ideas: for example, *GBA* treats Brecht's "Kleines Privatissimum für meinen Freund Max Gorelik" (*GBA*, 23:27–29) as draft material for *Kleines Organon* rather than as the personal type of *tête-à-tête* communication its title suggests (*GBA*, 23:445). The notes to the theoretical volumes of the new edition correctly refer to "theoretische Texte [. . .], die sich lediglich der Briefform bedienen" (*GBA*, 25:584). Some served the function of offering Brecht a safety valve, but beyond any use of the fictive letter as a private way of letting off steam or dealing with theoretical problems of the moment, one finds the more important function of rhetorical vehicle. That the epistolary and dialogic genres overlap and are intended to be mutually complementary can be seen from the corpus of poems referred to as "Gedichte aus dem *Messingkauf*" and the dramaturgical poetry in *Theaterarbeit*.[8] Some of these are in the form of letters; others masquerade as addresses to sympathetic or neutral audiences or homages to a particular actor or actress. As with the lecture, some kind of fictive addressee is required by such "Appellstrukturen." According to §58 of *Kleines Organon*: "die kleinste gesellschaftliche Einheit ist nicht der Mensch, sondern zwei Menschen" (*GBA*, 23:88).

## The Dramaturgical Poems

The theoretical poems have been largely overlooked by those interested in Brecht's dramatic theory, although as Berger and Bostock point out, they have the distinct attraction of being "immediately useful" and able to "explain — far more clearly than most commentators have done — many of Brecht's theories about the theatre" (Berger and Bostock 1961, 3). However, before Brecht's poems are examined, a word of caution is called for.

There are works by Brecht, including *Die Dreigroschenoper, Die Maßnahme, Der gute Mensch von Sezuan,* and *Der kaukasische Kreidekreis,* where elevated language, above all poetry and song, implies privileged status. When Shen Te speaks in verse in *Der gute Mensch von Sezuan* or the Singer in *Der kaukasische Kreidekreis* rises above the register of prose dialogue, they speak with heightened insight and assume the status of "Mitwisser des Stückeschreibers" (*GBA*, 12:330). The contrast between poetic diction and prose register in such cases signifies an ability to function as Olympian commentator on the immediate situation. But there is no such valorized hierarchy of registers in Brecht's dramaturgical writings. A theoretical statement made in a poem is not axiomatically more significant than one in prose. If some individual poems express points with particular clarity, lapidariness, or sophistication, this remains a matter of local accomplishment, not generic privileging. Nevertheless, one striking feature of the dramaturgical poems is their undoubted ability to apply fresh bold images to familiar abstract ideas. This is the case in the following extracts, the first on the idea that social disasters are by no means comparable to natural catastrophes but result from what Brecht once called "menschliche Machenschaften," and the second on "Historisierung":

---

[8] The editor's observation "in den Gedichten erschienen außerdem [i.e. apart from those in *Versuche* 14] 'Zum *Messingkauf* gehörige Gedichte'" (*GW*, 9:18*) offers no indication of the criteria for the proposed second category nor does it reveal whether the two groups, taken together, account for all 38 poems in *GW*, vol. 9.

Ich sehe da auftreten Schneefälle.
Ich sehe da nach vorn kommen Erdbeben.
Ich sehe da Berge stehen mitten im Wege
Und Flüsse sehe ich über die Ufer treten.
Aber die Schneefälle haben Hüte auf.
Die Erdbeben haben Geld in der Brusttasche.
Die Berge sind aus Fahrzeugen gestiegen
Und die reißenden Flüsse gebieten über Polizisten.
("Lied des Stückeschreibers," *GBA,* 14:299)

Da sagte ich zu mir:
Alles wandelt sich und ist nur für seine Zeit.
Also gab ich jedem Schauplatz sein Kennzeichen
Und brannte jedem Fabrikhof seine Jahreszahl ein und jedem Zimmer
Wie die Hirten dem Vieh seine Zahl einbrennen, daß es erkannt wird.
("Und so schnell wechselte zu meiner Zeit," *GBA,* 14:301)

Even in poems where the points made are not necessarily new, poetic formulations often make them more vivid than their prose equivalents, as a comparison between the first extract above and §19 of *Kleines Organon* would show. Some of the poems we shall be considering have been recognized as dramaturgical milestones: what Knopf refers to as "die groß angelegten Theorie-Gedichte, die als Gedankengedichte eine ganze Philosophie zur Kunst und Lebenskunst ausbreiten" (*BHB,* 2:464). But most remain neglected.

The publication history of Brecht's dramaturgical poems is far from straightforward. Few appeared in print during his lifetime, and their publishing fortunes since 1956 have been chequered. The 1967 *Gesammelte Werke* (*Werkausgabe*) included thirty-eight poems in the section "Gedichte 1938–1941" under the heading "Gedichte aus dem *Messingkauf*" (*GW,* 9:769–98). These the editor declared to be "alle *Messingkauf*-Gedichte" (*GW,* 9:18\*). A full inventory of the works in question can be found in Willett and Manheim 1976 (504–5) with each title annotated to indicate which had first appeared in *Theaterarbeit* (1952) and *Versuche* 14 (1955) and which not. As Willett and Manheim indicate, "the *Messingkauf* poems," which could at that time only refer to those published in *GW* as "Gedichte aus dem *Messingkauf*," are a relatively heterogeneous group: "a mixture of (a) poems written before the [*Messingkauf*] dialogue plan had been formulated, (b) poems written with this plan in mind (around 1938–40), (c) poems written after Brecht's return to Germany for [. . .] *Theaterarbeit* (1952) and (d) various other poems on theatrical subjects" (504). Willett and Manheim also point out that "at the same time there are some excellent theatre poems, mainly dealing with specific actors or productions, which were never included under this head" (505). To this I would merely add that some of the poems in (d) are also of considerable dramaturgical significance.

By contrast to *GW*, *GBA* admits a restricted corpus of seven poems under this rubric. These are offered both in an appendix to the *Messingkauf* complex (*GBA*, 22:857–69) and in the *GBA* poetry volume devoted to "Sammlungen, 1938" (*GBA*, 12:317–31). According to the editorial principles set out in the notes to both volumes, the seven *Versuche* poems have the distinction of being authorized as *Messingkauf* poems by Brecht himself. Poems that only appeared under that title in *Theaterarbeit* are accorded a different status, since strictly speaking, even if Brecht must have had a hand in this collective enterprise, the sole editors named on the title page are the Berliner Ensemble and Helene Weigel. The remaining so-called "Gedichte aus dem *Messingkauf*" are treated by *GBA* as individual items: "Die im *Messingkauf*-Material überlieferten Gedichte können [. . .] nicht als Bestandteile der vorliegenden Sammlung behandelt werden und erscheinen als Einzelgedichte" (*GBA*, 12:453), the point being that we have no documented evidence that Brecht intended to publish all so-called "Gedichte aus dem *Messingkauf*" as a separate collection or was even going, at some stage, to integrate them into *Der Messingkauf*. *GBA*'s solution of restricting the corpus to an authenticated minimum has the merit of purism, but it at the same time severs from their immediate genetic context a number of poems written at the time when Brecht was embarking on the *Messingkauf* project, some of which benefit from being seen within that framework. It also uncouples some poems written for *Theaterarbeit* in 1951 and 1952 and explicitly presented as being "aus dem *Messingkauf*" from the unfinished *Messingkauf* project. Apart from such demarcation problems, one is also left with the paradox that none of the seven poems in the small *Versuche* 14 and *GBA* corpus is mentioned anywhere in the *Messingkauf* plans. As *GBA* puts it: "Die Besonderheit dieser Sammlung besteht darin, daß — trotz ihres Titels — kein Gedicht im Kontext der Schriften zum *Messingkauf* zu finden ist oder durch entsprechende Hinweise Brechts dort zu lokalisieren wäre" (*GBA*, 12:452). To which must be added the further irony that the only poem to be explicitly located in the *Messingkauf* complex — "Neulich habe ich meinen Zuschauer getroffen" (*GBA*, 22:755) — has never enjoyed the status of being categorized as a "Gedicht aus dem *Messingkauf*," even though a MS inscription ("MK4") indicates that it was to be assigned to the "Vierte Nacht" (*GBA*, 12:452).

Mercifully, in the present context taxonomic concerns of this kind can remain in the wings, given that a significant number of poems, and a number of significant poems, belonging to both the largest (*GW*) and the smallest (*Versuche* 14 and *GBA*) corpora, benefit from being subsumed under the substantially larger category of what I have chosen to refer to as Brecht's "dramaturgical poems." This does not mean that the two groups are identical. As we have seen, some of the poems in the *Messingkauf* complex cannot, strictly speaking, be deemed "dramaturgical." Even of the seven works accepted by *GBA* as belonging unequivocally to *Der Messingkauf* not all number among Brecht's most important theoretical works. Nor does even the larger *GW* corpus give an adequate sense of the range and diversity of Brecht's "poems on the theatre." As a consequence, what follows will be confined to a selection of the most important dramaturgical poems, and while taking cognizance of their various publication contexts, it will not be bound by this aspect. The works to be looked at are, as Knopf has observed, "insofern für Lyrik ungewöhnlich, als sie wie etwa die *Studien,* die lyrische Kritik betrieben, Theatertheorie zum Thema haben, ein weiteres Feld, das [Brecht] für die Lyrik erschlossen hat und die Vielfalt seiner Möglichkeiten dokumentiert" (*BHB,* 2:461).

## "Brief an das Arbeitertheater 'Theatre Union' in New York, das Stück 'Die Mutter' betreffend"

By a quirk of circumstance, the first major theoretical poem by Brecht was never intended for *Der Messingkauf,* although it did appear among the poems in the Malik edition and in *Theaterarbeit.* In the second half of 1935, possibly as early as August when he first set eyes on Paul Peters's unsatisfactory, freely adapted translation of *Die Mutter,* Brecht wrote a draft of "Brief an das Arbeitertheater 'Theatre Union' in New York, das Stück 'Die Mutter' betreffend" ("Letter to the Workers' Theater Theatre Union in New York re. the Play 'The Mother,'" *GBA,* 14:290–93). The work exists in various versions incorporating numerous revisions, which suggests its importance for Brecht. What is also clear and, along with the existence of these various versions, speaks for a slightly later completion date, is that the work retains few vestiges of the aggrieved polemical tone or the specific recriminations that characterize Brecht's immediate correspondence with the Theatre Union. Yet this "Briefgedicht," had it been sent as a letter, would have effectively driven a wedge between the main body of the Theatre Union collective and its leadership; if that had been its purpose, however, a poem written in German would seem a strange instrument to choose. Instead of engaging in polemics, Brecht first attempts to set out his original intentions and to think his way into the minds of the people who had so signally failed to understand his epic treatment of Gorky's novel. In this "know-thine-enemy" sense, parts of the poem have something in common with the various study notes on the Stanislavsky System considered in the previous chapter. Yet there is one crucial difference. In the case of the Stanislavsky, Brecht was merely analysing the assumptions of his adversaries, but with little hope of converting them to his cause. In the case of the Theatre Union, as opposed to the dyed-in-the-

wool, apolitical Stanislavskians, Brecht does appear to assume that such politically well-intentioned people might still have their eyes opened to Epic
Theater's advantages. This combination of didactic and conciliatory stance
may explain why the poem was included in the Malik *Gesammelte Werke,* for
Brecht could expect to encounter similar disputes with ideological allies in
other countries during his continuing years of exile.

The compound "Arbeitertheater" in the poem's title is crucial to its
strategy when it comes to the treatment of its ostensible readership. Because
his nominal addressees are fellow socialists, Brecht does them the courtesy of
taking them through *Die Mutter,* explaining the rationale behind its innovative approach and the political significance of Pelagea Wlassowa's metamorphosis. Clearly, it is vital that people like the grass-roots members of the
Theatre Union should understand the work's ideological premises and purpose. The fact that they are only familiar with a garbled version of the
play — Brecht refers to it as a "Bearbeitung" ( *GBA,* 24:164) rather than a
translation — makes such a return to first principles imperative.

The poem speaks to the ordinary members of the Theatre Union in the
comradely familiar plural form of address: "So seht ihr," "seht, wie," "ich
sehe euch / Das kleine Stück lesend." In English such an effect would normally be reflected by the insertion of words like "comrades" or "brothers,"
but, as we shall see, Brecht reserves the noun "Genossen" for more strategic
effect in part 4. In one sense, the failure to produce nuances that could be
easily reflected in English does not matter; for what we have is a German
poem, as far as we know not translated into English at the time, which, while
seeming to speak to a very circumscribed American audience, reaches out
generally to *the kind of* theater people the playwright wants to help to understand the methods and intentions behind *Die Mutter.* The particularizing details in the title — signalling that it is a business letter "re." ("betreffend")
the 1935 production of *Die Mutter* by the Theatre Union in New York, addressed to the collective, not just the play's producer or translator as most of
Brecht's earlier complaints had been — should not seduce us into restricting
the poem to its source context. The fact that we hear as much about the earlier Berlin production as about the New York fiasco takes the material out of
and beyond the immediate context, as does our awareness that we, its
readers, are not members of the Theatre Union. Without the "Konkreti-
sierung" specified in the title, what one would be left with is the model of a
situation where an epic playwright is addressing an artistically reactionary
(Stanislavsky-trained) theater group, in an attempt to help them appreciate
the damage their approach does to Epic Theater and to urge them to have
the courage of their political convictions and return to the original material.
Add the title, and what one has is the historical specificity which also invariably underpins Brecht's conception of the typical. For this reason it is more
constructive to assume that a poem deriving from the disagreements with

the Theatre Union is now intended as a paradigm illustrating the classic faults of a "Naturalist" response to Epic Theater.

The first stanza of "Brief an . . ." establishes a number of vital facts about *Die Mutter:* (i) that it is not just a stage adaptation of a famous work of Russian fiction (although written "Nach dem Buch des Genossen Gorki"), but is also based on authentic contemporary documents ("viele Erzählungen proletarischer Genossen aus ihrem / Täglichen Kampf," "Erzählungen" here meaning firsthand reports);[9] (ii) that the play's "kärgliche Sprache" is appropriate to the dignity of its subject matter and is a matter of well weighed words representing a deliberate attempt to avoid the pathos of "Revolutionsromantik";[10] (iii) that this particular story, chosen from countless "alltäglich erscheinenden / Tausendfachen Vorgängen in verächteten Wohnungen / Unter den Vielzuvielen," is no less momentous than chronicles of the deeds of the great men and women of history and demands to be treated with equal respect; and (iv) that Pelagea Wlassowa's life and behavior are — or rather during the course of the play *become* — exemplary:

> Für meine Aufgabe hielt ich es, von einer großen historischen Gestalt
> zu berichten
> Dem unbekannten Vorkämpfer der Menschheit.
> Zur Nacheiferung.

Within Brecht's and Gorky's construct, Wlassowa doubles first as the archetypal downtrodden "proletarische Mutter" and then the unknown "Vorkämpfer" for humanity (read: socialism). (The *Theaterarbeit* version uses the feminine form "Vorkämpferin.") However, although required for propaganda purposes to serve as the nameless, unsung personification of the masses, she also has to be named and particularized in order to become an adequately concretized figure for the audience to appreciate as she goes the long "gewundenen Weg ihrer Klasse." This is not the kind of "Historisierung" that Brecht describes in the essays of the mid-1930s. Wlassowa does not become a "historische Gestalt" simply by dint of being methodically

---

[9] The reference is to Brecht's further Weimar Republic sources, not just to Gorky's own source documentation from the Nizhny-Novgorod region. However, Brecht seems to be reticent about the fact that the main source for *Die Mutter* is not Gorky's novel, but a contemporary adaptation for the German stage: Günther Weisenborn's and Günther Stark's *Die Mutter* (1931). In fact, Stark and Weisenborn are later named, along with Slatan Dudow and Hanns Eisler, as "Mitarbeiter" (*Theaterarbeit*, 170). On the relationship between the two adaptations, see Thomas 1973 and Kepka 1984–85.

[10] "Revolutionary romanticism" was one of the requisite ingredients of a work of true Socialist Realism; see Zhdanov 1950.

"historisiert und milieurisiert" in the way it was suggested characters in *An American Tragedy* could be. Rather, it is because of her representative role as an oppressed figure who grows in political stature to become capable of exemplary revolutionary behavior. In notes to the play, Brecht stressed the political significance of such a person's beginning to study her condition: "Die kleine Szene [. . .], in der die Wlassowa ihre erste Lektion in der Ökonomie empfängt, ist keineswegs nur ein Ereignis in ihrem eigenen Leben; es ist ein historischer Vorgang: unter dem ungeheuren Druck des Elends beginnen die Ausgebeuteten zu denken" (*GBA*, 24:172).

In "Über die epische Schauspielkunst: *Der Wechsel*," the actor asks "Was soll also geschehen, wenn wir eine kleinbürgerliche Familie dieses Jahrzehnts darstellen?," upon which his dismissive reference to the petty bourgeoisie is ignored and he is given a lesson in the "Historisierung" of history's hitherto anonymous masses. His follow-up question ("Wird der Mensch selber so nicht allzu unwichtig?") receives a reply largely in terms of abstract principles and predictable clichés:

> Im Gegenteil. Er wird geehrt, indem alle Veränderungen, die an ihm und durch ihn sichtbar sind, festgestellt werden. Er wird ebenso ernst genommen wie die Napoleons früherer Zeit. Sieht man eine Szene "Der Arbeiter soundso wird von seinem Boß zum Hungertod verurteilt," dann hat dies nicht weniger Bedeutung zu haben, als eine Szene "Napoleon wird bei Waterloo geschlagen." Ebenso einprägsam sollen die Gesten der zu dieser Szene vereinigten Personen sein, ebenso sorgfältig ausgewählt der Hintergrund. (*GBA*, 22:671)

Yet this later explanation of how the unpersons of history should be presented is far less incisive than the equivalent juxtaposition of great figures from the past and the anonymous masses in "Fragen eines lesenden Arbeiters" (Questions from a Worker Who Reads). Here, a critical contrast is established between the fêted rulers of previous millennia and the unacknowledged masses who were forced to carry out their orders:

> Wer baute das siebentorige Theben?
> In den Büchern stehen die Namen von Königen.
> Haben die Könige die Felsbrocken herbeigeschleppt?
> Und das mehrmals zerstörte Babylon
> Wer baute es so viele Male auf? In welchen Häusern
> Des goldstrahlenden Lima wohnten die Bauleute?
> Wohin gingen an dem Abend, wo die chinesische Mauer fertig war
> Die Maurer? (*GBA*, 12:29)

Yet while memorably impassioned, even this rapid-fire battery of questions amounts to little more than a series of rhetorical variations on the central point that the past has been monopolized as the history of great men. The poem about *Die Mutter,* by contrast, thanks to the concentration on the detail of one particular illustration, is able to give a more extensive answer to the actor's question than the one in "Fragen eines lesenden Arbeiters." In Pelagea Wlassowa's case, going "the way of her class" means more than remaining content with her role as one of "die Vielzuvielen" upon whom all history depends, even though others assume the historical credit. As the political significance of her learning to read suggests, this is the dialectical point at which Wlassowa, by intervening, becomes in a new sense exemplary and is no longer merely representative in her victimhood. Brecht's theoretical writings seldom had to confront the idea of a protagonist being offered up to an audience "Zur Nacheiferung." His theoretical comments on *Die Mutter* unfortunately concentrate so much on the play's epic features that the implications of Wlassowa's exemplary development for the problem of the audience's identification with her are not pursued.

When the first two parts of "Brief an . . ." appeared in *Theaterarbeit* in 1952, they bore the caption "Die Fabel," yet they offer a far more positive valorization of the plot material than the neutral noun "Fabel" suggests. Indeed, with the second part of the poem, factual plot-description gives way to a mythification of Wlassowa as the "mother" of the Revolution — less the abortive 1905 one than the definitive event of 1917 that her metamorphosis prefigures. Whereas the Theatre Union is shortly to be accused of betraying the approach taken in Brecht's original play, we are reminded that, after the death of her son, Wlassowa is not reduced to the status of helpless mourning mother, but rises to the heroic stature of "Vorkämpfer[in] der Menschheit":

[. . .] nun steht sie schon
Im dichtesten Getümmel der unaufhörlichen
Riesigen Klassenschlacht. Immer noch Mutter
Mehr noch Mutter jetzt, vieler Gefallenen Mutter
Kämpfender Mutter, Ungeborener Mutter, räumt sie
Jetzt im Staatswesen auf. Gibt den Herrschenden Steine
In das erpreßte Mahl. Reinigt Waffen. Lehrt
Ihre vielen Söhne und Töchter die Sprache des Kampfes
Gegen den Krieg und die Ausbeutung, Mitglied einer Heeresmacht
Über den ganzen Planeten, Verfolgte und Verfolgerin
Nichtgeduldete und Unduldsame. Geschlagene und Unerbittliche.
(*GBA,* 14:291)

Abandoned is the promised "kärgliche Sprache," a controlled poetic diction that Brecht had until then used in the poem. He no longer presents the poem's story like a "Bericht," which in part 3 he claims that *Die Mutter* itself is.[11] Brecht's poem from now on makes its point about the symbolic transformation of Pelagea Wlassowa in the familiar cadences of revolutionary rhetoric. Because Wlassowa's behavior is presented as worthy of emulation, the elevated tone employed to establish her political exemplariness becomes hymnic in the manner of the *Solidaritätslieder* of *Die Maßnahme* and *Kuhle Wampe*.

The pivotal contrast comes in part 4, where the Theatre Union is charged with having exploited her image as literal (rather than politically symbolic) mother for crude emotional effect:

> Statt um Bewunderung
> Werbt ihr um Mitgefühl mit der Mutter, die ihren Sohn verliert.
> Den Tod des Sohnes
> Legt ihr schlau an den Schluß. So nur, denkt ihr, wird der Zuschauer
> Sein Interesse bewahren, bis der Vorhang fällt. Wie der Geschäftsmann
> Geld investiert in einen Betrieb, so, meint ihr, investiert der Zuschauer
> Gefühl in den Helden: er will es wieder herausbekommen
> Und zwar verdoppelt. (*GBA,* 14:292–93)

Five years earlier, the dominant contrast in Brecht's theoretical writings had been between "Gefühl" and "Ratio." The kind of "Ratio" emphasized in the *Mahagonny* notes still figures in part 3 of the poem (in the verbs "prüfen" and "studieren"), but there is now a new emphasis on two different kinds of emotional response: an unproductive investment in sympathy for a grieving mother and elation at her metamorphosis leading to a desire to emulate her. The primitive teleology of the New York production, with its postponement of Pawel's death to the very end of the play, was calculated to pander to a basic urge in audiences to reach out emotionally to the mother left behind, a raw, instinctive emotion that could receive no constructive political direction at this late stage in the work. In contrast, Brecht places the news of Pawel's death back in scene 11 and has the information relayed by a chorus of revolutionary workers, thus leaving neither the mother alone with her grief nor the audience rendered helpless by unchanneled commiseration. Brecht's approach leaves a third of the play within which Pelagea Wlassowa could reassess her priorities and rationally commit herself to the revolutionary cause. It would take Brecht some time to adequately theorize the difference between permissible and impermissible feelings in Epic Theater. Witness his claim in a journal entry for 23 November 1938 that "Bei streng epischer Darstellung kommt eine Einfühlung erlaubter Art zustande" (*GBA,*

---

[11] Cf. Knopf's remarks on "die Sprache dieser Inhaltsangabe, die sich an den antiken Hexameter anlehnt, das epische Versmaß, das sich in der Schilderung von Schlachten und ihren Helden bewährt hat" (Knopf 1980a, 122).

26:326), a crucial insight, but one that was to remain no more than an isolated aperçu for some time to come. "Über rationellen und emotionellen Standpunkt" (*GBA*, 22:500–502) of the same year restricts its comments on categories of emotion in Epic Theater to one short paragraph. The earlier poem's contrast between an incitement to "Bewunderung" and "Nacheiferung" and the cheap exploitation of unusable "Mitgefühl" for the helpless, bereft mother already points in a more fruitful direction, although Brecht never theorized the underlying issues adequately, even in *Kleines Organon*.

In the "Anmerkungen [1933]" to the Berlin production of *Die Mutter,* Brecht makes the following claim:

> Diese [nichtaristotelische Dramatik] bedient sich der *hingebenden Einfühlung* des Zuschauers keineswegs so unbedenklich wie die aristotelische und steht auch zu gewissen psychischen Wirkungen, wie etwa der Katharsis, wesentlich anders. So wie sie nicht darauf ausgeht, ihren Helden der Welt als seinem unentrinnbaren Schicksal auszuliefern, liegt es auch nicht in ihrem Sinn, den Zuschauer einem suggestiven Theatererlebnis auszuliefern. Bemüht, ihrem Zuschauer ein ganz bestimmtes praktisches, die Änderung der Welt bezweckendes Verhalten zu lehren, muß sie ihm schon im Theater eine grundsätzlich andere Haltung verleihen, als er gewohnt ist. (*GBA*, 24:115)

The points made here, although important, remain non-specific and are once more largely presented *ex negativo*. Nothing in the 1933 notes can match the clarity of the later poem's contrast between the Theatre Union's exploitation of a mother's grief — "nur angedeutet" in the original play (*GBA*, 24:121) — and the "Bewunderung" the audience is meant to feel for Wlassowa as she resolutely goes the political way of her class. While Brecht's 1933 notes make *Die Mutter* seem closer to *Die Maßnahme* by suggesting that the thrust of the work's didacticism centers on the political practicalities of underground subversion ("den Zweck, ihren Zuschauern gewisse Formen des politischen Kampfes zu lehren" [*GBA*, 24:110]), the 1935 poem puts the emphasis squarely on the way Wlassowa transcends the confines of her nuclear family and her emotional environment to embrace a sense of solidarity with the extended family of international socialism, thereby becoming "Mitglied einer Heeresmacht / Über dem ganzen Planeten," teaching others "die Sprache des Kampfes / Gegen den Krieg und die Ausbeutung." Pelagea Wlassowa is the *Mahagonny* notes' "veränderliche[r] und verändernde[r] Mensch" *par excellence* (*GBA*, 14:291).

Parts 1 and 2 of "Brief an . . ." highlight the main features of the original Berlin production, paying particular attention to Wlassowa's political representativeness, but they say little about the overall methods employed in Epic Theater. True, much can be extrapolated from the critique of the deferral of Pawel's death until very late in the action. And when it comes to "stage business," we hear of the gradual transformation of Wlassowa's modest kitchen into a hive of revolutionary activity: "So beginnen die Wände zu fallen um ihren Herd." But it is only with part 3 that the rationale behind the work's sparse style is explained. The danger of the wrong kind of *gravitas* conjured up by the phrase "wie ein Bericht aus großer Zeit" and the ever-threatening pathos of "Revolutionsromantik" are offset by the suggestion that the style of *Die Mutter* will be "heiter und lustig" and "maßvoll / In den traurigen Dingen," that is, in no respect emotionally self-indulgent. In contrast to the later image of the Theatre Union's audience "investing" in characters in order to reap emotional dividends as the play nears its dénouement, part 3 employs a different monetary image: just as the often-deceived poor test a coin with their teeth to find out whether it is counterfeit, so working-class audiences are expected to weigh the characters' words and gestures to see if they ring true. Body language and verbal behavior will also have to be scrutinized. Only after such testing can a character's lines be seen to be "verbürgte Worte," words underwritten by experience. The remainder of part 3 establishes the framework supplied by Epic Theater within which such an appraisal can take place: minimalist décor ("Wenige Andeutungen / Zeigten die Schauplätze an"), the requisite pieces of sociopolitical information ("die Photographien / Der großen Gegner [. . .] projiziert auf die Tafeln des Hintergrunds. / Und die Aussprüche der sozialistischen Klassiker") and the necessary economy of verbal presentation to give the audience the kind of contemplative breathing spaces not found in the hectic pace of conventional drama ("Die Muße, [. . .] zu studieren und sich das eigene Verhalten / Zurechtzulegen") (*GBA*, 14:291–92).

What Brecht evokes at some length here is the authoritative "Modell" of the 1931 Berlin production. The act of first establishing such a yardstick is a clear departure from his usual "gestische Reihenfolge," whereby he first establishes what is wrong with existing "Aristotelian" theater before identifying Epic Theater's panacea. Brecht's well-tested dramatic paradigm dialectically showing correct behavior through a demonstration of mistaken responses (cf. those of the Young Comrade in *Die Maßnahme*) is refined in the theorizing of *Die Mutter*: correct and inappropriate production styles are juxtaposed to offer an illustration based on the " *Nicht — Sondern*" model.

Although he uses the comradely intimate German plural in his words to the Theatre Union, Brecht does not employ the standard socialist address "Genossen" until part 4, at the point where he is about to identify their crassest blunders. Placed here, the term implies that whatever criticisms are being voiced are intended in a spirit of comradely constructiveness. Apart from the reference to "Genosse Gorki," the word "Genosse" is employed a second time when the poem encourages the Theatre Union people to go back to the drawing board to rethink their conception of how the play needs to be produced. Criticism and encouragement thus form two parts of the same section, the one would not have been offered without the counterbalancing optimism that his readers could be convinced of the necessity of epic production techniques.

Having on other occasions shown no comparable understanding for *Mother*'s hapless translator or the New York production's inexperienced producer, Brecht now tries to think his way into the Theatre Union's collective mind upon finding themselves confronted with a work so radically different from the usual fare:

> Genossen, ich sehe euch
> Das kleine Stück lesend, in Verlegenheit.
> Die kärgliche Sprache
> Scheint euch ärmlich. So wie in diesem Bericht
> Drücken sich, sagt ihr, die Leute nicht aus. Ich las
> Eure Bearbeitung. Hier fügt ihr ein "Guten Morgen" ein
> Dort ein "Hallo, mein Junge." Den großen Schauplatz
> Füllt ihr mit Hausrat. Kohlgeruch
> Kommt vom Herd. (*GBA*, 14:292)

The understanding with which their sense of the play's poverty of detail is evoked quickly gives way to a satirically presented spectrum of countermeasures: as if the insertion of a "Guten Morgen" and the occasional "Hallo, mein Junge," a surfeit of stage clutter, or even the odor of boiled cabbage wafting into the auditorium were enough to transform a work of Epic Theater into a vehicle for Stanislavskian "Naturalism." Yet for all the lampooning, there can be few theoretical works by Brecht where such sympathy is expressed for those who fail to grasp, let alone respect, his methods.

The reference in part 4 to the German original's "kärgliche Sprache" draws a parallel between the play and the poem "Rede an . . .," inasmuch as the latter is at times couched in similarly unemotional language. Like *Die Mutter,* much of "Brief an . . ." is stylistically "ein Bericht": an account of the principles according to which the first version of the play had been written and of the Berlin production. The poem could even be read as an attempt to accustom the reader to the laconic register and simplicity of style with which Paul Peters and the actors had experienced such difficulty. But the Theatre Union's problems with the play will hardly be replicated in the reception of the poem, the simple reason being that, unlike *Die Mutter,* it reflects at length on its own style and explains why a theatrical work with a restricted number of mimetic features is necessary to the task in hand.

Brecht's "Brief an . . ." first appeared three years after the New York controversy. (The Malik Verlag that published it was also the publisher of Gorky's works in German translation.) The volume in which it appeared also contains a revised version of Brecht's play, now entitled *Die Mutter: Leben der Revolutionärin Pelagea Wlassowa aus Twersk*; in other words, Brecht was placing his play within the socialist canon even in this respect (Brecht 1938, I:149–218). The juxtaposition of a prudently revised version and a poem on how and how not to stage a work of Epic Theater was a shrewd move. As long as Brecht was dependent on the production vagaries of his exile predicament and had to take account of the hold of the Stanislavskians in America, a didactic poem combining elements reminding its readers of an exemplary production with the cautionary account of a stylistic betrayal was an appropriately realistic response. In this respect, the poem serves the same function as Brecht's later "Mutter Courage in zweifacher Art dargestellt" (*GBA*, 23:408–10). Yet whereas the sections of the poem devoted to the Theatre Union's mistakes at best resemble a cautionary tale, they also serve as a demonstration of the advantages of an epic treatment. This explains why "Rede an . . ." makes only relatively dispassionate reference to Brecht's various bones of contention with the Theatre Union concerning the uncomprehending way the work had been mutilated.[12] And it also accounts for why the poem ends, not on a recriminatory note, but with a rallying call:

> [. . .] Aber warum
> Fürchten, was neu ist? Ist es schwer zu machen?
> Aber warum fürchten, was neu ist und schwer zu machen?
>
> (*GBA*, 14:293)

The terms in which Epic Theater are presented here echo the description of communism in the final lines of "Lob des Kommunismus" in *Die Mutter* itself: "Er ist das Einfache / Das schwer zu machen ist" (*GBA*, 3:286). In other words, the challenge of confronting the aesthetically new (Epic Theater) also has political implications, an idea taken up in the image of the suspicious person who has always been deceived and exploited and for whom life is an experiment — something that politically radical theater should also be.[13]

---

[12] For example, the deletion of the "Bibelszene" and the "Antikriegspropagandaszene" (see *GBA*, 24:139) and such attenuating changes as the one from "Lob des Kommunismus" to "Lob des Sozialismus" and from "Ich bin eine Bolschewikin" to "Ich bin eine Revolutionärin." Also the Theatre Union's "Russifizierung der Kostüme" (*GBA*, 24:171). Brecht describes his original Russian setting as serving "beinahe als Verkleidung für die Darstellung deutscher Verhältnisse zur Beeinflussung deutscher Verhältnisse" (*GBA*, 24:199). Even if the New York production had been adequately "episiert," which it never was, it is difficult to imagine what the specifics of its parabolic framework would have been.

[13] The link between communism and Epic Theater is made in "Einige Irrtümer über die Spielweise des Berliner Ensembles": "Wenn der Kommunismus das Einfache ist,

The poem concludes with a point Brecht was to make again in the prose notes to *Die Mutter* of 1938: namely that proletarian theater should have the courage to lead its audience rather than pander to reactionary expectations and tastes.[14] In the poem's call to courage, pusillanimous theater people are exhorted to have the courage of their convictions:

> Warum sollte er das Neue fürchten anstatt das Alte? Aber selbst wenn
> Euer Zuschauer, der Arbeiter, zögerte, dann müßtet ihr
> Nicht hinter ihm herlaufen, sondern ihm vorangehen
> Rasch vorangehen, mit weiten Schritten, seiner endlichen Kraft
> Unbedingt vertrauend. (*GBA*, 14:293)

The subtleties of the poem's concluding lines contrast sharply with the simpler statement in the prose notes. Using the same antithesis ("vorangehen"/ "hinter [. . .] herlaufen"), the prose version simply declares that the proletarian theater should *keep ahead of* its audience.[15] In the poem, the proletarian audience is expected to be ahead of the game as a matter of course. That this may not always in practice be the case is allowed for by a strategically placed conditional: "Selbst wenn / Euer Zuschauer, der Arbeiter, zögerte." Yet the final effect in either case is to snatch victory from the jaws of the New York defeat. If the *Arbeitertheater*'s audiences do turn out to be as Aristotelian and reactionary as translator and producer had assumed, then they must be untypical of their class. (We are, in other words, back in the same labyrithine territory of *exceptions* and *rules* that Brecht's *Die Ausnahme und die Regel* [The Exception and the Rule, 1932] had explored.) Theater has an obligation to lead from the front, and, paradoxically, theory has a parallel duty to tell theater that it should lead the way, as the appropriate form of drama for "die Ausgebeuteten [und] immer Getäuschten." Whether it shows the reactionary they were wrong about what form revolutionary theater should take or gives the more progressive factions the theater they need, Brecht's theater is emphatically self-sanctioning. There is no such double ratification in the prose version of the idea that Epic Theater must lead from the front.

das schwer zu machen ist, wird es mit seinem Theater nicht anders sein" (*GBA*, 23:336).

[14] "Wenn *ein* Theater, so ist das proletarische Theater in der Lage, seinem Publikum voranzugehen, anstatt hinter ihm herzulaufen" (*GBA*, 24:170). These notes, published in vol. 2 of the Malik *Gesammelte Werke* (219–50), represent a revised version of "Anmerkungen [1933]," expanded to take account of the New York experiences.

[15] "Diese Verse lassen einen unwillkürlich an den Vorwurf denken, den Lenin einem begabten und von ihm geschätzten Dichter gemacht hat: 'Er läuft hinter dem Leser her, dabei müßte man dem Leser etwas voraus sein'" (Fradkin 1974, 275). The reference is to Maxim Gorky, "V. I. Lenin," *Sobranie sochineniy* 17 (Moscow: Gasudarstvennoe izdatelstvo chudozhestvennoi literatury, 1952), 45.

Almost a decade and a half after its original publication in London, Brecht's first dramaturgical poem made a reappearance in *Theaterarbeit: Sechs Aufführungen des Berliner Ensembles* (East Berlin, 1952), a publication designed to ensure Brecht's ideas a wider readership,[16] although this proved not to be the case. Such books, Brecht was to complain, "[gehen] bei uns [. . .] sang- und klanglos vorüber" (*GBA,* 30:125), to which an editorial note in *GBA* adds: "Die staatlichen Stellen fördern die Verbreitung dieses Buches aus dem 'formalistischen Brechtkreis' bewußt nicht" (*GBA,* 30:530). This is the reason behind both Brecht's efforts to draw attention to the publication and the eventual second edition with a larger print-run in the 1960s.

Although the subtitle of the 1952 volume puts the emphasis specifically on the Berliner Ensemble's work, in the case of *Die Mutter* substantial space is devoted to earlier productions. Ruth Berlau's chronologically ordered survey in fact covers five over a period of twenty years. However, the poem "Brief an . . .," which treats the first two of them, was certainly not included simply in order to avoid stirring up old controversies. The desire to deemphasize earlier polemics and recriminations explains why initially only the first two sections of the 1935 poem are used in *Theaterarbeit,* for they allow Brecht to focus on the main features of the original play. These sections now appear under the title "Die Fabel" (*Theaterarbeit,* 121).[17] Only at the bottom of the page does one find, in a minuscule typeface and tucked away in parenthesis, an indication of the original context: "Aus einem Brief Bertolt Brechts an das New Yorker Arbeitertheater 1935." It would not have been politic in the Stalinist GDR to make too much of the fact that it concerned an attempt to guarantee an appropriate staging of *Mother* in capitalist America; even reference to an "Arbeitertheater" might not have been sufficient insurance against attack. A further and possibly not unrelated reason for only including a portion of the 1935 poem in the part of *Theaterarbeit* devoted to specific productions was that it helped emphasize the continuities between the 1932 and the 1951 Berliner Ensemble production. When writing to Suhrkamp in

---

[16] In a broadcast "Gespräch über das Buch *Theaterarbeit*" of 1952, Brecht explains: "Wir wollen auf der Bühne das wirkliche Leben beschreiben, und zwar so, daß, der es sieht, fähiger wird, dieses Leben zu meistern. Das ist für die Theater eine sehr schwierige Aufgabe, und die Theater müssen also ihre Erfahrungen gegenseitig benutzen. Um sie aber benutzen zu können, müssen sie ihre Erfahrungen notieren. Und das haben wir versucht mit dem Buch *Theaterarbeit*" (Hecht 1975, 112).

[17] In "Einige Probleme bei der Aufführung der *Mutter*" (1951), Brecht emphasizes that the play differs from "Agitproptheater" (and, he might have added, from the earlier "Lehrstücke") by virtue of treating "wirkliche Menschen mit einer Entwicklung" and possessing "eine durchgehende echte Fabel" (*GBA,* 24:199). The stress on these features in 1951 may have been intended to align the play with the some of the formal requirements of a work of Socialist Realism.

September 1948 to suggest that the *Versuche* series be reactivated, Brecht remarked that this would reinforce the impression of a "Kontinuität, die ja faktisch ist in meinem Fall" (*GBA*, 29:470). *Die Mutter* was, Brecht pointed out in October 1952 in a letter to the Staatliche Kommission für Kunstangelegenheiten, "eine der schönsten Aufführungen des Ensembles, das Gegenstück zu *Mutter Courage*, positiv und sozialistisch" (*GBA*, 30:142). He even adds that Gorky had read and authorized the adaptation. The inclusion in *Theaterarbeit* of an enthusiastic account of the Berlin production by the Stakhanovite "Held der Arbeit" Hans Garbe ("Über die Aufführung," 168–70) was also meant to deflect any charge of "formalism," as was the surprising inclusion of a piece by Brecht's longstanding adversary Fritz Erpenbeck and an amicable conversation between Brecht and Friedrich Wolf on the differences between Epic and Dramatic Theater.

The first two parts of the poem set out much information that cannot be considered a summary of the work's plot, but rather concerns its "Entstehungsgeschichte." What had, in the context of the Theatre Union's production, been a way of showing how far the New York group had departed from the playwright's original intentions here becomes a useful documentation of how the play had come into being. *Theaterarbeit* sets out the first two parts, beginning "Als ich das Stück *Die Mutter* schrieb" and "So seht ihr also," on a single page, with the second of them being repeated on the following pages (122–29), now cut up into smaller sections and juxtaposed with photographs from the 1951 Berlin production (the 1932 and Leipzig ones were less copiously documented). The effect is one of textual duplication for the purpose of estrangement, as well as moving from overall background information to a detailed textual-visual focus on individual parts of Pelagea Wlassowa's story.

The pictorial sequence contrasts two images of Helene Weigel's Wlassowa: that of the suffering mother: "seht, wie zuerst / Ihr die Kopeke fehlt am Lohn ihres Sohnes; sie kann ihm / Seine Suppe nicht schmackhaft kochen" (122) and that of the emblematic revolutionary mother of the people, now holding a red flag and no longer alone with her parochial worries but standing firm among her male and female comrades (129). On this final page of the sequence, text and image are no longer kept separate, but are superimposed (just as Brecht had initially deployed the backcloth's hammer and sickle images separately, only to superimpose them iconically later on in scene 8 of *Die Mutter* [*GBA*, 24:117]). On the final *Theaterarbeit* page, the text printed in white on the dark surface of the photograph serves as a visual "Verfremdung" of the preceding, more conventional black-on-white typography. As elsewhere in the text-and-image sequence, Brecht does not simply work with extracts from his 1935 poem, he also introduces further "Historisierung" in the form of captions for many of the pictures. Thus the final triumphant one, going beyond the time frame of Gorky's novel and the main part of Brecht's adaptation, announces: "1917 ergreift das russische Proletariat die Macht. Im Zug der demonstrierenden Arbeiter geht Pelagea Wlassowa, *Die Mutter*." The kind of prefigurative function later read into Gorky's location of Pelagea Wlassowa's story in the 1905 Revolution (Gorky's novel dates from 1906–7) is now made explicit through the reference to the overthrow of Russian Czarism, with no doubt a further oblique reference to what GDR propaganda liked to term the "Befreiung" of East Germany in 1945. Indeed, if the poem entitled "Versuch Nr. 1 zur *Mutter*" (*GBA*, 15:243–45) is by Brecht, and there is some doubt about this (cf. *GBA*, 15:455), then it would take such a thought one stage further. For the work invokes a picture of bustling contemporary industrial East German citizens in the cadences of Brecht's earlier poem "An die Nachgeborenen" ("Ihr aber, die ihr heute / Den Kampf der Mutter betrachtet / In ihrem Morgen als eurem Heute stehend"). It presents the GDR as the world Brecht's Wlassowa was trying to bring about:

> Ihr nun, Anwender dessen, was unser Stück zeigt
> Nämlich dies: daß neue Formen den neuen Inhalten
> Zu geben sind
> Werdet nicht zögern, auf der Bühne zu begrüßen
> Was täglich in euren Schächten, Bauhöfen und Werkhallen
> Ihr beweist. (*GBA*, 15:244–45)

It is no longer the cautious American theater workers who are being encouraged to grasp the moment, but the audiences of the 1951 East Berlin production.

While the presence, in the part of *Theaterarbeit* exclusively devoted to *Die Mutter*, of an abridged version of "Ein Brief . . ." stresses a measure of continuity between Brecht's radically experimental work in the early 1930s and its continuation in the GDR, the relegation of parts 3 and 4 of the poem to a much later section helps relativize the impact of one of the more disastrous episodes of Brecht's exile years. At the same time it piously insinuates that any such antagonistic misunderstandings are out of place in the new GDR. The rest of the poem eventually appears over two hundred pages later in the section on the advantages of working with "Modelle." As one heading puts it: "Das Modellbuch warnt vor falscher Darstellung" (298). A note to the extracts from the poem, stating that the two accompanying illustrations are of "die [. . .] Aufführung durch die Theatre Union in New York," adds misleadingly: "Die geplante naturalistische Inszenierung wurde aufgegeben und der Wunsch des Stückschreibers nach Benutzung des Modells erfüllt" (334). Two well-chosen photographs of the New York stage sets are intended to corroborate this cosmetic version of what had actually happened in 1935. Placing the parts of "Brief an . . ." that document the controversy in the midst of a serial account of five productions, all allegedly abiding faithfully by the Brechtian "Modell," rewrites theater history. A major disappointment now reads like a signal victory for Epic Theater.

*Theaterarbeit*'s presentation of the Gorky adaptation looks calculated to align Brecht's work much more with socialist aesthetics than had been the case in 1932; Gorky was in fact only appropriated by the Zhdanovites as a Socialist Realist *avant la lettre* in the late 1930s. Even if Brecht's epic version of Gorky's novel would, if examined closely, soon dispel any suggestion of political correctness by association, there is little in the text and illustrative material in *Theaterarbeit* to make the underlying aesthetic disagreements centered on the "Formalismusdebatte" too glaringly obvious. And since many of the productions documented in *Theaterarbeit* involve adaptations of works by other writers (Gorky's *Vassa Shelesnova* [id., 1901], Lenz's *Der Hofmeister* [The Tutor, 1774], Hauptmann's *Der Biberpelz* [The Beaver Coat, 1893] and *Der rote Hahn* [The Red Cock, 1901]), the volume is able to position the Berliner Ensemble's more important Gorky adaptation favorably in relation to what was already becoming the whole vexed issue of the new socialist canon and the embryonic nation's cultural heritage ("Erbe"). Even if "Rede an das Arbeitertheater 'Theatre Union' in New York, das Stück 'Die Mutter' betreffend" had to be mutilated before it could find an acceptable place in *Theaterarbeit,* there is invariably a logic behind the measures taken. To make its mark effectively in the new GDR climate, the poem had to be cut up, redistributed and refunctionalized. Nothing comparable happened to any of Brecht's other dramaturgical poems during the two decades between 1935 and the writer's death.

## "Über alltägliches Theater"

Two further major dramaturgical poems date from the second half of 1935: "Über alltägliches Theater" (On Everyday Theater) and "Rede an dänische Arbeiterschauspieler über die Kunst der Beobachtung" (An Address to Danish Worker Actors on the Art of Observation). Although only the latter specifies an addressee, it is often assumed that they were both written with the same "Arbeiterschauspielgruppe" in mind,[18] namely the R.T. group, Ruth Berlau's Revolutionært Teater, popularly known as the Red Theater (Röde Teater). When published as part of a series of seven "Gedichte aus dem *Messingkauf*" in *Theaterarbeit* (where it is dated 1930; *Theaterarbeit,* 401) and as the twenty-sixth "Versuch" in *Versuche* 14 (1955), "Über alltägliches Theater" was given pride of place and put in first position. But the far larger group of thirty-eight "Gedichte aus dem *Messingkauf*" (*GW,*

---

[18] Cf. *GBA,* 12:451 on this point.

9:760–98) transposes "Rede an . . ." to first place.[19] It might be tempting to think of Brecht, having used the first poem to set out his misgivings about *Die Mutter*'s treatment, now writing a further dramaturgical poem devoted to the work of his Danish co-workers who had got right what the Theatre Union had so completely bungled. But this seems unlikely. Even the indications that Brecht's "Über alltägliches Theater" and "Rede an . . ." might both be addressed to the same — or in one case, *any*— specific theater group remain largely circumstantial. Whereas the Theatre Union was named in Brecht's earlier poem, the reference now is merely to Danish worker-actors. But as with "Brief an . . .," a more serious case can be made for treating "Rede an . . ." as a "Rollengedicht," with the target readership being once again much broader than the one indicated in the title.

"Über alltägliches Theater" (*GBA*, 12:319–22) is Brecht's most important statement in poetic form on the subject of "Verfremdung." In a letter of September 1938 to the American Guild for German Cultural Freedom setting out his reasons for applying for an extension to his current stipendium, Brecht refers to a number of works-in-progress: "einige theoretische Aufsätze [. . .], darunter zwei mir wichtig erscheinende Arbeiten über das Theater: 'Die Straßenszene' [. . .] und 'Theorie des Verfremdungseffekts,' worin ich die Schauspielkunst des Epischen Theaters darstelle [possibly a reference to the embryonic 'Kurze Beschreibung . . .']" (*GBA*, 29:111). The importance of the first of the projects mentioned can be gauged from the intention to include it in *Der Messingkauf* and also by the reformulation of the "street-theater" idea in related writings, including "Kurze Beschreibung." In a subsequent journal entry for 6 December 1940, Brecht gives some indication of just how important the parallels between "Verfremdung" in the theater and in everyday life were becoming for his thinking:

> Anschließend an die Untersuchungen in der "Straßenszene" müßte man andere Arten alltäglichen Theaters beschreiben, die Gelegenheiten aufsuchen, wo im täglichen Leben Theater gespielt wird. In der Erotik, im Geschäftsleben, in der Politik, in der Rechtspflege, in der Religion usw. Man müßte die theatralischen Elemente in den Sitten und Gebräuchen studieren. Die Theatralisierung der Politik durch den Faschismus habe ich schon ein wenig bearbeitet. Aber dazu müßte man das "elementare Ausdrucksbedürfnis" unserer Ästhetiken einzirkeln. Die "Straßenszene" bedeutet einen großen Schritt entgegen der Profanisierung, Entkultisierung, Säkularisierung der Theaterkunst. (*GBA*, 26:443)

[19] The English translation of Brecht's *Poems on the Theatre* correctly puts "On the Everyday Theatre" in first place (Berger and Bostock 1961, 5–9), but, perhaps to lend the volume's ending more weight, places "An Address to Danish Worker Actors on the Art of Observation" in penultimate position (15–21).

The last two sentences are crucial. Not only do they emphasize that examples of the cognitive value of "Verfremdung" can be found in many walks of life, they also use this fact to engage in what Benjamin and Brecht both saw as a necessary "Profanisierung" of art (cf. Benjamin's term "Entauratisierung" in "Das Kunstwerk im Zeitalter seiner technischen Reproduzierbarkeit"[20] and Brecht's repeated attacks on "das Kultische" in Stanislavskian theater). We shall see in the following chapter just what one of Brecht's examples came to mean in the case of "Über die Theatralik des Faschismus." However, it is worth recalling here that an effective practical contribution had already been made with *Furcht und Elend des III. Reiches,* a work which, on the analogy of chemistry's periodic table, Brecht described as a "Gestentafel" ("eben die Gesten des Verstummens, Sich-Umblickens, Erschreckens usw. unter der Diktatur" [*GBA,* 26:318]). The remark that follows immediately on from this explanation — "Der Schauspieler tut jedenfalls gut, die 'Straßenszene' zu studieren, bevor er eine der kleinen Szenen spielt" — could just as well have referred the actor to "Über alltägliches Theater." Indeed, the initial impression made by the poem is of its similarity to "Die Straßenszene. *Grundmodell einer Szene des epischen Theaters (1940)."* One of the poem's illustrations of "jenes Theater [. . .], das auf der Straße sich abspielt" offers a cameo of the situation explored in detail in "Die Straßenszene."[21] The bringing together of the words "alltäglich" and "Theater" (like the theoretical essay's almost oxymoronic compound "Straßenszene") is the overture to a number of confrontations between the world of the theater and life going on outside its confines.

[20] Walter Benjamin's "Das Kunstwerk im Zeitalter seiner technischen Reproduzierbarkeit" (Benjamin 1972–89, I, 2 [1974], 471–508) presents the thesis that in the modern age of mechanical reproductions works of art, including film and photographic reproductions, have undergone a "Funktionsänderung" (486). Once it is capable of being multiply reproduced, Benjamin argues, the work of art loses its "aura." This auratic quality, defined as a product of uniqueness, permanence, and distance (480–82), is shown to have been superseded by mass art forms available to all. Benjamin's picture of a paradigm change from auratic to non-auratic art forms had an influence on Brecht's conception of Epic Theater as a "Profanisierung" of the cultic aspect of Stanislavskian drama.

[21] According to *GBA,* 22:1021, the "alltägliches Theater" of life on the street was a popular topic in the late Weimar Republic. Brecht was probably familiar with a piece in the *Berliner Illustrierte Woche* of 29 May 1930, entitled "Schauspieler in der Straße," in which the words and behavior of a huckster tie salesman are analysed. The "Schalverkäufer" evoked near the end of Brecht's poem and the tie salesman in "Die Straßenszene" (*GBA,* 22:380) appear to be indebted to "Schauspieler in der Straße."

Seht dort den Mann an der Straßenecke! Er zeigt, wie
Der Unfall vor sich ging. Gerade
Überliefert er den Fahrer dem Urteil der Menge. Wie der
Hinter der Steuerung saß, und jetzt
Ahmt er den Überfahrenen nach, anscheinend
Einen alten Mann. Von beiden gibt er
Nur so viel, daß der Unfall verständlich wird, und doch
Genug, daß sie vor euren Augen erscheinen. Beide
Zeigt er aber nicht so, daß sie einem
Unfall nicht zu entgehen vermöchten. Der Unfall
Wird so verständlich und doch unverständlich, denn beide
Konnten sich auch ganz anders bewegen, jetzt zeigt er, wie nämlich
Sie sich hätten bewegen können, damit der Unfall
Nicht erfolgt wäre. ("Über alltägliches Theater" [*GBA*, 12:319–20])

This succinct introduction to the principles underlying "Verfremdung" and
the "*Nicht — Sondern*" model is made in fewer words than "Die Straßenszene" takes to complete its general exposition before proceeding to the
street-scene scenario.[22]

Given that "Die Straßenszene" was at one stage intended for inclusion
in *Der Messingkauf,* it is possible to view "Über alltägliches Theater" as a
preliminary exploration of ideas to be worked out more fully in "Die
Straßenszene" (dated both 1938 and 1940).[23] But the poem is far more than
just a preliminary sketch; it contains a higher density and subtler range of
points than found in "Die Straßenszene." Even the central idea that a
"Modell" can be a vehicle for "Verfremdung" is presented in a more
differentiated manner: "Von beiden [Perspektiven] gibt er [the accident's
eye-witness] / Nur so viel, daß der Unfall verständlich wird, und doch /
Genug, daß sie vor euren Augen erscheinen." The interlinked elements of
recognizability and defamiliarization brought out here are made to resemble
a juggling with variables, a method not adopted in "Die Straßenszene."

---

[22] Voges's analysis of the street-scene model demonstrates that it is not to be read
naturalistically as an illustration of "Verfremdung" and Epic Theater derived from a
real-life situation (as it is interpreted by Fiebach 1978), but is a complex construction
so organized as to make the aesthetic points required. Hence, according to Voges:
"Das 'Original' dieses Modells ist das neue Theater" (Voges 1985, 220). The constructedness of the model is more in evidence in the long prose form of "Die
Straßenszene" than in the brief sketch of its value in "Über alltägliches Theater."

[23] Margarete Steffin had written "Juni 1938" on an early draft (cf. *GBA*, 22:1021),
whereas *Versuche* 10 (1950): 123 dates it "1940." The dates presumably refer to different versions.

In the early part of "Über alltägliches Theater" Brecht sets himself a complex series of interlocking objectives. He needs to establish a contrast between the dangers of an ivory-tower theater ("In großen Häusern, unter künstlichen Lichtsonnen / Vor der schweigenden Menge") and "Das alltägliche, tausendfache und ruhmlose / Aber so sehr lebendige, irdische, aus dem Zusammenleben / Der Menschen gespeiste Theater, das auf der Straße sich abspielt" (*GBA*, 12:319). Reality, the poem must show, is out there among ordinary people, not in the citadels of high culture, a fact theater forgets at its peril. The dominant contrast between the theater of the street and the elitist institution is as absolute as that between Stanislavskian and oriental theater in "The Fourth Wall of China." This is why it is assumed that conventionally trained professional actors will take exception to the suggestion that they should learn their trade from the man in the street:

> Ihr aber sagt nicht: der Mann
> Ist kein Künstler. Eine solche Scheidewand aufrichtend
> Zwischen euch und aller Welt, werft ihr euch
> Nur aus der Welt. Hießet ihr ihn
> Gar keinen Künstler, so könnte er euch
> Gar keinen Menschen heißen, und das
> Wäre ein größerer Vorwurf. Sagt lieber:
> Er ist ein Künstler, weil er ein Mensch ist. (*GBA*, 12:321)

Brecht's near-syllogistic method is deliberately provocative. Even the link between the image of reactionary actors putting up a "Scheidewand" between themselves and reality and the fourth wall that Epic Theater has torn down is designed to goad. The emphasis on "das Alltägliche," so economically encapsulated in this poem, is central to much of Brecht's theorizing of "Verfremdung" in the 1930s, but it is presented with a different "Gestus" in different contexts. In "Die Straßenszene" there is no such element of provocation, evidently because the implied reader is not some stubborn actor, but someone already receptive to Epic Theater. Hence the open, factually presented admission that "der Vorgang [i.e. the "action-replay" of the accident] ist offenbar keineswegs das, was wir unter einem Kunstvorgang verstehen" (*GBA*, 22:272), even when at the same time various attempts are made to show that there is much artistry in the theater of the street (*GBA*, 22:378–79).

While illustrating the importance of observing street life, Brecht's poem has to maintain a distinction between registering surface detail and advocating a more penetrating kind of observation. "Das Alltägliche" cannot be confused with "das Natürliche"; if it were, one of his most important aesthetic principles concerning "echter Realismus" would be undermined. The contrast between merely replicating surface reality and a more interpretive form of observation comes both in the form of statement and illustration. "Nicht wie Papagei und Affe / Ahmen diese nur nach der Nachahmung willen, gleichgültig / Was sie da nachahmen, nur um zu zeigen, daß sie / Gut nachahmen können" is a jibe at both stage-set *trompe-l'œil* and Stanislavskian acting (though it has been suggested [Buck 1971, 21] that there may be a debt to Nietzsche's *Morgenröthe*). The images of actors as glorified parrots or monkeys denigrate. Brecht's contrast word here is the adjective "würdig," not just suggesting that a dignity of purpose has to be restored to the theater, but again taking up an idea from the *Mahagonny* notes that when they are in the theater actors and audience alike have to behave not in a spirit of escapism but in a manner worthy of them as social beings with a critical faculty and a sense of justice. Unlike the parrots and aping monkeys among the contemporary theatrical fraternity, epic actors, for that reason, need to have a "Zweck im Auge."

Most of the poem's other skirmishes with Stanislavskian theater take up and give further emphasis to the theater/street contrast of the early lines. When theater becomes associated with the irrational realm of cult, incense and initiation, of "restlose Verwandlung" purporting to be an aesthetic form of transsubstantiation, and a *unio mystica* between actor and role, the contrast between the world of the stage and life on the street becomes even starker. The theater has been transformed into a temple to Unreason, and it needs to be rescued by people coming in off the street.

The sins of the Stanislavskians are evoked mainly by means of various references to what the man in the street does *not* do:

> Und mit Staunen
> Mögt ihr eines betrachten: daß dieser Nachahmende
> Nie sich in einer Nachahmung verliert. Er verwandelt sich
> Nie zur Gänze in den, den er nachahmt. Immer
> Bleibt er der Zeigende, selbst nicht Verwickelte. (*GBA*, 12:320)

A particularly elusive passage:

> Jener
> Hat ihn nicht eingeweiht, er
> Teilt nicht seine Gefühle
> Noch seine Anschauungen. Er weiß von ihm
> Nur wenig. (*GBA*, 12:320)

is clarified in the English translation where "Jener" is rendered by "the person he plays" (Berger and Bostock 1961, 6). The ensuing vocabulary of cultic initiation ("Einweihung"), the smell of incense ("Weihrauch") and the image of actor and character merging to form "ein Drittes" is so indebted to Moscow Art Theater jargon that the very image of everyday theater in the street makes the need for such cravings seem preposterous. The theater of everyday life is not only held up as a model for serious political theater to emulate, but also makes certain contemporary practices appear doubly laughable. Thus, the "geheimnisvolle Verwandlung" that the actor undergoes as he moves from dressing room to stage is subjected to ridicule: "ein Schauspieler / Verläßt den Ankleideraum, ein König / Betritt die Bühne, jener Zauber / Über den ich die Bühnenarbeiter, Bierflaschen in Händen / So oft habe lachen sehen, passiert hier [i.e. on the street] nicht" (*GBA*, 12:321). Whereas much contemporary theater, with its arcane rituals and its obsession with transforming character, actor, and audience into a symbiotic entity, is a place of mystification, everything happening in the street is open to inspection and confirms commonsense. Here, there is no "Schlafwandler," no "Hoher Priester beim Gottesdienst," no effect of "Rausch."

The poem's first contrasting illustration of "alltägliches Theater" is a socially charged one.[24] Given that Stanislavsky's *An Actor Prepares* also contains an everyday illustration from a street accident to show what his kind of apolitical actor could learn from the situation (Stanislavsky 1988, 170), it may well be that Brecht's *Straßenszene* model was written as a counterargument to the passage in the Emotion Memory chapter there.

> zeigt sie
> Seine Redeflut vorführend
> Wie er versucht, das Gespräch abzubiegen
> Von der Wasserleitung, die geborsten ist. (*GBA*, 12:319)

We find the same critical distance in the image of the skeptical drunk seeing through the preacher's glib promises of bountiful rewards in the afterlife. Yet the intercalated sexual example of boys showing giggling girls how young girls resist their advances and "dabei / Geschickt die Brüste zeigen" renders all the more duplicitous and transparent the subterfuges dealt with in the

---

[24] The acuteness and brevity of this poetic example contrasts with its plodding counterpart in "Die Straßenszene": "Wir begegnen häufig Demonstrationen alltäglicher Art, die vollkommenere Imitationen sind, als unser Unfall an der Straßenecke sie nötig macht. Sie sind meist komischer Natur. Unser Nachbar (oder unsere Nachbarin) mag uns das habgierige Verhalten unseres Hauswirts 'zum besten geben.' Die Imitation ist dann oft ausgiebig und variantenreich. Bei näherer Untersuchung wird man aber doch feststellen, daß auch die anscheinend sehr komplexe Imitation nur ganz Bestimmtes im Verhalten unseres Hauswirtes 'aufs Korn nimmt.' Die Imitation ist eine Zusammenfassung oder ein Ausschnitt, wobei sorgsam solche Momente ausgelassen sind, in denen der Hauswirt unserem Nachbarn als 'ganz vernünftig' erscheint, welche Momente es doch natürlich gibt. Er ist weit entfernt, ein Gesamtbild zu geben; das würde gar keine komische Wirkung haben" (*GBA*, 22:374).

two more serious examples on either side of it. In each case, surface reality will not be understood if it is only slavishly imitated. The actor has to show what Brecht elsewhere calls "die Vorgänge hinter den Vorgängen" (*GBA*, 22:519). Allegedly, that is what happens in street scenes, even if there the end result often remains purely an act of exposure. The statement made about the street "actor" — "Dieser / Weiß, daß von seiner Genauigkeit vieles abhängt, ob der Unschuldige / Dem Verderben entrinnt, ob der Geschädigte / Entschädigt wird" — scarcely finds any equivalent in the examples at the start of "Über alltägliches Theater." Nevertheless, we are led to understand that the ideal Brechtian actor will already have a more politically interventionist purpose than the poem's illustrations indicate. This means that even "alltägliches Theater," like Mei Lan-fang's Chinese theater, has limitations as a model. Once more, radical politicization is required. If one compares the illustrations here with the central accident paradigm in "Die Straßenszene," one finds that the poem's material already carries more political weight. While the later essay vaguely claims that the "Demonstration" under discussion has "gesellschaftlich praktische Bedeutung" (*GBA*, 22:373) and will lead to "Kritik" of some kind (*GBA*, 22:371), the carefully worded formulations do little to disguise the fact that the socially practical dimension of a road accident and the kind of behavior the demonstration highlights are not as obviously political as the poem's examples. "Die Straßenszene" has to embroider on a rather contrived series of additional details that *might* emerge in one particular scenario and only then, as the final sentence concedes, would it have managed to politicize the situation effectively:

> Die Demonstration wird z.B. beherrscht von der Frage des *Schadenersatzes* usw. Der Chauffeur hat seine Entlassung, den Entzug des Führerscheins, Gefängnis zu befürchten, der Überfahrene hohe Klinikkosten, Verlust seiner Stelle, dauernde Verunstaltung, womöglich Arbeitsuntauglichkeit. Das ist das Feld, auf dem der Demonstrant seine Charaktere aufbaut. Der Überfahrene kann einen Begleiter gehabt haben, neben dem Chauffeur kann ein Mädchen gesessen haben. In diesem Falle tritt das *Soziale* besser in Erscheinung. Die Charaktere werden reicher gezeichnet werden können. (*GBA*, 22:374)

Because this is a pared-down model, there is never any suggestion that a Marxist might be driving the car and that it has run over a capitalist — or even a Stanislavskian actor! For all Brecht's ingenuity in suggesting the possibility of a sociopolitical dimension to the accident, just how unconvincing this passage is can be gauged from the fact that it is seldom mentioned in discussions of "Die Straßenszene." The examples in "Über alltägliches Theater" are less contrived.

With a forthrightness that stands out amidst the poem's general obliqueness, the point that street theater's methods will require further politicization is conceded at the end of "Über alltägliches Theater":

> Aber damit wir uns verstehen: selbst wenn ihr verbessertet
> Was der Mann an der Straßenecke macht, machtet ihr weniger
> Als er, wenn ihr
> Euer Theater weniger sinnvoll machtet, aus geringerem Anlaß
> Weniger eingreifend in das Leben der Zuschauer und
> Weniger nützlich. (*GBA*, 12:322)

The reason why this poem deserves pride of place in any dramaturgical sequence should by now be apparent. It has much to say about the importance of the non-Stanislavskian systems of preparation required of the epic actor. In this respect, it needs to precede both the vital processes of familiarizing oneself with the script and the collective rehearsal stage. For ideological reasons, it anchors the proposed approach in a "theater" of everyday life (praxis) and, without belaboring the point, implies that the principal models of everyday theater from which much can be learnt are working-class. (Who else conducted so much of their business in the street in the 1930s?) By means of a series of rhetorical antitheses (temple vs. street; cloistered theater vs. real life outside; vanity concerning skill in accurate imitation for its own sake vs. imitation with a political purpose; professional actor vs. rounded committed member of the human race; perhaps also evening vs. daytime) it efficiently identifies the main goals and methods of Epic Theater, while attacking, often by innuendo, the theoretical assumptions of "Aristotelian" theater. The work thus serves as a prologue to the other "Gedichte aus dem *Messingkauf*" — or for that matter to most of Brecht's subsequent dramaturgical poems.

## "Rede an dänische Arbeiterschauspieler über die Kunst der Beobachtung"

There were inevitably times when Brecht had to correspond with theater groups. February 1938 sees him setting out four pages of comments to a German emigré group based in Copenhagen. Unlike the Döbeln troupe, whose only reply seems to have been in the guise of a fictive dialogue, the Copenhagen group were involved in a real exchange of letters. Brecht takes issue with specific aspects of their staging of *Die Gewehre der Frau Carrar*: "Liebe Genossen, ich habe Euch versprochen, nachdem ich die positiven Seiten der Aufführung [. . .] besprochen habe, auch (zum Zweck der Verbesserung) die negativen zu besprechen" (*GBA*, 29:74). There is even a follow-up response to their own constructive "Selbstkritik" (*GBA*, 29:76).

Under such circumstances, Brecht can freely express himself in German and expect to be replied to in his native tongue. But the same situation did not obtain in the R.T. group with whom he could probably only communicate via Ruth Berlau. It is therefore unlikely that he would have addressed them directly in a German poem. Once again, as with "Brief an das Arbeitertheater 'Theatre Union' in New York, das Stück 'Die Mutter' betreffend," in the case of "Rede an dänische Arbeiterschauspieler über die Kunst der Beobachtung," we appear to be dealing with a form of "Rollengedicht" in which Brecht plays the part of "der Stückschreiber," a playwright this time making a speech to a group of actors. We, his readers, are in turn assigned the part of collective addressees. The rationale behind such a strategy is that all actors, not just the R.T. group, and indeed everyone interested in contemporary theater, will benefit from Brecht's thoughts on "die Kunst der Beobachtung," for "die Beobachtung ist ein Hauptteil der Schauspielkunst" (*Kleines Organon*, §54).

According to Ruth Berlau (Witt 1964, 65), the poem (*GBA*, 12:322–27) was written after Brecht had seen the R.T. rehearsing *Die Mutter*, so there is one sense in which it did start out in life as a companion piece to "Brief an. . . ." (First published in *Theaterarbeit*, the work is there dated 1934 [*Theaterarbeit*, 408].) But this time "Brecht" speaks with a multiplicity of voices, something that had not happened in the earlier poem, where the authority of a firm *persona* had been required to underwrite the criticism. At one stage, while illustrating the principle of "Historisierung," the poem invokes Brecht's own historical situation as exiled poet-dramatist, thus personalizing and hence defamiliarizing the usual relationship between author/director and cast. Putting the material in brackets adds a typographical "Verfremdung" to the invitation to the addressees to adopt a fresh perspective:

> (Selbst was hier geschieht, eben jetzt, bei uns, könnt ihr
> So als Bild betrachten: wie euch der landflüchtige
> Stückschreiber unterweist in der
> Kunst der Beobachtung.) (*GBA*, 12:326)

Elsewhere what was until then the lyrical "Ich" assumes the first person plural in order to act as spokesman for the less emancipated faction in the audience (as if they were unable to formulate their own inert dissatisfaction with an outmoded kind of theater that is not *their* theater):

> Wir aber, die Zuschauer
> Auf den niederen Bänken, sitzen verglasten Auges und glotzen
> Nunmehr in eurem Griff, auf eure Grimassen und Zuckungen
> Etwas nachempfindend geschenkte Freude und
> Unhemmbare Sorge. (*GBA*, 12:323)

The poem's controlling voice not only gives expression to the sentiments of those "Auf den niederen Bänken," but also suggests that their growing sense of dissatisfaction with such theater is also shared by the Epic playwright-poet. An alternative reading of this shift of perspective would be to assume the poem is made up of a montage of independent perspectives and voices. The spectrum of possibilities is hinted at during the course of the poem by three contrasting phrases: "in eurem Griff [glotzen]," "nach Kenntnissen greifen," and "eingreifen."

From the stanza ending "Wem also von euren Zuschauern / Sollt ihr folgen, Schauspieler? Ich schlage euch vor: / Den Unzufriedenen" (*GBA*, 12:324), the main *persona* begins to assume the role of authoritative political and dramaturgical mentor, rather than mere mouthpiece of unarticulated dissatisfaction. What follows is an orchestration similar to that in some of the radio discussions. The initial down-to-business "Wie aber / Nun dies anstellen?" appears to echo the famous title *What is to be done?* (Chto delat') used by both Chernyshevsky and Lenin in classic theoretical works of interventionist socialism. Yet before the more magisterial voice establishes and positions itself intertextually, there are moments of apparent indecision. After the poem's rousing invocation of the new world view (starting "Habt ihr denn / Nicht gehört"), we are told: "So ungefähr kommt's von den Bänken. Freilich *nicht alle* / Stimmen da zu" (my emphasis), while in the next line we are assured that "die meisten" still sit there in a state of ideological disarray. Later, the speaking voice slips back into uncertainty: "Ich sehe euch / *Alle, die Besten von euch,* schon gierig nach Kenntnissen greifen" (my emphasis). Yet three lines later the "Alle" appears to be further relativized by "schon studieren / Viele von euch die Gesetze des menschlichen Zusammenlebens." Not all these statements are mutually incompatible. Experience had certainly taught Brecht that it was possible to be studying the "Gesetze des menschlichen Zusammenlebens" and yet lag artistically behind the times, and the ratio of "die Besten" to "die meisten" may have simply been left indeterminate for encouragement. Nevertheless, the poem gestures towards the idea, already hinted at in "Rede an . . .," that actors, like audiences, should not merge into some collective monolith. Some may already be aware of the advantages of Epic Theater, others will remain unreconstructed Stanislavskians, and some still hover undecided. Such a lack of homogeneity is emphasized by the dispute that has broken out among the working-class members of the audience. Now the real conflict is not about two diametrically opposed conceptions of effective theater, but between two ideologies. Affirmative theater is rejected by those who know they are masters of their own fate and demand to see this fact reflected in a new form of drama. Speaking on their behalf, the Brechtian "Ich" once more expresses his own misgivings:

Lauter Opfer spielt ihr uns vor und tut, als wäret ihr
Hilflose Opfer fremdartiger Mächte und eigener Triebe.
Die Freuden werden ihnen, als wären sie Hunde, von unsichtbaren
Händen plötzlich zugeworfen wie Brocken, und ebenso
Plötzlich legen sich Schlingen um ihre Hälse, die Sorgen, die
Von oben kommen. (*GBA*, 12:323)

The poem's core objection to fatalism is voiced by contemporary theater's disappointed audiences. It is the people in the cheaper seats who are shown to bring the good news to the actors onstage:

Habt ihr denn
Nicht gehört, daß es ruchbar geworden ist
Wie dieses Netz von Menschen gestrickt und geworfen ist?
Überall schon von den hundertstöckigen Städten
Über die Meere, durchfurcht von menschenreichen Schiffen
In die entfernten Dörfer wurde gemeldet
Daß des Menschen Schicksal der Mensch ist! (*GBA*, 12:323)

Some of these lines echo Galilei's triumphant hymn to the dawning new age in *Leben des Galilei*; it is apt that the poem was published in *Versuche* 14 alongside that play. Other readers will recognize the final line as also appearing in "Fünf Schwierigkeiten beim Schreiben der Wahrheit" (*GBA*, 22:79). In both works, the idea of Man's being primarily at the mercy of his fellow men rather than of some form of fate (and thus able to defeat that adversary in a way that he could not, if up against a suprapersonal force) had its roots in Brecht's response to fascism. "Fünf Schwierigkeiten" and *Leben des Galilei* both date from the latter half of the 1930s. But the idea was already to be found in the original Berlin version of *Die Mutter* where, in scene 11, after she has received the news of Pawel's death and is being consoled by a group of God-fearing peasants, Pelagea Wlassowa is told: "der Mensch braucht Gott. Er ist machtlos gegen das Schicksal." To which she replies: "Wir [i.e. we communists] sagen: das Schicksal des Menschen ist der Mensch" (*GBA*, 3:313). In other words, what the poem "Rede an . . ." presents as the empowering gospel of socialist solidarity, radiating across the globe from the USSR and at the same time rising up from the proletarian seats in the theater to the actors onstage, is already at the very heart of the political message of *Die Mutter*. Either Brecht was so pleased with the formulation that he simply recycled it on a number of subsequent occasions or, more likely, he is implying that the R. T. actors, despite being "Arbeiterschauspieler," have become so preoccupied with their theatrical work that they have failed to take sufficient notice of what Brecht's play is saying to them and their audiences in their capacity as human beings. If the latter, then this second "Gedicht aus dem *Messingkauf*" is working with a variation on the "Künstler"/"Mensch" distinction made in "Über alltäg-liches Theater."

The solution that the poem offers to such artistic narcissism is to learn "*die Kunst der Beobachtung*" ("Angewandt auf die Menschen"). Epic actors must become "Forscher" and acquire a thorough "Menschenkenntnis" through enlightened observation; or as §55 of *Kleines Organon* puts it, "[der Schauspieler] muß sich das Wissen der Zeit über das menschliche Zusammenleben aneignen, indem er die Kämpfe der Klassen mitkämpft" (*GBA*, 23:86). The interventionist aspect to the poem's presentation of "die Kunst der Beobachtung" is made vivid by the application of horticultural imagery to the actor's activities: first in the general statement "Schärferen Auges überblickt / Der Obstzüchter den Apfelbaum als der Spaziergänger," and then dramatized in the consternation of the actors themselves: "Wie / Sollen wir, immer nur die / Obsttragenden Bäume, nun selbst die Gärtner werden?" (*GBA*, 12:326). The idea of Man being master of his own fate has given way to a dual defamiliarizing contrast: first, between the fruit grower and the passerby and then — boldly suggesting the leap of vision required of actors and audiences alike — between fruit trees and the *fruit-growers* into whom the trees must transform themselves overnight. Treating politicization and interventionist thought as processes familiar from nature is not intended to make them appear "natural" in a pejorative sense. Rather, it shows how great a paradigm change is needed before the passive victim becomes the master of his or her own fate and the "Papagei"-like actor can exercise the same stewardship over society as the fruit-grower has over the orchard's pro-duce. The stanza that conjures up the image of the fruit-bearing trees them-selves becoming gardeners ends with the assurance that actors who are also workers are well on their way to such an act of self-transcendence. They have the opportunity to school themselves in observation at their places of work and are not only "Arbeiterschauspieler," but are preparing through observa-tion to be "Schauspieler der Arbeiter, lernend und lehrend."

The main challenge that the central part of Brecht's poem has to con-front is that of finding a way to bridge the gap between the assertion that observation is a central factor in the class struggle and the conclusion's sug-gestion that such preparation will lead to the requisite politically interven-tionist form of art:

> Mit eurer Gestaltung eingreifen in alle Kämpfe
> Von Menschen eurer Zeit und so
> Mit dem Ernst des Studiums und der Heiterkeit des Wissens
> Helfen, die Erfahrung des Kampfs zum Gemeingut zu machen und
> Die Gerechtigkeit zu Leidenschaft. (*GBA*, 12:327)

The rhetoric of these final lines, even the surreal image of the trees becoming fruit growers, will ring hollow, if the central parts of the poem's treatment of "die Kunst der Beobachtung" fail to prepare the ground for such high-flown sentiments. Much depends on what kind of observation Brecht wishes his actors — and the poem's readers — to engage in. It is clearly very different from that at the center of "Über alltägliches Theater," although both forms are part of the process of *building up*[25] a form of theater worthy of the outside world. Strictly speaking, what is being described is not a matter of *observation,* since the poem's readers are hardly expected to wait, for example, until the next traffic accident occurs, before they register what happens in its aftermath. Rather, they are being invited to *recall* phenomena that they may have frequently witnessed in the past and to consider their implications for a political theater of distance. In other words, cumulative experience is being invoked in the guise of observation, yet the process equally involves ideation on the reader's part. In "Rede an . . .," by contrast, the emphasis is on actual observation as a political weapon: "Man wird dich beobachten, um zu sehen / Wie gut du beobachtet hast."

The initial contrast between actors whose main preoccupation appears to be literally "making an exhibition of themselves" in a self-centered narcissistic sense — "beharrlich / Fordern einige [!], ihr solltet / Keinesfalls nur euch zeigen, sondern / Die Welt" — is taken up by the injunction in the third stanza to rethink their function:

Darum
Fordern wir nun von euch, den Schauspielern
Unserer Zeit, Zeit des Umbruchs und der großen Meisterung
Aller Natur, auch der menschlichen, euch
Endlich umzustellen und uns die Menschenwelt
So zu zeigen, wie sie ist: von den Menschen gemacht und veränderbar.
                                        (*GBA*, 12:323)

Ingeniously, a parallel is established between "Aristotelian" theater's alleged obsession with the depiction of "Leute, die im Griff des Schicksals sind" and the predicament of the audiences of such plays. For just as the protagonists tend to display fatalistic attitudes and behave like passive victims, so such works leave their audiences emotionally in the grip (the phrase "im Griff" is used in both contexts) of the actors. Even if the assumption that audience

---

[25] Compare Brecht's use of the term "Aufbau" in "Aufbau einer Rolle: Charles Laughton" (*GBA*, 25:7–69), "Aufbau einer Szene" (*GBA*, 25:472–77), "Aufbau eines Helden" (*GBA*, 25:418–20), and in the poem "Sprechübung für Schauspieler" (*GBA*, 15:34–36), this last being another example of Brecht's use of the "Rollengedicht" genre.

response and audience politics are reciprocally related may be a little too tidy, the passivity suggested by the phrase "im Griff [sein]" contrasts effectively with the dynamic phrase "*gierig* nach Kenntnissen *greifen*" (my emphasis) in the final stanza.

There is little in this part of the poem that would be particularly new to anyone familiar with Brecht's discursive dramatic theory from the *Mahagonny* notes onwards, although striking images and lapidary formulations make for a more vivid picture. But one assumption underlying the advice to actors deserves attention because Brecht's writings have never before presented it so forcefully. I am referring to the "Umstellung" demanded of actors in this poem which does not merely involve them in honing their skills of critical observation all the better to mediate the world view of the (Epic) dramatist, but, more important, having to cultivate a "Beobachtung der Welt" that will educate them politically to the point where they are able to corroborate and endorse the playwright's ideological assumptions, if they have not already done so. (Arguably, this gives a further political twist to the "Papagei"/true actor contrast of the previous poem.[26]) Unlike the Stanislavskian actor, who can, as the occasion demands, totally transform him/herself into any character or deliver a polished performance in a play from any period, "Rede an . . ." puts the emphasis on political, rather than merely artistic, education. What in Stanislavsky's *An Actor Prepares* and *Building a Character* was a matter of technical preparation now becomes first and foremost a matter of ideological education through correct observation of the world.

"Um zu beobachten / Muß man vergleichen lernen. Um zu vergleichen / Muß man schon beobachtet haben." Just what kind of *comparative* observation underlies such a dialectic becomes clear from the poem's main illustrations of constructive observation. We are told, for example, that the observer should be able to differentiate between the behavior of various people as they pay their taxes, even if everybody pays them reluctantly, and see the difference between the person paying taxes and the tax collector, despite the fact that both are victims of the selfsame system. Like "vergleichendes Blättern," comparative observation, it is claimed, will highlight

---

[26] In "Der nur Nachahmende" (c.1945), Brecht makes a comparable point about mere imitation:

DER NUR NACHAHMENDE, der nichts zu sagen hat
Zu dem, was er da nachahmt, gleicht
Einem armen Schimpansen, der das Rauchen seines Bändigers nachahmt
Und dabei nicht raucht. Niemals nämlich
Wird die gedankenlose Nachahmung
Eine wirkliche Nachahmung sein. (*GBA*, 15:166)

contradictions in people's actions: the imperious, overbearing guest at the same time shows signs of fear; the dejected woman, unable even to afford shoes for her first child and now pregnant again, still possesses enough untapped reserves of courage to overturn kingdoms. The poor man who is sick is caught in a double bind ("[erfahrend], daß er nicht mehr gesund wird [. . .] Daß er aber gesund würd, wenn er nicht / Arbeiten müßte"), but he is nevertheless not defeated by his predicament, but gradually radicalized by it. Observation, as these examples suggest, is conceived of as something more than a meticulous noting of large numbers of individual details; it is the ability to decode phenomena from an activist, class-conscious perspective.

The phrase "die Kunst der Beobachtung" may have seemed neutral and primarily aesthetic when first encountered in the poem's title. But by the time the full political ramifications of a statement like "Schlecht beobachtet der, der mit dem Beobachteten / Nichts zu beginnen weiß" have been explained, the reader is in no doubt about the ideological nature of such observation. If Brecht was ostensibly still addressing the R. T. group (though negative phrases like "ausgestellt zu werden / Als Sehenswerte," the repeated "Was soll das?" and "Was nützt das?" combined with the eventual "Genug! Das genügt!" make the likelihood seem remote), then any differences between the R. T. and the Theatre Union would begin to look perilously minimal. No doubt Epic Theater was anathema to the Theatre Union, but the extent to which the second poem takes its Danish "Arbeiterschauspielgruppe" to task for lacking an adequate political purpose would appear to deliver an even more devastating criticism of actors who share Brecht's goal but do not see the means to achieve it. In this respect, "Rede an . . ." gives us some sense of the gulf between Brecht's ideal political dramaturgy in action and the kinds of ensemble, even politically well-intentioned ones, with whom he was obliged to work during the exile period. To publish it first in *Theaterarbeit* is, however, to suggest that it is a work of unfinished business, rather than some historical document left over from the "Inzwischenzeit."

## Miscellaneous Poems

"Reinigung des Theaters von den Illusionen" (On Purging Theater of Illusions, *GBA*, 15:170–71) is part of a complex of poems on theater dating from shortly after the end of the Second World War. As the notes to the poem put it: "[es wurde geschrieben] im Zusammenhang mit ersten Überlegungen, nach Europa zurückzukehren und im deutschen Sprachraum zu inszenieren" (*GBA*, 15:409). It forms part of a series of loosely related poems, including "Das Theater, Stätte der Träume" (Theater, Home of Dreams), "Das Zeigen muß gezeigt werden" (Showing Has to Be Shown), "Über die Einfühlung" (On Empathy), and "Über die kritische Haltung"

(On Adopting a Critical Stance), all included in *GW* as "Gedichte aus dem *Messingkauf*." The original MSS were in some cases numbered to indicate position in a planned cycle, but the project seems to have been abandoned at an early stage. "Reinigung des Theaters von Illusionen" is marked "Zweites Gedicht," but so too at one stage was "Das Zeigen muß gezeigt werden." I do not propose to discuss these works in the same detail as the major dramaturgical poems of the mid-1930s, but will examine certain features, concentrating in particular on any new ideas to be found in them and on their strategies for expressing various dramaturgical points in innovative ways, especially by placing them in the new post-1945 context.

"Reinigung" begins with an evocation of the postwar world for which it was written. It gives a more concrete "Historisierung" of that world than is to be found in any of the other dramaturgical poems of the time, or, for that matter, in Brecht's theoretical writings in general, with the exception of the foreword to *Antigonemodell 1948* (*GBA*, 25:73–81). Brecht's poem sets the scene for what he provocatively calls a "Reinigung des Theaters von den Illusionen," that scene being one of large-scale physical destruction and cultural trauma at the end of the Second World War. In this respect, one can appreciate why he wanted it to appear near the beginning of the contemplated sequence, almost as a prologue. Its highly specific historical situating meant that it could serve as an overture to other, seemingly narrower theater poems. Unlike the contrast in "Über alltägliches Theater" between an anachronistic, ivory-tower bourgeois theater and the bustling proletarian world on the streets, the contrast is now, more pressingly, between ruined German theaters still living in the past and the forward-looking, yet war-torn Soviet Zone of Occupation trying to resurrect itself and needing, but not always receiving, appropriate cultural assistance from its actors and other theater people who should, according to Brecht's earlier "Brief an . . .," form culture's vanguard.

The poem's initial emphasis on "zerfallende Häuser" symbolizes the fact that the theater world's buildings, like the majority of actors and the plays still being staged in them, are now little more than cultural relics from a bygone and politically defeated age. Literally, of course, like so many buildings in Germany immediately after the defeat of the Nazi regime, the few remaining theaters were, if not destroyed, badly in need of rebuilding and renovation. Whether interpreted symbolically or literally, the image creates a greater sense of historical urgency and of the price now being paid for living in a world of theatrical and political illusions than informed "Über alltägliches Theater." The demeaning picture of audiences waiting breathlessly and desperately ("süchtig") for escapist drama with happy endings contrasts shockingly with the changed world outside, which is not so much bustling as crippled and trying to pick itself up and make a fresh start:

Überall anderswo
Sind die Menschen schon bereit, ein solches glückliches
Ende zu bereiten den Verwicklungen, welche sie erkannt haben
Als von Menschen bereitet, also von Menschen beendbar.
(GBA, 15:170)

This anodynely propagandistic image of the "liberated" East Germans as "Menschen [. . .] schon bereit, ein solches glückliches/ Ende zu bereiten, den Verwicklungen" of recent years employs dramatic terms to suggest that real happy endings will now be made possible by the creation, under Moscow's tutelage, of a new state. When it comes to seeing the world through red-tinted spectacles, this introduction only meets its match in the first scene of *Der kaukasische Kreidekreis,* the one set in the Soviet Union. While some of what follows reads like a reprise of "Über alltägliches Theater," the immediate post-1945 context gives greater force to the attack on culinary theater (although the term itself is no longer used). Indeed, the lines also read like a calculated counterpiece to the image of the hypnotized Weimar Republic audiences lampooned at the end of *Die Dreigroschenoper,* people content to settle for contrived operatic endings and untroubled that these seldom occur in real life. The world outside the theater, Brecht's poem of some fifteen years later proclaims, is starting to make happy endings a political reality, and yet, unable to grasp this, reactionary audiences still hunger after vicarious gratification. Phrases like "im schrecklichen Ende," "Unglück" and "in euren zerfallenden Häusern" suggest that Brecht thinks that bourgeois theater's day of reckoning has finally come and why.

The need for a *tabula rasa* implied by the title's cleansing image makes deliberately subversive play with Aristotelian vocabulary as mediated to German classicism by Lessing's *Hamburgische Dramaturgie.* In §4 of *Kleines Organon,* engaging in a lengthy polemical campaign against the powerful hold of tragedy over twentieth-century audiences and appropriating Lessing's Aristotelian terms, Brecht was soon to present the phenomenon of catharsis as evidence that too much theater bore traces of having evolved from "das Kultische," a useful term allowing him to attack Aristotle and Stanislavsky in one fell swoop (while also hinting at a further analogy in the cultic, irrational aspects of National Socialism's "ästhetisierte Politik," as Benjamin saw it): "jene Katharsis des Aristoteles, die Reinigung durch Furcht und Mitleid, oder von Furcht und Mitleid, ist eine Waschung, die nicht nur in vergnüglicher Weise, sondern auch recht eigentlich zum Zwecke des Vergnügens veranstaltet wird. Mehr verlangend vom Theater oder ihm mehr zubilligend, setzt man nur seinen eigenen Zweck zu niedrig" (*GBA,* 23:67). As we shall see in the next chapter, this argument is part of a broad frontal attack on the debilitating effects of tragedy and catharsis on modern theater. By contrast, "Reinigung des Theaters von den Illusionen" makes its case from a more immediate historical vantage-point.

The combined aesthetic and contemporary historical connotations of "Reinigung" are signs of just how inventively the campaign is now being waged. The main point here is that as long as it continues to peddle the "enjoyable" experience of being *purged* of fear and pity, postwar German theater will remain a kind of Augean stable, waiting to be *cleansed* of its detritus: the variety of poisons and potions in "der unreine Topf" mixed to induce "die alte billige Rührung." The Aristotelian concept of "purgation," already the subject of much debate (see Wimsatt and Brooks 1970, 36–37), has now acquired further associations of clearing away the rubble, detoxification and even denazification. The image that follows — of reactionary audiences still anxious to identify with the sufferings ("Leid") of some great military leader from a distant or legendary past, when the handiwork of real generals lies in the rubble all around them — is one embodiment of the central contradiction upon which "Reinigung des Theaters von den Illusionen" is constructed. The illusions of which theater has to be purged are both those of the theater of empathy and those of the recent fascist past. It is above all because of the latter that it has become necessary to pull down the "schlechtgeleimte Häuser," theaters in which opiates are still being pushed and where little seems to have changed. To compound our sense of the unworldliness of such theater, we learn how transposable ("transportabel") even the commodified emotions being marketed there are (an idea satirized in the phrase "Zwei Pfund Mimik"). Actors in a love scene are said to ape behavior they have eavesdropped on while observing their "gequälte Dienstboten" (itself a barbed social detail in the new, supposedly classless society). The actor charged with conveying a general's anguish has to put himself in the right frame of mind by recalling the last time his salary was cut. (Hardly what Stanislavsky meant by Emotion Memory!) Such pathetic exercises have little to do with "die Kunst der Beobachtung" advocated in the Danish poem, for the falseness, or facile "Transportabilität," of the emotions parroted onstage puts the theater's "schlechtgeleimte Welt" at a double remove from the stark reality the audience has just left behind on their way into the foyer. They have undergone an unworthy transformation comparable to the one "Über alltägliches Theater" showed the actor undergoing between dressing-room and stage. The main criticism of such strategies is that there are enough issues and events in the real world calling out for the audience's response, without people allowing themselves to be duped into irrelevant escapist emotionalism or actors needing to engage in trite exercises in Emotion Memory. That the concept of transposable emotions — or even the difference between the positive use of "Transportabilität" when applied to techniques that can be appropriated and politicized in Epic Theater and the pejorative connotation when used to ridicule the strategies of Emotion

Memory — figures so seldom in Brecht scholarship is again in part attributable to the fact that the non-discursive theoretical works that invoke them are rarely quarried for their dramaturgical insights.

"**Darstellung von Vergangenheit und Gegenwart in einem**" (Portrayal of Past and Present in One [*GBA*, 14:372–73]) begins with one of the standard objections from the standpoint of historicizing Epic Theater to the presentation of events onstage in order to give the impression that they are actually happening at the time of staging. "Das, was ihr darstellt, pflegt ihr so darzustellen / Als geschehe es jetzt."[27] However, the subsequent addition of the phrase "Jetzt und nur einmal" takes the accusation on to a new plane. Because of this sense, not only of immediacy, but of uniqueness, audiences are lulled into feeling at liberty to escape their real identities by pretending that what they are witnessing is a slice of reality unfolding. The solution offered this time is not the usual "Episierung" that narrates events as if they had happened in the past. It is the recommendation that the audience's relationship to the "jetzt" of the stage-action should be "vielfältig": they should remain conscious of the fictive pre- and post-history of what appears to be happening at the moment so that it is perceived as "aus dem Vorher kommend und ins / Nachher gehend." As a corollary, any sense of uniqueness to the illusion of events happening in the present should be countered by the actor's ability to suggest that what is being seen has been enacted repeatedly ("daß dieser Augenblick / Auf eurer Bühne oft wiederholt wird, gestern erst / Spieltet ihr ihn, und auch morgen soll / Sind da nur Zuschauer, wieder die Vorstellung sein"). Most important of all, the audience should themselves remain similarly conscious of their own prehistory and future, as well as their present capacity as audience ("Er sitzt nicht nur / In eurem Theater, sondern auch / In der Welt"). Although we are offered no practical suggestions as to how this can be achieved, a more sophisticated conception of temporal "Episierung" has been established than can be found in Brecht's earlier theoretical writings. Instead of hopes being pinned mainly on creating an effect of "Antiillusionismus," the audience is to be reminded of so many competing facts that, as a consequence, divided attention — and hence critical distance — is assumed to be the only possible result. Again, because this "Vielfalt" of relationships between audience and stage "present" is only treated satisfactorily in this one particular poem, the idea seldom figures in the secondary literature on Brecht's audience theory.

---

[27] The work represents a variation on Schiller's remark to Goethe (letter of 26 December 1797): "der Erzähler weiß schon am Anfang und in der Mitte das Ende, und ihm ist folglich jeder Moment der Handlung gleichgeltend." On drama and the present, see Schiller's "Über die tragische Kunst" in *Werke*, Nationalausgabe, 20, (Weimar: Hermann Böhlaus Nachfolger, 1962), 165.

**"Über die Einfühlung"** (*GBA,* 15:173), on a subject which one would have thought Brecht had explored from every conceivable angle by the time this work was written around 1945, nevertheless approaches its topic — exemplified in the effect of an actor's portrayal of a "Bauer" — from a fresh perspective. Only as a result of "mangelnde Urteilskraft," it is claimed, can an actor portray his character with such conviction that he even believes himself that he is a "Bauer" and no longer an actor. "Aber Schauspieler und Zuschauer / Können glauben, sie seien Bauern, wenn / Was sie fühlen, gar nicht das ist / Was ein Bauer fühlt. / Je echter ein Bauer dargestellt ist / Desto weniger kann der Zuschauer meinen / Daß er selber ein Bauer ist." The charge here is not the usual one that empathy is the opposite of, or prevents, critical distance, it is that blanket empathy leads to an essentialist leveling of differences between audience and character onstage: that audiences are persuaded to identify with the inauthentic, that is, with what remains so ahistorical and generalized that social differences are blurred, rather than with genuinely realistic, "historicized" depictions. To put down a marker to the effect that empathy is based on a false premise of this kind[28] was a bold move on the part of someone preparing the ground for a return to what had now become the Soviet Zone of Occupation. For the campaigns that would rage there to Brecht's disadvantage would not only be between the proponents of Socialist Realism and the formalists but would also bring the theater of critical distance on to a collision course with the wider aesthetic of emotional identification.

**"Über die kritische Haltung"** (*GBA,* 15:174) contains the *locus classicus* on criticism as a form of "eingreifendes Denken." The poem represents a response to the widespread misconception that criticism is invariably negative and unproductive (the Nazis would have said "zersetzend"). The reason suggested for such a misunderstanding is a dangerous one to point to in the East Germany of the time: "Das kommt, weil sie [people who hold such a view] im Staat / Mit ihrer Kritik nichts erreichen können." The counterargument falls into two parts. First, the claim that "Durch bewaffnete Kritik / Können Staaten zerschmettert werden," a historically understandable position in 1945, although the lines in all probability involve an allusion to Marx's *Zur Kritik der Hegelschen Rechtsphilosophie.*[29] But then, taking up the nature imagery of the 1935 poem "Rede an . . .," less destructive images of productive criticism are offered than that of destroying states:

---

[28] The links between such essentialism and the thinking behind Stanislavskian theater are spelt out in "Stanislavski's 'System'" (Counsell 1996, 26–29).

[29] "Die Waffe der Kritik kann allerdings die Kritik der Waffen nicht ersetzen, die materielle Gewalt muß gestürzt werden durch materielle Gewalt" (Marx-Engels 1958–68, 1:385).

Die Regulierung eines Flusses
Die Veredelung eines Obstbaumes
Die Erziehung eines Menschen
Der Umbau eines Staates
Das sind Beispiele fruchtbarer Kritik.
Und es sind auch
Beispiele von Kunst. (*GBA,* 15:174)

The imagery and examples chosen are seductive. Few readers are likely to react to them with the words Andreas uses in scene 1 of *Leben des Galilei*: "Nehmen Sie nicht lauter solche Beispiele, Herr Galilei. Damit schaffen Sie's immer. [. . .] Mit Beispielen kann man es immer schaffen, wenn man schlau ist" (*GBA,* 5:194). It is not by chance that "Der Umbau eines Staates" (rather than "Zerschmettern" or the standard term "Befreiung" or even "Besiegung") comes at the end of the asyndetic enumeration, for "Umbau" still contains the element of construction (also present in the GDR's legendary "Aufbaujahre"). Nor can it be fortuituous that it is in the very last line of the poem where we hear that these are also examples of art, not just of fruitful criticism in general. Arguably, the third example is closest to the interventionist agenda of Epic Theater, though what is stressed in all these illustrations is the identity of what might to many seem a mental activity that leads on to positive achievements. The gulf between the figurative and the pragmatic, between theory and praxis, might occasion certain difficulties, if one were to apply these sentiments to Brecht's own "eingreifendes Theater." But here at least is a model of the way in which the poet wanted his readers to think about the social purpose of Epic Theater; and it is a model predicated on arguments made in Marx's eleventh "Feuerbach-Thesis" of a century before.[30]

After the publication of *Theaterarbeit,* the flow of dramaturgical poetry slowed to a trickle. *Versuche* 14 merely republishes earlier poems and no further ones were added to the ever growing *Messingkauf* complex. Brecht's use of poetry for theorizing purposes thus peaked at three important junctures: in the mid-1930s, in the wake of the Theatre Union experience; in the mid-1940s, as preparation for a return to Germany (conceivably in part as a drafting of ideas that would be reformulated in *Kleines Organon*[31]); and at the time in the early fifties when it became clear that the prose contents be-

---

[30] "Wobei [Brecht] aus dem 'nicht-sondern' der Feuerbach-These ein 'nicht nur-sondern' macht" (*BHB,* 4:13).

[31] Given Brecht's tendency to use poems to sketch out material for scenes in later plays, it would be possible to interpret some of the works written around 1945 as systematic preparations for either *Kleines Organon für das Theater* or the ongoing *Messingkauf* project.

ing assembled for *Theaterarbeit* needed to be supplemented with further points made in poetic form — this at a time when Brecht probably knew that *Der Messingkauf* would never be completed. Not all of these dramaturgical poems of two decades relate to productions of single works; sometimes two or three of Brecht's plays are mentioned or alluded to in them, and because of this one finds the editors of various Brecht editions making rather arbitrary decisions about which section of his writings they belong in. The shorter poems on the theater tend to concentrate on practical staging matters (lighting, curtains, make-up, stage props, the actor's preparation and relationship to his/her lines) and seldom stand back to look at more general dramaturgical and aesthetic issues. Hence, when Siegfried Unseld published his anthology of Brecht's *Schriften zum Theater* in 1957, most of these works were put in the "Theater-Praxis" section. Unlike these and many of Brecht's other theater-poems, which are often little more than personal tributes, "Gelegenheitsgedichte," or *aides-mémoire* in verse form, the poems looked at in the present chapter are centrally concerned with general artistic principles rather than myopic detail. Key issues such as the importance of an ideological value center for an actor's observation of society and for effective role preparation, major differences between Stanislavskian and Epic Theater, the importance and impact of "Historisierung," and the role of emotions in the theater are all well to the fore. What is more, the dramaturgical poems treat such questions in ways that often differ quite substantially from the discussion of them in the theoretical writings in prose. And they find succinct and memorable figurative language and employ an impressive range of images and "Modelle" that only occasionally find their equivalent in the other theoretical writings.

# 4: Preparations for East Berlin: *Kleines Organon für das Theater* (1948)

IN APRIL 1948, Brecht informed the American Academy of Arts and Letters that he could not come to accept in person an award from it, as he was "at present living in Switzerland" (*GBA*, 29:447). During November and December 1947 and for most of 1948 he and Helene Weigel were staying at Feldmeilen near Zurich in connection with the staging of his *Antigone* "Bearbeitung" at the Chur Stadttheater, "eine Art preview für Berlin," as he explained to his son Stefan (*GBA*, 29:440). The *Antigone* production was not the only activity undertaken at the time with East Berlin in mind. In July Brecht wrote to Max Frisch: "Ich schreibe im Augenblick an einem 'Kleinen Organon für das Theater'" (*GBA*, 29:454). His journal entry for 18 August records that he was:

> mehr oder weniger fertig mit *Kleines Organon für das Theater*; es ist eine kurze Zusammenfassung des *Messingkauf*. Hauptthese: daß ein bestimmtes Lernen das wichtigste Vergnügen unseres Zeitalters ist, so daß es in unserm Theater eine große Stellung einnehmen muß. Auf diese Weise konnte ich das Theater als ein ästhetisches Unternehmen behandeln, was es mir leichter macht, die diversen Neuerungen zu beschreiben. Von der kritischen Haltung gegenüber der gesellschaftlichen Welt ist so der Makel des Unsinnlichen, Negativen, Unkünstlerischen genommen, den die herrschende Ästhetik ihm aufgedrückt hat. (*GBA*, 27:272)

In December 1948 he signed a publishing contract with the Kulturbund and *Kleines Organon* appeared in *Sinn und Form* in January 1949, the year of the founding of the German Democratic Republic.

In a discussion with Werner Hecht some time after Brecht's death, Helene Weigel explained the background to the above entry:

> WEIGEL. Die Schweiz, das war unsere Vorbereitung auf Berlin. Ich habe den Brecht gedrängt, daß er seine theoretischen Schriften ordnet. Da gab es so viel Angefangenes. Du brauchst ein Programm, hab ich gesagt, daß sie sehen, was du willst. Er war davon nicht begeistert, aber er hat eingesehen und das *Organon* geschrieben.

HECHT. Ach, das haben Sie angeregt?

WEIGEL. Ich bin froh, daß er es gemacht hat. Er war wirklich am Anfang verärgert von dem Vorschlag. Immer schleppte er viele Seiten Theorie mit herum und wollte sie ordnen. Aber er kam nie dazu, er hat sich davor auch etwas gedrückt, weil die Notizen tatsächlich sehr unübersehbar waren. Dennoch wußte er immer ganz genau, was er wollte. (Hecht 2000, 68)

Brecht's putting on record the idea that *Kleines Organon für das Theater* (Short Organum for the Theater) was a condensed version of *Der Messingkauf* shows him now more consciously writing with "die Nachgeborenen" in mind. In truth, the claim that the one work is "eine kurze Zusammenfassung" of the other needs to be treated with caution. The very suggestion that *Kleines Organon* had a main thesis is one pointer; the material comprising the *Messingkauf* complex is far too diffuse to be guided by any single "Hauptthese." Also, the specific way in which *Kleines Organon* treats theater as "ein ästhetisches Unternehmen," coupled with the extent to which the work evidently needs to find a way of defending socially critical drama from the charges of abstraction (formalism?) and negativity (not sharing Socialist Realism's idealized picture of society?) again draws attention to divergences, not common ground.

Hecht offers the most detailed account to date of the relationship between *Der Messingkauf* and *Kleines Organon* (Hecht 1972, 122–26). While stressing that *Kleines Organon* is "eine selbständige Arbeit" he claims: "Die Vorrede [zum *Organon*] scheint geradezu ein Bericht über die nächtlichen Gespräche zu sein" (121). On the treatment of Marxism, he concludes that "der Gegenstand wird [im *Messingkauf*] noch *in der Debatte* vorgestellt, im *Kleinen Organon* hingegen geht Brecht *vom Ergebnis der Debatte* aus" (124). Perhaps influenced by Brecht's Feldmeilen journal entry, he even suggests: "man könnte versucht sein zu sagen, das *Kleine Organon* [. . .] fasse die Dialoge des *Messingkaufs* als Thesen zusammen" (125). And how did the one work grow out of the other? According to Hecht: "Wenn er das *Kleine Organon* eine 'kurze Zusammenfassung des *Messingkaufs*' nannte, so hat er den früheren zweifellos nicht als 'Vorlage' benutzt. Es handelt sich um eine Zusammenfassung aus der Erinnerung" (126). Like Brecht himself, Hecht is in part concerned with the genetic aspect of the relationship. For others, the focus has been on differences of a more general order. Particularly striking, as Willett points out, is the generic dissimilarity: "if the *Messingkauf* was derived from *Galileo* the new work seems to relate both formally and stylistically to the *Novum Organum* of Francis Bacon" (*BT*, 205). This is not just one further difference, but a crucial contrast. The numbered paragraphs of the *organon* mode were probably chosen to ensure a more disciplined progression of propositions and subjects than could be found in *Der Messingkauf*'s seemingly open-ended amalgam of dialogue, essay, fragment, and poetry. Given the sprawling, unevenly developed elements that make up the *Messingkauf* project (what Weigel probably had in mind when she referred to "so viel Angefangenes" and so little completed), it would be just as difficult to imagine a "Zusammenfassung" of it as it would be to propose any single "Hauptthese."

The 1980 *Brecht Handbuch* points to a key methodological difference, with the purpose of suggesting that the later "Zusammenfassung" is a formal regression: "während der *Messingkauf* versucht hat, eine komplexe neue Form zu entwickeln, die bereits auf eine 'Überwindung' des alten Theaters zielt, ist das *Organon* [. . .] ein formaler Regress: hier wird in handliche (und 'lehrhafte') Sätze gefaßt, was der *Messingkauf* dialektisch und diskutierend entwickelt hat; das *Organon* — als Sammlung abgezogener Kernsätze — verweist auf eine Haltung, die nicht mehr davon überzeugt ist, daß der *Messingkauf* so ohne weiteres durchzusetzen ist" (Knopf 1980a, 458). We shall return to this assessment in the next chapter, when considering *Der Messingkauf*'s "Dialogform" (although this appears to be at odds with the more differentiated account of the tentative "dialogic" quality of *Kleines Organon* in the new *Handbuch* [*BHB*, 4:321–29]). Other differences between the two works also bring into question any notion of the one work's being a "Zusammenfassung" of the other: above all the sheer amount of new material *Kleines Organon* adds to the *Messingkauf* discussions, as well as the elements Brecht jettisons. For example, *Der Messingkauf*'s parochial concern with German Naturalism is only sporadically in evidence in *Kleines Organon* (§30 being the exception); and its distinction between "K-Typus" and "P-Typus" theater (a substantial ingredient in *GW*, but only cursorily alluded to in *GBA*) fails to come into its own in *Kleines Organon*. Even the significance of the neologism "Thaëter" (*GBA*, 22:761) is too obliquely touched on in *Kleines Organon* to reflect the reason for coining the term, convincingly set out in *Der Messingkauf*. Moreover, references in *Kleines Organon* to the advantages of an aesthetic framework within which to treat "die diversen Neuerungen" of Brechtian theater and to the unfortunate way in which "die herrschende Ästhetik" had been suspicious of socially critical drama establish a markedly different referential context from the one obtaining for *Der Messingkauf*. Mittenzwei, who on the whole has no difficulty with the "Zusammenfassung" thesis, concedes: "so waren doch einige Gesichtspunkte, wenn nicht neu, so doch weiter ausgebaut" (Mittenzwei 1987, 2, 263). While Brecht had his reasons for wishing to highlight continuities in his work, a new factor has entered the equation: one which makes the positioning of *Kleines Organon* in relation to his earlier dramaturgical pronouncements a far more delicate undertaking. "Notwendig machte sich eine Zusammenfassung seiner methodischen Überlegungen schon deshalb, weil Brecht vermeiden mußte, daß man ihn im Lichte seiner Ansichten vor 1933 vorstellte. [. . .] Deshalb betonte er im Vorwort zum *Organon* deutlicher als im *Messingkauf* die Veränderungen in seiner Ästhetik" (Mittenzwei 1987, 2, 263). While Mittenzwei talks of "Veränderungen in seiner Ästhetik," Brecht himself stresses that *Kleines Organon* is only now finally working within an aesthetic framework: "In den gelegentlichen theoretischen Äußerungen, Ausfällen, technischen Anweisungen, publiziert in der Form von Anmerkungen zu Stücken des Verfassers, wurde das Ästhetische nur beiläufig und verhältnismäßig uninteressiert berührt" ("Vorwort," *GBA*, 23:65). Such a grudging remark may risk under-representing just how often Brecht had touched on wider aesthetic questions in his previous writings. Little indication is given of where he had done so, although his various engagements with Aristotle's *Poetics*, Horace's *Ars poetica*, Lessing's *Hamburgische Dramaturgie* and Schiller's dramaturgical writings, as well as the aesthetics of Hegel and Lukács, constitute obvious points of contact. Nevertheless, when a character in "[V-Effekte, Dreige-spräch]" (*GBA*, 22:399) objects that spending too much time on "der Begriff '*das Tragische*'" amounts to a "längere[s] Verweilen in ästhetischen Gefilden," the participants tellingly take the point and quickly move on.

Although wanting to avoid being simplistically identified with the *Mahagonny* notes or the radical "Lehrstück" experiments, Brecht had not changed his spots in the way suggested in the "Vorrede" to *Kleines Organon*. If he had, how could the *Organon* be a "Zusammenfassung" of ideas dating back more than half a decade? As *BHB*, vol. 4 demonstrates, there are marked continuities between the themes of the *Organon* and the fragmentary material in *Der Messingkauf*. The ideas in §37 read like a condensed version of "Vergnügungstheater oder Lehrtheater?" And §§47–59 are primarily indebted to a series of essays dating from the 1930s, above all "Verfremdungseffekte in der chinesischen Schauspielkunst" and "Kurze Beschreibung einer neuen Technik der Schauspielkunst, die einen Verfrem-dungseffekt hervorbringt." Even the lead concept of a new Marxist Theater of the Scientific Age has its roots as far back as "Dialog über Schauspiel-kunst" of 1929–30 (cf. *GBA*, 21:279 and *BHB*, 4:317).

# The Genesis of "Kleines Organon": "Entstehungsgeschichten"

"Während des Krieges tritt anscheinend eine Pause in den theoretischen Erwägungen Brechts ein [. . .]. Es war während der Emigration in USA an anderes zu denken, und außerdem war Brecht [. . .] des vielen Theore-tisierens müde geworden" (Hultberg 1962, 167). In fact, despite the claims of the war effort and a certain lack of impetus caused by having no adequate

US readership for his theoretical views, Brecht made a number of attempts during the early and mid-1940s to pull his dramaturgical statements together and to produce new ones that could jointly form the basis for a major analytical survey of what at the time he still thought of as "non-Aristotelian" or "Epic Theater." Often the spur appears to have come from third parties. In 1946, the New York publishers Reynal & Hitchcock, then preparing Eric Bentley's *The Playwright as Thinker* for publication, contemplated bringing out a selection of Brecht's plays in English, with an introduction by Bentley himself. As Brecht's letter to him of 27 February makes clear, Bentley was to be entrusted with the lion's share of responsibility for selecting the plays, commissioning and vetting translations, handling related correspondence, and organizing publicity. In the event, the project failed to materialize, but one of its offshoots, according to Lyon and Fuegi 1976 and Lyon 1980, was a clearer awareness on Brecht's part of the need for a major theoretical statement, both for the American context and in preparation for the return to Europe.

Brecht reported to Elisabeth Hauptmann, in a letter of July-August 1946: "ich habe nachgedacht, was in einer *Einleitung* zu den gesammelten Stücken stehen müßte, damit die Leser eine profitable Einstellung bekommen können (und ich setze dabei voraus, daß Bentley nicht als Kritiker, sondern als Erklärer schreiben will)" (*GBA*, 29:387). The four ensuing paragraphs outlining what had to appear in Bentley's introduction bear little direct relation to the material in *Der Messingkauf* or *Kleines Organon*, but at least a sense of what was called for was beginning to crystallize. Brecht expresses disappointment that Bentley cannot visit him that summer to be briefed on his role as "Erklärer." As compensation, he promises Hauptmann: "Ich werde ihm jedoch eine kleine Sammlung meiner theoretischen Schriften vorbereiten" (*GBA*, 29:388). In August he sends his "[Notizen zur Einleitung einer Stücke-Ausgabe]" (*GBA*, 23:57–58). But Bentley planned to come at the task from a different angle. He sends Brecht *The Playwright as Thinker*, hoping in that way "to engage the dramatist in an exchange of letters he could publish" (Lyon 1980, 162), but also because he needed clarification of certain points before writing his introduction. Brecht played for time: "Ihre Aufforderung, ich solle von Ihrem Buch ausgehen, ist legitim; ich lese es mit wirklichem Vergnügen und langsam" (*GBA*, 29:388). For the moment, though, he remains more interested in quibbling with points in Bentley's study, which he nonetheless recommends should be translated into German.

According to Hans (John) Viertel, one of Brecht's collaborators at the time and son of Californian exiles Berthold and Salka Viertel, Brecht showed him a draft of *Kleines Organon* in the summer of 1946. If such an early version did exist,[1] it could be interpreted as evidence of Bentley's success in encouraging Brecht to set out his dramatic theory in one major authoritative document. His awareness that even "a sympathetic collaborator and promoter of his works like Bentley did not understand his theories to Brecht's satisfaction" (Lyon 1980, 163) could have spurred Brecht into action. Yet even if this were so (and there are competing genetic scenarios[2]), the emphasis was still on the need to present himself to *American* audiences. That much is clear from Bentley's jibe: "Like Shaw, you are more eager to explain your politics and your morality than your art. This is your privilege. But I warn you that you will never make any further advance in America unless you can dispel the illusions and doubts that at present surround your kind of enterprise" (quoted in Lyon 1980, 163).

Knopf (1980a, 458) dismisses the "US first draft" thesis on two main counts: first, the fact that the Feldmeilen journal entry refers unequivocally

---

[1] Reference to John Viertel's claim was first made in Lyon and Fuegi 1976. According to Lyon 1980, "no extant documents confirm his claim (Brecht kept no journal in 1946 [. . .]), but circumstantial evidence suggests that Viertel, a reliable informant on Brecht's American exile, might be right" (164). Such "circumstantial evidence" as there is includes a letter of August 1946 to Bentley, in which Brecht invokes "die Experimente Francis Bacons" in defense of Epic Theater against "die übliche neutralisierende Behandlungsweise" and "die beruhigenden Hinweise, es handle sich um Vorläufiges, Provisorisches, Unverbindliches": "(So sind die Experimente Francis Bacons nicht das Entscheidende, sondern die definitive Einführung des Experimentierens in die Wissenschaft)" (*GBA*, 29:397). A robust counterposition has recently been adopted in the *Kleines Organon* section of *BHB*, vol. 4: "Die Behauptung John Fuegis [in *Brecht & Co.*], beim *Kleinen Organon* handle es sich um 'eine direkte Entgegnung auf Eric Bentleys *The Playwright as Thinker*' [. . .] ist ebenso haltlos wie seine Einschätzung, die Schrift sei auf Grund 'Bentleys Ansporn' [. . .] entstanden" (*BHB*, 4:316). But what is here dismissed as "Fuegis Überschätzung der Rolle Bentleys bei der Entstehung von B.s Schrift" (*BHB*, 4:317), and, as expressed here, rightly censured, is only part of a wider and more cautiously presented picture, which can be found in Lyon and Fuegi 1976 and Lyon 1980. While noting that "zahlreiche andere [Ansätze] aus dem *Kleinen Organon* lassen sich bereits in früheren theoretischen Schriften B.s ohne weiteres nachweisen" (*BHB*, 4:317), the author of the *BHB* section on *Kleines Organon* nevertheless claims "konkrete [?] Vorarbeiten für den Text" do not predate January 1948. It is now unlikely that we will ever be able to identify the "viele Seiten Theorie" that Weigel found Brecht carrying about the Feldmeilen house, and whether they already reflected the influence of Bacon signaled in Brecht's August 1946 letter to Bentley or were merely uncoordinated fragments.

[2] Bentley writes: "I would welcome two things: a brief account of your philosophy of art, and [. . .] an account of Epic Theatre that deals with some of the difficulties raised by Edmund Fuller some years ago and, more recently, by myself" (quoted in Lyon 1980, 165). The reference is to Fuller 1938.

to 1948 as the work's time of writing, and second, because the form of the *Organon* and its status as a drastic departure from the method of *Der Messingkauf* suggest a later stage of composition. *Kleines Organon* is too unlike *Der Messingkauf* for a draft of it to have existed in 1946. But since no such draft is available for scrutiny, its arguments and methodology must remain as much matters of speculation as the question of whether or not it ever existed. Given that there is also no reference to such an early draft in Brecht's published writings, the grounds for skepticism seem strong and the circumstantial evidence for its existence somewhat tenuous. Yet if the real issue were not Viertel's claim to have set eyes on an early draft of the *Organon* but the possible existence of a sheaf of draft theoretical essays of the kind Weigel saw Brecht carrying around, then the role of possible US catalysts may not be quite so cut-and-dried.

A further episode in *Kleines Organon*'s complex "Entstehungsgeschichte," set at a slightly earlier stage than the one Lyon and Fuegi focus on, has Brecht responding with similar dissatisfaction to Max Gorelik's *New Theatres for Old*. In this case, there is a modicum of supporting documentation. Brecht's journal entry for 4 March 1941 reads:

> *Gorelik* schickt mir sein Buch über modernes Theater. Er behandelt episches Theater sehr fähig und vorsichtig, wenn es auch ein wenig nach Karbol riecht, da er seine Vorliebe für Laboratorien nicht verleugnen kann. Es wird mir klar, daß man von der Kampfstellung "hie ratio — hie emotio" loskommen muß. Das Verhältnis von ratio zu emotio in all seiner Widersprüchlichkeit muß exakt untersucht werden, und man darf den Gegnern nicht gestatten, episches Theater als einfach rationell und konteremotionell darzustellen. (*GBA*, 26:467)

For some time during 1944, with the defeat of Nazi Germany now only a matter of time, Brecht had been considering producing "eine umfangreichere Darstellung seiner Theatertheorie" (*GBA*, 23:445). A series of pieces were written in quick succession, most with consecutively numbered sections, giving the impression that they were conceived as forming part of a larger project. That the first of these[3] was "Kleines Privatissimum für meinen Freund Max Gorelik" has led to the assumption that Brecht had become aware of the need for some authoritative theoretical clarification by the rather selective and less than acceptable treatment of his work in *New Theatres for Old*. Gorelik had at one time been that rare animal, a well-disposed American supporter of Brecht's theater. But he had over the years mellowed,

---

[3] The pieces, all in *GBA*, vol. 23, are: "Kleines Privatissimum für meinen Freund Max Gorelik" (37–39), "Zweites der kleinen Gespräche mit dem ungläubigen Thomas" (39–41), "[Dramatik der großen Stoffe]" (41), "[Charaktertragik und Situationstragik]" (42), and "[Neue Anweisungen für das Theater]" (55).

becoming a convert to Stanislavskianism, as Brecht noted in his journal for 12 June 1944:

> [Ich] sagte Gorelik, daß er sich verändert habe, und gab ihm ein paar Thesen. Wieder kam er mit "ein Drama braucht Spannung, climax und identification," er könne nicht verstehen, wenn er sich nicht einfühle. Ich sprach gegen eine Wand, als ich auseinandersetzte, wie wenig durch Einfühlung in einen Betroffenen zu verstehen ist. Er kann von dem Interesse am "to sell the story" nicht weggebracht werden. Und am Verkauf von shocks und Emotionen. (*GBA*, 27:191)

Brecht's 1944 pieces can, in the light of this, be read as pilots for *Kleines Organon*, especially those parts dealing with what is there referred to as "das Theater, wie wir es vorfinden." The fact that *Kleines Organon* ended up looking like a composite version of some of Brecht's earlier theoretical writings, above all from the late 1930s, is explained in the "Vorrede" by reference to recent history and in particular the deprivations of exile: "die Häufung von Neuerungen bei dem Fortfall praktischer Demonstrations-möglichkeiten in der Nazizeit und im Krieg legen nun den Versuch nahe, diese Spezies Theater auf seine Stellung in der Ästhetik hin zu prüfen oder jedenfalls Umrisse einer denkbaren Ästhetik für diese Spezies anzudeuten" (*GBA*, 23:66).

Although the series of new theoretical drafts had begun with a not-so-private "Privatissimum" containing a number of references to the contemporary American cultural scene,[4] there is evidence that the context for the reception of Brecht's theoretical project had changed between 1944 and 1948. In the case of the more Eurocentric *Kleines Organon*, it would have been difficult to read the reference to a dominant aesthetic as applying to the United States. "Artistisch betrachtet," Brecht once declared, "ist [der Striptease-Akt] immer noch das Beste, was das amerikanische Theater hervorgebracht hat" (*GBA*, 23:52). In the draft pieces following on from "Kleines Privatissimum," he continues to make dismissive remarks in the same provocative vein about Broadway and the "culinary" nature of American theater in general. But despite the hold of the Stanislavsky System, he refrained from conjuring up the bogeyman of an American "aesthetic." The

---

[4] There are references to Hollywood, Broadway, Clark Gable, Louis B. Mayer and MGM, the Theatre Guild, and the progressiveness of American fiction in contrast to theater; also some shrewd observations on William (Wilhelm) Dieterle's historical film biographies for Warner Brothers (*The Story of Louis Pasteur* [1936], *The Life of Emile Zola* [1937]), and *Dr Ehrlich's Magic Bullet* [1940]), a biopic about the man who discovered the syphilis antidote Salversan. The latter made the theme of Ibsen's *Ghosts* obsolete, according to Brecht. His discovery is also of relevance to the reference to Ibsen's work in §34 of *Kleines Organon*.

alleged hostility towards theater displaying a "kritische Haltung" referred to in the Feldmeilen journal entry was hardly part of some constructible American aesthetic. As Lyon and Fuegi have shown, what rankled with Brecht was American theater's compulsive need for a comfortingly unquestioning form of realism combined with obligatory happy endings. But any battle between Brecht and the theater of his host country was one-sided. There could be no bilateral conflict in the mid-1940s because the American theater Establishment was largely unaware of Epic Theater's existence. The remarks in *Kleines Organon* about an ingrained hostility to any form of critical theater are as much, if not more, pertinent to a liberated Eastern Europe, gradually coming into the orbit of Zhdanov's doctrine of Socialist Realism. In addition to his stance in the "Expressionismusdebatte," Brecht's various essays dating from 1938–39 — on Lukács's predilection for the nineteenth-century historical novel, on forms of realism and the jejune doctrine of Socialist Realism ( *GBA,* 22:423–45, 456–57, 460–66) — make it clear that he had been aware for some time just where conflicts were likely to arise upon his return to East Germany. Within such an Eastern bloc framework, even the juxtaposition of a verb like "aufdrücken" with the phrase "die herrschende Ästhetik" becomes more sinister than would have been the case, even despite McCarthyism, had Brecht still been writing primarily with contemporary American theater in mind.

According to the *GBA* note to the Feldmeilen journal entry: "Brecht plant bereits während der Arbeit an *Galileo* in Kalifornien eine Darstellung seiner Theatertheorie in der Form des Baconschen Organons. In der Schweiz regt ihn Helene Weigel dazu an, die Arbeit fertigzustellen, um sie für den Start der beabsichtigten theaterpraktischen Arbeit in Berlin als Konzept zur Verfügung zu haben" ( *GBA,* 27:531). The operative word here is "fertigstellen." Other commentators, by contrast, refer to *Kleines Organon* either as "im Sommer 1948 verfaßt" (for example, Mittenzwei 1987, 2:262) or state as incontrovertible fact that it "entstand [. . .] im Sommer 1948" ( *BHB,* 4:316). We are dealing here not just with rival claims about the date of the amorphous work's first drafting and who was the catalyst, but with competing views of why the work was written. In Mittenzwei's opinion, Weigel convinces Brecht that, in the light of the *Kulturpolitik* of the Soviet Zone of Occupation, it was "wichtig [. . .], mit einem programmatischen Anspruch aufzutreten" (Mittenzwei 1987, 2:262). Bentley's advice, by contrast, is clearly given with an American reception in mind. Granted that Brecht in exile had in the past as often as not prepared theoretical statements for the country he was going to rather than the one he was in, Weigel's account becomes all the more persuasive, although this does not totally discount the part played by either Bentley or Gorelik in bringing Brecht back to the drawing board and being the catalyst for preliminary work towards such a project. Nevertheless, even draft material from the Californian period that ended up in *Kleines Organon* would have needed to be substantially recast by 1948 if it was to have the desired impact in East Berlin. Witness the draft "Vorrede" to the *Organon* in which Brecht declares:

> *Die nachfolgenden Notizen über ein neues Theater sammelnd,* kommt es dem Verfasser zu Bewußtsein, sie können aufgenommen werden als eine Antwort auf die hin und wieder aus seinem unglücklichen Land ertönenden Rufe nach Neuem auf verschiedenen Gebieten. Er gibt daher lieber schnell die Versicherung ab, daß sie einfach im Verlauf seiner Arbeit niedergeschrieben sind, nachdem er nahezu zwanzig Stücke verfaßt, mit einer Reihe von Theatern verschiedener Nationalität gearbeitet, einiges Theoretische veröffentlicht und dieses falsch interpretiert gelesen hat. ( *Nachlass,* quoted *GBA,* 23:459–60, my emphasis)

Brecht's denial that he is merely responding to recent calls from his "unglückliches Land" for some appropriate mission statement and his assertion that the *Organon* "Notizen" were written in response to "false interpretations" or, one might surmise in this particular case, the kind of misplaced emphases that both *New Theatres for Old* and *The Playwright as Thinker* offered seem somewhat disingenuous. Even if he was not responding to a call, Weigel was right in thinking that Brecht needed to return to Berlin with a high-profile program. But the most revealing comment concerns the admission that the material had been accumulating over a long period of time "im Verlauf seiner Arbeit." This suggests a gestation period that contradicts the "1948 abgefaßt" hypothesis.

Knopf's point that significant qualitative differences between *Der Messingkauf* and *Kleines Organon* are *prima facie* evidence of a substantial elapse of time between the two works is not to be dismissed lightly, even if it is difficult to translate the suggestion into a mechanism for gauging just where the main bulk of draft *Kleines Organon* material should be placed on a spectrum stretching from 1939–40, the first period of intensive work on *Der Messingkauf,* and 1944, the time of Brecht's alleged response to *New Theatres for Old,* or 1946, when John Viertel recollected seeing a first draft of *Kleines Organon,* or even 1948, the year *Kleines Organon* was undoubtedly ready for the press. What is beyond dispute, even as early as the time of the contretemps with Gorelik, was that Brecht would eventually return to Europe, in all probability East Berlin, and that he was well aware of the need to equip himself with an up-to-date theoretical passport.

## The "Vorrede" and the Rhetoric of Positioning

Despite the emphasis on theater as a "Stätte der Unterhaltung," from its title onwards *Kleines Organon* displays much concern with the category of usefulness: both the work's own utilitarian value for practioners of Epic Theater and theater's politically didactic function within society. Indeed, "Organon" means "instrument." Unfortunately, to substitute the Latin "Organum" for the Greek "Organon," as English discussions of the work often do, risks implying too exclusive an indebtedness to Francis Bacon's *Novum Organum* of 1620. Brecht may have even deliberately opted for the Greek term because it was used collectively for Aristotle's various writings on logic or he may have done so because it also occurs in the title of the standard German translation of Bacon's *Novum Organum*.[5] Whichever the main referential framework, Brecht's *Organon* was obviously intended as a helpful tool "*für* das Theater." Although Bacon himself repeatedly referrred to Aristotle's *organon* concept, as has been demonstrated (Knopf 1980a, 459) his predilection for the aphoristic is a matter of destroying long-established systems in order to introduce doubt and combine theory with practice in new experimental ways that Galilei's work had already prefigured. Hence, one could apply Brecht's description "nicht-aristotelisch" to the *Novum Organum-Kleines Organon* relationship, in the sense that the one work is a *Kontrafaktur* of the other. Although this might suggest that *Kleines Organon* was essentially a Baconian work conceived to apply to theater the principles the *Novum Organum* had established for modern scientific enquiry, Brecht's theoretical work in some respects nevertheless remains close to the "philosopher's handbook" quality of Aristotle's collective writings on logic. It has even been argued that *Kleines Organon* is "formal stark von Bacon beeinflusst" (*BHB*, 4:318), while the *Novum Organum* ("das sich formal an Aristoteles' *Organon* anlehnt und sich inhaltlich damit auseinander setzt") stands in a more ambivalent relationship to Aristotle's work. But such a picture foregrounds surface structural affinities at the risk of failing to do justice to the difference between an authoritative Aristotelian *organon* and a similarly organized Baconian inductive *organum*. Any attempt to present Brecht's numbered sections as "aphorisms" (e.g. *BHB*, 4:175, 318) misleadingly suggests a formal indebtedness only to Bacon, whereas the work in many respects stands more at the watershed between its two models. Indeed, the implicit association with Bacon's *Novum Organum* communicates much more a sense of being at the onset of a paradigm change. This may explain why, according to Strehler, in a discussion with Italian students Brecht referred, in what looks like a Freudian slip, to "das, was ich im *Neuen Organon* sagte" (cited in *BHB*, 4:329).

---

[5] Brecht knew Bacon's Latin work, in J. H. von Kirchmann's German translation (Bacon 1870); an annotated copy is in his *Nachlassbibliothek*. In the German, any connotative difference between "Organon" and "Organum" has been lost.

As is appropriate for a work intended as a tool or user's manual, the *Organon* begins with a clarity of exposition and an air of step-by-step methodological caution: "In der Folge wird untersucht, wie eine Ästhetik aussähe, bezogen von einer bestimmten Art, Theater zu spielen, die seit einigen Jahrzehnten praktisch entwickelt wird" (*GBA*, 23:65). This is "induktive Theorie" in the same sense as Gorelik's *New Theaters for Old* had emphasized that Brechtian theater was "inductive theater." Nevertheless, the authoritative tone of the "Vorrede" tends to mask some of the more problematic features of Brecht's method in the work. At issue is not the at times self-consciously experimental nature of the undertaking: the attempt to imagine how an aesthetic *would look* when extrapolated from a certain form of theater, that is, Epic Theater seen as Theater for the Scientific Age. Evidently, such an aesthetic is presented in a way that seeks to avoid becoming apodictic or dogmatically prescriptive. But with Brecht about to return to East Berlin, there is a sense in which the *Organon,* notwithstanding its cautiously inductive discourse, is at the same time so formulated as to assume the confidence of both an aesthetic and a program, yet without appearing to overtly challenge the Eastern bloc's aesthetic orthodoxies.

Brecht's aim was an aesthetic framework that would be the key to an understanding of "die diversen Neuerungen" (*GBA*, 27:272) associated with Epic Theater. Hence, the prefatory paragraph's assertion "es wäre zu schwierig, etwa die Theorie der theatralischen Verfremdung außerhalb einer Ästhetik darzustellen." Earlier theoretical writings by Brecht had of course shown this not to be true. But setting aside such local presentational difficulties, the main problem thrown up by the "Vorrede" lies neither in the inductive, calculatingly non-prescriptive and yet firm approach nor in the unresolved question of whether what had earlier been theorized as "Epic Theater" was about to be integrated into a pre-existent aesthetic or whether the outlines of a new aesthetic were being extrapolated from the practice of Epic Theater. Rather, it concerns the restricted scope of what is about to be formulated. Even if most aesthetics of drama have to some degree been "bezogen von einer bestimmten Art, Theater zu spielen," it was generally the case, at least until the Romantic period, that their very prescriptiveness or broad consensual referentiality made them applicable to whole periods and genres and binding for entire cultural communities. Uncharitably, one might question the value of an "aesthetic" based not so much on Epic Theater in general as on one playwright's work or his perception of how plays by other dramatists needed to be produced. Brecht could be charged with not having responded in the right spirit to Bentley's accusation that he gave the appearance of talking about theater in general, but "you brushed aside all modern art except your own kind" (quoted in Lyon 1980, 163). In his defense, one could argue that Brecht is not just writing about his own work, but about what he hopes will become the theater of the modern age. Viewed tactically, the prominence of the term "Ästhetik" in the "Vorrede" is also intended to imply the emergence of a new aesthetic with more than enough substance to be seen as the alternative to "die herrschende Ästhetik" within the Soviet sphere of influence.

What Brecht sees as the main thesis of *Kleines Organon*, "daß ein bestimmtes Lernen das wichtigste Vergnügen unseres Zeitalters ist, so daß es in unserm Theater eine große Stellung einnehmen muß," figures far less prominently in the *Messingkauf* fragments, yet it had been a theme in Brecht's theoretical writings for more than a decade and a half and would remain so until the final year of his life (cf. "[Über Kunstgenuß]," *GBA*, 23:385–86). What is new in *Kleines Organon* is the linking of such an assumption with an approach to theater as an "ästhetisches Phänomen": "Behandeln wir das Theater als eine Stätte der Unterhaltung, wie es sich in einer Ästhetik gehört, und untersuchen wir, welche Art der Unterhaltung uns zusagt!" (*GBA*, 23:66). A journal entry for 25 February 1941 concerning the *Messingkauf* complex already notes: "In der ästhetischen Sphäre, die übrigens keineswegs als 'über' der doktrinären gelegen auszusehen ist, wird die Frage des Lehrhaften eine absolut ästhetische Frage, die sozusagen autark gelöst wird. Das Utilitaristische verschwindet hier in eigentümlicher Weise: es taucht nicht anders auf als etwa in der Aussage, Nützliches sei schön. Die praktikablen Abbildungen der Realität entsprechen lediglich dem Schönheitsgefühl unserer Epoche" (*GBA*, 26:457).[6]

The prologue's suggestion that it is apt for an aesthetic to treat theater as first and foremost a place of entertainment is by no means as self-evident as the argument appears to assume. Horace's *Ars poetica* retains a more differentiated position on the subject: "Aut prodesse volunt aut delectare poetae / aut simul et iucunda et idones dicere vita" (lines 333–34). In the influential *L'Art poétique* (1674) of Nicolas Boileau, the case is made for pleasurable entertainment and utilitarian pragmatism in equal measure, rather than on behalf of mere pleasure: "Qu'en savantes leçons votre muse fertile / Partout joigne au plaisant le solide et l'utile" (4, 87–88). In general, from the Renaissance and German Baroque until the last third of the eighteenth century, the notion of usefulness, now given a specifically Christian interpretation, predominates, with pleasure being at times reduced to the status of a necessary compromise between lofty moral purpose and catering to more self-indulgent literary appetites. The preface to Grimmelshausen's

---

[6] The final sentence here, with its claim that what is "praktikabel" (i.e. critical pictures of an oppressive society that can be subsequently translated into direct "interventionist" action; he elsewhere talks of "exekutive Kritik" in the same sense) is a central plank in Brecht's conception of theater as "eingreifendes Denken." Whether intervention amounts to changing the way people think or changing their world, or both, receives different emphases in Brecht's theoretical writings on theater.

*Simplicissimus Teutsch* (1668), for example, refers to the novel as "Überauß lustig / und männiglich nutzlich zu lesen" (the standard Baroque formula, as usual reversing the order of *prodesse* and *delectare* in Horace, but allowing for a combination of pleasure and usefulness rather than a choice between the two). The preface to Grimmelshausen's sequel, *Trutz Simplex: Oder ausführliche und wunderseltsame Lebensbeschreibung der Ertzbetrügerin und Landstortzerin Courasche* (1670), a novel Brecht had particular reason to take to heart because of his own dramatic treatment of the Courage figure, resorts to a similar formula: "Eben so lustig / annehmlich un nutzlich zu betrachten / als Simplicissimus selbst."[7]

A century later, the time-honored Horatian pairing was beginning to lose currency. Bodmer's *Critische Abhandlung von dem Wunderbaren in der Poesie* (1740) had exclusively stressed the pleasures of the imagination. Yet while the *pleasurable* aspect might have appealed to Brecht, he would no doubt have wanted to substitute "learning through discovery" for "the imagination." Baumgarten's *Aesthetica* (1750) argued that art is neither *utile* nor *dulce*, but there is no evidence that Brecht ever read this founding work of German aesthetics. Hagedorn uses the word "das Gefällige" (the closest one comes to Brecht's own "das Wohlgefällige"), while underlining the importance of "das Gesellschaftliche." And although Brecht's published writings refer to eleven of Nietzsche's books, *Die Geburt der Tragödie aus dem Geiste der Musik* (The Birth of Tragedy from the Spirit of Music, 1872), the work that furnished the most original aesthetic theory for Brecht's own century, is not among them. Brecht shows little or no interest in the period when the *prodesse-delectare / utile-dulce* paradigm is being superseded by other paradigms, some foregrounding pleasure or at least non-didactic purposes. Yet there is one exception to this reluctance to place *Organon* within a post-Renaissance tradition of aesthetics. That is to say, there are distinct parallels between parts of *Kleines Organon* and Schiller's *Über den Grund des Vergnügens an tragischen Gegenständen* (On the Cause of Pleasure in Tragic Subjects, 1792), where theater's purpose is seen as "die Hervorbringung [des] Vergnügens," "ein Zweck [. . .], der schlechterdings nur durch moralische Mittel erreicht werden könne, daß also die Kunst, um das Vergnügen als ihren wahren Zweck vollkommen zu erreichen, durch die Moralität ihren Weg nehmen müsse."[8] Brecht's journal for 1 September, the month after he had completed *Kleines Organon*, reads:

---

[7] On this point I am indebted to Ehrenzeller 1973, esp. 130–31, and Voßkamp 1973, in particular the discussion of the Christian implications of "Nutzen und Belusten / prodesse & delectare, wie Horatius redet" in Sigmund von Birken's preface to *Die Durchleuchtige Syrerinn Aramena* (70–71).

[8] See Kesting 1956, Hultberg 1962 (170–71) and Kobel 1992 (129–30). Kobel gives a detailed account of the similarities between Schiller's treatment of "das Moralische"

Lese jetzt amüsiert Schillers "Vergnügen an tragischen Gegenständen."
[*sic*] Er beginnt, wie ich im "Organon," mit dem Vergnügen als dem
Geschäft des Theaters, wehrt sich wie ich gegen Theorien, die das
Theater für die Moral einspannen (und dadurch adeln) wollen, bringt
aber dann sogleich alles in Ordnung, indem er das Vergnügen ohne
Moral sich nicht denken kann, d.h. das Theater genügt der Sittlichkeit
nicht etwa, indem es eben vergnügt, sondern kann angeblich gar nicht
vergnügen, wenn es nicht moralisch ist. Das Moralische muß also nicht
vergnüglich sein, damit es ins Theater darf, sondern das Vergnügen
muß moralisch sein, damit es ins Theater darf. Ich selber mache freilich
etwas recht Ähnliches mit dem Lernen, wenn ich es einfach zu einem
Vergnügen unserer Zeit mache. (*GBA*, 27:273)

It is as if Schiller's essay had offered Brecht a defamiliarizing strategy for observing his own method in *Kleines Organon*. But his amusement at discover-
ing that in (once again) declaring learning to be the source of greatest
pleasure he had ended up treating the relationship of usefulness to pleasure
in much the same way as Schiller had treated "das Moralische" is no damn-
ing moment of destructive honesty. Rather, it was part of an awareness that
he belonged to a long and venerable aesthetic tradition traceable back to
Horace's *Ars poetica*. The admission in no way undermines the position
adopted in the "Vorrede" to *Kleines Organon*, according to which the state
of society's and theater's "Kult des Schönen" and "Abneigung gegen das
Lernen und [. . .] Verachtung des Nützlichen" makes such a stand necessary.
The prologue's contrast between "die herrschenden moralischen oder
geschmacksmäßigen Vorschriften" and Epic Theater's "Neigung zu
gesellschaftlichen Tendenzen" legitimizes such a position.

In the light of Mittenzwei's suggestion that *Kleines Organon* was in part
written to prevent Brecht's being associated upon his return to East Berlin
with his earlier, Weimar Republic theories, it could be argued that the
"Vorrede" more than once risks giving hostages to fortune: first, by quoting
a passage from the *Mahagonny* notes reminding readers of his declared intention at that time "aus dem Reich des Wohlgefälligen zu emigrieren"
(*GBA*, 23:66). The passage, the concluding part of the notes, reads:

> *Für Neuerungen — gegen Erneuerung!*
> Die Oper "Mahagonny" ist vor drei Jahren, 1927, geschrieben. In den
> anschließenden Arbeiten wurden Versuche unternommen, das
> Lehrhafte auf Kosten des Kulinarischen immer stärker zu betonen. Also
> aus dem Genußmittel den Lehrgegenstand zu entwickeln und gewisse
> Institute aus Vergnügungsstätten in Publikationsorgane umzubauen.
> (*GBA*, 24:84)

---

and "Vergnügen" and Brecht's discussion of the relationship between learning and
pleasure.

This sounds like the austere Brecht of the "Lehrstücke" period casting aside "das Kulinarische" (even in the parodied form in which it had appeared in *Mahagonny* and *Die Dreigroschenoper*), and seeing the necessary alternative to it in "das Lehrhafte," but not the kind of "lustvolles Lernen" that he would theorize in the 1933 notes to *Die Mutter*. In the *Kleines Organon* "Vorrede," not only has "das Kulinarische" been confusingly equated with "das Wohlgefällige," but the motives for writing didactic works and even the integrity of the final paragraph of the *Mahagonny* notes also appear to have been brought into question. The reason for this declaration is now trivialized as no more than a kind of smokescreen, with the purpose "sich die Ästheten der Presse vom Leibe halten [zu] können." But this rewrites literary history. In the absolute sense suggested above, Brecht had never carried out his intention of emigrating from the realm of enjoyment; and in any case no one can *partly* emigrate or do so *half-heartedly*. From at the latest *Die Mutter* onwards, the equation of "Lernen" with "Vergnügen" meant that he had only emigrated in the eyes of some of his least understanding detractors. If the throwaway reason given for ending the *Mahagonny* notes seems more question-begging than illuminating, it is surprising that Brecht chooses to draw attention to this passage. Perhaps the intention was to offer a "Verfremdung" of his present position in the light of earlier misconceptions of just what depths of unapologetic didacticism Epic Theater could sink to. No doubt, the contrast between the figurative idea of "emigrieren" and another metaphor, just as palpably indebted to the exile experience — "uns in diesem Reich [des Wohlgefälligen] niederzulassen" — was inserted to conjure up the picture of a Brecht, having spent an unconscionably long time in exile in the capitalist West, now a reformed man. The Prodigal Son has returned to his true home, would seem to be the message. But the twist is that the Prodigal Son of the prologue's extended metaphor claims to be returning, not to the realm of Socialist Realism, but to "das Reich des Wohlgefälligen." *BHB*, vol. 4 rightly points to the humor in *Kleines Organon,* and one might add: particularly in the "Vorrede," some of whose effects have been described as "schelmisch" (*BHB*, 4:321). There is much play with the readers' expectations here, both those of prejudiced readers who still equate Brecht with the austerity of his late Weimar works and of people for whom he is still the Brecht of *Die Dreigroschenoper.* Some of this playfulness can be seen in his repeated prediction that such an assumed change of heart will be met with dismay by those who always thought they had found his Achilles heel. Yet such teasing nevertheless risks introducing an unnecessarily confrontational element, patronizingly predicting, as it seems to do, that general consternation will be the response to any such *volte-face* and that almost everyone would be happier if he were to continue making the same mistakes he is assumed to have made in the past. If Brecht's ostensible return to "das Reich des Wohlgefälligen" is deemed to have occurred by the time *Kleines*

*Organon* appeared, this can scarcely be taken literally, assuming that the implication is that East Berlin itself was such a realm. That would indeed be "schelmisch," given the highly prescriptive Socialist Realist aesthetic being imposed by the *Kulturpolitiker* of the new Stalinist regime. As all this suggests, the prologue to *Kleines Organon* plays a series of cunning games with the image of the East Germany Brecht would like to be returning to, rather than his actual destination.

Only the reader attuned to the ironies and playfulness of this "Vorrede," itself an enjoyable and subtly enlightening piece of complex writing, will appreciate that Brecht is saying something very different from what he seems to be confessing. It is surely not by chance, then, that the later paragraph in which the phrase "Stätte der Unterhaltung" first occurs begins with the words "Widerrufen wir also [. . .]." After all, the idea of a tactical recantation must already be tinged with a certain sense of situational irony, coming from the man who wrote scenes 13 and 14 of *Leben des Galilei*. Brecht is not in any simple sense a lost soul recanting what is presented as his earlier misguided position on entertainment as a cultural luxury in dark times. This has been indicated at a number of earlier places in the prologue: in the diagnosis of theater's "Entleerung von allem Wissenswerten" as "ein Verfallsmerkmal," with the claim that "die falschen Abbildungen des gesellschaftlichen Lebens auf den Bühnen [. . .] entlockten ihm [Brechtian theater] den Schrei nach wissenschaftlich exakten Abbildungen" and the observation "den Kult des Schönen, der betrieben wurde mit der Abneigung gegen das Lernen und der Verachtung des Nützlichen, lehnte es verächtlich ab." Despite these pointers, the one thing Brecht is reluctant to do at this early stage is to make too explicit the link between a general conception of the theater as a "Stätte der Unterhaltung" and the joy of learning for the children of the Scientific Age. He is keeping his powder dry until the claim can be made as part of an unfolding historical-cum-dialectical account of how Epic Theater came to assume the role of Theater of the Scientific Age.

Such maneuvering might have been less multi-layered if there were a sense in which Brecht had actually "emigrated" from the realm of the enjoyable in the late 1920s and early 1930s, or at least if there were adequate evidence to suggest he himself believed he had done so. In reality, the contrast in the prologue to *Kleines Organon* between Brecht then and Brecht now is more a rhetorical strategy, and as such an illustration of the role of wit in the realm of "das Wohlgefällige." Well before "Vergnügungstheater oder Lehrtheater?" (1935) — the essay usually associated with Brecht's views on the relationship between entertainment and didacticism — one finds him making the key point, in respect of *Die Mutter,* that any simple distinction between learning and enjoyment in the theater is based on a false dichotomy:

Einer der Haupteinwände der bürgerlichen Kritik gegen die nicht-aristotelische Dramatik vom Typus der "Mutter" stützt sich auf eine ebenfalls rein bürgerliche Trennung der Begriffe "unterhaltsam" und "lehrreich." Danach ist die "Mutter" vielleicht lehrreich (wenn auch nur [. . .] für einen kleinen Teil der möglichen Zuschauer), aber bestimmt nicht unterhaltend (nicht einmal für diesen kleinen Teil). Dieser Trennung nachzugehen ist nicht ohne Reiz. Es mag über-raschen, daß hier eine Degradierung des Lernens schlechthin beab-sichtigt ist, indem es nicht als Genuß vorgestellt wird. In Wirklichkeit wird natürlich der Genuß, indem er so sorgfältig von jedem Lehrwert entleert wird, degradiert. Aber man braucht sich nur umzusehen, welche Funktion das Lernen in der bürgerlichen Gesellschaftsordnung hat. [. . .] Die Erinnerung an die schreckliche Qual, unter der die bürgerliche Jugend ihr "Wissen" eingetrichtert bekommt, hält den zu seiner "Unterhaltung" ins Theater Gekommenen ab, sich wieder behandeln zu lassen wie einer, "der auf der Schulbank sitzt." Die Haltung des Lernenden ist diffamiert. (*GBA*, 24:134)

The "Vorrede" specifically associates emigrating from the realm of the enjoyable with the *Mahagonny* notes, yet even if this puts the emphasis on opera's need to find a new, politically constructive function, few commen-tators have ever equated the principal works of Epic Opera with un-adulterated didacticism or systematic expulsion of the enjoyable from the theater.[9] Moreover, the above remarks about learning and enjoyment, in-spired by the mixed reception of the original Berlin production of Brecht's Gorky adaptation, are more concerned with painful memories of authoritar-ian classroom situations or the general anti-intellectual antipathy towards learning *per se*. Any talk of an "emigration" only makes sense when read as a reflection of the bourgeoisie's perception of the Brecht of the final years of the Weimar Republic. By the same token, any programmatic U-turn back to the realm of the enjoyable by the time of *Kleines Organon* would only be in the eyes of those who have either failed to understand Brecht's works, were unfamiliar with his dramatic theories, or were in any case laboring under their prejudices about what activities are enjoyable and the feeling that all learning was anathema.

The section entitled "Das Lehrtheater" in "Vergnügungstheater oder Lehrtheater?" reiterates many of the prejudices that been explored two years before in the notes to *Die Mutter* in *Versuche* 7: didactic situations are pa-tronizing, learning is not enjoyable because of the draconian or boring con-

---

[9] This will only be the case if Brecht's "Lehrstücke" are seen as a subcategory of Epic Theater in general. On the relationship between the "Lehrstück" and Epic Theater, see *BHB*, 4:81–86.

texts with which it is associated and as a result it is automatically seen as the opposite of theater's purpose, which is held to be essentially escapist.

> Nach allgemeiner Ansicht besteht ein sehr starker Unterschied zwischen Lernen und sich Amüsieren. Das erstere mag nützlich sein, aber nur das letztere ist angenehm. Ich habe also das epische Theater gegen den Verdacht, es müsse eine höchst unangenehme, freudlose, ja anstrengende Angelegenheit sein, zu verteidigen. Nun, ich kann eigentlich nur sagen, daß der Gegensatz zwischen Lernen und sich Amüsieren kein naturnotwendiger zu sein braucht, keiner, der immer bestanden hat und immer bestehen muß. (*GBA*, 22:110–11)

As also happens in "[Unterhaltung und Unterhalt]" (*GBA*, 22:117), the historicizing point is made that class interests determine which kinds of learning are enjoyable and which not, hence the whole question is more explicitly politicized: "Für die verschiedenen Volksschichten spielt das Lernen eine sehr verschiedene Rolle" (*GBA*, 22:111). For those who have "ein ungeheures praktisches Interesse am Lernen" (*GBA*, 22:112) and realize that they are disempowered without access to information, acquiring knowledge becomes "lustvolles Lernen, kämpferisches und fröhliches Lernen" (ibid.). Having established and played in its title with the notion of a false (bourgeois) antithesis, the essay "Vergnügungstheater oder Lehrtheater?" does not return to the choice implied by the "oder" in the title. The two subsequent sections ("Theater und Wissenschaft" and "Ist das Theater eine 'moralische Anstalt'?") proceed as if the answer can be taken for granted. The role of science in a Theater for the Scientific Age[10] coupled with the argument that such theater is more concerned with sociopolitical than bourgeois aesthetic and moral issues is based on the assumption that for such theater's ideal audience *learning* and enjoyment go hand-in-hand. This may explain why in "The German Drama: Pre-Hitler" of 1935 Brecht's discussion of the "Lehrstück" includes the claim that "learning-play" (rather than "teaching" or "didactic play") is "the nearest English equivalent I can find" (*GBA*, 22:941). Brecht now refuses to exclude even the austere

---

[10] An undated note from the 1950s, probably by Hans Bunge, reads: "Seit einigen Jahren ist Brecht immer weniger zufrieden mit der Deutung, die dem Begriff 'episches Theater' gegeben wird [. . .]. Seine Darstellung des ihm vorschwebenden Theaters des neuen Zeitalters erscheint ihm jetzt zu allgemein, zu technisch, zu formal. Er arbeitet an einer theoretischen Überführung aller hauptsächlichen Züge des epischen Theaters in Züge der materialistischen Dialektik. Auf diese Weise hofft er, den Begriff 'episch' zwar beizubehalten, ihn aber mehr oder weniger zu einem wirklich formalen erklären zu können, so daß die epische Form eben nur die Form des materialistisch-dialektischen Inhalts wird" (*Nachlass,* quoted in *GBA*, 23:569). A "Nachtrag" to §4, written in 1954, refers to the fact that the concept "Epic Theater" has been discarded; the term itself plays a relatively minor role in *Kleines Organon*.

"Lehrstücke" from the realm of enjoyable learning: "If there were not such entertaining learning, then the entire theatre would not be able to instruct. For theatre remains theatre even while it is didactic, and as long as it is good theatre it is also entertaining. In Germany, philosophers discussed these learning-plays, and plain people saw them and enjoyed them, and also discussed them" (*GBA*, 22:942–43). If even the "Lehrstücke" and *Die Mutter* are illustrations of the fusion of instruction and entertainment, it is difficult to imagine where the "Emigration aus dem Reich des Wohlgefälligen" is to be found. It would be more appropriate to assume that the idea reflects less Brecht's actual view of a certain period of his work than common misconceptions about the sacrifice of audience appeal being the price to be paid for writing didactic works. The "Vorrede" to *Kleines Organon* positions the work by seeming to lock horns with what it presents as a widespread perception. As no doubt it needed to at the time.

## "Welche Art der Unterhaltung"?

Anyone who had read no more than the first twenty paragraphs of *Kleines Organon* would probably assume that the work was guided by a different "Hauptthese" from the one mentioned in the Feldmeilen journal entry. For Brecht repeatedly stresses that *in general* theater's overriding function is to entertain, rather than moving quickly on to the more nuanced proposition that "ein bestimmtes Lernen" constitutes "das wichtigste Vergnügen unseres Zeitalters." The simple equation of the theater with giving pleasure becomes something of a leitmotif threading together a series of *ex cathedra* assertions about the nature and purpose of all drama, with the idea becoming increasingly politicized the more it is developed within the context of the "Scientific Age" of Marxism-Leninism.

One salient feature of the *Organon*'s early sections is the attempt to offer "eine Bestimmung des Minimums [. . .] die Beschreibung der allgemeinsten Funktion der Einrichtung 'Theater'" (§2). This accounts for the level of generality of such pronouncements as the following:

"'Theater' besteht darin, daß lebende Abbildungen von überlieferten oder erdachten Geschehnissen zwischen Menschen hergestellt werden, und zwar zur Unterhaltung" (§1). "Vergnügung [. . .] ist die nobelste Funktion, die wir für 'Theater' gefunden haben" (§2). "Seit jeher ist es das Geschäft des Theaters wie aller andern Künste auch, die Leute zu unterhalten. [. . .] Weniger als alles andere brauchen Vergnügungen eine Verteidigung" (§3). "Jene Katharsis des Aristoteles [. . .] ist eine Waschung, die nicht nur in vergnüglicher Weise, sondern recht eigentlich zum Zwecke des Vergnügens veranstaltet wurde." (§4)

Only with §§5–7 does a greater differentiation and concretization enter the argument, something that Brecht needs if he is to advance beyond variations on his equation "Theater = Stätte der Unterhaltung." He does so in the distinctions between "einer hohen und einer niedrigen Art von Vergnügungen" (§5), between "schwache (einfache) und starke (zusammengesetzte) Vergnügungen" (§6), and in the argument that "Vergnügungen der verschiedenen Zeiten waren natürlich verschieden, je nach der Art, wie da die Menschen gerade zusammenlebten" (§7), of which only the final aspect is illustrated: not just by alluding to historically and culturally different kinds of enjoyment ("Der von Tyrannen beherrschte Demos des hellenischen Zirkus mußte anders unterhalten werden als der feudale Hof des vierzehnten Ludwig"), but by considering the implications for different forms of replication: "Das Theater mußte andere Abbildungen des menschlichen Zusammenlebens liefern, nicht nur Abbildungen anderen Zusammenlebens, sondern auch Abbildungen anderer Art." §8 goes on to link historical modes of "Abbildung" to the way in which theater's stories are told and to changing function, from reconciling the ancients to their fate or glorifying some Baroque or neo-classical conception of stoic self-transcendence to allowing the audience to participate in the "Selbstbespiegelung des sich frei austobenden neuen Individuums" of the Elizabethan era. The claim in §9 that our pleasure in such "Abbildungen" seldom depends on the "Grad der Ähnlichkeit des Abbilds mit dem Abgebildeten" echoes the point in the *Mahagonny* notes that culinary enjoyment is directly dependent on the degree of unrealness of the "Abbilder" offered (*GBA*, 24:77). At the same time, it also prepares the ground for the *Organon*'s defense of "Verfremdung" rather than faithfully mimetic modes of replication, a stand that will become crucial not long after Brecht's return to East Berlin.

However, before progressing to a demonstration of the importance of "Historisierung" and "Verfremdung," Brecht inserts three provocatively challenging claims: (1) our openness to the works of so many earlier traditions (a problem for Marxism that is also addressed in Marx's *Grundrisse*) raises the suspicion that this is because of a contemporary lack of orientation rooted in the fact "daß wir [Brecht diplomatically includes himself alongside his readers in the various indictments that follow] die speziellen Vergnügungen, die eigentliche Unterhaltung unseres eigenen Zeitalters gar noch nicht entdeckt haben" (§11); (2) we are not hindered in our enjoyment of the works from bygone cultures by their inaccuracies and improbabilities because we transfer our attention to other compensatory features (§12); and (3) "wir bemächtigen uns der alten Werke vermittels einer verhältnismäßig neuen Prozedur, nämlich der Einfühlung, der sie nicht allzuviel geben" (§12). Obviously, Brecht could have proceeded to the establishment of a connection between a theater of enjoyment and the sort of "lustvolles Lernen" particular to the Scientific Age without touching on any of these issues. Nevertheless, to suggest that our relationship to the classics is suspect because a sophisticated reception of them has given way to crude empathy and to argue that such identificatory behavior or a displacement concern with "sprachliche Schönheiten" or "Eleganz der Fabelführung" (§12) makes us oblivious to the works' errors and discrepancies — the very features that Brecht's adaptations for the Berliner Ensemble will be designed to bring out — and above all, to suggest that a misguided reception of works of the past has something to do with the fact that the significance of the Theater of the Scientific Age has yet to be fully acknowledged represents a massive three-pronged attack on a broad cultural front. By the logic of these claims, Stanislavskian theater becomes even more questionable and the role of tradition (later enshrined in the GDR's "Erbe" debate[11]) is put within a new, more critical framework. And the possibility has been aired that certain kinds of apolitical pleasure derived from various historically diverse cultural sources have in some respect become anachronisms. In other words, Brecht thereby succeeds in denigrating virtually all past and present alternatives to his own theater before proceeding to the panacea. As with "Über experimentelles Theater," the sequence of argument gives the impression that the need for a *critical* theater is derived inductively from a methodical assessment of what is wrong with contemporary drama. The chief difference from the Stockholm lecture lies in the extent to which the main four attacking paragraphs (§§9–12) apply as much to the theater of the GDR and the Soviet Union as they do to Western trends, past or present.

Instead of moving directly on to the new kind of theater, *Kleines Organon,* in an act of "Historisierung" of its theory,[12] first sets out the phases in

[11] Apart from launching Socialist Realism, the First Soviet Writers' Congress (Moscow, 1934) tackled the question of the new Soviet literature's relationship to literary traditions of the past and debated which forms of pre-twentieth-century realism and socialist writing were part of Socialist Realism's "inheritance." Karl Radek's speech "Contemporary World Literature and the Task of Proletarian Art" (Scott 1935, 73–142) was instrumental in establishing the outlines of the campaign to identify Socialist writing's true inheritance. International Socialism's so-called "Erbedebatten" of the 1930s, spearheaded by Radek and Lukács, concentrated on two tasks: the promotion of an acceptable proto-Socialist tradition in classicism and nineteenth-century realist fiction and the denigration of all forms of decadent, experimental writing. Hence the Expressionism-, realism-, and formalism-debates within German Marxist cultural politics (see Gallas 1971, Schmitt 1973, and Bloch 1973) were part of a broader debate about Socialist literature's inheritance ("Erbe"). The main implications of the "Erbedebatte" for the GDR are examined in Schlenker 1977 and Träger 1981.

[12] Unlike the technique of "Historisierung" in the mature plays, in Brecht's dramatic theory "Historisierung" tends to be applied less to the present than to the past. As a consequence, it remains largely a matter of the adequate intellectual contextualization of historical phenomena. When it comes to the present, Brecht is content in his theo-

which the new Scientific Age had come into being and the obstacles it had to confront. The pattern delineated, one of promising breakthroughs followed by limited reversals, is made memorable in Brecht's own biographical illustration of the idea:

> Ich, der dies schreibt, schreibe es auf einer Maschine, die zur Zeit meiner Geburt nicht bekannt war. Ich bewege mich in den neuen Fahrzeugen mit einer Geschwindigkeit, die sich mein Großvater nicht vorstellen konnte; nichts bewegte sich damals so schnell. Und ich erhebe mich in die Luft, was mein Vater nicht konnte. Mit meinem Vater sprach ich schon über einen Kontinent weg, aber erst mit meinem Sohn zusammen sah ich die bewegten Bilder von der Explosion in Hiroshima. (§16)

Like so much in this part of *Kleines Organon,* the sentiments are worthy of Brecht's Galilei. Although the January 1949 staging of *Mutter Courage und ihre Kinder* at the Deutsches Theater in East Berlin was to be the nearest production in time to the *Sinn und Form* publication of *Kleines Organon* (with the result that the play and the *Organon* were often discussed in tandem, as if they represented a perfect match between theory and practice), the spirit that informs the theoretical work remains palpably that of *Leben des Galilei.* "Unser Zusammenleben als Menschen — und das heißt: unser Leben — ist in einem ganz neuen Umfang von den Wissenschaften bestimmt" (§14) could just as well have been said by Galilei.

In *Kleines Organon,* from the Renaissance and seventeenth century onwards, science is credited with assuming the task of making the earth "bewohnbar." However, the rising bourgeoisie is charged with censoring and rationing dangerous knowledge: "Was der Fortschritt aller sein könnte, wird zum Vorsprung weniger, und ein immer größerer Teil der Produktion wird dazu verwendet, Mittel der Destruktion für gewaltige Kriege zu schaffen" (§18). The bourgeoisie are presented as putting obstacles in the way of new work in an area that would subject their destructive hegemony to scrutiny: "ein anderes Gebiet [. . .], nämlich das der Beziehungen der Menschen untereinander bei der Ausbeutung und Unterwerfung der Natur" (§17). The disastrous consequence of this policy — "Der neue Blick auf die Natur richtete sich nicht auch auf die Gesellschaft" — is only stressed at the stage (in §§17–18) where the *Organon* is on the point of heralding the eventual arrival of "die neue Wissenschaft, die sich mit dem Wesen der menschlichen Gesellschaft befaßt und die vor etwa hundert Jahren begründet wurde" (§19), that is: circa 1848, the year of the *Communist Manifesto.* This Marxist-Leninist "Gesellschaftswissenschaft" (§23) is the justification for Brecht's presentation of people in the twentieth century as

---

retical writings to historicize the aesthetic values of late bourgeois culture; there is no attempt to see his own reaction within a relativistic, historically transient framework.

"Kinder des wissenschaftlichen Zeitalters." According to §20, this break-through in widening the purview of science to the social field brings with it a "neue Produktivität": "Es treffen sich aber Wissenschaft und Kunst darin, daß beide das Leben des Menschen zu erleichtern da sind, die eine beschäftigt mit ihrem Unterhalt, die andere mit ihrer Unterhaltung" (§20). The utilitarian, non-"culinary" nuances of Brecht's "Unterhaltung" only emerge when the enjoyment that comes from mental and political productivity is fully defined; and this is done more in a spirit of prophecy than as a matter of historical record: "In dem Zeitalter, das kommt, wird die Kunst die Unterhaltung aus der neuen Produktivität schöpfen, welche unsern Unterhalt so sehr verbessern kann und welche selber, wenn einmal ungehindert, die größte aller Vergnügungen sein könnte" (§20). Similarly, in §23: "Ein Theater, das die Produktivität zur Hauptquelle der Unter-haltung macht, muß es auch zum Thema machen und mit ganz besonderem Eifer heute, wo der Mensch allenthalben durch den Menschen gehindert wird, sich zu produzieren." That final phrase, "sich zu produzieren," echoed in the last paragraph of the *Organon*, far transcends the application of the sciences, be they "Naturwissenschaften" or "Gesellschaftswissenschaft," to production. It implies a form of "Produktivität" that eradicates "Entfrem-dung" and finds its apotheosis in the individual's coming to fruition in meaningful work and social interaction. (Brecht is here on the whole merely reflecting Marx's and Engels's position on man's social potential, as set out in *Die deutsche Ideologie* and *Zur Kritik der Politischen Ökonomie*.) Much of Brecht's confidence stems from the ability to treat all such assumptions within the framework that regards Marxism-Leninism as a *science*. The whole argument in this part of *Kleines Organon* would be undermined if the scien-tific integrity of Marxism-Leninism as a hard science were ever open to doubt in the arguer's mind.

Because the new productivity initially manifests itself in the form of in-terventionist criticism (§22 reiterates the images of regulating a river, plant-ing a tree and grafting shoots onto a fruit tree), it combines an improvement in the "Unterhalt" (social conditions) and in the means of self-realization. The argument works with a contrast between the narrower, capitalist term *Produktion*, which according to §18 was monopolized by one particular class and used for the purposes of large-scale destruction, and *Produktivität*, an idea not tied to industrial production, but enjoying overtones of discovery, social amelioration, constructive criticism, and self-fulfillment. The requi-site Theater of the Scientific Age is thus aligned with the project of "die Kritik, d.h. die große Methode der Produktivität, zur Lust machend" (§25). At one simple but crucial level, that "Lust" is equated with the idea of audi-ences being "unterhalten mit der Weisheit, welche von der Lösung der Probleme kommt" (§24).

Revisited in the light of §§19–23, Brecht's remarks in the prologue about his return to the realm of pleasure can now be seen to have deliberately aroused false expectations. The new pleasure combines that of consciously belonging to the new Scientific Age and, in its supreme form, of partaking of the fulfillment brought about by "Produktivität," rather than mere material "Produktion." There appears to be an admission to this effect at the beginning of §24 when, having invoked the new joy of "Produktivität," *Kleines Organon* forms a bridge between §23's concluding statement that "das Theater muß sich in der Wirklichkeit engagieren, um wirkungsvolle Abbilder der Wirklichkeit herstellen zu können und zu dürfen" and the claim at the beginning of §24: "Dies erleichtert es aber dann dem Theater, so nahe an die Lehr- und Publikationsstätten zu rücken, wie ihm möglich ist." With this, Brecht again alludes to the passage from the *Mahagonny* notes quoted in the "Vorrede," although he now does this to bring out certain shifts in nuance. The radicalness of the earlier idea of "umbauen" may have gone, but the difference between moving theater as close as possible to a society's "Lehr- und Publikationsstätten" and transforming "gewisse Institute [including theater] aus Vergnügungsstätten in Publikationsorgane" is small enough to suggest that the position adopted in *Kleines Organon* is not evidence of some damascene conversion and return to the fold, but a continuing domicile in the same realm. For those desperate for an alternative scenario, one in which Brecht the Prodigal Son returns to the family, the work can present the image of a changed Brecht (although the plan "gewisse Institute [. . .] in Publikumsorgane umzubauen" risks seeming heretical in the new GDR context). For those more sensitive to what he is really saying here (and what he has repeatedly said in the past), a coded message of this kind will reinforce the impression that subtle changes of emphasis, not huge tectonic shifts, are taking place.

By the end of the first twenty-five paragraphs (or sections), the task of establishing a historical scheme within which the Theater of the Scientific Age can be legitimized has been accomplished. Epic Theater has been demonstrated to be the epitome of "wohlgefälliges Theater" and the underlying concept of entertainment has been historicized and "milieurisiert" in respect of theater. And relating the new theater to the "neue Gesellschaftswissenschaften" means that the aesthetic has been given its due philosophical grounding. These tasks having been achieved with more breadth of vision and more rigor than in Brecht's previous theoretical writings, *Kleines Organon* is in a strong position to move on to matters theatrical on the microlevel and justify its status as an "Organon *für* das Theater."

§26 expostulates once more on the irrelevance of what is dismissively referred to as "das Theater, wie wir es vorfinden" by showing it pandering to the need for escapist entertainment rather than encouraging "lustvolles Lernen." The caricature of mesmerized, virtually catatonic audiences reads like a calculated reprise of the paragraph beginning "Herausstürzend aus dem Untergrundbahnhof" in the *Mahagonny* notes (*GBA*, 24:81). Nevertheless, major changes of emphasis register the way Brecht's thinking has developed further, even if many audiences are in a time lock. There is also a difference of method. In *Kleines Organon*, audience behavior is critically presented using the "*Nicht — Sondern*" technique explained in §57 (*GBA*, 23:87). The approach, a variation on the "Glotzen" / "Sehen" distinction in scene 1 of *Leben des Galilei*, depends on a series of antonyms: "Sie haben freilich ihre Augen offen, aber sie schauen nicht, sie stieren, wie sie auch nicht hören, sondern lauschen" (§26). Such parallelism and antithetical structuring, reminiscent of the Psalms, leads to an even more devastating critique of audience inertia, since it is now measured against the alternative. Although enjoyment is mentioned, these various activities or modes of inactivity are judged in terms of productivity: "Schauen und Hören sind Tätigkeiten, mitunter vergnügliche, aber diese Leute scheinen von jeder Tätigkeit entbunden und wie solche, mit denen etwas gemacht wird" (§26). As far as appropriate and impermissible modes of audience behavior are concerned, Brecht may have in some respects been here before — almost twenty years ago — but the new focus on "Produktivität" represents a substantial advance on the undifferentiated distanced audience response that is offered as the solution in the essays of the early 1930s.

A parallel is established between the behavior and expectations of modern audiences who go to the theater to surrender to escapist experiences and the fantasies of a child about to go on a fairground merry-go-round:

> Der Zuschauer wünscht in den Besitz ganz bestimmter Empfindungen zu kommen, wie ein Kind sie wünschen mag, wenn es sich auf eines der Holzpferde eines Karussells setzt: der Empfindung des Stolzes, daß es reiten kann und daß es ein Pferd hat; der Lust, daß es getragen wird, an andern Kindern vorbei; der abenteuerlichen Träume, daß es verfolgt wird oder andere verfolgt usw. Damit das Kind all das erlebe, spielt die Pferdeähnlichkeit des Holzvehikels keine große Rolle, noch stört die Beschränkung des Rittes auf einen kleinen Kreis. Alles, worauf es den Zuschauern in diesen Häusern ankommt, ist, daß sie eine widerspruchsvolle Welt mit einer harmonischen vertauschen können, eine nicht besonders gekannte mit einer träumbaren. (§28)

This passage acts as a ridiculing "Verfremdung" of the mind-set of Aristotelian theater's audience, for once delivered without recourse to Brecht's usual culinary, narcotic or hypnotic metaphors. Whereas §26 had merely registered the audience's behavior from the perspective of an outside observer, the "Karussell" version disinters what is going on in their minds. Their expectations are presented as being little more than those of an immature child, excited by the thought that in climbing onto the merry-go-round it will be in possession of a make-believe horse and have the feeling of being able to control it, while at the same time being entranced by the way it is carried along, as if by magic, past the onlooking children. Exhilarating childish fantasies of being chased or being in hot pursuit of others, have, like all the other forms of enjoyment associated with the "Karussell," little to do with the degree of verisimilitude to the experience or even the fairground replica's "Pferdeähnlichkeit." The whole fairground apparatus is there to pander to the "träumbare Welt" of infantile delusion. This is the full extent of the image's connotations and satirical thrust in *Kleines Organon*. The focus is emphatically on the audience of non-Aristotelian theater, one that prefers to exchange a fantasy world for the one it feels forced to inhabit. We are here offered no equivalent metaphor for the attitudes of the new audience, made up of the children of the Scientific Age. For, staying with the merry-go-round image, it would be difficult to imagine what the alternative equivalent of such childish willing suspension of disbelief would be. For this, one has to look in Brecht's earlier theoretical writings.

Long before *Kleines Organon*, Brecht had written about the "Karussell-[or K-]Typus des Theaters," at that time contrasting it with what he called the "P-" or "Planetarium-Typus." A journal entry for 12 February 1939 reads: "der Philosoph besteht auf dem P-Typ (Planetariumtyp, statt K-Typ, Karuselltyp), Theater nur für Lehrzwecke, einfach die Bewegungen der Menschen (auch der Gemüter der Menschen) zum Studium modelliert, das Funktionieren der gesellschaftlichen Beziehungen gezeigt, damit die Gesellschaft eingreifen kann" (*GBA*, 26:327–28). The juxtaposition, with its emphasis firmly on the advantages of the planetarium-type of theater, was at one stage to have formed part of *Der Messingkauf* (cf. *Der Messingkauf*, Plan A 2: "Zweite Nacht," *GBA*, 22:695). However, in *GBA* the various essays centering on this pair of schematic models[13] are relegated to the status of "Vorarbeiten zu einer größer geplanten Arbeit" (*GBA*, 22:1023) and published independently, on the grounds that the ideas were never worked out in detail in *Der Messingkauf* (*GBA*, 22:1024). Although all four essays make a distinction between K and P types in their titles, only the last two explain the implications of the contrast. The first amounts to little more than a sketch on the relationship of literature to science, but the second, with its suggestion that any rigorous science/literature distinction may be misleading and its concern with the theater of "Einfühlung," does gesture towards a two-part model designed to evaluate diametrically opposed types of theater.

[13] The essays and drafts, all dating from c.1938, are: "Die Dramatik im Zeitalter der Wissenschaft [1] (*K-Typus und P-Typus*)" (*GBA*, 22:385), "Die Dramatik im Zeitalter der Wissenschaft [2] (*K-Typus und P-Typus*)" (*GBA*, 22:386–87), "K-Typus und P-Typus in der Dramatik" (*GBA*, 22:387–89), and "[K-Typus und P-Typus und die Krise der Einfühlung]" (*GBA*, 22:390–92).

Only in the final two essays, though, does the contrast between the two types become central. "K-Typus und P-Typus in der Dramatik" starts with the "Planetarium-Typus" as a metaphor for certain features of the Epic Theater before looking back to pre-existing theater of entertainment. The long second paragraph advocates as a model for contemporary theater an "allbekannte Einrichtung für astronomische Demonstrationen." As a way of showing human behavior, it is seen as being "zu schematisch" (*GBA*, 22:387), although this is a criticism that can also be leveled at the "Karussell" model. The even more detailed description of the "K-Typus" given here, about four times as long as that in *Kleines Organon*, is less concerned with the child's perspective than with establishing a series of parallels between the merry-go-round model and Aristotelian theater. Much emphasis is placed on the make-believe aspect ("das uns in fiktive gefährliche Umgebungen schleppt. Fiktiverweise reiten, fliegen, steuern wir selber. Durch Musik wird eine Art sehr leichten Trancezustandes erzeugt," "die Fiktion, selber zu dirigieren"). The model is associated with both the moment of "Einfühlung" and that of "Fiktion" (ibid.). Later, "die Dramatik vom K-Typus" is parenthetically explained as "(die Einfühlungs-, Fiktions-, Erlebnisdramatik)" and "die Dramatik vom P-Typus" as "(die kritische, realistische Dramatik)" (*GBA*, 22:389). The terms of the ensuing juxtaposition of characteristics of the two types — the one surrendering the audience unwittingly to the world, the other making the world yield itself up to the audience's mastery — plays off an adult's picture of astronomy against a child's world of fantasy and escapism. In *Leben des Galilei*, astronomy is also associated with ridding the heavens of metaphysics (cf. the people's image in scene 10 of "Galileo Galilei, der Bibelzertrümmerer!" [*GBA*, 5:262]). This association is absent from the theoretical planetarium model; if there is any implicit allusion to secularization, it merely comes in the analogy between the movement of the planets and social and political behavior patterns. However, in the last essay, "[K-Typus und P-Typus und die Krise der Einfühlung]," the accusation that the P type is usurping science's responsibilities is countered with the objection that it would be more pertinent to accuse the K type of taking over "die Geschäfte der Religion" (*GBA*, 22:390). This final essay, arguably elliptical to the point where it can only be fully understood in the light of the previous piece, makes little attempt to elaborate on the suggestion that various spheres of responsibility are being usurped by the two types of theater. Although in the final two essays Brecht tries to endow his contrasting models with a degree of philosophical and political significance, the attempt remains both sketchy and rather contrived. This may explain why, when he returns to the "Karussell" idea in *Kleines Organon*, he detaches it from the contrasting "Planetarium-Typus," thereby allowing his source idea to gain in vividness through the way it lends perspective to the degree of willing suspension of disbelief with which the child approaches the carousel ride. By restricting the image to the gullibilty of traditional theater audiences, it achieves an essentially satirical effect.

With the final essay, the model becomes too allegorized and loses some of its cognitive value. The suggestion that the "Karussell-Typus" demands of the actor "daß er sich selbst zeigt" and of its audiences that they see themselves in what is being shown, whereas the "Planetarium-Typus" demands of the actor "daß er andere zeigt" and that the audience see not themselves but others in the depicted characters is not something convincingly derived from the dual model's associative imagery. Instead it is clumsily imported into the metaphors defining the two types. It is this interpretive overloading in the final essay that makes the third the most plausible handling of the model and ensures that it is closest to the treatment of the "Karussell" image in *Kleines Organon*. Even if the other essays had at one stage been spin-offs from the *Messingkauf* project, what happens to the "Karussell" image in *Kleines Organon* has less to do with any mechanical "Zusammenfassung" than with a prudent piece of later editing. The "K-Typus" may be about an experience that undeniably involves pleasure, but it is unproductive pleasure and hence unworthy of contemporary adult audiences. Moreover, as has recently been pointed out, the "P-Typus" image fails to supply an adequate model for explaining Epic Theater: "der bildhafte Vergleich lässt unberücksichtigt, worum es [Brecht] im Theater vorrangig ging: um die Demonstration von Eingriffsmöglichkeiten, um die Veränderbarkeit der dargestellten Realität" (*BHB*, 4:201). The planetarium model may explain the movement of the planets, but it can hardly make them change their orbits in the interventionist way that Epic Theater was meant to function.

Unlike these preliminary essays, *Kleines Organon* treats the "K-Typus" in isolation and — a characteristic feature of Brecht's recent suspicion of spurious, invented jargon — simply evokes a picture of the child's merry-go-round experience, without deriving a label denoting an abstract category from the vivid extended image. A certain newfound confidence is in evidence in Brecht's distancing of himself from "the whole apparatus of scientific terminology with which he surrounded his theatre [which] was in large measure a rhetorical device to bestow special status on his proposals" (Speirs 1987, 46). Instead, an act of simple reconstruction of the child's naïve world is engaged in in order to strike a blow against the general abuse of empathy in Stanislavskian theater. Equally significantly, the dramaturgical associations of the "Karussell" image in *Kleines Organon* are more implied than stated and remain more tied to the source experience than was the case in the last two of Brecht's preliminary essays.

In the short paragraph immediately following the conjuring up of the child's merry-go-round experiences a link is made to contemporary theater with the bald statement "Solcherart ist das Theater, das wir für unser Unternehmen vorfinden" (§29). In one respect, it is a strange assertion. Brecht, about to come back to East Berlin with a highly developed alternative theater and an ever-growing international reputation, should not, in theory at least, have to feel constricted by "das Theater, wie wir es vorfinden." (It is not clear whether Brecht already — or ever — equated the theater of Socialist Realism with the "Karussell-Typ.") Presenting the dilemma of having to choose between K type theater and the Theater of the Scientific Age may have been an "Aesopian" way of implying that Brecht was all too aware of the chasm that separated his work from the "herrschende Ästhetik" of the world he was about to enter. The desire to stress this may even explain §30's backward glance to the failures of late nineteenth-century Naturalism. As in "Über experimentelles Theater," the movement is once again damned with faint praise: praise for taking a stand against "gewisse gesellschaftliche Übelstände" and in some (unspecified) instances even against "die Gesamt-struktur der Gesellschaft," for having felt "die Brise wissenschaftlichen Geistes," and for having tried to offer "etwas getreuere Abbildungen des menschlichen Zusammenlebens." Yet the attempt is dismissed as a well-intentioned failure. The resultant "Abbildungen," it is claimed, make the world *palpable* ("sichtbar") but not *comprehensible* in terms of its socio-political mechanisms ("sichtig," a neologism[14]). The only examples of Naturalism's inability to get below the surface of society's problems come in §34, where he strongly criticizes the choice of relatively soft targets in Ibsen's *Ghosts* and Hauptmann's *Die Weber* for treating society as little more than "Milieu" and for focusing narrowly on the "Empfindungen, Einblicke und Impulse der Hauptpersonen." The choice of works appears to imply that circumstances — the currently incurable nature of syphilis and the failure of the Silesian weavers' ill-conceived revolt of 1844 — have been allowed to assume the role of Fate, whereas they are both examples of changeable circumstances. These particular works are put alongside *Oedipus, Othello,* and *Wallenstein,* not only to illustrate the audience's error in identifying with the central characters' sufferings in their fate-like predicaments, but also to suggest that their ephemeral *Problematik* consigns them to a bygone age. Brecht's quarrel is now not primarily with German Naturalism as a historical phenomenon. Just as he chose the term "Aristotelian" to suggest the millennia-old obsolescence of many principles still in evidence in contemporary theater, so his use of "Naturalismus" (and the adjective "natura-

---

[14] "[Brecht] verwendet hier mit 'sichtig' einen Ausdruck, der laut Duden aus der Seemannssprache stammt und bedeutet, dass man 'eine klare Sicht hat.' Da [Brecht] den Begriff als Gegensatz zu 'sichtbar' aufbaut, muss aber angenommen werden, dass der Ausdruck [hier] eine eigene Bedeutung hat [. . .]. Im Kontext ließe sich der Unterschied wie folgt ermitteln: 'Sichtbar' meint, mit den Augen wahrnehmbar, während 'sichtig' darüber hinaus Einsicht, Erkennen (von Zusammenhängen etc.) bedeutet" (*BHB*, 4:324).

listisch"), not as a period concept but in a typological sense, is intended to suggest that much contemporary theater is an anachronism in the Scientific Age. There are times when appearing to fight the battle with surface mimesis via a critique of historical Naturalism allows Brecht to avoid openly engaging in polemics with the Stanislavskians immediately after his return to East Berlin. The presentation (in §54) of the new theater's alleged goal as "vom Abklatsch zur Abbildung zu kommen" works with a further pair of rhetorical contrasting terms, but neatly avoids confining the issue to the German Naturalist movement. And there are times when attacking certain forms of "Abbild" may suggest an association with the mechanically constricting "Abbildtheorie" which so dogged the evolution of Marxist thought.[15] In effect, Brecht's picture of a contemporary theater dominated by the Naturalist aesthetic is as much a matter of caricature as the association of that same theater's audience with the child on the "Karussell" or the attack in the "Vorrede" on theater as a shady collection of "Verkaufsstätten für Abendunterhaltung" (*GBA*, 23:65). Much non-Brechtian theater is thus presented as harnessed to an obsolete aesthetic and pandering to infantile needs. Change is required.

## "Abbildungen anderer Art"

Much of the following part of *Kleines Organon* (§§35–52) has Brecht returning to more familiar territory, being concerned, as it is, with explaining the principle, though again seldom the techniques, of "Verfremdung." A particularly striking feature of this account is the extent to which "Verfremdung" is now explained in connection with the process of "Historisierung" (in "The Fourth Wall of China" the two ideas were discussed at different ends of the same essay) and the role of the latter in facilitating the avoidance of audience empathy. Ironically, by the time "Historisierung" in the theater is explained, it may not be such an unknown process to the *Organon*'s readers, for it has been a regular feature of the work's own method. The notion of different forms of aesthetic pleasure for different periods has already been historicized through the account of the aesthetic repercussions of "das wissenschaftliche Zeitalter" and the importance of the different sociopolitical

---

[15] In 1935, in response to Judin and Fadeyev 1934 (details: *GBA*, 22:925), Brecht observes that "eine bloße Widerspiegelung der Realität läge, falls sie möglich wäre, nicht in unserem Sinne. Die Realität muß kritisiert werden, indem sie gestaltet wird [. . .]" ("[Über das Programm der Sowjetschriftsteller]" (*GBA*, 22:136). The theoretical background to this is outlined in the section on "reflectionist theory" in Eagleton 1976, 45–50 and was originally expounded in Lenin's *Materialism and Empirio-Criticism*.

roles of science in different epochs. Even various categories of audience response have been seen in historical context.

In §28, a reference is made to what Brecht believes to be a guiding principle of Aristotelian theater according to which "die Mittelpunktsfiguren
müssen allgemein gehalten werden, damit der Zuschauer sich mit ihnen
leichter identifizieren kann." Obviously, this is unlikely to be a conscious
precept; indeed, it looks as if it may have even been derived *ex negativo* from
Brecht's earlier thinking about "Historisierung" (cf. the poem "Über die
Einfühlung" [*GBA*, 15:173]) rather than from an encounter with specific
contemporary plays. As we saw in the last chapter, the subject of one part of
that poem is the reaction of the audience to an actor's trying to play the part
of a "Bauer" convincingly. The conclusion drawn there — "Je echter ein
Bauer dargestellt ist / Desto weniger kann der Zuschauer meinen / Daß er
selber ein Bauer ist" — already points towards the fact that a high degree of
specificity in character portrayal is an important weapon in the fight against
the audience's identifying with the character. In §39 he takes up this idea:
"Wenn nun eine Person historisiert der Epoche entsprechend antwortet und
anders antworten würde in andern Epochen, ist sie da nicht 'jedermann
schlechthin'? Ja, nach den Zeitläuften oder der Klasse antwortet hier jemand
verschieden." This emphasis on "Historisierung" and specificity as factors in
creating a distanced response is also present in Brecht's requirement that
characters and problems have to be "*historisiert* und *sozial milieurisiert*"
("Zweiter Nachtrag zur Theorie des *Messingkaufs*," *GBA*, 22:701). Not in
the documentary, Naturalist sense deriving from Taine's categories of *race,
moment,* and *milieu,* but because, as the "Nachtrag" says of the second
process, such social "Milieurisierung" is interventionist: "[es] stellt ständig
die momentane Gesellschaftsordnung in Frage und zur Diskussion."

The discussion in §42 of the "Spielweise, welche zwischen dem ersten
und zweiten Weltkrieg am Schiffbauerdammtheater in Berlin ausprobiert
wurde" observes that "die Effekte verhinderten zweifellos die Einfühlung."
However, the past tense, justified by the period in question's being an early
phase when great hopes were being placed in a process of "Verfremdung"
(though the term did not yet belong in Brecht's vocabulary), hints that
"Verfremdung" has now become part of the wider framework supplied by
"Historisierung." "Historisierung" is the subject of a series of sections of
*Kleines Organon,* starting in §36 with "Das Feld muß in seiner historischen
Relativität gekennzeichnet werden können. Dies bedeutet den Bruch mit
unserer Gewohnheit, die verschiedenen gesellschaftlichen Strukturen
vergangener Zeitalter [. . .] zu entkleiden" and running through to §39
where "Historisierung" is linked with the equally significant concept of
"Widerspruch." Given that the ordering principle governing *Kleines Organon* is one of movement from the general to the particular, one can
appreciate why the discussion of "Historisierung" precedes that of "Ver-

fremdung." As we saw in chapter 2, there were a number of earlier contexts in the 1930s in which Brecht was beginning to explore the potential of "Historisierung," foregrounding it to the point where it possibly even looked as if it were becoming an umbrella concept for "Episches Theater" and "Verfremdung." It is only in *Kleines Organon*, however, that the relationship of "Historisierung" to "Verfremdung" is clearly established, together with their importance for controlling audience response and their relationship to what had earlier been presented in a deceptively simple "*Nicht — Sondern*" model. Section 39 marks a deepening of the process and gives a sense of the demands placed on the actor when compared with Brecht's earlier comments on how Dreiser's *An American Tragedy* could be historicized. What is at stake now is no mere representativeness either in epochal or class terms, but a sense of the various cross-currents that go to make up the historicized figure: "lebte er zu anderer Zeit oder noch nicht so lang oder auf der Schattenseite des Lebens, so antwortete er unfehlbar anders, aber wieder ebenso bestimmt und wie jedermann antworten würde in dieser Lage zu dieser Zeit." Until here, the emphasis has been on certain circumscribed forms of typicality highlighted by the process of "Historisierung." Brecht goes on to add further complicating factors, still using the same demonstration model of how in different historical circumstances someone might respond to a particular question:

> Ist da nicht zu fragen, ob es nicht noch weitere Unterschiede der Antwort gibt? Wo ist er selber, der Lebendige, Unverwechselbare, der nämlich, der mit seinesgleichen nicht ganz gleich ist? Es ist klar, daß das Abbild ihn sichtbar machen muß, und das wird geschehen, indem dieser Widerspruch im Abbild gestaltet werden wird. Das historisierende Abbild wird etwas von den Skizzen an sich haben, die um die herausgearbeitete Figur herum noch die Spuren anderer Bewegungen und Züge aufweisen. Oder man denke an einen Mann, der in einem Tal eine Rede hält, in der er mitunter seine Meinung ändert oder lediglich Sätze spricht, die sich widersprechen, so daß das Echo, mitsprechend, die Konfrontation der Sätze vornimmt. (§39)

So far, the passage has been using a question-and-answer strategy to explore how someone in a certain period might answer, but then it appears to problematize its own aporia about the typical by considering respects in which the person "mit seinesgleichen nicht ganz gleich ist." The defamiliarizing idea of the echo bringing together various layered, contradictory utterances dominates the paragraph's final effect, combining, as it does, lucidity with eeriness. As the next paragraph points out, such a process of applying "laufend fiktive Montagen an unserm Bau" is close to the effect of "Verfremdung," one where "ein aktuelles Verhalten etwas 'Unnatürliches' bekommt" (§40).

A theatrical "Abbild" that emphasizes the contradictions, historical tensions, and variables is thus not only a matter of "Historiserung"; it at the same time defamiliarizes the material. And when the next paragraph compares the process of "fiktive Montagen" with earlier metaphors for "eingreifendes Denken" and "fruchtbare Kritik," the way ahead is open for Brecht's latest detailed explanation of the "Verfremdungseffekt."

In *Kleines Organon,* the principle of "Verfremdung" still receives substantially more attention than the process of "Historisierung," even if the latter has now been fully integrated into Brecht's theoretical construct. Two defining statements, one in §42 and the other in §43, reach back to earlier accounts of the process. The first takes up the work's initial definition of theater as consisting of "lebende Abbildungen von [. . .] Geschehnissen zwischen Menschen" with the explanation: "*Eine verfremdende Abbildung ist eine solche, die den Gegenstand zwar erkennen, ihn aber doch zugleich fremd erscheinen läßt*" (my emphasis). This new emphasis on "Verfremdung" being a form of "Abbild[ung]" was probably intended to suggest common ground between the theater of estrangement and the reflectionist aesthetic of Socialist Realism. The second defining characteristic mentioned is no longer concerned with the cognitive potential of the "Abbild," but with the strictly interventionist aspect of "Verfremdungen": "Die neuen Verfremdungen sollten nur den gesellschaftlich beeinflußbaren Vorgängen den Stempel des Vertrauten wegnehmen, der sie heute vor dem Eingriff bewahrt." Considerable effort now goes into stressing the difference between Brechtian "Verfremdung" and its antecedents: "Die alten V-Effekte entziehen das Abgebildete dem Eingriff des Zuschauers gänzlich, machen es zu etwas Unabänderlichem" (§43). This distinction, between apolitical and politically interventionist forms of "Verfremdung," represents an attempt to ward off the response from detractors that defamiliarization is nothing new, that there has always been an estranging tradition in philosophy, literature, and the visual arts.[16] As long ago as 1936, when the device was being tentatively explored in "Verfremdungseffekte in der chinesischen Schauspielkunst," Brecht had been anxious to identify continuities and differences between earlier forms of the device and its function in Epic Theater. But whereas it had suited his purposes then to place himself in the oriental

---

[16] Brüggemann (1973, 322) and the *Brecht Handbuch* (*BHB,* 4:319) suggest that Brecht was indebted to Bacon's *Novum Organum* for aspects of his thinking about "Verfremdung." *BHB,* vol. 4 draws attention to the following passage from Kirchmann's translation of Bacon: "das Staunen ist ein Abkömmling des Seltenen. Jedes Seltene ruft ein Erstaunen hervor, selbst wenn es aus der Art ganz gewöhnlicher Eigenschaften stammt. / Dagegen wird das, was mit Recht Bewunderung verdiente, weil es in seiner Art von anderen Arten starke Abweichungen zeigt, sobald es häufiger auftritt, im allgemeinen wenig beachtet."

tradition, in *Kleines Organon* the emphasis is on the demarcation of the device in its politicized form.

In some parts of his exposition of "Verfremdung," Brecht simply finds fresh formulations for the ideas of the past decade or more. Although the Hegelian "bekannt ist nicht erkannt" has remained one of the phrases most readily associated with his defamiliarizing technique, §44's "wer mißtraut dem, was ihm vertraut ist?" has a fresh and equally lapidary quality. In the context of "das Veränderbare," §33's innovative play with the idea of what is traditionally assumed to be "nicht kritisierbar" ("die Götter," "die Katastrophe") reflects the false consciousness underlying people's general inertia *vis-à-vis* the familiar. In §45 he goes on to describe "jener fremde Blick" as "so schwierig wie produktiv," which should have given an opportunity for Brecht finally to relate "Verfremdung" to the guiding principle of enjoyment, but again nothing explicit is made of such a connection. Brecht must have sensed this omission, though, because in a "Nachtrag" to §45 we are assured that the Theater of the Scientific Age "vermag die Dialektik zum Genuß zu machen. Die Überraschungen der logisch fortschreitenden oder springenden Entwicklung, der Unstabilität aller Zustände, der Witz der Widersprüchlichkeiten usw., das sind Vergnügungen an der Lebendigkeit der Menschen, Dinge und Prozesse, und sie steigern die Lebenskunst sowie die Lebensfreudigkeit" (*GBA*, 23:290).

Instead of any simple suggestion that "Verfremdung" is a matter of theatrical pleasure, what the reader is offered in the main body of *Kleines Organon* is a series of variations on Brecht's usual key points about "Verfremdung": that it involves "alles so zu begreifen, daß wir eingreifen können" (§46) or, in the same paragraph, the importance for "Verfremdung" of the "*Nicht — Sondern*" model: "Wie er ist, muß er nicht bleiben; nicht nur, wie er ist, darf er betrachtet werden, sondern auch, wie er sein könnte. Wir müssen nicht von ihm, sondern auf ihn ausgehen." Of all the attempts to define or redefine "Verfremdung" in *Kleines Organon,* it is principally the one in §45 that is calculated to integrate it into the framework of a theater for the new Scientific Age. Taking up the previous paragraph's reference to "eine Technik der Verfremdungen des Vertrauten," illustrated by the anecdote about Galileo and the swinging candelabra, it declares: "Welche Technik es dem Theater gestattet, die Methode der neuen Gesellschaftswissenschaft, die materialistische Dialektik, für seine Abbildungen zu verwerten. Diese Methode behandelt, um auf die Beweglichkeit der Gesellschaft zu kommen, die gesellschaftlichen Zustände als Prozesse und verfolgt diese in ihrer Widersprüchlichkeit" (§45). This is the closest *Kleines Organon* comes to the definition of "Verfremdung" as a dialectical process of "verstehen — nicht verstehen — verstehen" ("Dialektik und Verfremdung," *GBA,* 22:401). But the combination of the Galileo anecdote and the assertion of the importance of a materialist dialectic for such a process makes it clear that the device is not only political because its goal is to change the world, but also because the presentational and diagnostic methods as well as the material to which it is applied are in themselves dialectical. Without actually using Engels's term, *Der Messingkauf* had implied that "falsches Bewußtsein" is the root cause of the initial incomprehension. Perhaps because he considered this was too dangerous a topic to handle in a treatise intended for East Berlin, no mention of this is made in the *Kleines Organon* "Zusammenfassung."[17]

The relationship of "Verfremdung" to "Antiillusionismus" and "Historisierung" is re-defined in §§51–52 where the three principles are now configured in a clear hierarchical relationship. To begin with, the actor's estrangement of the figure played is presented in historicizing terms: an actress plays her part "als ob die Frau die ganze Epoche zu Ende gelebt hätte und nun, aus der Erinnerung, von ihrem Wissen des Weitergehens her, das äußerte, was von ihren Äußerungen für diesen Zeitpunkt wichtig war, denn wichtig ist da, was wichtig wurde." (Even if the point was meant to refer to *Mutter Courage und ihre Kinder,* it is more convincingly illustrated by *Leben des Galilei.*) Only when the dominant relationship between "Verfremdung" and "Historisierung" has been established does Brecht return to his earlier, more mechanical conception of actor-role estrangement as a form of "Antiillusionismus." Here, too, the formulation puts most weight on the political process of "Historisierung" and plays down estrangement's simpler (anti-

---

[17] Friedrich Engels's letter of 14 July 1893 to Franz Mehring, author of *Über den historischen Materialismus,* responding to Mehring's treatment of his and Marx's concept of "Ideologie" relates ideology to false consciousness in the following passage: "Ideology is a process accomplished by the so-called thinker consciously, it is true, but with a false consciousness. The real motives impelling him are unknown to him, otherwise it would not be an ideological process at all. Hence he imagines false or apparent motives. [. . .] He works with mere thought material which he accepts without examination as the product of thought, he does not investigate further for a more distant process independent of thought; indeed, its origins seem obvious to him, because as all action is produced through the medium of thought, it also appears to him to be ultimately based on thought" (Marx-Engels 1934, 511). As Alvin W. Gouldner explains: "'false consciousness' [. . .] is neither a deliberate nor an accidental mistake, but, rather, a wrong view produced systematically by the speaker's social position within the whole. [. . .] The idea of a false consciousness means that not all persons or groups are — whatever their good will — able to see the whole and its contradictions and speak the truth about them." False consciousness is seen as part of "Marx's epistemology [which] involves an ideological 'critique' that attempts to show that what persons know of the whole is either aided or distorted by their social position and by the everyday life experiences and interests that this systematically generates. Marxist critique culminates in showing how persons' consciousness or knowledge is not autonomous but always depends on their social location" (Gouldner 1985, 240–41).

Aristotelian) function of destroying illusions: "Eine solche Verfremdung einer Person als 'gerade dieser Person' und 'gerade dieser Person gerade jetzt' ist nur möglich, wenn nicht die Illusionen geschaffen werden: der Schauspieler sei die Figur, und die Vorführung sei das Geschehnis" (§51). Now, "Antiillusionismus" is not simply a weapon in Epic Theater's armory of adversarial responses to surface *mimesis* and unproductively empathic audience behavior. It is the precondition for more important political perspectives on the material portrayed.

§52 also goes beyond Brecht's previous treatments of "Antiillusionismus" by introducing what it refers to as "eine weitere Illusion [. . .]: die, als handelte jedermann wie die Figur." At issue is not theatrical essentialism in the sense that characters in a play are assumed by the audience to be Everyman figures, illustrating values and behavior common to people at all times. (This had already been dealt with in "Verfremdungseffekte in der chinesischen Schauspielkunst," where it had been presented as the opposite of Brechtian "Historisierung.") Brecht now takes one step further the dissection of any "Illusion" of consonance between character and "das Allgemein-Menschliche" or the assumptions of the age and suggests that it would be wrong to expect consonance even at the level of an individual character's behavior:

> Es ist eine zu große Vereinfachung, wenn man die Taten auf den Charakter und den Charakter auf die Taten abpaßt; die Widersprüche, welche Taten und Charakter wirklicher Menschen aufweisen, lassen sich so nicht aufzeigen. Die gesellschaftlichen Bewegungsgesetze können nicht an den "Idealfällen" demonstriert werden, da die "Unreinheit" (Widersprüchlichkeit) gerade zu Bewegung und Bewegtem gehört.

Within such a dialectical framework, "Antiillusionismus" acquires a far more overtly political function, one less likely to be understood in purely theatrical terms. Onto the schematic " *Nicht — Sondern*" model has been grafted the more particularizing notion of a variable contradictoriness between behavior and character. Typicality, according to *Kleines Organon* (modifying Engels's strictures to Margaret Harkness on her novel *A City Girl*), is not so much a matter of truth of detail as the truthful reproduction of typical characters under typical circumstances. And that can, without necessarily having to, involve a contradictory relationship between character and behavior. The claim is no doubt advanced with the errors of Socialist Realism in mind.

Apart from the emphasis on acting, the most helpful feature of the *Organon*'s account of "Verfremdung" is the relating of the process to contradiction. This reaches its climax in §45, but has been gestured towards elsewhere: in §6's suggestion that certain mediations of pleasure are "widersprüchlicher und folgenreicher" than others, in §28 (the "Karussell" section) with the assertion that audiences coming into K-type theater are exchanging "eine widerspruchsvolle Welt" for "eine harmonische," in §64's image of the preparing actor's sense of amazement at "die Widersprüche in den verschiedenen Haltungen" he has to display, and in the discussion of *Hamlet* in §64. Knopf's *Brecht Handbuch: Theater* (1980a) treats the plays under the rubric of *Eine Ästhetik der Widersprüche* (the work's subtitle). For many of *Sinn und Form*'s East German readers in 1949, just emerging from the rigors of one totalitarian regime's jargon and gradually being conditioned to and by another's, the dialectical materialist discourse of Marxism-Leninism will have been made a little more palatable by being presented as the highlighting of social processes *in their contradictoriness*. Nevertheless, it could be objected that the centrality of contradiction to Brecht's method of characterization, to his themes, and to his theatrical methods still remains understated. Point 5 of "Dialektik und Verfremdung" (1938) had already identified the systematic highlighting of elements of "Widersprüchlichkeit" as a key factor in the process of defamiliarization (*GBA*, 22:401–2). And even where the term is not used, it is implicit in many works preceding *Kleines Organon*, including "Die dialektische Dramatik" (*GBA*, 21:431–43) and "Dialektik" (*GBA*, 21:519). But it will only receive its due when Brecht moves on to reconceptualize his experiments as "Dialektisches Theater," for example, in "*Mutter Courage, in zweifacher Art dargestellt*" (1951), part of "Die Dialektik auf dem Theater." There he states: "Die dem Publikum tief fühlbare Tragik der Courage und ihres Lebens bestand darin, daß hier ein entsetzlicher Widerspruch bestand, der einen Menschen vernichtete, ein Widerspruch, der gelöst werden konnte, aber nur von der Gesellschaft selbst und in langen, schrecklichen Kämpfen" (*GBA*, 23:409–10).

In 1955, in response to a questionnaire from *Neue Deutsche Hefte*, Brecht voted Mao's essay *On Contradiction* the "best book" he had read in the past twelve months (*GBA*, 30:585).[18] When in that same year he came to write a "Nachtrag" to §53 of the *Organon*, Brecht quoted Mao to the effect that of the two components that make up any contradiction, one is always the primary element. Even if this undeveloped idea was the uneasy indication of an all-too-recent encounter with one of the classics of Marxist theory, Lenin's thoughts on dialectics in *Under the Banner of Marxism* had been known to Brecht since the early 1930s.[19] And the fact that he had stuck an abbreviated version of Lenin's "There is no such thing as abstract truth,

---

[18] Mao Tse-tung (1893–1976). The German translation of his essay on contradiction (*Über den Widerspruch*) was published in the GDR in 1954. Brecht studied it while working on his adaptation *Hirse für die Achte* (see *GBA*, 30:371).

[19] V. I. Lenin. 1925. "Unter dem Banner des Marxismus" ["Pod znamya marksisma"], in *Unter dem Banner des Marxismus*, 1:9–20. Brecht's attention was drawn to Lenin's proposal for a society of materialist friends of Hegelian dialectics by Adoratzky 1931.

truth is always concrete" to a beam in his Svendborg house suggests that at the time of his Danish exile he must have been familiar with Lenin's *One Step Forwards, Two Steps Back* from which the statement comes. But despite Brecht's familiarity with the ABC of Marxism-Leninism, it is likely that Sternberg and Korsch were the main sources of his ideas on the role of contradiction within materialist dialectics, mainly through private discussions.

Given Brecht's belief that "lebendig [ist] nur, was widerspruchsvoll ist" ("Dialektische Züge," *GBA*, 23:305), it is hardly surprising that he associates contradiction with truth to life. This is why he censures as "bürgerlich" works where all contradictions, inconsistencies, and disharmonies have been ironed out: "Die Darstellungen des bürgerlichen Theaters gehen immer auf die Verschmierung der Widersprüche, auf die Vortäuschung von Harmonie, auf die Idealisierung aus" (*GBA*, 23:294). Brecht's concern with a theater of contradiction is, of course, more than just an anti-bourgeois stance or a desire to capture the complexities of the real world. At root it is profoundly ideological. At the highest level of generality, it has to do with productivity or the lack thereof. According to Mao, "some contradictions are characterized by open antagonism, others are not."[20] Which is a shorthand way of saying that under capitalism contradictions were antagonistic (i.e. in the medium term destructive) whereas under communism they would be part of the healthy ongoing discourse of self-criticism and the improvement of the system. The classic statement on this subject is to be found in Lenin's declaration that "antagonism and contradiction are not [. . .] one and the same. Under socialism, antagonism will disappear, but contradictions will remain,"[21] which does not tie Brecht's theater, as it had been in the past, to antagonistic contradictions inherent in various forms of capitalist society. The first scene of *Der kaukasische Kreidekreis* (The Caucasian Chalk Circle, 1944), set in the USSR, and Strittmatter's *Katzgraben* are cases in point. But apart from being a justification of his own approach, the *Organon*'s emphasis on contradictoriness at the same time allows Brecht to insinuate that the Moscow Art Theatre's productions of nineteenth-century Russian classics, above all Chekhov, were just as committed to a "Verschmierung der Widersprüche" as was Western bourgeois theater. Whether the distinction is between "antagonistic" and "non-antagonistic" contradictions (Mao) or "antagonism" and "contradiction" (Lenin), the implications for an understanding of Brecht's "Widerspruchstheater" are largely the same. It is mainly through highlighting contradictions, in events, characters, and whole epochs and societies, that the world's changeability will be communi-

---

[20] "On Contradiction," Mao, 1968, 70.

[21] "Remarks on N. I. Bukharin's *Economics of the Transitional Period*," quoted in Mao 1968, 71.

cated and intervention encouraged: "Gezeigt werden soll die Veränderbarkeit des Zusammenlebens der Menschen (und damit die Veränderbarkeit des Menschen selbst). Das kann nur geschehen dadurch, daß man das Augenmerk auf alles Unfeste, Flüchtige, Bedingte richtet, kurz auf die Widersprüche in allen Zuständen, welche die Neigung haben, in andere widerspruchsvolle Zustände überzugehen" (*GBA*, 23:299). Hence, "der Dialektiker arbeitet bei allen Erscheinungen und Prozessen das Widerspruchsvolle heraus, er denkt kritisch, d. h. er bringt in seinem Denken die Erscheinungen in ihre Krise, um sie fassen zu können" (*GBA*, 25:416). Such a process is clearly not totally unrelated to the deployment of the "*Nicht — Sondern*" model, although Brecht is now more anxious to emphasize contradiction's relationship to dialectics: "Das Theater entwickelt sich wie alles andere in Widersprüchen. (Das Studium der Dialektik empfiehlt sich [. . .])" (*GBA*, 23:314).

## Theater Praxis Theorized

Käthe Rülicke claimed a considerable role in encouraging Brecht in the early 1950s to add a series of "Nachträge" to *Kleines Organon*:

> Den Nachträgen voraus gingen Gespräche, in denen ich der Ansicht war, daß Brecht im *Organon* die Hauptsache, die Dramaturgie, vergessen hätte. Brecht fand: nicht vergessen, aber als selbstverständlich vorausgesetzt, und er bezeichnete diese Nachträge im Gegensatz zum *Organon* — als Beschreibung einer bestimmten Art, Theater zu spielen. (letter to Hans Bunge, *Nachlass,* quoted *GBA*, 23:567–68)

In 1968 Rülicke published her own attempt to compensate for the *Organon*'s sins of omission: her study of *Die Dramaturgie Brechts*. Nevertheless, it is debatable whether *Kleines Organon* could, in the light of its overall succinctness, be accused of devoting proportionately little space to "die Beschreibung einer bestimmten Art, Theater zu spielen." In §§70–74 Brecht considers at some length the role of set-designers, mask-makers, musicians, and choreographers in ensuring that the entire burden does not fall on the actor ("nicht alles muß der Schauspieler machen, wenn auch nichts ohne Beziehung auf ihn gemacht werden darf" §70). Even the major topic in the final part of the *Organon,* the relationship of "die Fabel" to "das Gestische," is presented largely in terms of the challenge these present to the actor. And "Historisierung," "Verfremdung," and "das Widersprüchliche" are also explained very much with the actor in mind. It is doubtful whether the "Nachträge" simply represent a response to Rülicke's complaints about the *Organon*'s omissions, for the correctives and addenda in the "Nachträge" cover a wide variety of issues, of which not all relate to matters of practical theater or are of a dramaturgical nature.

In Hultberg's assessment, the paragraphs in *Kleines Organon* on "Verfremdung" and Brechtian methods of production "bringen nichts wesentlich Neues" and those on *Leben des Galilei* and *Hamlet* "dienen nicht der theoretischen Klärung der Probleme" (Hultberg 1962, 176). Ironically, his main objection to many of the passages on acting and staging techniques in the *Organon* is the diametrical opposite of Rülicke's: "auch die letzten Paragraphen über die Dekoration, die Gesänge und die Choreographie gehören mehr zu Brechts Theaterpraxis als zu seiner Theorie" (ibid.). There is clearly some substance to this final charge, just as certain theater poems were not included in chapter 3 of the present study on the grounds that they were concerned with narrowly pragmatic issues of the kind mentioned above. But there is a substantial difference between Brecht's various poems on the subject of, say, lighting, the role of curtains, or make-up in Epic Theater and the equivalent passages in *Kleines Organon*. Once the poems have been removed from the *Messingkauf* context, as in *GBA* they largely have been, they can only deal with their material in isolation, deprived of the support of an overall theoretical context of the kind that *Der Messingkauf* would eventually have provided. In *Kleines Organon,* on the other hand, practical issues are invariably treated within the wider conceptual frameworks supplied by the discussion of "Verfremdung," "Historisierung," and "Antiillusionismus," or the attempt to elaborate an aesthetic for the Scientific Age. In this respect, their contribution is that of practical illustrations of general dramaturgical and aesthetic points. Purism of the kind advocated by Hultberg is not desirable. Whatever example one has in mind — be it from the writings of Aristotle, Horace, Gottsched, Lessing, Diderot, or Nietzsche — it would be difficult to find a theoretical work that remains rigorously theory-bound and makes no reference to actual plays or to practical matters. *Kleines Organon* represents a judicious response in part to the need Brecht felt in the immediate postwar period to recapitulate his earlier attempts at theorizing acting and production techniques in the writings of the late 1930s, especially those that came in the wake of his detailed study of the published work of Stanislavsky. Yet even though there is more of a pragmatic strand to the discussion than some have conceded, the *Organon* nevertheless tends to foreground general principles and characteristics of a type of theater rather than dwell on practical illustrations. That would remain the task of Brecht's occasional essays on individual productions and of his four *Modellbücher*.

Much of the material in §§54–62, that is, up until the discussion of "gestisches Material," could well have borne the title *Die Arbeit des Schauspielers an der Rolle,* had it not been preempted by Stanislavsky. In §§54–57 he further develops some of the salient points made in the *Messingkauf* poem "Rede an dänische Arbeiterschauspieler über die Kunst der Beobachtung." The tautology that unthinking mimesis represents ("bei bloßer Nachahmung käme höchstens das Beobachtete heraus") is once more at the center of the discussion, but now with a sharper focus on the political weakness of such "Naturalism." Theater that merely seeks to replicate the actual world is rejected as being "nicht genug [. . .], da das Original, was es aussagt, mit zu leiser Stimme aussagt" (§54). The metaphor of speaking in subdued tones is an inspired choice, for whereas the *Messingkauf* fragments had presented the need for "Verfremdung" with an emphasis mainly on the audience's "Unwissenheit," the image of speaking *sotto voce* prepares the way for the suggestion that it is above all the actor who must lend his or her interpretive voice to reality. The seemingly apodictic "ohne Ansichten und Absichten kann man keine Abbildungen machen" (§55) is not some general maxim or personal memorandum from the playwright to himself. It is addressed first and foremost to the actor. "Will der Schauspieler nicht Papagei oder Affe sein, muß er sich das Wissen der Zeit über das menschliche Zusammenleben aneignen" (§55). This means abandoning the position of Olympian observer of mankind's foibles and political errors; the art of observation has to be a matter of "die Wahl des Standpunktes" (§56), both during the act of observation and in the subsequent preparation to depict onstage what has been observed. As "Das *Kleine Organon* und Stanislawskis System" was to put it in 1953, the year of the Stanislavsky Conference: "[*Kleines Organon*] versucht, Parteilichkeit bei der Darstellung von Menschen auf der Bühne durchzusetzen. Aber natürlich von Menschen, runden, widerspruchsvollen, realen Menschen" (*GBA,* 25:581).

In the ensuing paragraphs, a series of further issues — the cultivation of observation, the "*Nicht — Sondern*" model, the highlighting of "gestisches Material" in individual scenes and the importance of "critical" acting — forms part of a new continuum, rather than being considered in too compartmentalized a fashion. In each case, it is the actor who binds the material together. The actor has to adopt a political standpoint, and any method of communicating the material to the audience has to be centered on this political view. But to talk of the actor in the generic singular risks becoming unhelpfully schematic. If whole ensembles of actors did what Brecht asked of "*the* actor," there would be a danger of such harmony between the cast that all tensions and contradictions would risk disappearing from the production concept. *Kleines Organon* does not always treat the actor generically, but the issue of ideological homogeneity as a potential danger is not confronted head-on. Brecht also says little about the interaction between the playwright's voice and that of the actor(s). Not because he has no interest in what in Wayne Booth's terms might be thought of as a "rhetoric of theater,"[22] but because he is trying to be faithful to his theoretical work's title. An *organon* "für das Theater" is to some considerable extent an *organon* for practical theater people, of whom the actor is the most important, not the playwright or some such academic construct as the "implied author."

In previous discussions of the actor's role in creating critical distance, Brecht tended to suggest in generalized, seemingly unpolitical terms that a refusal to identify with his or her character on the actor's part would create critical distance in the audience. As we saw in chapter 2, there are times when he makes it look like little more than an artistic decision on the actor's part whether or not a character was to be played from the inside or the outside or from a position that reflected both perspectives. The relatively apolitical way in which the actor's distancing rehearsal strategies are treated in "Kurze Beschreibung," even the full title's implication that what is at stake is little more than a matter of a "neue Technik," is one example of Brecht's reluctance to pay enough attention to the necessary politicization of the actor. What may have been prudent reticence during the years of Scandinavian and American exile would clearly not do for East Berlin. Hence, Brecht makes good the omission in *Kleines Organon* (as in some of the "Gedichte aus dem Messingkauf"). Here, he argues that for the "Akt der Nachahmung" to become the product of "ein Denkprozeß" (§54), the actor "muß [. . .] sich das Wissen der Zeit über das menschliche Zusammenleben aneignen, indem der die Kämpfe der Klassen mitkämpft" (§55). What these fine words mean in practice can best be seen in §57, where Brecht explains what needs to happen when the actor begins to read the script and adopt the requisite political stance to the part. The paragraph contains a number of by now familiar recommendations: actors should not try to *understand* their roles too quickly; they should cultivate the defamiliarizing "Haltung des sich Wundernden"; they should look for ways to communicate such a stance to the audience by the application of the "*Nicht — Sondern*" model to the material and show that things are changeable because they did not have to be

---

[22] Booth 1963 explores the way a wide variety of what he terms "rhetorical" devices (ones that persuade the reader to adopt a particular evaluative stance to a fictional character or event) play a substantial part, alongside the narrator, in controlling the values of a work's reception. The sum total of these devices is hypostatized as "the implied author." While Booth is concerned with factors contributing to a cumulative "rhetoric," drama has traditionally been assumed to involve situations where no one figure is the author's *raisonneur* or the work's focalizer and where complexity and irony result from the dialogic interplay between the views of various figures. Given that §§70–74 of *Kleines Organon* go beyond the actor, or ensemble of actors, to consider the role played by stage set, costume and music in Brechtian drama, it would be instructive to assess the interaction between these elements using Booth's methodology.

the way they were (in this respect, §57 really is a "Zusammenfassung" of ideas from *Der Messingkauf* and "Kurze Beschreibung"). But Brecht makes two important new points about acting: one concerning the actor as an individual, the other about the actor's place within an ensemble, which is the closest he comes to offering an appropriate corrective to the earlier schematizing discussion of "der Schauspieler" in the generic singular.

The first point is a variation on the concluding image of the discussion of "Historisierung" in §39. There we were told that a historicized image needs to retain a degree of imprecision: the actor's historicizing of his lines will ensure that the audience becomes aware of contradictory factors and tangential echoes of other possibilities; the words spoken should not come across as too definitive. In §57, without any direct reference to "Historisierung," he recommends that the actor refrain from firming up his or her role too definitively, but instead endeavor to retain the flavour of earlier tentative, questioning phases in the preparation process: "er muß, mit dem Text, diese seine ersten Reaktionen, Vorbehalte, Kritiken, Verblüffungen memorieren, damit sie in seiner Endgestaltung nicht etwa vernichtet werden, indem sie 'aufgehen,' sondern bewahrt und wahrnehmbar bleiben; denn die Figur und alles muß dem Publikum weniger eingehen als auffallen." Again, the remarks are kept at the level of abstract principle, with no indication of the means by which such an effect can be achieved. Perhaps the right questioning state of mind is the only essential requirement and individual actors will have their own strategies for communicating "das Skizzenhafte." Given that Brecht elsewhere uses possibly misleading phrases like "Aufbau der Figur" (§58) and "zurechtgemachte Vorgänge" (*GBA*, 23:292), this is one of the more illuminating treatments of the dangers of an over-definitive style of acting. Perhaps it was itself delivered in too subdued a tone, for whereas virtually every discussion of Brechtian staging speaks at length about décor, lighting, curtains, body language, and anti-illusionist devices, one seldom finds any engagement with the content of §57 of *Kleines Organon*.

Brecht's second point (§§58–59) concerns collective work and comes in the shape of a timely reminder that the individual actor is part of a group (he even uses the word "Partner" rather than "Mitschauspieler" to refer to the other actors with whom an actor works): "das Lernen des Schauspielers muß zusammen mit dem Lernen der anderen Schauspieler, sein Aufbau der Figur mit dem Aufbau der andern Figuren vorgenommen werden." The point is partly made as an attack on the tyranny of the "star" system (Brecht had, after all, just come back to Europe after spending a number of years in the vicinity of the Hollywood film studios, but the situation was not much different in Europe). *Kleines Organon* refers to "[die] Unsitte unserer Theater [. . .], daß der herrschende Schauspieler, der Star, sich auch dadurch 'hervortut,' daß er sich von allen andern Schauspielern bedienen läßt: er macht seine Figur fürchterlich oder weise, indem er die Partner zwingt, die ihren furchtsam oder aufmerksam zu machen usw." (§59). Whereas "Kurze Beschreibung" focuses on a series of strategies tested and tried in rehearsal to distance individual actors from their roles, now, in §59, these become methods of combating the tyranny of the "star" system in order to create the right synergy for politically synchronized ensemble work. In case this still risks sounding too much like a matter of empty rituals, Brecht goes on in §60 to point out that individual actors, who have by then subjected their parts to "zahllose Aufbauakte," need to deconstruct what they have built up. They will have to acquire the ability to do this at the stage when they begin to interact with other actors and are thus able to see their parts from both the inside and the outside. Without measures to counteract it, the "star" system would not merely be disadvantageous to the rest of the cast; even the dominant actor would be unable to learn about his or her part by seeing it from a defamiliarizing perspective. For reasons which we must now turn to, the alternative to the demeaning image of "der herrschende Schauspieler" being *served* by all the other lesser actors is the possibility of *serving the plot*: "Schon um diesen Vorteil allen zu gewähren und dadurch der Fabel zu dienen, sollten die Schauspieler die Rollen auf den Proben mit ihren Partnern mitunter tauschen." The aim is no longer the mere technical creation of the critical distance between actor and role. It involves a situation where the actor is the servant of "die Fabel," rather than the focal point in an introspective drama of individual psychology. What this means will be seen to depend more on a definition of "plot" than on the notion of "serving."

## "Die Fabel" and "das Gestische"

Plot ("die Fabel") becomes a central concept in *Kleines Organon,* despite the fact that it had relatively little prominence in Brecht's previous theoretical writings.[23] Plot is now linked to the playwright's idiosyncratic concept of "das Gestische," to such an extent that one could argue that a recentered plot without an adequate emphasis from the actor on the "gestisches Material" informing it would be the equivalent of observation without an adequate political vantage point.

　　"Die Fabel ist nach Aristoteles — und wir denken da gleich — die Seele des Dramas" (§12) is one of the most frequently cited and most deceptive passages in *Kleines Organon.* It appears to show Brecht, the self-appointed arch anti-Aristotelian, for once wholeheartedly agreeing with Aristotle. This

---

[23] The exception is "Dialog über Schaulspielkunst." Here the actor is advised to concentrate on "nicht so sehr den Menschen, sondern die Vorgänge" (*GBA,* 21:279). On this and other continuities between *Kleines Organon* and Brecht's earlier theoretical writings, see *BHB,* 4:317–18.

is a rare occurrence in Brecht's theoretical writings. Even where Aristotle's *Poetics* had suggested that imitation is the basis of the pleasure derived from all forms of art, Brecht chose not to mention this in his account of theater's primary pleasure-giving function in the early paragraphs of the *Kleines Organon*. "The plot," according to Aristotle, "is the principal part — the soul, as it were — of tragedy" (Aristotle 1953, 16). Brecht's and Aristotle's formulations seem to say the same thing, and yet when it comes to the overriding importance of "die Fabel," Brecht's declared agreement with Aristotle is not without its complexities. "Nach Aristoteles," as one commentator points out, "geht die Fabel aus dem Charakter der Figur hervor [. . .]. Dagegen setzt das *Kleine Organon*: 'Es ist eine zu große Vereinfachung, wenn man die Taten auf den Charakter und den Charakter auf die Taten anpaßt; die Widersprüche, welche Taten und Charakter wirklicher Menschen aufweisen, lassen sich so nicht aufzeigen' (*GBA*, 23:85)" (*BHB*, 4:318).

As Wimsatt and Brooks remind us, Aristotle's "statement (*Poetics* VI) that the plot (*muthos*) is the soul and first principle (*arche kai psuche*) of tragedy" has remained a "question vigorously debated by the exegetes" (Wimsatt and Brooks 1970, 1, 37), usually because in many dramas it is difficult to disentangle plot from character in any meaningful way; they are each only conceivable in terms of the other. But Brecht in any case so redefines plot and character as to renegotiate the relationship between the elements involved. In doing so, he isolates what Aristotle merely posits as one of *six* elements of tragedy (also including character, verbal expression, the imitation of intellect, spectacle and song-writing), thus omitting any reference to the typological scheme to which it belongs. To confound matters, he also detaches plot from the specific context of tragedy, about which he always had substantial misgivings,[24] in order to make it "die Seele des Dramas" (§12) or "das Herzstück der theatralischen Veranstaltung" (§65). A further complicating factor is that while for Aristotle "plot" meant a single action of a certain magnitude, for Brecht it consisted of a multiplicity of actions within a discontinuous epic construct.[25] Thus, it already looks suspiciously as if the Aristotle with whom Brecht is apparently in such rare accord is to some extent a figure of Brecht's own fashioning.

---

[24] In the letter to his son Stefan in which he announces his work on *Kleines Organon*, Brecht also mentions the changes he is making in his *Antigone* adaptation "Änderungen [. . .], um die griechische 'moira' (das Schicksalhafte) herauszuschneiden" (*GBA*, 29:440).

[25] "Aristoteles ist [. . .] Verfechter einer 'geschlossenen' Handlung [. . .], 'episodische' Fabeln lehnt er prinzipiell ab [. . .]. Wiederum argumentiert hier der [Brechtsche] Text konträr: 'Die Teile der Fabel sind also sorgfältig gegeneinander zu setzen, indem ihnen ihre eigene Struktur, eines Stückchens im Stück, gegeben wird'" (*BHB*, 4:318).

On the basis of other utterances by him, one might have expected Brecht to have good cause to privilege plot over what Aristotle would have called the "imitation of character." Although the key question of the centrality to Brecht's plays of the generic parable, or *Modellstück*, method is not addressed in *Kleines Organon* any more than it is in the other major theoretical writings, there is, as Klaus-Detlef Müller has demonstrated, an important link between the emphasis on "die Fabel" and Brecht's parabolic approach to sociopolitical problems. In addition, although *Kleines Organon* frequently uses the word "Charakter" in the modern sense, the concept is of substantially less importance to Brecht than that of "Verhalten." According to Käthe Rülicke, "Brecht sprach [. . .] auf den Proben fast nie über den Charakter einer Figur, sondern über ihre Art, sich zu verhalten; er sagte beinahe nie, was ein Mensch *ist*, sondern was er tut" (Hecht 1963, 107). On one occasion, in connection with work on *Der kaukasische Kreidekreis*, he even declared: "Man sollte niemals vom Charakter einer Figur ausgehen, denn der Mensch hat keinen Charakter" (Hecht 1966, 72).[26]

Brecht comes to his approval in §12 of Aristotle's stress on the importance of *muthos* by way of a jeremiad concerning the way theater had over the years marginalized plot-related matters: "Unsere Theater haben gar nicht mehr die Fähigkeit oder die Lust, [. . .] Geschichten [. . .] noch deutlich zu erzählen, d. h. die Verknüpfung der Geschehnisse [an Aristotelian concept[27]] glaubhaft zu machen." The root reason, according to *Kleines Organon*, is not merely a growing obsession with psychological problematics and individual feelings as the center of drama, but the harnessing of such interests to the pursuit of a theater based on empathy as the mainspring of audience response. When properly handled, an emphasis on the story line can thus disregard the psychological aspect of drama and lead to a more suprapersonal, political approach to problems. Yet having preemptively introduced the idea of "die Fabel" as "die Seele des Dramas" (presumably selecting only one of Aristotle's two terms so that he can imply that this is a worthier "soul" than any introspective concern with the souls of the characters onstage), Brecht does not return to the idea until §§64–65, that is, over three-quarters of the way through *Kleines Organon*. He now takes it in an entirely new direction, not only going beyond any semblance of

[26] Having declared in 1954 that "die Eigenschaften der Menschen werden betrachtet als Möglichlichkeiten des Verhaltens; untersucht auf ihre Abhängigkeit von allgemeinen gesellschaftlichen Vorgängen in der näheren oder ferneren Umwelt," Brecht adds in parenthesis: "Auch bei dieser Betrachtungsart bleiben Charaktere sichtbar." ("[Dialektisches Theater]," *GBA*, 23:303).

[27] On this, see *BHB*, 4:327. Although Brecht is using a term from Aristotle's *Poetics* here, what he means by "Verknüpfung" is better expressed by the cause-and-effect model to be considered in *Der Messingkauf.*

agreement with Aristotle, but also interpreting the German concept of plot ("Fabel") in a series of unmistakably Brechtian ways. Even here, though, any conceivable link between "die Fabel" and audience pleasure remains no more than implied. It is only with "[Vergnügungen auf dem Theater]" (*GBA*, 23:302–3), dating from 1954, the year of the "Nachträge," that Brecht makes a sufficiently detailed case for plot's importance as a major factor in a play's enjoyability.

In *Kleines Organon*, the litmus test of Brecht's claim concerning the centrality of the plot to his kind of theater comes in §63 where, in order to bring out what he refers to as "das gestische Gehalt" of a work, an attempt is made to offer a form of renarration-cum-interpretation of the first two scenes of *Leben des Galilei*. This exercise in identifying the action's "gestisches Gehalt" becomes meaningful in the context of §61's explanation of the elusive term "gestischer Bereich": "der Bereich der Haltungen, welche die Figuren zueinander einnehmen," including "beschimpfen," "komplimentieren," and "belehren," all gestural factors identified as being "von einem gesellschaftlichen 'Gestus' bestimmt."[28] Two features of this explanation are noteworthy: first, that it is specifically addressed to actors and hence concerns the implications of "gestisches Material" for role preparation: and second, that the as yet understated nature of the political content of what Brecht has referred to as a social "Gestus" becomes central to his re-interpretation of the meaning of "die Fabel." In the *Organon*'s account of certain details in the first two scenes of *Leben des Galilei* one finds much material with political implications. For example (§63), Galilei's demonstration of the heliocentric theory to Andrea is carried out "mit einer Hast [. . .], da sie nicht bezahlt wird," and the way in which Galilei offers a new treatise to his academic masters displays a servility characteristic of someone used to being put in his place ("[der] die Zurück- und Zurechtweisungen gewohnt

---

[28] There is only a tenuous connection between the concepts "gestischer Bereich" and "gestisches Gehalt" in *Kleines Organon* and the "gestische Sprache" explored in "Über reimlose Lyrik mit unregelmäßigen Rhythmen," first published in *Das Wort* 3 (Moscow, 1939): 122–26. "Gestische Sprache," as outlined in that essay (*GBA*, 22:357–64), is largely a matter of what linguists now term *iconic* word order: i.e. the sequencing of a series of statements or ideas in a single sentence to reflect the logical or temporal relationship of elements to one another. Brecht's classic illustration is the biblical "Wenn dich dein Auge ärgert: reiß es aus!" (*GBA*, 22:360), also discussed in "Über gestische Musik" (*GBA*, 22:329). Unfortunately, as has been demonstrated (Heinze 1992, 121) Brecht often fails to distinguish between "Gestus" (in the sense of "Gestik") and "sozialer" or "gesellschaftlicher Gestus" (*GBA*, 22:330, 617), meaning a phenomenon's latent sociopolitical content. This is even true of what has been called (*BHB*, 4:226) his "classic" definition of the term as "ein Komplex von Gesten, Mimik und (für gewöhnlich) Aussagen, welchen ein oder mehrere Menschen zu einem oder mehreren Menschen richten" (*GBA*, 22:616).

ist"). The assumption, made explicit at the beginning of §64, is that by sifting through the sociopolitical implications of such elements ("solch gestisches Material auslegend"), the actor will gradually adopt the right attitude to the role.

The terms "Gestus," "gestisches Gehalt," and "gestischer Bereich" possess two separate, but related areas of meaning in *Kleines Organon*. "Der gestische Bereich," according to §61, refers on one simple level to something as straightforward as meaningful gestures between characters onstage. Brecht cites "Körperhaltung, Tonfall und Gesichtsausdruck," as well as types of transactional relationships such as aggression, admiration, or showing a person something. The "gestisches Gehalt" of the behavior of two characters towards one another is in this sense a matter of making the audience aware of their social relationship: who dominates over whom, what class people belong to, the circumstances in which their actions are being performed, and the prehistory and subsequent repercussions of what is being observed. As that last point implies, an Epic actor has to reveal to the audience that he or she knows far more than the character being played in a certain scene, with the result that our awareness of a contrasting series of "Grundgesten" behind individual incidents can highlight key behavioral contradictions within people[29] or even whole societies. On a second level, as Brecht's analysis of the first two scenes of *Leben des Galilei* shows, "gestisches Gehalt" can, more specifically, be a matter of latent sociopolitical content. Hence, "die Titel sollen die gesellschaftliche Pointe enthalten" (§67): in other words, it is ultimately what is significant with a view to things that need to be changed in society. "Gestisches Material," facilitating the foregrounding of a scene's "gestisches Gehalt," is therefore utterly dependent on the actor's ability to find the right political vantage point from which to portray a character.

Set against such a background of assumptions, "plot" becomes mainly important in *Kleines Organon* when interpreted as the vehicle for "gestisches Material." This crucial fact is most clearly expressed in one of the "Nachträge": "Die *Fabel* entspricht nicht einfach einem Ablauf aus dem Zusammenleben der Menschen, wie er sich in der Wirklichkeit abgespielt haben könnte [i.e. something more in keeping with what Aristotle meant by the term], sondern *es sind zurechtgemachte Vorgänge, in denen die Ideen des Fabelerfinders* [. . .] *zum Ausdruck kommen*. So sind die Figuren nicht einfach Abbilder lebender Leute, sondern *zurechtgemacht und nach Ideen geformt*" (*GBA*, 23:292, my emphasis). When Brecht discusses the importance of plot in §65, he shows just how different his position on the sub-

---

[29] As has been pointed out (*BHB*, 4:319), Brecht incorporates Lessing's idea of "gemischte Charaktere" (*Hamburgische Dramaturgie*) into his notion of politically significant internal contradictions.

ject is from Aristotle's. For Brecht, plot is important, not primarily in the Aristotelian sense that there is a pleasure to be derived from the sheer unfolding of a play's story line or the organization of a dominant intrigue, but because the story has been adjusted ("zurechtgemacht") to allow it to serve as a vehicle for the mediation of "alles, was diskutierbar, kritisierbar, änderbar sein kann" (§65). And this is said, not with reference to plot's parabolic potential, but with an eye to the "gestisches Material" that needs to be highlighted in each sub-unit of a scene. ("Blocking" in Epic Theater rehearsals thus acquires a substantially different function than it had in Stanislavskian theater.) When §67 declares that "das Publikum ja nicht eingeladen werde, sich in die Fabel wie in einen Fluß zu werfen, [. . .] man muß mit dem Urteil dazwischenkommen können," the structural difference between Aristotle's and Brecht's conceptions of plot once again becomes clear. Instead of plot for plot's — or entertainment's — sake, plot is interpreted by Brecht as material shaped to an end: the result of "die Auslegung der Fabel und ihre Vermittlung durch geeignete Verfremdungen" (§70). This is true both of "die Fabel in ihrer Gänze" (§64), which is mainly a matter of a play's parabolic potential, and of plot understood as an aggregate of significant details, the "Gesamtkomposition aller gestischen Vorgänge" in a given scene or set of scenes (§65). In *Kleines Organon,* most of Brecht's practical suggestions concerning techniques for bringing out the "Grundgestus" of "die Fabel" relate to plot as "Einzelgeschehnis" (§66), in other words, whatever is going on in what §67 refers to as "die Teile der Fabel," the "Stückchen im Stück," not to the plot of an entire work in Aristotle's sense (cf. §§66–67). This has to be so, since Brecht's preference for discontinuous, interacting story lines inevitably diminishes the importance of a play's overall plot. The concern with "gestisches Material," with the political semiotics of "[das], was *zwischen* den Menschen vorgeht" (§65), the semiotics of behavior rather than character and feelings, and the need to integrate the socially significant "Gestus" of individual scenes within what §65 refers to as "die Gesamtkomposition aller gestischen Vorgänge" are factors that imply that for Brecht what is important is not the plot itself, but a particular way of instrumentalizing it. Some of the formulations in *Kleines Organon* hint at this (e.g. §§70, 61), but none does so with the explicitness of the "Nachtrag" just quoted. When Brecht's discussion of the centrality of plot is associated with the challenge of creating plausible situations ("die Verknüpfung der Geschehnisse glaubhaft [. . .] machen"), he means plausible in terms of the interlocking series of politically significant "Grundgesten" in the individual segments of scenes, not in traditional terms of psychological motivation. Hence "die Fabel," what Brecht requires of plot, and what he means by "die Seele des Dramas" again differ considerably from what the *Poetics* meant; and they do so for the reason given at the end of *Kleines Organon*: "wir stehen zu dem Abgebildeten anders als die vor uns" (§13). Yet it is unlikely, given the East German readership that *Kleines Organon* was primarily written for, that the work would benefit from severing this illusory link to the "wohlbehütetes Erbe"; the Moscow-based *Das Wort,* co-edited by Brecht, had promised the German people they would become the rightful heirs to this "wohlbehütetes Erbe" after the defeat of fascism (*Das Wort* 1 (1936): 4). In any case, the *Organon*'s focus is primarily on the implications of privileging and politicizing the plot for the actor, obviously not a topic to be found in the *Poetics.* Yet the dismissive reference in *Kleines Organon* to catharsis as the goal of a plot's teleology in a certain kind of tragedy still begs questions about the role of feelings in drama, especially since the place of the emotions in Epic Theater has always been one of the most contentious issues in the reception of Brecht's theoretical writings and in polemical reactions to the plays.

## The Emotions

In the same letter to Hans Bunge in which she claims credit for the fact that the "Nachträge" paid more attention to dramaturgical matters, Käthe Rülicke writes: "Brecht hatte die Absicht, weitere Nachträge über die Rolle des Gefühls [. . .] zu schreiben" (quoted in *GBA,* 23:568). Whether he felt he had not done sufficient justice to the subject in the main body of *Kleines Organon* or was merely acting on a suspicion that this subject would represent the main point of attack is now impossible to determine. But feelings are certainly one of the areas where Brecht's later thinking, as articulated in *Kleines Organon,* does differ substantially from that expressed in the early 1930s.

As early as §4, catharsis is provocatively presented as "eine Waschung, die nicht nur in vergnüglicher Weise, sondern recht eigentlich zum Zwecke des Vergnügens veranstaltet wurde." Here "recht eigentlich" seems to mean "exclusively," and the suggestion that there could be any serious function to the process of purgation appears to be discounted. Given such a reading and in light of the arguments of §§7–8, one might have thought that this would have been sufficient reason simply to consign catharsis to the status of a phenomenon of a bygone age. But Brecht's repeated diatribes against Aristotelian theater suggest that the fight must go on. The above statement is immediately followed by the words: "Mehr verlangend vom Theater oder ihm mehr zubilligend, setzt man nur seinen eigenen Zweck zu niedrig an," which has the effect of reducing catharsis to the status of a "niedrige Art von Vergnügung." This is done on the grounds that the emotion involved blocks ideological insights. Cathartic effects, like tragedy itself, are treated as if they were either politically affirmative or merely escapist. In §9 Brecht conjures up the far more critical image of an audience prepared to overlook the inconsistencies of classical or neo-classical tragedy for the sake of emotional self-indulgence: "Auch wir übersehen gern derlei Unstimmigkeiten, wenn wir an den seelischen Waschungen des Sophokles oder den Opferakten des Racine [. . .] schmarotzen dürfen, indem wir versuchen, der schönen oder großen Gefühle der Hauptpersonen dieser Geschichten habhaft zu werden." What might conventionally have been viewed as "high" or "great" drama with an ethical or religious purpose to justify the cathartic effect is summarily relegated to the category of "niedrige Vergnügungen," ones where emotions are expended without the achievement of "[jene] Produktivität [. . .], welche [. . .] die größte aller Vergnügungen sein könnte" (§20). Brecht's polemical substitution of the word "Waschung" for "Reinigung" is no doubt intended to censure both the passivity of the audience undergoing the process and also impute to them the hypocritical feeling of being morally cleansed by the dramatic experience. "Waschung" is as materialistic and satirical a metaphor as the one that gave rise to the term "kulinarisch." As we saw in chapter 3, Brecht also alludes to catharsis in his poem "Reinigung des Theaters von den Illusionen," dating from the same period as *Kleines Organon*. This time, however, he uses Lessing's more elevated phrase "Reinigung durch Furcht und Mitleid." But in neither context is there an adequate exploration of the connotations, nature, and function of catharsis in antiquity or even a coherent case for its being out of place in the modern world. Given the importance of the polemical term "Aristotelian theater" in Brecht's theoretical writings and his claim that *Kleines Organon* will treat Epic Theater within the framework of aesthetics, this is a surprising omission. In a plan dating from the 1939–41 period for the contents of the Second Night of *Der Messingkauf*, Brecht does note that one topic should be "die Poetik des Aristoteles" (*GBA*, 22:695), but there is no detailed discussion of the *Poetics* in the parts that were written.

Four years before, in a discussion of catharsis ("Zweites der kleinen Gespräche mit dem ungläubigen Thomas," *GBA*, 23:40), Brecht has his interlocutor refer to "die kathartischen Nervenschocks" that modern audiences have come to expect of mainstream (Aristotelian) theater. The phrase is borrowed from Gustav Freytag's[30] diagnostic presentation of modern tragedy, in which he states that it is designed to produce "mächtige

---

[30] Gustav Freytag (1816–1895), minor German dramatist mainly famous for his novel *Soll und Haben* (1855). When Brecht met the American writer John Howard Lawson, the author of an early attack on him in *Theatre Workshop*, in July 1943 ("den Lawson, der über Dramaturgie geschrieben hat"), his immediate reaction was: "reaktionäres Zeug, 'zurück zu Gustav Freytag'" (*GBA*, 27:157). Lawson's *The Theory and Technique of Playwrighting* (1936) was clearly being compared with Freytag's *Die Technik des Dramas* (1863), an attempt to explain and systematize the rules of classical drama, as set out in Aristotle's *Poetics*, for the nineteenth century. For accounts of both works, see Carlson 1993, 257–59, 382.

Spannungen, [die] das Nervenleben ergreifen": "Diese merkwürdige Ergriffenheit von Leib und Seele, das Herausheben aus den Stimmungen des Tages, das freie Wohlgefühl nach großen Aufregungen ist genau das, was bei dem modernen Drama der Katharsis des Aristoteles entspricht" (Freytag 1965, 79–80). It is not possible to see from the dialogue fragment alone whether Freytag is being invoked in order to be rejected or to be built on dialectically. If nothing else, his psychiatric-cum-medical account of what Aristotelian catharsis has been debased to in modern times would give Brecht enough points of agreement for a detailed discussion of catharsis then and now. But of course Freytag is not attacking "die Katharsis des Aristoteles," but merely its equivalent in the modern world; and his "modern world" is almost a hundred years before Brecht's. And rather than "Katharsis — aber Neuerungen!" in the spirit of the formulation in the *Mahagonny* notes, his call was for a return to the basic principles set out in the *Poetics* and a systematization of them to the point where they could be more rigorously observed in the late nineteenth century. If an expanded version of Brecht's "Zweites Gespräch" had succeeded in showing why Freytag's was a quixotic program, then the result might well have been the missing detailed analysis of the relationship of Aristotelian theater to the ideas in Aristotle's *Poetics* and a demonstration of why neither Aristotle nor Freytag was relevant to the Scientific Age, its problems and its solutions.

In fact, in *Kleines Organon* Brecht makes less of the dangers of a theater based predominantly on catharsis than he had in his earlier writings. He takes them as read. To some extent, of course, anything he says about "Verfremdung," "Antiillusionismus," or even non-identificatory acting techniques is predicated on his views about the way certain emotions create a passive audience and hinder the application of reason and hence block political insight. But few sections or groups of paragraphs in the *Organon* have the specific task of continuing Brecht's longstanding fight against what the *Mahagonny* notes had summed up with the one blanket term "Gefühl." §34 does admittedly refer dismissively to the kind of theater in which "wir [the audience] die Empfindungen, Einblicke und Impulse der Hauptpersonen aufgezwungen bekommen." And with §35 a window has already been left open to the possibility of a "Theater [. . .], das Gedanken und Gefühle verwendet und erzeugt, die bei der Veränderung des Feldes selbst eine Rolle spielen."

*Kleines Organon* has reached the stage where a decisive breakthrough is required if Brecht is not to remain the victim of his earlier false dichotomies and thus once more play into the hands of his old enemies.[31] A year later,

---

[31] Old adversaries, among them Fritz Erpenbeck, now editor-in-chief of the pro-Stanislavsky periodical *Theater der Zeit*, and Alfred Kurella, tended to respond more

with "Friedrich Wolf — Bert Brecht: Formprobleme des Theaters aus neuem Inhalt," he makes it clear that clarifying his thinking on the role of feelings in Epic Theater is vitally important:

> Es ist nicht der Fall — wiewohl es mitunter vorgebracht wurde — daß episches Theater, das übrigens — wie ebenfalls mitunter vorgebracht — nicht etwa einfach undramatisches Theater ist, den Kampfruf "Hie Vernunft — hie Emotion (Gefühl)" erschallen läßt. Es verzichtet in keiner Weise auf Emotionen. [. . .] Die "kritische Haltung," in die es sein Publikum zu bringen trachtet, kann ihm nicht leidenschaftlich genug sein. (*GBA*, 23:110)

In *Kleines Organon,* it is mainly in connection with "Historisierung" that Brecht introduces the thesis that Epic Theater involves both thoughts and feelings, although what is new here is not the simple claim that both have a role to play in Brechtian theater, but the Feldmeilen thesis that a particular configuration of the two is a characteristic of the Theater of the Scientific Age. Even in §35, feelings are no longer axiomatically associated with escapist "culinary" theater (what *Der Messingkauf* dismisses as "Unterhaltung (der ablenkenden Art)" [*GBA*, 22:700]). Brecht now concedes that virtually all situations and actions involve both thoughts and feelings. Thus, *feelings* that help bring about change are put alongside *ideas* that change the world. Any crude antithesis, such as the contrast between Aristotelian theater's exploitation of feelings and the strategic evocation of "virtuous emotions" (Speirs 1987, 30), has given way to greater discrimination. The argument (§§48–49) now centers on the actor's attitude to the character portrayed. The idea is taken up in the warning "nur sollten seine eigenen Gefühle nicht grundsätzlich die seiner Figur sein, damit auch die seines Publikums nicht grundsätzlich die der Figur werden." There may be little that is new in what is said here about the political rationale behind the epic actor's relationship to his part or in what emerges from the following paragraph's discussion of the way Laughton played Galilei. However, integrating these ideas, originally set out in "Kurze Beschreibung," into the framework of the Theater of the Scientific Age is a bold move. Emotion *versus* reason and blacklisted *versus* "virtuous" emotions cease to be the presiding antitheses, for there is no longer any "schema" based on the usual simplifying antithesis. Nor are the dangers of emotion and the advantages of reason presented in compartmentalized arguments as they were in many of the earlier theoretical utterances.

The concluding section of *Kleines Organon,* §77, returns to the subject of enjoyment in order to move the main frame beyond theater as an

---

to their own critical image of *Mutter Courage und ihre Kinder* and to Brecht's writings of the early 1930s than to the substance of *Kleines Organon.* On the work's reception, see *GBA,* 22:460–61.

aesthetic experience to the politics of the real world: "Die Abbildungen müssen nämlich zurücktreten vor dem Abgebildeten, dem Zusammenleben der Menschen, und das Vergnügen an ihrer Vollkommenheit soll in das höhere Vergnügen gesteigert werden, daß die zutage getretene Regeln in diesem Zusammenleben als vorläufige und unvollkomme behandelt sind." The highest pleasure comes not from any myopic pleasurable contemplation of theater's depictions of the world, but from the audience's awareness, a result of the process of "Historisierung," of the provisional and imperfect nature of what the *Organon* refers to as "the rules" of the world itself. The implication is that the *laws* of a Marxist-Leninist conception of history, "Gesetze" that had been or still will be repeatedly invoked in the *Messingkauf* complex, dictate that the *rules* governing specific societies are but provisional. In the Scientific Age, the greatest pleasure, emotional as well as intellectual, is said to come from the recognition of the dialectical nature of social phenomena. Yet theater is still for Brecht to some considerable extent the instrument of that recognition and the final words of the *Organon* return the theater to the realm of a new form of "heiteres Betrachten" ("heiter" and "leicht" are key words in this part of the argument), a form of observation that is nevertheless part of a process of intervention in the affairs of the world: "In seinem Theater mag [der Zuschauer] seine schrecklichen und nie endenden Arbeiten, die ihm den Unterhalt geben sollen, genießen als Unterhaltung, samt den Schrecken seiner unaufhörlichen Verwandlung. Hier produziere er sich in der leichtesten Weise; denn die leichteste Weise der Existenz ist in der Kunst."

Two paragraphs earlier, the *Organon* had reminded us "daß es ihre Aufgabe ist [i.e. the task of all the arts that contribute to the theater], die Kinder des wissenschaftlichen Zeitalters zu unterhalten, und zwar in sinnlicher Weise und heiter" (§75). In light of this statement, one might inquire of Brecht's theoretical work whether it also successfully responds to a comparable imperative to give pleasure, above all "in sinnlicher Weise," which in this context means the blending of pleasure with instruction. If the paragraphs of *Kleines Organon* are intended as prolegomena to an "Ästhetik des wissenschaftlichen Zeitalters," then arguably they too should communicate the sensuous pleasure of learning through discovery that epitomizes the best of Brechtian theater. Certainly, some passages do seek to convey the spirit of "lustvolles Lernen" combined with a sense of newfound power brought about by knowledge and the awareness that conditions are impermanent and hence changeable. In §56, a short postscript to the argument that "ohne Ansichten und Absichten kann man keine Abbildungen machen," Brecht conveys just such a mood of elation when describing the triumphant sense of potential that the actor's "Wahl des Standpunkts," his adoption of the right political stance towards the material, brings with it: "Wie die Umgestaltung der Natur, so ist die Umgestaltung der Gesellschaft ein Befreiungsakt, und es sind die Freuden der Befreiung, welche das Theater eines wissenschaftlichen Zeitalters vermitteln sollte." That such a theater can accomplish this is left in no doubt by works such as *Leben des Galilei* and *Der kaukasische Kreidekreis*. It is hardly surprising that the Galilei play is referred to so frequently in the *Organon*: its hero's words quoted in §69, a scene of discovery from it evoked in §72, and scenes from it analyzed in §49 and §63, the longest section in the entire work. There is, however, a conceptual fuzziness to the treatment of "eingreifendes Denken" at some points in *Kleines Organon*. For example, §23 declares that "das Theater muß sich in der Wirklichkeit engagieren, um wirkungsvolle Abbilder der Wirklicheit herstellen zu können und zu dürfen." But an interventionism that both precedes and legitimizes Epic Theater while at the same time being the goal and end product of Epic Theater is something of a viciously circular conception.

Whether *Kleines Organon* itself achieves a comparable synthesis of reson and emotion is a more open question. By declaring it to be an "organon," Brecht seems to position *Kleines Organon* decidedly on the rational side of the dialectic, although this does not prevent there being significant fluctuations in tone and method. The "Vorrede" is measured and cautiously paced, though also communicating with much humor its sense of purpose and a patient concern with basic principles. But Brecht later discusses certain aspects of the actor's task and experiences, the need to convey the complexities of "Historisierung" or the way in which the phases of building up an artist's relationship to a part eventually feed into the fine detail: here a sense of the pleasure of discovery is powerfully conveyed to the reader through the quality of the prose. In general, however, the sense of intellectual pleasure, the savoring of formulations and images, permeates the fabric of *Kleines Organon* at a more local level. It comes, for example, in the flamboyant hyperbole of the confession in the "Vorrede" that "der abgeschmackte Kulinarismus geistloser Augen- oder Seelenweiden" had provoked in the author of the *Organon* "den Schrei nach der schönen Logik des Einmaleins"; and in the unfolding of the satirical implications of the "Karussell" image in §28. It is there in the impatience for a *tabula rasa* captured in the final rhythms of §33: "Barbarische Belustigungen! Wir wissen, daß die Barbaren eine Kunst haben. Machen wir eine andere!" And one finds it again, not just in word plays like those on "begreifen" and "eingreifen" (§46), or "sichtbar" and "sichtig" (§30), or the prologue's play with the Prodigal Son metaphor, or Brecht's Marxist-atheist *bon mot* "Haben wir nicht gesehen, wie der Unglaube Berge versetzt hat?" (§32) with its "take" on 1 Corinthians 15:2, but also in the verbal gusto with which the inflated acting style that Germany has inherited from the Third Reich is lampooned in a passage of advice about how a Brechtian actor should not perform: "Seine Sprechweise sei frei von pfäffischem Singsang und jenen Kadenzen, die die

Zuschauer einlullen, so daß der Sinn verlorengeht. Selbst Besessene darstellend, darf er selber nicht besessen wirken; wie sonst könnten die Zuschauer ausfinden, was die Besessenen besitzt?" (§47). It can also be found in the wit underlying such phrasing as: "Unser Tun hat nichts von einem fröhlichen Sich-Umtun, und um uns auszuweisen, verweisen wir nicht darauf, wieviel Spaß wir mit etwas gehabt haben, sondern wieviel Schweiß es uns gekostet hat" (§75). This sensual pleasure at what language can do shades across into the general enjoyment of the "Gestus des Zeigens," which is also deployed in a gleeful, at times mock-histrionic or quasi-Biblical form at a number of junctures. We have already encountered it in the passage about the theater of the barbarians; and it is prevalent in the middle sections of the *Organon,* especially at the point of transition between the existing "Theater, wie wir es vorfinden" and the Theater of the Scientific Age. For example: "Dennoch, schreiten wir fort! Gefallen wie gesprungen! Wir sind offenbar in einen Kampf gekommen, kämpfen wir also!" (§32); "Schreiten wir fort, indem wir untersuchen, wie [. . .]" (§57), "Gehen wir, um zum gestischen Gehalt zu kommen, die Anfangsszenen eines neueren Stückes durch, meines *Leben des Galilei*" (§63). It would be unrealistic to expect a work of some 30 pages to sustain a synthesis of elated intellectual discovery and verbal pleasure consistently in each paragraph. Not even *Leben des Galilei* does that in more than a third of its scenes. However, when compared with the more sober expository tones of "Über experimentelles Theater," "Kurze Beschreibung," or the *Messingkauf* dialogue sequences, *Kleines Organon für das Theater* comes closer to illustrating its own thesis than any of Brecht's previous theoretical works had done.

# 5: "Viel Theorie in Dialogform": The *Messingkauf* Project (1939–1956)

B RECHT'S JOURNAL FOR 12 February 1939, recording how productive he had recently been, ends with the words: "Viel Theorie in Dialogform *Der Messingkauf*" (*GBA*, 26:327). Weeks, even months earlier, most probably shortly after the completion of *Leben des Galilei* in November 1938,[1] Brecht had sketched out a series of dialogue fragments. He would continue to return to the *Messingkauf* project for more than a decade and a half. In the early 1950s, a fresh burst of activity augured well after a series of stops and starts. Among the pre-published results were a number of significant pieces, including the "Übungsstücke für Schauspieler" in *Versuche* 11 (1951), a miscellany of "Reden" and poems for *Theaterarbeit* (1952), and a small collection of "Gedichte aus dem *Messingkauf*," published in *Versuche* 14 (1955). As late as 1956, the year of his death, Brecht had not totally abandoned work on *Der Messingkauf*. The project of a civilized exchange of ideas about theater and society and different ways of depicting the world had been started in the dark days of the Soviet purges and the Moscow "Expressionismusdebatte" (conducted by Lukács, Gábor, and various other orthodox leftwing *Kulturpolitiker* on the editorial board of the journal *Das Wort*), which was hardly a debate at all as the one side subjected the other, in the person of Brecht himself, a fellow editor of *Das Wort*, to a campaign of personal vilification, but without ever mentioning him by name. Those who think Brecht's plans for the Fourth Night of *Der Messingkauf* were utopian may need to remind themselves that even the events of the First Night would have seemed unreal at that time. At the height of the later but equally vicious "Formalismusdebatte" in the GDR, Brecht would return to work on *Messingkauf* material for inclusion in *Theaterarbeit*.

---

[1] Earlier datings assume that "Verfremdungseffekte in der chinesischen Schauspielkunst" (1936), "K-Typus und P-Typus in der Dramatik" (1938), and "Die Straßenszene" (1938), all mentioned in early plans, still form part of *Der Messingkauf*. Hecht, for example, believed that the essay on Chinese acting continued to belong to the project, hence the dating of *Der Messingkauf* as "1937 bis 1951" (*GW*, 16:449). The proposed chronology is undermined by an inconsistency between his claim that the essay was written in 1937 and the correct, though tentative, reference to its appearance in English translation in 1936 (*GW*, 16:7\*).

Among Brecht's theoretical writings, *Der Messingkauf* is unique, and not solely on account of its protracted genesis. No other theoretical work by Brecht was as wide-ranging or innovative. The various overlapping — and often conflicting — plans, the vast array of fragments and, sadly, the handful of near-complete sections add up to a deeply problematic corpus, reminiscent of the result of the "Teilbausystem" in Kafka's *Beim Bau der chinesischen Mauer.* A staggering accumulation of dialogue fragments, embryonic speeches, half-written essays, poems, and rehearsal pieces had gradually built up in Brecht's files. Yet this was to form but part of the ever-expanding work. "*Der Messingkauf* liegt in Unordnung" (*GBA*, 27:170), Brecht noted in September 1943, once more about to put the project on the back burner, where it was to stay, on and off, for a long time. Publishing an interim "Zusammenfassung" in *Kleines Organon* proved little more than a stopgap solution. True, it ensured that a resumé of Brecht's current theoretical position became available in time for his return to East Germany in October 1948. Yet had the series of ambitious plans that stand like monuments to *Der Messingkauf*'s various genetic phases[2] come to full fruition, Brecht would have been better equipped on his return to East Berlin to continue with his writing and directing activities and to ensure an adequate reception of Epic Theater. New work would have been underwritten by an adequate exposition of his current aesthetic thinking and a more pragmatic consideration of contemporary theater work than the scope of either "Kurze Beschreibung" or *Kleines Organon* had permitted. Whether this would have shielded him from the misunderstandings and cultural polemics awaiting him not long after he settled in the GDR is another matter. But Brecht's Marxist credentials would have been less open to suspicion (especially in the West), his position within the vitriolic "Erbe-Debatte"[3] would have been established, and the extent to which theory and practice had moved on since the days of *Mahagonny,* with which, despite *Kleines Organon,* he was still too often identified, would have been impossible to ignore.

*Der Messingkauf,* pursued "mit unterschiedlicher Intensität und größeren Unterbrechungen" (*GBA*, 22:1110), remained a systemically amorphous

---

[2] The notes to *Der Messingkauf* (*GBA*, 22:1110–17) distinguish four main stages: an "Entstehungsphase" (February 1939 until early 1941); a renewed burst of activity (summer 1942 until 5 September 1943); the resumption of work (c.1945), largely as a result of the impetus derived from collaborating with Charles Laughton on *Galileo*; and a final, more sporadic period of activity lasting from the time of *Kleines Organon* (1948) to the publication of *Theaterarbeit* (1952). A detailed genetic account of the principal phases and the ever-changing shape of *Der Messingkauf* is given in *BHB*, 4:192–220; the main features of the fragment's treatment in *GBA* are set out on pages 192–94.

[3] See Brüggemann (1973, 178–211) on Brecht's role in the "Erbe" debate.

project about which its author's judgments continually fluctuated. There were times when waning enthusiasm tipped over into resignation. Picking up the reins again in October 1940, Brecht confessed: "Wenn ich zur Abwechslung den *Messingkauf* aufschlage, ist es mir, als werde mir eine Staubwolke ins Gesicht geblasen. Wie kann man sich vorstellen, daß dergleichen je wieder Sinn bekommt?" (*GBA*, 26:413–14). Extensive pictorial documentation of the Wehrmacht's preparations for an invasion of Britain following hard on the heels of this passage shows Brecht's skepticism to be primarily motivated by free Europe's imperilled predicament. Throughout July and August, his journal repeatedly gives shape to a tension between an awareness of the threat of Nazi invasion and the dogged sense of purpose with which the playwright pursued his political-cum-aesthetic concerns. This is noticeable in the juxtaposition of thoughts on Wordsworth's poetry with photos of civilians undergoing gasmask-training (24.8.40), the insertion of pictures of a bomber's cockpit and hand grenades into a series of entries on the Greek epigram (28–29.8.40), and the way in which a seemingly innocent production decision ("Brot und Milch oder Reis und Tee für die *Sezuan*-Parabel") follows press photographs of chaotic scenes on the beaches at Dunkirk (*GBA*, 26:396–97), while thoughts on Boswell's *Life of Samuel Johnson* sit incongruously next to a war map of Great Britain demonstrating the island's vulnerability to air and sea attack (*GBA*, 26:414–15). Despite Brecht's constant awareness of living in dark times,[4] the looming Nazi threat never caused him to abandon *Der Messingkauf*. In 1945, now in California, he returned to the project with redoubled enthusiasm, yet was still unable to bring sufficient system into the "Unordnung" that had caused him such despair two years before. Once *Kleines Organon* had been seen through the press, any need to complete what was supposed to be Brecht's crowning theoretical achievement became less pressing, in part because his energies were now taken up with practical theater work and bouts of internal GDR aesthetic wrangling, but also because *Theaterarbeit* and the various "Modellbücher" had taken over the role of interim status reports. By this time, *Der Messingkauf* had become both the most rewarding and frustrating of all of Brecht's major theoretical enterprises.

The nature of this grandiose project and Brecht's failure to complete it go hand in hand. We have seen how some of the earlier theoretical essays resorted to various "epic" structuring devices and new inventive forms of "Theorieverfremdung." Now going a step further, *Der Messingkauf* attempts to expound, illustrate *and perform* theory by means of an ingenious presen-

---

[4] The Philosopher's "Rede über die Zeit" (*GBA*, 22:733), beginning with an echo of Brecht's poem "An die Nachgeborenen" ("Bedenkt, daß wir in einer finsteren Zeit zusammenkommen"), gives a powerful sense of the state of the world and thus justifies the current reassessment of theater's obligations.

tational strategy largely dictated by the theatrical medium that is at the same time the work's subject-matter.

## The Project's Fictive Context: Method and Antecedents

Brecht's first outline establishes the *setting* of *Der Messingkauf* (only "Über experimentelles Theater" had, as a lecture, a "setting" in this sense). The location is "ein großes Theater [. . .] nach der Vorstellung." The *plot* (and this is also his first theoretical writing to have one) begins thus: "ein Philosoph [ist] gekommen, um sich mit den Theaterleuten zu unterhalten." According to Hecht, Brecht "[bemühte sich], die Theaterleute als echte Widersacher zu gestalten, als hervorragende Vertreter des alten Theaters" (Hecht 1972, 116). In reality, the group comes across as less monolithically reactionary than this implies and the label "Vertreter des alten Theaters" would be an insult to some of the dialogue's participants. The complexity of Brecht's new, less adversarial paradigm is made clear in the initial explanatory comments on the list of *dramatis personae*:

DIE PERSONEN DES MESSINGKAUFS

*Der Philosoph* wünscht das Theater rücksichtslos für seine Zwecke zu verwenden. Es soll getreue Abbilder der Vorgänge unter den Menschen liefern und eine Stellungnahme des Zuschauers ermöglichen.

*Der Schauspieler* wünscht, sich auszudrücken. Er will bewundert werden. Dazu dienen ihm Fabel und Charaktere.

*Die Schauspielerin* wünscht ein Theater mit erzieherischer gesellschaftlicher Funktion. Sie ist politisch.

*Der Dramaturg* stellt sich dem Philosophen zur Verfügung und verspricht, seine Fähigkeiten und Kenntnisse zum Umbau des Theaters in das Thaeter des Philosophen zur Verfügung zu stellen. Er erhofft sich eine Neubelebung des Theaters.

*Der Beleuchter* gibt das neue Publikum ab. Er ist Arbeiter und mit der Welt unzufrieden. (*GBA*, 22:696)

These are people who, in different ways and to varying degrees, have much to learn from one another. The principle outlined in the section "Ausführungen des Philosophen über den Marxismus," according to which "die Lehre kritisiert die menschliche Praxis und läßt sich von ihr kritisieren" (*GBA*, 22:717), applies as much to this theatrical microcosm as it does to the political world at large. This holds true even in the case of the Philosopher; witness the reference to his ruthlessness. It is glaringly obvious when it comes to the Actor lost in his professional self-absorption. And it is arguably also a characteristic of the politicized Actress with her single-minded concentration on the didactic, and of the *Dramaturg*[5] obsessed with changing the theater rather than the world. It even applies to the Lighting Technician (also in places referred to as the Stagehand), the group's token worker, because despite his political dissatisfaction with the world, he is associated with a narrow specialization offering little sense of a solution to the dramatized problems his lighting illuminates, and also because his only concern is with getting the sets changed as soon as possible so that he can go home. Yet for all their shortcomings, the diverse participants in the discussions to follow are, with the exception of the Philosopher, people with valuable hands-on experience of the theater: "Sie haben teilgenommen an den Bemühungen um ein Theater des wissenschaftlichen Zeitalters [i.e. they are *not* Hecht's cardboard cut-out "Vertreter des alten Theaters"]. Jedoch hat die Wissenschaft dadurch wenig gewonnen, das Theater aber allerhand eingebüßt" ( *GBA,* 22:695). This frustrated sense of underachieving is in evidence in the *Dramaturg*'s satirical litany of examples that follows the sad admission "wir scheuen vor keiner Neuerung zurück":

> Alle ästhetischen Gesetze sind längst über Bord geworfen. Die Stücke haben bald fünf Akte, bald fünfzig, mitunter sind auf einer Bühne gleichzeitig fünf Schauplätze aufgebaut, das Ende ist glücklich oder unglücklich, wir hatten Stücke, wo das Publikum das Ende wählen konnte. Außerdem spielen wir einen Abend stilisiert, den andern ganz natürlich. Unsere Schauspieler sprechen Jamben so geschickt wie den Jargon der Gosse. Die Operetten sind häufig tragisch, die Tragödien enthalten Songs. Den einen Abend steht auf der Bühne ein Haus, das in jeder Kleinigkeit, bis auf die letzten Ofenröhre, einem echten Haus nachgebildet ist, am nächsten deuten ein paar bunte Balken eine Weizenbörse an. Über unsere Clowns werden Tränen vergossen, vor unsern Tragödien hält man sich den Bauch. Kurz, bei uns ist alles möglich, ich möchte sagen: leider. ( *GBA,* 22:775)

The above catalogue contains a number of topical allusions: to Karl Kraus's mammoth *Die letzten Tage der Menschheit,* Alfons Paquet's simultaneous stage sets, Brecht's *Der Jasager* and *Der Neinsager,* Leo Lania's *Konjunktur,* Walter Mehring's *Der Kaufmann von Berlin,* as well as a host of other post-Expressionist plays and modish agitprop productions. As if we had not heard

---

[5] The term *Dramaturg,* still used in modern German (unlike its earlier English equivalent "Dramaturge"), has no counterpart in modern English. It signifies: the literary and artistic director of a theater, responsible for planning programs of performances, script editing, and advising on the choice of costumes, scenery, and lighting. From the time of Lessing's *Hamburgische Dramaturgie,* the *Dramaturg* has often been responsible for writing dramaturgical or aesthetic statements about the company's work.

it before, the impression is of a frenetic obsession with novelty, causing contemporary theater to become permissive to the point of losing all sense of direction. The *Dramaturg* recalls having once put on "ein Stück über die Kommune" (*GBA*, 22:714), and a note suggests that this is probably a reference to Nordahl Grieg's *Nederlaget* (premièred under Ruth Berlau's directorship in Copenhagen in 1937).[6] Yet what this says about the *Dramaturg* is unclear. Has he been otherwise involved in left-wing political theater, as Berlau had been, or is he an alter ego of the Brecht who will go on to write *Die Tage der Kommune*? That this remark remains politically unproductive suggests that even the *Dramaturg* is in need of inspired leadership. A philosopher, not a *Dramaturg* or even a playwright, is entrusted with the task of giving the right political impetus.

The fact that the participants come together after a performance on the very stage where they are now sitting[7] suggests that the experiences of that evening have strengthened their resolve to reassess their work. Whether their dissatisfaction implies that the East German groups with which Brecht worked while drafting later sections of *Der Messingkauf* were less open to Epic Theater than he wished is a moot point. But it may be significant that the Actor informs the Philosopher: "Immer noch steht deinem Thaeter[8] unser Theater sehr im Weg" (*GBA*, 22:756) and that this occurs in a fragment

---

[6] Margarete Steffin's German translation of the Norwegian's play was published in *Das Wort* in 1938. However, in a letter to Helene Weigel of 25–26 February 1949 (*GBA*, 29:501), Brecht rejected the work as "erstaunlich schlecht" ("zeig das niemandem mehr"), yet still rescueable. If the allusion is correct, this does not speak well for the *Dramaturg*'s past track record.

[7] An early exchange identifies the play staged that evening: "PHILOSOPH [. . .] Nimm den heutigen Abend! Als dein Lear seine Töchter verwünschte" etc. (*GBA*, 22:709). Given the number of references to *King Lear* in *Der Messingkauf*, especially the extended discussion (*GBA*, 22:806–7) and the role that it played in earlier explanations of "Historisierung," there is no reason to assume that this detail no longer formed part of the setting.

[8] A dialogue fragment attributed to the Philosopher and headed "Das Thaeter" explains: "Unser Thaeter wird sich vom Theater, diesem allgemeinen, alterprobten, berühmten und unentbehrlichen Institut, außerordentlich unterscheiden [. . .]. Ein wichtiger Unterschied [. . .] wird der sein, daß es nicht für ewige Zeiten eröffnet werden soll. Nur der Not des Tages, gerade unseres Tages, eines düsteren zweifellos, soll es dienen" (*GBA*, 22:761). Later, "Thaeter" is defined as entailing pleasure for didactic purpose: "DER PHILOSOPH Ich benötige aber Nachahmungen von Vorfällen aus dem Leben für meine Zwecke. Was machen wir da? DER DRAMATURG Von ihrem Zweck [der Unterhaltung] getrennt, ergäben die Nachahmungen eben nicht mehr Theater, weißt du. DER PHILOSOPH Das wäre mir unter Umständen dann weniger wichtig. Wir könnten ja, was dann entstünde, anders nennen, sagen wir: Thaeter" (*GBA*, 22:779).

dating from the earliest phase of work on *Der Messingkauf.* No comparable sentiment is to be found in fragments written after Brecht's return to East Berlin.

The agenda seems to be clear: "Aus einer Kritik des Theaters wird neues Theater" (*GBA*, 26:196). At the same time, the debates sparked off by the Philosopher's arrival are already theater on theater, or to be more precise, a form of "Verfremdungstheater," staking out the aims, political *raison d'être*, and possibilities of the genre. This is made explicit from the outset. After some banter about whether or not the stage set should be left standing for the duration of the discussion ("Wir müssen unsern Freund auch bitten, die Kulissen nicht allzu rasch abzubauen, da sonst zuviel Staub aufgewirbelt wird"), the *Dramaturg* spells out the aptness of the location:

> Du [siehst] als Philosoph ja ganz gern hinter die Kulissen, und du als Schauspieler hast, wenn schon kein Publikum, so doch wenigstens seine Stühle im Rücken. Während wir über das Theater sprechen, können wir hier das Gefühl haben, dieses Gespräch vor einem Publikum zu führen, also selber ein kleines Stück aufzuführen. Auch haben wir die Gelegenheit, ab und zu, wenn dies unsern Gegenstand klären sollte, einige kleine Experimente zu veranstalten. (*GBA*, 22:773)

The pertinent and yet defamiliarizing[9] setting is the enabling condition for "viel Theorie in Dialogform." But it is also justified by the inclusion of a series of "Übungsstücke für Schauspieler" in the overall plan for *Der Messingkauf.*[10] Even some of the work's poems and "*Reden*" have a double

---

[9] An accompanying note reads: "Die Schauspieler gestört in der Illusion durch die Kulissen" (*GBA*, 22:719).

[10] The "Übungsstücke für Schauspieler" are not theoretical statements, but rehearsal procedures, involving "Parallelszenen" from daily life, invented to create a new relationship to classical works on the actor's part: e.g. "Der Mord im Pförtnerhaus *(Zu Shakespeares "Macbeth," II, 2)*" (*GBA*, 22:830–33) and "Der Streit der Fischweiber *(Zu Schillers "Maria Stuart," 3. Akt)*" (*GBA*, 22:834–39). There are also "Zwischenszenen" to *Hamlet* (*GBA*, 22:840–47) and an exercise in speaking verse onstage: "Der Wettkampf des Homer und Hesiod" (*GBA*, 22:847–52). Brecht stresses the practical value of such exercises for the actor (especially in terms of a new relationship to the plot), rather than their theoretical implications. The "Parallelszenen" are introduced with the explanation: "Die folgenden Übertragungen [...] in ein prosaisches Milieu sollen der Verfremdung der klassischen Szenen dienen. [...] Die Übertragungen stellen das Interesse an den Vorgängen wieder her und schaffen beim Schauspieler außerdem ein frisches Interesse an der Stilisierung und der Verssprache der Originale, als etwas Besonderem, Hinzukommendem" (*GBA*, 22:830). The *Hamlet* pieces "sollen eine heroisierte Darstellung des Hamlet verhindern. [...] Die Zwischenszenen für 'Romeo und Julia' sollen [...] die Darsteller des Romeo und der Julia instand setzen, diese Charaktere widerspruchsvoll aufzubauen" (*GBA*,

structure of address, inasmuch as they can be delivered to an audience (real or imagined), while at the same time forming part of the onstage exchanges. As the project moved beyond any simple discussion format, a new multi-genre fragmentariness and (often unintentional) discontinuity created a situation where only a selective montage of pieces could still be performed before a live audience. That this was in some way feasible is demonstrated by the Ensemble's ninety-minute stage production for the Theater am Schiff-bauerdamm's "Brecht-Abend Nr. 3" (première: 12 October 1963).[11]

As we saw from some of the poems in chapter 3, the *Messingkauf* project was by no means simply "Theorie *in Dialogform.*" (Willett's English title, *The Messingkauf Dialogues,* is misleading.) In the two published versions of the material: in *Schriften zum Theater/GW*[12] and *GBA,* the ratio of dialogue to non-dialogue varies from approximately equal to one third to two-thirds. The incorporation into Hecht's edition of various essays later denied a place in the *GBA* version accounts for further differences in ratio. The publication in *GBA,* vol. 22 of a substantial hitherto unpublished corpus of draft material, as well as a number of "Gedichte aus dem *Messingkauf*" (there were none in the *GW,* vol. 16 version of *Der Messingkauf*), also creates a different generic mix. It therefore seems ironic that in 1951, by which time the increasing river of draft *Messingkauf* outpourings threatened to burst its banks and widen out into much more than the planned work "in Dialogform" referred to in the Danish journal, Brecht should declare once more that *Der Messingkauf* was a *dialogue,* a "Viergespräch über eine neue Art, Theater zu spielen" or a "Gespräch über neue Aufgaben des Thea-

---

22:840). The specific sequence ("Es wird eine [Shakespeareszene] gespielt, dann eine improvisierte Szene aus dem Alltagsleben mit dem gleichen theatralischen Element, dann wieder die Shakespeareszene" [*GBA,* 26:354]) replicates the dialectic of "verstehen — nicht verstehen — verstehen" described in "Dialektik und Verfremdung" (*GBA,* 22:401).

[11] Details can be found in the *Messingkauf* "Rezeption" section (*GBA,* 22:1123), "Die Trompete und das Messing" (Hecht 1972, 133–39) and the "Dickschädel" episode of *Helene Weigel* (Hecht 2000, 84–85). Werner Hecht, Matthias Langhoff, Manfred Karge and Manfred Wekwerth were responsible for the "Bühnenfassung" based on the *GW* version of *Der Messingkauf.* The stage adaptation ran for over 100 performances, mainly at the Theater am Schiffbauerdamm in East Berlin but also as guest performances in the GDR and abroad, although an embargo was subsequently placed on further performances. A radio version entitled *Dialoge aus dem "Messing-kauf,"* based on the East Berlin "Bühnenfassung," adapted and produced by Klaus Schöning, was broadcast by the Westdeutscher Rundfunk in the series "Hörspiele im WDR" on 18 November 1968.

[12] The "Lese-Fassung" in Volume 5 of *Schriften zum Theater* is, according to *BHB,* 4:193, "ein Produkt der Herausgeberin Elisabeth Hauptmann." *GW* offers a "text-revidierte" version of it. The *GBA Registerband* (806) lists the main differences.

ters."[13] Whether this was a private injunction to himself apropos the need to return to the generic purity of the original conception or was simply the most economic way to refer to what was virtually becoming a piece of "progressive Universalpoesie" in Friedrich Schlegel's sense is impossible to say. In Hecht's assessment, "was nach 1942 für den *Messingkauf* geschrieben wurde, fügt sich nicht mehr in den ursprünglichen Dialograhmen ein" (Hecht 1972 121), but in truth Brecht had never set out to write an exclusively single-genre piece: "von Anfang an hat Brecht die Absicht, auch Essays in den *Messingkauf* aufzunehmen. So sieht er den Aufsatz *Abstieg der Weigel in den Ruhm* (möglicherweise schon Ende 1938 begonnen) während der Arbeit am *Messingkauf* 1939 in der Vierten Nacht [. . .] vor" (*GBA*, 22:1112). The "Übungsstücke für Schauspieler" also belonged to the complex by 1940. Brecht seems to have always entertained irreconcilable intentions, as far as the question of the genre, or genres, to be used was concerned: "Ihm ist daran gelegen, den Ertrag seiner zahlreichen, häufig bruchstückhaften kleineren theoretischen Texte über das Theater in einem größeren Werk zu ordnen und zusammenzufassen. Dazu scheint ihm die Gesprächsform gute Möglichkeiten zu bieten, andererseits will er aber [. . .] auch vorhandene Arbeiten verwenden. So entsteht ein großes Projekt in Dialogform, das auch andere Gattungen zuläßt" (*GBA*, 22:1110).

Various repercussions of this tension between a homogeneous work of "Theorie in Dialogform" and one encompassing a number of genres and text types are worth noting. For example, the fact that when it came to pre-publishing some of the material in *Theaterarbeit*, Brecht permitted a number of poems and speeches to be included, but no dialogue. Individual poems and short speeches were easier to separate off for independent publication, but their exclusive use is nevertheless at odds with the picture of *Der Messingkauf* presented in *Versuche*. Equally surprisingly, during the crucial 1945 period, when substantial new sections were being produced, little dialogue was added (on this, see *GBA*, 22:1116), although Brecht was not averse to incorporating sequences of poetry into draft "Reden" (e.g. *GBA*, 22:812–13). More surprisingly, the "Nachträge zum *Messingkauf*," one of the most important parts of the project, were set out in numbered, *Organon*-like prose sections, with no use being made of the discussion format. To be sure, the "Nachträge," being concerned with general issues of principle, are more suited to treatment in discursive prose. Yet given the early date of composition, one might have expected the "Nachträge," if "Nachträge" they really are,[14] to be in the form of a retrospective discussion (a "post-

---

[13] *Versuche* 11 (1951), 108 and *Versuche* 14 (1955), 104.

[14] The "Nachträge" are not postscripts in the way that the numbered parts of the "Anhang" to "Kurze Beschreibung" are. They came into being so early on that there

performance" discussion analogous to the scenario of *Der Messingkauf* itself). So one is left with the paradox that even in the late 1930s, when Brecht was still enthusing about "Theorie in Dialogform," he at the same time contemplated the inclusion of more of his earlier theoretical essays into the corpus than would be envisaged later on.

Both main editions of *Der Messingkauf* offer ample evidence of the coexistence of dialogue, poetry and prose within the wider theoretical matrix, and in the case of *GBA,* even fragments whose generic status is unclear.[15] Possible reasons why the material is in different genres when different topics are discussed have not to my knowledge been put forward, although Hecht tends to favor the assumption that existing material, "zunächst lediglich in Prosafassungen," was awaiting transformation into dialogue (Hecht 1972, 246–47). In some instances, however, there may be more serious underlying reasons. Thus, to return to an example already cited, there could be a link between Brecht's desire to make a forceful statement about Helene Weigel's acting in "Abstieg der Weigel in den Ruhm" (*GBA,* 22:796–98) and the choice of discursive prose as the medium. Such a move could well have been influenced by the wish to put on the record facts about the actress's epic achievements that were, in Brecht's eyes, non-negotiable. Or, to view the issue in more general terms: while Brecht may have seen certain attractions to putting the substance of various already written theoretical fragments into the mouths of the discussion's respective interlocutors, choices had to be made about what material would work well — or more plausibly — as part of a larger perspectivized dialogue and what would not. Any consideration of such a possibility would require not just functional distinctions between the role played by dialogue, essayistic, poetic and "Rede" genres in *Der Messingkauf,* but also a more sophisticated discrimination between types of dialogue — both in this work and in Brecht's theoretical writings in general.

The journal entry about theory in dialogue form is followed by the parenthetical "(angestiftet zu dieser Form von Galileis *Dialogen*)" (*GBA,* 26:327). Nevertheless, this remark about the importance of Galileo's dialogues[16] needs to be treated circumspectly. Brecht's attention was undoubt-

---

was as yet too limited a body of theory to supplement. In places, they read more like plans for further drafts.

[15] Two of the Philosopher's fragmentary speeches (B, 11–12, *GBA,* 22:710–11) are described as "vermutlich Monologteile der geplanten Rede [des Philosophen über die Unwissenheit]" (*GBA,* 22:1118). The terms "Monologteile" and "geplante Rede" reflect the passages' ambiguity. Thematically they could just as well be drafts of the discussions of the First Night, not yet "dialogisiert." Their apodictic tone often suggests that only the Philosopher could say certain lines, but whether in the body of the discussion or as part of a "Rede" is open to question.

[16] *Dialogo sopra i due massimi sistemi del mondo, tolemaico, e copernicano* (1632) and *Discorsi e dimostrazione matematiche intorno a due nuove scienze attenenti alla me-*

edly drawn to the advantages of "dialogisierte Theorie" while he was researching the parts of the play which have Galilei engaged in scientific discussion with his collaborators and when he was looking for a quotation from the *Discorsi* with which to conclude the recantation scene. But this does not mean that *Der Messingkauf* employs the mode in a way strictly comparable to that used by the historical Galileo. To take an obvious detail, no figure in *Der Messingkauf*, not even the Actor, plays the traditional role of Fool allocated to Simplicio in Galileo's *Dialogo*. A genuine Simplicio figure would surely have made a more robust attempt to defend Aristotelian theatre. True, there are times when the Actor serves as foil to the Philosopher, but he is also allowed to make intelligent points and is seldom a mere token antagonist or a way of ridiculing adversaries. Already there appears to be a discrepancy between Brecht's acknowledgment of the part played by Galileo's writings in his realization of the importance of dialogue as an effective medium for theorizing and the way in which the participants interact in the *Dialogo* and *Discorsi*, on the one hand, and *Der Messingkauf*, on the other. In any case, as we have seen, within just over eighteen months, while again working on *Der Messingkauf*, Brecht would choose to highlight the importance of Diderot's *Jacques le fataliste* and Kivi's *Seitsemän veljestä* for his grasp of the advantages of what he calls "die Art, Zwiegespräche einzuflechten" (*GBA*, 26:430). And he does so in a journal entry only two weeks before his summary of the content of the First Night of *Der Messingkauf*.

Buehler describes *Der Messingkauf* as being "in der Art des Platonischen Dialogs," but makes nothing of the point, apart from a reference to Brecht as "seine Ansichten durch die Figur des Philosophen äußernd" (Buehler 1978, 129). In fact, a later table of *Messingkauf* contents (circa 1945) refers to this longer-standing dialogue tradition. Part (a) of the section "Der V-Effekt" reads: "[Der V-Effekt] im täglichen Leben (Grammatik, Sokratischer Dialog)" (*GBA*, 22:793). That the specific grammar of everyday discourse can defamiliarize is not something new in Brecht's writings, but it is Handke's version of the "*Nicht — Sondern*" model that offers more examples of grammar's potential in this respect. And the bold suggestion that one finds instructive examples of Socratic dialogue in everyday contexts seems like a dazzling flash of lateral thinking about an idea, but it is then set aside presumably for later development. Brecht did, however, describe his Galilei, a figure very close to the Philosoph of *Der Messingkauf*, as having a "Sokratesgesicht" (*GBA*, 29:181). And one Brecht scholar, seeing in Mutter Courage echoes of "Brecht's Socratic contrariness," also suggests that

---

*canica ed i movimento locali* (1638), known to Brecht in Arthur von Oettingen's translation: *Unterredungen und mathematische Demonstrationen über zwei neue Wissenszweige, die Mechanik und die Fallgesetze betreffend*, 2 vols, Leipzig: Englemann, 1890–91.

"Brecht's model, as is made manifest in *The Messingkauf Dialogues,* was Socrates" (Thomson 1997, 14, 12).

In the first paragraph of his *Kalendargeschichte* "Der verwundete Sokrates," the completion of which is also recorded in the journal entry of 12 February 1939 announcing the start of work on *Der Messingkauf,* Brecht succinctly characterizes the Socratic method. This method was familiar to him from his study of the *Symposium* when he was in search of material for his fictional account of Socrates at war. Given the authority with which it is set out in Brecht's story, it might be considered one further putative model for the method of *Der Messingkauf.* "Der verwundete Sokrates" (Socrates Wounded, 1938) introduces its protagonist via a traditional association, based on the metaphor of midwifery, as "der Sohn der Hebamme, der in seinen Zwiegesprächen so gut und leicht und unter so kräftigen Scherzen seine Freunde wohlgestalter Gedanken entbinden konnte und sie so mit eigenen Kindern versorgte, anstatt wie andere Lehrer ihnen Bastarde aufzuhängen" (*GBA,* 18:410). Even though the two thinkers are arguing to very different ends, the terms in which the fifth-century B.C. Greek philosopher is described could in many respects apply to Brecht's Philosopher. The Socratic *elenchus* (literally: "cross-examining"), a series of question-and-answer routines by which Plato's Socrates tests the assumptions of his interlocutors and discovers inconsistencies in their thinking, is not without parallels in *Der Messingkauf.* Many of the exchanges orchestrated by Brecht's Philosopher, for example the exploration of the Fourth Wall convention, to be looked at below, have more in common with the Socratic method of theorizing than the historical Galileo's presentational strategies. This is not to lay claim to the Philosopher as a Socratic figure; he is no more this than he is simply the Marxist Brecht in disguise.[17] Yet any

---

[17] Given that *Der Messingkauf* at one stage points to the role of the *raisonneur* in Naturalist drama (*GBA,* 22:770), the issue could be summed up by asking whether the Philosopher is Brecht's *raisonneur.* N.B. Hecht's claim "natürlich ist der Philosoph nicht etwa identisch mit Brecht" and "der Philosoph des *Messingkaufs* erinnert somit viel eher an jenen Typ, den Brecht in seinem Text *Über die Art des Philosophierens* beschreibt" (Hecht 1972, 110–11). On two occasions in *Der Messingkauf* a distinction is made between the Philosopher and Brecht. In the first, the Philosopher asks what "der Stückschreiber" [*sic*] has to say about changing the text of plays (*GBA,* 22:745). In the second, the Actor asks the Philosopher: "Sagte der Augsburger etwas über seinen Zuschauer?" To which comes the reply "Ja. Folgendes," followed by the Philosopher's reciting of Brecht's poem "Neulich habe ich meinen Zuschauer getroffen" (*GBA,* 22:754–55). Hecht also suggests that at one point the "Rede des Dramaturgen (aus *Der Messingkauf*)," (*GBA,* 22:856–57) "macht den Dramaturgen zu einer Art Sprachrohr des Stückeschreibers" (Hecht 1972, 121). First published in *Theaterarbeit,* the "Rede des Stückeschreibers über das Theater des Bühnenbauers Caspar Neher (Aus: *Der Messingkauf*)" (*GBA,*

conclusion about how he conducts his discourse has implications for our image of the other participants' roles and status in *Der Messingkauf.* Does Brecht's Philosopher, like Plato's Socrates, reason from a hypothesis, unlike Aristotle, who invariably started from premises "known" to be true? If Socrates's *elenchus* had a tendency to demolish rather than build constructively upon the opponent's position, this might give us a purchase on any possible appropriation of the Socratic method on Brecht's part. At the very least, we can surmise that Plato's Socrates, the historical Galileo of the *Dialogo* and *Discorsi*, and even the Diderot of *Jacques le fataliste*, while all making extensive use of dialogue in diverse theorizing contexts, do so in different ways. To which method Brecht's dialogue fragments approximate is still a matter for investigation. But one can posit differences of kind between, at the one end of the spectrum, an authoritarian, manipulative form of dialogue where there is one dominant interlocutor, for example, Herr Keuner (the author's *raisonneur*, as it were), as is the case with the Socrates of the *Symposium* and the *Phaedo*,[18] and a less orchestrated, free exchange of ideas (which may or may not be extensively in evidence in *Der Messingkauf*), at the other.

No such distinction is allowed for in "Die Trompete und das Messing," where Hecht postulates a series of "Vorläufer des *Messingkaufs*": "Die im *Messingkauf* gewählte Form des Dialogs hatte Brecht schon in den zwanziger Jahren für theoretische Untersuchungen benutzt. Ausgangspunkt waren Gespräche mit Fachleuten, die er, vor allem im Rundfunk, geführt hat" (Hecht 1972, 118–19). The reader is referred to a broadcast discussion between Brecht, Alfred Kerr, and the Theaterintendant Richard Weichert (Radio Berlin, 15 April 1928).[19] In the case of the surviving dialogue sketch for this "Dreigespräch,"[20] we are even told that "Brecht [hat] in seinen Notizen Kerrs Beiträge ausgespart"; we also hear of Brecht's "Notizen zu diesem (oder über dieses) Dreigespräch" (Hecht 1972, 118), the limping formulation suggesting uncertainty as to whether these are rigidly prescriptive planning notes or the record of a discussion already transmitted. Hecht also cites dialogues in which Brecht's interlocutors are not identified, as well as "eine größere Niederschrift" of one where Ihering's contribution had been pre-scripted on the basis of a recent publication. Yet none of these re-

---

22:853–55) even has Brecht appearing "als agierende Person im *Messingkauf*" (*BHB*, 4:218).

[18] One of the Herr Keuner stories from Brecht's *Kalendergeschichten* is on the subject of Socrates and epistemology ("Sokrates," *GBA*, 18:444–45).

[19] "Die Not des Theaters" (*GBA*, 21:229–32). A note refers to an original broadcast on the "Deutsche Welle" (Frankfurt a. M.-Stuttgart, 11 April 1928; *GBA*, 21:690).

[20] "Die Not des Theaters: *Ein Dreigespräch zwischen Dichter, Theaterleiter und Kritiker*" (*GBA*, 21:690–92).

markable features, the kind we noted many examples of in chapter 3, prompts any consideration of the differences between the radio discussions of the Weimar period[21] and Brecht's use of dialogue in *Der Messingkauf*. The claim that, in the case of the early exchanges, "die Dialogform bot die Möglichkeit, die Probleme von verschiedenen Standpunkten aus zu betrachten und zu untersuchen" (118), fails to acknowledge the manipulativeness of Brecht's radio discussions, and they were invariably *Brecht's* and no-one else's. The leading question in the present context is, therefore, whether things had changed by the time of *Der Messingkauf* and if the discussions in the theater would resemble "das Auditorium der Staatsmänner" that an early plan intended theater itself to become (*GBA*, 22:697).

We have already encountered Knopf's view that *Kleines Organon* represented a regression to *ex cathedra* pronouncements by comparison with the subtler interchange of views in *Der Messingkauf*. His subsequent, extremely positive discussion of this "komplexe neue Form" spells out the main advance in the medium's handling in Brecht's greatest theoretical project:

> *Der Messingkauf* [ist] als "Theorie" einzigartig und bis heute in seiner Bedeutung weder erkannt noch durch andere Theatertheorien erreicht [...]. *Der Messingkauf* [...] realisiert die Theorie praktisch. Er setzt den Philosophen auf das Theater (realisierte Metaphor vom "Philosophen auf dem Theater"[22]) und konfrontiert ihn mit Theaterpraktikern;

---

[21] Manipulated dialogue is not just a feature of Brecht's early theorizing. According to a note to "Einige Irrtümer über die Spielweise des Berliner Ensembles" (January 1955): "Brecht verteilt die Argumente, auf die es ihm ankommt, in individualisierender Weise auf die einzelnen Gesprächsteilnehmer. Die Namenskürzel sind zwar die Initialen der genannten Mitarbeiter des Berliner Ensembles, aber nach deren übereinstimmender Erinnerung gibt Brecht ihre Meinungen nicht authentisch wieder" (*GBA*, 23:581). "Hemmt die Benutzung des Modells die künstlerische Bewegungsfreiheit?" (*Theaterarbeit*, 309–14), ostensibly a discussion between Brecht and Erich Alexander Winds, *Intendant* of the Städtische Bühnen Wuppertal, is annotated in *GBA* as follows: "Brecht hat durch Ruth Berlau von der Kritik erfahren, der Winds wegen seines Entschlusses zu einer Modellinszenierung ausgesetzt ist. Ein 'Gespräch' dieser Art hat Brecht mit Winds nicht geführt. Die ihm durch die Zeitungskritiken bekannten und von Ruth Berlau zugetragenen Probleme formuliert er um als 'Fragen' des Intendanten, auf die er dann 'Antworten' gibt" (*GBA*, 25:537–38).

[22] In all probability the reference is to "Der Philosoph im Theater" (c.1939: *GBA*, 22:512), an impassioned plea for a rapprochement between theater people and philosophers: "Tatsächlich behandeln die Theaterleute Dinge, welche die Philosophen sehr interessieren müssen, nämlich das menschliche Benehmen, menschliche Anschauungen und Folgen menschlicher Handlungen." This is one of a number of sketches containing what the *GBA* notes refer to as "direkte oder indirekte Überlegungen zum *Messingkauf*" (*GBA*, 22:1063).

> [. . .] das Theater verwandelt sich für vier Nächte in ein Diskussions-
> forum, das sich (die Zuschauer im Rücken) der Öffentlichkeit ausstellt.
> Zugleich realisiert sich dabei die Theorie nicht mehr monologisch —
> *und damit möglicherweise einseitig, apodiktisch —, sondern dialogisch;*
> *das bannt sowohl die Gefahr der bloß theoretisierenden, womöglich nur*
> *innersprachlichen Argumentation, dient aber auch der Überprüfung, der*
> *"demokratischen" Kontrolle und zielt darauf, die anderen zu überzeugen*
> *(nicht zu überreden): "persuasive Kommunikation"* [Habermas], *wie das*
> *heutige Stichwort lautet).* (Knopf 1980a, 453, my emphasis)

Apart from the accolade implicit in invoking Jürgen Habermas's *Theorie des kommunikativen Handelns,* Knopf uses other equally positive descriptive phrases in respect of *Der Messingkauf*'s form of dialogue, including "'Zusammen-Spiel' von Kontrahenten" and "dialektisch und diskutierend," while rightly stressing the pragmatic nature of the onstage discussions as "in Sprache umgesetzte reale Erfahrungen" (453). The source of these remarks, Knopf's 1980 *Brecht Handbuch,* was presumably based on Elisabeth Hauptmann's earlier "Lese-Fassung" which, by definition, has the effect of making the dialogue appear more seamless and predominant than in *GBA.* Yet leaving aside differences in editorial practice, it is important to approach the *GBA* edition bearing in mind Knopf's position on the radically innova-tive nature of the work's dialogue. I am thinking in particular of the sugges-tion that, as exploited in *Der Messingkauf,* it prevents theoretical statements from becoming overly monologic or one-sided, with the concomitant risk of becoming apodictic; also his assertion that the dialogue format facilitates a democratic to-and-fro of ideas. In other words, his view that the fragmenta-tion of ideas across a spectrum of participants (even though there are times when only the Philosopher and the *Dramaturg* hold center stage) creates a genuinely constructive exchange of ideas between people with a common purpose, but with diverse perspectives, varied professional specializations, and assorted ideological interests.

## The First Night (1): Premises, Aims, and Approaches

Brecht did not record a comment on the specific implications of having his fictive "Theaterleute" meet with the Philosopher over a period of four nights. Possibly, the resultant four-part structure was meant to impose disci-pline on the material, as had been the case with the division of *Kleines Or-ganon* into short units. The post-performance meetings also have the author-ity of an exchange of views based on immediate experience, as well as em-phasizing the essential relationship between theory and practice. Being peo-ple with demanding commitments, the stage's representatives and the visiting Philosopher need to budget their time. Yet if the length of the longest draft version of the first Night of their encounters is anything to go by, the full *Messingkauf* would have far exceeded anything capable of being contained within a single evening's performance time. Any combination of discussion, speeches, poems, and work with the "Übungsstücke" would have come closer to the scale of Wagner's *Ring* cycle than that of a Berliner Ensemble "Brecht-Abend." To put the project in perspective, the *Messingkauf* material published in *GBA*, vol. 22 is 174 pages long, already two and a half times the length of the script of the English version of *Leben des Galilei*, a work clearly constructed with an eye to how much could be encompassed within one evening's theater. The various ambitious plans for the full four Nights, of which the final one was to have been the work's apotheosis, force one to the conclusion that, if completed, *Der Messingkauf* could only have been received on the page or, if on the stage, only in some draconian adaptation. And if the entire work had ended up as expansively organized as many of the plans required, any adaptation would risk doing serious damage to the designed interplay of elements. Of course, it is also possible to treat the four incomplete Nights of the surviving fragment as analogous to the loosely structured, quasi-autonomous elements in an epic work. Under such circumstances, a notion of sequentially variable and even subtractable parts would offer a "Brechtian" justification for the work's posthumous "Lese-" and "Spiel-Fassungen," with the "users" of *Der Messingkauf* intended, in *Gebrauchsliteratur* fashion, to utilize it eclectically, selecting parts and testing them for their "Materialwert." Such considerations are academic. The First Night was the only section to exist in continuous dialogue form — as Fragment B 115 (*GBA*, 22:773–80) — and performances of the "Lese-Fassung" were firmly discouraged on principle until the late 1990s. Any treatment of *Der Messingkauf* as an example of epic discontinuity would, in any case, ride roughshod over the reader's continual awareness of the shortfall between heroic conception and the sum of the extant fragments.

A plan from the 1939 to 1941 period gives an overview of the ground to be covered during the various Nights. It is no more than an interim scheme; one should not assume that it would necessarily remain the blueprint for later phases of *Der Messingkauf*. For a start, the essays highlighted below, which were at that time scheduled for inclusion in *Der Messingkauf*, do not appear in later conceptions. However ephemeral, the plan nevertheless gives some sense of the work's intended scope and innovativeness by comparison with Brecht's previous theoretical writings:

A2

*DER MESSINGKAUF*

*Erste Nacht*
Begrüßung des Philosophen im Theater / die Geschäfte gehen flott /
Flucht aus der Wirklichkeit ins Theater / es gibt Altes und es gibt
Neues / der Film als Konkurrenz / der Film ein Test der Gestik / die
Literarisierung / die Montage / die Wirklichkeit / der Kapitalismus,
pokerfaced man / die Wirklichkeit auf dem Theater / die Bedürfnisse
des Philosophen / der Appell / das Engagement

*Zweite Nacht*
Die Poetik des Aristoteles / das Emotionenracket / die neuen Stoffe /
der Held / **K-Typus und P-Typus** / **Theatralik des Faschismus** /
die Wissenschaft / Gründung des Thaeters

*Dritte Nacht*
**Die Straßenszene** / der V-Effekt / das Rauchtheater / die Übungen
/ "Furcht und Elend" / die Shakespeare-Varianten

*Vierte Nacht*
Zurückverwandlung in ein Theater / Chaplin / die Komödie / die
Jahrmarktshistorie / **die chinesische Schauspielkunst** / die fröhliche
Kritik / die Lehrer (*GBA*, 22:695–96)

Even this outline omits a number of key topics, such as dialectical
theater, the relationship of didacticism to entertainment, "das Gestische,"
epic acting, and the use of parables and models as part of the process of
"Historisierung." Some of its items are signalled so cryptically that it is difficult to imagine just how they would have come across in final form. But the
ultimate difficulty stems from the fact that this plan, like so many subsequent
ones, was never fully implemented.

At almost every juncture, Brecht's *Messingkauf* contains textual gaps.
The feeling of fragmentariness is compounded in the new edition by the way
the material has been chronologically subdivided to give a sense of the main
genetic stages of work on the project. At every phase and substage of work
on *Der Messingkauf*, the four-part template offers little more than an approximate accommodating frame for a series of short fragments, autonomous pieces (essays and "Reden"), some assigned to an individual Night,
but coexisting alongside unassigned draft material. Ambiguity reigned right
to the end: a plan dating from the final period, "IV. *Messingkauf* (Wünsche
des Stückeschreibers)" (*GBA*, 22:829), documents Brecht's intention to
include the 1939 essay "Rollenstudium" (*GBA*, 22:600–604). The corres-
ponding *GBA* note ("in den *Messingkauf* nicht aufgenommen" [*GBA*,

22:1136]) leaves it unclear whether this was the result of a later conscious decision not to incorporate the material or a failure to follow up on the proposals listed as "Wünsche des Stückeschreibers." The condition of this work-in-progress is that of a monumental superfragment, a memorial to indecision about what is to be abandoned and what retained, what pieces in the jigsaw puzzle have still to be written, to which Night the floating material should be allotted, how many genres there should be, and in what configurations. During the initial phase of laboring on *Der Messingkauf,* Brecht comes across two quotations in Levin Schücking's *Charakterprobleme bei Shakespeare* and transcribes them without comment, although doubtless aware of their bearing on some of the problems he is having with the project: "In einem Schauspielmanuskript von 1601 sind mehrere Varianten angeführt, und am Rand bemerkt der Verfasser: 'Die eine oder andere dieser Änderungen, wählt die euch am besten scheint' und 'Wenn diese Formulierung schwer verständlich oder nicht für das Publikum geeignet ist, kann die andere genommen werden'" (*GBA,* 22:736). The predicament evoked here, seldom a problem in Brecht's earlier theoretical writings, poses major difficulties for editor, reader, and commentator alike. The order in which elements occur in *GBA* is not, as the editors rightly make clear, intended to reconstruct a "vermutlicher Arbeitsprozeß" (*GBA,* 22:1144), because none can be retrospectively imposed on much of the material. Nor, given that the *Messingkauf* corpus is set out according to the four approximate genetic phases and within them, where possible, according to the Four-Night scheme, can any satisfying sense of overall structural wholeness emerge.

The published condition of the *Messingkauf* project inevitably imposes limitations on how it is used and received. In the last (but not definitive) version of the First Night, there are longer sequences of dialogue that can be explored integrally. But the presence of draft essays and "Reden" means that a systematic treatment of even the dialogue sections of the work would not be a meaningful approach. Certain themes run across a number of Nights and are not fully worked out in any particular one; nor are they restricted to the dialogue portions of *Der Messingkauf.* It will therefore be necessary, in what follows, to extrapolate what Brecht says on certain subjects and treat the material, at least in part, independently of its place in the notional matrix. Before going on to do this, however, we need to address some of the preliminaries that had to be dealt with in the First Night.

One task of the First Night was to explain the work's title. Its meaning is not self-evident; hence readers who knew the "Gedichte aus dem *Messingkauf,*" "Übungsszenen," and "Reden" prepublished in *Versuche* and *Theaterarbeit* had still to wait until 1963, when volume 5 of *Schriften zum Theater* was published, to learn just what the term signified. Yet the "Messingkauf" title had already been in place by February 1939. It is confirmed in the sketch "Thema der Ersten Nacht," from the 1942–43 phase, where it occurs as the last of six headings indicating contents, the others being: "Theater und Wirklichkeit, Zwecke der Kopien, Illusion, Der Naturalismus, K-Typus und P-Typus" (*GBA*, 22:767). It is clear to Brecht that the title needs to be explained within the main body of the discussions about theater's purpose and its methods, if the Philosopher's wishes concerning a socially interventionist theater are to be met. Although it is conceivable that the above list was meant to indicate the sequence in which topics were to be covered, the title is eventually explained much nearer the start of the first encounter. Not surprisingly, it is the Philosopher who sets out what is implied by the compound noun "Messingkauf," for the underlying simile is his and his alone.

> Ich möchte [. . .] betonen, daß ich mich als Eindringling und Außenseiter hier fühle in diesem Haus voll von tüchtigen und unheimlichen Apparaten, als jemand, der hereingekommen ist, nicht um Behagen zu empfinden, ja sogar ohne Furcht Unbehagen erzeugen würde, da er mit einem ganz besonderen Interesse gekommen ist, dessen Besonderheit man gar nicht genug unterstreichen kann. Ich fühle diese Besonderheit meines Interesses so stark, daß ich mir wie ein Mensch vorkomme, der, sagen wir, als Messinghändler zu einer Musikkapelle kommt und nicht etwa eine Trompete, sondern bloß Messing kaufen möchte. Die Trompete des Trompeters besteht aus Messing, aber er wird sie kaum als Messing verkaufen wollen, nach dem Wert des Messings, als soundso viele Pfund Messing. So aber suche ich hier nach meinen Vorfällen unter Menschen, welche ihr hier irgendwie nachahmt, wenn eure Nachahmungen freilich einen ganz anderen Zweck haben als den, mich zu befriedigen. Klipp und klar: ich suche ein Mittel, Vorgänge unter Menschen zu bestimmten Zwecken nachgeahmt zu bekommen, höre, ihr verfertigt solche Nachahmungen, und möchte nun feststellen, ob ich diese Art Nachahmungen brauchen kann. (*GBA*, 22:778)

Clearly, the Philosopher sees himself as a "Messingkäufer" in a sense that the other participants in the group do not apply to themselves.[23] Perhaps because he is the dominant participant in the dialogue, there is no discussion of the image's appropriateness.

An Editorial Note to *The Messingkauf Dialogues* (1965) refers to the work's "cryptic title" (for which the literal translation "Buying Brass" is offered). Elsewhere, readers of *Brecht on Theatre* are informed that the idea "derives from the analogy with a man who buys a brass instrument for the

---

[23] Although Hecht refers to "die heutigen Messingkäufer" in the context of his Berliner Ensemble collaborators (Hecht 1972, 135), there is no evidence of the term's being used in this way during Brecht's lifetime.

metal it is made of rather than for the music it makes. The theatre, in other words, is being cross-examined about its content, from a hard headed practical point of view" (*BT,* 170). Such an explanation supplies information that even the German original cannot mediate through the title alone. But the deferral of an explanation in *Der Messingkauf* itself is for a good reason: i.e. to let the title function as a hermeneutic challenge. Even when the idiosyncratic connotations of the brass-buying simile are revealed, it is still left to the reader to test the appropriateness of the image to the project. Admittedly, it soon becomes clear that the brass buyer stands for the Philosopher and that brass buying is an image for a Marxist utilitarian approach to the value of Epic Theater, as well as an expression of the Philosopher's sense of entering a world to which his political values are as yet alien. Even then, the simile's referential possibilities are not exhausted. The presence of "Übungsstücke" based on classical works of literature permits a narrow reading[24] according to which the Philosopher is encouraging the theater people to revisit Greek drama and the plays of Shakespeare and German classicism in order to test great works for their "Materialwert," that is, what is still worth salvaging for the modern world. (In the *Mahagonny* notes, Brecht had used the metaphor of sieving in a comparable sense.) In one of the early passages that point forward to the "Übungsstücke," the Philosopher says of the canon's false depictions of reality: "Ihr könnt seine Interpretationen [i.e. the playwright's] ja zum Teil wegstreichen, Neues einfügen, kurz, die Stücke als Rohmaterial verwenden" (*GBA,* 22:708). Yet despite this, the Philosopher introduces his brass-buying simile within a much wider framework than as an antidote to any "Einschüchterung durch die Klassizität" (*GBA,* 23:316). The main context is not that of the theater people approaching classical works as a scrap-metal merchant might a brass instrument, but of the Philosopher's own turning to a progressive theater troupe, *in his capacity as philosopher,* in order to assess how much of their work will stand the "Messingkauf" test of material value. In terms of the simile, this means the value as raw metal for ideological purposes of the instrument, or here: the *Apparat.* The bold "Messingkauf" image, an alienation device, involves a process of double historicization. While reassessing the classics in a spirit of Brechtian "Historisierung," the discussion's participants are at the same time obliged to look at themselves from the perspective of those who come after. According to one of the "Nachträge," "Bei der *Historisierung* wird ein

---

[24] Hecht places disproportionate emphasis on this narrower meaning of the "Messingkauf" simile — applying it to the testing of the classics — and fails to do justice to the spirit in which the Philosopher approaches the theatre itself. (Hecht 1972, 126–33) In the "Materialwert" essays, Brecht the playwright approaches canonical works with a new utilitarian criterion, whereas in *Der Messingkauf* the value of the "Übungsstücke" and "Parallelszenen" is for the actors as they prepare their roles.

bestimmtes Gesellschaftssystem [now read: "Theaterapparat"] vom Standpunkt eines anderen Gesellschaftssystems [here read: "kulturpolitisches
Apparat"] aus betrachtet" (*GBA*, 22:699). The brass-buying simile works
with an image calculated to challenge essentialist assumptions about aesthetic values; the imprecise nature of its referentiality is also part of a process
of estrangement.

Although the "Messingkauf" trope was new in 1939, Brecht's concern
with "Materialwert" goes back to the Weimar years.[25] In "Die Trompete
und das Messing," Hecht seeks to trace the "Messingkauf" image to early
examples in Brecht's writings of a contrast between utilitarian value ("Materialwert") and traditional idealist criteria of aesthetic value (Hecht 1972,
108–9). The best-known occurs during Polly Peachum's "wedding" celebra-
tions in *Die Dreigroschenoper,* when Macheath tries to impress his gang and
lift the tone of the occasion by extolling the virtues of connoisseurship
("Habt ihr denn keine Ahnung von Stil? Man muß doch Chippendale von
Louis Quatorze unterscheiden können"). Trauerweiden-Walter responds
like the Philistine he is: "Sieh dir mal das Holz an! Das Material ist absolut
erstklassig" (*GBA*, 2:243). Hecht speaks of "der Vandalismus des Trauerweiden-Walter," while making it clear that this sequence entails more than
a mere throwaway comic one-liner. At stake, Hecht claims, is Brecht's own
new utilitarian aesthetic,[26] here presented in an estranged form (but then,

[25] Discussions of the idea are to be found in Brüggemann (1973, 21–34), Voigts
(1977, 93–98), and *BHB*, 4:196–97. Voigts charges Hecht with misrepresenting
the "Materialwert" concept as a "durchgängiges Motiv" in Brecht's writings, a
criticism taken up in *BHB*, vol. 4: "Die Ausführungen des Philosophen sind zu
Unrecht mit [Brechts] sogenannter 'Materialwert'-Theorie aus den 20er Jahren in
Zusammenhang gebracht worden." The differences between the "Messingkauf"
simile and Brecht's "Materialwert" approach are seen to be the following: "Während
sich die Materialwert-Theorie auf Stücke des klassischen Repertoires bezog und nach
deren 'Gebrauchswert' für ein aktuelles Theater fragte [. . .], interessiert den
Philosophen die Institution Theater und die Frage, inwieweit deren Mittel einem
neuen gesellschaftlichen Zweck zugeführt werden können" (*BHB*, 4:196–97). While
Hecht is rightly criticized for positing loose continuities, the presence of
"Übungsstücke" and "Parallelszenen" in *Der Messingkauf* suggests that the "Materialwert" paradigm has been radically refashioned, rather than completely abandoned.

[26] Werner Mittenzwei explores what he terms Brecht's "Materialästhetik" exclusively
within the framework of the playwright's "Lehrstück" period (Mittenzwei 1976,
241–45). In a dissenting piece, Hans-Dieter Krabiel cautions against such restriction:
"Es gibt gute Gründe, [Brechts] theoretische und praktische Bemühungen um ein
neues Theater seit Mitte der 20er-Jahre insgesamt als fortgesetzten Versuch zu
werten, den Gebrauchsstandpunkt in diesem Bereich durchzusetzen. Seine Polemik
gegen das zeitgenössische Theater enthält im Kern immer den Vorwurf, es habe
keinen Gebrauchswert mehr" (*BHB*, 4:38).

much of this defamiliarizing wedding scene functions as a comment on the nature of theatrical conventions).

In "Forderungen an eine neue Kritik" (c. 1929) (*GBA*, 21:331–32), Brecht announced that "die ästhetischen Maßstäbe sind zugunsten der Maßstäbe des Gebrauchswerts zurückzustellen"; the new criterion should be "Wem nützt sie [i.e. "die Schönheit"]." Around the time of *Die Dreigroschenoper*, he wrote two essays on "Materialwert."[27] The second and more important, entitled "Der Materialwert," tries to imagine how civilized Rome must have reacted to the Vandals' "barbaric" treatment of its precious cultural artifacts which, in their ignorance, they valued solely for the raw material from which they were made: "Holz zum Beispiel gibt Feuer, für das Geschnitzte daran hatten [die Vandalen] keine Augen" (*GBA*, 21:288). To the Romans, Brecht reasons, such an attitude must have seemed like deliberate iconoclasm, "ungeheurer ästhetischer Fanatismus." To subvert such an automatic, culturally conditioned response, "Der Materialwert" implies that the Vandals should be seen as exemplary for the way they rigorously selected from Roman civilization only that which they materially needed. (Brecht, the Marxist, proposes treating the bourgeois *Theaterapparat* in the same way.) Both "Materialwert" essays contain a dash of provocation. At one point, "Der Materialwert" compares the naive practicality of the historical Vandals with the barbaric cultural vandalism of the German Army's subjecting Rheims Cathedral to intense bombardment near the start of the First World War. Shifting his ground drastically while not changing the subject, he goes on to claim that he once considered staging a work by Friedrich Hebbel (1813–63), but had second thoughts on the matter: "Ich habe [. . .] mit drei Worten Hebbels Monumentalwerk *Herodes und Mariamne* zum alten Gerümpel geworfen" (*GBA*, 21:288). A nineteenth-century German classic had evidently failed the "Messingkauf" test! Brecht admits that his only interest would have been in the work's "Materialwert," meaning no more than "die grobe Handlung" — and that, only after the last act had been amputated. But, trusting his better judgment, he had dismissed Heb-

---

[27] Brecht's "Materialwert" (*GBA*, 21:285–86) offers a spirited defence of the director Leopold Jessner's "wohlüberlegte Amputationen und effektvolle Kombinationen mehrerer Szenen" in his attempt to bring out the "Materialwert" of Goethe's *Faust*, thus transforming it into "Jessner's *Faust*," a *Faust* for the Weimar Republic. While this had the effect of making Jessner "der von der Presse gefeierte Anführer des derzeitigen Vandalentums auf dem Theater," Brecht is at the same time defending practices that resemble his own. This first essay, for reasons not unconnected with the *Dreigroschenprozeß*, devotes much space to the charge of literary plagiarism that results from such controversial methods of appropriation. By contrast, "Der Materialwert" (*GBA*, 21:288–89) concentrates on the central implications of the utilitarian approach.

bel's play (he elsewhere uses a noun that mocks its paltry "Materialwert" as no more than that of a "Gipsrelief"[28]). Such "Gipskauf" would have been preposterous, when judged by the standards of a "Messingkäufer."

At this stage of Brecht's thinking, "Materialwert" meant little more than "Gebrauchswert," a popular term in the writings of "Neue Sachlichkeit" intellectuals of the Left.[29] By the time of *Der Messingkauf,* however, particularly because of the Philosopher's dialectical materialist philosophy, it has acquired a sharper edge, as well as becoming more differentiated.[30] Absence of "Materialwert" (encoded class content that a Marxist interpretation could highlight to make selected works of past literature of use in the present) becomes one more reason for rejecting Hebbel or partially rescuing Schiller's *Wallenstein* as in some sense "verwendbar."[31] In *Der Messingkauf* the Philosopher is exploring much more than just the untapped ideological "Materialwert" of the bourgeoisie's classical literary canon. To keep with the metallurgical metaphor, he is *assaying* longstanding theatrical conventions

---

[28] "[Stirbt das Drama?]" (*GBA,* 21:133). In this review for the *Vossische Zeitung* (4 April 1926), Brecht has yet to apply the criterion of "Materialwert." His response remains little more than general polemic: "wir, die wir doch viel gesunden Appetit auf Theater haben, müssen gestehen (und uns dadurch unbeliebt machen), daß zum Beispiel so billiges und gestammeltes Zeug wie dieses Gipsrelief *Herodes und Mariamne* uns nicht mehr befriedigen kann."

[29] See John White 1982 and Midgley 2000, 7–94. Voigts argues that "der oft zitierte Vergleich der Kunst mit den Gebrauchsgegenständen der Vandalen führt irre [. . .], Brecht wollte trotz des Begriffes 'Material' keine 'Verwendbarkeit' der Kunst" (Voigts 1977, 94). Just what his motives were for positioning himself within a Neue Sachlichkeit debate about utilitarian art during the mid-1920s is disputed, but by the time of the "Übungsstücke" and the *Messingkauf*-project, the simile has become less misleading.

[30] The *Brecht Handbuch* comments on the difference between some of the remarks in *Der Messingkauf* and the polemical stance of the "Materialwert" essays: "Eine zu große Neigung zu ändern kann 'das Studium des Textes leichtsinnig machen'; 'aber die Möglichkeit, zu ändern und das Wissen, daß es nötig sein kann, vertieft wiederum das Studium.' [*GBA,* 22:745] Die Sätze belegen, wie entschieden sich [Brechts] Auffassung in diesem Punkt seit der 'Materialwert'-Theorie der 20er-Jahre verändert hat" (*BHB,* 4:205). *BHB,* 4:214 notes further differences.

[31] Just how early the concept became politicized can be seen from Brecht's 1934 piece "Das Proletariat ist nicht in einer weißen Weste geboren" (*GBA,* 22:63–67): "Die Basis unserer Einstellung zur Kultur ist der Enteignungsprozeß, der im Materiellen vor sich geht. Die Übernahme durch uns hat den Charakter einer entscheidenden Veränderung. Nicht nur der Besitzer ändert sich hier, auch das Besitztum. Und das ist ein verwickelter Prozeß. Was von der Kultur also verteidigen wir? Die Antwort muß heißen: jene Elemente, welche die Eigentumsverhältnisse beseitigen müssen, um bestehenzubleiben" (*GBA,* 22:64).

and styles of acting, forms of experimentation, and even Epic Theater itself. The immediate consequence may be that the brass-buyer, the person looking for "Materialwert" in areas generally considered sacrosanct, can come across as Philistine. But his objective is much more than the slaughter of sacred cows; by challenging the established criteria of artistic value, the Philosopher's inquisitive approach demonstrates the need for a new aesthetic worthy of the Theater of the Scientific Age. The "Messingkauf" image is the boldest act of linguistic "Verfremdung" in the title of any of Brecht's theoretical writings.[32]

On the whole, the promised testing comes in the form of the Philosopher's asking the theater people to explain and justify their practices. The ultimate effect, apart from putting many of these anachronistic conventions under the magnifying glass, is to force them to measure their theater work using the yardstick of the Philosopher's ideology, while he asks what help their kind of theater can give him. Throughout *Der Messingkauf*, the project has this double agenda: to test, and find wanting, certain theater practices, and to explain the solution: Epic Theater's method of engaging dialectically with society. It is the same double purpose that had already characterized the two-column schema in the *Mahagonny* notes.

# The First Night (2): Naturalism's Place within the Unfolding Dialogue

Brecht began work on *Der Messingkauf* less than a year after Stanislavsky's death. The theater magician was dead, but not laid to rest. In a journal entry for 15 September 1947 Brecht could still complain: "Bemerkenswert ist, wie die Deutschen das System der progressiven russischen Bourgeoisie der Zarenzeit so ganz und gar unberührt konservieren können" (*GBA*, 27:247). It is therefore not surprising that one of the first fragments for the project, entitled "Naturalismus," has the *Dramaturg* taking issue with "die Hauptwerke des Stanislawski" (*GBA*, 22:703) rather than with "die Poetik des Aristoteles." No works are named, so it is best to assume that what he has in mind is the Russian director's achievements in general. In other words, Naturalism is being generically identified with a contemporary *style of production,* not with classic productions and certainly not in any straightforward sense with the nineteenth-century European movements of that name. Even though the *Dramaturg* sets about criticizing Stanislavsky for being a mu-

---

[32] The image reappears near the end of the *Messingkauf* complex, in a discussion of Shakespeare's *Richard III*. It comes in the Guest's (i.e. the Philosopher's) words: "so zeigen Trompeter Messing und der Apfelbaum im Winter Schnee. Ihr verwechselt zwei Dinge: daß man etwas bei euch findet und daß ihr etwas zeigt" (*GBA*, 22:820).

seum piece ("einige seiner Aufführungen [laufen] nun schon über 30 Jahre ganz unverändert"), what are referred to as his "Naturalist" productions with their "minutiös ausgeführten Gesellschaftsschilderungen" and their obsession with "die Erforschung des Seelenlebens einiger Einzelpersonen" (*GBA*, 22:703–4) function, in this first fragment of dialogue, largely as a foil to the Philosopher's proposed Theater of the Scientific Age. The suggestion that these ossified productions can be compared "mit durch tiefe Spatenstiche gewonnenen Erdklößen, von Botanikern zum Studium auf den Untersuchungstisch gebracht" satirizes their inappropriateness for the contemporary world as well as offering a scientific variant on the "Messingkauf" simile. Thus, even Stanislavsky's achievements possess "Materialwert," inasmuch as they can be dug up and dissected for people to learn from their mistakes. So far, *Der Messingkauf* simply covers old ground. The political case against *trompe l'œil* Naturalism's fixation with surface detail had already been made in "Über experimentelles Theater." But now broad-brush polemic gives way to a certain evenhandedness. The *Dramaturg* puts forward a number of claims in Stanislavsky's defense (his works are documents of their time, have value as material for social scientists, serious "gesellschaftliche Impulse" towards social reform emanated from them) as well as reminding his listeners of Naturalism's failures, although in the process blurring any distinction between period concept and qualititative term. Naturalism's approach, it is claimed (with a play on words), treated society's ills as so "natürlich" that they scarcely elicited any critical response; their painstaking fidelity to surface detail was more a matter of replication than interpretation and the *causes célèbres* championed by Naturalist playwrights were short-lived (by now, the distinction between Stanislavsky's production style and the work of the Naturalist dramatists has become blurred). The fragment concludes in obituary mode by treating Stanislavsky as the personification of Naturalism. It is spoken by the *Dramaturg,* which suggests that it cannot be the last word on the subject, but rather the reaction of a disappointed former devotee:

> Seine Figuren blieben nicht weniger flach, als seine Handlung banal blieb. Der künstlerische Tiefgang war nicht größer als der soziale. Von den Werken Stanislawskis blieben die weniger eingreifenden und mehr beschreibenden länger und wirkten künstlerischer, offen gestanden auch sozial bedeutender. Aber auch sie zeigten keine einzige große Figur und keine einzige Fabel, die denen der Alten an die Seite gestellt werden könnte. (*GBA*, 22:705)

This passage is as much a comment on Stanislavsky's audiences and the plays he put on as a verdict on the producer's work. Even the *Dramaturg* acknowledges the strengths as well as the weaknesses of the Stanislavsky system, logically presented as a phase of modern theater to be overcome. The sense of a need to go beyond the achievements of stage Naturalism, while remaining conscious of its contextual value, raises the question of why, at this relatively late stage of Brecht's theorizing, the phenomenon should be chosen as the starting point for *Der Messingkauf*. Two factors, though not real reasons, are mentioned in the discussion. First, the claim that "wenn die Kritiker nach realistischen Meisterwerken gefragt werden, nennen sie immer naturalistische Werke" (*GBA*, 22:769), which makes Naturalism a way forward to a serious discussion of "realism." Second, the assumed link between mimesis and an appeal to feeling in contemporary theater: "DER PHILOSOPH [. . .] wozu ahmt ihr sie [die Wirklichkeit] also nach? DER SCHAUSPIELER Um die Menschen mit Leidenschaften und Gefühlen zu erfüllen, um sie aus ihrem Alltag und ihren Vorfällen herauszureißen" (*GBA*, 22:777). But this is only part of the story. The focus on Naturalism was also intended to serve positioning purposes, for, as in "Über experimentelles Theater," the discussion works forward from shared notions of experiment and the "Verwissenschaftlichung" of drama and once more prepares the ground for a phaseological conception of German drama's "Weg zum Epischen Theater." Perhaps Brecht simply wanted to present himself as Stanislavsky's grave digger. But tilting at what the fragment itself dismisses as a redundant anachronism was a problematical move in more than one sense. A careful reading of what Stanislavsky says about "the art of mere reproduction" in *An Actor Prepares* (Stanislavsky 1988, 19–20) shows him to be explicitly anti-Naturalist (on this, see Benedetti 1982, 11, and Counsell 1996, 26); but acknowledging this would run counter to Brecht's purpose. Yet, contemplating eventually returning to Eastern Europe, Brecht knew that by mounting one more attack on one of the Soviet Union's cultural icons he would be entering the arena of Zhdanovist *Kulturpolitik*. Instead of forming part of a broader ideological dissection of Aristotelian drama and a defense of Epic Theater, it risked placing Brecht at the center of cultural disputes internal to Marxist aesthetics. When he returned to Naturalism in the 1942–43 phase of work on *Der Messingkauf*, Brecht moved beyond what had to some extent looked like unfinished business from the late 1930s.

Naturalism remains a major ingredient in the two 1942 plans for the First Night: in the first plan, on its own, in the second in the configuration "Der Naturalismus. Wissenschaftliches Zeitalter" (*GBA*, 22:767). After the Philosopher has been welcomed, the first dialogue fragment sets out the case against Naturalism in non-specific terms, with as yet little focus on the Stanislavskian subform. In the second fragment, it appears as part of a more illuminating "Naturalismus — Realismus" antithesis (*GBA*, 22:769). The criterion with which the Philosopher-"Messingkäufer" now approaches various forms of theater concerns their ability to engender critical response. A preliminary note reads: "Beschreibung aristotelischen Theaters. Unmöglichkeit einer kritischen Haltung." The charge concerns audience response: "Durch Hineinversetzen in einen Menschen das Getriebe nicht mehr zu überblicken [. . .]. Das Getriebe zu handhaben von diesem Standpunkt aus unmöglich" (*GBA*, 22:768). The attack is twofold: (a) a distanced perspective is not possible and (b) for that reason an *interventionist* response is not brought about. The charge "Unmöglichkeit einer kritischen Haltung" could also be leveled at Naturalism, be it historical (much of the argument here is conducted in the past tense) or typological. Initially, the *Dramaturg* is content to assert that "die Abbildungen des Naturalismus führten zu einer Kritik der Wirklichkeit." The Philosopher's rejoinder ("Zu einer ohnmächtigen") and his subsequent *post mortem* on the demise of historical Naturalism and the mimetic approach are so phrased as to associate his interlocutors with Stanislavskian bad habits in the past: "Eure naturalistischen Abbildungen waren schlecht gemacht. Darstellend wähltet ihr einen Standpunkt, der keine echte Kritik ermöglicht. In euch fühlte man sich ein, und in die Welt richtete man sich ein. Ihr wart, wie ihr wart, und die Welt blieb, wie sie war" (*GBA*, 22:769). (They can hardly be talking about the performance of *King Lear* that evening, nor could actors talking on a stage in the late 1940s carry the blame for the faults of a Naturalism that was past its heyday some half a century earlier.) *Dramaturg* and Philosopher initially talk at cross-purposes because they have irreconcilable conceptions of "echte Kritik." The Philosopher's rejection of empathy as critically unproductive grafts comments made about Aristotelian theater onto the rejection of Naturalism, although elsewhere in Brecht's theoretical writings the two tendencies are by no means synonymous; Aristotelian drama is generally charged with escapism, Naturalism in its historical form is accused not of this, but of not going far enough. For the *Dramaturg*, a Naturalist "Abbildung," inasmuch as it duplicates a situation calling for change, *is* already a critical response. For the Philosopher, depiction divorced from an adequate "Standpunkt" will fail in interventionist terms and is hence condemned to remain affirmative.

Traditional literary history has tended to present Naturalism as coming after Realism, or, in some cultures, coexisting with it. However, such a picture again hardly suits Brecht's dialectical-cum-phaseological purpose. Brecht's imposition of the arbitrary starting point of Naturalism on his narrative has the advantage of making the debate focus primarily on the shortcomings of a certain kind of mimesis. Naturalism is dismissed as neither fish nor fowl by the Actor (not usually the most incisive of participants, but nevertheless speaking from experience). To which the *Dramaturg* replies: "Der Naturalismus konnte sich nicht sehr lang halten. Er wurde beschuldigt, den Politikern zu flach und den Künstlern zu langweilig zu sein, und verwandelte sich in den *Realismus*. [. . .] Der Realismus [. . .] legt weniger Gewicht darauf, mit dem Leben ohne weiteres verwechselt zu werden. Dafür will er die Realität tiefer fassen" (*GBA*, 22:769). This construct, according to which Naturalism's defects bring about a counter-tendency (realism), which in turn leads to a corrective (genuine realism), is schematically dialectical, which has the advantage of allowing Brecht to see dramatic developments within a cultural-historical framework of inevitable patterns, while at the same time presenting aesthetic shifts in emphasis within the wider theater-society relationship. If Naturalism is judged in terms of its sociopolitical efficacy, then, by implication, Epic Theater must be as well.

One of the main criticisms of what the Actor mockingly calls Naturalism's "Arrangements der 'Wirklichkeit'" is that they create little more than a semblance of verisimilitude: "der Naturalismus [nahm] niemals eine genaue Wiedergabe [vor], sondern [täuschte] nur eine genaue Wiedergabe vor" (ibid.). Anyone familiar with what John Osborne has called Naturalism's "pedantry,"[33] the ostentatious pauses and elliptical dialogue, the wilful longueurs, token snippets of regional dialect, and "Sekundenstil," would probably agree with such a verdict. But all Brecht has done so far is condemn historical Naturalism on its own terms. The subsequent criticism — "Man sah von der Wirklichkeit so viel (und fühlte auch ebensoviel), als man am Ort selbst sah (und fühlte), also sehr wenig. [. . .] bekam also nicht mehr als außerhalb des Theaters" (*GBA*, 22:769–70) — would have been taken by some Naturalists as a compliment. But the syntax and tone of the above sentence make it clear that this is meant as a fundamental criticism. This is the prime charge against all slavishly mimetic theater, not just historical Naturalism or the anachronistic Stanislavskian production approach, and hence it is the underlying justification for a theater of defamiliarization, although the argument will have to proceed gradually via a distinction between a mere *semblance* of realism[34] and genuine realism before it gets there. Before that, the fragment presents an argument already used in the poem "Über die Einfühlung" to the effect that empathy is only possible because characters are "schematisch" rather than differentiated and individualized. Paradoxically, what is mistaken in such instances for its realism is in fact the converse. The

---

[33] The phrase (Osborne 1971, 105) arises in connection with the fussy stage set and meticulous production details of Gerhart Hauptmann's *Einsame Menschen*.

[34] In the first phase of *Der Messingkauf*, these accusations were set out in more detail and voiced by the *Dramaturg:* "Die naturalistischen Aufführungen erweckten die *Illusion*, man befinde sich an einem realen Ort. [. . .] Daß es sich *nur* um Illusion handelte, sah man deutlicher an den naturalistischen Stücken als an den naturalistischen Aufführungen. Die Stückeschreiber arrangierten natürlich die Vorgänge ebenso fleißig wie die nichtnaturalistischen. Sie kombinierten, ließen weg, veranstalteten Zusammentreffen von Personen an unwahrscheinlichen Stellen, vergröberten die einen Vorgänge, verfeinerten die andern usw. Sie machten halt, wo die Illusion, man habe es zu tun mit der Realität, Gefahr lief, verletzt zu werden" (*GBA*, 22:718).

talk is now of false realisms, probably including Socialist Realism, and historical Naturalism has for the moment been left behind.

Two final fragments from the 1942–43 phase return to the subject of Naturalism. The first is an aphoristic remark (no doubt intended for the Philosopher to say): "Du bekommst mehr als nur Nachbildungen / das ist weniger" (*GBA*, 22:791). This criticism of Naturalism's images of the world ("Nachbildungen"), that more surface detail means less insight and hence less incitement to direct action, has been running as a subtext through most of the previous fragments on Stanislavskian theater and Naturalism. (There is never any suggestion of a political link between Stanislavsky's theatrical work during the Csarist period and the triumph of Soviet socialism, nor could there be.) The critique is so strikingly set out in the dialogue that follows that one might regard the one-sentence fragment as a thesis to be expounded.

The second fragment contains some of the *Messingkauf* project's most hard-hitting observations on the subject of Naturalism. The Philosopher begins by reprising his main charge against Naturalism's failure to be politically interventionist enough: "selbst wenn der Zuschauer sich eindenken oder einfühlen kann in solche Helden, wird er doch noch nicht instand gesetzt, die Realität zu meistern" (ibid.). The pairing of "sich eindenken" with "sich einfühlen" remains a lost opportunity, since "sich eindenken" could have led to a more differentiated model of audience response; and the phrase "die Realität meistern," while the underlying Marxist agenda remains implicit, is measurably more to the point than earlier circumlocutions ("praktikable Weltbilder," "praktikable Definitionen," a theater for "praktische Zwecke"). From here on, the discussion breaks new ground. The *Dramaturg*'s impetuous "Ich sehe, der Realismus soll auch preisgegeben werden" and his automatic defense of what he naively takes to be what the Philosopher means by "realism" call out for a clearer discrimination of types of realism:[35]

> Es scheint nur das, was ihr Realismus nanntet, kein Realismus gewesen zu sein. Man hat einfach als realistisch erklärt, was bloße Wiedergabe photographischer Art der Realität war. Nach dieser Definition war der Naturalismus realistischer als der sogenannte Realismus. Dann hat man ein neues Element hineingebracht, die Meisterung der Realität. Dieses

---

[35] A related note, Brecht's "Naturalismus und Realismus in den Darstellungen des Berliner Ensembles" (1953), makes it clear that the Naturalism/Realism contrast also applied to styles of acting. That this is not theorized in *Der Messingkauf* may have something to do with the difficuties Brecht was experiencing with some of the Ensemble's actors: "In der Tat befindet sich das Ensemble [. . .] in einer kritischen Phase seiner Entwicklung, in der es die naturalistische Spielweise einiger seiner besten Schauspieler in eine realistische überführen muß" (*GBA*, 23:264).

Element sprengte den Naturalismus, auf Grund dessen allein man von Realismus gesprochen hatte. (*GBA*, 22:792)

Expressionism plays no role in this truncated account; nor is there any indication of the specific features of historical Realism, whether in drama or fiction, that made Naturalism's photographic mimesis appear "realistischer" than Realism itself. But of course, to give Realism a capital "R" in this way is to suggest that the Philosopher is primarily concerned with period concepts, when he is often not. Realism *of some form*, "typological realism" in the Philosopher's schematic account, has given way to an ostensibly more faithful form of "photographic" realism (in Naturalism), after which a "new element," the yardstick of ability to facilitate "die Meisterung der Realität," dethrones Naturalism (although, paradoxically, elsewhere in *Der Messingkauf* "der Naturalismus" still lives on in its Stanislavskian subform as more than mere pretender to the throne), while a new mode of "echter Realismus" takes over. When referring to "was ihr Realismus nanntet," the Philosopher is tacitly accusing the theater people of being unable to distinguish between Naturalism and either historical Realism or Epic Theater's genuine realism. A valorized concept of "echter Realismus," enabling reality to be both "wiedererkannt" and "durchschaut" in preparation for its mastering, is an ahistorical, typological phenomenon masquerading as part of an inevitable historical process. The schema "Naturalismus" — ("Realismus") — "Echter Realismus" reflects neither the periods of German literary history nor that of modern European drama. Unfortunately, the idea that the power to master "reality" is a corollary of the ability to perceive the laws of history becomes lost amongst the polemics against Naturalism and false realisms, empathy and "sich eindenken," as well as schematic characterization. The fragment ends with its strongest point, one that would surely have had to be integrated into any systematic justification of "Verfremdung": "Es müssen die Gesetze sichtbar werden, welche den Ablauf der Prozesse des Lebens beherrschen. Diese Gesetze sind nicht auf Photographien sichtbar.[36] Sie sind aber auch nicht sichtbar, wenn der Zuschauer nur das Auge oder das Herz einer in diese Prozesse verwickelten Person borgt" (*GBA*, 22:792).

[36] This is a reformulation of Brecht's much-quoted declaration that "die Lage wird dadurch so kompliziert, daß weniger denn je eine einfache 'Wiedergabe der Realität' etwas über die Realität aussagt. Eine Fotografie der Kruppwerke oder der AEG ergibt beinahe nichts über diese Institute. Die eigentliche Realität ist in die Funktionale gerutscht" (*Der Dreigroschenprozeß*, *GBA*, 21:469). The main improvement in the later version lies in the linking of insight to the laws of cause and effect.

One recurrent feature of these fragmentary discussions of Naturalism is the level of abstraction at which they are conducted.[37] This may partly be because we are looking at material intended for the First Night (*Kleines Organon* begins with a similar establishment of first principles). The step-by-step exploration of the deficits of Naturalism and Realism that Brecht was planning would have paved the way for presenting Epic Theater as a teleological necessity. The Philosopher's final speech in the above fragment does not yet introduce the term "Verfremdung." Nevertheless, his declaration "daß die Realität auf dem Theater wiedererkannt wird, ist nur eine der Aufgaben des echten Realismus," coupled with his emphasis on the new element ("die Meisterung der Realität"), defines the goals and rationale of "Verfremdung," even if *Der Messingkauf* has still to consider the legitimacy and methods of defamiliarization adopted. A further cluster of fragments explores the phenomenon of "Entfremdung" (without using Marx's term) in order to put into context Epic Theater's turning to the "V-Effekt" as the main panacea.

In an early, one-sided "dialogue," "Ausführungen des Philosophen über den Marxismus" of 1939, Brecht had already linked the cause-and-effect model with "Historisierung" in his discussion of the betrayal motif in Schiller's *Wallenstein*. Following an analysis of the play's alleged errors comes the exchange:

| | |
|---|---|
| DRAMATURG | Was würde ein Marxist machen? |
| PHILOSOPH | Er würde den Fall als historischen Fall darstellen, mit Ursachen aus der Epoche und Folgen in der Epoche. |
| DRAMATURG | Und die moralische Frage? |
| PHILOSOPH | Die moralische Frage würde er ebenfalls als eine historische Frage behandeln. (*GBA*, 22:717) |

Such a claim rests on an "Epochenbegriff" that brackets pairs of causes and effects as if they were the determinants of a new conception of drama's evolution. This constricting paradigm would need to be expanded to embrace patterns of socioeconomic cause and effect across larger units of history and to map them onto the historical model if it were to be more than a schema.

---

[37] Despite a passing reference to Stanislavsky's production of Chekhov's *The Cherry Orchard* (*GBA*, 22:718), on only one occasion, in "Inhalt der Ersten Nacht des Messingkaufs," does Brecht give a detailed indication that he means European Naturalism rather than just German Naturalist drama. This comes in the claim that "der Naturalismus (der Goncourts, Zolas, Tschechows, Tolstois, Ibsens, Strindbergs, Hauptmanns, Shaws) markiert die Einflußnahme der europäischen Arbeiterbewegung auf die Bühne" (*GBA*, 22:1113). Even here, the generic use of names displays a tendency to abstract from literary history.

Throughout Brecht's mature theoretical writings on drama, a term to which he repeatedly alludes, while never using it directly, is Friedrich Engels's concept of "falsches Bewußtsein," as explained in his letter of 14 July 1893 to Franz Mehring. This may be part of a general policy on Brecht's part to offer Marxist diagnoses, but to avoid rebarbative jargon. (For example, Brecht's "Lied vom Flicken und vom Rock" in scene 3 of the 1938 version of *Die Mutter* began life as "Verurteilung des Reformismus" (*GBA*, 14:525), but the Marxist concept was subsequently edited out.) Likewise, the preference for the term "Widerspruch" and the "*Nicht — Sondern*" model over "Dialektik" and for "eingreifendes Denken" rather than a theory/practice model, as well as the sparing use of "Basis" and "Überbau," were all part of this tendency towards user-friendly explanations, coupled with the attempt to defamiliarize jargon. In preparing the ground for the account of "Verfremdung" in *Der Messingkauf,* Brecht adopts a similar strategy. During the first phase of work on the project, he writes a series of fragments on the subject of "Unwissenheit," meaning *inter alia* epistemological shortsightedness, the lack of mental agility required to make the leap from effects and symptoms to the underlying sociopolitical causes and the absence of political curiosity allegedly shown by many people living under capitalism. Two of these fragments bear titles ("Aus der 'Rede des Philosophen über die Unwissenheit'" and "Aus der 'Rede des Gastes über die Unwissenheit der vielen' vor den Theaterleuten" [*GBA*, 22:710, 712]). Others, usually attributed to the Philosopher, are untitled and hence may have been intended either for his speech or for integration into the general dialogue.[38] In the *GW* "Lese-Fassung," the material begins with the second "Rede" fragment, where the Philosopher employs an almost biblical "Gestus" of address: "Laßt mich euch berichten, daß die Ursachen der Leiden und Gefahren der Unzahl der Leidenden und Gefährdeten unbekannt sind" (*GBA*, 22:712). That the fragments appear in a different order in the two editions is less material to what follows than the fact that these pieces, originally assigned to the First Night, do not form part of the later "zusammenhängende Dialogfassung" of the First Night (Fragment B 115, *GBA*, 22:1114). It is, however, worth bearing in mind that the *GBA* notes also refer to it merely as "die teilweise Zusammenfassung der Ersten Nacht" (*GBA*, 22:1115), thus not precluding the eventual integration of other (earlier) fragments, including those on "Unwissenheit." Indeed, they

---

[38] In *GW*, these fragments are brought together under the title "[Über die Unwissenheit]" and subheaded "Aus der 'Rede des [Philosophen] über die Unwissenheit der vielen' vor den Theaterleuten" (*GW*, 16:524–29). Since each individual fragment is separately attributed to the Philosopher, this gives the misleading impression of someone having a conversation with himself rather than addressing a group of listeners.

allow for a cumulative, rather than self-renewing model of the draft material accruing from *Der Messingkauf*'s various genetic phases. According to such a model, early fragments need not be thought of as having been abandoned when new, longer sequences have come into being. Instead, they acquire the status of fragments still waiting to be inserted. Given the importance of the "Unwissenheit" pieces, this is what one would expect to happen, for they relate to a number of key topics broached on the First Night as well as preparing the ground for material that Brecht was considering for inclusion in the Second Night: among them "K-Typus und P-Typus," "der V-Effekt," "die Wissenschaft," and "Gründung des Thaeters" (*GBA*, 22:696).

There are no doubt circumstances where it is right to assume that a process of working from fragments to larger units of text would involve ongoing decisions about the status of individual unfinished items. Under such circumstances, some material would be edited out and other fragments would be gradually incorporated into the body of the work (possibly after being put into dialogue form). In such a situation, the ultimate importance of earlier draft elements would be demonstrated by their retention at the next stage of composition. It is characteristic of Brecht's method, however, that this does not happen in the case of the "Unwissenheit" fragments. A corpus of material that forms part of the Philosopher's critique of Naturalism and represents one of the most vigorous justifications of "V-Effekte" to be found anywhere in Brecht's theoretical writings only appears in fragments dating from the first stage. This could mean one of two things. Either (and this seems less likely) Brecht failed to appreciate the significance of what he had written and deliberately allowed these passages to be superseded by other arguments, or he decided that they had made their point effectively enough for them to be held in waiting for some later stage of integration. He may also have wished to reconsider his theoretical position on the aesthetic implications of "falsches Bewußtsein" and "Entfremdung" in advance of his return to Stalinist East Germany. Whatever the reasons for the "Unwissenheit" material's being put on hold, it is there in the *GW* "Lese-Fassung." It is in the *GBA* complex, too, although probably less because of a general editorial policy regarding *Nachlass* material, which required a focus on "die letzte Bearbeitungsstufe" (*GBA Registerband*, 808), than in order to give some sense of the project's complex step-by-step development.

What the "Unwissenheit" fragments draw attention to is more than the simple fact of (political) ignorance, a predicament that was presented using a series of well-chosen images. For example:

> Sie wissen, warum der Stein so und nicht anders fällt, wenn man ihn schleudert, aber warum der Mensch, der ihn schleudert, so und nicht anders handelt, wissen sie nicht. [. . .]. Jedesmal, wenn ich von dieser Insel wegfahre, fürchte ich, daß das Schiff im Sturm untergehen

könnte. Aber ich fürchte eigentlich nicht das Meer, sondern die mich unter Umständen auffischen.[. . .] Wir alle haben sehr unklare Vorstellungen davon, wie unsere Handlungen sich auswirken, ja, wir wissen nur selten, warum wir sie unternehmen. (*GBA*, 22:710–11)

Ignorance is linked with powerlessness and fear, especially fear of one's fellow men. More than simply registering defective political consciousness, which is assumed to be synonymous with the inability to understand the dialectical patterns of cause and effect in society and in history, the fragments suggest people do not even know *that* they do not know: "Nicht daß man nicht alle Glieder der Kette sieht, ist schlimm, sondern daß man die Kette nicht sieht" (*GBA*, 22:722). Or if not totally blind, they have only a vague inkling that there must be more to be grasped:

> Unsere Abhängigkeit auf allen Seiten in allen Entscheidungen ist uns nur dumpf fühlbar. Irgendwie hängt alles zusammen, fühlen wir, aber wie, wissen wir nicht. So erfährt die Menge den Brotpreis, die Kriegserklärung, den Mangel an Arbeit wie Naturereignisse, Erdbeben oder Überschwemmungen. Lange Zeit scheinen diese Naturereignisse nur Teile der Menschen zu betreffen oder den einzelnen nur in einem kleinen Teil seiner Gewohnheiten. Erst spät zeigt es sich, daß das alltägliche Leben unalltäglich geworden ist, und zwar das Leben aller. Irgend etwas ist unterlassen, irgend etwas falsch gemacht worden. Die Interessen großer Schichten sind bedroht worden, ohne daß diese großen Schichten sich als Interessenverbände in dieser Sache zusammengetan haben. (*GBA*, 22:711–12)

In the first phase of *Der Messingkauf,* this picture of "Unwissenheit" might be thought of as a prelude to the "Ausführungen des Philosophen über den Marxismus" (*GBA*, 22:716–18). But it also belongs to the complex of ideas that serve as the justification for a "scientific" theater involving the use of various forms of "Verfremdung" to enable audiences to see the real chains of causality. The embryonic "Unwissenheit" material, coming as it does immediately after the critique of Naturalism, risked directing attention too quickly to the problem of the audience's epistemological limitations. Or perhaps, like the Philosopher's speech on Marxism (which no longer figures in the next phase of the project), it would have moved too precipitately to political solutions. If this were the danger, it might account for the next major shift in direction: to a detailed consideration of the achievements of Erwin Piscator.

## A Test Case: The Piscator Thread

The *GW* "Lese-Fassung" of *Der Messingkauf* creates the impression of a series of highly organized parallel discussions of the work of three important playwrights. This is achieved by drawing together a series of disparate fragments and imposing similar umbrella titles on the dialogues thus foregrounded: in the Second Night, "[Das Theater des Shakespeare]" and "[Das Theater des Piscator]," and in the Third, "[Das Theater des Stückeschreibers]." In reality, there is no such ordered sequence of discussions of the achievements of either Shakespeare or Piscator, and *Der Messingkauf* is in its entirety, either directly or indirectly, about "das Theater des Stückeschreibers." Because Piscator is of even more importance to the substance of *Der Messingkauf* than he was for "Über experimentelles Theater," the present section traces the thread of Piscator fragments through the phases of work on *Der Messingkauf* in order to explore why Brecht keeps returning to Piscator's innovations and their relationship to his own theater work.

The affinities between Epic Theater and Piscator's so-called Political Theater is a topic already present in notes from the first phase. A fragment headed "Verhältnis des Augsburgers zum Piscator" (*GBA*, 22:763) figures among texts not yet assigned to a particular Night. The material gives no clue as to which category the contents might have been subsumed under, although the phrase "das politische Theater" occasionally occurs in plans and fragments dating from this phase. Two of the subjects appearing in a plan for the Second Night — "die neuen Stoffe" and "Gründung des Thaeters" (*GBA*, 22:695) — also suggest that an acknowledgment of Piscator's importance for non-Aristotelian theater would not have been amiss there, assuming that Piscator received credit as a director who favored new subjects and that the neologism "Thaeter" denoted more than just Brecht's Epic Theater.

Many of the claims in "Verhältnis des Augsburgers zum Piscator" create a highly perspectivized picture of Piscator's achievements *as measured against Brecht's own*. If the points had been integrated into a discussion, they would have probably been attributed to the Philosopher. He is certainly the most likely mouthpiece for the opening claims that "der Piscator machte vor dem Augsburger politisches Theater" and "die Umwälzung im Jahre 18, an der beide teilnahmen, hatte den Augsburger enttäuscht und den Piscator zum Politiker gemacht. Erst später kam der Augsburger durch Studium zur Politik" (*GBA*, 22:763). Since "durch Studium" refers to Brecht's encounter with *Das Kapital* and Lenin's works, as well as with the thoughts of Sternberg, Korsch, and Benjamin, Piscator is being damned with grudging praise. Brecht's ideological credentials, it is implied, were sounder than Piscator's. A similar combination of acknowledgment and undermining comes in the following assertion: "Obwohl der Piscator niemals ein Stück, kaum je eine Szene selber schrieb, bezeichnete ihn der Augsburger doch als den einzigen fähigen Dramatiker außer ihm" (ibid.). While giving credit where due (note the low-key word "fähig"), Brecht simultaneously relativizes Piscator's work, almost making it seem as if the former's status depended on the latter's guarded recognition. Something similar happens in the case of the token evenhandedness with which Brecht establishes that "die eigentliche Theorie des nichtaristotelischen Theaters und der Ausbau des V-Effekts ist dem Augsburger zuzuschreiben, jedoch hat vieles davon auch der Piscator verwendet und durchaus selbständig und original." Piscator is being assigned the role of John the Baptist to Brecht, theater's Savior. Piscator may have been the first to create Political Theater, but he is said to have derived many of his most incisive effects from "der Augsburger," a Brecht who, and now the knife is turned, has an ideologically far greater weapon in the shape of "Verfremdung." Another patronizing assertion, "der Augsburger arbeitete für den Piscator die meisten großen Stücke durch, schrieb auch Szenen für sie, einmal einen ganzen Akt. Den *Schwejk* machte er ihm ganz," is so weighted in Brecht's favor that it would have proved difficult to translate its substance into a register of "persuasive Kommunikation." The final division of the spoils ("Vor allem war die Wendung des Theaters zur Politik Piscators Verdienst, und ohne diese Wendung ist das Theater des Augsburgers kaum denkbar") displays the very apodictic quality that, according to the 1980 *Brecht-Handbuch,* should have been obviated by the new dialogue paradigm. On balance, this paragraph communicates a need to put the record straight to Brecht's advantage. The approach belongs in spirit more to the method of the orchestrated radio discussions of the 1920s, which may explain why the *Messingkauf* complex keeps coming back to the vexed question of the Brecht-Piscator relationship without ever successfully translating the material into dialogue.[39] True recasting into plausible discussion would have meant offsetting one's own strong opinions and long held assumptions by having interlocutors question them; and would have required the ability to present theoretical propositions in an ironic manner that entries in Brecht's exile journals were never called upon to do.

*Der Messingkauf* returned to the issue of Piscator's significance in 1945 with two new passages on the subject. The first, entitled "Piscator," reads like a continuation of the earlier assessment: "Die Anhänger des Piscator stritten eine Zeitlang mit denen des Augsburgers darüber, wer von den beiden die epische Darstellung gefunden hätte. Tatsächlich wandten sie sie beide gleichzeitig an, in verschiedenen Städten, der Piscator mehr im Bühnenmäßigen (in der Verwendung von Inschriften, Chören, Filmen usw.), der Augsburger im Schauspielstil" (*GBA,* 22:794). Whereas Piscator's innovations are itemized (perhaps suggesting that they have not been prop-

---

[39] In an allusion to *Trotz alledem!* the *Dramaturg* credits Piscator with being "der erste, der es für nötig fand, im Theater *Beweise* vorzubringen. Er projizierte auf große Leinwände authentische Dokumente. Viele warfen ihm sogleich vor, er verletze die Regeln der Kunst. Sie habe ihr eigenes Reich aufzubauen, sagten sie" (*GBA,* 22:720), but sadly the brief note is not dignified with transformation into a contribution to the discussion.

erly acknowledged hitherto), Brecht's are taken for granted, leaving us in no doubt that he is already the greater of the two rivals.

In *GBA,* the above passage is prefixed by the cipher "B 127," the B assigning it to the amorphous category "ausgeführte Dialoge, Übungsstücke, Gedichte und Schriften" (*GBA,* 22:1144). So too is the longer companion piece that follows, "Aus der 'Beschreibung des Piscatortheaters' in der 'Zweiten Nacht,'" which not only has a title (suggesting that it was possibly written for prepublication in *Versuche*), but is also, for reasons which will become apparent, assigned to the *Dramaturg.* Both Piscator pieces are preceded by A 21, a short three-line note on the relationship of philosophy to literature (A signifying "Pläne bzw. Übersichtsdarstellungen oder sonstige Notizen," *GBA,* 22:1144). But even the first Piscator fragment is scarcely much longer. Indeed, comparison of these three categorizations shows just how resistant many of the *Messingkauf* fragments are to ordering within a binary system.[40] The reference in B 127 to disputes between Piscator's supporters and Brecht's contains the seeds of an unwritten dialogue about who did what first and where the contribution of each ultimately lies. Its two-sentence structure — with an elaboration of the statement "stritten eine Zeitlang" followed by the authoritative sounding "tatsächlich," implying a resolution to the altercation — looks like a more generalized indication of the root question and the correct answer than the following piece. There the issue is explored by the *Dramaturg,* once more playing the role of someone prone to prejudice and apt to leap to hasty conclusions. What he says could not have been said by the more reliable Philosopher.

Two features of "Aus der 'Beschreibung des Piscatortheaters' in der 'Zweiten Nacht'" distinguish it from the earlier statements about Brecht's ally and rival, and both relate to the fact that it is the *Dramaturg* who is speaking. First, there is the aspersion cast on his artistic integrity by the malicious reference to how Piscator's work was financed: "Er bekam das Geld von einem Bierbrauer [. . .]. Es waren mehr als eine Million Mark, was er für seine Experimente ausgab" (*GBA,* 22:794). This snide jibe differs in character from the claim in "Über experimentelles Theater" that Russian avantgarde and Stanislavskian theater had received Soviet state funding, whereas Brecht's received no such subvention. Piscator, by contrast, stands accused of being a "kept" dramatist, though the remark is, of course, the *Dramaturg*'s and not Brecht's. There is a link between such theater tittle-tattle and the point concerning the Piscator collective's experiments with mechanical innovations: such machinery costs money, but privileged Piscator can afford

[40] If A 21 is a plan for the contents of the Second Night, one might equally well reason that B 127 is, at a lower level of generality, one for the material to be covered in the Piscator-Brecht component of *Der Messingkauf,* part of which has already been worked out as B 128.

it. The illustrations are not taken from Piscator's greatest achievements, that is, *Trotz alledem!* and his production of Ernst Toller's *Hoppla wir leben!* but from *Schwejk,* the play Brecht claims he himself had written:[41]

> Er machte den Fußboden beweglich, indem er zwei breite Bänder darüber legte, die, von einem Motor getrieben, zum Laufen gebracht werden konnten, so daß die Schauspieler marschieren konnten, ohne vom Fleck zu müssen. So konnte er ein ganzes Stück in Fluß bringen. Es zeigte den Marsch eines Soldaten zur Front, durch Rekrutierungsbüro, Klinik und Kaserne, über Landstraßen, durch Lager, in Scheunen, in die Schlacht. [. . .] Für dasselbe Stück verwendete er als Rückwand einen gezeichneten Film, in dem die Oberen verspottet wurden. Überhaupt führte er den Film ins Theater ein und machte so die Kulisse zur Schauspielerin. (*GBA*, 22:794–95)

Although some attempt is made to describe the function of the protagonist in the play, the impression given is that the one thing the *Dramaturg* remembers about the production is its new-fangled gadgetry. (One could imagine how Brecht would have felt if its use of a revolving stage was the only thing audiences associated with *Mutter Courage!*) This impression of a certain *déformation professionelle* on the *Dramaturg*'s part is reinforced by an allusion to a further production by Piscator: *Rasputin, die Romanows, der Krieg und das Volk, das gegen sie aufstand,* after the play by Alexei Tolstoy and Pavel Shchegolev: "In einem andern Stück baute er, auf zwei einander schneidenden Drehbühnen, viele Schauplätze, auf denen mitunter zu gleicher Zeit gespielt wurde. Dabei senkte sich der Bühnenboden zugleich mit dem Dach" (*GBA,* 22:795). The two most likely interpretive possibilities here are either that the *Dramaturg*'s blinkered view of Piscator's significance is a thesis to which another character (the Philosopher?) would offer the necessary corrective, or that the *Dramaturg*'s assessment is largely on target and will thus serve as the starting point for a discussion of epic ways of using the stage, the ideological limitations of Piscator's brand of Political Theater, visual effects in general, or, continuing on from the Stockholm lecture, the relationship of Piscator's and Brecht's work to *experimental* theater. Speaking more for the latter is the fact that what the *Dramaturg* emphasizes is not so dissimilar to the assessment of Piscator's importance in "Über experimentelles Theater."[42] But that assessment was made in 1939. Both Brecht and Piscator have moved on.

---

[41] I.e. the Piscator-Lania-Gasbarra-Brecht 1928 adaptation of Max Brod's and Hans Reimann's stage version of Hašek's novel.

[42] Or for that matter Max Brod's published recollections of Piscator's staging of the Brod-Reimann adaptation of Hašek's *Švejk.* Cf. Brod's "Piscator und Schwejk" (*Die Weltbühne,* 25 (1929), 844.

When the last of the *Messingkauf* pieces on Piscator was published in *GW,* it was positioned immediately after "Aus der 'Beschreibung des Piscatortheaters' in der 'Zweiten Nacht.'" Whatever the editorial reasons for such a move,[43] this obscures the relationship between the two pieces. "Aus der 'Beschreibung des Piscatortheaters' in der 'Zweiten Nacht'" was the personal view of just one character, someone whose aim is described in "Die Personen des *Messingkaufs*": "*Der Dramaturg* stellt sich dem Philosophen zur Verfügung und verspricht, seine Fähigkeiten und Kenntnisse zum Umbau des Theaters in das Thaeter [*GW* has "Theater"] des Philosophen zur Verfügung zu stellen" (*GBA,* 22:696). Yet while the *Dramaturg* may be anxious to put himself at the Philosopher's disposal, he is nevertheless often identified with "Theater," rather than "Thaeter." His judgments on the work of such a pioneer as Piscator may be of negligible importance. We saw evidence of his untrustworthiness in "Aus der 'Beschreibung des Piscatortheaters' in der 'Zweiten Nacht,'" indeed the very title of that fragment might be read as suggesting that any claims he made were intended to form part of some larger whole. To remove the title of a comparable passage ("'Das Theater des Piscator,' aus dem *Messingkauf*") and attribute it to the *Dramaturg,* as the "Lese-Fassung" did (*GW,* 16:595), gives rise to misleading expectations. The differentiated judgments and wealth of detail in *Der Messingkauf*'s final assessment of Piscator's work, which *GBA* places among the "Texte ohne Zuordnung zu den Nächten," suggest that it is unlikely that this passage could still be attributed to the *Dramaturg.* The new, more definitively formulated title ("Das Theater des Piscator") suggests a very different status. Now the record is to be set straight, presumably by the Philosopher.

The slur concerning Piscator's plutocratic benefactors is repeated in this version ("das Theater des Piscator, geführt von den Geldern eines Bierbrauers und eines Kinobesitzers"[44]), but is offset by a reference to box-office policy — a sizeable proletarian subscriber list that cut back profits from ticket receipts and the expense of the elaborate stage machinery used in productions. The allusion to Piscator's private funding, the only part of "Das Theater des Piscator" that might have been assigned to the *Dramaturg,* is immediately counterbalanced by an approving reference to the Piscator collective's working methods: "Ein Kollektiv von Dramatikern diskutierte auf der Bühne in einer Art Dauerdiskussion, und die Diskussion setzte sich

[43] The *GW* notes to *Der Messingkauf* declare an editorial intention to make "die 'Nahtstellen'" between the various fragments used in its reconstruction "sichtbar" (*GW,* 16:4*), which might account for the added title, but not the misattribution.

[44] The first allusion is to the brewery magnate Ludwig Katzenellenbogen, friend of Tilla Durieux, who played the Czarina in Piscator's *Rasputin.* The cinema owner remains unidentified.

fort durch die ganze große Stadt in den Zeitungen, Salons, Kaffeehäusern und Stuben" (*GBA*, 22:814). Piscator is praised for having changed "das Theater als Kunstinstitut" (*GBA*, 22:815), for providing "Anschauungsunterricht" (ibid.), for the topicality of his revues and plays, and for working innovatively with placards, film, projected documentation, and epic methods of "Literarisierung." It is almost as if these achievements were singled out for praise because they reflected some of the ideas about changing the "Apparat" and experiments in staging techniques that had also been Brecht's own. Comment on Piscator's subject matter is on the whole more equivocal. Given Brecht's views on "Historisierung" and the fact that the Philosopher's "Thaeter" "[soll] nur der Not des Tages, gerade unseres Tages, eines düsteren zweifellos [. . .] dienen" (*GBA*, 22:761), the following hardly sounds like a resounding compliment: "[Piscators] Theater war aktuell, nicht nur, wo es Tages-, sondern auch, wo es Jahrtausendfragen behandelte" (*GBA*, 22:814). Later allusions to "ein Stück, das die Grausamkeit des Geburtenzwangs zeigte" (Carl Credé's *§218: Frauen in Not* [1929]) and "ein Stück über die chinesische Revolution" (Friedrich Wolf's *Tai Yang erwacht* [1931]) help corroborate the idea of contemporary relevance and appropriate documentary "Anschauungsmaterial" (*GBA*, 22:815). But of all Piscator's productions, that of Credé's work could just as well have been used as evidence of a penchant for sentimentalized Naturalism; and the superficial documentary method of Wolf's work may be highlighted to suggest that the material had been more probingly treated by another work about which Piscator had been critical: Tretiakov's *Brülle China!* (in Meyerhold's production of 1930).[45] If this is the underlying charge, then Piscator stands condemned by one of his own principles, for he was known to have spoken out strongly against Naturalism in the theater.[46]

The most important paragraph of "Das Theater des Piscator," the concluding one, consists of a further revealing amalgam of praise and implied criticism. Initially hailed as "einer der größten *Theaterleute* aller Zeiten" (my emphasis), that is, a man of the theater, not a dramatist, Piscator is again praised for his technical innovations: "Er hat das Theater elektrifiziert und fähig gemacht, große Stoffe zu bewältigen," although whether this means that he himself is to be credited with having addressed these large themes or merely credited with having put the new resources at Brecht's disposal is left

---

[45] Trading in "detail, not elucidation" was Piscator's charge against Tretiakov's and Meyerhold's work (*Moskauer Rundschau*, 5 October 1930, quoted in Willett 1978b, 125). Meyerhold counterattacked with the claim that although Piscator wanted revolutionary theater, he confined himself to revolutionizing "the material aspect of theater technique" (Stefan Priacel: "Meyerhold à Paris," [Interview] *Monde* [*sic*], Paris, 7 July 1928).

[46] Piscator 1980, 210–11 and Buehler 1978, 52–55.

unsaid. What remains clear is that certain limitations to Piscator's theatrical interests are about to be subjected to a critical review, starting with an extremely waspish comment:

> Für die Schauspielkunst hatte er zwar nicht so wenig Interesse, wie seine Feinde behaupteten, aber doch weniger, als er selber sagte. Vielleicht teilte er ihre Interessen nicht [the implication being that Piscator had enemies in acting circles], weil sie seine nicht teilten. Jedenfalls hat er ihnen keinen neuen Stil gegeben, wenn er auch nicht schlecht vorspielte, besonders die kleinen scharfen Rollen. Er gestattete mehrere Spielarten zugleich auf seiner Bühne und zeigte dabei keinen besonderen Geschmack. Es schien ihm leichter, die großen Stoffe kritisch zu bewältigen vermittels ingeniöser und grandioser szenischer Prästationen als vermittels der Schauspielkunst. Seine Liebe zur Maschinerie, die ihm viele vorwarfen und einige allzu hoch anrechneten, zeigte er nur, soweit sie ihm gestattete, seine szenische Phantasie zu betätigen. (*GBA*, 22:816)

When writing about estrangement in oriental theater, Brecht, the theoretician who does set much store by acting, at the same time engages in an act of self-presentation. Here, too, much of what he says about Piscator reads as an estranged version, a variant of the "*Nicht — Sondern*" model, of the theoretical position Brecht adopted on the importance of acting and an ensemble style. But the main case against Brecht's rival rests on the charge that his technical innovations are confined to purveying information, rather than facilitating necessary critical perspective. An earlier comment in the same piece, to the effect that "Der Hintergrund, ehemals — und in den benachbarten Theatern noch immer der unbewegte Geselle — wurde zum Star des [Piscator-]Theaters und spielte sich groß an die Rampe" (*GBA*, 22:815), is also significant in this connection. In the more obvious, literal sense, Brecht accuses Piscator of misguidedly making the stage machinery take center stage. And in light of what Brecht has to say in *Kleines Organon* about the deficiencies of a star-centered form of theater as opposed to ensemble playing, this is hardly a compliment. It is not by chance that Brecht has a tendency to mimic this displacement of priorities in his own writings on Piscator, by making so much of the machinery and paying so little attention to the topics that Piscator took on. The idea of the "Hintergrund als Star" also works on another level of signification. That is to say, what Piscator presents as the essential information the audience needs to be given is not what Brecht calls "die Vorgänge hinter den Vorgängen als Vorgänge unter Menschen" (*GBA*, 22:519). Even the earlier suggestion that Piscator's many montage effects "zerrissen Fabel wie Charakterführung der Personen" (*GBA*, 23:815) is probably condemnatory, coming from a dramatist who argues: "Auf die *Fabel* kommt alles an, sie ist das Herzstück der theatralischen

Veranstaltung" (*GBA*, 22:92). The damaging undercurrents to the apparent praise, the gap between what is said and what left unsaid, the continuous implied contrast between Piscator and Brecht, combine to make the essay speak with more than one voice. Although not (yet) "dialogisiert," it nevertheless diminishes Piscator's significance, while at the same time favoring Brechtian theater. There is a strong hint here of the two disputing factions that were mentioned in the previous Piscator piece, and again the same sense of knowing that only one of them can be "tatsächlich" correct.

## "Verfremdung" Revisited

"In der Mitte der V-Effekt" was the concluding sentence in the original February 1939 journal entry about Brecht's embryonic *Messingkauf* project (*GBA*, 26:328). A snatch of dialogue from the first period of work on *Der Messingkauf* suggests that an account of "Verfremdung" was to follow soon after the shortcomings of Naturalism and the theater of empathy had been sufficiently vilified. The first sentence presents an image of the "traffic" between stage and auditorium that anticipates a later communications theory approach to theater:

> DRAMATURG  Aber die Verbindung zwischen oben und unten ist gekappt! Das Kabel ist durchschnitten, wenn die Einfühlung unterbrochen ist! Oder existiert da eine andere Verbindung, denn es muß doch Interesse erregt werden hier oben?
>
> PHILOSOPH  Wir kommen zum V-Effekt. (*GBA*, 22:720)

Brecht had already attempted to explain what the alternative form of communication would be in an essay probably dating from earlier the same year: "[V-Effekte. Dreigespräch] *GBA*, 22:398–401) (also known as "[Dreigespräch über das Tragische]"). Given that the participants are Karl, Thomas, and Lukas, names used for another draft *Messingkauf* dialogue of the time ("Theatralik des Faschismus"), it is conceivable that "V-Effekte" formed part of the *Messingkauf* complex. Indeed, given how concerned a later part of the discussion is with the interplay between comic and tragic elements in *Furcht und Elend des III. Reiches,* a work also referred to in *Der Messingkauf* (*GBA*, 22:799–80), the likelihood increases.

It is not hard to see why the *GW* editor saw the discussion as being primarily about "das Tragische," whereas the *GBA* title puts emphasis on the term "V-Effekte," given the way Karl's first speech establishes a clear connection between "Verfremdung" and comedy ("Solche Verfremdungseffekte, wie du sie benützt, findet man im niedersten Schwank" [*GBA*, 22:398]). The connection between comedy and defamiliarization is discussed more than once in Brecht's writings, at times with insufficient emphasis on the political purpose of Brechtian "Verfremdung" or, as is the case with Karl's first speech, in the form of an unsubstantiated claim that comedy invariably involves the "Verfremdung einer gesellschaftlichen Haltung." Karl's suspicion, "dann kommt es mir vor, als hättet ihr einfach aus der Komödie soundso viele Elemente genommen und sie in das ernste Stück gesteckt," gives rise to fundamental misgivings: "wird da nicht die Tragödie ruiniert?" (ibid.), as if, for the sake of a few convenient distancing devices, something as sacrosanct as a tragic conception of the world — as well as the preeminent position of tragedy within drama — were being abandoned. The direction the discussion then takes concerning the effect of comic interludes in Shakespearean tragedy strengthens the assumption, in light of the role of the Shakespearean "Zwischenszenen" in *Der Messingkauf,* that the "Dreigespräch" was probably written for incorporation in the larger work. If so, then the central relationship between "Verfremdung," comedy and tragedy/the tragic would have finally received its due, for later on in the discussion Thomas sets out the main objections to tragedy on the part of Epic Theater's practitioners:

> Nun ist es ganz richtig, daß die tragische Stimmung der Alten dadurch sehr gestört würde, daß die gesellschaftliche Grundlage des Schicksals eines Helden nicht mehr als etwas Dauerndes, von den Menschen nicht Abänderbares, für alle Menschen Bestehendes betrachtet und dargestellt würde, wie es durch die Spielweise der Neueren zweifellos geschähe. Damit wir mit dem Helden verzweifeln können, müssen wir sein Gefühl der Auswegslosigkeit teilen, damit wir erschüttert werden können durch seine Einsicht in die Gesetzmäßigkeit seines Schicksals, müssen wir ebenfalls, was in seinem Fall passiert, als unverrückbar gesetzmäßig einsehen. Eine Spielweise, die die gesellschaftliche Grundlage als praktikabel und historisch (vergänglich) darstellt [. . .], muß die tragische Stimmung entscheidend stören. Jedoch ist nicht gesagt, daß damit durch die neue Spielweise keine tragische Stimmung mehr entstehen könnte. Diese Spielweise ist allerdings nicht an ihrer Hervorbringung interessiert. [. . .] Aber sie würde tragische Stimmung zulassen, wenn eine Darstellung, welche die Historizität und Praktikabilität der gesellschaftlichen Grundlage berücksichtigt, eine solche Stimmung hervorrufen würde. (*GBA,* 22:399–400)

Thomas explains that any hostility towards tragedy on the part of Epic Theater is by no means categorical: the tragic element still appears "an bestimmten Stellen und in bestimmter Form [. . .]. Aber nicht im allgemeinen" (*GBA,* 22:401). Given how many of Brecht's plays problematize notions of tragedy and fate, it is surprising how understated the topic is in his theoretical writings. Admittedly, critiques of "Einfühlung" often pay regard to the phenomenon of characters onstage being presented as *victims* of circumstances ostensibly beyond their control. Yet even when the topic of emotion in the theater leads on to the Aristotelian concepts of "fear" and "pity," as happens with some of the *Messingkauf* fragments, the subject is seldom pursued in any detail.

Untypically, an interchange between Lukas and Thomas virtually allows the former to belittle the Epic Theater's predictable position and force Thomas (the dialogue's Philosopher figure) to respond. Lukas, who fears that Thomas's ultimate goal is "eine Liquidierung der Tragödie" (*GBA,* 22:399) in the interests of a far-distant utopian goal, describes what he takes to be Thomas's position in such a way that it reads like a satire of how Brecht himself was often misrepresented.

> Bei euch wird die Grundstimmung des Tragischen also aufgehoben? Das erstaunt mich nicht. Ich sehe da diesen utopischen Geist am Werke, diesen recht flachen Optimismus, der davon ausgeht, daß man durch die Abschaffung gesellschaftlicher Mißstände ohne weiteres eine allgemeine, gleichmäßige und harmonische Glückseligkeit aller Menschen garantiert bekäme; welcher Optimismus dann dazu führt, daß man auch schon während des Kampfes gegen die Mißstände die leidende Menschheit und den leidenden einzelnen als nur vorläufig und vorübergehend leidend mit einigem Gleichmut anhört, wenn er klagt. (*GBA,* 22:399)

This could be a tactical move, a preemptive strike on Brecht's part to enable him to work forward from caricature to his real position. The result, read this way, would be dialogized theory of a more subtle calibre than that in the radio discussions. But caricature is at the same time also a form of "Verfremdung." By estranging his own position through a cleverly simplified version of it, Brecht is more likely to achieve a hyper-alert state of mind in the reader at the point where Thomas sets out his actual position. And this he proceeds to do.

Thomas makes three important new points. First, that in Shakespearean drama "die Darstellung des Tragischen durch Züge gewinnt, die sonst in der Komödie ihren Platz haben. Freilich wird die Grundstimmung des Tragischen auch bei ihm nicht etwa durch die komischen Züge aufgehoben. Eher verstärkt sie sich durch diese Lebensnähe" (*GBA,* 22:399). What remains unarticulated is the implication of this statement for an understanding of Epic Theater. If "das Tragische" is still present in residual form, then presumably a comparable effect of reciprocal intensification can still be achieved. Even more revealing than the direction in which the Shakespearean analogy was leading is the new emphasis on comedy's "Lebensnähe." With this, Brecht goes beyond locating the source of many "Verfremdungseffekte" and gives them greater legitimacy with the claim that they represent life.

A second new factor comes with Thomas's response to the accusation that he displays a "merkwürdige Gleichgültigkeit gegen das Problem der Tragik." (Lukas, by contrast, appears to have a vested interest in staving off "the death of tragedy.") Thomas responds to this charge with a clever maneuver followed by a point of breathtaking substance: "Das hoffe ich. Ich weiß, in den Stücken der Alten und den zeitgenössischen, die ihnen folgen, wird es dem Zuschauer nicht überlassen, seine Gefühle zu wählen. Was er bekommt, sind nicht Ausschnitte aus dem menschlichen Zusammenleben schlechthin, sondern tragische Schauer" (*GBA*, 22:400). Comedy, and by extension "Verfremdung," have already been praised for their "Lebensnähe." Now a comparable operation is carried out on tragedy as it is accused of producing something articifial: "tragische Schauer" or Freytag's "Nervenschocks." The avoidance of the word "Furcht" and the use of "Schauer," with connotations of Jacobean drama, "Schauerromantik," and even the horror film, is as much an estranging caricature of Lukas's position as Brecht had once offered of John Howard Lawson's! To emphasize the audience's inability to choose their feelings, Thomas continues with figurative language designed to stress the unworldly artifice of what Lukas calls "das Tragische": "Für sie wird einiges Vorgefallenes zusammengemixt in einer Mischung, die tragische Schauer erzeugt, oder andere Emotionen" (ibid.). (It is worth bearing in mind that at one stage the Philosopher, by referring to Pavlov's conditioned reflex experiments with dogs, questions the way in which the theater tends to treat its audiences: "Menschen sind keine Hunde, wiewohl ihr auf dem Theater sie als solche behandelt" [*GBA*, 22:714]). The claim that Aristotelian drama creates and channels the audience's emotions in a restrictive way, whereas Epic Theater does not ("das ist nicht Sache der Neueren, welche [. . .] die Emotionen des Zuschauers nicht auszubestimmen wünschen" [*GBA*, 22:400–401]), should have been challenged by Lukas. But by now he has served his purpose and there will be no detailed exploration of the differences between Aristotelian and Epic Theater using the criterion of the audience's degree of emotional freedom.

The third key point introduced by Thomas concerns the factors leading to what he calls "tragische Schauer" in Aristotelian drama. Lukas's distinction — "Bei den Alten traten die tragischen Schauer ein, wenn ein Mensch seiner Natur folgte. Bei euch Neueren hat er wohl gar keine Natur?" — leads to the gnomic exchange that concludes the "Dreigespräch," as if leaving issues hanging in the air were more than just an accidental aspect of some of the *Messingkauf* fragments:

*Thomas:*    Oh, doch, wenn Sie wollen. Nur: er kann ihr dann auch nicht folgen.

*Lukas:*    Das nenne ich nicht Natur.

*Thomas:*    Und wir nennen es Natur.

*Karl*:        Das ist sehr philosophisch. (*GBA*, 22:401)

Brecht has established a connection between the methods of comedy and "Verfremdung," as well as pointing to the *Schwank* (elsewhere it is the *commedia dell'arte* and the *Volksstück* as an important influence on his estranging devices. He has pointed to a key contrast between the worldview upon which "Verfremdung" is predicated and that of tragedy. He further tries to explain "Verfremdung" by juxtaposing it, not with an artistic tendency to which it is specifically indebted, but one that might be adduced by people who think they understand what "Verfremdung" is.

In one *Messingkauf* fragment the Philosopher is asked: "Verwendet nicht auch der *Surrealismus* in der Malerei eine Verfremdungstechnik?" (*GBA*, 22:824). This is a significant departure. On the whole, up until now Brecht has been content to draw attention to earlier examples of "Verfremdung" in areas he holds in high regard, including traditional Chinese acting, Japanese Nô theater, the *Volksstück,* and the paintings of Breughel the Elder.[47] The introduction of Surrealism into the explanation of "Verfremdung" is a move of a different order. Calling the Surrealists "sozusagen die Primitiven einer neuen Kunstform" implies that they are part of "Verfremdung"'s heritage, though not in any straightforward way. In fact, the distance between Surrealism and "Verfremdungstheater" is as great as that between Brechtian "Verfremdung" and the concept of defamiliarization in Russian Formalism. Not surprisingly, the Philosopher's subsequent emphasis on the shock factor in Surrealism is more a matter of differences than similarities:

> Sie versuchen den Betrachter zu schockieren, indem sie seine Assoziationen aufhalten, enttäuschen, in Unordnung bringen, etwa dadurch, daß eine Frau an der Hand statt Finger Augen hat. Sowohl dann, wenn es sich um Symbole handelt (Frau sieht mit Händen), als auch dann, wenn nur einfach die Extremität nicht der Erwartung nach ausläuft, tritt ein gewisser Schock ein, und Hand und Auge werden verfremdet. Gerade indem die Hand keine Hand mehr ist, entsteht eine Vorstellung *Hand,* die mehr mit der gewöhnlichen Funktion dieses Instruments zu tun hat als jenes ästhetische Dekorativum, das man auf 10 000 Gemälden angetroffen hat. (*GBA*, 22:824–25)

Shock effects are not normally part of Brecht's arsenal; as Grimm has shown (Grimm 1959, 13), he learnt to his cost in early productions that to disturb the audience in this way could be counterproductive in a didactic play. Yet while making Surrealism sound politically suspect as far as the rela-

---

[47] A discussion of Breughel's *Karl der Kühne nach Murten* was planned for *Der Messingkauf* (*GBA*, 22:802).

tionship of means to end was concerned (the effect, according to the Philosopher, "endet, was die Wirkung betrifft, in einem Amüsement durch den besagten Schock"), he turns a loose analogy into a practical distinction. At the same time, Brecht grants Surrealism's "Verfremdungen" a certain ability to comment symbolically on social conditions. "Oft freilich sind diese Bilder nur Reaktionen auf die untotale Funktionslosigkeit der Menschen und Dinge in unserm Zeitalter, d.h. sie verraten eine schwere Funktionsstörung. Auch die Klage darüber, daß alles und jedes zu funktionieren habe, also alles Mittel und nichts Zweck sei, verrät diese Funktionsstörung" (*GBA*, 22:825). Brecht had only a marginal interest in Surrealism and avant-garde painting, so it is likely that the subject is invoked for largely demarcation purposes. On one level, the Philosopher can suggest that Surrealist pictures have a defamiliarizing function and even exemplify the problem of lost function in modern society. But such an aspect brings it closer to defamiliarization in Shklovsky's less restricted, apolitical sense (one of his main illustrations is defamiliarization in Tolstoy's novels). Brecht is only allowing his Philosopher to make this point in order to show that Brechtian "Verfremdung" should not be confused with the Surrealists' tricks of the trade. While both may be rejected by orthodox Marxist aesthetics as formalist, Brecht's techniques, despite surface similarities, have a very different (political) agenda. While not making distinctions of this order when discussing antecedents of "Verfremdung" in the work of artists he admires, when it comes to movements and "formalist" tendencies with which it would be unhelpful for him to be identified, he invokes the same "new element" that had formed part of his critique of Naturalism: "die Meisterung der Realität" (*GBA*, 22:792).

## Theater and "alltägliches Theater"

In Brecht's "Dritter Nachtrag zur Theorie des *Messingkaufs*" a connection is made between the wartime world in which many of the *Messingkauf* fragments were written and some of the work's theoretical preoccupations (a connection made elsewhere in the project by the detailed discussion of certain features of *99%*, the 1938 Paris production of *Furcht und Elend des III. Reiches* (*GBA*, 22:799–80).

> Das Bedürfnis des Zuschauers unserer Zeit nach Ablenkung vom täglichen Krieg wird ständig vom täglichen Krieg wieder reproduziert, streitet aber ebenso ständig mit dem Bedürfnis, das eigene Schicksal lenken zu können. Die Scheidung der Bedürfnisse nach Unterhaltung und nach Unterhalt ist eine künstliche. In der Unterhaltung (der ablenkenden Art) wird der Unterhalt ständig bedroht, denn der Zuschauer wird nicht etwa ins Nichts geführt, nicht in eine fremde, sondern in eine verzerrte Welt, und er bezahlt seine Ausschweifungen,

die ihm nur als Ausflüge vorkommen, im realen Leben. Nicht spurlos gehen die Einfühlungen in den Gegner an ihm vorüber. Er wird sein eigener Gegner damit. Der Ersatz befriedigt das Bedürfnis und vergiftet den Körper. (*GBA*, 22:700)

The idea is not developed, but there are a number of points of contact between Brecht's theoretical considerations and the war-ridden times in which they were written.

Among the unprocessed material dating from the first phase of *Der Messingkauf*, there is an English newspaper cutting captioned "Song Greets Churchill Back to Commons": "ein Lied," according to an editorial note, "dessen Zusammenhang mit dem *Messingkauf* nicht ermittelt werden konnte" (*GBA*, 22:1112). This is true, in the sense that one can only speculate as to what use Brecht intended to make of the incident. Circumstances suggest, however, that the song must have been "For he's a jolly good fellow" (whose chorus "And so say all of us" would have reflected the cross-party solidarity of the war-time coalition government); and Brecht's interest in the incident was in all probability as an example of the "Theatralik" he wished to investigate, not just in fascism, but in daily life and politics in general, according to a journal entry for 10 October 1942:

Für den *Messingkauf* wäre auszuarbeiten das Thema *angewandtes Theater*, d.h. es müßten einige Grundbeispiele des Einander-Etwas-Vormachens im täglichen Leben beschrieben werden sowie einige Elemente theatralischer Aufführung im privaten und öffentlichen Leben. *Wie* Leute andern Leuten Zorn zeigen, weil sie es für schicklich oder vorteilhaft halten, oder Zärtlichkeit oder Neid usw. usw. Wichtig die auch im privaten Leben geübte Gruppierung in den verschiedenen Situationen. Wie werden die Distanzen gewechselt bei einem Ehekrach [. . .]. Es ist nämlich von der größten Bedeutung, daß es für (teilweise unbewußtes, aber doch) Theater angesehen wird, was die Menschen machen, wenn sie soziale Ränge usurpieren oder zugestehen, in ihrem Ausdruck und Verhalten mehr oder weniger bedingten Sitten Rechnung tragen usw. Wenn es da Natürliches gibt, ist es änderbare Natur. (*GBA*, 27:126)

The setting of Churchill's reception (the British House of Commons, an institution with arcane codes and rituals), the specific moment (the return of a revered national leader after a period of illness) and the way affection is expressed (through a song which combines spontaneity, boyish enthusiasm, and memories of schooldays) would have offered Brecht a fruitful, though rather different field for analysis than the ones he chose to pursue in the framework of *Der Messingkauf*. What he did concentrate on was even more strongly influenced by the political events of the moment than the circumstances surrounding Churchill's return to the Commons.

A fragment from the first phase of work on *Der Messingkauf* takes up some points from the poem "Über alltägliches Theater" and prepares the ground with a caveat:

SCHAUSPIELER Aber ist es nicht nötig, das Theater herauszuheben aus der Straße, dem Spielen einen besonderen Charakter zu verleihen — da es ja eben nicht auf der Straße und nicht zufällig und nicht durch Laien und nicht angeregt durch einen Vorfall stattfindet?

PHILOSOPH All diese Umstände heben es genügend heraus, denke ich. Alle diese Unterschiede, die zwischen Theater und Straße bestehen, sollen ja auch besonders herausgehoben werden. Da soll beileibe nichts weggeschminkt werden! Aber wenn man die beiden Demonstrationen noch so sehr unterscheidet, so muß doch der theatralischen wenigstens etwas von der ursprünglichen Funktion der alltäglichen bleiben. Gerade durch das Unterstreichen der Verschiedenheit, des Professionellen, Vorbereiteten usw. erhält man diese Funktion frisch. (*GBA*, 22:731–32)

The original plan for the contents of *Der Messingkauf* (*GBA*, 22:695) includes a piece designated as "Theatralik des Faschismus" (Second Night) as well as the earlier (1938) essay "Die Straßenszene" (Third Night). Taking its cue from this initial plan,[48] *GW* puts the dialogue "Über die Theatralik des Faschismus" in the Second Night and has "Die Straßenszene" immediately preceding it. There are good reasons for this move: the two essays are thematically linked by the idea of "alltägliches Theater" and "Über die Theatralik des Faschismus" specifically refers back to "Die Straßenszene"[49] (hence the material could hardly be postponed until the Third Night).

---

[48] In "Probleme der Edition von Brecht-Texten," Hecht elucidates the *GW* editorial policy concerning variants: "Für die Leseausgaben wurde im Falle von Varianten diejenige als 'gültig' angesehen, die als die letzte innerhalb eines verfolgbaren Arbeitsprozesses identifiziert werden konnte" (Hecht 1972, 233). There is no such clear statement concerning the contents of *Der Messingkauf* in the *GW* edition.

[49] Since "Die Straßenszene" was not published until 1950, it is likely that the allusion is to an as yet unwritten dialogue based on the ideas in that essay (completed in 1938). The fictive nature of such dialogues is often an obstacle when one asks which theoretical works the participants are referring to. In "Dialog über eine Schauspielerin des epischen Theaters" (*GBA*, 22:353–55), the Actor's introductory remark —

Wir haben eine kleine Szene an einer Straßenecke gefunden, in der der Augenzeuge eines Verkehrsunfalls den Passanten das Verhalten der Betroffenen vorführte. Aus seiner, des Straßendemonstranten, Art zu spielen, haben wir einige Züge hervorgehoben, die für unser Theaterspielen Wert haben können. Wir wollen jetzt eine andere Art theatralischer Darbietung betrachten, die ebenfalls nicht von Künstlern und nicht zu künstlerischen Zwecken, aber in tausendfacher Weise und in Straßen und Versammlungshäusern veranstaltet wird. Wir wollen die Theatralik im Auftreten der Faschisten betrachten. ( *GW*, 16:559)

The speaker, another Thomas, gives the impression that the ground covered by the prose version of "Die Straßenszene" has already been the subject of a discussion between himself and someone called Karl.[50] The implication must be that Brecht intended to recast "Die Straßenszene" as a dialogue that could be integrated into the ongoing exchange between the two men (which would eventually be reassigned to the Philosopher's interlocutors in the final form of *Der Messingkauf*). Thus, while Brecht has already started recasting some of his older ideas in dialogue form, he is as yet uncertain as to who the participants should be. Thomas sounds like a precursor of the Philosopher, but his ideological and intellectual position is less clearly defined than those of the source of the "Ausführungen des Philosophen über den Marxismus" ( *GBA*, 22:716–18).

In *GBA*, neither "Über die Theatralik des Faschismus" nor "Die Straßenszene" appears among the materials belonging to the 1939–41 period. The notes to "Über die Theatralik des Faschismus," now published elsewhere in the same volume ( *GBA*, 22:561–69), present the piece as "nicht für den *Messingkauf* bearbeitet" ( *GBA*, 22:1075). Any explicit connection between the essay and subsequent phases of the *Messingkauf* project has been ruled out, yet the 1941–43 plan does allow for a fragment on "Einfühlung" ( *GBA*, 22:784–86), which is the umbrella concept under which "Über die Theatralik des Faschismus" treats Hitler's oratory; a later plan of contents dated circa 1945 refers to a section to be entitled "Krise und Kritik der Einfühlung" ( *GBA*, 22:793). A related piece, "'Rede des Schauspielers über die Darstellung eines kleinen Nazis': aus dem *Messingkauf*," which *GW* includes as a coda to the "Theatralik des Faschismus" essay in *GW*, vol. 16, is now put in *GBA* among the passages not yet assigned to any particular Night. As the notes point out, "Unklar ist, ob Brecht mit Themen in den

"Ich habe Ihre Schriften über das epische Theater gelesen" — leaves the author of the accompanying notes ( *GBA*, 22:1013) ruminating on whether this refers to recent published writings such as "The Fourth Wall of China" and "The German Drama: Pre-Hitler," both at that time only available in English translations, or whether he means the much earlier theoretical works.

[50] The ubiquitous Thomas, Karl, and Lukas were also the participants in "V-Effekte, Dreigespräch" ( *GBA*, 22:398–401).

Plänen, die Titel von bereits ausgearbeiteten Schriften tragen, [a description which surely applies to both "Über die Theatralik des Faschismus" and "Die Straßenszene"] [. . .] generell eine Übernahme solcher Texte in den *Messingkauf* beabsichtigt" (*GBA*, 22:1112). Even if these pieces were not scheduled to form part of the 1945 plans for *Der Messingkauf,* we still need to take account of Brecht's intention, expressed as late as 10 October 1942, to explore "das Thema *angewandtes Theater*" (*GBA*, 27:126). The remark suggests that he still has a structure into which the "Theatralik" essay could be inserted. This entry, in particular the terms used in it to explain the concept of "angewandtes Theater," makes it seem less likely that "Über die Theatralik des Faschismus" had already been ruled out in some form or another. By 1945 an analysis of Hitler's histrionics and their hold on the German people might soon become of less topical concern. But in earlier phases of the *Messingkauf* project, to apply dramaturgical expertise to the most dangerously histrionic manifestation of fascism to date was to give a clear illustration of how theater could become "eingreifendes Denken," this time in both a positive and a negative sense. A diary entry for 12 February 1939 talks of highlighting "das Funktionieren der gesellschaftlichen Beziehungen [. . .], damit die Gesellschaft eingreifen kann" (*GBA*, 26:327–28), which gives some indication of just how vital an essay of this kind could have been to a positive counter agenda at an earlier stage of the Second World War.

Unlike "Die Straßenszene," written in June 1938 as an autonomous piece and only subsequently considered for inclusion in *Der Messingkauf,* "Über die Theatralik des Faschismus" began life intended for the *Messingkauf* complex, but was eventually dropped. (It was not published as a freestanding piece until 1993.) If one of the principal arguments for *GBA*'s favoring the "Fassung früher Hand" is "die Brechts Werk angemessene Historisierung" ("Editionsbericht," *GBA Registerband,* 807), then "Über die Theatralik des Faschismus" can arguably benefit from consideration within the context of the early phases of work on *Der Messingkauf.*

"Über die Theatralik des Faschismus" presents Hitler's speeches as examples of an emotive rhetorical "Theatralik," effectively exploited but "nicht zu künstlerischen Zwecken" (*GBA*, 22:562). While it might seem logical to categorize "Die Straßenszene" as centering on "einen gewöhnlichen, tausendfachen Vorgang, aus dem Leben gesucht, den man im allgemeinen nicht als theatralischen bezeichnet, weil er nicht unter Künstlern sich abspielt und keine künstlerischen Zwecke verfolgt" (*GBA*, 22:561), to treat Hitler's oratory in the same way is more of a calculated, but necessary act of "Verfremdung." "Über die Theatralik des Faschismus" is at one point declared to be "sehr verschieden von dem Theater, das der Augenzeuge des Unfalls an unserer Straßenecke macht" (*GBA*, 22:565), different in that the latter represents a common-sense attempt to explain a dramatic event in retrospect and via demonstration techniques, whereas Hitler's "Theatralik" has the very opposite effect because of its goal: "die *Einfühlung* des Publikums in den Agierenden [. . .] dieses Mitreißen, dieses alle Zuschauer in eine einheitliche Masse Verwandeln, das man von der Kunst fordert" (ibid.). Hitler, in other words, is an accident whose horrifying repercussions are still to be revealed, whereas "Die Straßenszene" is about an accident that has happened and now needs to be calmly reconstructed. Through this contrasting of "Die Straßenszene" with the "Theatralik des Faschismus" a "*Nicht — Sondern*" model is deployed, to be followed by another as Thomas juxtaposes the way in which one might sensibly have expected a genuinely serious political speaker to behave (without emotion, "mit einem gewissen Ernst," using rational argumentation and not projecting his own personality) with the various "Tricks" with which Hitler decks out his public performances. In contrast to the impersonality of enlightened discourse, Hitler presents himself as "eine Einzelperson, ein Held im Drama" (*GBA*, 22:566). And the kind of drama in which he performs is so manipulated as to bring about mass audience-identification with the charismatic demagogue: "Worauf es ihm ankommt, ist, den Zuschauer, der sich in ihn einfühlt, zur Haltung eines Argumentierenden zu verführen" (*GBA*, 22:567). Which does not mean that Hitler attempts to seduce the aroused crowds with real arguments, but simply that his *Gestik* makes them feel they are participating in rational debate. "Die Herstellung der Einfühlung" (*GBA*, 22:568) has been little more than the product of an illusion. This demythologizing of Hitler's rally performances, with its emphasis on his repertoire of seemingly uncontrived "Kunstgriffe" and the "Gesetzlichkeiten, nach denen sein Auftreten sich abspielt," is offered as a critical insight that will defuse the usual mesmerizing effect. The immediate and obvious answer to Karl's question "Wie soll ich an das Theater denken, wenn das Leben so schrecklich ist?" (*GBA*, 22:562) is that the threats of contemporary life will be understood and hence more avoidable if understanding his methods and agenda leads to the mastering of the threats Hitler represents. As Thomas puts it, "Wir wollen [. . .] eine andere Art theatralischer Darbietung betrachten, die ebenfalls nicht von Künstlern und nicht zu künstlerischen Zwecken, aber in tausendfacher Weise und in Straßen und Versammlungshäusern veranstaltet wird" (*GBA*, 22:562). Hitler, who was known to have taken acting lessons from a third-rate professional,[51] is shown to employ cheap theatrical tricks for political purposes; and in demonstrating this, Brecht offers "den Schlüssel zur Meisterung einer unklaren Situation." This is no longer merely theater turning to the contemporary world for its subject matter, it is theater using

---

[51] According to Brecht's source — Olden, 1935, 88 — this is a reference to the Munich Hofschauspieler Fritz Basil. The fact is also the basis for the parodistic scene 6 of *Arturo Ui*, as well as Brecht's article "My Most Unforgettable Character" (*GBA*, 20:59–62), submitted, without success, to the *Reader's Digest*.

its professional expertise to unmask the pseudo-theater of the aestheticized politics of the moment.

In one sense, "Über die Theatralik des Faschismus" does resemble "Die Straßenszene," inasmuch as its exploration of the theatricality of fascist demagoguery serves as a *model*. But rather than being a model of the *modus operandi* of Epic Theater, as "Die Straßenszene" was, its case is that Hitler works with various strategies to create "Einfühlung" among his followers and that such "Aristotelian" politics are deeply dangerous because "Einfühlung" is the enemy of all rational understanding:

> Karl: Ich sehe natürlich, welche Gefahr es ist, sich in ihn [Hitler] einzufühlen, da er das Volk auf einen gefährlichen Weg bringt. Aber ich denke mir, daß du im Grunde nicht nur darauf hinauswillst, daß es gefährlich sein kann, sich in einen Agierenden einzufühlen (wie es gefährlich ist, sich in diesen einzufühlen), sondern daß es gefährlich ist, ganz gleichgültig, ob er wie jener, einen auf einen gefährlichen Weg bringt, oder nicht. So ist es doch?
>
> Thomas: Ja. Und zwar schon deshalb, weil die Herstellung der Einfühlung es dem, der ihr verfällt, unmöglich macht, noch zu erkennen, ob der Weg gefährlich ist oder nicht. (*GBA*, 22:568)

Fascism's "Theatralik" is therefore shown to be the diametrical opposite of "Thaeter." By which token, if the application of theatrical terms to Hitler's demagogic performances is a form of "Verfremdung," with the dictator functioning as a political illustration of the dangers of total identification (the equivalent of a Stanislavskian "restlose Verwandlung" of the audience, but probably not in this case of the actor), then the cognitive advantage of the illustration, apart from its historical immediacy, is that it demonstrates in extreme terms just where emotional "Einfühlung" can in the end lead. "Gegenseitige Verfremdung" is also at work here. What is at stake, however, is something more than a series of narrowly aesthetic issues. "Angewandtes Theater" means theater applied to life, in this case bringing to bear principles of observation that will reveal the source of a ruthless demagogue's rhetorical appeal and undermine it. Theater theory ceases to be merely an aesthetic matter when applied in this way, and ironically, like the histrionics it dissects, it is artistic knowledge serving non-aesthetic purposes. This is a less benign variation on Brecht's dictum that "alle Künste tragen bei zur größten aller Künste, der Lebenskunst" (*GBA*, 23:290).

The dialogue's conclusion ties these two aspects of the material, its artistic value and its pragmatic value in respect of life beyond the theater's walls, a little too neatly together:

*Thomas:* [. . .] Darum ist die theatralische Darbietung, wie sie durch den Faschismus gegeben wird, kein gutes Beispiel eines Theaters, wenn man von ihm Darstellungen haben will, die den Zuschauern den Schlüssel für die Bewältigung der Probleme des gesellschaftlichen Zusammenlebens aushändigen.

*Karl:* Es ist schwierig, zu diesem Schluß ja zu sagen. Er verwirft eine Praxis der Theater, die durch Jahrtausende geübt wurde.

*Thomas:* Meinst du, die Praxis des Anstreichers ist neu? (*GBA*, 22:569)

Hitler appropriates the identificatory techniques of a type of theater that would never have been in a position to prevent him from winning hearts, if not minds. In one fell swoop, the workings of a false "Theatralik" have been exposed, Aristotelian drama has received a further broadside and the aims and methods of Epic Theater have been further sanctioned within a dialogue that might itself lay claim to being called "epic."

## "Einfühlung" and Its Consequences

"Über die Theatralik des Faschismus" draws a forceful analogy between the demagogic abuse of audience identification and the manipulative effects of Aristotelian theater. The essay's removal from the *Messingkauf* project risked leaving this ultimate theoretical work without a major statement of Brecht's current thinking on why emotional identification was politically so dangerous. To compensate for this omission, an essay entitled "Einfühlung" was added to the First Night[52] materials during the 1941–43 phase (*GBA*, 22:784–86). This replacement piece is Brecht's most authoritative statement on the subject since the unpublished "Thesen über die Aufgabe der Einfühlung in den theatralischen Künsten" of circa 1935 (*GBA*, 22:175–76); whereas the theses merely hint that the status of "Einfühlung (Identifikation)" will have to be rethought in light of Epic Theater's advances, the new essay attempts to carry out that task. As yet it only refers to the methods and goals of Epic Theater in an indirect manner. It will not be until the next phase of the project that "Einfühlung" receives fuller critical treatment within the context of Epic Theater: in B 161 (an unassigned piece). While the faults of the Stanislavskian approach are often presented in magisterial essay form, the circumscribed role "Einfühlung" plays within the preparatory

---

[52] A plan from this time, entitled "Thema der Ersten Nacht" (*GBA*, 22:767), indicates two items that might have served as a peg for the essay: "Illusion" and "Der Naturalismus."

stages of Epic Theater was for a long time neglected. Brecht eventually goes on to integrate the material into a more complex exchange of ideas between Philosopher, Actor and *Dramaturg.*

The *Messingkauf* essay on "Einfühlung" begins by *historicizing* Stanislavsky's contribution to theater: first, by questioning its hegemony with a brief prefacing paragraph on "die epische Spielweise," its aims, and its objectives (*GBA,* 22:784), and subsequently by introducing Stanislavskian theater as "die vorläufig letzte theoretisch durchgeplante Spielweise des bürgerlichen Theaters" (*GBA,* 22:784–85). Much of the unfolding argument, even the terminology, is familiar from Brecht's earlier writings. Now, however, some half a dozen years after *Mother,* we find a number of fresh angles and a more nuanced assessment of Stanislavsky's importance, as well as indications of a recognition of the reasons why he cannot simply be demonized.

Before once more outlining the basic principles of Method Acting, Brecht again credits Stanislavsky with being one of the first to systematize his procedures in print ("Stanislawski, dem das Verdienst zusteht, diesen Akt [der restlosen Verwandlung] beinahe wissenschaftlich exakt untersucht und angegeben zu haben"). But this key sentence, echoing Brecht's letter to Piscator of July 1936, follows up the praise with a devastating charge of essentialism: "[Stanislawski hält es] nirgends für nötig, [sein Theater] gegen Kritik irgendwelcher Art zu verteidigen: er ist auf solche Kritik überhaupt nicht gefaßt. Die Einfühlung scheint ihm ein Phänomen, das eben ganz untrennbar zur Kunst gehört, so untrennbar, daß von Kunst überhaupt nicht gesprochen werden kann, wo sie nicht zustande kommt" (*GBA,* 22:785). There are two distinct aspects to this charge. First, Brecht classifies failure to question the legitimacy of "Einfühlung" as a severe weakness because the method will consequently remain insufficiently theorized and assessed in terms of its sociopolitical function. Second, he challenges Stanislavsky's allegedly unquestioning association of empathy with all art — which here means all *theater* — on the erroneous assumption that any serious attack on "Einfühlung" is tantamount to aesthetic heresy. This may lie behind Brecht's use of the neologism "Thaeter" at a number of points in the *Messingkauf* project, in the sense that he is not confusing Epic Theater with all theater, but presenting it as "Thaeter": an alternative theater to that of the bourgeois establishment. The "Historisierung" of Stanislavskian theater at the beginning of the essay was clearly intended to show that "Einfühlungstheater" and theater *per se* are not synonymous. In a shrewd countermove, Brecht draws attention to the invidious situation people who want to criticize the Stanislavskians put themselves in: "Wer dieser Auffassung widersprechen will [. . .], befindet sich zunächst in einer schwierigen Lage, da er nicht leugnen kann, daß das Phänomen der Einfühlung tatsächlich im Kunsterlebnis schlechthin vorkommt" (*GBA,* 22:785). This is an important concession on Brecht's part, since from this point onwards he has to present his case with more differentiation than an argument rejecting empathy in its entirely would need to employ. It might be easier, as Brecht admits, for someone with serious misgivings about "Einfühlung": "wenn er einfach behaupten könnte, [das Phänomen] sei überhaupt aus der Kunst zu entfernen. Und doch verliert das Phänomen der Einfühlung einen Großteil seiner Bedeutung, wenn es erst an jenen Platz (keinen außerhalb) der Kunst verwiesen ist, wo es einer neuen Theorie gemäß hingehört" (ibid.). As the reference to a new theory of drama suggests, the real issue is not the place of "Einfühlung" within Stanislavsky's theory, but the more pressing question of just what the theory of Epic Theater needs to do with the insight that the phenomenon can never be banished from either performances or rehearsals.

Brecht refers back to the essay's earlier claim that Stanislavskian theater employs "eine Technik, welche die *Wahrheit* des Spiels garantieren soll" (ibid.), "Wahrheit" being a loose portmanteau term for verisimilitude, a semblance of social and historical authenticity and plausibility. The main need now is to make a distinction between where "Wahrheit" can be achieved and where any suggestion of it is misleading. Brecht concedes that Stanislavskian preparation techniques guarantee a measure of truth-to-life and remove an unwanted "stagey" artificiality: "Alle falschen Töne, jedes Sich-Vergreifen des Schauspielers in der Geste oder der Maske kann vollständig vermieden werden" (*GBA*, 22:786). This may seem a generous acknowledgment, but in fact it amounts to little more than praise for the Stanislavsky School's working with a latterday form of behavioral Naturalism. But this is only Brecht's starting point. Had the essay been "dialogisiert," a second voice would have had to come in to take the argument in a more productive direction. There follows a substantial misgiving: "Es ist jedoch nicht schwer, einzusehen, daß eine solche Wahrheit nicht schon ohne weiteres alle Fragen beantwortet, die gestellt werden können" (ibid.). In thus delimiting the "truth" of Stanislavskian performance, Brecht weighs in with an allusion to "Die Straßenszene": "Auf solche Weise ist jeder beliebige Vorgang zwischen Menschen an einer wirklichen Straßenecke 'wahr' und zugleich unverständlich. Der Zuschauer sieht hier, wie bei Nachbildung auf dem Theater, Zorn und vielleicht auch noch seine unmittelbare Ursache" (ibid.). Faithful replication, as the discussion in the First Night had shown, is of virtually no political value. Truth of this kind has little to do with true realism. The allusion to "Die Straßenszene" highlights the difference between surface respect for detail and the insight that only some form of "Modell" can bring. Brecht moves on to a more damaging criticism of Stanislavskian surface "truth" with his reference to the cause-and-effect model that was brought so much to the fore during the discussions of the First Night. In reality, he now objects: "die Ursachen treten, wie jedermann heute weiß, in Reihen auf, indem sie wieder Ursachen haben, und der Vorgang an der

Straßenecke und seine 'wahre' Nachbildung auf dem Theater haben beide eine sehr kurze, überblickbare Ursachenreihe, *der Kausalnexus ist ärmlich, primitiv, auf dem Theater ist er sogar noch erheblich ärmlicher als an der Straßenecke*" (ibid., my emphasis). More impoverished, because the hold of "Einfühlung" over the theater leads to a foreshortening of genuine inquiry into the causal nexus and an undemanding concentration on the emotional value of events: "[Der Zuschauer] gerät selber in Zorn oder Eifersucht, versteht sozusagen gar nicht mehr, wie man nicht in Zorn oder Eifersucht geraten könnte, und wird so desinteressiert am Kausalnexus dieser 'natürlichen,' d.h. gegebenen, nicht weiter zu untersuchenden Emotionen" (ibid.). This would have been the point at which to explain whether cause-and-effect patterns are also demonstrated by using simple models, but the essay breaks off here,[53] although a discussion from the circa 1945 phase of *Der Messingkauf* once more takes up the question of what Epic Theater can offer as an antidote to Aristotelian theater's obsession with total "Einfühlung." The difference between the "Epic" strategies outlined in "Die Straßenszene" and "jeder beliebige Vorgang zwischen Menschen an einer wirklichen Straßenecke" has been brought out, but in very simplified terms (hence the eventual subtitle's reference to "Die Straßenszene" as no more than a "*Grundmodell*"). What Brecht now needed to do in *Der Messingkauf* was to return to the strategies of Epic Theater and theorize these more systematically in the light of the different forms of "Wahrheit" to which theater can aspire.

He had a number of preliminary sketches and notes he could build on, of course. In January and February 1941, in the wake of "Kurze Beschreibung," his various theoretical sketches include a number of attempts at coming to terms more rigorously with the challenge of a theater of identification.[54] These might all be considered preparatory studies for *Der Messingkauf*, and, in a more permissive reading, part of the *Messingkauf* complex. The most important of these, which may be why it is written up in the Fin-

---

[53] An excuse is offered: "Es ist immer sehr schwierig, ein Bild zu finden, das unmißverständlich ausdrückt, was man meint. Am nächsten scheint mir folgender Vergleich zu kommen" (*GBA*, 22:786). In the event, Brecht's solution was to discontinue the search for a persuasive image and return to the implications of this essay for the rehearsal situation, which meant taking Stanislavsky on in his own territory.

[54] "Einige Andeutungen über eine nichtaristotelische Dramatik" (*GBA*, 22:680), "[Wirkung epischer Schauspielkunst]" (*GBA*, 22:680–81), "[Keine Erregung von Emotionen]" (*GBA*, 22:681–82), "Über das Merkwürdige und Sehenswerte" (*GBA*, 22:682–83,) "Über das schrittweise Vorgehen beim Studium und Aufbau der Figur" (*GBA*, 22:684–85), "Kann der Schauspieler, schrittweise vorgehend, mitreißen?" (*GBA*, 22:686), "Über die Auswahl der Züge" (*GBA*, 22:686–88), and "Die Verschiedenheit um der Verschiedenheit willen dargestellt" (*GBA*, 22:688–89).

nish journal for 11 January 1941, makes a crucial distinction, in the context of Epic Theater, between the permissible — indeed necessary — role played by "Einfühlung" for *the actor* at rehearsal stage, a form of short-term identification, and another kind, in Aristotelian theater, where the actor's identification with the role, *during performance,* influences the audience's feelings in such a way that the players too cannot help but identify with the character portrayed. For this latter process, one to be avoided, Brecht will go on to use a more clearly defined conception of "Suggestion" than was to be found in the *Mahagonny* "Schema." First, though, comes the distinction between rehearsal and performance practices:

> Anlagend die Rolle der *Einfühlung* auf dem nichtaristotelischen Theater: die Einfühlung ist hier eine Maßnahme der *Probe*. Voraus geht das *Einrichten* der Rolle (der Schauspieler legt sich alle Äußerungen, Verrichtungen, Reaktionen zurecht, so daß sie ihm bequem liegen, wobei er noch nicht eine besondere Figur kreiert, wenn er auch einige allgemeinste Eingenschaften anlegt). Dann kommt, im Grund sprungweise, die Kreierung der Figur (wobei er seine Erfahrungen hinzuzieht, bestimmte Menschen kopiert, Züge verschiedener Menschen kombiniert usw.). Schon das Einrichten der Rollen kann einen Abschluß dadurch erfahren, daß der Schauspieler sich selber einfühlt, zunächst in die Situationen (wie er selber in solcher Lage sich verhielte). Beim Kreieren der Figur kann er wieder eine Einfühlung vornehmen, nunmehr in die Person, die er darstellen, kopieren will. Jedoch ist auch diese Einfühlung nur eine Phase, eine Maßnahme, die ihm zu vollerer Erfassung eines Types verhelfen soll. (*GBA*, 26:454)

A number of crucial points emerge here, contrasting with the simple psychic distancing-oriented treatment of the subject in "Kurze Beschreibung," and, because they only partially find their way into *Der Messingkauf,* they have tended to be associated with the later Brecht of the East Berlin Stanislavsky Conference period in the early 1950s. At that time too, for instance in the *Katzgraben* notes, we find him emphasizing the importance of "Einfühlung" at the rehearsal stage:

> *Hurwicz:*  [. . .] Aber Sie sind ja gegen Einfühlung, Brecht.
>
> *B:*  Ich? Nein. Ich bin dafür, in einer bestimmten Phase der Proben. Es muß dann nur noch etwas dazukommen, nämlich die Einstellung zur Figur, in die ihr euch einfühlt, die gesellschaftliche Einschätzung. (*GBA*, 25:439)

Although the way the point is illustrated makes it seem like the fruit of the *Katzgraben* rehearsals, it was an insight formulated more than ten years earlier, and recorded then in more differentiated detail. There, in a journal entry, particular attention is drawn to the fact that "Einfühlung" is a deliberate *measure,* only to be adopted at the preparatory stage. Moreover, there is a clearer sense of requisite phasing to the process: first, a feeling of one's way into a certain *situation* (a marked contrast to Brecht's earlier remarks on the subject where it was often difficult to know just what the actor was empathizing with: a character, characters in the plural in a predicament, or a given situation[55]). Particular importance is attached to the *caveat* that follows:

> Wichtig aber ist, daß die jeweilige Einfühlung ohne Suggestion stattfindet, d.h. es soll nicht auch ein Zuschauer zur Einfühlung veranlaßt werden. Dies ist schwierig, aber möglich. Dem Schauspieler des jetzigen Theaters allerdings ist eigene Einfühlung und Verleitung des Zuschauers zur Einfühlung (suggestive Einfühlung) identisch. Er kann sich schwer das eine ohne das andere vorstellen und das eine schwer ohne das andere praktizieren. In Wirklichkeit kommen die beiden Maßnahmen getrennt vor, und ihre Kombination ist eine besondere Kunst. [. . .] Der Schauspieler des jetzigen Theaters kann sich auch Wirkung ohne Einfühlung und Wirkung ohne Suggestion nicht vorstellen. (*GBA*, 26:454–55)

By deflecting attention to the Stanislavskian-Aristotelian actor for whom "suggestive Einfühlung" and powerful acting are inseparable, Brecht manages to skate over the fact that, even as late as the time of "Kurze Beschreibung," he was still basing his practical recommendations on the assumption that the actor's relationship to his part would automatically generate a mirror relationship in the audience. Now a more nuanced picture emerges: empathy at the rehearsal phase on the actor's part is a *technique,* and what is more, one to be applied in stages. While Brechtian rehearsals may derive some of their methods from Stanislavsky, the new use of "Einfühlung" still represents a means to a radically different performance goal. What Brecht calls "suggestive Einfühlung," that is, a less conscious effect and more an unthinking actor-part relationship — or in the case of the Stanislavsky School a highly cultivated one — is the result of carrying forward unquestioning role identification from the rehearsal stage to performance, and this tends to result in uncritical identification on the audience's part. By distinguishing between "Einfühlung" as a legitimate rehearsal technique and "suggestive Einfühlung" as an unproductive result of a certain kind of Aristotelian performance, Brecht can now make a clear distinction between what is permissible as a means and what is unacceptable as another

---

[55] Since empathizing with a *situation* inevitably means empathizing with a person in such a predicament, it is easy to understand why Brecht introduces "Situationen" into the picture.

kind of end.[56] While the distinction between what is helpful at the rehearsal stage ("Einfühlung" on the actor's part) and what is counterproductive during performance (a "suggestive Einfühlung" contagious to the audience) is an advance, it is still expressed in "*Nicht — Sondern*" terms. Moreover, it fails to generate a more sophisticated account of the spectrum of emotions that do take place during the performance of a play. This unfinished business will be postponed until a much later dialogue: "Einige Irrtümer über die Spielweise des Berliner Ensemble (*Kleines Gespräch in der Dramaturgie*)" (*GBA*, 23:323–38).

With good reason, the two figures who dominate the subsequent (Socratic) discussion of "Einfühlung" and acting in B 161 are the Actor and the Philosopher. Not for the first time, the Actor is allowed to present a caricature of the latter's position; this caricature then invites a series of clarifications. Characteristically, the discussion begins with the Actor's trying to goad the Philosopher: "Sicher doch, du willst nicht sagen, daß ich eine Figur nachahmen soll, in die ich mich nicht im Geiste hineinversetzt habe?" (*GBA*, 22:822). The Actor refers loosely to his relationship to the part "bei den Proben," whereas the Philosopher focuses on a more specific task: "die Figur aufbauen." The Philosopher's contributions to the discussion repeatedly clarify some of the simpler points made in the earlier "Einfühlung" sketch, partly by creating a complex taxonomy of preparatory operations and partly by introducing a whole new series of contrasts. The Philosopher takes up the Actor's new verb "sich hineinversetzen" (he will later use another pair of antithetical terms to posit a contrast between Stanislavskian "Sicheinfühlen" and Epic Theater's "Sichhineinversetzen"); he does so in order to show the Actor that the opening question cannot be answered in the simple terms in which it was posed. Before one can immerse onself in a character ("in ihre Körperlichkeit, in ihre Denkweise"), the character has to be "vorgestellt," and this demands "Phantasie" on the actor's part since the stage figure is not

---

[56] A cautionary phrase from elsewhere in *Der Messingkauf,* "ein paar vorsichtige Äußerungen abstrakter Art" (*GBA*, 22:760), also applies here. But Brecht's comments on John Ford's film version of *The Grapes of Wrath* illustrate the dangers of "suggestive Einfühlung." His diary for 22 January 1941 records: "Wir sehen den Film nach *Steinbecks* 'Grapes of Wrath.' Man sieht noch, daß es sich um ein großes Buch handeln muß, und die Unternehmer wollten wohl nicht 'die Kraft aus ihm nehmen.' Sie kochen das Thema in Tränen weich. Wo nicht 'suggestives Spiel' vorherrscht, gibt es starke Wirkungen (die Traktoren als Tanks gegen die Farmer, der faschistische Streichbrechercamp, die Autofahrt durch die ganzen Staaten auf Arbeitssuche, das Begräbnis des alten Farmers). Das Ganze eine interessante Mischung von Dokumentarischem und Privatem, Epischem und Drrramatischem [sic], Informativem und Sentimentalem, Realistischem und Symbolischem, Materialistischem und Idealisierung" (*GBA*, 26:460).

necessarily always a given nor someone once observed and now reconstructed from memory. Whereas "Illusion" — the feeling that one *is* the character — will shortly be associated with "Unverstand," "Phantasie" is an unreservedly positive term. Such a creative act of ideation, of imaginatively thinking one's way into a character, is, the Philosopher cautions, only "eine der Operationen des Aufbaus der Figur." Once accomplished, it will have to be followed by a rewinding of the process ("nur ist nötig, daß ihr es versteht, euch dann wieder hinauszuversetzen," the unfamiliar new verb acting as a "Verfremdung" of the line of thought the Actor has so far been content to follow). Because a whole series of operations is required, the Actor's vague phrase "bei den Proben" is unhelpful, given that he invariably fails to specify *which stage* of the rehearsal process he is talking about. The discussion is moved forward more constructively from role to situation, when the Philosopher makes a distinction between "eine Vorstellung von einer Begebenheit vermitteln" and "eine Illusion erzeugen" — the verbs are important as they distinguish between communicating necessary information and creating a false illusion, in the sense of "suggestive Einfühlung" into what is in any case no more than a theatrical fiction. The Actor, who has protested that people overestimate the extent to which actors do *become* their parts, is corrected. His references to inappropriate thoughts that invade the actors' minds while they are acting onstage and thus prove that total identification with the role is not what happens during a performance are dismissed as irrelevancies: "Sie mögen eure Einfühlung stören, aber sie vertiefen die des Publikums" (ibid.). To avoid being sidetracked, the Philosopher takes the discussion back to the danger for the audience of a theater based on illusions. By this stage, a new (for Brecht) terminological distinction is proposed between "Sichhineinversetzen," a deliberate stage in the imaginative process of building up the part (later followed by a requisite "Sichhinausversetzen"), and an uncontrolled, and hence counterproductive "Sichhineinfühlen," dangerous in that it leads to the "Illusion" in the audience that they are watching events in real life happening before their very eyes.

As so often in Brecht's theoretical writings, the case against "Einfühlung" is made by means of a series of antithetical concepts: "Sichhineinversetzen" / "einfühlen," "Phantasie" / "Unverstand" or "Illusion," "bei den Proben" / "bei den Operationen der Aufbau der Figur." As if this were not complicated enough, the Actor is allowed to push the Philosopher into a further distinction by confronting him with a dogmatic conclusion ostensibly drawn from the argument so far: "Das Sichhineinversetzen in die Person soll also nur bei den Proben vor sich gehen und nicht auch beim Spielen?" (*GBA*, 22:822–23). The Philosopher's reply involves a rhetorical strategy that works particularly well in the dialogue context, but would have been more difficult to integrate into an essay. For the Philosopher first says what he would like to say, then gives his reasons for caution and finally signals his withdrawal from what he has been toying with as a tenable position:

> Ich könnte einfach antworten: beim Spielen sollt ihr euch nicht in die Person hineinversetzen. Dazu wäre ich durchaus berechtigt. Einmal, da ich einen Unterschied zwischen Sicheinfühlen und Sichhineinversetzen gemacht habe, dann weil ich wirklich glaube, die Einfühlung ist ganz unnötig, vor allem aber, weil ich fürchte, durch eine andere Antwort, wie immer sie sei, dem ganzen alten Unfug wieder ein Türlein zu öffnen, nachdem ich das Tor vor ihm verschlossen habe. Gleichwohl zögere ich. (*GBA*, 22:823)

It may seem surprising to hear the nearest person *Der Messingkauf* has to a *raisonneur* suggesting that he would ideally like to advocate a more sophisticated position. This looks like Brecht, the former scourge of the Stanislavsky School, stating that he does not want his argument to become too differentiated only because it might reopen the old Pandora's box full of misunderstandings of Epic Theater. Yet this is what he proceeds to do with his example of "schwache Einfühlung" during a rehearsal when tired actors delivered their lines with little conviction, a strangely maverick illustration, then discounted with "ich muß aber sagen, daß die Schauspieler niemals wagen würden, so vor Publikum zu spielen" (*GBA*, 22:823). Given that the phrase "Gib ein Beispiel!" has become something of a leitmotif in *Der Messingkauf*, it is worth noting here that what Brecht has done this time is to give half an example and then discuss it in ambivalent terms, before retreating to the more familiar "certainties" of his earlier theorizing with the confession "wenn ich sicher sein könnte, das ihr den ungeheueren Unterschied zwischen dem neuen Spiel und dem alten, das auf voller Einfühlung beruht, als kaum weniger ungeheuer sehen könntet, wenn ich ganz schwache Einfühlung für möglich erkläre, dann würde ich es tun" (ibid.). This is not simply prevaricating, Brecht is using the dialogue mode to good effect by leaving the matter for the reader/audience to take further. The Philosopher shares his strategic problems with his listeners; he implies that they may not be artistically mature enough for what he would like to say to them; yet he says it anyway. A risqué, new concept ("ganz schwache Einfühlung") has been injected into the discussion. The Actor is given an opportunity to engage in thought games with it, but does not rise to the bait; instead, the *Dramaturg* is allowed to close the speech off from any further onstage debate: "DER DRAMATURG: Können wir so sagen: so wie man jetzt diejenigen Dilettanten heißt, die keine Einfühlung zustande bringen, wird man vielleicht einmal diejenigen Dilettanten heißen, die nicht ohne sie auskommen? Sei ganz beruhigt. Du nimmst deiner Spielweise in unseren Augen ihr Befremdliches mit deinem weisen Zugeständnis nicht" (*GBA*, 22:823–24). This bland attempt at a reconciliation of positions, reflecting a desire to put the Philosopher's mind at rest on an issue that has not been the real point in his long preceding speech, gives a further ironic twist to the problem of using dialogue for Socratic purposes. The Philosopher may be allowed to play games with his listeners, but they are not permitted to reply in kind. When the Actor is permitted the gauche comment "Ich glaube, du hast eine übertriebene Meinung, *fast eine Illusion* darüber, wie tief wir Schauspieler des alten Theaters uns in die Rollen einfühlen" (*GBA*, 22:822, my emphasis), the Philosopher is given the pleasure of puncturing the rather contrived play on "Illusion" by pointing out that an actor trying to check that a prop is correctly positioned, how a particular gesture should be delivered or worrying about whether he can avoid the comedian's attempt at distracting him from his role is in fact engaged in the preservation of the audience's illusions, not in serious resistance to "Einfühlung." It should be noted that the Actor was also present at the discussion of audience illusion in the Third Night ("Wie ist es mit der vierten Wand?" *GBA*, 22:802–3), yet does not appear to have come away any the wiser.

The exchange beginning "Wie ist es mit der vierten Wand?" is a striking example of the role played by what might be called "Socratic 'Verfremdung'" in Brecht's theorizing. If that "Verfremdung" has achieved its purpose in the relevant sequences of *Der Messingkauf,* the Actor's ideas in the discussion we have just been looking at will have become substantially more difficult to identify with. The Philosopher's principal weapon against this particular convention is Socratically feigned ignorance. If, of all the participants in the *Messingkauf* dialogues, he is the closest to Brecht's position, he still shows no familiarity with the arguments of "Verfremdungseffekte in der chinesischen Schauspielkunst," with its allusion to the fourth-wall convention in its English title. When the *Dramaturg* begins the exchange with the question "Wie ist es mit der vierten Wand?" he asks "Was ist das?" (*GBA*, 22:802). His disingenuous naivety forces *Dramaturg* and Actor to try to put into words the illusionist conventions that center on the missing fourth wall. In doing so they employ imagery that of itself makes the degree of deception involved seem ridiculous:

DER DRAMATURG  Für gewöhnlich spielt man so, als ob die Bühne nicht nur drei Wände, sondern vier hätte; die vierte da, wo das Publikum sitzt. Es wird ja der Anschein geweckt und aufrechterhalten, daß, was auf der Bühne passiert, ein echter Vorgang aus dem Leben ist, und dort ist natürlich kein Publikum. Mit der vierten Wand spielen heißt also so spielen, als ob kein Publikum da wäre.

DER SCHAUSPIELER  Du verstehst, das Publikum sieht, selber ungesehen, ganz intime Vorgänge. Es ist genau, als ob einer durch ein Schlüsselloch eine Szene belauscht unter Leuten, die keine Ahnung haben, daß sie nicht unter sich sind. In Wirklichkeit arrangieren wir natürlich alles so, daß man alles gut sieht. Dieses Arrangement wird nur verborgen. (*GBA*, 22:802)

In this modern version of the *elenchus,* Brecht has his Actor unwittingly reveal more about the dubiousness of the convention than do even the *Dramaturg*'s words. The estranging image of the audience peeping through a keyhole (a satirical "Verfremdung" of the fourth-wall aperture) not only makes such behavior look unnatural; it also imports overtones of illicitness. For in a theater of emotional appeal where "ganz intime Vorgänge" are being watched voyeuristically, the potential for prurience of such a situation is a further metaphor for the kind of "unworthy" behavior Brecht repeatedly castigated. Perhaps the fourth-wall convention matches the suspect appeal to the audience's baser instincts, but the Philosopher lampoons such an illusory situation with his suggestion that, since no one peeping through a keyhole would applaud what they are watching, perhaps the audience should wait until they reach the cloakroom before signalling their appreciation, thus breaking the spirit of such an irrational "verwickelte geheime Abmachung."

The Actor himself draws attention to the central contradiction in the convention with his admission that "in Wirklichkeit" the actors do not consistently behave as if the audience were not there. His point that everything is so arranged "daß man alles gut sieht" stands as a token for all the other secret concessions to an audience that is treated as being both there and not there: compromises the Actor believes to be necessary for a "realistic" play. Although not mentioned, many other features of the fourth-wall convention also take cognizance of the audience: where actors face when speaking, how they project, configurations of characters — seated, standing, or at table — and visual tableau effects, all give the lie to the *Dramaturg*'s reference to "so spielen, als ob kein Publikum da wäre." But the one isolated point about ensuring that the audience can see everything is sufficent to satirize the undemanding nature of such audiences — "undemanding" in the sense that they are content with Naturalist replicas rather than demanding Epic Theater.

The contrivance and contradictions underlying the convention are well brought out in this discussion. Applause in the right places is permitted, yet rationalized as confirmation of the fact that the actors have, until this point, succeeded in upholding the illusion "daß es den Schauspielern gelungen ist, so aufzutreten, als sei es nicht vorhanden!" (*GBA*, 22:802). This evidence of the complex interplay between artificial conventions and gestures of verisimilitude leads on to a familiar exchange concerning the differences between simulated and "echter" Realism. The Philosopher uses a well-chosen verb ("wegschminken") to condemn the illusion upon which the fourth-wall convention operates. By contrast, Epic Theater presents reality's face without any figurative makeup. The fourth wall is a synecdoche for the entire reportoire of conventions of an illusionism designed for those who prefer to confuse semblance with reality. It is the Worker who interrupts with "Ich bin für realistisches Spiel," and when the Actor later proudly boasts "wir spielten hier bisher nicht für Krethi und Plethi," the association of one kind of convention with reaction and the other with class progress is made explicit. The Philosopher, with a little help from the Worker, has forced the *Dramaturg* and the Actor to see the irrationality and unproductiveness of their conventions.

## The *Messingkauf* "Nachträge"

"Den *Messingkauf* durchflogen," Brecht's journal for 8 August 1940 begins, although just how much draft material he could have marshalled by then obviously depends on how many old essays are still thought of as part of the project. The result of this interim review is a series of "Nachträge," all dated 8 August, which add up to an impressively searching corrective. Unlike the retrospective "[Nachträge zum *Kleinen Organon*]" (*GBA*, 23:289–95), written between 1952 and 1954, that is, well after that complete work's publication, the *Messingkauf* "Nachträge" are as much a matter of intent as past achievement. This explains why the *GBA* notes to the volume in which *Der Messingkauf* appears can refer to the "Nachträge" as offering "[einen] zusammenfassenden Rückblick" (*GBA*, 22:1113), while those to the first *Journale* volume emphasize their forward-looking aspect: "Die Notierungen [. . .] dienen Brecht zur Selbstverständigung über die weitere Arbeit am *Messingkauf*" (*GBA*, 26:657). The *GW* edition, treating the *Messingkauf* "Nachträge" as if their function were similar to that of those to the *Kleines Organon*, puts them at the end of *Der Messingkauf* (*GW*, 16:651–57). *GBA*, on the other hand, places them chronologically immediately after the preliminary plans. Yet no matter how ambiguous the function of these Janus-headed pieces, the length and quality of the observations in them reflect a renewed surge of enthusiasm about the whole project. It would be difficult to find a dozen pages anywhere else in the *Messingkauf* complex as rich in original points and well-formulated explanations.

The first "Nachtrag" concentrates on "den Verkehr zwischen Bühne und Zuschauerraum," or more specifically: "die Art und Weise, wie der Zuschauer sich der Vorgänge auf der Bühne zu bemächtigen hat" (*GBA*, 22:697), where "sich bemächtigen" could signify *receive, process* or *act on*.

To claim "die Theorie ist verhältnismäßig einfach" may be wishful thinking, but at the outset the first "Nachtrag" does list the main charges against Aristotelian drama succinctly and clearly. They are: (once more) that empathy militates against critical insight, now referred to using the anglicized noun "Kritizismus"; and that the way in which such theater manipulates contrived plots deprives works of adequate referentiality and leaves them deriving their impact from "theatrical" effects rather than any ability to engage with the real world. In contrast to the simple charge of "Irrealität" leveled at "die dramatische Form des Theaters" in the *Mahagonny* notes, a key concession is made here in that it is recognized that even in the theater of "Einfühlung," a certain modicum of plausibility and hence referentiality is required if empathy is to be ensured. The point is made in such a way as to prepare the ground for a justification of Epic Theater: "Handlungen, die an das wirkliche Leben erinnern, werden dazu allerdings benötigt, und sie müssen einigermaßen wahrscheinlich sein, damit die Illusion zustande kommt, ohne welche die Einfühlung nicht gelingt. Jedoch ist es keineswegs nötig, daß etwa auch die Kausalität der Vorgänge in Erscheinung tritt, es genügt vollständig, wenn sie nicht bezweifelt zu werden braucht" (*GBA,* 22:698). That gap, between a theater of "Handlungen" in which a deceptive veneer of causality is seldom brought into question and a "Fabel"-oriented parable that acts as the vehicle for displaying genuine sociopolitical patterns of causality, marks the crude divide between Aristotelian (or even Naturalist) drama and Epic Theater. Never before in Brecht's writings has thematized causality played such a major role as a criterion for distinguishing between different forms of theater. In order to demonstrate that the plausibility of a dramatic replica ("Abbild") involves issues of referentiality and the audience's ability to test what they are shown against their experience in the world outside, Brecht inserts a claim that, although part of the subtext of *Der Messingkauf,* is never made explicit in any of the fragments: "Nur derjenige, welcher hauptsächlich an den Vorgängen des Lebens selber interessiert ist, auf die in den Theatern angespielt wird, sieht sich in der Lage, die Vorgänge auf der Bühne als Abbilder der Wirklichkeit anzusehen und zu kritisieren." "Kritizismus," in the present context, denotes not just theater's ability to criticize the world outside, but the audience's ability to evaluate plays politically in terms of their images of the world. So far, what has been said does little more than identify further reasons for rejecting one kind of theater and espousing a new one. Unfortunately, the following significant rider finds little reflection in the *Messingkauf* fragments. "Solches tuend, verläßt er den Bezirk der Kunst, denn die Kunst sieht ihre Hauptaufgabe nicht in der Verfertigung von Abbildern der Wirklichkeit schlechthin." The allusion could be to the classical conception of art's autonomy or to its idealizing, transfiguring function. While this claim is overstated, it is questionable whether the Philosopher ever manages to inject the same degree of provocation into his exchanges with the theater people. The assumption about what the "Bezirk der Kunst" actually is represents a caricature of what Brecht saw as a bourgeois aesthetic.

"Es ist nicht ganz gerechtfertigt, beim aristotelischen Theater von 'Vorgängen, die der Zuschauer auf der Bühne abgebildet sieht,' zu sprechen. In Wirklichkeit sind Spiel und Fabel des aristotelischen Theaters nicht dazu bestimmt, Abbilder von Vorgängen im Leben zu geben, sondern das ganz festgelegte Theatererlebnis (mit gewissen Katharsiswirkungen) zustande zu bekommen" (*GBA*, 22:697–98). With this assertion, a number of further issues are factored into the equation and the "traffic" between stage and auditorium begins to appear more complex. As a result, Aristotelian drama appears to have a tendency to remain centripetal, while Epic Theater comes across as centrifugal, inasmuch as its parabolic material is designed repeatedly to confront its audience with the world beyond the stage. Whereas *Der Messingkauf* devotes considerable space to the strengths and limitations of Naturalism, this "Nachtrag" marks an attempt to swing the argument away from the Stanislavsky legacy and back to the central antithesis of Aristotelian/Epic Theater. One problem with the extensive space devoted to Naturalism in *Der Messingkauf* is that the work fails to demonstrate the nature of the alleged connection between Naturalism and "gewisse Katharsiswirkungen," not least because specific examples are not adduced; and again neither Aristotle's nor Lessing's writings on the subject are treated in sufficient analytical depth. Moreover, the kind of limited and ultimately ineffective referentiality that Naturalism can be charged with is very different from the "Irrealität" Brecht sees in Aristotelian theater. Hence, the complaint in the first "Nachtrag" that "Spiel und Fabel des aristotelischen Theaters [sind] nicht dazu bestimmt, Abbilder von Vorgängen im Leben zu geben" (*GBA*, 22:698) would need substantial reformulation before it could be applied to any Naturalist aesthetic. By once more tapping into the discourse of Marxist aesthetics with the concept "Abbild," Brecht gives the impression that he is seeking solutions to problems that have been traditionally the preoccupation of socialist writers. He thus insinuates that the Socialist Realists have not been so distant in their approaches from the writers of historical Naturalism.

The next step is to establish that a true "Abbild" is one that does justice to the causal nexus and that only the "V-Effekt" can do so. "Er besteht darin, daß die Vorgänge des wirklichen Lebens auf der Bühne so abgebildet werden, daß gerade ihre Kausalität besonders in Erscheinung tritt und den Zuschauer beschäftigt" (*GBA*, 22:698). There are a number of strands here, and *Der Messingkauf* only partly manages to bring them together successfully.[57] A distinction between "Abbilder" that are character-centered and those that are plot-driven is one that could without difficulty be reconciled with Brecht's earlier distinction between a theater of emotional gratification and one of political learning, or brought into alignment with the emphasis on "die Fabel" in *Kleines Organon*. A successful highlighting of patterns of causality, as demanded in the first "Nachtrag," has yet to be related to the definition of "Verfremdung." No doubt it would have been relatively easy to demonstrate that a plot-oriented work has distinct advantages when it comes to revealing sequential patterns of causality. However, the link between plot-centeredness and "Verfremdung" and also the reasons why "Verfremdung" is particularly equipped to highlight chains of cause and effect as yet seem more like working hypotheses than proven facts. Conceivably, all that is being said is that "Verfremdung" will produce the kind of questioning response that will make the audience more likely to ask *why* things happen as they do. Brecht returns to the issue of causality in the final "Nachtrag": "Um Gesetzlichkeiten festzustellen, muß man die natürlichen Vorgänge sozusagen verwundert aufnehmen, d.h. man muß ihre 'Selbstverständlichkeit' auflösen, um zu ihrem Verständnis zu gelangen" (*GBA*, 22:701–2). While this may seem little more than a variation on the earlier point, the final "Nachtrag" does make some illuminating points about epic structure's role in helping the audience to achieve insight into socioeconomic causality.

The picture of epic structure given in the *Mahagonny* notes is now explicitly presented as a feature of an estranging process or, at least, as something working symbiotically with "Verfremdung." Our ability to compare what the play shows with events in life is made easier because of the epic fragmenting of plot: "Die Fortführung der Fabel ist hier diskontinuierlich, das einheitliche Ganze besteht aus selbständigen Teilen, die jeweils sofort mit den korrespondierenden Teilvorgängen in der Wirklichkeit konfrontiert werden können, ja müssen. Ständig zieht diese Spielweise alle Kraft aus dem Vergleich mit der Wirklichkeit, d.h. sie lenkt das Auge ständig auf die Kausalität der abgebildeten Vorgänge" (*GBA*, 22:701). Epic structure is no longer merely a *countermeasure*, a way of preventing the buildup of emotional identification that in Brecht's opinion vitiates Aristotelian theater. Now it is a direct means to a specific form of "Verfremdung" allowing the chains of causality that are concealed in the real world to become visible (hence Brecht's use of the phrase "die Kausalität der *abgebildeten Vorgänge*"). Epic Theater's double task, of offering the audience insights by means of a discontinuous structure that gives them the space to measure

---

[57] It is not clear, for example, whether Brecht's cause-and-effect model would respect Engels's advice (in his letter to Mehring of 14 July 1893) to avoid "the common undialectical concept of cause and effect as rigidly opposite poles, the total disregarding of interaction" (Marx-Engels 1934, 512).

"das Abbild" against "das Abgebildete" while at the same time working with a skeletal *continuum* designed to highlight lines of causality, is now integrated into a revised conception of "Verfremdung." The new feature is more than just distanced observation or being *prevented from* being taken in by surfaces; it links "Verfremdung" to a cognitive reward specifically in terms of the audience's being given the opportunity to arrive at an overview in respect of the causal nexus.

The second "Nachtrag," beginning "Einige Punkte können das Auftreten der materialistischen Dialektik in der Theorie zeigen" (*GBA*, 22:699), broaches issues that initially appear to bear little relation to the subjects in the first one. A certain continuity is supplied by the fact that the second "Nachtrag" offers a more nuanced treatment of the notion of causality. The "few points" are in fact four: 1) the dialectical nature of the "V-Effekt," 2) the contradiction between empathy and distanciation as constituent elements of acting, 3) "Historisierung," and 4) the failure of "die aristotelische Dramaturgie" to reveal the role of "objective" contradictions in processes (the list is marked "Nicht fertig"). The references to estrangement and "Historisierung" offer nothing that was not already in the essays of the late 1930s. But the other two points mark something of a breakthrough. The suggestion that "der Widerspruch zwischen Einfühlung und Distanzierung wird vertieft und wird ein Element der Darstellung" is one of Brecht's rare acknowledgments that aesthetic distance is a variable factor because contradiction is not a static phenomenon. Here, the idea that the interplay between the two is a matter of dialectical contradiction means that moving constantly between the two possibilities is perceived as acting's equivalent of "gegenseitige Verfremdung." Even more important, it is evidence that Brecht is on the verge of integrating a conception of dialectical structure into his model of audience response, even though he does not follow through on this insight in much of *Der Messingkauf*. The "Übungsstücke" may be built on a structure of estranging juxtaposition, but Brecht still has some way to go to an explicitly dialectical conception of acting and audience response. As far as the *Messingkauf* project is concerned, the failure to register "objektive Widersprüche in den Prozessen" is seen as one of the blind spots of Aristotelian drama. The issue plays only a small role in *Der Messingkauf*, but Brecht attempts to compensate for this with his various essays collectively entitled "Die Dialektik auf dem Theater" (*GBA*, 23:386–413). When first published in *Versuche* 15 (1957), 79–104, they were introduced with the statement: "Hier wird versucht, die Anwendung materialistischer Dialektik auf dem Theater zu beschreiben. Der Begriff 'episches Theater' scheint immer mehr einer solchen inhaltlichen Ausarbeitung bedürftig." Although these pieces overlap chronologically with the final phase of work on *Der Messingkauf* and follow the direction indicated by the second "Nachtrag," they were never intended to form part of *Der Messingkauf*. Rather, they offer a complementary account of the political aesthetic underlying Brecht's final phase of work as a director.

As we saw in the discussion of "Über die Theatralik des Faschismus," Brecht was beginning to draw parallels between the thought control methods of the National Socialists and the techniques of Aristotelian and Naturalist theater. In this respect, *Der Messingkauf* is engaging in the same process of "confronting" the theater with the real world that his fourth "Nachtrag" sees as the task of Epic Theater. When contrasting the impact of Epic Theater with the effect Aristotelian works have on their audiences, Brecht formulates the difference using defamiliarizing political terms: someone watching Epic Theater "wird nicht völlig 'in Bann gezogen,' seelisch nicht gleichgeschaltet, nicht in eine fatalistische Stimmung dem vorgeführten Schicksal gegenüber gebracht" (*GBA*, 22:701). In similar fashion, he presents the Theater of the Scientific Age in terms relating dramatic advances to historical context: "Das neue Theater ist einfach ein Theater des Menschen, der angefangen hat, sich selbst zu helfen. 300 Jahre Technik und Organisation haben ihn gewandelt. Sehr spät vollzieht das Theater die Wendung" (*GBA*, 22:700). The points made so far will eventually be elaborated in *Kleines Organon*. But in the third "Nachtrag" Brecht already indicates some directions in which this train of thought needs to be taken. First, he refers to "der V-Effekt" as a "soziale Maßnahme" (ibid.), not only making the general point that "Verfremdung" is more than just an alternative artistic device for addressing "den gesellschaftlichen Menschen," but also bringing out the specifically Marxist dimension of "Produktion" by presenting it as an example of collective self-help. Second, by contextualizing "Verfremdung" as *the* defining feature in an aesthetic of the Theater of the Scientific Age, he succeeds in integrating theatrical advances within a model of historical progress, an idea also fleshed out in more detail in the early parts of *Kleines Organon*. In the *Messingkauf* complex, more so than in *Kleines Organon*, "Verfremdung" does remain "in der Mitte": "Das Theater, das mit seinem V-Effekt eine solche staunende, erfinderische und kritische Haltung des Zuschauers bewirkt, ist, indem es eine Haltung bewirkt, die auch in den Wissenschaften eingenommen werden muß, noch kein wissenschaftliches Institut. Es ist lediglich ein Theater des wissenschaftlichen Zeitalters" (*GBA*, 22:702).

## "Messingkauf" and Marxism

A fragment from the first phase of work on *Der Messingkauf* has the Philosopher explaining his ideological mission to the representatives of the theater not long after his arrival among them on the First Night.

> Die Wissenschaft sucht auf allen Gebieten nach Möglichkeiten zu Experimenten oder plastischen Darstellungen der Probleme. Man

macht Modelle, welche die Bewegungen der Gestirne zeigen, mit listigen Apparaturen zeigt man das Verhalten der Gase. [. . .] Mein Gedanke war es nun, eure Kunst der Nachahmung von Menschen für solche Demonstrationen zu verwenden. Man könnte Vorfälle aus dem gesellschaftlichen Zusammenleben der Menschen, welche der Erklärung bedürftig sind, nachahmen, so daß man diesen plastischen Vorführungen gegenüber zu gewissen praktisch verwertbaren Kenntnissen kommen könnte. (*GBA*, 22:715)

We do not know how far apart they were written, but only three fragments later come the "Ausführungen des Philosophen über den Marxismus" (*GBA*, 22:71–81). Those gathered are told:

Die marxistische Lehre stellt gewisse Methoden der Anschauung auf, Kriterien. Sie kommt dabei zu gewissen Beurteilungen der Erscheinungen, Voraussagen und Winken für die Praxis. Sie lehrt eingreifendes Denken gegenüber der Wirklichkeit, soweit sie dem gesellschaftlichen Eingriff unterliegt. Die Lehre kritisiert die menschliche Praxis und läßt sich von ihr kritisieren. Die eigentlichen Weltanschauungen jedoch sind Weltbilder, vermeintliches Wissen, wie alles sich abspielt, meist gebildet nach einem Ideal der Harmonie. Für euch ist der Unterschied, über den ihr euch anderweitig unterrichten könnt, wichtig, weil ihr eure Nachahmungen von Vorfällen beileibe nicht als Illustrationen zu etwaigen, von den Marxisten aufgestellten Sätzen bilden sollt, deren es [. . .] viele gibt. Ihr müßt alles untersuchen und alles beweisen. Die Klärung eurer Vorfälle kann nur durch andere Vorfälle geschehen. (*GBA*, 22:716–17)

In "Theorie der Pädagogien," written at the time of the *Mahagonny* notes, Brecht declares that "in Wirklichkeit die Politiker Philosophen und die Philosophen Politiker sein müssen. Zwischen der wahren Philosophie und der wahren Politik ist kein Unterschied" (*GBA*, 21:398). At the time this was meant as an attack on "die bürgerlichen Philosophen" who distinguish between contemplative people and people of action and a warning against leaving political matters to "den Tätigen"; "Die Lust am Betrachten allein ist für den Staat schädlich, ebenso aber die Lust an der Tat allein" (ibid.). However, while, in the context of *Der Messingkauf,* having an interventionist philosopher (in Lenin's sense) come to the theater seeking help for his "Zwecke" may look like a continuation of some of the principles set out in "Theorie der Pädagogien," the subtext is now radically different. Events in Europe and the Soviet Union in the 1930s radically changed assumptions about the role of the state in regimenting the arts for didactic and state-serving purposes. This explains the caution with which the Philosopher presents his aim and hints at the danger of interference to the theater people. In many respects his mission overlaps with Brecht's own, and he is wise to try to dissociate himself from the threat of state interference, even if he is clearly a Marxist and the country in which the dialogues will take place is recognizably a socialist state. He is wise to suggest that his theater-oriented agenda at the same time is intended to serve as a model of one particular form of "Art und Weise des Zusammenlebens unter den Menschen" (*GBA*, 22:773). The differences between the idealistic rationale behind the "Messingkauf" program to create a "Theater der Staatsmänner" and the realities of GDR *Theaterpolitik* would become increasingly obvious during the coming years. But the model in *Der Messingkauf* is not directed simply at a utopian future in the ruthless way that *Die Maßnahme* had been. It is about dealing with the problems of the present, and these are not merely centered on rival forms of theater or on the relationship between theater and politics.

The (Marxist) Philosopher himself offers various models during the course of the *Messingkauf* encounters: models of "Unwissenheit," of the true cause-and-effect patterns of "die Vorgänge hinter den Vorgängen," and illustrations of the damage done, both in and outside the theater, by an obsession with surface, "photographic" Naturalism and misplaced emotions. However, the two principal "Grundmodelle des epischen Theaters" that Brecht at the outset intended to integrate into *Der Messingkauf*— that of the "Straßenszene" and the "P-Typus des Theaters" — both stand at a tangent to the Philosopher's real purposes. Klaus-Dieter Krabiel has argued that the "P-Typus" model, based on an analogy between the planetarium and the theatre, is deeply flawed: "Im Planetarium werden lediglich bestimmte Bewegungsabläufe demonstriert, der bildhafte Vergleich lässt unberücksichtigt, worum es [Brecht] im Theater vorrangig ging: um die Demonstration von Eingriffsmöglichkeiten, um die Veränderbarkeit der dargestellten Realität" (*BHB*, 4:201). As we saw in chapter 4, the charge that the "P-Typus" model of Epic Theater lacks this vital component[58] could just as well be leveled against the "Straßenszene." They were dropped from *Der Messingkauf*, it has been argued, because they are primarily models of types of theatre approaches, neither of which offers an effective enough replica of a philosophically grounded "dialektisches Theater." The *Dramaturg* seems to sense this because, in answer to the Philosopher's "Man macht Modelle, welche die Bewegung der Gestirne zeigen," he says: "Ich vermute, daß man diese Demonstrationen nicht einfach ins Blaue hinein veranstalten

---

[58] Krabiel draws attention to the note to the Second Night that follows the phrase "Der P-Typus" with "Widerspruch: der nicht nur betrachtende, sondern auch agierende Mensch als Zuschauer" (*GBA*, 22:719). According to Krabiel: "der 'Widerspruch,' der hier angemeldet wird, richtet sich zweifellos gegen den Vergleich des neuen Typus von Dramatik mit einem Planetarium [. . .]. [Dies] erklärt, warum [Brecht] den Vergleich im *Messingkauf* und auch sonst später nicht mehr verwendet hat" (*BHB*, 4:201).

kann. Irgendeine Richtung muß man haben, nach irgendwelchen Gesichtspunkten muß man die Vorfälle auswählen" (*GBA*, 22:715). This has been inserted as a cue to allow the Philosopher to offer the theatre people an account of the requisite organizing principle (Marxism): "Es gibt eine Wisenschaft über das Zusammenleben der Menschen. Es ist eine große Lehre über Ursache und Wirkung auf diesem Gebiet. Sie kann uns Gesichtspunkte geben." But then, less predictably, the Philosopher draws their attention to an example of what, in his eyes, theater in turn has to offer Marxism:

> Ich muß eine Einschränkung machen. Diese Lehre beschäftigt sich vornehmlich mit dem Verhalten großer Menschenmassen. Die Gesetze, welche diese Wissenschaft aufstellte, gelten für die Bewegung sehr großer Einheiten von Menschen, und wenn auch über die Stellung des einzelnen in diesen großen Einheiten allerhand gesagt wird, so betrifft auch dies eben für gewöhnlich nur die Stellung des einzelnen eben zu diesen Massen. Wir aber hätten bei unseren Demonstrationen es mehr mit dem Verhalten der einzelnen untereinander zu tun. (*GBA*, 22:715–16)

In bringing together a small group of theater practitioners within the confines of the stage space and engaging with them in the discussion of subjects of vital importance to them, but about which they are not in agreement, the Philosopher's strategy already starts out as an exploration of "das Verhalten der einzelnen untereinander" within the wider context of a highly politicized "Massengesellschaft." As this suggests, the Four Nights were themselves conceived to demonstrate theater's ability to reconcile the macroscopic concerns of politics and ideology, while at the same time, by virtue of the exploitation of a well-chosen microcosm, showing that theater was uniquely constituted to meet the Philosopher's requirements.

Although much of the discussion in *Der Messingkauf* has the task of demonstrating the political advantages of Epic Theater, it would not have suited Brecht's purposes to have the Philosopher visit an Epic Ensemble. In theory at least, for the dialectical interaction between the Philosopher and the representatives of theater to be successful, the theater people have to look more in need of the Philosopher's guidance than any tidily parabolic version of the Berliner Ensemble would have been. At the same time the Philosopher has to trust that the traffic between them will make them an appropriate object of his pressing attentions. He tries to allay their suspicions by indicating that he has no intention of simply exploiting them as artistic means to his political end. They, on aesthetic grounds alone, have yet to be convinced: "Du willst für besondere Zwecke gewisse Künste einsetzen, und zwar so, daß einiges, was bisher als Hauptsächliches bei der Kunst betrachtet wurde, wegfällt. Unsere Künste sollen als bloße Fertigkeiten verwendet werden. [. . .] Die Zwecke, die du nennst, sind überaus ernst. Das Theater aber ist etwas Spielerisches. Soll auch dieses Spielerische aufgegeben werden?" (*GBA*, 22:716). How much "persuasive Kommunikation" does then take place within the *Der Messingkauf*? Even granted that we are dealing with a large-scale fragment, what is the relationship between goal and achievement on the Philosopher's part, or the dialogic and the monologic on Brecht's?

Brecht's first acknowledged model for *Der Messingkauf* was Galileo's use of the dialogue for theorizing, and in these dialogues two world systems and their representatives were in dispute. In *Der Messingkauf,* the equivalent of the Copernican position, the Marxist Philosopher, is as unequivocally right as his seventeenth-century counterpart was. But there is a sense in which, if one compares this scenario with the way Brecht's plays handle conflicts between enlightened and reactionary forces, the constituent parts of the *Messingkauf* complex end up looking more like *Mutter Courage und ihre Kinder* than *Leben des Galilei.* The people who have much to learn from the Philosopher seldom appear to do so adequately during the dialogues (and that is arguably the only place where they could be shown to learn: speeches, poems, fragments do not involve the interaction necessary for a dramatized learning process to take place.) On the first evening, the theater people being subjected to the "Messingkauf" test have high expectations of their encounter with the Philosopher. They listen politely, explain their own practices and the conventions of their theater world, but are seldom shown to have changed in the way that characters in Brechtian Epic Theater often do. There are three ways of reading such a situation. It could be seen as a more subtle deployment of the "*Nicht — Sondern*" paradigm, in the sense that instead of having a schematic confrontation between someone in search of Epic Theater and a representatively Stanislavskian theatre company, Brecht has constructed an encounter between someone who shares his political ideology, but takes part in discussions mainly about Stanislavskian Naturalism and surface realism with theatre people who have not yet reached their potential. (In other words, the balance between the various synergies is not yet right.) An alternative reading would assume a strategy comparable to that adopted in *Mutter Courage und ihre Kinder.* When questioned by the dramatist Friedrich Wolf about the fact that Courage fails to learn from her experiences in the play, Brecht famously replied: "Wenn jedoch die Courage weiter doch nichts lernt — das Publikum kann, meiner Ansicht nach, dennoch etwas lernen, sie betrachtend" (*GBA,* 23:109).[59] The reader of *Der*

---

[59] When this discussion was first published with the title "Formprobleme des Theaters aus neuem Inhalt" in January 1949 in *Volk und Kunst,* the "Monatsschrift des Bundes Deutscher Volksbühnen," it was schematically presented as an encounter between a representative of Epic Theater and a representative of Dramatic Theater: "Hier nehmen zwei Dichter, die diese Formen am deutlichsten vertreten, [. . .] selbst

*Messingkauf* — or, if the "Bühnenfassung" is performed, the audience — could be expected to be learning more quickly from the Philosopher than do the theater's representatives. They would be able to appreciate the fine differentiations between the various people onstage and between those representing the theater in *Der Messingkauf* and the two types of theater that form the basis of the exchanges (Stanislavskian and Epic). The third possible reading involves more emphasis on the fragmentary nature of the project and in particular the amount of work the Fourth Night still has to perform if the Philosopher's wishes are to be met. Brecht evidently has high hopes of what will be achieved during the Fourth Night. But the project becomes bogged down in documenting what it is opposed to, just as Brecht had earlier expended more energy on his satirical variations on the "Karussell-Theater" model than on the "Planetarium-Typus."

These features of *Der Messingkauf* are not unrelated to another aspect of the project: the relative understatement of the Philosopher's Marxism and the concentration on matters theatrical. A note in Brecht's journal for 12 February 1939 reads: "Aus einer Kritik des Theaters wird neues Theater. Das ganze einstudierbar gedacht, mit Experimenten und Exerzitium. In der Mitte der V-Effekt" (*GBA*, 26:328). One might have expected to read "In der Mitte der Marxismus." Perhaps the American context gave him reason for playing down the political subtext to *Der Messingkauf* that Müller and Voges have seen as always implicit even in seemingly dramaturgical and aesthetic discussions. By the time he took up work again on the *Messingkauf* project in the early GDR years, Brecht clearly had other reasons why he should not seem to be putting the dominant Socialist Realist aesthetic in question with a counteraesthetic, even though, in his practical work with the Berliner Ensemble, he was continuing to do precisely that.

---

in einem Gespräch zu dem Problem Stellung. Unsere Leser werden es begrüßen, wenn wir [. . .] zwei der wesentlichen Dramatiker unserer Zeit zu diesem aktuellen Theaterproblem das Wort erteilen" (editorial preface, quoted in *GBA*, 23:471).

# Works Consulted

## Primary Literature: Works by Bertolt Brecht

1930–33. *Versuche* 1–7. Potsdam: Kiepenheuer.

1938. *Gesammelte Werke.* 2 vols. London: Malik.

1949–57. *Versuche* 9–15. Frankfurt a. M.: Suhrkamp; Berlin-Weimar: Aufbau.

1957. *Schriften zum Theater: Über eine nicht-aristotelische Dramatik.* Ed. by Siegfried Unseld. Frankfurt a. M.: Suhrkamp.

1961. *Theaterarbeit: 6 Aufführungen des Berliner Ensembles.* 2nd revised and enlarged edition. Ed. by Berliner Ensemble and Helene Weigel. Berlin: Henschel.

1967. *Gesammelte Werke: Werkausgabe in 20 Bänden.* Ed. by Werner Hecht. Frankfurt a. M.: Suhrkamp.

1988–2000. *Werke: Große kommentierte Berliner und Frankurter Ausgabe.* 30 vols + *Registerband.* Ed. by Werner Hecht, Jan Knopf, Werner Mittenzwei, and Klaus-Detlef Müller. Berlin-Weimar: Aufbau; Frankfurt a. M.: Suhrkamp. Paperback edition (same pagination) 2003.

## English Translations of Theoretical Works by Brecht

1936. "The Fourth Wall of China: An Essay on the Effect of Disillusion in the Chinese Theatre." Trans. by Eric Walter White. *Life and Letters To-Day* 6:116–23.

1961. "On the Experimental Theatre." Trans. by Carl Richard Mueller. *Tulane Drama Review* 6, no. 1:3–17.

1961. *Poems on the Theatre.* Trans. by John Berger and Anna Bostock. Northwood: Scorpion.

1964. *Brecht on Theatre: The Development of an Aesthetic.* Trans. and ed. by John Willett. London: Methuen; NewYork: Hill and Wang.

1965. *The Messingkauf Dialogues.* Trans. by John Willett. London: Methuen.

1976. *Bertolt Brecht: Poems 1913–1956.* Ed. by John Willett and Ralph Manheim. London: Eyre Methuen.

2003. *Brecht on Art and Politics.* Ed. and trans. by Tom Kuhn and Steve Giles. London: Methuen.

## Other Sources

"*L'ABC de la guerre.*" In *Brecht 98: Poétique et politique,* ed. by Michel Vanoosthuyse. Montpellier: PUF.

*Alternative,* 8. 1965. [Collective volume on the Bertolt Brecht-Karl Korsch relationship.]

Adler, Meinhard. 1976. *Brecht im Spiegel der technischen Zeit: Naturwissenschaftliche, psychologische und wissenschaftstheoretische Kategorien im Werk Bertolt Brechts: Ein Beitrag zur Literaturpsychologie.* Berlin: Nolte.

Adoratzky, Vladmir Viktorovich. 1931. "Marxismus-Leninismus und Dialektik." *Unter dem Banner des Marxismus* 3:321–23.

Albers, Jürgen. 1977. "Das Prinzip der 'Historisierung' in der Dramatik Bertolt Brechts." Diss., Universität Saarbrücken.

Aristotle. 1953. *Aristotle's "Poetics" and "Rhetoric."* Introd. by T. A. Moxon. London: Dent.

Arnold, Heinz Ludwig, ed. 1972. *Text + Kritik: Sonderband Bertolt Brecht 1.* Munich: Richard Boorberg.

Avineri, Shlomo. 1968. *The Social and Political Thought of Karl Marx.* Cambridge: Cambridge UP.

Backes, Dirk. 1981. "*Die erste Kunst ist die Beobachtungskunst*": *Bertolt Brecht und der Sozialistische Realismus.* Berlin: Kramer.

Bacon, Francis. 1870. *Franz Baco's "Neues Organon."* Trans. and annotated by Julius Hermann von Kirchmann. Kirchmann's Philosophische Bibliothek, 32. Berlin: Heimann.

Barthes, Roland. 1977. "Diderot, Brecht, Eisenstein." In *Image — Music — Text: Essays selected and translated by Stephen Heath,* 69–78. London: Fontana.

Bauland, Peter. 1968. *The Hooded Eagle: German Drama on the New York Stage.* Syracuse: Syracuse UP.

Baxandall, Lee. 1967. "Brecht in America, 1935." *The Drama Review* 12 no. 1:69–87.

Ben Chaim, Daphna. 1981. *Distance in the Theatre: The Aesthetics of Audience Response.* Ann Arbor-London: UMI.

Benedetti, Jean. 1982. *Stanislavsky: An Introduction.* London: Methuen.

Benjamin, Walter. 1972–89. *Gesammelte Schriften.* Ed. by Hermann Schweppenhäuser and Rolf Tiedemann. 7 vols. Frankfurt a. M.: Suhrkamp.

———. 1978. *Versuche über Brecht.* Frankfurt a. M.: Suhrkamp.

Bennett, Susan. 1997. *Theatre Audiences: A Theory of Production and Reception.* London: Routledge.

Bentley, Eric. 1946. *The Playwright as Thinker: A Study in Modern Drama.* New York: Reynal and Hitchcock.

———. 1964. "Are Stanislavsky and Brecht commensurable?" *Tulane Drama Review* 9:69–76.

———, ed. 1968. *The Theory of Modern Stage: An Introduction to Modern Theatre and Drama.* Harmondsworth: Penguin.

———. 1981. *The Brecht Commentaries, 1943–1980.* London: Eyre Methuen.

Berg, Günter, and Wolfgang Jeske. 1998. *Bertolt Brecht.* Sammlung Metzler, 310. Stuttgart: Metzler.

Biszrtray, George. 1978. *Marxist Models of Literary Realism.* New York: Columbia UP.

Bloch, Ernst. 1973 [First published 1935]. *Erbschaft dieser Zeit.* Frankfurt a. M.: Suhrkamp.

———. 1960. "Zur *Dreigroschenoper.*" In *Bertolt Brechts "Dreigroschenbuch": Texte, Materialien, Dokumente.* Ed. by Siegfried Unseld. 195–97. Frankfurt a. M.: Suhrkamp.

Böckmann, Paul. 1961. *Provokation und Dialektik in der Dramatik Bert Brechts. Kölner Universitätsreden,* 26. Krefeld: Scherpe.

Boleslavsky, Richard. 1978. *Acting: The First Six Lessons.* New York: Theatre Art Books.

Bölsche, Wilhelm. 1887. *Die naturwissenschaftlichen Grundlagen der Poesie: Prolegomena einer realistischen Ästhetik.* Leipzig: Reissner.

Booth, Wayne C. 1963. *The Rhetoric of Fiction.* Chicago, IL: Chicago UP.

Brauneck, Manfred, and Christine Müller, eds. 1987. *Naturalismus (Manifeste und Dokumente zur deutschen Literatur, 1880–1900).* Stuttgart: Metzler.

Brecht-Zentrum der DDR. 1986. *Brecht 85: Zur Ästhetik Brechts.* Berlin: Henschel.

Brooker, Peter. 1988. *Bertolt Brecht: Dialectics, Poetry, Politics.* London-New York-Sydney: Croom Helm.

———. 1994. "Key Words in Brecht's Theory and Practice of Theatre." In *The Cambridge Companion to Brecht,* ed. by Peter Thomson and Glendyr Sacks, 185–200. Cambridge: Cambridge UP.

Brüggemann, Heinz. 1973a. "Bert Brecht und Karl Korsch." *Jahrbuch der Arbeiterbewegung* 1:177–81.

———. 1973b. *Literarische Technik und soziale Revolution: Versuche über das Verhältnis von Kunstproduktion, Marxismus und literarischer Tradition in den theoretischen Schriften Bertolt Brechts.* Reinbek bei Hamburg: Rowohlt.

Buck, Theo. 1971. *Brecht und Diderot oder Über Schwierigkeiten der Rationalität in Deutschland.* Tübingen: Niemeyer.

Buck-Morss, Susan. 1977. *The Origins of Negative Dialectics: Theodor W. Adorno, Walter Benjamin, and the Frankfurt Institute.* New York: Free Press.

Buehler, George. 1978. *Bertolt Brecht — Erwin Piscator: Ein Vergleich ihrer theoretischen Schriften.* Abhandlungen zur Kunst-, Musik- und Literaturwissenschaft, 250. Bonn: Bouvier.

Bullough, Edward. 1957. "'Psychical Distance' as a Factor in Art and an Aesthetic Principle." In *Aesthetics: Lectures and Essays,* ed. by Elizabeth M. Wilkinson, 91–130. London: Bowes & Bowes. Originally appeared in 1912 in the *British Journal of Psychology* 5:87–118.

Bunge, Hans. 1970. *Fragen Sie mehr über Brecht: Hanns Eisler im Gespräch.* Munich: Rogner & Bernard.

Burnshaw, Stanley. 1935. "The Theatre Union produces *Mother*." *New Masses* (3 December): 27–28.

Busch, Walter. 1982. *Cäsarismuskritik und epische Historik: Zur Entwicklung der politischen Ästhetik Bertolt Brechts, 1936–1940.* Europäische Hochschulschriften 1, 522. Bern-Frankfurt a. M.: Lang.

Carlson, Marvin. 1993. *Theories of the Theatre: A Historical and Critical Survey, from the Greeks to the Present.* 2nd expanded edition. New York: Cornell UP.

Casebier, Allan. 1977. "The Concept of Aesthetic Distance." In *Aesthetics: A Critical Anthology,* ed. by George Dickie and Richard J. Selafani, 783–99. New York: St Martin's Press.

Chiarini, Paolo. 1957. "Lessing und Brecht: Einiges über die Beziehungen von Epik und Dramatik." In *Sinn und Form: Zweites Sonderheft Bertolt Brecht,* ed. by Deutsche Akademie der Künste, 188–203. Berlin: Rütten & Loening.

Claas, Herbert. 1977. *Die politische Ästhetik Bertolt Brechts vom Baal zum Caesar.* Frankfurt a. M.: Suhrkamp.

Cook, Bruce. 1982. *Brecht in Exile.* New York: Rinehart & Winston.

Counsell, Colin. 1996. *Signs of Performance: An Introduction to Twentieth-Century Theatre.* London, New York: Routledge.

Crumbach, Franz Hubert. 1960. *Die Struktur des epischen Theaters: Dramaturgie der Kontraste.* Braunschweig.: Pädagogische Hochschule.

Davies, Peter. 2000. *Divided Loyalties: East German Writers and the Politics of German Division, 1945–1953.* MHRA Texts and Dissertations, 49; Bithell Series of Dissertations, 24. London: MHRA.

Delabar, Walter, and Jörg Döring, eds. 1998. *Bertolt Brecht: 1898–1956.* Berlin: Weidler.

Dial, Joseph Franklin. 1975. "The Contribution of Marxism to Bertolt Brecht's Theatre Theory: The Epistemological Basis of Epic Theatre and Brecht's Concept of Realism." Diss., Cambridge, MA: Harvard U.

Dickson, Keith A. 1978. *Towards Utopia: A Study of Brecht*. Oxford: Clarendon.

Diderot, Denis. 1959. *Œuvres Esthétiques*. Ed. by Paul Vernière. Paris: Garnier.

Döblin, Alfred. 1963. *Aufsätze zur Literatur*. Ed. by Walter Muschg. Freiburg i. Br.-Olten: Walter.

Dreiser, Theodore. [n.d.] *Amerikanische Tragödie: Nach dem Roman von Theodore Dreiser: Für die Bühne eingerichtet von Erwin Piscator*. Wiesbaden-Berlin: Ahn & Simrock.

———. 1925. *An American Tragedy*. New York: Horace Liveright.

Dümling, Albrecht. 1985. *Laßt euch nicht verführen: Brecht und die Musik*. Munich: Kindler.

Duroche, L. L. 1967. *Aspects of Criticism: Literary Study in Present-Day Germany*. The Hague: Mouton.

Eagleton, Terry. 1976. *Marxism and Literary Criticism*. London: Methuen.

Eckhardt, Juliane. 1985. *Das Epische Theater*. Darmstadt: Wissenschaftliche Buchgesellschaft.

Eddershaw, Margaret. 1996. *Performing Brecht: Forty Years of British Performances*. London- New York: Routledge.

Ehrenzeller, Hans. 1973. *Studien zur Romanvorrede von Grimmelshausen bis Jean Paul*. Bern: Francke.

Ellis, John M., and David G. Mowatt. 1965. "Language, Metaphysics and Staiger's Critical Categories." *Seminar* 1:122–25.

Fankhauser, Gertrud. 1971. *Verfremdung als Stilmittel vor und bei Brecht*. Tübingen: Elly Huth.

Fei, Faye Chungfang. 1999. *Chinese Theories of Theater and Performance from Confucius to the Present*. Ed. and trans. by Faye Chungfang Fei. Ann Arbor: Michigan UP.

Feuchtwanger, Lion. 1928. "Brecht dargestellt für Engländer." *Die Weltbühne*, 4.9. Reprinted in *Brecht as they knew him*, ed. by Hubert Witt, 17–22. London: Lawrence & Wishart, 1974.

Fiebach, Johann. 1978. "Brechts *Straßenszene*: Versuch über die Reichweite eines Theatermodells." *Weimarer Beiträge* 24:123–47.

Fischer, Matthias-Johannes. 1989. *Brechts Theatertheorie: Forschungsgeschichte — Forschungsstand — Perspektiven*. Europäische Hochschulschriften 1, 1115. Frankfurt a. M.-Bern-New York-Paris: Lang.

Flaschka, Horst. 1976. *Modell, Modelltheorie und Formen der Modellbildung in der Literaturwissenschaft*. Forum litterarum, 6. Cologne-Vienna: Böhlau.

Flashar, Hellmut. 1974. "Aristoteles und Brecht." *Poetica* 6:17–37.

Fradkin, Ilja. 1974. *Bertolt Brecht: Weg und Methode.* Leipzig: Reclam.

Freytag, Gustav. 1965. *Die Technik des Dramas.* Darmstadt: Wissenschaftliche Buchgesellschaft.

Fuller, Edmund. 1938. "Epic Realism: An Analysis of Bert Brecht." *One Act Play Magazine,* 1124–30.

Gábor, Andor. 1932. "Zwei Bühnenereignisse." *Die Linkskurve* 11–12:20–22.

Gaede, Friedrich. 1972. *Realismus von Brant bis Brecht.* Munich: Francke.

Galilei, Galileo. 1987. *Schriften, Briefe, Dokumente.* Ed. by Anna Mudry. 2 vols. Munich: Beck; Berlin: Rütten & Loening.

Gallas, Helga. 1971. *Marxistische Literaturtheorie: Kontroversen proletarisch-revolutionärer Schriftsteller.* Neuwied-Berlin: Luchterhand.

Gersch, Wolfgang. 1974. *Film bei Brecht: Bertolt Brechts praktische und theoretische Auseinandersetzung mit dem Film.* Munich: Hanser.

Giles, Steve. 1997. *Bertolt Brecht and Critical Theory: Marxism, Modernity and the "Threepenny Opera" Lawsuit.* Berne: Lang.

Giles, Steve, and Rodney Livingstone, eds. 1998. *Bertolt Brecht: Centenary Essays.* German Monitor, 40. Amsterdam-Atlanta, GA: Rodopi.

Goethe, Johann Wolfgang von. 1948–60. *Gedenkausgabe der Werke, Briefe und Gespräche.* Ed. by Ernst Beutler. Zurich-Stuttgart: Artemis. Vol. 20: *Der Briefwechsel zwischen Goethe und Friedrich Schiller,* introd. Karl Schmid (1950).

Gorelik, Max. 1937. "Epic Realism: Brecht's Notes on the *Threepenny Opera.*" *Theatre Quarterly* 3:29–40.

Gorelik, Mordecai. 1940. *New Theatres for Old.* New York: Samuel French.

Gorky, Maxim. 1949–56: *Sobranie sochineniy.* Moscow: Gasudarstvennoe izdatelstvo chudozhestvennoi literatury.

———. 1962. *Mother.* Trans. by Margaret Wettlin. Introd. by Avrahm Yarmolinsky. New York: Collier.

Gottsched, Johann Christoph. 1962. *Versuch einer Critischen Dichtkunst vor die Deutschen.* Darmstadt: Wissenschaftliche Buchgesellschaft.

Gouldner, Alvin W. 1985. *Against Fragmentation: The Origins of Marxism and the Sociology of Intellectuals.* New York, Oxford: Oxford UP.

Grimm, Reinhold. 1959. *Bertolt Brecht: Die Struktur seines Werkes.* Nuremberg: H. Carl.

———. 1961. "'Verfremdung': Beiträge zu Ursprung und Wesen eines Begriffs." *Revue de la littérature comparée* 35:29–40.

———. 1961. "Vom *Novum Organum* zum *Kleinen Organon*: Gedanken zur Verfremdung." In *Das Ärgernis Brecht*, ed. by Willy Jäggi and Hans Oesch, 45–70. Basel-Stuttgart: Basilius.

———. 1963. "Das Huhn des Francis Bacon." In *Strukturen: Essays zur deutschen Literatur*, 198–225. Göttingen: Vandenhoeck & Ruprecht.

———. 1965. "Die ästhetischen Anschauungen Bertolt Brechts: Notizen zu dem Buch von Helge Hultberg." *Zeitschrift für deutsche Philologie* 84, Sonderheft, 90–111.

———. 1984. "Der katholische Einstein: Brechts Dramen- und Theatertheorie." In *Brechts Dramen: Neue Interpretationen*, ed. by Walter Hinderer, 11–32. Stuttgart: Reclam.

Habermas, Jürgen. 1981. *Theorie des kommunikativen Handelns*. Frankfurt a. M.: Suhrkamp.

Halliwell, Stephen. 2003. *The Aesthetics of Mimesis: Ancient Texts and Modern Problems*. Princeton, NJ: Princeton UP.

Hampton, Charles C., Jr. 1971. "'Verfremdungseffekt.'" *Modern Drama* 14:340–54.

Hansen-Löve, Aage A. 1978. *Der russische Formalismus: Methodologische Rekonstruktion seiner Entwicklung aus dem Prinzip der Verfremdung*. Veröffentlichungen der Kommission für Literaturwissenschaft, 5. Vienna: Verlag der österreichischen Akademie der Wissenschaften.

Hartung, Günter. 1982. "Einleitung in Brechts Ästhetik." *Weimarer Beiträge* 6:70–83.

Hecht, Werner, ed. 1963. *Materialien zu "Leben des Galilei."* Frankfurt a. M.: Suhrkamp.

———, ed. 1966. *Materialien zu "Der kaukasische Kreidekreis."* Frankfurt a. M.: Suhrkamp.

———. 1972. *Sieben Studien über Brecht*. Frankfurt a. M.: Suhrkamp.

———, ed. 1975. *Brecht im Gespräch: Diskussionen, Dialoge, Interviews*. Frankfurt a. M.: Suhrkamp.

———, ed. 1986. *Brechts Theorie des Theaters*. Frankfurt a. M.: Suhrkamp.

———. 1987. "Grund der Empörung über eine 'ganz unerträgliche Behandlung': Brechts Stanislawski-Studium 1953." *Maske und Kothurn*, 33:75–87.

———. 1997. *Brecht Chronik 1896–1956*. Frankfurt a. M.: Suhrkamp.

———. 2000. *Helene Weigel: Eine große Frau des 20. Jahrhunderts*. Frankfurt a. M.: Suhrkamp.

Hegel, Georg Wilhelm Friedrich. 1969–71. *Werke*. Ed. by Eva Moldenhauer and Karl Markus Michel. 20 vols. Frankfurt a. M.: Suhrkamp.

Heinze, Helmut. 1992. *Brechts Ästhetik des Gestischen: Versuch einer Rekonstruktion*. Heidelberg: Carl Winter.

Heller, Heinz-B. 1975. *Untersuchungen zur Theorie und Praxis des dialektischen Theaters: Brecht und Adamov*. Europäische Hochschulschriften 1, 704. Frankfurt a. M.: Lang.

Helmers, Robert, ed. 1984. *Verfremdung in der Literatur*. Darmstadt: Wissenschaftliche Buchgesellschaft.

Hentschel, Ingrid et al., eds. 1997. *Brecht & Stanislawski und die Folgen: Anregungen bei der Theaterarbeit*. Berlin: Henschel.

Herhoffer, Astrid. 1998. "Brecht: An Aesthetics of Conviction?" In *Bertolt Brecht: Centenary Essays*, ed. by Steve Giles and Rodney Livingstone, 211–26.

Hill, Claude. 1975. *Bertolt Brecht*. Boston: Twayne.

Hinck, Walter. 1966. *Die Dramaturgie des späten Brecht*. Palaestra 229. Göttingen: Vandenhoeck & Ruprecht, revised edition.

Holz, Arno. 1896. "Zola als Theoretiker." *Freie Bühne für modernes Leben*, 1:101–4.

Horace. (Quintus Horatius Flaccus) 1962. "Von der Dichtkunst, an die Pisonen." Trans. by Johann Christoph Gottsched. Original Latin: Q. Horatii Flacci: *De arte poetica ad pisones*. In Gottsched 1962, 10–64.

Hultberg, Helge. 1962. *Die ästhetischen Anschauungen Bertolt Brechts*. Copenhagen: Munksgaard.

Ihering, Herbert. 1929. *Reinhardt, Jessner, Piscator oder Klassikertod?* Hamburg: Rowohlt.

———. 1959. *Bertolt Brecht und das Theater*. Berlin: Rembrandt.

Innes, C. D. 1972. *Erwin Piscator's Political Theatre: The Development of Modern German Drama*. Cambridge: Cambridge UP.

Ivernel, Philippe. 1999. "L'Œil de Brecht: À propos du rapport entre texte et image dans le *Journal du travail et l'ABC de la guerre*." In *Brecht 98: Poétique et politique*, ed. by Michel Vanoosthuyse. Montpellier: PUF.

Jäger, Manfred. 1995. *Kultur und Politik in der DDR: 1945–1990*. Cologne: Edition Deutschland Archiv.

Jameson, Fredric. 1998. *Brecht and Method*. London-New York: Verso.

Jauß, H. R. 1974. "Levels of Identification of Hero and Audience." *New Literary History*, 283–317.

Jendreiek, Helmut. 1969. *Bertolt Brecht: Drama der Veränderung*. Düsseldorf: Bagel.

Jeske, Wolfgang. 1984. *Bertolt Brechts Poetik des Romans*. Frankfurt a. M.: Suhrkamp.

Jesse, Horst. 1996. *Brecht in Berlin*. Munich: Das freie Buch.

Jessner, Leopold. 1979. *Schriften: Theater der zwanziger Jahre*. Ed. by Hugo Fetting. Berlin: Henschel.

Jones, D. R. 1986. *Great Directors at Work: Stanislavski, Brecht, Kazan, Brook*. Berkeley-Los Angeles, CA: California UP.

Judin, Petr, and Aleksander Fadeyev. 1934. "Sozialisticheski realizm — novy metod sovietskoi literatury." *Pravda*, 8 May.

Jürgens, Martin. 1982. "Zum Prinzip der Montage in Bertolt Brechts 'soziologischen Experimenten.'" *Zeitschrift für Literaturwissenschaft und Linguistik* 12:88–105.

Kagan, Moissej. 1971. *Vorlesungen zur marxistisch-leninistischen Ästhetik*. Berlin: Dietz.

Kautsky, Karl. 1933. *Neue Programme*. Vienna: E. Prager.

Kebir, Sabine. 2000. *"Abstieg in den Ruhm"*: *Helene Weigel: Eine Biographie*. Berlin: Aufbau.

Kellner, Douglas. 1980. "Brecht's Marxist Aesthetic: The Korsch Connection." In *Bertolt Brecht: Political Theory and Literary Practice*, ed. by Betty Nance Weber and Hubert Heinen, 29–41. Manchester: Manchester UP.

Kepka, Ania. 1984–85. "The Relationship of Brecht's *Die Mutter* to Its Sources: A Reassessment." *German Life and Letters* 38:233–48.

Kesting, Marianne. 1956. "Gedanken zum epischen Theater." *Merkur* 10:1127–32.

———. 1959. *Das epische Theater*. Stuttgart: Urban.

Klotz, Volker. 1957. *Bertolt Brecht: Versuch über das Werk*. Berlin-Zurich: Artemis.

———. 1968. *Geschlossene und offene Form im Drama*. Munich: Kohlhammer.

Knopf, Jan. 1974. *Bertolt Brecht: Ein kritischer Forschungsbericht: Fragwürdiges in der Brecht-Forschung*. Frankfurt a. M.: Fischer-Athenäum.

———. 1980a. *Brecht Handbuch: Theater. Eine Ästhetik des Widerspruchs*. Stuttgart: Metzler.

———. 1980b "'Eingreifendes Denken' als Realdialektik: Zu Bertolt Brechts philosophischen Schriften." In *Aktualisierung Brechts*, ed. by W. F. Haug et al, 57–74. Berlin: Argument.

———. 1993. "Elegische Warnungen vor dem 'eigenen' Faschismus: Bertolt Brecht." In *Verrat an der Kunst? Rückblicke auf die DDR-Literatur*, ed. by Karl Deiritz and Hannes Krauss, 81–88. Berlin: Aufbau.

———. 1995. *"Kleines Organon für das Theater."* In *Lexikon literaturtheoretischer Werke*, ed. by Rolf Günter Renner and Engelbert Habekost, 192–94. Stuttgart: Kröner.

————. 2000. *Bertolt Brecht.* Stuttgart: Reclam.

————, ed. 2001. *Brecht Handbuch.* Vol. 1: *Stücke.* Stuttgart-Weimar: Metzler.

————, ed. 2001. *Brecht Handbuch.* Vol. 2: *Gedichte.* Stuttgart-Weimar: Metzler.

————, ed. 2002. *Brecht Handbuch.* Vol. 3: *Prosa, Filme, Drehbücher.* Stuttgart-Weimar: Metzler.

————, ed. 2003. *Brecht Handbuch.* Vol. 4: *Schriften, Journale, Briefe.* Stuttgart-Weimar: Metzler.

————, ed. 2003. *Brecht Handbuch.* Vol. 5: *Register, Chronik, Materialien.* Stuttgart-Weimar: Metzler.

Kliuyev, Viktor. 1966. *Teatral' no-esteticheskie vzglyady Brechts: Opyt estetiki Brechts.* Moscow: Nauka.

Kobel, Jan. 1992. *Kritik als Genuß: Über die Widersprüche der Brechtschen Theatertheorie und die Unfähigkeit der Literaturwissenschaft, sie zu kritisieren.* Frankfurt a. M.-Berlin: Lang.

Kock, Klaus. 1981. *Brechts literarische Evolution: Untersuchungen zum ästhetisch-ideologischen Bruch in den "Dreigroschen"-Bearbeitungen.* Munich: Fink.

Koestler, Arthur. 1978. *Janus.* New York: Random House.

Koller, Gerold. 1979. *Der mitspielende Zuschauer: Theorie und Praxis im Schaffen Brechts.* Zürcher Beiträge zur deutschen Literatur- und Geistesgeschichte, 50. Zurich-Munich: Artemis.

Korsch, Karl. 1966. *Marxismus und Philosophie.* Ed. by Erich Gerlach. Frankfurt a. M.: Suhrkamp.

Krabiel, Klaus-Dieter. 1993. *Brechts Lehrstücke: Entstehung und Entwicklung eines Spieltyps.* Stuttgart: Metzler.

Lachmann, Renate. 1970. "Die 'Verfremdung' und das 'Neue Sehen' bei Viktor Sklovskij." *Poetica* 3:226–49.

Lada, Ismene. 1996. "Emotion and Meaning in Tragic Performance." In *Tragedy and the Tragic: Greek Theatre and Beyond,* ed. by M. S. Silk, 396–413. Oxford: Clarendon.

Lawson, John Howard. 1936. *The Theory and Technique of Playwriting.* New York: Putnam.

Lessing, Gotthold Ephraim. 1990. *Hamburgische Dramaturgie.* In *Werke und Briefe in zwölf Bänden,* ed. by Wilfried Barner. Frankfurt a. M.: Deutscher Klassiker Verlag.

Ley, Ralph. 1979. "The Corrective Continued: Bacon, Science and the Epistemological Nature of Epic Theater." In *Brecht as Thinker: Studies in Literary Marxism and Existentialism,* 195–225. Ann Arbor: Applied Literature Press.

Licher, Edmund. 1984. *Zur Lyrik Brechts: Aspekte ihrer Dialektik und Kommunikativität.* Europäische Hochschulschriften 1, 732. Frankfurt a. M.: Lang.

Lindner, Burkhardt. 1972. "Brecht/Benjamin/Adorno: Über Veränderungen der Kunstproduktion im wissenschaftlich-technischen Zeitalter." In *Text + Kritik: Sonderband Bertolt Brecht* 1, 14–36. Munich: Richard Boorberg.

———. 1975. "Avantgardeistische Ideologiezertrümmerung: Theorie und Praxis des Brechtschen Theaters am Beispiel des Faschismusparabeln." In *Arbeitsfeld: Materialistische Literaturtheorie. Beiträge zu ihrer Gegenstandsbestimmung,* ed. by Klaus-Michael Bogdal, Burckhardt Lindner, and Gerhard Plumpe, 229–66. Frankfurt a. M.: Fischer-Athenäum.

Ludwig, Karl-Heinz. 1975. *Bertolt Brecht: Philosophische Grundlagen und Implikationen seiner Dramaturgie.* Abhandlungen zur Kunst-, Musik- und Literaturwissenschaft, 177. Bonn: Bouvier.

———. 1976. *Bertolt Brecht: Tätigkeit und Rezeption von der Rückkehr aus dem Exil bis zur Gründung der DDR.* Kronberg/Ts.: Scriptor.

Lukács, Georg. 1923. *Geschichte und Klassenbewußtsein: Studien über marxistische Dialektik.* Berlin: Malik.

———. 1932. "Aus der Not eine Tugend." *Die Linkskurve* 11–12:15–24.

———. 1955. *Goethe und seine Zeit.* Berlin: Aufbau.

Lunn, Eugene. 1982. *Marxism and Modernism: An Historical Study of Lukács, Brecht, Benjamin and Adorno.* Berkeley-Los Angeles: California UP.

Luthardt, Theodor. 1955. "Vergleichende Studie zu Brechts *Kleines Organon für das Theater.*" Diss., Friedrich-Schiller-Universität, Jena.

Lyon, James K. 1975. "Der Briefwechsel zwischen Bertolt Brecht und der New Yorker Theatre Union von 1935." *Brecht Jahrbuch* 1975, 136–55.

———. 1980. *Bertolt Brecht in America.* Princeton, NJ: Princeton UP.

———. 1995. "Brecht in Postwar Germany: Dissident Conformist, Cultural Icon, Literary Dictator." In *Brecht Unbound: Presented at the International Brecht Symposium held at the University of Delaware February 1992,* ed. by James K. Lyon and Hans-Peter Breuer, 76–88. London: Associated UP.

Lyon, James K., and John Fuegi. 1976. "Bertolt Brecht." In *Deutsche Exilliteratur seit 1933,* vol. 1: *Kalifornien,* part 1, ed. by John M. Spalek and Joseph Strelka, 268–98. Bern-Munich: Francke.

Mao Tse-tung. 1968. "On Contradiction." In *Four Essays on Philosophy,* 23–78. Peking: Foreign Languages Press.

Markwardt, Bruno. 1967. *Geschichte der deutschen Poetik.* 5 vols. Berlin-Leipzig: de Gruyter.

Martin, Carol, and Henry Bial, eds. 2002. *Brecht Source Book*. London-New York: Routledge.

Marx, Karl, and Frederick Engels. 1934. *Selected Correspondence, 1846–1895*. Ed. and trans. by Dona Torr. London: Martin Lawrence.

Marx, Karl, and Friedrich Engels. 1958–68. *Werke*. Ed. by Institut für Marxismus-Leninismus beim ZK der SED. Berlin: Dietz.

Mews, Siegfried, ed. 1997. *A Bertolt Brecht Reference Companion*. Connecticut: Greenwood Press.

Mews, Siegfried, and Herbert Knust, eds. 1974. *Essays on Brecht: Theater and Politics*. Chapel Hill: North Carolina UP.

Midgley, David. 1988. "Communism and the Avant-garde: The Case of Georg Lukács." In *Visions and Blueprints*, ed. by Edward Timms and Peter Collier, 52–65. Manchester: Manchester UP.

———. 2000. *Writing Weimar: Critical Realism in German Literature, 1918–1933*. Oxford: Oxford UP.

Mierau, Fritz. 1976. *Erfindung und Korrektur: Tretjakows Ästhetik der Operativität*. Berlin: Akademie.

Mitchell, Stanley. 1974. "From Shklovsky to Brecht: Some Preliminary Remarks towards a History of the Politicisation of Russian Formalism." *Screen* 15:74–81.

Mittenzwei, Werner. 1967. "Die Brecht-Lukács-Debatte." *Sinn und Form* 19:235–69.

———. 1969. "Erprobung einer neuen Methode: Zur ästhetischen Position Bertolt Brechts." In *Positionen: Beiträge zur marxistischen Literaturtheorie in der DDR*, 9–100. Leipzig: Reclam.

———. 1969. *Gestaltung und Gestalten im modernen Drama: Zur Technik des Figurenaufbaus in der sozialistischen und spätbürgerlichen Dramatik*. Berlin-Weimar: Aufbau.

———. 1976. "Die Spur der Brechtschen Lehrstück-Theorie: Gedanken zur neueren Lehrstück-Intepretation." In Steinweg 1976, 225–54.

———. 1977. *Wer war Brecht? Wandlung und Entwicklung der Ansichten über Brecht im Spiegel von "Sinn und Form."* Berlin: Das europäische Buch.

———. 1987. *Das Leben des Bertolt Brecht oder Der Umgang mit den Welträtseln*. 2 vols. Frankfurt a. M.: Suhrkamp.

Morley, Michael. 1972. "Invention Breeds Invention: Brecht's Chronicle of the Dialectical Principle in Action." *Brecht heute* 2:105–20.

Mueller, Roswitha. 1989. "The *Lehrstück*: Learning for a New Society." In *Bertolt Brecht and the Theory of Media*, 123–43. Lincoln-London: Nebraska UP.

Müller, Joachim. 1958. "Dramatisches und episches Theater: Zur ästhetischen Theorie und zum Bühnenwerk Bertolt Brechts." *Wissenschaftliche Zeitschrift der Friedrich-Schiller-Universität* (Gesellschafts- und sprachwissenschaftliche Reihe, 8), 365–82.

———. 1966. "Dramatisches, episches und dialektisches Theater." In *Episches Theater*, ed. by Reinhold Grimm, 154–91. Cologne-Berlin: Kiepenheuer & Witsch.

———. 1976. "Brechts Gedichte aus dem *Messingkauf*." *Sprachkunst* 7:90–116.

Müller, Klaus-Detlef. 1967. *Die Funktion der Geschichte im Werk Bertolt Brechts: Studien zum Verhältnis von Marxismus und Ästhetik.* Tübingen: Niemeyer.

———. 1972. "Der Philosoph auf dem Theater: Ideologiekritik und 'Linksabweichung' in Bertolt Brechts *Messingkauf*." In Arnold, 1972, 45–71.

———. 1990. "Brechts Theatermodelle: Historische Begründung und Konzept." In *Bertolt Brecht: Actes du Colloque Franco-allemand tenu en Sorbonne (15–19 novembre 1988)*, ed. by Jean-Marie Valentin and Theo Buck, 315–32. Bern-New York: Lang.

Müller-Schöll, Nikolaus. 1999. "Theater im Text der Theorie: Zur rhetorischen Subversion der Lehre in Brechts theoretischen Schriften." *Brecht Jahrbuch* 24:265–75.

Mumford, Meg. 1995. "Brecht Studies Stanislavsky: Just a Tactical Move?" *New Theatre Quarterly* 11:241–58.

Münzberg, Otto. 1974. *Rezeptivität und Spontaneität: Die Frage nach dem ästhetischen Subjekt oder soziologische und politische Implikationen des Verhältnisses Kunstwerk-Rezipient in den ästhetischen Theorien Kants, Schillers, Hegels, Benjamins, Brechts, Heideggers, Sartres und Adornos.* Frankfurt a. M.: Lang.

Naimark, Norman M. 1995. *The Russians in Germany: A History of the Soviet Zone of Occupation, 1945–1949.* Cambridge, MA: Harvard UP.

Nørregaard, Hans Christian. 1993. "Bertolt Brecht und Dänemark." In *Exil in Dänemark: Deutschsprachige Wissenschaftler, Künstler und Schriftsteller im dänischen Exil nach 1933*, ed. by Willy Dähnhardt and Birgit S. Nielsen, 405–62. Heide: Westholsteinische Verlagsanstalt Boyens.

Nössig, L., J. Rosenberg, and B. Schrader, eds. 1980. *Literaturdebatten in der Weimarer Republik: Zur Entwicklung des marxistischen literaturtheoretischen Denkens, 1918–1933.* Berlin: Aufbau.

Olden, Rudolf. 1935. *Hitler the Pawn.* London: Gollancz.

Osborne, John. 1971. *The Naturalist Drama in Germany.* Manchester: Manchester UP; Totowa, NJ: Rowman & Littlefield.

Pavis, Patrice. 1984. "On Brecht's Notion of *Gestus*." In *Semiotics of Drama and Theatre*, ed. by Herta Schmid and Aloysius Van Kesteren. Amsterdam-Philadelphia: John Benjamins.

Philpotts, Matthew. 2003. "'Aus so prosaischen Dingen wie Kartoffeln, Straben, Traktoren werden poetische Dinge': Brecht, *Sinn und Form*, and Strittmatter's *Katzgraben*." *German Life and Letters* 50:56–71.

———. 2003. *The Margins of Dictatorship: Assent and Dissent in the Work of Günter Eich and Bertolt Brecht.* British and Irish Studies in German Language and Literature, 34. Oxford, Bern: Lang.

Pike, David. 1985. *Lukács and Brecht.* Chapel Hill-London: North Carolina UP.

———. 1992. *The Politics of Culture in Soviet-Occupied Germany, 1945–1949.* Chapel Hill-London: North Carolina UP.

Piscator, Erwin. 1968. *Schriften.* Ed. by Ludwig Hoffmann. Vol. 1: *Das politische Theater*. Vol. 2: *Aufsätze, Reden, Gespräche*. Berlin: Henschel.

———. 1980. *Theater — Film — Politik: Ausgewählte Schriften.* Ed. by Ludwig Hoffmann. Berlin: Henschel.

Pracht, Erwin. 1969. "Bertolt Brecht über die soziale Funktion der Kunst." *Weimarer Beiträge* 1:46–73.

Radek, Karl. 1935. "Contemporary World Literature and the Task of Proletarian Art." In Scott 1935: 73–162.

Rapoport. [Iosef Makvejevich] 1936. "The Work of the Actor." *Theatre Workshop* 1:5–40.

Rasch, Wolfdietrich. 1963. "Bertolt Brechts marxistischer Lehrer: Zum ungedruckten Briefwechsel zwischen Bertolt Brecht und Karl Korsch." *Merkur* 17:988–1003.

Reich, Bernhard. 1970. *Im Wettlauf mit der Zeit: Erinnerungen aus fünf Jahrzehnten deutscher Theatergeschichte.* Berlin: Henschel.

Ritter, Hans Martin. 1986. *Das gestische Prinzip bei Bertolt Brecht.* Cologne: Prometh.

Rollka, Manfred. 1971. "Bertolt Brechts Radiotheorie." *Rundfunk und Fernsehen* 19:145–54.

Rosenbauer, Hansjürgen. 1970. *Brecht und der Behaviorismus.* Bad Homburg v.d.H.-Berlin-Zurich: Gehlen.

Rülicke-Weiler, Käthe. 1966. *Die Dramaturgie Brechts: Theater als Mittel der Veränderung.* Berlin: Henschel.

Ruoff, Karen. 1976. "Tui oder Weiser? Zur Gestalt des Philosophen bei Brecht." In *Brechts Tui-Kritik: Aufsätze, Rezensionen, Geschichten*, 17–52. AS 11. Karlsruhe: Argument.

————. 1980. "Das Denkbare und die Denkware: Zum Problem des eingreifenden Denkens." In *Aktualisierung Brechts,* ed. by W. F. Haug et al, 75–84. AS 50. Karlsruhe: Argument.

Salm, Peter. 1971. *The Poem as Plant: A Biological View of Goethe's "Faust."* Cleveland, OH: Case Western Reserve UP.

Schaefer, Heinz. 1956. "Der Hegelianismus der Bert Brecht'schen Verfremdungstechnik in Abhängigkeit von ihren marxistischen Grundlagen." Diss., Technische Universität Stuttgart.

Schevill, James. 1961. "Bertolt Brecht in New York." *Tulane Drama Review* 6:98–107.

Schirokauer, Arno. 1931. *Der Kampf um den Himmel.* Berlin: Gundel.

Schlenker, Wolfram. 1977. *Das "Kulturelle Erbe" in der DDR: Gesellschaftliche Entwicklung und Kulturpolitik.* Stuttgart: Metzler.

Schmitt, Hans-Jürgen, ed. 1975. *Die Expressionismusdebatte: Materialien zu einer marxistischen Realismuskonzeption.* Frankfurt a. M.: Suhrkamp.

Schöne, Albrecht. 1958. "Bertolt Brecht: Theatertheorie und dramatische Dichtung." *Euphorion* 52: 272–96.

Schoor, Uwe. 1992. *Das geheime Journal einer Nation: Die Zeitschrift "Sinn und Form," Chefredakteur Peter Huchel, 1949–1962.* Berlin: Lang.

Schöttker, Detlev. 1989. *Bertolt Brechts Ästhetik des Naiven.* Stuttgart: Metzler.

Schreckenberger, Hugo, ed. 2003. *Ästhetiken des Exils.* Amsterdamer Beiträge zur neueren Germanistik, 54. Amsterdam-Atlanta GA: Rodopi.

Schubbe, Elimar. 1972. *Dokumente zur Kunst-, Literatur- und Kunstpolitik der SED.* Stuttgart: Seewald.

Schumacher, Ernst. 1955. *Die dramatischen Versuche Bertolt Brechts, 1918–1933.* Berlin: Rütten & Loening.

Schürer, Ernst. 1971. *Georg Kaiser und Bertolt Brecht: Über Leben und Werk.* Frankfurt a. M.: Lang.

Scott, H. G. 1935. *Problems of Soviet Literature: Reports and Speeches at the First Soviet Writers' Congress.* Moscow: Cooperative Publishing Society of Foreign Workers in the USSR.

Seidel, Gerhard. 1978. "Dialog mit Brecht." *Neue Deutsche Literatur* 26:109–15.

Seliger, Helfried. 1974. *Das Amerikabild des Bertolt Brecht.* Bonn: Bouvier.

Shookman, Ellis. 1989. "Barthes's Semiological Myth of Brecht's Epic Theater." *Monatshefte* 81:459–75.

Sokel, Walter H. 1973. "Figur — Handlung — Perspektive: Die Dramentheorie Bertolt Brechts." In *Deutsche Dramentheorien: Beiträge zu einer historischen Poetik des Dramas in Deutschland*, ed. by Reinhold Grimm, 2:548–79. Frankfurt a. M.: Athenäum.

Speirs, Ronald. 1987. "Theories of Theater." In *Bertolt Brecht*, 35–48. Basingstoke: Macmillan; New York: St. Martin's Press.

Staiger, Emil. 1968. *Grundbegriffe der Poetik*. Zürich-Freiburg i. Br.: Atlantis. Revised edition.

Stanislavsky, Konstantin Sergeyevich. 1988. *An Actor Prepares*. Trans. by Elizabeth Reynolds Hapgood. London: Methuen.

———. 1988. *Creating a Role*. Trans. by Elizabeth Reynolds Hapgood. London: Methuen.

———. 1989. *My Life in Art*. Trans. by J. J. Hopkins. London: Methuen.

———. 1989. *Stanislavsky's Legacy*. Trans. by Elizabeth Reynolds Hapgood. London: Methuen.

Steinweg, Reiner. 1972. *Das Lehrstück: Brechts Theorie einer politisch-ästhetischen Erziehung*. Stuttgart: Metzler.

———, ed. 1976. *Brechts Modell der Lehrstücke: Zeugnisse, Diskussion, Erfahrungen*. Frankfurt a. M.: Suhrkamp.

Sternberg, Fritz. 1925. *Der Imperialismus*. Berlin. Reprint, Frankfurt.a. M.: Suhrkamp, 1971.

———. 1963. *Der Dichter und die Ratio: Erinnerungen an Bertolt Brecht*. Göttingen: Sache & Pohl.

Streisand, Marianne. 2000. "Stimmung bei Brecht: Über die Produktion von Stimmungen und Atmosphären in der Theaterarbeit des späten Brecht." *Zeitschrift für Germanistik* 10:562–78.

Striedter, Jurij. 1966. "Transparenz und Verfremdung." In *Immanente Ästhetik, ästhetische Reflexion: Lyrik als Paradigma der Moderne*, ed. by Wolfgang Iser, 263–96. Poetik und Hermeneutik 2. Munich: Fink.

———, ed. 1969. *Texte der russischen Formalisten*. Vol. 1: *Texte zur allgemeinen Literaturtheorie und zur Theorie der Prosa*. Munich: Fink.

Strittmatter, Erwin. 1955. *Katzgraben: Szenen aus dem Bauernleben*. Berlin: Aufbau.

Styan, J. L. 1973. *Drama, Stage and Audience*. Cambridge: Cambridge UP.

Subik, Christof. 1982. *Einverständnis, Verfremdung und Produktivität: Versuche über die Philosophie Brechts*. Klagenfurter Beiträge. Vienna: Verlag Verband der wissenschaftlichen Gesellschaften Österreichs zur Philosophie.

Subiotto, Arrigo. 1975. *Bertolt Brecht's Adaptations for the Berliner Ensemble*. London: MHRA.

Sudakov, Ilya. 1937. "The Actor's Creative Work." *Theatre Workshop* 1:7–42.

Suvin, Darko. 1984. *To Brecht and Beyond: Soundings in Modern Dramaturgy.* Sussex: Harvester; New Jersey: Barnes Noble.

Tatlow, Antony. 1977. *The Mask of Evil: Brecht's Response to the Poetry, Theatre and Thought of China and Japan: A Comparative and Critical Evaluation.* European University Papers, XVIII/12. Bern-Frankfurt a. M.-Las Vegas: Lang.

Tatlow, Antony, and Tak-Wai Wong, eds. 1982. *Brecht and East Asian Theatre.* Hong Kong: Hong Kong UP.

Thalheimer, August. 1923. "Über den Stoff der Dialektik." *Die Internationale* 5:270–71.

————. 1928. *Einführung in den dialektischen Materialismus.* Berlin-Vienna: Verlag für Literatur und Politik.

Thiele, Michael. 1991. *Negierte Katharsis: Platon — Aristoteles — Brecht.* Frankfurt a. M.-Bern: Lang.

Thomas, Emma Lewis. 1973. "The Stark/Weisenborn Adaptation of Gorky's *Mother*: Its Influence on Brecht's Version." *Brecht heute / Brecht today* 3:57–63.

Thomson, Peter. 1997. *Brecht: "Mother Courage and Her Children."* Cambridge: Cambridge UP.

Träger, Claus. 1981. *Studien zur Erbetheorie und Erbeaneignung.* Leipzig: Reclam.

Voges, Michael. 1985. "Gesellschaft und Kunst im 'wissenschaftlichen Zeitalter': Brechts Theorie eines episch-dialektischen Theaters." In *Bertolt Brecht: Epoche — Werk — Wirkung,* ed. by Jörg-Wilhelm Joost, Klaus-Detlef Müller, and Michael Voges, 201–52. Munich: Beck.

Voigts, M. 1977. *Brechts Theaterkonzeptionen: Entstehung und Entwicklung bis 1931.* Munich: Fink.

Völker, Klaus. 1969. "Brecht und Lukács: Analyse einer Meinungsverschiedenheit." *alternative* 67/68, 134–47.

Völker, Klaus, and Hans-Jürgen Pullem. 1983. *Brecht Kommentar zum dramatischen Werk.* Munich: Winkler.

Voßkamp, Wilhelm. 1973. *Romantheorie in Deutschland: Von Martin Opitz bis Friedrich von Blanckenburg.* Stuttgart: Metzler.

Wagner, Peter. 1970. "Das Verhältnis von 'Fabel' und 'Grundgestus' in Bertolt Brechts Theorie des epischen Theaters." *Zeitschrift für deutsche Philologie* 89:601–15.

Weber, Carl. 1994. "Brecht and the Berliner Ensemble: The Making of a Model." In *The Cambridge Companion to Brecht,* ed. by Peter Thomson and Glendyr Sacks, 167–84. Cambridge: Cambridge UP.

Weisstein, Ulrich. 1962. "Cocteau, Stravinsky, Brecht and the Birth of Epic Opera." *Modern Drama* 5:142–53.

———. 1972. "Soziologische Dramaturgie und politisches Theater." In *Deutsche Dramentheorien: Beiträge zu einer historischen Poetik des Dramas in Deutschland,* vol. 2, ed. by Reinhold Grimm, 516–47. Frankfurt a. M.: Athenäum.

———. 1972. "Vom dramatischen Roman zum epischen Theater." In *Episches Theater,* ed. by Reinhold Grimm. Neue Wissenschaftliche Bibliothek, 15. 36–49. Cologne-Berlin: Kiepenheuer & Witsch.

———. 1986. "Brecht und das Musiktheater: Die epische Oper als Ausdruck des europäischen Avantgardismus." In *Kontroversen, alte und neue: Akten des VII. Internationalen Germanisten-Kongresses,* ed. by Albrecht Schöne, vol. 9., 72–85. Tübingen: Niemeyer.

Wekwerth, Manfred. 1957. "Auffinden einer ästhetischen Kategorie." In *Sinn und Form: Zweites Sonderheft Bertolt Brecht,* 260–68.

———. 1973. *Schriften: Arbeit mit Brecht.* Berlin: Henschel.

White, Eric Walter. 1935. "Bertolt Brecht." *Life and Letters To-Day* 13:65–76.

White, John J. 1971. "A Note on Brecht and Behaviorism." *Forum for Modern Language Studies* 7:249–58.

———. 1982. "The Cult of 'Functional Poetry' during the Weimar Period." In *Weimar Germany: Writers & Politics,* ed. by Alan Bance, 91–109. Edinburgh: Scottish Academic Press.

———. 1998. "Brecht and Semiotics, Semiotics and Brecht." In *Bertolt Brecht: Centenary Essays,* ed. Giles and Livingstone, 89–108.

———. 2005. "Bertolt Brecht's *Furcht und Elend des III. Reiches* and the Moscow 'Realism' Controversy." *Modern Language Review* 100: 157–80.

Willett, John. 1959. *The Theatre of Bertolt Brecht: A Study from Eight Aspects.* London: Methuen.

———. 1978a. *The New Sobriety: Art and Politics in the Weimar Republic.* London: Thames and Hudson.

———. 1978b. *The Theatre of Erwin Piscator: Half a Century of Politics in the Theatre.* London: Eyre Methuen.

———. 1984. *Brecht in Context: Comparative Approaches.* London: Methuen.

Wimsatt, W. K., and C. Brooks. 1970. *Literary Criticism: A Short History.* 4 vols. London: Routledge & Kegan Paul.

Wirth, Andrzej. 1957. "Über die stereometrischen Strukturen der Brechtschen Stücke." In *Sinn und Form: Zweites Sonderheft Bertolt Brecht*, 346–86.

Witt, Hubert, ed. 1964. *Erinnerungen an Brecht*. Leipzig: Reclam.

Wizisla, Erdmut, ed. 1998. *"... und mein Werk ist der Abgesang des Jahrtausends": 22 Versuche, eine Arbeit zu beschreiben*. Berlin: Akademie der Künste.

Wöhrle, Dieter. 1980. "Bertolt Brechts 'Dreigroschenprozeß': Selbstverständigung durch Ideologiezertrümmerung." *Sprachkunst* 11:40–62.

Wolf, Friedrich. 1968. *Briefwechsel: Eine Auswahl*. Berlin-Weimar: Aufbau.

Wu Zuguang, Huang Zuo-lin, and Mei Shaowu. 1981 (1984). *Peking Opera and Mei Lan-fang: A Guide to China's Traditional Theatre and the Art of Its Great Master*. Beijing: New World Press.

Wulbern, Julian H. 1971. "Ideology and Theory in Context." *Brecht heute* 1:196–204.

Yun, Mi-Ae. 2000. *Walter Benjamin als Zeitgenosse Bertolt Brechts: Eine paradoxe Beziehung zwischen Nähe und Ferne*. Palaestra 309. Göttingen: Vandenhoeck & Ruprecht.

Zhdanov, Andrei Aleksandrovich. 1950. *On Music, Literature and Philosophy*. London: Lawrence & Wishart.

Žmegač, Viktor. 1969. *Kunst und Wirklichkeit: Zur Literaturtheorie bei Brecht, Lukács und Broch*. Bad Homburg v.d.H.-Berlin: Gehlen.

Zutshi, Margot E. 1981. *Literary Theory in Germany: A Study of Genre and Evaluation Theories, 1945–1965*. Europäische Hochschulschriften 1, 427. Bern-Frankfurt a. M.-Las Vegas: Lang.

# Index

As an integral part of his work as a political playwright, Bertolt Brecht concerned himself extensively with the theory of drama. He was convinced that the Aristotelian ideal of bringing the audience to catharsis through identification with a hero and the resultant experience of terror and pity worked against his goal of creating a Marxist theater of critical distance and political insight. He did not want his audiences to indulge in emotional escapism, but required them to respond with a combination of skeptical distance and intellectual curiosity to what they were being shown, and it was in pursuit of this goal that his main theoretical thrusts — his famous "Verfremdungseffekte" (de-familiarization devices) and epic theater, among others — were conceived.

*Bertolt Brecht's Dramatic Theory* is the first detailed study in English of Brecht's writings on the theater to take into account the substantial new material first made available in the recent German edition of his collected works. It offers in-depth analyses of Brecht's canonical essays on the theater, ranging from his notes of 1930 on the innovative opera *Mahagonny* to the unfinished *Messingkauf* project of the late 1940s and early GDR years. Close readings of the individual essays are supplemented by surveys of the connotations and changing status within Brecht's dramaturgical oeuvre of key theoretical terms, including epic and anti-Aristotelian theater, de-familiarization, historicization, and dialectical theater.

Brecht's distinct contribution to the theorizing of acting and audience response is also examined in detail, with each theoretical essay and concept being placed within the context of the aesthetic debates of the time, subjected to a critical assessment, and considered in light of subsequent scholarly thinking. In many cases, the playwright's theoretical discourse is shown to employ methods of "epic" presentation and techniques of de-familiarization that are corollaries of the dramatic techniques for which his plays are justly famous.

JOHN J. WHITE is Emeritus Professor of German and Comparative Literature at King's College, London. He is the co-author, with Ann White, of *Bertolt Brecht's* Furcht und Elend des Dritten Reiches: *A German Exile Drama in the Struggle against Fascism* (Camden House, 2010).

Should become the standard reference in English for understanding Brecht's difficult and seemingly contradictory statements. . . . A book that will now be the definitive resource on this topic. Essential.

CHOICE

White's presentation excels in close readings of strategically chosen texts in five chronologically arranged chapters. . . . This is a solid volume with abundant explanatory footnotes, comprehensive bibliography, and detailed index.

GERMAN QUARTERLY

John J. White's thorough, many-faceted account of the sources and evolution of Brecht's ideas and how he sought to realize them provides a wealth of astute analysis useful to theatrical practitioners, to teachers and scholars of literature, and, in part at least, to social scientists.

GERMAN STUDIES REVIEW, 2006

*Bertolt Brecht's Dramatic Theory* is the first detailed study in English of Brecht's writings on the theatre to take into account the substantial new material first made available in the recent German edition of his collected works. . . . [A work] suggesting new possibilities for Brecht scholars and others interested in his works.

GERMANIC NOTES AND REVIEWS

This is an encyclopaedic undertaking whose philological rigour marks the study as a major work of *Germanistik*.

MODERN LANGUAGE REVIEW

[A] nuanced, thorough, and stimulating investigation cum critical evaluation of Brecht's theorizing on theater. . . .

MONATSHEFTE

Brecht was obliged to calibrate his statements for particular audiences and situations. . . . Temperamentally . . . [he] was disposed to be poetically indirect rather than to strive for maximum transparency. John J. White deserves considerable credit both for taking on the challenge of analyzing Brecht's theory as a whole, and for doing so in a manner that never loses sight of those complexities.

TEXT AND PRESENTATION

CPSIA information can be obtained at www.ICGtesting.com
Printed in the USA
LVOW11s0333140814

398814LV00001B/120/P